THE

WILLARD J. GRAHAM SERIES

IN ACCOUNTING

BOOKS IN
THE WILLARD J. GRAHAM SERIES IN ACCOUNTING

CONSULTING EDITOR   ROBERT N. ANTHONY   *Harvard University*

ANDERSON, SCHMIDT, & MCCOSH   *Practical Controllership*   3d ed.

ANTHONY   *Management Accounting: Text and Cases*   4th ed.

ANTHONY   *Management Accounting Principles*   rev. ed.

ANTHONY, DEARDEN, & VANCIL   *Management Control Systems: Text, Cases, and Readings*   rev. ed.

BARR & GRINAKER   *Short Audit Case*   rev. ed.

FREMGEN   *Accounting for Managerial Analysis*   rev. ed.

GORDON & SHILLINGLAW   *Accounting: A Management Approach*   4th ed.

GRIFFIN, WILLIAMS, & LARSON   *Advanced Accounting*   rev. ed.

GRINAKER & BARR   *Audit Practice Case*

GRINAKER & BARR   *Auditing: The Examination of Financial Statements*

HAWKINS   *Corporate Financial Reporting: Text and Cases*

HENDRIKSEN   *Accounting Theory*   rev. ed.

HOLMES, MAYNARD, EDWARDS, & MEIER   *Elementary Accounting*   3d ed.

HOLMES & OVERMYER   *Auditing: Principles and Procedure*   7th ed.

HOLMES & OVERMYER   *Basic Auditing Principles*   4th ed.

KENNEDY & MCMULLEN   *Financial Statements: Form, Analysis, and Interpretation*   6th ed.

LADD   *Contemporary Corporate Accounting and the Public*

MAURIELLO   *The Irwin Federal Income Tax Course: A Comprehensive Text*

MEIGS, LARSEN, & MEIGS   *Principles of Auditing*   5th ed.

MIKESELL & HAY   *Governmental Accounting*   4th ed.

MOORE & STETTLER   *Accounting Systems for Management Control*

MURPHY   *Advanced Public Accounting Practice*

MURPHY   *Auditing and Theory: A CPA Review*

NEILSON   *Interactive Computerized Accounting Problems Set*

NEUNER   *Cost Accounting: Principles and Practice*   8th ed.

NICHOLS   *Programmed Cost Accounting: A Participative Approach*

NIELSEN   *Cases in Auditing*

O'NEIL, FARWELL, & BOYD   *Quantitative Controls for Business: An Introduction*

PATON   *Corporate Profits*

PYLE & WHITE   *Fundamental Accounting Principles*   6th ed.

SALMONSON, HERMANSON, & EDWARDS   *A Survey of Basic Accounting*

SCHAFER   *Elements of Income Tax—Individual*

SCHRADER, MALCOLM, & WILLINGHAM   *Financial Accounting: An Input/Output Approach*

SHILLINGLAW   *Cost Accounting: Analysis and Control*   3d ed.

SPILLER   *Financial Accounting: Basic Concepts*   rev. ed.

STAUBUS   *Activity Costing and Input-Output Accounting*

VATTER   *Accounting Measurements for Financial Reports*

WELSCH, ZLATKOVICH, & WHITE   *Intermediate Accounting*   3d ed.

WILLIAMS & GRIFFIN   *Management Information: A Quantitative Accent*

Practical
controllership

PRACTICAL CONTROLLERSHIP

DAVID R. ANDERSON, C.P.A.
Formerly Controller, The Stanley Works

LEO A. SCHMIDT, C.P.A.
Professor Emeritus of Accounting
The University of Michigan

ANDREW M. McCOSH, C.A.
Professor of Management Accounting
University of Manchester

 Third Edition • 1973

RICHARD D. IRWIN, INC. *Homewood, Illinois* 60430
IRWIN-DORSEY LIMITED *Georgetown, Ontario*

Third Edition

First Printing, February 1973

ISBN 0-256-00008-5
Library of Congress Catalog Card No. 72–92414
Printed in the United States of America

PREFACE

More than a quarter of a century has elapsed since the publication of the first edition of this book, shortly after the end of World War II. The intervening years have been a period of technological development and economic growth unprecedented in world history. Prosperity, as measured by industrial production and gross national product, has shown a rapid growth, with only a few relatively short pauses in the uptrend. The standard of living, at least in the developed countries, has reached a new high level; and scientists in all disciplines are predicting the early arrival of the time when man's major problem will be how to utilize his leisure time, rather than how to feed, clothe, and house himself and his family. By these signs it would appear that we should be well on our way to achieving the best of all possible worlds.

There is, however, another side to the coin. Our progress has been accomplished at the cost of a severe inflation that carries the threat of an ultimate collapse in the economy. The economic gap between the have and the have-not nations has widened, and the have-nots are envious and resentful. We have suddenly realized that, in our enthusiasm for growth and ever more growth, we have been abusing our natural resources; almost overnight, pollution of the environment has become a prime political and social issue. The stability of our social order has been shaken by the revolt of disadvantaged groups and the alienation of many of our most intelligent young people, and this upheaval has been accompanied by an alarming increase in violence and crime. We are warned by some prophets that the accelerating rate of change in all aspects of human living is carrying us out of the industrial age into a "post-industrial" or "super-industrial" society, and that our economic and social structures must be modified—in ways not too clearly defined—if we are to avoid collapse and chaos.

Business managers have been, and are, at the very center of this ferment. They have applied the fruits of technological progress to step up drastically the production and distribution of goods and services, and in the process they have expanded their operations on a global scale. By research in business practices they have evolved new tech-

niques in all phases of their management functions—product development, production, marketing, organization and personnel administration, and—most germane to the subject of this book—the planning and
control of all of the firm's activities. Increasingly, they are recognizing
their responsibility for the social consequences of their decisions and
are taking an active part in programs designed to remedy the ills that
are plaguing our society. Accountants and financial executives are immediately concerned with proposals for a redefinition of the objectives
of accounting, the adoption of uniform accounting standards, and more
complete disclosure of the details of corporate operations and of corporate management's plans and forecasts for the future. Perhaps of even
greater importance, they are beginning to think in terms of the special
contribution they can make to the evolution of social accounting and
long-range social planning.

Through all of these developments there has been little, if any, substantive change in the basic nature of the controllership function. There
has, however, been a significant change in emphasis. Forward planning
of operations, which was treated extensively in both the first and revised
editions of this book, has assumed increasing importance and has become more formalized, with a whole new body of philosophy and practice. The advent of successive generations of computers has speeded
up and, to a great extent, simplified the mechanical processes of recordkeeping and reporting; at the same time it has created new problems
of administration and of internal control and internal audit. This computer revolution, together with the rapid advances in operations research, has put into the hands of the controller powerful new tools that
are especially useful in the forward-planning phases of his responsibilities.

In recognition of these changes in the relative emphasis on the various phases of the controllership function, the material in this edition
has been reorganized. It is presented in five parts, as follows:

I.   The Controllership Concept
II.   Basic Techniques
III. Operational Planning and Control
IV.   Long-Range Planning
V.   Advanced Techniques

Parts I, II, and II represent a revision and updating of material in the
second edition; discussion of mathematical techniques and the use of
the computer has been added, where appropriate, with cross-references
to the chapters in Part V. The chapters in Part IV deal with the theory
and practice of long-range planning, with particular emphasis on the
financial aspects of planning and the role of the financial officer. Part V,
which is completely new, provides a working background in the basic
principles of the computer and its application to business problems.

In this, as in the previous editions, emphasis is laid on the importance of conforming to sound theoretical principles and at the same time adapting the procedures followed to the needs and capacities of the organization and the individuals composing it. To quote from the introduction to the second edition: "On the one hand, we may err in following theory too literally, assuming that all apparent deviations from the expected normal way of doing things must be wrong or stupid. On the other hand, it is just as serious an error to take the attitude that we have moved into the 'practical, facts of life' area where the textbook theory just does not fit and must therefore be discarded." It cannot be repeated too often that the adaptation of theory to the practical situation is an essential element in the art of controllership.

A significant organizational development during the last decade, which is discussed in Chapter I, has been the increase in the number of executives holding the title of vice president—finance. This development has not, in our opinion, resulted in any deterioration in the status of the controller as a member of the management group—rather, it has facilitated his extending his influence in the areas of forward planning and financial policy formulation. Controllership is still, we believe, a distinctive function, and we have, therefore, retained the title of *Practical Controllership* for this edition.

A word is in order as to the role of the controller in the new business climate that is evolving out of the current flux of growth and change. It is beyond the scope of this book—indeed, beyond the authors' competence—to predict how the forces of change will eventually affect our economic and social environment. We believe, however, that under any economic and social structure there will be a need for the controllership function. The controller may be hard-pressed to keep abreast of the times, both technically and in his comprehension of the shifting priorities among his responsibilities; but if he is successful in doing this he will be "where the action is," and he will continue to be in a position to make a positive contribution to business management and to social progress.

January 1973   DAVID R. ANDERSON
                                                  LEO A. SCHMIDT
                                                  ANDREW M. McCOSH

Memorandum to instructors—problems and cases

With this, the third, edition of *Practical Controllership,* a new kind of flexibility in use is provided. Hitherto, it has been traditional to include both problems and cases with the text in a single volume. This has tended to restrict the choice of cases open to instructors, and has also implied that new case material can be built into the book only when the text is revised. Accordingly, in response to many instructors' suggestions, there are no cases in this volume. Instead, a series of recommended lists of cases will be offered to adopting instructors. Each of these recommended cases has been published by the Intercollegiate Case Clearing House, Soldiers Field, Boston, Massachusetts 02163. Naturally, any instructor is free to devise his own case list, or not to use cases at all if that is his preference. Those who want to use one of the recommended case lists, or parts of them, may obtain the lists by writing to the Clearing House.

The use of cases in connection with the book is intended to give the student maximum opportunity for independent thinking. The "problems," which are incorporated in this volume, are, in general, based directly on material in the text itself, while the purpose of the case is to put the student as nearly as possible into a practical business situation. Often the case will present information that is superfluous, or, on the other hand, it may give inadequate information. The question of whether or not the information given is adequate, the possible reasons for its inadequacy, what could be done retroactively in actual business to dig out the information when it is needed, or what should have been done originally to have it available when needed—these are all questions collateral to the direct-action problem in the case. Consideration of these aspects of information is another phase of the training of the student to handle himself in the imperfect and practical world. It is one of the elements of strength in the case method that, if properly handled, can add greatly to the real training of the future controller.

Acknowledgment is due to Mr. S. Robert Gramen and Mr. Louis W. Petro, both of the University of Michigan, and Mr. Peter Quinn, of the Manchester Business School, for their assistance in preparing many of the problems and case lists and the corresponding solutions and discussions in the Instructors Manual.

CONTENTS

Part III
OPERATIONAL PLANNING AND CONTROL

strengths and weaknesses. Summary of objectives. Basic assumptions. Plans. Profit and loss statement. Highlight summary and major check points. The long-range plan and the annual budget. Planning effort more important than "the plan." Practicalities of the five-year plan. Summarization of venture plans. Measurement of actual venture performance against long-range plans.

Problems 567

Appendixes

Part I

The controllership concept

1 DESCRIPTION OF THE CONTROLLERSHIP FUNCTION

CONTEXT AND DEFINITION

This book, like its two earlier editions, recognizes that controllership is still in a state of evolution. We are pleased to see evidence of a maturing of the concept in both academic and applied areas.

The most obvious evolutionary development in recent years is the growing tendency to reorient the functions of the controller and that of the treasurer and sometimes the secretary, through the use of the new job title Vice President–Finance. This tendency has several interpretations. One acceptable interpretation is that the controller is being given a promotion from the strictly staff function of controllership to additional line duties, a circumstance which is well expressed by the joint title Vice President–Finance–Controller. This interpretation, like other new arrangements, is backgrounded by recognition of the very real difficulty experienced in drawing the line between the pure controller function and the decision-making line functions. The controller's information function has long been recognized as extending beyond the collection of information to the reporting and interpreting thereof. Often the interpretation of information—analysing its significance for the concerned line official—is tantamount to determining the line official's action, even though the controller makes a conscientious effort to confine himself to interpreting and to avoid the actual making of the decision. The apparent easy way out of this difficulty is to give the controller line authority. While the combination of staff and line functions does have one desired effect, it is a step away from functional differentiation, and it may be in broader aspects unfortunate. It is hardly likely that, having made a decision with his line hat on, the controller–vice president will thereafter be entirely objective in reporting information which would reflect adversely on the wisdom of his own decision while wearing

3

his controller hat. The fact that the incumbent clearly recognizes his two-hat capacity should help materially in avoiding criticism and his own appreciation of the difficulties may sharpen his performance in both areas. As an aid to this differentiation and recognizing the fact that the most organizations still separate the job of the controller from line responsibility, except, of course, within his own department, our analysis in the following pages will be in terms of "pure" controllership.

An organization shift which is apparently closely related to that discussed above occurs when the previous controller is moved up to a new position, that of Vice President–Finance, and another person moves into the controller job. If the new vice president in effect becomes a supercontroller, with the controller actually only an assistant controller, we are right back in our previous situation. If, however, the new vice presidency is a promotion to straight line authority over broader finance responsibilities and if the essential duties of the controller are fully assumed by the new incumbent the situation is organizationally clean.

Frequently, a new position, Vice President–Finance is created and filled by some one other than the controller either from outside the business or by promotion from within. Usually the controller and the treasurer report to this new officer instead of directly to the chief executive officer. This arrangement is again clean as to functional organization.

In addition it should be pointed out that the title Vice President–Controller does not always carry the intent of line authority. The person with this title may still have staff authority only, the purpose of the title, thus used, being to express the rank of the holder in the management heirarchy, indicating clearly that he is a member of the top management team as is discussed later in this chapter.

Specific controllership positions

An extremely practical situation faces the controller at the time he assumes the job either by promotion or by coming in from the outside. Regardless of the theoretic concepts or of what may be shown by survey methods as the controller's proper sphere, the duties of the particular job are usually fixed by custom of the particular job, by the bylaws of the corporation, and/or specific resolutions of the board of directors. In the absence of a special contract of employment with the corporation these customs and provisions will govern and should be carefully considered before taking the job. Frequently, these previous arrangements are out of date or they may have been ill conceived in the first place. They may (a) represent past or present peculiarities of the business, (b) historical conditions no longer relevant, (c) reflections of past power struggles of individuals, (d) the tailoring of the job to special capacities of previous incumbents, or still other reasons.

In any case, the prospective controller should take advantage of the fluidity of the situation and bargain for a proper statement of his position and duties. The trade-off will be between a statement in broad, safe generalities and much more detailed commitments. If there has been a history of conflict and rivalry in the firm involving previous controllers it may be especially important to get a firm statement of authority and responsibility. The assistant who is being advanced to the major position will have the advantage of knowing the detailed involvements of the situation. The man from the outside will have more independence and trading power. Either should check his understanding of the ideal controllership concept against the practical conditions of the job to put himself into the best long-run position.

Definitions of controllership

In an important sense definition of the controllership function is the basic purpose of this book. No dictionary can help us, however, and it would serve no good purpose to attempt our own airtight one-sentence definition. Our interest in the subject lies in the ramifications, the evolving nature, the borderline issues, the relations to other concepts, which will obviously take space and many words to explore.

It will be well to begin this broad task of definition by examining several attempts to characterize the central concept of controllership in fairly simple terms. For instance the statement that "the controller is the figure partner on the management team" is a nontechnical but quite effective approach. If we follow this by explaining what we mean by "figure" and also put forth an adequate picture of the "team work" of top level management with each member contributing his special abilities, we have a fair beginning. Such an approach to the definition of controllership would be the proper one to use in making a presentation to the local Rotary. It informs without presuming to be airtight or complete.

The first edition of this book contained a pungent, short characterization of controllership as follows: "If we eliminate from consideration miscellaneous, occasional, and special assignments, it becomes apparent that the really essential duties of controllership are all aspects of one basic function—designing and operating the records of the business and reporting and interpreting the information which they contain." Here again we might seem to have a single sentence definition, or at least a characterization of controllership. Again the statement standing entirely alone is not adequate. But this statement, with its assumed background and with its implications properly developed, will be found to be fair and useful in building toward an adequate concept of controllership.

The opening phrase ". . . eliminate . . . miscellaneous, occasional, and special assignments . . ." needs discussion at this point. This phrase is useful in that it recognizes the fact that the controller's job as it is found in actual practice turns out to be not only the exercise of the pure controllership function but the performance of a lot of other small, necessary duties which are from time to time wished upon the controller simply because there is no one else around the place as capable of assuming those duties. This statement is not idle flattery of our friends, the incumbent controllers. We must recognize the fact that in any business there are occasional special tasks which do not fall naturally into the job description of normal organization units. Top administration must assign such jobs to someone who has the ability to adjust quickly and easily to the new requirements. Most important to such an adjustment is the ability to see this task against the entire business background, and no one else is as fully equipped in this respect as the controller. So, "Joe Controller, it's your baby."

Various attempts have been made to define the controller's job by surveying the activities of controllers on the job in representative firms. Such efforts are very useful in "getting the picture" of actual conditions, but they carry the danger of confusing the incidental, occasional, and miscellaneous with the essential. This is what the quotation from our first edition aims at. The point is obviously important in establishing a scholarly, professional, understanding of the controllership concept, and it may also have great and immediate practical importance for the practicing controller who wants to keep himself clear of petty ancillary duties so that he can do the best job of his prime function. Occasional controllers, being empire builders at heart, have wished themselves into the anomalous situation by grabbing for additional responsibilities surrounding their own proper areas.

The second part of the quotation referred to is a direct, positive statement of the material content of the controller's job "—designing and operating the records of the business—reporting and interpreting the information which they contain." Note that the ground staked out is the *records* of the business, not merely the debit and credit dollar system, though that of course is still the backbone of the records. In today's techniques "records" include devices in which the record may be a magnetic bit as well as holes in cards or ink on paper. Note also that reporting and interpreting are given coordinate prominence with designing and recording. Note finally that all of this leads to the word *information*. A full explanation and implementation of these elements would constitute a very acceptable definition of the controllership concept.

This definition finally provides an excellent frame for the clarification of what was meant in our opening statement asserting evidence of a maturing trend in the controllership concept. For a long time there has been a recognized shifting of emphasis from the designing and operating of the record system to the reporting and interpreting phase. This shifting has continued and is being stepped up to a more critical attitude toward interpretation and toward the whole meaning of information in management. Controllers are discovering that fancy devices for interpreting the same ancient data will no longer suffice. They realize that a new look at the very nature of the information to be accumulated is needed. The analysis must start with the management needs to be served. This requirement goes far beyond lip service to the fine word management. It must really get to the shifting, changing, problems of management in the strange new world. If this means the abandonment of some old restrictions and concepts, so be it. As never before, it is necessary for the controller as a part of the team to leave his own cubicle and to consult with line management to be sure that he is constantly up to date on the relevant, determining issues.

If our erstwhile unified business has grown into a diversified conglomerate, reporting and interpreting needs take on a whole new slant. If our computer goes on-line, real-time, the change comprises more than a change in techniques of getting the same old information. There may be vast new possibilities in the situation which change the pattern of possible information service to management.

Development in related fields such as operations research and quantitative methods in general open new possibilities which the controller must be ready to incorporate into his whole information system. The purpose of these devices is to get more useful information out of the available basic data. In this sense they may be regarded as a strengthening of the reporting and interpreting functions, for these have always involved the arrangement of data so as to bring out the significant relationships between various elements. However the new mathematical devices do so much more in bringing out these significant relationships that it might not be unrealistic to visualize them as an entirely new element in the definition—*manipulation**—a separate step between reporting and interpreting.

If manipulation is not to be recognized as a unique step in the definition it must certainly be respected as a new and vital element in the final step *interpreting*. This book, our third edition, is happy to adapt our basic definition of controllership to embrace this new element. Whatever we decide on the exact semantics of the issue, there can be no doubt that the practical utilization of the new techniques is one of the signs of the maturity of the controller.

New developments in the science of communication theory constitute another element which may measure the maturity of the controller. Information which is not truly *communicated* is hardly information. This issue is elusive but very real. The studies and writings in communication

---

* Manipulation in common parlance often has a derogatory connotation which is *not* intended in our use of the word.

theory to date are seldom illustrated by financial statements, but the principles apply significantly. The difficulties of communication identified by the experts are especially pertinent in the field of management accounting.

If we consider only the final, major, occasion of communication in the area, the annual statements, we can demonstrate the major difficulties. First, the information sought to be communicated is complicated far beyond the information which is commonly used in demonstrations of communication theory. Second, the difficulties of encoding are very great. By this we have in mind the lack of uniformity of representational devices. Third, the audience, the statement recipients, are enormously varied in their needs and capabilities, ranging from the janitor's widow to the investment analyst! These difficulties parallel, in exaggerated form, exactly the difficulties visualized by the communication experts in their much simpler illustrations. Furthermore communication is not limited to the major statements but is of the essence of the thousand and one reports and forms which move from man to man and office to office throughout the firm.

Communication theory breaks the communication process into its constituent elements and by this means focuses attention on the real nature of the difficulties. This is the method of science and it bears results which, with patience and imagination can be applied in the controllership area with gratifying results. A study of available writings in the field of communication science is a must for the "homework" of the controller.

Central concept—information

From what has been said about the attempts at a simple definition of controllership and about the possible maturing of the concept, it becomes evident that the core idea is information and the controller's responsibility therein. If we visualize the entire field of information which could be of any possible consequence to any part of management, we can study the controllership concept, in terms of what segments of this entire area the controller's responsibility can and should embrace. Some of the areas are obviously the controller's, especially the dollar measurements within the typical accounting framework. Some very large areas are obviously not his responsibility. They include great areas of information in science, law, politics, ethics, philosophy, and engineering which must be left to the line executives—and they will have their own controversies on the division of responsibilities within these areas. There remain great areas of information between these clear cases where the controller and others may have to argue and compromize as to responsibility and control. In these areas a sure way to be wrong is to be too categorical. Here the answer as to the controller's responsibility is not "yes" or "no" but "maybe," "sometimes," "in certain respects," and very usefully, "yes, insofar as."

The "maybe" and "sometimes" approach recognizes the fact that circumstances vary enormously. It is conceivable, for instance, that in some fairly simple manufacturing situations it might be within reason to state that all information regarding production will be reduced to accounting control in terms of dollars and necessarily related quantitative measures. In more complicated situations, a production control department may reasonably handle much of its own direct working information.

However, the "insofar as" approach to settling information responsibilities is more often useful since it consciously tries to draw the line of demarcation. Information pertaining to research, for instance, is not the controller's responsibility except insofar as it is appropriate to measure the costs thereof. This measurement will extend to total costs, period by period, breakdowns to the pattern of projects (pure research, future products, current production improvements, etc.). It will or may involve the several elements of research costs: government-sponsored and other outside contracts, own company research. Anyone of these divisions may be broken down to specific projects. Beyond such general terms, one would have to know the individual company situation to make further intelligent analysis. The present purpose is to demonstrate the usefulness of the "insofar as" approach. The controller generally does not pretend to any knowledge of or responsibility for research except insofar as costs are involved. There might, of course, be circumstances in which the controller might try to measure the benefits derived from specific research projects to match against his cost breakdowns but this in most cases will be a judgmental matter beyond quantitative measurement. Even on the cost side, there will, of course, be plenty of controversy left as to just how far he should go in measuring the elements of costs, just what if anything shall be done to allocate general costs to projects, etc.

Even the question of degree of refinement can be most effectively approached under our "insofar as" thinking. At this point the rationale should be that the refined breakdown devices are desirable "insofar as management has any significant use for such detail." No possible theory can solve this type of problem, unless we wish to twist the words to say that the management action, or use criterion, *is* our theory for these myriads of border line cases.

It may be tempting to establish the simple test of quantifiability for the controller's responsibility for information. In a negative way this test seems to have a certain degree of validity. Information which is inherently nonquantifiable such as legal principles, ethical judgments, etc., is seldom the controller's responsibility. On the other side of the coin the rule is not so clear. The controller's responsibility does not extend to all quantifiable information. Certain kinds of technical information must by their very nature be collected initially by the employees of line divisions. Market research data constitute a good example. Such data may be in quantity terms but so intimately involved in market strategy that the marketing department itself can do a more adequate job of marshaling, reporting and interpretation than the controller could do.

The actuarial department of an insurance company provides another good example of quantitative information for which the controller should certainly not be responsible. In this case the highly technical nature of the information argues that it be maintained in the actuarial department. Some of this technical information on policy premium and reserves, for instance, eventually becomes accounting data for inclusion in reports to the insurance commissioner and requires close cooperation of the controller and actuary for proper handling. The personnel department may wish to keep a substantial amount of its quantitative information in its own files, though the running record of wages, withholdings, etc., will be in payroll under the controller.

At the present time we find the placing of the computer techniques in a problematic situation. Substantial parts of computer hardware and time are devoted to rather routine record keeping and certainly should be the controller's responsibility. Other chunks of time and hardware are engaged in highly technical efforts for engineering and research and should clearly be in the hands of personnel with statistical or mathematical backgrounds. Between those clear cases are vast areas in which the aggressive and knowledgeable controller ought to stake out his claims. There is no easy right answer to this problem. It is posed here merely as one more illustration of the complicated nature of information problem.

The entire information area must be viewed as a ragged continuum from the clear case of accounting dollars to the completely nonquantitative abstractions. Custom has made parts of this area the controller's province, but it is to be hoped that something more rational than custom or whim will in the long run determine borders of his area.

The foregoing discussions have assumed that the usefulness of information to management is obvious. As a matter of fact, the true nature of management use of information is of the essence of this whole book, and the issue will be raised again and again in many ways. At this point, a very general though fundamental caution on the point may be appropriate.

Usefulness should not mean that someone somewhere has *said* that he thinks some information is useful. That is not enough. The real test of the situation is that there must be a *high probability* that the information in question *will influence action*. What we are trying to avoid in this statement is the criterion of mere management interest in or affection for some facet of information. There is no denying that the controller may be on a delicate spot if some prestigious person in the administration directly requests information which is unlikely to pass the action test. The controller will be in a strong position if, before specific controversy arises, he can get top management's blessing on the principle that *probability of action thereon* shall be the criterion of information usefulness.

The management accounting versus financial accounting "controversy"

As top man for the entire accounting responsibility, the controller has a special interest in what to many persons looks like a rather basic controversy between two segments of the accounting profession, that is the apparent differences between "financial" and "management" accountants. The following analysis does not aim to prove either point of view right or wrong, but hopes to shed a little more light on the real nature of each point of view and thus aid our major purpose of more successfully implementing the total service of the controller toward all legitimate purposes.

By and large the financial accounting approach is that of the public accountants aiming at the very practical problem of assurance of proper custodianship of their client businesses and the clear reflection of the "facts of the case" in their certified statements. Going beyond this generalization and examining the myriad detail issues which make it real, we find that the determining aim of public accounting is the use and enforcement of "good accounting theory." By and large good accounting theory is the material of financial accounting textbooks in contra distinction to the content of the management accounting books. This does not mean that the books came first and that the financial accountants are following book principles. What it does mean is that the financial viewpoint is older than the management viewpoint and the original texts were written by scholars who had absorbed their ideas from the accounting that was then in vogue.

THE LOGIC OF ACCOUNTING

To get to the bottom of the difference between the financial and management accounting viewpoints, we will in the next few pages do some basic research. This research consists of some highly critical reading of selected statements from accounting "literature." We will do this reading with a *second-level consciousness* directed at the *reasoning behind the direct statements made*. We will find that the writers often assert this or that finding, truth, or gospel, without any obvious proof or reasoning. This is not necessarily poor writing, it simply means that the writer expects the reader to supply the reasoning from the general context, and in simple situations this may suffice. At other times the writers, a little more conscious of their logic, give informal clues to their reasoning process by a word or two from which the reader can reconstruct the writer's more complete thinking. Thus if the writer says method A is better than method B "because it is more conservative," he is really using the assumption that conservatism is obviously desirable and that it clinches the argument. Another writer may state that method A is to be preferred over other methods "because it is the only one allowed by income tax regulations." This is a very practical argument. Note that the writer uses it to select the "preferred" method which is a little less than saying this method is right and that all others are wrong. Yet many readers will read the intention of rightness-wrongness into such a statement. A careful thinker will certainly not be willing to accept the dictum that only those methods which get by the tax man are right.

Frequently, an argument is made by appeal to some specific authority. Someone, some day may argue, "Method A is right because that's the way Anderson-Schmidt-McCosh handled it on page xx." While this would be flattering to the present authors, we still feel it our duty to point out that such an appeal is only as good as the specific authority in the context in which the statement was made and that it might be easy to find opposing authorities. The appeal to authorities is a weak argument.

The quoted examples illustrate the desirability of going behind the immediate statement of an argument to discover the basic thinking—the reference to the controlling consideration—which is supposed to clinch the specific case at issue. The three examples all used premises which might be good enough under certain conditions, but they are certainly not the kind of thinking which we should hope to find as the basis for a profession.

The search for viable premises

Challenging the implied premise upon which an argument is based has the effect of driving the proponent back to more defensible ground. If this process is intelligently followed, it should finally uncover some premise which is entirely acceptable to both parties to the argument. When men of good will argue in this way—for the sake of clarification and enlightenment instead of for mere head-bashing—they make real progress toward the establishment of a sound procedure.

Now let us look at a few more statements in which the reasoning is fairly apparent:

1. "To neglect to recognize a wage accrual would misstate the current liability total significantly."

2. "Taking depreciation on a ten-year basis simply does not square with the known twenty-year life of the machine."
3. "Research cost should be allocated to those ventures which benefit from it."
4. "The purpose of the allowance for bad debts is to correct the balance sheet valuation of accounts receivable to the probable realizable amount."
5. "Pricing raw materials out at LIFO is aimed at producing true economic costs of production."
6. "Even twenty-year bonds owned by the business should be shown as current assets if management intends to sell them in a relatively short time."
7. "An item described as 'Unamortized 1962 Fire Loss' should not be shown as an asset in the December 31, 1970, balance sheet."
8. "Amounts expended in December to advertise the January clearance sale are an asset as of December 31 because the expected benefit has not yet been received."

The writers of these textbook statements are all pounding away at basic theory. Their reasoning is implied by words which are not formally argumentative. Only the last item contains the fighting word "because." In each case, however, close inspection reveals what the writer had in mind, and we can visualize what his further defense would have been if his statement had been challenged.

Major premise I

Actually, there is one safe, fundamental ground upon which these eight statements are ultimately based. Behind each of these statements there lies the assumption that there is *an objectively observable fact* (event, situation) of business life which must be portrayed clearly in accounting language. This accounting language comprises a few definitions (asset, liability, capital, income, and expense) and a fairly simple system of interrelationships. These definitions and relationships are themselves the product of long and patient observation and categorization of business situations and events.

Out of this thinking we can formulate the major premise which underlies the foregoing statements and upon which all accounting theory is based. It may be simply stated as follows: *As between any two methods that method is preferred which most clearly portrays the objectively observed facts of business.* The particular words used can of course be varied: "any two methods" can be expanded to "two or more methods." No harm is done if "correct" is substituted for "preferred." The premise can be cited as "the clear portrayal principle," and if "portrayal" is too formal we can talk about "getting the clearest picture possible," or we can insist on "the closest possible correspondence between the accounting representation and the observed phenomena." Although the words may vary, the *concept is vital.*

It is important that we differentiate clearly between such a statement of the general premise controlling our thinking and the assertions which describe the particular phenomena to which it is being applied. There may, of course, be disagreement about what the specific observed facts are. Simply poor observation, variations of interpretation colored by previous experience, or mere failure of communication may be the cause of disagreement. Technically, these are *minor premise* difficulties. Recognizing this, the adversaries should repeat their observations until agreement is reached on the specific observed facts.

It may be useful to point out that this approach is similar to that of the natural sciences. In our field of accounting, the phenomena observed are those of business rather than segments of nature, though, of course, we can argue that business itself is merely a very special segment of the activity of nature's most important creature—man.

It is at least interesting and possibly important to point out that accounting could have been developed as a *pure science,* an unadulterated effort to get a clear understanding of this complicated phenomenon called business without any thought that such effort might be useful in the actual conduct and control of what was happening. This would have been parallel to the toast said to be dear to the hearts of mathematicians: "Here's to pure mathematics, may it never be worth a damn to anyone." It is unlikely that any accountant, even the theory-inclined accounting professor, has ever used this as a toast to accounting. Much of mathematics has a way of becoming useful, to the distress of the pure mathematician. Accounting is so obviously and immediately useful that is stretches the imagination to visualize it as a "pure" science.

Basic theory and management accounting

The above observation, the inherent usefulness of accounting, underlies the relationship of or distinction between financial and management accounting.

Professor William Andrew Paton is regarded by many as the preeminent accounting theorist of the past 50 years. Yet this theorist has always been extremely impatient with even the implication that management accounting was something distinct from any good accounting. When such an implication touched his own writings, usually thought of as characteristically theoretical, his reaction was vigorous and vocal. "Why that's plain silly! There is management accounting on every page of this book!

In this statement, properly analyzed, we have the real crux of the financial accounting versus management accounting question, and it goes right back to the pure versus applied aspect of accounting. If there is one thing that practical management really needs above all others it is a clear portrayal of the facts as they are! This is what Paton has in mind when he says there is management accounting on every page in his books. There has been no writer who has stuck more rigidly to the insistence that accounting must portray facts as they are. That is good theory, and incidentally very good management accounting in a truly basic sense.

Why then does the apparent difference between the viewpoints continue to exist? The answer lies in the fact that the management accountants utilize a second area of reasoning which goes beyond the principle of correct portrayal. Again a careful reading of and listening to accounting writing and conversation enables us to identify the real nature of this second reasoning process.

Major premise II

There are many situations in practical accounting in which the clear portrayal premise will not give a decision between two competing methods. In these situations the problem is not that one method shows the truth and the other a falsehood, but rather that there are two truths which are competing for recognition, and the circumstances are such that the accountant must decide which of the truths he wishes to present. The accountant in this case raises the question: Which of these truths is the more important to management? Which will guide management to the safer, more intelligent, business decision? Put into more formal language this thinking becomes another broad major premise: *As between two proposed methods that method is preferred (or correct) which will the more surely guide management toward making the wiser decision.* Again the particular wording may vary greatly. It could be stated: As between competing accounting methods, management needs should dictate the method selected. Most briefly the concept can be characterized as "the management impact principle."

The use of this premise might seem to put a tremendous burden on the accountant. He apparently assumes that he is wise enough to see the way the management decision should go and he selects the method which will push management in that direction. This is in fact the way in which the aggressive, confident accountant often works, and for a great many simple situations it is entirely proper. For more complicated situations the accountant should explain the two methods and their probable impacts as clearly as possible to management and then after full consultation make his selection of method. A few illustrations are needed to demonstrate the management impact principle.

First a very safe "oldie." Business A had a $50,000 bank balance on December 30. On December 31, the treasurer wrote and mailed

$30,000 worth of checks, all of which were outstanding at the close of the year's business. The problem is how to show the situation in the December 31 balance sheet. Consulting our lawyer we find that the *legal fact* is that the $30,000 of outstanding checks are a liability. Consulting our business sense we find the fact that we have spent the money and that our effective bank balance is $20,000. Here we have two sets of "facts," either of which can be clearly portrayed, competing for recognition. Accountants generally select the practical business fact and ignore the legal fact. Why? This decision is made on the basis of the major premise outlined above. Obvious management impact is the guidance the accounts might give the treasurer when he begins to write checks on the next business day. The legal fact that the $30,000 of outstanding checks are a liability, that we could stop payment on them and proceed to write another $50,000 worth of checks, is of very little significance to management under anything like normal conditions.

Second illustration, somewhat parallel to the above: On December 15, the business "buys" a $100,000 piece of real estate on a land contract paying $5,000 down and agreeing to pay $5,000 per month. The payment of the twentieth $5,000 amount will pass the title. Again as in the case of the outstanding checks we have two truths, two sets of facts. Legally, on December 31 the business has a $5,000 asset which can be properly described as "Equity in Real Estate under Land Contract Purchase Plan." Practically, the management may conceive of the situation as a $100,000 purchase with a $95,000 liability. Again the accountant must decide which of the competing facts to show in the accounts and statements. Probably the majority of accountants would elect to follow the legal interpretation in this case instead of the practical businessman's viewpoint. Are we inconsistent in following the law in this case and ignoring it in the case of the outstanding checks? The clear portrayal premise is of no help here. The selection must be made on the basis of the probable impact on management.

Certain readers may disagree with the decision made in either of these illustrations. Our purpose here is not to argue for either decision but to point out the logical basis on which it must have been made. It should be noted that while we may be fully agreed on the major premise of desirable management impact there is still room for disagreement at the level of the particular or minor premise facts. Someone may really feel that the businessman would be better off, management-wise, to see the outstanding checks as liabilities. One could also make a good case to the effect that many businessmen would be better off to recognize the $95,000 of unpaid installments of the land contract as a liability. These differences are *minor premise* differences; the major premise used is still the management impact principle.

A third illustration demonstrating the use of the management impact premise lies in the valuation of inventory. Here we have a variety of possible accounting answers: Cost, market, cost or market—whichever is lower. Cost may mean several different things: FIFO cost, LIFO cost, moving average cost, actual cost of specific units on hand. Each of these is subject to different interpretations when we get down to actual detailed application. Does cost include freight in or not? What about costs of unpacking? Do we add interest for necessary time of aging for certain goods? What rate? It should be quite apparent that the problem is the choosing of one method from many possibilities all of which are real, or true, and more or less objectively determinable. Over the years the writings on inventory valuation have been voluminous and the debates heated. Sometimes these debates proceed more by vivid declamation than by logic, but where the reasoning can be discovered it will be found to be the application of the management impact premise. A special difficulty involved in the inventory valuation debate is the fact that many writers seem to be trying to establish a general rule which will fit all situations whereas the conditions of inventory vary enormously from business to business. Thus it is quite likely that one of the competing methods would be right for one business while a quite different method might be right for another. This statement does not involve an inconsistency, but merely recognizes that the minor premise conditions differ from case to case. The choice of methods must be made separately for each set of conditions. In every case the thinking should be in terms of what is really best for the particular management concerned. The old lower-of-cost-or-market valuation of inventory has persisted in small business, especially in retailing. We might be satisfied to state that this is justified "because it is conservative" but it would be better to dig behind this statement to point out what the management impact would be under the various patterns of market price behavior which might be encountered. Prices might be stable, steadily rising, steadily falling, erratic, suddenly up near end of year, suddenly down near end of year, and so forth. The inventory value shown in the accounts and statements might influence management in dividend (or withdrawals) policy, in price setting, in the rate of purchases, and in still other ways. Insofar as we can see through to these management impacts, in small retailing at least, the cost-or-market method comes out very well indeed. The experience of thousands of small businessmen, especially retailers, has kept this method the favorite without the benefit of theorizing, but it is quite certain that the most careful analysis as suggested here would have come out with the same result. The complete analysis would involve hundreds of tryouts of the management impact under all probable conditions of price movement, inventory expansion–contraction, homogeneous or heterogeneous inventory, cash stringency or plushness, easy or tough competition, and so forth. If under a considerable majority of such assumed conditions management of the small retail establishment would seem to be best advised under the cost-or-market inventory we would consider the method proven to be the best for such circumstances.

In contrast to the retailers, manufacturers have quite generally adopted the LIFO method of inventory valuation. It would indeed be an interesting exercise to try to visualize all the varying conditions of volume movement, price movement, competitive circumstances, and so forth for a "typical" manufacturer and to try to follow the impact of LIFO and other methods through to the recognition of management impacts. Way too complicated to attempt? Yet that is exactly what has been going on in the thousands of arguments which have swung the manufacturers to this method. An occasional argument that LIFO represents the "real facts" turns out to be not an argument under the clear portrayal premise but an assertion that LIFO represents the facts that management really needs.

A fascinating situation to work with in the light of our two major premises would be that of the wholesaler of some large unit items—say four or five models of color TVs. These are bought by dozens and sold by ones, twos, or threes. At time of purchase the actual cost of each item is marked on the crate. The purchase price varies considerably, generally upward to be realistic during the accounting period, and the quantity on hand at the end of the period covers at least two or three shipments of each model. How is the ending inventory to be priced?

Under our first major premise, clear portrayal of the actual observable facts, it might seem obvious that we should accept the actual cost as marked on each crate of the units on hand at the end of the period. Note, however, that this basis would give varying results in inventory valuation depending upon the physical movement of the crates out of the warehouse. If the warehouseman is under management orders to move the crates on a strict first-in–first-out pattern we would get a very different inventory value (and net profit!) than if the warehouseman followed a probably more convenient last-in–first-out physical pattern. Imagine also the results we would get if in some month, with a wide variation in purchase costs, the warehouseman was "sore" at the manager. He knows that the manager is on a month-to-month bonus plan based on the month's profits, so he (warehouseman) calmly picks all the highest cost crates for the month's issues. The month-end inventory comprises all the low-cost crates; the profit depends on the pique of the warehouseman!

Since the units in each model are identical regardless of date of receipt, is there any sense in pricing the end inventory differently for each pattern of physical movement? Is there a conflict of major premises in this situation? Or does it again require a very careful observation of and selection among several sets of "facts," among which the marked-on prices because of their high visibility are merely one potentially misleading element? If we visualize the company controller arguing this situation with the company's CPAs, it will certainly make the point that the parties had better be clear as to the possible major premise involved.

One more swing into a controversial topic will be useful. For twenty-five years or more the full costers and the variable costers have been arguing. Does this problem fall under the clear portrayal premise? An honest look at the observable facts in any manufacturing industry reveals a highly intricate pattern of costs running more or less in a continuum from fully variable to fully fixed. Both the full costers and the variable costers see this picture fully. Thus, by and large, their differences are not differences in their observations but rather a difference in the desirable emphasis in presentation. Both controversialists know that there are variable costs and that there are full costs.

Though the proponents are not usually careful to state their major premises, a critical reading of their arguments reveals that the real difference between them is simply whether management will be better served to concentrate its attention on variable or on full costs, and this is clearly a management-impact argument. A simple decision one way or the other in this argument is just not in the cards. For certain purposes, management *must* use direct costs and for other purposes and under other conditions management *must* use full costs. Under any one particular set of circumstances, we get a bona fide argument, clearly under the management impact principle between the two methods. This is good and as it should be, but no one seeing the whole picture can reasonably espouse either direct or variable costing with the complete abandonment of the other.

Summary: Major premises I and II

Summarizing to this point: Reasoned thinking in the accounting area goes back to either of two fundamental considerations, the clear portrayal of objective observation or the desirable impact on management. In general, the first of these is the characteristic method of accounting theory, though it would be an oversimplification to *limit* accounting theory to this method. The second is the method of management accounting. We cannot find any serious line of demarcation between these two methods in the actual practice of accounting. Certainly, the financial accountants understand and practice management accounting. Certainly, also, the management accountants are generally good theorists, in our sense of recognizing the usefulness of clear portrayal. The initial difference is the greater tendency of the management accountants to reason under the management impact premise. As their confrontation with business goes from simple illustrative situations, such as we have been using, to the greater complications of today's actual business problems they deal with vastly more intricate observations. Their problem is still the selection of what to present and what to leave out and how to marshal the selected elements. The controlling consideration remains the management impact now in a different magnitude but not of a different kind.

The first phase of the increased magnitude of the management problem takes the form of expanded, more detailed objective observations. These are of two kinds: finer breakdowns of events within the business itself and the expanding recognition of outside events which bear upon the business process. A clear illustration of the greater detail from within the business is the breakdown of the total wages cost in manufacturing into the various aspects of wages—the growing number of fringe benefits occasioned by luxuriating union wage contracts on the one hand, and on the other hand the greater detail with regard to the utilization of the labor, that is the array of variances from budget and standard. 'This is a far cry from the simple wages expense of early accounting. Similarly, the old original sales expense becomes in modern business a great range of distribution costs broken down by product, area, salesman and customer. Any question as to the pattern of these breakdowns either as to "kind" category or as to degree of detail is rather obviously not a question of clear portrayal but of management usefulness or impact.

The greater use of detailed information from outside the business is exemplified in even fairly simple situations by the use of outside standards of trade associations in analytical juxtaposition with the results in "our own" business. This trend extends with enormous variations through the use of census data, market research, and possibly even to commercial spying on competitors. At the fringes of this trend there will in practice be conflict between the responsibility of the controller and that of various operating units—but that is nothing new.

Manipulation: A new element?

Closely related to the acquisition and presentation of greater depth and detail of information is the growing *manipulation* of material information from all sources. This would be considered by many to be the heart of the new management accounting. We can consider the development of percentage analyses from the underlying dollar figures as the earliest type of manipulation. Graphic presentation, break-even point analysis, and so forth, all the way to operations research and other refined mathematical techniques are all a part of this effort, by manipulation, to bring out ever more significant relationships buried in the basic data.

The practitioner might well be impatient with the pedagog's insistence that all this advanced technique is governed by a simple principle characterized as the management impact premise. But there can be little doubt that two practitioners in dispute as to method will, in a final showdown, each claim that his method will be more useful to the line man or to the front office. An appreciation that this is the final test, practically as well as theoretically, should be useful in avoiding a lot of less than conclusive sparring.

New emphasis on teamwork

A peculiarity of today's management accounting situation is the fact that many forefront management efforts, especially operations research, are in the hands of teams of men from radically different backgrounds. Engineers, mathematicians, psychologists, public relations experts, and others are being brought together to produce results which are often superior to those which would be likely to result from any single group. Such different backgrounds are almost certain to carry into the joint effort varying generalizations, principles, objectives, which in initial phases of the cooperation will seem to clash, or at least to be inconsistent. In more technical terms, these various parties are using different major premises each of which was quite satisfactory in its own area, but which may seem untenable to team members from other areas. Full intelligent discussion will take the form of challenging the stated premises and necessitate a search for premises fully acceptable to all team members. Here again, as within the special area of accounting, the final, broadly acceptable major premise will be found, however stated, to be the usefulness to management. An appreciation of this rationale should speed up the process of zeroing in on the true issues and most useful solutions. There will always be plenty of disagreement at the level of the minor premises—that is the actual, specific, effect of various proposed courses of action, but it will help enormously if the parties in the discussion recognize this pattern of logic and the fact that there is agreement on the statement of the overall objective.

The third major premise

The two major premises presented above should function as a means of keeping the entire map of the forest before the controller lest the thousands of individual trees on which he must work obscure his larger view. Possibly the total balance of his thinking can be somewhat further assured by outlining a third possible major premise which gives the view from the mountaintop.

There can be little doubt that just as clear portrayal is good for management, we can similarly feel quite certain that effective management decisions within business generally redound to the benefit of society as a whole. We propose here that there may be situations in which neither clear portrayal nor management impact seems to be at stake but in which we can trace a broad social impact of the accounting decision. The controller may find this level of thinking useful in making specific decisions, but he may find it even more pertinent when he finds himself trying to understand, or indeed when he finds himself actually responsible for the broader profession-wide decision-making processes. Such occasions would arise when important matters of accounting policy are being considered by formal legal authorities or by informal but prestigious groups, that is by the courts, the SEC, or other government regulatory bodies, or by the Financial Accounting Standards Board.

At this level we should expect that the controlling major consideration would be the true, long time consequences not only to the particular businesses making the decisions but also to the entire social melange of which these businesses are a significant part. We can formalize the major premise as follows: *As between two (or more) methods, that method should prevail whose long-time results would be most desirable for society as a whole.* Again, the premise could be worded in many different ways, but the core idea is clear and can be most readily characterized as *the social impact major premise.*

In arguments under this premise there will again be plenty of room for differences at the minor premise level just as there was under our two earlier major premises. Society is a conglomerate of groups whose interests are diverse; the long run benefits may clash with the short run; benefit to one person or group may mean detriment to others. The total net, social benefit will be difficult to appraise in particular instances, but there can be little quarrel with the principle that insofar as we can see our way clear we would prefer to maximize the benefit.

While simpler and more immediate social consequences may sometimes be involved, the principal social impact of possible alternatives will usually be the effect on *resource allocation.* Wise resource allocation is the most basic problem of political economy just as it is the most basic problem of the individual business unit. Accountants have very generally followed what they deemed to be the commonly accepted accounting principles. There is a strong effort today to drive them to even more conformity. This will make the social impact of their decisions, for good or bad, even more pronounced than heretofore.

Illustration from lumber industry

A fairly simple example from the past may be useful at this point. The lumber industry in its years of heyday largely ignored depletion of its major natural resource as a cost in its product costing. We suggest that the radical alternative of depletion of *value* might have been the right method. We regard the industry-wide failure to recognize depletion as a cost of production as error. This error brought the apparent costs of lumber to the producer to an unwise low figure on the books of the intramarginal as well as on the books of the marginal producer. Under these conditions it is unlikely that the selling prices of lumber were a proper guide for the allocation of the nation's lumber resources. The cities grew fast and flimsily of wood as more substantial materials were neglected, and for the last fifty years society has been paying for the error in terms of lumber scarcity and high prices.

There may be those who will argue that the more rapid growth of the cities, spurred by the too cheap lumber, was a highly desirable development and well worth the later inconvenience of scarcity and high prices. Note that this turn of the argument is disagreement at the *minor* premise level and still utilizes the "desirable social impact" as its major premise.

Illustration from pollution control

Today's greatly heightened interest in the pollution control problem presents an interesting demonstration of the social impact of accounting—again the *failure* of proper accounting in the past. In today's emotion-laden atmosphere, the popular argument is trying to fix the blame. Far more important would be the calm effort to understand what has actually happened as a basis for deciding what can be done to rectify past damage and to prevent still worse future damage. Our own interest is still more abstruse—to visualize the impact which accounting thought and procedures may have had on bringing the industry and pollution problem to its present state.

Good accounting assumes that the cost of product should include increments representing the consumption of all asset values necessary to that production. Naive accounting of the past often failed to recognize even depreciation of plant. Failure to recognize depletion of natural resources was even more common. We have come a long way from such simple error. In general all assets (i.e., *owned resources*) concerned in production are acknowledged costs, though we still have considerable differences as to the timing or scheduling of such costs into production. We now begin to realize that production in many industries has involved the use (consumption, destruction) of *assets not owned* but in the public realm, such as the air about us and the water in the streams and lakes to which there is no personal title. Since they were not owned, since they had no cost, and since their consumption would have been extremely difficult to measure in our dollar terms, accountants simply ignored them as of no consequence to product cost.

Occasionally, the despoiling of the nonowned asset—fresh air for instance—carried with it the destruction by emitted fumes of nearby private property such as an orchard or other crops. In this instance, a successful suit for damages by the neighbor sustaining the loss did bring the cost into the picture in a dollar measurable amount and, if not into product cost, at least on to the books as a recognizable quantity. If as a result of such a damage suit, corrective measures were taken to prevent future damage, the cost of such measures would clearly become a cost of production.

The larger problem of the damage to the general atmosphere (or streams or lakes) is parallel. The difference is that the "damage suit" is not a simple court case but the trial of public opinion and of resulting legislation, possibly backed up by private or class damage suits, injunction procedures and so forth. The required measures for future control will involve substantial capital outlay and subsequent operating charges which will naturally flow into product costs and most certainly be reflected in the sales prices of the product.

What the total significance or cost of past damage to the public realm has been by the joint negligence of industries, municipalities and John Q. Public himself will never be adequately measured. (Lake Erie is forever ruined! Who can measure that?) How this responsibility should be shared by the contributors to the damage is likewise an extremely difficult problem. The more radical thinking tries to blame industry for the bulk of the damage and hopes to collect from industry the bulk of the cost of corrective measures. This rationale has the ring of plausibility but it overlooks some essential accounting and economic facts—which bring us right back to our topic of accounting and major premise number three—the social impact.

If we can visualize the Financial Accounting Standards Board or its predecessors of 50 or 75 years ago considering the air pollution problem we should be able to throw some real light on the present situation. The far-seeing members of the board might have argued that there was a cost involved in the use of the atmosphere for the riddance of waste products—particles and noxious gases. If capital expenditures and current costs had been incurred to prevent such damage, there is no question that current production costs would have included the proper proportion thereof, and if this had been done on an industry-wide basis these costs would have been reflected in the sales prices and thus passed on to the public as any other legitimate costs.

If, however, no technological measures had been available for the time being to *prevent* that damage, it would certainly have been good accounting to accrue the liability toward the inevitable day of reckoning when industry would be expected to make good the damage. It is acknowledged that the dollar measurement involved would have been extremely difficult. Now here is the delicate point: The debit resulting from the accrual of the liability (if recognized on an industry-wide basis) should have then been treated as a production cost and again passed on to the public in the sales price.

Under our social impact major premise, this would have been good accounting in terms of its probable impact. For one thing, it would have been a strong incentive to install control devices as soon as they became available. Second, charging the cost to the customer through the sale price is the only real way by which the cost could be covered. If in specific cases the cost would have been too high to recover through sales, those units of industry would have been abandoned (or never started) and we would have had rather different but more intelligent allocation of resources.

What we have argued above is simply that early recognition of the true cost of pollution through the accounts would have had desirable social consequences.

Incidentally, the rationale of the above argument becomes the soundest possible defense for today's industry against the assessment of enormous amounts to make good past damage. Since the cost was *not* recognized, it was *not* included in product costs and *not* passed on to the public through sales prices. Put another way: The sales prices of products were too low since they did not cover these costs. The public benefited temporarily (for 50 or 75 years) by those low prices. The erroneous accounting and erroneous pricing did *not* result in excessive profits. The corporations are *not* presently possessed of enormous funds really belonging to the public which can now be used to clean up the mess as some popular thinking seems to imply.

This argument obviously involves the delicate relationships of costs and selling prices which economists so dearly love to belabor. "Marginal costs determine selling prices." True! But the cost of pollution—the use, the abuse, the destruction of natural resources was simply not recognized by anyone as a cost, and it simply did not get into the accountants', the economists', or the businessmen's conscious processes, marginal or otherwise. The economist will still be right, of course,—in the *very long run!* Eventually, after our one hundred year error lag, the real facts will impose themselves, become conscious facts, and finally enter the cost and price picture. Our point simply is that, over the years, accounting which recognized the social impact might have produced far more timely desirable social results.

Conglomerate reporting and the social impact major premise

One of the "hottest" topics of the day is the form and degree of detail which shall be expected or required in the reporting of profit segments of conglomerates. The arguments for more detail as put forward by the analysts in behalf of investors are all based on an obvious application of the social impact major premise, i.e., the business-investment community *needs* this information for the intelligent allocation of capital resources.

The individual investor can see the problem in terms of his own management requirements, which coincide closely with the social impact point of view.

Managements of corporations have tended to resist the pressure for revealing more segment detail for fear of revealing confidential matters with resulting competitive handicap. This may be a well founded fear in some instances. The apparent *opposition* of results under the social impact and management impact major premises here involved is fascinating to consider. We do not presume to make a substantive evaluation of the point. We merely suggest that the argument will proceed most effectively if the logical framework is clearly appreciated.

Further exploration of the possible conflict of major premises will certainly be important and interesting. It is unlikely, however, that such conflicts will be more than temporary or apparent. As in the above case, a thorough analysis of the apparent conflict will become a guide as to a really satisfactory solution of an initially difficult problem. For instance the solution of the conglomerate reporting problem will not be a simple "tell all" or "hide all," but rather a patient consideration of exactly what information can and must be revealed in what pattern, what degree of detail, and in what timing. Efforts to date have been handicapped by the attempt to formulate a too-simple rule which could be made the basis of regulation to fit all cases. The conditions from company to company are just too diverse for such simple rule-writing. What we are saying is that conglomerates *are conglomerates*. Their very nature is diversity and nothing less than a very patient examination of each case on its merits with both company and investor points of view fully considered will give viable answers.

CONTROLLERSHIP IN TERMS OF GENERAL PURPOSES

In preceding sections of this chapter, we have approached the concept of controllership by examining some simple, direct attempts at definition; we have approached it in terms of the logic of its thinking processes. In this section we preview another approach—that of the general purposes which controllership serves in the fully mature business. Some of these have already been touched on incidentally to the making of other points. The fully exhaustive treatment will require attention throughout the rest of this book.

The purposes of controllership break into two groups of which the first are traditional, routine, accepted. The second group are three purposes which are commonly thought of as constituting the controller's distinctive contribution to management. The following outline will serve to show the overall pattern.

Outline of controllership purposes
1. Traditional
   a) Routine services
   b) Property control
   c) Statements and reports
      —for management and owners
      —for outside parties—legal reporting
2. Management information service
   a) Control
   b) Venture measurement
   c) Forensics

The routine traditional services include accounting for accounts receivable and payable, payroll, and cash and property records which may be thought of as bookkeeping in even the sizeable firm. Fortunately, most of this work has been so routinized and mechanized that it goes smoothly most of the time. While the controller is technically responsible for these subfunctions he seldom need be aware of them. However, when something goes wrong or when circumstances change so that the routine needs to be amended, the controller's responsibility is again activated. Even these problems are usually handled by the systems section of the controller's department, with the controller himself called upon for only the more significant and crucial decisions.

The importance of changing circumstances has been dramatically demonstrated in the last ten years, the change being the advent of practical electronic data processing. Insofar as electronic techniques have taken over routine record keeping and have now settled back into a new routine phase we are back again in bookkeeping, with magnetic spots taking the place of holes in cards or pencil marks. The routine is delegated, but responsibility for the existence of an adequate routine remains the controller's.

The work of the systems section is the active force in guaranteeing that the enormous routine requirements are being accomplished by the most modern and economic methods. The internal audit section polices the operations to insure that the techniques laid down by systems are being faithfully followed. Together these two sections are the controller's method of carrying his responsibility for routine service.

Item 1 *b*) of the outline puts property control, or safeguarding the assets, as a purpose of the controller. This provision needs a more cautious statement. Actually safeguarding the company's assets is every executive's and every employee's responsibility. Specifically, the safeguarding of assets is also a function of the company's security section possibly including a company police force and fire department. We have already pointed out that the treasurer's function is custodianship of assets. Why then this provision for property control as a purpose of the controller?

A necessary part of the process of safeguarding assets comprises documents and records designed and operated and handled in certain ways without which the assets could not be protected. This becomes the function of the controller in cooperation with the treasurer, the legal department, the security section and others. The point can be more accurately stated as follows: Property control, safeguarding the assets, is the controller's function *insofar as* this can be accomplished through the design of information documents and the laying down of rules for handling them.

Our very useful phrase "insofar as" lays down the working rule for the necessary interfunctional cooperation for property control. It will be found useful in setting up proper routines initially and also in fixing the responsibility for negligence where it occurs. Property control will be treated much more fully in Chapter 2.

Item 1 *c*) "Statements and reports" is a very broad topic as anyone acquainted with accounting knows, and it will be fully treated in later chapters. Here it is necessary to view it as one of the purposes the controller must serve. We should be aware at this point that some of the statements are repetitive, formal, and conformable period after period. Especially so are the statements going to the owners, the stockholders. These are the typical reports of financial accounting custodianship, balance sheet, income statement, and funds statement. Even in these more or less routine statements, however, there are still some real problems. The Financial Accounting Standards Board and its predecessor committees and boards have long been making determined efforts to improve the content and form, to eliminate certain practices which have been potentially misleading, and to improve the probability of correct understanding by the typical reader.

Statements to operating management are tremendously varied because they are normally tailored to the nature and circumstances of individual businesses. The point to be made here is that the information produced by the controller gets across to management only through the routine or special statements. The matter of planning the entire statement system is a worthy task in itself over and above its specific information content. Statements to owners and management merge over into the statements to outside parties issued under various degrees of necessity and pressure including finally the reports specifically required by law. This topic, considered worthy of an entire subsequent chapter, is discussed in Chapter 3.

Part 2 of the outline, the controller's responsibility for measures directly related to management use, will be taken up specifically in Chapter 4. The nature of these topics is such, however, that full implementation of Part 2 is in a real sense the subject matter of the rest of this book.

2 THE PROPERTY CONTROL FUNCTION

The general problem

The protection of the property of a business in the sense of care and economy in use is the concern and responsibility of every employee. Every line executive is certainly charged with the proper and efficient use of the equipment in his organization unit, and to this end he is expected to exercise direct control over his immediate employees. This responsibility ranges all the way from the technical direction of employees operating and caring for highly complicated scientific equipment down to the requirement of proper economy in the use of standard common supplies of all kinds. A thorough appreciation of this principle and a consistently high morale in its application can have a very substantial effect on the ultimate well-being of a business. Contrast such a situation with one in which the business is riddled from top to bottom with virtual disregard for economy. Such a condition might well cause heavier cumulative losses than overt fraud.

The protection of property in this sense is everyone's duty, but the controller cannot let the matter rest with the placid assumption that the duty will be recognized and honored simply as a moral obligation. Analysis of the situation based simply upon observation of the facts of business life brings out the fact that the responsibility of individuals for property can be strongly reinforced by the marshaling of information regarding that property. This fact puts the responsibility for the protection of property—insofar as it can be accomplished through information, that is through record design and operation—clearly into the hands of the controller. This important subfunction of constrollership was commented on in general in Chapter 1. Its considerable development—implementation—is the purpose of this chapter.

A second aspect of property control is the protection of the assets of the business from actual theft or any form of fraudulent misappropriation. Here again there should be a widespread sense of responsibility

29

among employees, especially those in executive positions. With respect to the prevention of actual physical theft of property, measures within the business may range from no specific provision at all to a highly developed system of security regulations and an organized company police. The controller normally has no direct responsibility for the physical aspects of the protective system; nevertheless, certain activities of the security force must be tied in closely with the organization of paperwork routines which are the controller's responsibility.

The validity and utility of this statement can be illustrated by referring to the problem of setting up the plant police or guard system. Visualize an extensive plant with five or ten gates through the high mesh fence. At each gate is stationed a 24-hour guard. Who shall be in control of these guards? Who shall prescribe their selection and training? Who shall lay down the rules regarding their inspection of homeward-bound employees' lunch boxes? Who shall regulate their possibly delicate relations to the public police? Who shall decide what arms, if any, they are to carry? Are these matters properly the responsibility of the controller? They are certainly a part of the problem of protection of property, but they are not the controller's problems.

On the other hand, full protection of property also requires that truck movements carrying product or equipment out of those gates should be properly authorized. Ideally, the gate guard should examine the invoice or other "property move document" authorizing the carrying-out of the gates of every truck load moved. What shall be the form of this document? Shall it be in duplicate, with one copy to be picked up by the guard? Who shall be authorized to approve apparently exceptional or emergency cases where no document is available? These questions obviously tie in closely with the entire paper-work pattern over which the controller must have jurisdiction, and under our rationale they would therefore be controller responsibility.

There are many other places in the organization of a complicated business where functions overlap or clash. The problem of organizing responsibility for and control over the plant guards may be accepted as a fair illustration of the careful thinking necessary in such instances.

We can pretty well summarize the plant-guard organization problem by the statement "*Insofar as* the plant guards must inspect, understand, and act on the basis of paper authorizations for property movement they will be under the functional responsibility of the controller."

There is no doubt that there will be occasional conflict between the personnel manager or plant superintendent who has general line control over the plant guards and the controller with regard to the details of the guards' responsibilities. The actual extent of our delicate "insofar as" concept can easily be misunderstood and misinterpreted in its application to the plant guards or anywhere else. These controversies will be settled preferably by amicable discussion between the immediate supervisors involved or, if that fails, by an up-the-line appeal to whatever general authority can make the settlement. This possible conflict of authority is no different from the hundreds of others in any complicated business organization structure. Every functional department or unit is in potential conflict with many others, no matter how well the organization is set up. Intelligent cooperation is the hallmark of a properly run business, and the frank recognition of areas of conflict of interest is an imperative element in the achievement of effective long-run cooperation.

When we move from the theft of physical properties to the area of fraud and misappropriation, we are clearly in the area for which the controller must assume principal responsibility. Cash and related assets which can be, and in the normal conduct of business are, converted into cash are extremely attractive properties which present a much higher degree of temptation to theft than do most physical assets. In their very nature, these assets are represented by, handled and manipulated through, paper recordkeeping. If they are to be protected, the steps to be taken are intimately connected with the record-keeping system, and that is clearly the controller's province.

The controller's techniques of property control

In itself the double-entry bookkeeping system affords an ingenious though often unappreciated tool to aid in the protection of property. The principle of debit and credit equality requires that a record be made of the origin and disposition of all property owned by the business. The observance of this principle does not in itself guarantee adequate protection for the business assets, but it does compel continuing attention to the problem by requiring the accountant to write into the record some kind of answer to the question: "Where did the property of the business come from, and what became of it?" In writing this answer the accountant also writes the history of the business. This history is the basic record used by the controller in fulfilling his legal-reporting and management functions, and it is also the framework upon which he builds the property-protection system.

The preceding paragraph indicates the basic terrain—the debit and credit accounting system—upon which the controller must construct his "routines, methods, and measures" to accomplish the purpose of property protection. In the final analysis, many of the actual devices used are so intimately related to the practical details of specific routines that it is difficult to visualize or to discuss them in the abstract. The remainder of this chapter will address itself to that task—to lay out the principles in a sufficiently clear and emphatic manner that the reader may have at least a running start when faced with the actuality of a specific installation.

Basic principles of property control

The practical way to come to grips with the problem before us is to visualize any business as two great flows: on the one hand, the great stream of revenues and related receipts and, on the other, the great stream of expense and related expenditures. At the confluence of these streams is the great pool of assets of which the officers and employees of the corporation are the custodians. The controller must be able to assure himself that all monies and other values related to the inflowing stream that the business *should have received* have indeed been received and that all such receipts have been properly recorded and thereby acknowledged by the responsible custodian within the business. With respect to the outflowing stream, he must assure himself that all monies and other values shown as parted with were indeed expended *for the purposes indicated* and that those purposes were the legitimate purposes of the business. Thus, in addition to protecting the assets owned (in the pool), there is the more difficult double responsibility with respect to each of the two transaction streams: first, the accurate record of what did occur and, second, the basic propriety of the occurrence itself.

Visualizing the business in this way should be a considerable help in learning to recognize the risks which, to be protected against, must be clearly understood. The controller must be able, though it may be distasteful to him, to assume the viewpoint of the would-be fraudulent employee, in order to discover the possibilities of improper conversion of the company's assets. Only by so being aware of these opportunities can he adequately protect the properties of the firm. By setting up safeguards against all probable risks, he removes temptation and "keeps the employees honest." This is a homely phrase, but the thought behind it, far from being a cliché, is very close to the basic idea of internal control, and we can hardly find a better or more succinct statement of purpose to use as a guide.

Practical rules of property control

Long experience has built up a few simple rules which are generally recognized as fundamental in the accomplishment of the general purpose of property protection against the temptations and risks of the practical conditions of business. These rules may be stated as follows:

1.   Set up the accounts so that the personal responsibility of individuals as custodians of the various assets of the company can be identified.

2.   Provide physical facilities and safeguards to prevent movement of property without the knowledge of the responsible custodians.

3.   Issue clear and definite instructions specifying on what authority each custodian can release property for which he is responsible—e.g., who can approve the payment of vendors' invoices, the issuing of raw

materials from the stockroom, the issuing of a "credit memo" canceling a customer's obligation, and so forth.

4. Organize the accounting routine so that, as far as possible, the work of every employee who handles property is subject to automatic check by some other employee or through records kept by some other employee.

5. Test the operation of these automatic checks from time to time.

6. Verify the existence of the various classes of property by physical examination and count at periodic intervals.

Internal control and internal audit

Close examination of the foregoing rules brings out the fact that the first four concern the setting-up of the "routines, methods, and measures," i.e., the building of the system aimed at forestalling fraud. These measures collectively comprise internal control or internal check. Rules 5 and 6 concern the subsequent supervision of the system to see that it is continuing to work as intended. These two rules are simply the realistic recognition of the fact that no system, no matter how well designed, will continue for long to work without supervision. The employees who must do the actual work have the normal human failings of laziness and mental density, on the one hand, and, on the other, a desire to "improve" the operation by ill-advised changes and short cuts, to say nothing about deviations carefully thought out to cover shortages and fraud. Actually, the word "policing," used in its proper sense, accurately describes the intent of rules 5 and 6, but, since this word has unpopular connotations, it is not commonly used. Under most circumstances the term "supervision" will be adequate as long as we are entirely clear as to the purpose necessarily served.

The term "internal audit" in general describes the operation of rules 5 and 6, though, of course, in practice the constructive phase of rules 1 through 4 and the supervision phase of rules 5 and 6 are very closely related. On the one hand, the systems man who lays out the original pattern of routines must have in mind the feasibility of subsequent policing, supervision, or auditing of those routines. Subsequently, in auditing the operation of the system, the professional internal auditor should be constantly on the alert for shortcomings in the system. These may be imperfections in the original design of the internal control devices, or they may be caused by the growth and change of the business which can easily cause even the best original devices to be outgrown or outmoded.

The original thinking on internal control systems dates back to manual methods of accounting. Adjustments necessitated by mechanical methods, "standard" posting machines, punched card methods, and computers have generally strengthened control. Routine accuracy is far greater with machine methods, and with imagination the automatic checks envisioned in rule 4 become more effective than checks under straight manual methods.

With the availability of electronic processing the trend away from human error or intentional distortion can be still further extended. This will require full understanding by the planners and programmers of the nature of possible frauds. The new risk will be that in the pressure to set up the routines to handle normal situations the planners may forget to provide for the intentional deviations constituting fraud. To the extent that electronic devices can extend farther back toward the capture of the original transaction than previous methods, electronics will provide a more complete safeguard. The petty crook will be driven out of the "books" and back to the raw transaction before it is picked up electronically. The really glamorous fraud would of course be that in which the programmer sets steps into the program itself to accomplish the fraud. Against such an eventuality, we can only argue that the controller himself, or perhaps the public accountant in his behalf, must have sufficiently detailed knowledge of electronic data processing for an occasional critical inspection of the programs in use. Interference with the normal operation of a program through the console constitutes another possible hazard. Fuller development of audit in the EDP environment is necessarily left to later chapters in this book.

The second area of fraud which will remain in the electronics era lies in those low volume areas which are simply not worth programming and which therefore will continue to be handled by manual methods. A manufacturing company's relatively infrequent transactions in its investment portfolio, its annual bonus payments to a dozen top executives, possibly a few hundred equipment acquisitions, a few bank loans and repayments, and scrap disposals are illustrations of typically low volume situations which will need protection through traditional means for a long time to come.

Organizing for internal control and audit

If the property-protection function is a subfunction of controllership, it follows logically that the organization unit responsible for this work should fall within the controller's department and that the persons involved must report to the controller. This point is emphasized here because the alternative argument is sometimes made that the internal auditor should report directly to the president, the treasurer, or possibly a vice president in order to be independent of the controller. The implication of this argument is that the internal auditor ought to be in such an independent position that he could check on and report on the controller's activities. This seems to the authors to be an unsound argument. In each of the functional areas final confidence must rest on some individual. The controller should be the final respository of confidence for his function.

There is of course the outside possibility that even the top administration of the business could be negligent or fraudulent. The answer to this possibility lies in the use of independent outside auditors making an annual audit and presumably possessing such a high level of ability and integrity that wrongdoing would be detected and reported, no matter at how high a level. Consideration of the problem at this level suggests the advisability of having the outside auditors technically employed by and reporting to the board of directors rather than to the controller, treasurer, president, or any other officer. The ultimate safeguard would follow English practice and have the outside auditors hired by and reporting to the stockholders at their annual meeting. The fact that most American corporations have not adopted these ultimate safeguard arrangements is evidence that, by and large, they have complete confidence in their officers. Placing the internal auditor under the controller is a part of this picture of confidence in the higher echelons of management.

In making the outside audit, every certified public accountant is trained to inquire closely into the adequacy of the company's internal control and audit system. As part of this inquiry he will ascertain the organizational position of the internal auditor. He will thus be aware of the theoretical risk involved in having the company auditor report to the controller, and he will be on guard against the remote possibility that this relationship may cover up any impropriety.

Perhaps it is almost obvious, but it should be stated "for the record," that the applications of internal control devices are generally much easier in fairly large businesses. The separation of duties which comes naturally in the effort to gain the efficiencies of large-scale operation in the office can be availed of to secure the automatic check of each employee's work by the work of some other employee. In smaller businesses, greater areas of responsibility must be left in the hands of each individual, and this makes the implementation of rule 4 much more difficult. The smaller business also finds the expenditure of much time or money on internal auditing disproportionately costly. The best counterbalancing safeguard is the close personal touch on the part of the controller. The bonding of every employee who is in a position of trust, which is desirable under almost all circumstances, should be especially insisted upon where it is impossible to maintain satisfactory internal controls.

Summarizing the problem—applications

We have argued that the protection of property is a proper subfunction of controllership, in that it is a normal extension of the controller's basic responsibility for the marshaling of information. In this chapter we have moved closer to the practical aspects of the problem by encouraging the reader to visualize business in terms of its two great streams of receipts and disbursements in order to recognize more clearly the possibilities of fraud. We have stated the rules of property control which constitute the practical guide lines for setting up the system and for supervising its operation. In the remainder of this chapter we shall demonstrate or test out these principles and the practical rules by applying them to a few of the leading circumstances met in typical business. These illustrations are by no means exhaustive; they will cover but a small segment of the business area, but it is hoped that they will demonstrate the manner in which, with an active imagination, the principles and rules may be applied in any practical set of circumstances.

The protection of cash

The protection of cash is almost as broad a topic as the entire problem of internal control. Actual cash on hand—that is, cash in the bank or currency in the cash register—is not particularly difficult to protect. Here the problem is custodianship, and practical rules 1 (setting up the accounts to tell us where the cash is—in whose charge) and 2 (furnishing the custodian with the proper physical facilities) give us the clues as to proper procedure.

It is when the cash is involved in the two flows, in and out, that it becomes a real problem. In the flow stages, cash and the records which facilitate its flow, are in the hands of a great many employees who cannot possibly be kept under immediate surveillance. At this point, too, as the flow of cash becomes involved with the flow of other assets, the problem of protection cannot be neatly compartmentized but must be studied against the whole complex of business and office routines. At various points, practical internal check takes the form of checking the handling and records of noncash assets against the related cash transactions. Generally, noncash assets are less attractive than cash, so that the real risk in protecting such other assets is at the point of their conversion into cash.

The discussion of the protection of assets cannot follow the simple sequence of the assets as listed in the balance sheet. In the business process, merchandise becomes accounts receivable or cash, and accounts receivable becomes notes receivable, cash, or bad debts, and in this process of shifting there are several danger spots. While it is cash which is usually wanted by the dishonest employee, his way of getting it may involve the manipulation of transactions and records at stages preceding the actual appearance of cash.

For instance, a common fraud in small business is to fail to post a sale on account to the customer's account and then to steal the cash received from the customer when he pays. The original failure to post to the customer's account paves the way for the theft of incoming cash. If the debit had gotten into the account, a credit would have had to be made when the cash was received, in order to prevent the sending out of a statement showing the amount as still due. A variation of this fraud would be to steal the incoming cash, fail to post the credit, and destroy the statement at time of mailing, to prevent the customer's becoming alerted to the shortage in his account. Eventually, the account balance could be gotten rid of by writing it off as a bad debt or as a sales return, or by shifting it to some other customer's account which was about to be written off as uncollectible. We can approach this series of related frauds from the angle of protecting merchandise, protecting accounts receivable, protecting cash, or preventing a bad-debts writeoff fraud. If the business is big enough to set up an office routine such that the employee who handles cash receipts has nothing to do with posting to the customers' accounts or cannot get his hands on the statements to be mailed to customers, these frauds become impossible for the single individual to perpetrate. If, in addition, we have airtight rules to the effect that accounts may be written off as bad only on the written authority of the credit manager and that credits for returned sales are made only on the written authority of a sales-adjustment department, we prevent a couple more variations of the fraud. The last two sentences are obviously applications of practical rules 4 and 3, respectively.

To commit these frauds in the more highly mechanized routines of larger businesses requires parallel adaptation. Though it would usually necessitate the collaboration of two or more employees, and thus become more difficult, this fact should not lull the controller into a false sense of security. Unfortunately the crooks are still with us. While it may seem severe to dig up the old adage "set a crook to catch a crook," it is true that the internal auditor must learn to think like a crook in order to set up the techniques of prevention.

Fraud in cash sales

Probably the commonest of all frauds in business and the one hardest to provide against is the "knocking-down" of cash sales by clerks or cashiers in retail businesses. When the drugstore customer buys a pack of cigarettes, hands the clerk the correct amount of cash, and rushes to catch his bus, it is very easy for the clerk to pocket the cash, without any record and without ringing the amount up on the cash register. This fraud might be caught by an eagle-eyed proprietor or supervisor who happen to be watching from a distance. However, the making of three or four small cash sales in a rush period with change carried in the clerk's hand or side pocket is considered perfectly normal in some stores and is countenanced to save the time of walking to and from the cash register between sales. The clerk is expected to ring up the sales at the first momentary pause in the rush of business or when he has to go to the cash register for change for a larger bill. Such a routine is very efficient in the sense of time economy if the business can rely on the honesty of the employee, but it is obviously wide open to temptation and should seldom, if ever, be allowed. The obvious answer is more cash registers at strategic points in the store and a mandatory ringing up of each sale separately. It should be noted that none of our four practical rules helps us much to prevent this simplest of all frauds, unless we stretch rule 3 regarding the authority for the release of assets to include exactly what must be done with the property (cash) received in exchange for the merchandise which has been released.

The modern cash register itself is designed to go as far as possible in preventing the cash-sale fraud. The pop-up index tabs are intended to help enforce the proper ringing up of cash through customer-audit of the transaction. If the customer strolls to the cash register with the clerk and glances at the visible pop-up index, there is considerable pressure on the clerk to ring up the correct amount of the sale. Once the amount has been correctly punched in, the register contains the locked-in total so that the clerk can be held responsible at the end of the day for the cash which has been received. Where several clerks operate out of one cash register, separate cash drawers may be provided, and the machine programmed to produce separate totals against which the cash received is checked at the end of the day. To prevent the clerks' getting into each other's cash drawers, the register can be equipped to ring bells of different tones for each drawer as it is opened. Very clearly, these provisions are an illustration of practical rule 2: "To provide physical facilities and safeguards to prevent movement of property without the knowledge of responsible custodians."

As has been implied in the foregoing remarks, there is no sure method of protecting the retail business against the occasional small cash-sale fraud or against the closely related frauds in which the clerk sells to his friends at less than the regular price or in which he gives his friends a long measure of goods which are sold in bulk. The simple theft of small items of merchandise by the clerk for his own use is in the same general category. It is a known fact, however, that these frauds and thefts often do not remain small but tend to grow and to explode into epidemic proportions. When this happens, it, of course, becomes serious in terms of its effect on gross margin and on net profits. Often the effect on the gross margin of the business as a whole or on the gross margin of some particularly affected department is the first real evidence that management has of such fraud. In most businesses it is possible to watch the percentage of the gross margin to sales quite closely department by department or by product lines. It will vary up or down as the effect of the known factors of changing prices or changing pricing policy. When the actually *attained* gross margin for a month or other period deviates significantly from the *expected* percentage, there should always be a serious effort to account for the difference. If the *attained* margin is less than the expected margin and if it cannot, on restudy, be specifically accounted for, there is reason for a suspicion of fraud of the simple knocking-down of cash sales or merchandise-theft variety. What is to be done depends on specific conditions. Possibly a tightening of the rules or close personal supervision will correct the situation, or it may be necessary to go so far as to call in a detective agency to apprehend the dishonest employees. Detectives specializing in this type of service commonly under the name of "shopping services" are wise in the ways of the crooks and skilled in the methods of detection and conviction.

Petty-cash procedure

Many firms find it necessary to permit small payments to be made in currency at one or more places in the organization, though it is a well recognized fact that it is much more difficult to protect such payments than payments by check. Each such currency payment center may best be protected by the device known as an imprest cash (or petty-cash) fund. One individual is made responsible for each fund. He is given initially a certain sum in currency ($50, or $100, $500, etc.), and he is thereafter held for the possession of money in that amount or vouchers indicating the legitimate purposes for which the money has been expended.

The vouchers may comprise small invoices, C.O.D. slips, specific receipts on the company's own forms, or still other evidences of the propriety of the disbursement. They should be in ink so that the amounts cannot be subsequently raised. Bonding companies are quite insistent on this apparently small point. As his fund approaches exhaustion, the petty cashier presents his paid vouchers to the company cashier, who reimburses him for the exact amount of the vouchers with a company check made out to the petty cashier. The petty cashier cashes this check and thus brings his fund again to its full initial amount. Under our practical rule 2 it is clear that the petty cashier must be provided with a locked drawer in which to keep his cash and vouchers. The account carried in the ledger showing "Petty Cashier—J. D. Wilson—$500" and similar accounts for any other petty cashiers in the firm are a simple illustration of practical rule 1. The regulations regarding the form of the petty-cash vouchers (in ink, signed, dated, amount not to exceed $10, etc.) are clearly an application of rule 3; and the fact that the petty-cash vouchers will be examined by the general cashier prior to reimbursement is clearly an application of practical rule 4.

It is very important that incoming cash receipts be *not* used for the making of payments of any kind. Many small businesses still do use receipts of cash in this way, and in so doing they lay themselves open to a whole range of frauds which are much harder to prevent or to discover under these conditions. Probably one of the most useful dictates in the whole armory of control is that "all cash receipts must be deposited in toto each day, and all cash disbursements must be made by check." The second half of this statement is, of course, amended by what has been said of the technique of petty-cash expenditures under an imprest system—which, in an effective sense, does run them through the check disbursement system. The first half of the statement clearly forbids the use of incoming cash for payments.

Securities

Some securities are highly negotiable—actually payable to bearer—others are so protected by registration of both principal and interest that the danger of theft is greatly decreased. It must also be realized that, while some securities are very temporarily held, others are purchased and held more or less permanently. The precautions that must be thrown about them therefore vary greatly.

The ledger accounts recording ownership of securities should, by their account numbers and titles, identify the conditions under which the securities are held (temporary, long-term, pension fund, sinking fund, and so forth), and also directly or indirectly they should identify the person (or persons) responsible as custodian. This is simply the application of the first rule. Application of the second rule, the provision of the necessary physical facilities, may take various forms. At its simplest, the custodian will have physical possession of the key to the strongbox containing the securities, or the securities may be held by a trust company under contract, naming the responsible employee who is authorized to have access, to withdraw, to pledge, and so forth. Rule 3 should also be specifically respected with regard to securities owned. The minutes of the directors should fix unmistakably the placing of the authority for the release of securities owned, for it is at the point of release (which usually means conversion into cash) that the chief danger of fraud lies. This written responsibility should be broad enough to cover the handling of proxies, the exercise or disposition of stock rights, disposition of fractional share rights involved in stock dividends received, and so forth, for here again, when there is action on the securities rather than static custodianship, there is opportunity for fraud.

Most commonly the responsibility for securities will reside in the company's treasurer, and in this case his specific rights and duties with regard thereto may be fixed by a charter provision which sets up the treasuryship in the first place. Whenever any deviation from this standard pattern becomes necessary, as, for instance, where some of the treasurer's responsibilities are delegated to one or more cashiers, such delegation should be formally provided for, at least by a recorded resolution of the executive committee, if not by a minute of the directors meeting.

In these various provisions the controller has a double interest. His first interest is to see that the provisions are set up as an integral part of the whole system of property protection. Second, the controller is interested, now through his internal auditor, to see that all these security provisions are followed out to the letter. Employees, pressed for time, are often tempted to take short cuts. Initially, these may be innocent attempts to bypass what may be regarded as unnecessarily strict rules, but once such short-cutting begins to "get by," the opportunities that are opened may easily lead to not-so-innocent practices and outright fraud.

Inventories

Inventory control, in the broad sense of inventory management, will be deferred to a subsequent chapter of this book. We are here concerned with the protection of inventory as part of the controller's overall responsibility for the protection of property. Sometimes the words "inventory control" refer to the still narrower concept "inventory accounting." These two last concepts—protection of inventory and accounting for inventory—are quite closely related, and this relationship is the heart of our present problem. Basically we are trying to answer the question: What can the controller do through the use of the accounts and related routines to guarantee the proper protection of inventories?

Theoretically, the problem should be fairly simple, for the applicability of the four practical rules of control is very clear in respect to inventory—in fact, they seem to have been phrased with the inventory situation in mind. Under rule 1, accounts can be set up to reflect the personal responsibility of individuals as custodians—every physically separate classification of inventory can be represented by a separate account in the ledger. Under rule 2, inventory can be physically locked up with the key in the custodian's hands. Release of inventory from the storeroom on written requisition only (rule 3) is a well-understood and widely practiced technique. And even the fourth rule—setting up the work of employees to check each other—can be implemented fairly easily for inventory. The difficulty in inventory control is the purely practical one that to tie all items of inventory up as tightly as the full use of the four rules indicate would hamstring the business. Whether we are talking about merchandise in a trading business, raw materials, goods in process, or finished goods in a manufacturing business or even the inventory of supplies in a service business, the really airtight control of inventories would be a serious handicap to the free flow of the business process. On the other hand, we certainly cannot relax all controls without risking very serious shortages. This dilemma calls for very nice balancing of the needs and disadvantages of any particular situation, and it is very easy for the controller to go too far in either direction in setting up the routines.

The principal clue to the solution of this dilemma lies in the recognition of the fact that the commodities making up any inventory vary widely as to physical characteristics, value, and convertibility. The inventory items sand, iron ore, and limestone are heavy, bulky, low in unit value, and would be almost impossible for a thief to convert into cash if he could haul them away. For these and other items of similar characteristics the four rules can be considerably relaxed. At the other extreme we can visualize the raw materials gold and platinum in the inventory of a jewelry manufacturer, as well as the completed items in his finished-goods inventory, gold watches and diamond rings in the inventory of a retail jeweler, and so forth. These items have the physical characteristic of easy portability, high unit value, and considerable convertibility. Such items must be closely guarded by all reasonable means. Between these extremes lie hundreds of thousands of other inventory items with every conceivable combination of characteristics and therefore with a very wide range of risk of misappropriation.

There are also other factors which bear on the problem. The physical conditions under which the property must be handled by employees is important. Within a plant which has its every entry and exist guarded, we may allow very free handling of most inventory items, which we could not allow on an outdoor construction job where the employee is free to leave in any direction at any time.

The type of employees and their traditional morale may be very significant factors, though these factors must be *very* carefully considered, as it is well known that it is the *trusted* employee who gets away with the big frauds.

After considering all these factors, the controller must finally weigh the *degree* to which the protective devices which he would like to install would slow down, or otherwise handicap, the business process. There will always be a certain area within which it is proper to take a calculated risk in order to facilitate the conduct of business. The men's clothing retailer cannot keep his supply of neckties under lock and key, nor can the auto manufacturer ask the man on the assembly line to sign for every part which comes into his possession for a moment before he hangs it on the frame passing his station.

Generally, where it appears to the controller that a retreat from strict accounting control of inventories is indicated, he should discuss the point frankly and openly with the line authorities in charge of the area in question. If the protection of the property cannot be by internal control techniques, the responsibility must pass to the line executives, superintendents, and foremen, and it should be made unmistakably clear to them that they do have this responsibility. The great danger is that the responsibility may be lost sight of somewhere between parties, each assuming the other to be responsible and no one actually being on guard.

The controller must be careful not to accept too readily the arguments of the factory manager and the line persons under him that materials must be loosely handled to facilitate the factory processes. It is well known that the typical shop man likes to have a large pile of his raw material, or the parts on which he is to work, ready at hand. He does not feel comfortable under close scheduling of materials movements and argues that experience has shown him the need of a big backlog. Actual examination shows much of this type of management to be simply a bad habit which can be changed, with proper planning and education, to a safer and more economical pattern of operations.

If at all possible, these matters should be settled between the controller's staff and the line authorities on an entirely congenial and cooperative basis. However, the channels are always open through the appeal to higher organization to get an authoritative ruling. The controller must not hesitate to use such force if he feels himself entirely in the right on crucial issues. In a very real sense we are back at the point with which we opened this chapter, that the protection of the property of a business is the responsibility of every employee. We are now, however, in a much better position to see how the overall responsibility can and must be divided between the controller and the line.

A closer look at practical rule 4

"Organize the accounting routine so that, as far as possible, the work of every employee who handles property is subject to automatic check by some other employee, or through records kept by some other employee." This is one of those fine statements which are easy to make, easy to understand in a shallow manner, and easy to parrot back on a written examination. However, this statement is not easy to implement in actual practice. Even our own reference to the use of rule 4 in preceding sections of this chapter will be found to be somewhat general and vague. A closer look at this rule and at the possibilities of its application is really necessary.

Most significant transactions, upon very careful examination, will be found to consist of three elements: (1) initiation or authorization; (2) custody of the asset or assets involved; (3) recording. A clear case is the purchase on account of a new type of raw materials. The transaction is initiated by the production planning department for materials not previously stocked. In this case we can visualize the formal authorization as a separate act when the purchasing agent sends out the order. Upon receipt of the goods, their custody initially is in the hands of the receiving department. After proper checking, custody goes to the raw-materials storeroom. Recording is by several persons in the accounting department—the voucher clerk, the stores clerk, the general bookkeeper. This transaction is clearly split among several persons along the lines of its three basic elements, and when it is thus organized it is quite safe from fraud—the several persons concerned automatically check one another.

Earlier in this chapter we mentioned the retail cash sale as a very difficult transaction to protect. Note that in this transaction the three elements are present, but in the very nature of the case they are all in the hands of a single individual, the salesclerk. Acting for the store, he authorizes the transfer of the merchandise to the customer; he has custody of the merchandise and of the cash received; he is the one who makes the record by punching the cash register. Many department stores try to break the cash sale into its elements by requiring the clerk, after writing a sales ticket, to present the ticket, the merchandise, and the cash to a wrapping and cashiering station where the goods are compared with the sales ticket for description, quantity, and price, wrapped, and handed to the customer. This opportunity to inspect the goods while momentarily in the wrapper's hands is an important aspect of custody. The change is made, and the cash received is rung up by the wrapper-cashier. Since the clerk knows that he is being checked, he is quite likely to "return the compliment" by checking the amount rung up by the cashier, so we may be quite certain that the record—the cash-register punch—is correctly made. Such a breaking down of the cash-sales transaction to its functional elements would be a great deterrent to the cash-sales fraud.

The issuance of office supplies from storage on the requisition signed by the office manager can be visualized as broken into its three elements. Signing of the requisition is the formal authorization; custody of the supplies shifts from the stores keeper to the office boy to the stenographer who is to use them; the record is the requisition itself (or a copy thereof) which carries to the bookkeeper the description of the supplies, the account to be charged as written in by the office manager, and the cost as entered by the storekeeper.

A favorite fraud in small business is the sale of scrap materials (metals, waste paper, and so forth) by the janitor, night watchman, or yard man to the junk dealer for cash. In some cases the transaction is simply not reported; in others it is reported but for a lesser amount than the actual sale. Here again the risk lies in the fact that all three elements of the transaction are in the hands of one employee—he authorizes the transfer, he has custody, and he makes (or neglects to make) the record or misstates it to his own advantage. In larger businesses the scrap is sold to the large salvage company (no longer a junk dealer) on the basis of open bidding for all the scrap to be produced for a calendar quarter or a whole year. This constitutes the authorization of the transfer. To get out of the gate, the salvage truck must show a weighing ticket from the company's own scales. A receipted copy of the weighing ticket goes to the bookkeeping department. Thus the custody and the record are provided for. The check comes through the mail to the cashier and is run through the cash receipts journal to be posted to miscellaneous accounts receivable. Fraud becomes much more difficult.

Obviously, the breaking of a transaction into its elements as described in these instances is far easier for the large concern than for the small. For some transactions it is much harder to accomplish than for others. In any case—this is the principle which this discussion aims to establish—a careful study of the three elements of the transaction is often the clue to the possible way of splitting a transaction for which, at first, there seemed no feasible solution. It should also be clear that the real purpose of internal control is better served by the splitting of the transaction along its basic element lines than by any other forced division of the total task.

Control by dollar value

Beyond the point at which responsibility for items of inventory can be enforced through use of the specific devices here provided, the controller can still exercise substantial control in terms of total dollar values. What this means can be illustrated in terms of office supplies. In a large organization such supplies may be tightly accounted for as they are being purchased, received, and put into the supplies storerooms. Thus far, the supplies are under complete accounting control, and it should be possible to prove a physical inventory against the book record in whatever degree of detail has been carried. After the point of issuance from stores, in reams, dozens, and boxfuls, no further detail responsibility is feasible, but the total value of the supplies issued to the office is charged to the account Office Expense–Supplies. The monthly totals of this account and the cumulative totals to date for the year now become the somewhat cruder, but still effective, control. These figures can be watched by comparison with previous similar periods and by comparison with budgeted amounts—adjusted for volume of activity in the best systems. Such scrutiny will not catch the petty pilferage of a few pencils or typewriter ribbons, but it will show up any really significant leakage or pronounced uneconomies in the use of supplies. This type of dollar control plus the direct, watchful supervision of the office manager or suboffice heads are often the best that can be provided.

Similarly in the manufacturing process, detailed, quantitative custodianship record keeping ceases for most raw materials at the point of requisition and issue from the storeroom. In this case the cost accounting for material on a dollar basis, often checked very closely against material-usage standards, takes over the control. The occasional theft of an attractive piece of raw material by an employee will not be caught, but any systematic stealing of disposable quantities or any significant losses through breakage or waste will most certainly show up in the variance analysis.

The devices we are now talking about are not usually thought about in connection with the controller's function of property protection but rather as a normal part of his major service to management and in the control of the productive process as such. At this point the two purposes merge and both may be admirably served by the same techniques.

Internal audit—The follow-up

Internal audit, policing, supervision, or follow-up, whatever we are pleased to call it, is an essential part of the whole scheme of property protection. In the small business the controller may have to assume direct responsibility. In larger businesses a staff of a dozen or more is not uncommon.

The first of the two rules of internal audit was stated near the beginning of this chapter, as follows: "Test the operation of these automatic checks from time to time." This task requires considerable imagination and experience. It may take the form of observation of on-going procedures; the examination of documents for initials, check marks, and other evidences of proper prior procedure. In manual systems, it involves the comparing of source documents with entries made in journals; test-checking of postings from journals or original media to general and subsidiary ledgers; and other routine comparisons which may be thought of as following the "audit trail." In more mechanized systems, the internal auditor tests independently run totals of original transaction documents against the totals of the formal machine runs. Specific EDP programs can be tested by trial runs of simulated original transactions with known results. Unless skill and imagination are behind these devices, however, they may become just so much wasted motion. Not only must the internal auditor know accounting, auditing, and office procedures, but he must know just how the checks and balances of the particular system are supposed to work. He must be a keen enough student of human nature to visualize where the system is likely to break down and what the early evidences of the breakdown would be. He must understand the changing business scene to visualize the impact of substantive changes upon the processing of the resultant data, so that he can give immediate warning if the methods which were adequate must be changed to meet the changing conditions. Ideally, he should have enough imagination and understanding to check the business processes not only against the mechanical rules of internal control but, through them, to fundamental considerations of operational efficiency and managerial policy.

The second phase of internal audit and the final (sixth) rule of the whole property-protection process is the periodic verification, by physical examination and count, of the existence of the various classes of property called for by the accounts.

The most obvious application of this rule is the checking of the raw-materials inventory of a manufacturing concern, where we typically find a perpetual inventory record for each kind of material. While the pricing of inventories is a complicated and controversial matter, there is no mystery about the keeping of a running balance of quantities. It is this quantity balance that the internal auditor seeks to verify by physical count of the actual material on hand. The usual plan is to do this job at odd times throughout the year, checking individual sections of the inventory so that the entire inventory may be covered about once every year or two. Good judgment often indicates that certain segments of the inventory which are particularly subject to theft should be checked oftener, perhaps two or three times per year, while other segments may be allowed to go unchecked for rather long periods. Certain items in almost every inventory are critical in the sense that a shortage therein would be especially serious. These items also merit frequent and exact checking.

A physical inventory of work in process is next to impossible in many industries. Here the auditor must be satisfied with checking the accounting record for propriety of procedures and for reasonableness of balances by comparisons with prior periods, budgets, and production schedules. In some special cases in which specific raw materials bulk large in the manufacturing process, the quantities in process are shown in the accounts and can be checked by physical examination.

In some industries, finished goods are delivered to customers immediately upon completion and thus do not present an item for inventory. Other industries stock their finished product and control it on the books in perpetual inventory accounts. These should be checked by physical examination and count.

Any inventory shortage or overage should be exhaustively investigated. Whether the explanation is error, unaccounted waste, or fraud, it is the business of the internal auditor to find the facts.

The total job of physical checking of inventories can often be divided with the outside auditors by prearrangement. While the CPA will wish his own men to do enough checking to assure him of the general reliability of the records, he will usually be glad to rely on the company auditor's check for substantial sections of the inventory, thus freeing this own time and energy for more productive tasks.

Wholesale merchandise inventories are generally under running inventory control and present about the same problems as the raw-materials inventories of manufacturing firms.

Retail merchandise inventories in small establishments are seldom under accounting control, so there is nothing to "check against." Since there usually is neither internal auditor nor controller in such businesses, the function of internal audit, if it is to be exercised at all, must be the responsibility of the accountant or someone in general management capable of visualizing the problem. In this case the task narrows down to precautions to assure the proper taking of the periodic physical inventory, followed by a really critical study of the gross margins which result when those inventories are used in the statements. This is the same point that was discussed in connection with the discovery of the cash sales "knockdown" frauds.

In larger retail firms, especially in department stores, merchandise inventories are usually under the control of some form of the retail method. In effect, the retail method is a perpetual inventory of merchandise by department totals rather than by individual items and carried in terms of retail prices (with some fine technical adjustments) rather than at cost. This book retail inventory can be checked against physical inventories priced as marked for sale on a department-by-department basis. Discrepancies may indicate error in the calculation of the book figures, error in the routine reporting of sales, the shortage of theft by outsiders (shoplifting), or fraud by employees.

The "inventory" of other assets

The principle of making an independent physical check of the existence of property can and should be extended to assets other than the usual inventories of materials. For such assets as cash and accounts receivable, the essential emphasis shifts from physical inspection to a critical review of technical evidence. There may be minor amounts of currency to be counted, but the principle task in "inventorying" the cash is the reconciliation of the bank accounts. In assuming this task, the internal auditor is proving that the relations with the bank are working as they are supposed to work and that the balance or balances shown by the accounts are actually in existence at the bank.

Doing the same job for accounts receivable usually requires verification of the balances by confirmation from the customers. Whether the auditor should make a 100 percent confirmation as of a certain date, a test percentage confirmation of an alphabetical segment, or of a scientifically selected random sample, or work his confirmation in conjunction with the outside auditor—these are details which will vary from business to business and possibly from year to year. In any case the internal auditor is working under the instruction of rule 6—the periodic verification by physical inventory and count—though the interpretation of the words "physical inventory and count" is being adjusted to the needs of the situation.

Rule 6 is extended also to the fixed plant properties. On the border between current supplies and fixed-asset plant lie the small tools. In many manufacturing plants the small tools are an exceptionally attractive item to the employees and therefore a very real headache to plant managers and auditors. The physical inventory of small tools can establish the probable extent of employee thefts but in itself does not prevent them. Prevention is in the very difficult area of employee morale. One case may be cited to illustrate how difficult control of small tools may become. A certain company, which incidentally is supposed to be noted for its high employee morale, took the precaution of etching the corporate name into the steel of every worthwhile small tool. Yet it has become a standing joke that a great number of employees show off their well-equipped basement workshops with no attempt to conceal the etched-in source of most of the tools. The authors of this text do not pretend to know the solution to this problem.

Moving into the area of heavier machine tools, the possibility of fraud takes on a very different aspect. Conceivably, foremen, night watchmen, and truckers working together could steal pretty substantial items of equipment. Such fraud has been perpetrated, and the inventory of equipment by the internal auditor might uncover the first evidence of it if it should occur. At this point the search for fraud is likely to be merely incidental; the auditor is more likely to be interested in such other matters as whether or not the proper records are being kept with respect to maintenance of equipment, depreciation of equipment, and the proper differentiation of capital and expense charges. These are matters of established management policy which can be badly neglected or distorted if not policed once in awhile. These considerations go beyond the simple concept of protection of property and merge into the area of the use of accounting information for management. This also is the proper province of the internal auditor, and if he can combine his checking for such matters with his efforts to inventory the plant assets, it is all to the good.

The final extension of the job of physical count and verification of properties would seem to be to the buildings and land. Does the internal auditor actually have any duties with respect to these long-lived assets? This is not a task requiring many current repetitions, but on occasion, as, for instance, when a controller takes a new job with a corporation, he would certainly want to assure himself of the fact that the accounts for all plant assets were a correct portrayal of the plant assets actually in existence and owned by the company. This inquiry should probably extend into the question of proper legal description and title. Under the impetus of defense contracting, there have been many complicated joint arrangements between the government and industry in which large quantities of equipment and even buildings are owned by the federal government but operated by industry. Under these conditions the necessity of checking into the correctness of plant accounting is evident. The widespread use of sale and lease-back arrangements, in which the lessee undertakes responsibility for maintenance, insurance, and taxes on plant buildings for long periods of time, further confuses the picture. In effect, the lessee has all the perquisites of ownership other than the actual title. There will be plenty of instances in the coming years in which management will be in danger of confusion as to which of its plants are owned and which leased unless the accounts and underlying legal records are very clear on this point.

It should be apparent after our detailed discussion of property protection and internal control that the actualities of the matter are more difficult to grapple with than the general principles involved. To get our feet firmly on the ground the best approach is graphic portrayal which we attempt in the next few pages.

Graphic portrayal of internal control relationships

To accomplish even an approximation to mastery of internal control, the student should overlook no possibilities. The graphic presentation of a typical internal control system is a technique with great possibilities. The flow-charting of an actual system is probably the most effective way to learn how it really works. Its advantages and its flaws can be made to show up far more clearly by this method than by any amount of word description. If changes are to be made in the flow routine, there is no better way to try them out in advance than against the background of the flow chart of present methods. If new employees are to be shown their place in the pattern of operations, there is no better way than by showing the position they are to occupy in a good flow chart. As outside auditors come into a business, especially in a first audit, an accurate flow chart of the company's procedures is the best possible aid to getting them sufficiently acquainted with the business to begin their work promptly and effectively.

The accompanying flow chart (Figure 2–1) for a hypothetical Park Equipment Company illustrates the major forms and procedures for its order-writing-shipping-billing-accounts receivable process. The business is large enough to have considerable division of office function and pretty fair internal check. It uses "standard" billing and posting machines (i.e., not punched-card equipment or electronic data processing). The chart is laid out in areas corresponding to the principal office divisions involved and is intended to be largely self-explanatory for a reader who has a reasonable familiarity with practical business requirements.

We can study this chart at three levels or for three purposes. Our

Figure 2-1
PARK EQUIPMENT COMPANY
Flow Chart of Order-Billing-Shipping-Accounts Receivable Procedures

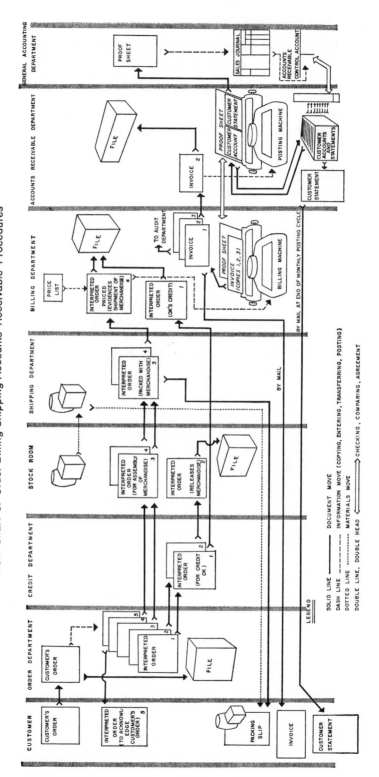

first interest in it should be for its substantive representation, that is, we should see it as an illustration of some of the principles and practices with which we have been concerned in this chapter. Second, we should examine closely the techniques of flow-charting used, that is, the manner of communicating graphically the facts of the situation. Third, we may get some very good training in the thinking behind internal control if we try to discover what some of the conditions within the business must have been to call for the particular procedures shown in the effort to protect the properties of the company. The next few paragraphs comprise a guided tour of the chart with these three approaches in mind.

The substance of the chart

The action of the chart begins with the receipt of an order from the customer. The order department "interprets" this order in the sense of putting it into the company's own numbering and description of items if these are not already clearly stated in the customer's order. This stage may also be used to eliminate items which are known to be permanently or temporarily out of stock. In some cases it may be necessary to communicate with the customer if his requirements are not clearly indicated. The customer's order thus analyzed is written up in five copies as an "interpreted order." Copy number 5 bears such printing that it may be sent to the customer as an acknowledgment of his order.

Copies 1 and 2 are sent to the credit department for approval of the customer's credit standing and assurance that the amount ordered does not obviously exceed his credit limit. If the decision on the limit were at all close, the credit department would have to get a special "pricing-out" from the billing department before giving final approval. This special procedure is not shown on the chart, and we may assume that this special situation is rarely encountered, otherwise the routine shown would be quite defective. This is an illustration of the all-important principle that the special circumstances of the business must be carefully considered in laying out its procedures and that such special factors and procedures can be studied effectively in terms of the flow chart.

Copies 3 and 4 of the interpreted order are sent to the stockroom. The credit department stamps its OK on copies 1 and 2 and sends copy 1 to the billing department. Copy 2 goes to the stockroom as notice to the stockman that he is to assemble the merchandise and release it to the shipping department. Copy 2 is filed in the stockroom as evidence of the proper release of the goods. Copies 3 and 4 accompany the merchandise to the shipping department, where copy 3 is used as a packing slip to go with the merchandise to the customer. Copy 4, which has been initialed by the shipping department, goes to the billing department to become the basis for invoicing and accounting.

The billing department checks copy 4 against copy 1, on which the credit has been OK'd, which it has held as its follow-up copy. The billing department then prices copy 4 and, from this priced copy, makes up the formal invoice in triplicate on any standard billing machine. Copies 1 and 4 are filed together in the billing department. The invoice forms enter the machine as continuous fanfold forms and are separated along the perforations for subsequent processing. The billing machine also produces a proof tape which develops the total of each day's billings to be used as a prelist check against the day's posting run in the accounts receivable department.

We are now following the completed invoices. Copy 1 of the invoice is sent by mail to the customer. Copy 3 goes to the auditing department (not shown), where it becomes the internal auditor's basic document for any checking which he considers necessary. Copy 2 goes to the accounts receivable department as the source of the charge to the customer's account.

A great many variations can be worked out for the accounts receivable posting. The method shown in the chart assumes that the account and monthly statement are filed together, are pulled from the file, inserted in the machine, posted, and refiled each time an invoice for the customer comes through. Some machines produce original impressions on both the account and the statement (as shown by their positioning in the machine in the chart), while others use carbon or N.C.R. paper to duplicate the posting through the statement to the account. In every case the posting machine produces a proof tape or sheet which shows all the postings of each day's run and produces a total for the day, which is checked, as shown, against the total of the day's billings and is the source of the day's entry into the sales journal or register. At the end of the month (or at some cycle mailing date if preferred) an adding-machine total is run of all the customers' balances and checked against the balance in the accounts receivable control account in the general ledger in the general accounting department, the control account having received its debit posting from the sales journal.

The techniques of the chart

The flow-chart techniques to be noted in the Park Equipment Company chart are the representation of areas (departments); the fact that the flow is generally from left to right and downward, which corresponds to normal reading habits; the aids to comprehension in the pictographs of merchandise, the files, and the accounting machines; and most important, if closely observed, the specialization of lines denoting the several kinds of relationships. The most common line used is the simple solid line indicating the movements of the documents physically between departments or from one stage or operation to another within a department. The line of small dashes denotes the transfer of information from one document to another. This occurred between the original customer's order and the interpreted order, between the price list and copy 4 of the interpreted order, between copy 4 and the invoice as produced by the billing machine, between copy 2 of the invoice and the statement and account as produced on the posting machine, between the proof sheet and sales journal, and between the sales journal and the accounts receivable control account. This relationship is especially important because it must be realized that each of these information transfers is not automatic but goes through the eyes-brain-fingers chain of the human operator, with all the opportunity for error which that sequence involves.

The comparison or checking operations, shown as double-line, double-headed "arrows," is also subject to the same hazard of reliance on human eyes and brain. This relationship is the very heart of internal check, as its obvious purpose is to catch the simple errors. The chart which is drawn to show these hazards clearly may often indicate the possibility of amended procedures which can eliminate some of them and thus make the entire process safer and usually more economical. The use of multiple carbon copies is itself a great safeguard—imagine the additional risk of error if five copies of the interpreted order were to be made manually! One of the great advantages of moving from procedures like those illustrated into punched-card techniques and on into electronic data processing is that these more advanced techniques substitute highly reliable mechanical devices for the extremely error-prone human machine. Parallel charts of the order writing-billing-accounts receivable procedure by manual, "standard" machine, punched card, and electronic processes indicate clearly the steps in which the human element is utilized. Each would show strikingly the successive elimination of this weakest link in the chain.

It is noteworthy that, while it has been possible in the past to organize manual and simple machine office procedures and to indoctrinate the employees who are to run them without the use of flow charts, the situation is quite different when the much more intricate procedures of punched cards and electronics are being planned. The art of flow-charting has been developed to a high degree of sophistication as an adjunct to the installation of such systems. It is also interesting to note that again and again it is realized that a substantial part of the savings involved is due to the more critical examination of basic procedures forced by studies preparatory to the installation of new methods. The point is driven home by the experience of one firm (possibly apocryphal) which claimed to have made substantial savings by the installation of punched-card methods—and then a few years later made additional savings by discarding punched-card methods and going back to standard machine methods. Similar savings by going into computer methods—and then back out of computer methods—may very well be encountered in the modern day!

The flow chart and varying conditions

We have already touched upon some of the differences in actual situations which would condition the procedures to be used. We have mentioned the possible problem of pricing out and credit OK. A related point is the fact that the acknowledgment of the customer's order was sent to him before his credit had been checked. This might prove embarrassing if shipment were then withheld for credit reasons. If this is likely to happen more than very rarely, it might be better to hold up the acknowledgment of the order until after the credit is OK'd. Alternatively, the printed wording on the acknowledgment might be such as to indicate that it is made conditional upon the credit check.

The chart as shown implies that the filing of copy 2 of the interpreted order under control of the stockroom is sufficient protection to the stockman under his responsibility as a custodian. If the merchandise involved is particularly valuable and subject to conversion, we might want to provide the stockman with an actual receipt signed by the shipping department representative who received the merchandise. On the other hand, even the precaution of filing copy 2 in the stockroom is dispensed with in many cases where the nature of the merchandise is such that airtight custodianship responsibility is no problem.

If the order received from the customer is usually very simple—say for a single item or for highly standardized merchandise—so that there is very little chance of misunderstanding, the order writing as a separate operation can be dispensed with and the invoice prepared directly from the customer's order in a sufficient number of copies to facilitate the whole subsequent office routine.

The mechanics of posting to detailed account receivable and statement depend on the frequency of transactions with each customer. Obviously, ten transactions a month would constitute a very different problem than that of one or two a year. It depends somewhat on whether the customer usually pays each invoice as a unit or whether he allows invoices to accumulate for a month and settles by a monthly check. This itself goes back to the nature of cash-discount terms offered, if any, and to the degree of tightness with which they are enforced.

In some businesses it is considered necessary to have available the complete history of the customer account relationship in a compact form such as the usual account receivable gives. In other cases, each sale to a customer is considered an entirely separate deal, with no need to refer to any preceding sales. Under this assumption, we may save a lot of work by simply filing a copy of the invoice as the charge to the customer's account, thus cutting out all the work and error possibility of the accounts receivable posting operation.

Obviously, these differences in situation and resulting office procedures would show up very differently in the flow chart. The point to be made here is that the attempt to draw an accurate flow chart is itself one of the best ways of discovering the possibilities of more efficient procedures.

The initial determination of what the procedures are to be and their revision as conditions change are an inherent responsibility of the controller, but in practice, of course, they will usually be delegated to a systems accountant who is a real specialist in such matters. When any change is contemplated, the primary consideration must be the facilitation of the actual business process. The consideration of economy of effort must be secondary, as must also be the ease of internal-check and internal-audit protection. Where conflict between these various purposes develops, the controller must exercise his best judgment in obtaining a balance between facility, economy, and safety.

Summary

This chapter has dealt with the very important subfunction of controllership—the control and protection of property. To fit the many devices aimed at this purpose most effectively together, it is necessary to visualize property as two great streams flowing into and out of the pool of property ownership. Most of the danger of loss and the most difficult problems of protection occur during the in-and-out flows, though protection of property during its varying lengths of stay in the pool must also be provided. Experience has indicated six practical rules or devices which together accomplish the protective function. Four of these, collectively known as "internal check" or "internal control," are devices which may be built into the business routine to give a very large measure of automatic protection. The other two, known generally as "internal audit," are procedures which police the internal check measures to see that they continue to operate as intended and that the actual property values are in fact as called for by the records.

The application of the rules was illustrated by reference to some of the typical situations encountered in business. Rule 4 was especially examined, and it was pointed out that its effective application relied upon an intimate study of the anatomy of the transaction. The relationship of special internal control devices to normal accounting procedures was discussed as control by dollar value. Particular aspects of the inventory problem were presented as they applied both to merchandise and to other assets.

The final section of the chapter encouraged the reader to view the problem of internal control in graphic terms. The illustrative flow chart served to tie down some of the points made earlier in the chapter and to introduce the reader to the problems and capacities of the graphic techniques in this area.

The subject of internal control deserves far more attention than can be given it in one chapter in any book. It is felt that this minimum treatment is a fair outline of the subject and should be a good beginning for the more intense study that every controller should give to the subject.

3 THE FUNCTION OF LEGAL REPORTING

DETERMINING THE PRINCIPLES OF ACCOUNTING

All writings, textbooks, periodicals, random brochures in the field of accounting try to make their impact on what is right in the area, that is, to determine the principles of accounting. The doers, the thinkers, and the talkers in the field who may never bother to write, constantly make their contributions under the implacable pressures of experience. Within the public accounting profession, in-house training has a large impact. Teachers contribute their bits and pieces. Complicating and threatening this free and undirected process there has been added within the last 50 years a new force—government control, regulation, protection, interference. Each involved governmental segment finds it necessary to prescribe forms of reporting which sooner or later, for good or bad, begin to impinge upon the actual underlying records—to determine the allowable accounting principles.

Against this background of anarchical freedom on the one hand and bureaucratic fiat on the other it has long been evident that a more systematic effort was necessary if accounting was to serve its various purposes effectively. The way out of the difficulty began slowly to take form in the efforts of the accountants' professional organizations. The American Institute of Certified Public Accountants, the Financial Executives Institute, the American Accounting Association, the National Association of Accountants, and others have labored at the tedious process of creating an acceptable consensus.

The most concerted and aggressive efforts have been those of the AICPA. The main threads of the Institute's efforts can be picked up very briefly as follows. In the formative period of the Securities Exchange Commission committees of the Institute consulting with SEC officials were influential in developing rules within desirable patterns. Later the Institute organized its Committee on Accounting Procedure which functioned for 20 years and expressed its findings in 51 bulletins. In 1959 this committee was succeeded by the Accounting Principles Board of

18 members which worked on a volunteer basis for thousands of man-days and produced 4 statements and some 21 published opinions on basic and increasingly controversial subjects. It is worthy of note that the Securities and Exchange Commission has generally cooperated sincerely with the APB in spite of their diverse sponsorships.

During 1970 and 1971 it became evident, however, that the sponsorship of a single group and the special point of view of the APB limited its total effectiveness. Other groups and their business backers were unhappy to accept pronouncements in whose creation they had no firm voice. This resulted in the creation of a study group which became known as the Wheat Committee after its chairman, Francis M. Wheat, a former SEC commissioner. This committee clearly identified the need of a more broadly based body to assume the responsibility of establishing acceptable accounting principles. Its suggestions for the establishment of a new body, the Financial Accounting Standards Board (FASB), was accepted in 1972 by the several concerned financial and accounting groups.

The FASB consists of seven full-time paid members with five year terms, and with an initial annual budget of approximately $3 million financed by contributions collected by the AICPA from the public accounting profession and by the Financial Executives Institute (FEI) from industry. Legal and financial control will be vested in the Financial Accounting Foundation (FAF), with nine trustees. The nine trustees will include the president of the AICPA; four CPAs in public practice, nominated by the AICPA; two financial executives, nominated by the Financial Executives Institute and the National Association of Accountants; one financial analyst, nominated by the Financial Analysts Federation and one accounting educator, nominated by the American Accounting Association.

The Foundation will appoint members of the FASB; four of the seven members will be CPAs drawn from public practice, the remaining three members will not need to hold CPA certificates but should possess extensive experience in the financial reporting field.

The Foundation will also establish a Financial Accounting Standards Advisory Council (FASAC) and appoint its approximately twenty members to one-year terms. The Foundation will be expected to consult with the several organizations and the SEC in its search for qualified Advisory Council appointees. Though the FASB and FASAC are legally parts of the FAF they will operate with full independence.

The hope and expectation is that this well-balanced structure will be accepted by business and government as the authority for determining accounting principles in the foreseeable future. Though our point of view in this book is that of the controller of an individual business, it is evident that in the discharge of his own functions, especially in his subfunction of legal reporting, he must keep a weather eye on the larger movements in the accounting area. In this respect the strategic position and work of the FASB will be of greatest importance.

We have indicated previously that the controller's responsibility for legal reporting should be viewed as a necessary subfunction of his inherent controllership function. This chapter will examine this basic fact somewhat more closely, giving necessary attention to the organization aspects of the problem in relation to the legal and secretarial functions. Presumably, the controller will proceed with more assurance in the performance of his duties if he realizes more clearly the forces which have made them what they are.

One way of treating the legal reporting function would be to proceed directly to the numerous occasions and specific forms with which the practicing controller will be concerned. It seems to us, however, that more will be gained by going further back into the subject, first to the basic question of servicing the legal function in business, and then to the legislative-legal background of the burgeoning government-business relationships. This we try to do in this chapter.

THE LEGAL-REPORTING FUNCTION AND
FORMAL ORGANIZATION

In visualizing the early development of business management in terms of breaking down the original total management function, we barely touched on the legal aspects. In even the simplest situations the owner-manager is constantly taking actions which have significant legal impacts. Purchases on account, sales on account, bank borrowings, the hiring of employees, the purchase of real estate—all these are legal actions in which the proprietor must know the rules and must guard his steps. As the various management functions are delegated, these legal responsibilities follow the delegation of the management functions to which they are related.

In every sale on account, the salesman is the representative of the business in making a legal contract. The purchasing agent binds the business legally in every credit purchase. So common are these legal aspects of business that we seldom even consider them as parts of the legal function. It is only when the smooth course of normal business relationships is somehow interrupted that we become aware of the legal problem involved. When the proprietor is hailed before the court because of his own or his employees' presumed legal slips or when he needs the services of the court to bring his customers, creditors, or employees into line or when he is involved in a damage suit, then he suddenly realizes the legal import of the situation. Theoretically, he could still retain his full legal function and go before the court in person. Practically, he realizes at this point his need of expert help, and so he delegates a substantial part of his legal function on a contractual basis to a hired attorney. Such "outside" delegation may be practiced to some extent for any of the functions, but it is most common for the legal function. Many businesses reach very considerable size before creating their own legal departments, and the two forms of providing technical legal service often continue side by side as business grows to very large size.

The controller is not particularly involved with this general aspect of the legal function and its possible patterns of delegation, beyond, of course, his awareness that his own actions and those of his employees have legal significance, as do those of any employees. There is, however, another rather special aspect of the legal function in which the controller does find himself much involved, and that is the whole gamut of legal relationships between the business and governmental agencies, especially the reporting requirements, which actually constitute a very large element of the government-business relationships.

Later sections of this chapter will consider particular legal-reporting requirements and the controller's responsibility therein. At this point we are more concerned with the problem of analyzing the development of this subfunction in general and in examining the rationale whereby it became the controller's responsibility.

The corporation, being an entity created by the state, is controlled in its general outlines by the statutes that provide for its creation. Specific statutory requirements and the pressure of precedent in the administration of the laws on incorporation have brought about a considerable degree of uniformity in the form of organization at the top of the corporate structure. Basic control is by an elected board of directors operating through officers as provided by the charter. Almost uniformly the charter specifies that these officers shall be a president, vice president, treasurer, and secretary.

Various combinations of these offices are made. "Vice president and treasurer" is a fairly common title; "vice president and secretary" is not uncommon. Most common is the combination of the offices of secretary and treasurer. No single-word title has ever been invented for this job; the title is still kept in the compound form, usually "secretary-treasurer," which is recognition of the fact that the two functions are differentiable. English practice, though stemming from the same basic legal roots as our own, has continued to place much more emphasis and importance on the secretary's function. In England, there is an organization called the Chartered Institute of Secretaries, which occupies an honored position parallel to the Chartered Accountants Association. It is bulwarked by courses of study, apprenticeship practices, and an examination as a condition of membership. The secretaryship of chartered companies is virtually always held by a member of the Chartered Institute of Secretaries. The position is considered to be of fully professional status. There is also an American association of corporate secretaries of fully professional status but it is less well known than its English parallel.

The function of the modern corporate secretary has developed from its original meanings. The two leading dictionary definitions of secretary are (1) "one who is entrusted with private or secret matters; a confidential officer or attendant," and (2) "a person who conducts correspondence, keeps minutes, etc., for another as for an individual, a corporation, a society, or a committee, and who is charged with the general conduct of the business arising out of such correspondence or the making of such records."[1]

In the small corporation of some years ago the function of the secretary was closely described by these definitions. Even today that part of the correspondence which is technically related to the corporate life and activity is handled by the corporate secretary. Notices of stockholders' meetings, directors' meetings, the minutes of these groups, dividend notices, proxy requests, and so forth, and the signing of the more significant contracts entered into by the corporation are all still recognized as secretarial duties.

When, however, in the modern corporation the correspondence takes the form of voluminous, technical, and detailed reports required by government and when the source data for these reports reach down into the details of the accounting and statistical systems of the corporation, we see the secretary standing back and turning over the task of assembling or writing such a report to the controller.

To summarize the argument of the last few pages: though, in a basic organization sense, legal reporting is secretaryship, a substantial part of its intellectual content is law. Behind these two elements and absolutely essential in their practical performance lie the tasks of collecting and marshaling vast arrays of technical data. This is the basis upon which the elements are joined and put into the controller's hands. Possibly a clear appreciation of this relationship—an understanding of its origin—may stand the controller in good stead when he faces the sometimes delicate problems of cooperation with the secretary and the legal counsel or when questions of organization shifts and changes are contemplated. Inevitably, as business grows and develops and as the problems of government control and aid and taxes are further complicated, there will be additional reports and elaborations of existing reports. Following the course already well marked, these will be the primary responsibility of the controller, but, realizing the origins and nature of his reporting task, he need never hesitate to seek the help of legal counsel, or should he feel in any way embarrassed when certain of his reports go out over the signature of the secretary.

---

[1] *New Century Dictionary of the English Language* (New York: Appleton-Century, 1948).

THE CONTROLLER AND THE BASIC LAW

Practically, of course, the controller must assume the responsibility for the detail of forms preparation for all legal reporting. He or his staff must remain abreast of every shift in the laws and regulations and of every required reporting form. The underlying accounting system must provide the necessary information to feed the legal forms directly or at least to provide categories that may be feasibly reworked to serve the legal forms.

Beyond these immediate requirements, however, the good controller should concern himself with the broader flow of social purposes which has evolved and which continues to evolve into the laws of which present reporting requirements are the practical manifestation. The great bulk of the "social legislation" and the supporting court interpretations thereof with which we are here involved has developed in the short period of 50 or 75 years. Extremists regard much of this legal evolution as the entering wedge of socialism-communism or on the other hand as a sop thrown to the proletariat to head off basic change. A more measured view is that these are refinements which take the rough edges off of the capitalistic system and give it an opportunity to work in a practical and humane manner. The sincere acceptance of this point of view creates an ambiance within which the business man and the controller can work with government controls in an honest and reasonably comfortable manner. Acceptance of this point-of-view has another deeply significant consequence. The study of the efforts, since 1900, to control business through statutes and legal decisions becomes the study of a greater drama than any playwright has ever assayed, which is well worth "reading" for its sheer interest alone.

For the controller, however, such a study has additional clearly practical reasons. While the reporting jobs may be 95% routine, there is always that final sticky point of interpretation, that special case, that different situation or that new development, not envisaged by the law, which requires a higher degree of judgment. For these situations the greatest safeguard is an appreciation of the basic background—the real intent of the law. The controller may make the decision himself or he may call for help. If he takes the problem to the company's legal counsel, his understanding of the background involvement will be very useful in presenting and discussing the problem. If the item should wind up in the court the controller's breadth will again be helpful to the lawyer in direct charge of the company's case.

A second, and even more important reason why the controller should prepare himself fundamentally in the evolution of legal control of business is that the process is still in evolution and that the best brains of the nation will be needed to guide the future of this process. As an individual, working directly with his representatives in Congress and in state legislatures he can make his judgment felt. Even more effectively, as a member of his professional organizations, primarily the Financial Executives Institute, he can bring his influence to bear where it really counts to keep the process practical and humane.

Such attempts to influence legislation frequently involve a powerful temptation to seek more immediate benefits for business at the expense of fundamental, necessary, and in the long run, inevitable controls aimed at broader benefits to all business and society as a whole. Understanding of the broad flow of social-legal forces will protect the individual or organization from being caught on the wrong side of the argument. To be thus caught with obviously short-run, or plainly selfish, reasons would rob the person or organization of real weight which will be necessary when the chips are down on basic issues.

The foregoing has been easy to say. Of course, we are all in favor of the long-run basic welfare of the system and against short-run selfish purposes! The crux of the matter lies in the fact that the controller must equip himself with a real understanding of the evolving processes of constitutional law. This sounds a little as though we are asking the controller to take a few years off to go through law school. Fortunately, this is not necessary. There are a few good books on the subject of government control of business which bring the whole matter of the developing constitutional process down to the business man's level without sacrificing the understanding of the basic issues. A few weekends with such a book[2] will give the controller a great boost in the right direction and, in addition, if he is sensitive, it will give him the pleasure of understanding the great drama of civilization in the process of making itself viable.

THE CONTROLLER AND ADMINISTRATIVE LAW

A special feature of government-business relationships of comparatively recent development is the creation and growth of importance of administrative law. Modern business has developed in such varied forms and the problem of necessary regulation has become so complicated that the old pattern of independent legislative, executive and judicial branches of government in direct contact with the citizenry is no longer feasible in many areas. Administrative law and the system of administrative commissions have developed to fill this need. The law in each case prescribes an area of control, and within this area combines limited legislative, executive, and judicial authority in the hands of a governing unit, the appointed commissioners.

It is easy for the business man who has just lost an argument with some commission to cavil against such an "unconstitutional combining

---

[2] A good one is John Philip Wernette's *Government and Business* (New York: Macmillan, 1969).

of the three elements of proper government!" It does often seem unfortunate that the writing and enforcing of the rules—the prosecuting—and the judging shall be in the same hands. The alternative, however, is virtually unthinkable. Without the interposition of the commission, the law itself would have to be written in the full detail for positive regulation, and every dispute and contest would have to be handled by the courts. Legislators (for this discussion applies to state as well as to the Federal jurisdictions) simply do not have the technical expertize to do this detailed job. The administrative commission, with all its possible drawbacks, is still a very fortunate, and, on the whole, effective invention for the purpose.

The move began with the Interstate Commerce Commission in 1887 followed by the Federal Trade Commission, the Federal Power Commission, the Federal Communications Commission, the Securities and Exchange Commission, the Civil Aeronautics Board, and others. In each case the commission is set up and given its initial assignment by a basic piece of legislation. As experience is accumulated the original law is amended many times with provisions for expanded powers and increased responsibilities. The commission writes its own system of rules and regulations which expand and get more complicated. Specific actions involving individual businesses are argued, decided, and reported. A certain number of cases are carried to the courts and the decisions handed down, sometimes after a series of appeals, and become a very considerable file of precedents which the lawyer (and controller?) must know if they are to guide the business affairs intelligently.

While some of the proceedings before the commissions inevitably take on the adversary attitude of court cases, the more desirable attitudes of advising, consulting, compromising should and do play a very large role. These attitudes are fully congruent with general purpose of control through administrative law—that is to allow the capitalistic system— profit-oriented, privately owned business—to operate in a humane and civilized manner. Henry Carter Adams, Chief Statistician of the Interstate Commerce Commission in its early days coined the expression "to fix the plane of competition" to describe the purpose of the ICC efforts to regulate the railroads. This phrase is essentially valid over a very large area of administrative control. Adams also must be given principal credit for realizing that control of the railroads could be based only on reliable information, and that such reliability could come only from an accounting and reporting system that was uniform in its essential structure. Other commissions, federal and state, have followed the pattern of the ICC. Unfortunately, almost any degree of uniformity, once achieved, tends to rigidity. There is no question that the business man's complaints about "strait-jacket" accounting enforced by various authorities are often well justified. The need to preserve a desirable flexibility while at the same time achieving necessary uniformity becomes a special type of challenge, and a very proper item for negotiation between the administrative authority and the controller.

THE CONTROLLER AND SPECIFIC REPORTING REQUIREMENTS

The remaining purpose of this chapter is to examine some of the more important reporting tasks which are commonly required of the controller. We cannot hope to cover the *substance* of these requirements—their mastery calls for professional specialization and long intensive study. We do hope to *place* each of these reporting requirements properly within the scope of the controller's concept and to visualize the impact which it has upon the general accounting framework. The difficulty of the subject—and its fascination—lies in its ever changing, broadening, and complicating nature.

Social security and related reports

Oldtimers remember the furor in accounting circles at the passing of social security and unemployment tax laws. These laws called for reporting requirements in such detail with regard to individual employees that they caused a virtual convulsion in payroll records and procedures. Many businessmen and accountants felt at the time that the burdens of the new record keeping were so onerous as to be intolerable. And so they would have been, had it not been for the new techniques of machine accounting which were developed to meet the new situation. About the same time or shortly thereafter, payroll deductions for other purposes (union dues, community chests, savings-bond drives, credit unions, hospitalization, pensions, and so forth) became much more common. Within a few years, the complications handled in payroll procedures far exceeded anything that would have been considered possible at an earlier date. Virtually, every one of these deductions means additional reports to be planned and scheduled. Fortunately, much of this reporting, once planned and set up, becomes so routine that it can be handled by down-the-line employees and, like many systems jobs, once accomplished, is hardly thought of as the controller's problem. It should be noted that, while many reports are legal in the sense of being required by statute, others find their origin in contracts such as the agreement for dues check-off with the labor union or the deduction for hospitalization under agreement with the "Blues" or other health care plans. Closely related are other purely voluntary plans such as community fund drives and savings bond plans which may involve temporary periods or only partial and changing groups of employees. Though these reports are not legal in the sense of required by law, they are controlled by legal and contractual considerations and must be tied into the general accounting structure with great care.

Income taxes

The most all-pervasive legal reporting requirement, of course, is the income tax situation—federal, state, and city. The state of Wisconsin had an income tax even earlier, but most accountants think of the income tax as originating with the first federal law of March 1913. The total impact of the income tax laws upon accounting is impossible to visualize. One great change it brought about was the education of business as to the fact of depreciation. Before the income tax, depreciation was for many businesses just "a theory" of no practical concern in the determination of net income. "You ain't laying out any cash so it ain't an expense!" It is sad that the educational value of tax depreciation rules has gone way beyond the mark of simple truth. Recent shifts in depreciation rules and the related investment credits have all been in the direction of earlier write-offs with no pretense of paralleling the fact. The complications of continuous reconciliation of tax depreciation and book depreciation ("keeping two sets of books") are well known and a good example of the impact, good or bad, of the tax law upon the basic usefulness of accounting. Hundreds of more elusive impacts of the tax regulations could be ferreted out. Most of them are relatively harmless, but the controller should remain on guard and sensitive to the way in which the tax considerations tend to push accounting principles around, sometimes for very significant amounts.

Actually this has become an important segment of the controller's interpretive function. In his dealings with top management he will often have to say, "Tax-wise we must do this, but don't let it obscure the real fact that . . . ."

The first clause of the above quote, "Tax-wise we must do this . . ." characterizes the extremely practical aspect of the controller's tax responsibility often thought of as tax planning. Tax planning itself is two-phase. The first phase is the advice the controller gives to management as to what to do and how and when to do it to put the business in the correct position for tax minimization. The second, and closely related, phase is the proper accounting for whatever has been done so that the advantage of the fact will not be thrown away by clumsy reporting.

It is a sad fact that so much thought and energy must be given by the controller and management to the tax impacts of so many moves. The second clause of the quote ". . . but don't let it obscure the fact that . . ." gets back to the happier matter of the positive use of information in running the business and this is, of course, the heart of the controller's function.

Organizing for the tax function

Organizing the tax function in the large corporation to give effect to its philosophical and practical aspects is essentially a matter of co-operation of various parties within the business, hopefully with the stern blessing of top management.

As stated in the brief discussion of the legal function in the opening chapter, the organization of federal tax work in any particular company may vary with the circumstances and the personnel available. Generally some form of tax committee will be the best method of bringing the various abilities within the business to bear on the problem. For instance, the secretary of the company may assume primary responsibility for all federal tax matters, with the assistance of a tax committee, which includes, besides the secretary, an assistant secretary, the controller, and an assistant to the controller The secretary acts as chairman of the committee, reporting to the president on all tax problems and questions of tax policy, representing the company in formal conferences with the Internal Revenue Service, and, in general, handling the legal and administrative aspects of the tax function. The assistant secretary has the responsibility for following in detail the laws, regulations, and court decisions and for answering specific questions that arise in day-to-day operations. The controller's assistant prepares the returns, assembles the necessary data from the various departments of the business, and acts as the company's direct representative when the returns are audited by the field agent of the Revenue Service. The controller, besides assuming general responsibility for the work of his assistant, outlines and develops any special accounting techniques or analyses that may be required, maintains outside contacts for exchange of information on new developments, participates in conferences with Internal Revenue Service representatives when necessary, and contributes to committee discussions a background of knowledge of company operations and accounting.

Although the meetings of such a tax committee may be on an informal basis, a meeting should be held at least once each month, and a summary record of discussions and conclusions should be maintained for permanent reference. It will be found that, through the exchange and interplay of the various points of view of the committee members, supplemented by consultations with the company's attorneys and public accountants as occasion arises, tax problems and tax-saving opportunities may be very thoroughly covered. This particular plan of organization might not be suitable in all situations, but, whatever the organization plan, it should provide somehow for coordinating and combining a knowledge of the tax laws and their administration, an understanding of the accounting techniques involved, and a full background on company policies and operations.

Incidentally, the controller may effectively utilize the meetings of the broad based tax committee as one opportunity to hammer home the pervasive problem of tax accounting versus management accounting—starting here to assure that the tax tail does not wag the business dog.

State and city income taxes

As of the present, forty-one states have income taxes. Income tax laws are being passed more and more by cities—some two hundred at a recent count—many of them in the comparatively small population range of 10,000 to 25,000 and most of them in the northeast and midwest sections of the country. State taxes on personal income vary from 2 or 3 of net income to as high as 14 percent, and there is a strong tendency to raise the rates once the low rate has put the government's foot in the door. State taxes on corporate income are generally in the 4 to 7 percent range, most of them at a single fixed rate, but several on a graduated basis as low as 1 or 2 percent on low incomes to as high as 8 percent on the highest level.

Recent popular pressures to relieve homeowners of the burden of property taxes—especially for education—are certain to accelerate the trend toward state and local income taxes.

Contemplating the problem of multiple income tax returns, there is a natural tendency to hope that difficulties can be kept at a minimum by writing the law for state and local units so that they may "piggyback" on the federal returns. This principle is quite commonly observed, but the need to recognize fine legal distinctions and the desire to tailor the law to special local situations generally makes simple "piggybacking" impossible.

Since the movement for city income taxes will inevitably spread, there is a tremendous opportunity for financial executives and certified public accountants to study the patterns of present city income tax laws and to be ready with advice to city legislators on the great needs of keeping the new laws simple, effective, and fair. This will be lobbying of the highest character—exactly the kind of good citizenship we hope for from high minded professional people.

The starting point for visualizing the relationships of federal, state, and city income taxes may well be an old fashioned multicolumnar work sheet on which a pair of columns for each of the three returns is added to the right of the normal 10 or 12 columns. Each of the tax returns is basically a repetition of the items in the accounting "Income" columns. The necessary differences in taxable revenues and allowable deductions can be made to stand out clearly in the comparative columns. For the really simple situation in which the entire business lies within a single tax jurisdiction, such a work sheet may actually be the best device for whipping out the tax returns. It would certainly be a boon in answering the questions of the tax auditor months or years later when the reconciliation of the state and city returns to the federal government will probably be the heart of the argument.

For the less than simple situation which cannot possibly be embraced in an actual work sheet, the work-sheet pattern of thinking may still be useful in organizing the multiple returns. Furthermore, looking forward to the practical problem of tax return preparation may be of considerable help in the early stages of legislative planning when there is still a chance of influencing provisions of the law. The warning by the professional accountant of the practical difficulties which certain legal provisions would cause for hundreds of taxpayers in the future should bear considerable weight in legislative deliberations.

For the large corporation with income producing activities spread in really numerous taxing localities, the problem of a great many separate tax returns may seem quite forbidding. An important part of the answer will be in the proper coding of basic data for computer manipulation. In most cases sales and cost data will be analyzed by regions for management control and, with foresight, it should be possible to articulate such management breakdowns, with the necessary tax area breakdowns. Such marshaling of the routine data is the strong forte of the computer system.

The computer systems man will immediately recognize that the most difficult part of such a system is the data control step; that is, ensuring that the code placed in each record is correct. Systems analysts and programmers can build restrictions into the program that will establish that the region code is one of the valid codes, but it is usually necessary to rely on careful supervision of clerical personnel to see that the code is exactly correct for the actual transaction. This difficulty is, of course, not unique to region codes, but is a critical feature of any computerized system.

Other taxes

The reporting of other taxes (retail sales, alcoholic beverages, tobacco products, insurance, public utilities, pari-mutuels, amusements, and so forth) is quite routine. Technically, the reporting of the supporting data is the controller's function, though once set up it becomes so routine as to be no problem. In all these areas there are from time to time changes in rates, court decisions on borderline cases, new laws, and so forth which may be serious responsibilities for the controller—with, of course, the close cooperation of the company's legal counsel. A sound device for catching these miscellaneous shifts in situation will be for the chairman of the tax committee to keep a routine question on his meeting agenda, "Has there been any development in the area of other taxes or other required reports of which we should be cognizant?"

Property taxes are not usually thought of as constituting a reporting problem, but the administration of the whole tax problem must certainly embrace them. Proper classification of real estate holdings as to situs within taxing jurisdictions is the legal department's responsibility, but it is just good sense for the controller to have a discrete interest in the matter. The simple question of whether the company's property is or is not within the city limits becomes in practice whether it is also properly within the school tax district, within the drainage area, within the harbor control board, and so forth. Personal property, especially inventory, may present a unique problem when inventories are held in several or many taxing jurisdictions. Since in many cases property taxes are assessed on inventories at a particular date each year—the dates being different in different jurisdictions—tax money can be easily thrown away or saved, by knowing the rules as to these crucial dates and by timing purchases, sales, deliveries, or transshipments in accordance with the company's perfectly legal advantage. The tax advantages of such control must be carefully balanced against the possible disadvantages in basic purchasing policy, adequate stocks, traffic costs, and so forth.

THE SECURITIES AND EXCHANGE COMMISSION

Of all the administrative commissions the Securities and Exchange Commission (SEC) occupies the most central, general, and significant position in terms of impact in accounting.

The modern phase of the problem of control of the securities industry and the involvement of accounting therein began with the Securities Act of 1933 and has progressed through additional acts of Congress to create the present huge structure of control. Paralleling the formal legal development has been the tremendous burgeoning of administrative regulations and the less obvious but very important growth of experience within the structure of the SEC.

The history and growth of the SEC can be traced in its admirable series of releases reporting in succinct form its activities over the years. Those releases that concern specific actions against individual companies—denials of registrations and objections to current reports and against brokers for illegal procedures are a dramatic demonstration of the necessity for control. The accounting releases are a distillation of SEC experience of a more general nature—its efforts to formulate rules and regulations for more general guidance of business and its accountants. Many of these accounting regulations, especially the earlier ones, read like accounting principles textbooks. These are striking evidence that in many cases the basic principles which we had thought of as "generally accepted" had not in fact penetrated into the jungles of practical business, and that they needed at least the force of administrative law to bring them into common use. Some of the deviations practiced by sizable business would have been grounds for flunking sophomores in the accounting principles course.

In this enlightened day many persons do not appreciate the comparative recency of jungle tactics in the securities business. Prior to the securities legislation of 1933 the investor had protection against overt fraud only through the difficult processes of common law action with some slight help from state laws aimed generally at the worst and most obvious "blue sky" rackets. The 1929 stock market collapse and the depression which followed pointed up the complete inadequacy of the state laws and the need for more sophisticated regulation obviously necessary at the federal level.

The Securities Act of 1933

This act provides that the issuer of new securities offered in interstate commerce or through the mails must obtain registration thereof from the SEC (originally from the Federal Trade Commission). This registration is based upon detailed financial information submitted to the SEC, with registration refused for reason of misstatements or omissions. After clearance of the registration a prospectus containing substantially the same information as in the registration must be made available to prospective buyers. It is understood and constantly reiterated that the SEC does not pass upon the value of the securities—only upon the adequacy of the information presented, upon which the buyer must form his own judgment. This is the principle of reliance upon full disclosure.

The Securities Exchange Act of 1934

This act created the Securities and Exchange Commission and gave it the responsibility for administering the 1933 Act and authority over the trading in securities after issue. In general all issuers whose stocks are traded in on the exchanges must submit annual and interim statements to the SEC and to the exchanges. The content of these periodic statements is prescribed in the SEC regulations and has evolved over the years into a formidable body of accounting principles and rules. The annual statements must be certified by certified public accountants. This is the provision which brings the accounting profession and the Financial Accounting Standards Board of the American Institute of Certified Public Accountants into the picture—a relationship of great implication and consequence.

Public Utility Holding Company Act of 1935

This act recognizes the special conditions obtaining in electric and gas utilities and the special temptations to manipulation of which the industry was guilty prior to its passage. Administered by a unit of the SEC, this law goes further than the information requirements of the basic 1933 and 1934 acts and gives the commission actual authority over intercompany service charges, certain aspects of physical integration, types of securities that may be issued in specific cases, and so forth. The act empowers the commission to prescribe uniform classifications of accounts for subject companies. Under this provision the SEC has been satisfied to require the use of Federal Power Commission (FPC) uniform accounts for those companies not already using the FPC system.

Trust Indenture Act of 1939

This act can be best understood as attempting to do for bondholders what the 1933 and 1934 acts do for stockholders. The act provides that the trustee for the bondholders in large issues, usually a corporation, must be independent, i.e., free of conflict of interest which might prevent it from truly representing the bondholders' interests. Again the SEC is given administrative responsibility for the act.

Investment Company Act of 1940

This act was necessitated by the considerable differences between investment companies and industrials. Again registration statements and periodic statements are provided for, and the act specifies that "the Commission . . . may issue rules and regulations providing for a reasonable degree of uniformity in the accounting policies and principles to be followed by the registered companies. . . ." The need for special refinements of definition in regard to the varying aspects of income determination in such investment businesses is obvious. It becomes especially important when one realizes the generally unsophisticated type of stockholder of investment companies and their need to understand the reported showing of income for tax purposes.

Chandler Act

This act gives the SEC one of its lesser-known responsibilities which is to advise the court and security holders in the case of companies being reorganized under Chapter X, of the National Bankruptcy Act. The Chapter X reorganization plan of any corporation which has a liquidated indebtedness of $3 million or more must be submitted to the SEC for investigation of its feasibility and fairness. The Commission's authority is purely advisory: to call attention to proposed security arrangements which its experience leads it to believe would be unsound, misleading, or otherwise injurious to the investing public.

Investment Advisors Act of 1940

The tremendous spread of stock ownership to literally millions of individuals has brought with it the business of selling investment advice involving thousands of investment advisors. The potential danger of fraud in this situation is apparent. The Investment Advisor's Act of 1940 makes an effort to head off the crudest of such dangers by requiring the registration of those who set themselves up as advisors and by requiring specifically that they disclose to clients any private connections they have with companies involved in their recommendations which could be interpreted as "conflict of interest" situations. In policing this situation the SEC may use injunction procedure and may refer evidence of violation to the Attorney General for criminal prosecution.

Securities Investor Protection Corporation Act of 1970

This act established the S.I.P.C., a corporation to be financed by assessments on its members, brokerage firms, to establish a fund to protect customers' accounts up to $50 thousand in event of the liquidation of an S.I.P.C. member. The $50 thousand claim limit is for cash *and* securities; however, not more than $20 thousand of the claim may be for cash.

The law was passed December 30, 1970, and provided that the fund be built up to $75 million within 120 days and to $150 million eventually. All brokers and dealers who are not exempt are required to pay an initial assessment of ⅛ of 1 percent of gross 1969 revenues from securities business. Assessments thereafter will be set at a minimum of ½ of 1 percent per annum until the fund totals $150 million. The act permits assessments of up to 1 percent per annum if it is necessary to build or maintain the fund and S.I.P.C. determines that such assessment will not materially harm S.I.P.C. members or their customers. Broker-dealers who are members of S.I.P.C. will be subject to financial responsibility inspections, the filing of certain reports, as well as the payments of assessments.

THE PROBLEM OF MULTIDIVISIONAL REPORTING

The latest reporting problem, and one that will be with us for a long time, is the proper reflection of the earnings of the multidivisional business most commonly spoken of as the conglomerate problem. Principally, the pressure for improved reporting in this area comes from investors through their spokesmen the investment analysts. Initially, the cause was the tremendous merger movement of the late sixties, and the justified feeling that the "clean" reporting of the erstwhile independent units was being lost in the merged reporting of the resulting conglomerate.

It soon became apparent, however, that the problem was not merely one of the recent consolidation. What the analysts really feel they need is the reporting of income segregated by sources, that is by distinguishable types of business activity regardless of how those separate activities happen to have gotten together under the corporate roof. Thus many large corporations, even though not significantly involved in recent mergers find themselves under pressure to reveal much more detail of their profitability pattern than they have given their stockholders and the public heretofore.

The sensitive, knowledgeable, accountant shudders at the difficulty of the problem, a difficulty which the public, the typical stockholder, and many analysts do not comprehend. For one thing, there are the enormous differences in the degrees of diversity among companies. One company may embrace distilling, Great Lakes shipping, and a Florida orange grove. Another has several models of automobiles, home freezers, and locomotives, and a third has 4,000 different items of automotive production and replacement parts. The routine accounting system of each of these companies will develop sufficient product profitability information for internal management needs. The distiller-shipping-citrus company may get very close to a net income for each of its three ventures. The automotive company's accounts may develop information quite close to a net income for its quite distinct freezer and locomotive ventures. However its several automobile models may be so closely related in engineering, manufacturing and sales processes, with substantial joint costs virtually unallocable, that the accounts cannot sensibly go beyond the concept of "contribution to overhead and profit" for each model. The auto parts manufacturer's accounts may be on the basis of standard cost for materials and labor with no attempt to distribute any overhead to its multiple products. The management of each of these companies knows quite well how far it can trust its breakdown figures for its own internal purposes, but to present these same figures to the various "publics" unschooled in the niceties and difficulties of accounting is practically a guarantee of confusion.

The situation of the auto parts manufacturer clearly demonstrates another practical difficulty, that is the determination of the degree of differences among the products which will justify differentiation for profit reporting. A first guess might be that "original equipment" and "replacement parts" would be a useful major breakdown but familiarity might show this distinction to have no significant counterpart in the actual manufacturing process of many of the items. Even if these two divisions were accepted as significant there would remain the question of the advisability of further breakdowns to engine parts, body parts, chassis parts and possibly to brakes, transmissions, bumpers, frames, etc. Obviously, without knowing a great deal about the actual operations of the manufacturer, we cannot even commence to set up sensible divisions. A more elusive though pertinent question is whether the breakdowns used by internal management, in *any* degree of fragmentation, will prove to be the ones useful to the investor. Internal accounting is heavily influenced by the technology of production, the pattern of organization, and considerations of control. The investor wants figures that he can compare significantly with figures of competing firms. He especially wishes to trace the profitability of the previously independent concern into the conglomerate of which it is now a part. It *may* be feasible for the conglomerate to continue to report on the merged business as a unit if in fact its operations are continued quite independently. Often, however, this simple pattern does not persist beyond the initial stage of merger. Some segments of the previously independent operation may be dropped entirely, or expanded greatly, or combined operationally into divisions of other merged units. The newly merged unit may quite properly be assessed with new elements of general overhead, or it may be relieved of certain costs (engineering, research, legal, sales, etc.) which it previously necessarily supported. All of these possible shifts tend to vitiate comparison with past performance or with other still independent competitors.

Another aspect of merger is that the very concept of profitability of the previous independent may disappear. Visualize the situation of Big Industrial acquiring Small Independent, a coal mine, or cement producer, or glass manufacturer, with the purpose of absorbing the entire production of the newly acquired unit into its own further production process. Big Industrial may, in its internal accounting, treat the supply unit as a profit center with a carefully compiled "transfer price" arbitrating between producer and consumer units within the firm. It would be naive, however, to assume that the "profit" thus shown by the coal, cement, or glass facility would be comparable to the previous history of profits or the profits of still independent coal, cement or glass producers. These are some of the difficulties—there are obviously many more—in the way of segmented profit reporting.

For a broad, documented view of how financial executives regard these difficulties, the reader is referred to the study of the problem by Professor Robert K. Mautz, financed by the Financial Executives Research Foundation and published in 1968 under the title Financial Reporting by Diversified Companies. The Mautz study stresses the two difficulties already involved in the foregoing discussion, common cost allocations and transfer pricing. Mautz also recognizes a third difficulty stressed by the industry representatives, that is the risks of revealing to competitors information which the business properly regards as confidential. For a real appraisal of these difficulties, it is necessary to visualize more exactly the form and content of the segmented reporting to be used.

Mautz points out that three bases for segmenting diversified companies for reporting purposes might be used: (1) the basis of legal organization according to corporate entities, (2) the basis of internal structure for control purposes, or (3) the basis of the product lines of industries in which the business operates. The first two bases are of concern to management, whereas some variation of the third will quite generally be the choice of investor-analyst.

To go all-out on the industry-product line basis would call for some standard classification of all possible products as a starting point. Such a standard is available in the Standard Industrial Classifications (SIC) prepared by the Technical Committee on Industrial Classification (representatives of various federal agencies supervised by the Office of Statistical Standards of the Bureau of the Budget). Close inspection of this tremendously detailed classification, however, shows clearly that, as Mautz concludes, it was not intended for and is not appropriate to the purpose here in mind. One difficulty with the SIC classification is that it is a combination of physical characteristics and end-use classes. Mautz quotes an illustration of this source of confusion:

Bicycles are considered to be used for transportation purposes, so companies manufacturing them are included in Major Group 37, "Transportation Equipment." Tricycles are used for fun and are therefore considered to be toys so they are included in "Major Group 39, Miscellaneous Manufacturing Activities." A company that makes tricycles would be assigned Number 3943, "Children's Vehicles, Except Bicycles." If the company also made bicycles, seemingly a closely related product, it would also receive Number 3751, "Motorcycles, Bicycles, and Parts." Thus with a relatively nondiversified product line, a company might carry two two-digit SIC numbers.

One wonders where unicycles and quadicycles would fit—and exercycles and pedal-driven paddle boats, all of which have significant physical similarities.

It is some relief to swing from the possibility of highly detailed segment reporting to the answers which Mautz got from 196 representative financial analysts on the point of how many segments could be utilized affectively. Of those responding, 87.3 percent indicated that they would prefer less than 12 segments, and over half (56.1 percent) said they would prefer less than 9 segments. Yet the fact that 12 or 9 or fewer segments were asked for—extremely vague judgments, under the circumstances—does put emphasis on the fact that the real question is the nature of the segments rather than their number.

It is our judgment that the useful basis of segmentation will be some adaptation of product line differentiation as seen in terms of the unique top management problems of each business. This means product lines as they must be visualized for forward planning for it is the future which the investor buys, and he is interested in segmented profit reporting of past accomplishment only as it casts light on the future.

Formal moves toward segmented profit reporting

Recognizing the inevitability of the movement toward multidivisional or segmented profit reporting the three major interested organizations have been very busy during the last few years on their several angles. There has been some polite sparring on the delicate questions of just what is to be done and who should take the initiative, but on the whole the relationship between the Securities and Exchange Commission, the American Institute of Certified Public Accountants, and the Financial Executives Institute has been cooperative in the situation which all three realize is complicated and important. Tracing the interchanges and moves is an education in how things get done at the business-professional level.

We have mentioned the work of Mautz, sponsored by the F.E.I. The practical outcome to date is that the SEC in its October 14, 1970, Release No. 8996 under the Securities and Exchange Act of 1934 adopted regulations essentially similar to the Mautz recommendations. This is again a very significant example of control through the administrative commission technique. The new provisions went into effect on January 1, 1971, as part of a revision of Form 10 under the 1934 Act. Similar provisions were made in other releases under the 1933 and other acts administered by the SEC. The sections with which we are here concerned are quoted in full.

From the SEC Release No. 8996, October 14, 1970

(c) (1) *Information as to lines of business.* If the registrant and its subsidiaries are engaged in more than one line of business, state, for each of the registrant's last five fiscal years, or for each fiscal year ending after December 31, 1966, or for each fiscal year the registrant has been engaged in business, whichever period is less, the approximate amount or percentage of (i) total sales and revenues, and (ii) income (or loss) before income taxes and extraordinary items, attributable to each line of business which during either of the last two fiscal years accounted for—

(A) 10 percent or more of the total of sales and revenues,

(B) 10 percent or more of income before income taxes and extraordinary items computed without deduction of loss resulting from operations of any line of business, or

(C) a loss which equalled or exceeded 10 percent of the amount of income specified in (B) above;

provided, that if total sales and revenues did not exceed $50,000,000 during either of the last two fiscal years, the percentages specified in (A), (B) and (C) above shall be 15 percent, instead of 10 percent.

If it is impracticable to state the contribution to income (or loss) before income taxes and extraordinary items for any line of business, state the contribution thereof to the results of operations most closely approaching such income, together with a brief explanation of the reasons why it is not practicable to state the contribution to such income or loss.

Instructions. 1.   If the number of lines of business for which information is required exceeds ten, the registrant may, at its option, furnish the required information only for the ten lines of business deemed most important to an understanding of the business. In such event, a statement to that effect shall be set forth.

2.   In grouping products or services as lines of business, appropriate consideration shall be given to all relevant factors, including rates of profitability of operations, degrees of risk and opportunity for growth. The basis for grouping such products or services and any material changes between periods in such groupings shall be briefly described.

3.   Where material amounts of products or services are transferred from one line of business to another, the receiving and transferring lines may be considered a single line of business for the purpose of reporting the operating results thereof.

4.   If the method of pricing intracompany transfers of products or services or the method of allocation of common or corporate costs materially affects the reported contribution to income of a line of business, such methods and any material changes between periods in such methods and the effect thereof shall be described briefly.

5.   Information regarding sales or revenues or income (or loss) from different classes of products or services in operations regulated by Federal, State or municipal authorities may be limited to those classes of products or services required by any uniform system of accounts prescribed by such authorities.

(2)   *Information as to classes of similar products or services.* State for each fiscal year specified in (1) above the amount or percentage of total sales and revenues contributed by each class of similar products or services which contributed 10 percent or more to total sales and revenues in either of the last two fiscal years, or 15 percent or more of total sales and revenues if total sales and revenues did not exceed $50,000,000 during either of the last two fiscal years.

Instructions. 1.   Paragraph (2) calls for information with respect to classes of similar products or services regardless of whether the registrant is engaged in more than one line of business as referred to in paragraph (1) above. However, this information may be combined, where appropriate, with the response to paragraph (1).

2.   Instruction 5 to paragraph (1) above shall also apply to paragraph (2).

(d)   If a material part of the business of the registrant and its subsidiaries is dependent upon a single customer, or a very few customers, the loss of any one of which would have a materially adverse effect on the registrant, the name of the customer or customers and other material facts with respect to their relationship, if any, to the registrant and the importance of the business to the registrant shall be stated.

(e)   If the registrant and its subsidiaries engage in material operations outside the United States, or if a material portion of sales or revenues are derived from customers outside the United States, appropriate disclosure shall be made with respect to the importance of that part of the business to the registrant and the risks attendant thereto. Insofar as practicable, furnish information with respect to volume and relative profitability of such business.

(f) Indicate briefly, to the extent material, the general competitive conditions in the industry in which the registrant and its subsidiaries are engaged or intend to engage, and the position of the enterprise in the industry. If several products or services are involved, separate consideration shall be given to the principal products or services or classes of products or services.

(g) The Commission may, upon the request of the registrant, and where consistent with the protection of investors, permit the omission of any of the information herein required or the furnishing in substitution therefor of appropriate information of comparable character. The Commission may also require the furnishing of other information in addition to, or in substitution for, the information herein required in any case where such information is necessary or appropriate for an adequate description of the business done or intended to be done.

To assume that these regulations are the final word on the subject would be naïve. For instance the basic paragraph (c)(1) deals with "lines of business" while (c) (2) repeats the regulations in terms of "classes of similar products or services," with a final provision that the two bases may be combined, *where appropriate.* This is rather obviously compromising between two approaches to the definition of significant segment.

The 10 percent limitation for large business with 15 percent for businesses under $50 million is another element of compromise. The breakpoint is sure to come up for possible revision as experience begins to accumulate—and pinch. The use of both of these percentages of the businesses's total to determine materiality of a line or product group is at best an arbitrary device. Many businesses would find 8 percent (or 13 percent) segments worthy of separate reporting while in other cases 11 percent (or 16 percent) segments might be of little interest. These percentage cutoffs are, however, at least definite enough to be identifiable. The alternative, more basically sound device of letting each management decide for itself what segments are significant would be simply unenforceable if managements should balk at the whole idea. Another real objection to the use of percentages in the present form is the fact that a small firm might find itself obligated under the 15 percent provision to report on some sensitive and competitive items while its very large competitor with a much greater absolute volume of the item can hide behind the 10 percent limitation.

One of the "saving" provisions of the regulation is the paragraph numbered (c)(1)(C) beginning "If it is impractical . . ." This provision is apparently intended for the situation in which the allocation of general overhead items to the several lines cannot be accomplished in a satisfactory manner. Without being specific (c)(1)(C) leaves open the possibility of developing segment profits to the point of "contribution to overhead and income" rather than to push on to a complete allocation and a meaningless net income.

Final paragraph (g) is the general saving provision certainly necessary at this early stage to make the regulation palatable to a wide range of business men. It would seem to be the only answer to the difficult situation envisaged in the second paragraph above. It might, on the other hand, become the Achilles' heel of the whole regulation if business quite commonly decides to be recalcitrant. Such is the difficulty of administrative regulation.

One possible requirement which was in the preliminary discussions, but which has happily been omitted, was the breakdown of total *assets* to correspond to the sales-profits reporting segments. This would have had considerable theoretical and practical interest to investors, making possible a very significant measure of profitability. However, the practical difficulties of such a requirement caused a thumbs down reaction from most parties. It is something to watch for in the future, when the simpler present requirements have been digested.

Other provisions of Release No. 8996

Two other provisions of Release No. 8996 will be welcome to investors though they will not be new to a great many companies.

Item 1.(b)
5.   If applicable and material for an understanding of such business, furnish the following information:
(A)   The dollar amount of backlog of orders believed to be firm, as of a recent date and as of a comparable date in the preceding fiscal year, together with an indication of the proportion thereof not reasonably expected to be filled within the current fiscal year, any seasonal or significant aspects of such backlog and the extent to which backlog is significant in the business of the registrant.

· · · · ·

(D)   The estimated dollar amount spent during each of the last two fiscal years on material research activities relating to the development of new products or services or the improvement of existing products or services which was company-sponsored and on that which was customer-sponsored, indicating the approximate number of professional employees engaged full time in each category of activity during each such fiscal year; and, ...

Backlog has always been a favorite bit of information for investors this provision will give backlog information the status that it deserves. Similarly investors have been placing more and more emphasis on research in attempting to gauge future prospects.

SEC Release No. 8996, and other recent releases contain a great many more provisions of interest to the financial executive—we cannot hope for full substantive coverage in this book. We do hope that the examples presented in this chapter demonstrate the importance—and drama—of the great cooperative effort for intelligent regulation which is going on before our eyes.

The three protagonists again and again clearly exemplify their separate, different, and matching functions. The SEC holding the legal responsibility strives mightily to put good accounting into enforceable legal terms. The F.E.I., often seeming to "drag its feet," is motivated by a full appreciation of the enormous difficulty of writing regulations to fit every situation and therefore constantly on the side of flexibility, provisions for voluntary adherence and safeguarding "outs" for the special case. The A.I.C.P.A., trying to consolidate the great influence of the CPA's, recognizes the positions of the other protagonists, grapples with the most difficult and immediate problems, and dares to come out with opinions which have no legal force but which are presumably binding on members of the A.I.C.P.A.

OTHER LEGAL REPORTING

We have treated at length of a few reporting situations requiring the controller's attention. The social security, income tax, and SEC group of laws have the most direct impact in accounting. Other legal reporting which must be considered by the controller trends off to more specific legal requirements and will justify a more direct leaning on the company's legal department. Specifically, there is the "Walsh-Healy Act," technically the Public Contracts Act of 1936, which attempts to regulate employment conditions in the public interest through government contract conditions. The Fair Labor Stanards Act of 1938 aims at the same purposes through conditions of employment under a liberal interpretation of interstate commerce. These laws are administered by the U.S. Department of Labor. They have rather specific record keeping requirements which, however, do not impinge on accounting theory.

Reports to the Federal Trade Commission (FTC) go back to the Federal Trade Commission act of 1914, one of efforts of the Wilson administration efforts to curb various malpractices considered as "unfair competition." The FTC has authority to require reporting (which could overlap that of the SEC) described in the law as

. . . to require, by general or specific orders, corporations engaged in commerce, excepting banks and common carriers . . . or any class of them, or any of them . . . to file with the Commission in such form as the Commission may prescribe annual or special, or both annual and special, reports or answers in writing to specific questions. . . .

The SEC is interested in the merger movement from the angle of protecting the investor from potential deceit and fraud, the FTC is interested in those same mergers from the angle of protecting the public from the dangers of monopoly, limiting of competition, collusive pricing, and so forth. That their procedures are similar is evidenced by new regulations issued by the FTC, announced in the May 10, 1969, Federal Register, calling for special reports relating to corporate mergers, of companies having assets of $10 million or more and combined assets of $250 million or more. Detailed financial data are required. These reports are informational only and do not imply acceptance of or rejection of the merger by the FTC.

Another important concern of business is its relation to the FTC under the provisions of the Fair Trade Practices Act of 1936, commonly known as the Robinson-Patman Act. This act tightened up and modernized previous state and Federal legislative attempts to prevent certain aspects of price competition which were considered basically destructive to normal and desirable competition. The "unfair" practice aimed at was that in which manufacturers or wholesalers gave such price concessions to large retailers—principally the chain stores—that these firms could undercut small retailers and drive them out of or at least handicap them severely in the final consumer market.

The act prohibits such price discriminations as will "injure, destroy, or prevent competition," but it does allow price differentials (a) necessary to meet the provable prices of others in the same market, and (b) where it can be shown that the actual costs of doing business with specific customers, because of volume or other factors, is lower. This last provision, proving the propriety of lower prices on the basis of lower costs has become known as "cost justification." It obviously becomes an exercise in accounting—to prove that the costs of serving one customer or group or classification of customers are less than for other typical customers. The pattern of what is and what is not sufficient evidence is gradually evolving from the cases on which the Commission has ruled. These cases have been brought together with very thorough commentary in a book, *Cost Justification*, by Dr. Herbert F. Taggart, published in 1959 by the University of Michigan Bureau of Business Research and kept up to date by a series of follow-up studies since then.

The sometimes nightmarish complications encountered in this area are another good illustration of the difficulty encountered in the attempt, by legislation and administrative commission techniques to make the capitalistic system work in a reasonably effective and humane manner.

An exhaustive analysis of legal reporting under all Federal and state laws would be a lifetime job. A realistic down-to-earth approach to the whole matter is to visualize the individual controller dealing directly with representatives of the Treasury Department and other government agencies for the purpose of explaining or verifying data submitted in reports and returns, answering requests for new information, and in some cases negotiating settlements and agreements. In many of these dealings the government representatives and the controller, as the representative of his company, are on opposite sides of an issue; sometimes the issue is a major one, as where a substantial tax liability is involved, and sometimes it is a relatively minor question, such as the amount of detail required in some report or questionnaire.

It is important to remember that the government field representatives with whom the controller deals do not as a rule have much to do with making law or policy—their duty is to administer laws and policies laid down by higher authority, and the great majority of them are anxious to perform that duty with fairness and with a minimum of disturbance to business. The controller should acquire an understanding of the law under which the various agencies operate, their general policies, organization, and lines of responsibility, and the scope of the assignments and instructions given to their field representatives. Differences of opinion or interest should be analyzed objectively in an effort to reach common ground or, if that is impossible, to agree on the nature of the issue and the facts involved, so that the case can be clearly presented for review by higher authority in the agency or by the courts. Such an approach does not imply any surrender of rights either by the company or by the government; it is simply the comon-sense way to a successful handling of the necessary working relationships between government and business.

In dealing with government representatives at the policymaking level, the same attitude of cooperation and frankness, with an objective effort to arrive at a mutual understanding of common problems, is unquestionably to the advantage of both business and the government. There are, of course, government policymakers who are hostile to business, and there are times when issues must be clearly drawn and carried, if necessary, to the highest lawmaking authority—the state legislature or the Congress. But these occasions are rare; the great majority of issues, at least in the controller's field of responsibility, can and should be settled as matters of administration. It is noteworthy that many business men who go into government service soon find themselves acquiring the "government viewpoint"; similarly, there are few government officials who will not acquire something of the "business viewpoint" if they are exposed to it. For this reason, the work of the committees appointed by the Financial Executives Institute, and the American Institute of Certified Public Accountants to confer with various government agencies on common problems has been and will continue to be of the utmost importance. The individual controller can obviously exert more influence on government policy by working through these committees than by his own unaided efforts; but by his attitude in his own dealings with government representatives he can help to create the background of mutual confidence and good will that is essential to the success of the committees' work.

4 IMPLEMENTATION OF THE MANAGEMENT CONCEPT

Chapter 1 of this book set up the basic concept of controllership in terms of definition and purposes. Chapters 2 and 3 treated two of the necessary subfunctions. It is the function of this chapter to move into the implementation of the three remaining major purposes served by controllership. These together constitute what is most commonly considered the area of information service to management.

DATA, INFORMATION AND MANAGEMENT

This somewhat overworked word, implementation, is still the best way to characterize the practical job that faces the controller. If we may assume that the philosophy of management accounting has been correctly visualized we can hardly escape the challenge of building an information framework which will enable us to put that philosophy to work. The angle of approach is different, but the problem again is very close to the basic controllership function as defined in Chapter 1—". . . designing and operating the records of the business and reporting and interpreting the information which they contain." This statement will become more and more meaningful as we get into the effort to tie up wishful thinking to the concrete details of method. "Information" is the good word in our entire effort. At this point another effort to refine the information concept is necessary. If we contemplate for a moment the enormous range of detailed "information" that *could* be collected regarding the operation of any business, we must realize that a great proportion thereof would never have the slightest trace of usefulness. Such collected words and figures might in themselves be clear representations of objectively observable facts, but unless they are going to have some *impact on management actions*, they are "mere data." Properly sorted out, the potentially *useful* data become *"information."*

While Webster may not agree specifically with this distinction between data and information, it is for our purposes a very useful distinction. In part, then, the task of setting up the controller's information system will be the cautious avoidance of mere data and the heightened attention to potential usefulness as the screening criterion in judging systems content. By and large the above distinctions are not really new; they have been in effect in most present accounting systems. An awareness of the real nature of the distinction is important when faced with the practical problem of the almost constant revisions going on in any live system. This will be especially true at the time when new EDP techniques become available with their enormous potential for collecting and storing. "Mere data" would still be useless though collected by a million dollar computer.

The problem in terms of statement usefulness

The issue of mere data versus information will generally arise in the redesign of the reports and statements because it is at this point that the use or nonuse, becomes most apparent. Everyone has run into the claim, often justified, that certain reports are produced period after period for no better reason than that they have always been part of the system. It seems to take a peculiar kind of fortitude to order the discontinuance of such reports. Delicate interpersonal relationships are at stake when a systems man suggests to the line official recipient of a report that it is probably useless and should be discontinued. He is dangerously near to seeming to accuse said official of having wasted the company's money in the past by continuing to receive said useless report. A more tolerable approach would usually be to ask the line official whether he would care to suggest improvements in the form or content of the report. This would allow the line man himself to get credit for discovering the fact that some or all of the content was no longer useful. If the case is really clear the net result will probably be the same—discontinuance—but with no delicate sensibilities abraded.

In actual practice, the elimination of "mere data" will often not be as gross a problem as the dropping of a whole report or even sections thereof. It may comprise the dropping of minor ancillary matters—dates, descriptive words, names, subtotals, detail figures, rulings, heading elements, etc. The motivating rationale should, of course, be the service and convenience of the report to the line recipient, not the saving in time and effort to the controller's division. This attitude is both basically sound, and incidentally good interpersonal relations for keeping the line men happy.

Premium on foresight

We have warned against useless data. Complementary to this warning is the acknowledgement that it is not possible to supply all the information needed for every business decision. Rationally stated, the task becomes: *to provide in advance, as far as feasible, the foreseeable information requirements.* The probable usefulness of information in any area does not manifest any clear cutoff, but constitutes a rough continuum. A particular problem may call for information which lies anywhere on this range, or, even with the best of planning, which may be outside of what has been foreseen and provided for.

In some instances, such information can be dug up by special ad hoc effort when needed. If such new information requirements are truly unique the controller may have to go to new sources entirely outside his present system. Frequently, however, the new information requirement may be in the nature of more detail or new relationships among facts already in the basic information system. Such special analyses will be feasible in direct proportion to the skill and imagination with which the underlying general pattern was designed. Built-in flexibility for long-run eventualities as well as the service of obvious, immediate needs can be attained only by the most conscientious attention to the purposes to be served.

INFORMATION COMES ALIVE IN TERMS OF PURPOSES

To get beyond lip service to the idea that the controller's function is information for management use it is necessary to examine much more critically the concept of the management-information relationship. To a personnel man, management is getting things done through people. To the marketing man, management is finding out what will sell, getting it, and selling it. To the finance man, management is putting out money under calculated risk conditions and expecting it to come back with an increment. The production man's management is the implementation of the "build a better mousetrap" philosophy. These are all valid viewpoints, but they are not directly useful for our purpose. More pertinent to our interest is the fact that in all of these areas the quintescence of management is the decision-making process.

Many business schools have picked up this approach, implemented it with thousands of specific cases involving decision making and have done a tremendous job in the training of business leaders. This approach aims at finding out what business is all about by examining it in the concrete—the sorts of things that business men are really doing. Such study or actual experience in the business area if backed by imaginative observation, leads to an awe inspiring appreciation of the enormous variety of situations in which decisions must be made—and every one of those decisions requires a large command of information. To set up an information system to enable the business to handle an infinity of discrete problems would be an infinite job. This is what the controller faces and it is, in the absolute sense, impossible.

The only hope, and the controller's practical procedure, is to classify the myriads of business problems to the point where he can see a pattern developing. If he can visualize business problems falling into groups with substantial similarities, he will have a reasonable chance to organize the information necessary for management. Different groupings of business problems have been offered from time to time. We are under no illusion that all business problems will fall neatly into the breakdown pattern here offered, but we have found that this pattern is the most useful in our very special problem of developing an information system with maximum chance of usefulness. Obviously, the system must get at the roots of things in aiming at the most all-pervasive problems and obviously too it must be flexible to allow greatest accommodation for differences in business situations. In actual use, the test of the system will be its ability to supply the information needed in particular decision situations either in a directly useful form or in a form from which it is possible by manipulation to derive the directly necessary information.

In setting up a particular system, the controller must have imagination to foresee to as great an extent as possible the practical problems which will face his management. In this task, he will be well advised to consult extensively with the line executives to get their help in foreseeing problem situations. If this quest is a blind search for any and all "problems that may arise in the future," it will not get very far. If, on the other hand, the controller conducts this quest with some knowledge of the patterns of problems that are likely to come up and searches for help to apply this general knowledge to the specific problems which the line can foresee, he will have a very good chance of setting up a vital system. Chapter 1 already suggested the basic outline of purposes. It remains now to dig further into the purposes to be served in order to plan the construction of the necessary information framework.

THE PROBLEM OF CONTROL

Our analysis of the usefulness of a breakdown of expenses in the accounts has already approached the problem of control at several points in this book. At this point, it is necessary to emphasize the ubiquitousness of this problem and to further examine its ramifications. No matter whether the business is trading, manufacturing or service, it will have a recognized departmental structure which will to a large extent follow functional lines. Each organization unit will have its tasks to perform and its legitimate costs to get its work done. What we did not emphasize before becomes important now. The organization is human beings. Some humans are inherently motivated by the conscientious ideal of giving the best possible service at the most economical cost to the employer. Unfortunately, the corporation cannot rely on this ideal motivation. In a period of prosperity, an occasionally lucky corporation could perhaps neglect formal technical control, but under normal, competitive conditions, neglect of control will soon find the corporation "bled white" by contagious inefficiencies, uneconomies, and possible fraud. Management must find ways, gentle or tough, to exact efficient, economical operation from every organizational unit. Direct methods of persuasion, exhortation, and the general maintenance of a high morale are highly desirable, but experience shows that they are not enough and that these mild methods must be backed up by unimpeachable measurements through the accounts. Only so can credit be given where credit is due —and fully documented blame where deserved.

While the accounting system must serve a variety of purposes, this purpose of control of expenses is central. The pattern of the expense accounts in the usual chart is most obviously aimed at this effect.[1] Its primary classification follows the organization and measures the total expenses unit by unit. The breakdown within the units by object of expenditure is designed to help the organization head in the discharge of his responsibility by showing him as clearly as possible the total of each expense under his jurisdiction. The ideal is fine, the real problem of control is making it work, and that is a matter of close attention to details, difficulties, "bugs" in the actual situation, and recognition of the human, interpersonal, factors.

Most importantly, the system must be set up simple enough, yet flexible enough, so that it can be thoroughly sold to the organization unit head who is being measured. He must understand its purpose, be convinced that it is fairly designed to do its job, and convinced also that it is accurate in its routine functioning. This selling job must begin with a careful explanation at the time the system is installed, but even more important it must be followed up by completely frank and fair use as the daily, weekly, or other periodic reports start rolling in. The form and tone of the reports must support the basic idea that control means not only putting the screws on by comparing the actual cost totals to past performance, budgeted standards, and so forth, but that the detail breakdown comparisons are really useful in helping the line man see exactly where the differences lie. To make this point effective the controller's representative handling the detail must always stand ready to listen to the line men's ideas as to the adequacy of the breakdown for each particular purpose. The foreman *and* his supervisor should be in on these discussions, and both must be satisfied. This places a considerable burden on the systems man, but it is the single most critical interpersonal issue in the whole control situation. There is a vast difference in final effect between achieving sincere cooperation of the line and what is too often found in practice—distrust and hatred of the whole system with ingenious efforts to beat it by a dozen devious dodges.

The systems man in contact with the line man must be alert for

---

[1] Chapter 7 takes on the full technical problem of setting up the actual accounts to accomplish the purposes here outlined.

any unusual situation. The best that any text can do for him is to call attention to a few of the most commonly met problem situations. One such situation is that in which a particular department or cost center needs a greater degree of breakdown in one or more of the standard objects of expenditure. Supplies would be the most obvious case. The foreman of the label printing department of a pharmaceutical manufacturer for instance wanted its supplies broken down as follows:

4011   Supplies
4011-1 Supplies—Plate Making—Offset
This account will be charged with supplies used in making plates for the offset press. This includes such items as acid, albumen, etc.
4011-2 Supplies—Plate Making—Rubber
This account will be charged with supplies used in making rubber plates. This includes such items as plastic matrix material, badelite, adhesive fabric, plate gum, etc.
4011-3 Supplies—Linotype
This account will be charged with supplies for the Linotype machine.

The first two digits, in this case 40, identify the Label Printing Department. The third and fourth digits, 11, are the general number for supplies. The -1, -2, -3 numbers are special kinds of supplies of considerable importance to this department and broken out at the request of the department head.

This particular breakdown reflects the foreman's intimate knowledge of conditions within his department and of the need to identify more exactly the wastes in supply usage, which the controller's representative unaided would not appreciate.

Closely related to the further breakdown of standard classifications is the recognition of the occasionally really unique item as such with full presentation rather than to force it into some distantly related account or into a catchall miscellaneous. If for instance the systems department has computer rentals expense, this should not be forced into utilities expense but should be set up as "computer rentals" in one of the open numbers of the object classification.

Another area which can develop friction if not properly handled is the charging of certain general expenses to the department on an allocated basis. This is entirely proper and necessary in accumulating total departmental costs as part of the full product costing scheme. Great care is necessary in interpreting the department expense reports in order not to confuse such items over which the department head has no control with the controllable items. The form of the report should reinforce the distinction, possibly by showing a subtotal for the controllable items and by relegating the noncontrollables to a below-the-line position on the statement. Some companies entirely eliminate the noncontrollable expenses from the reports used for expense control though they do, of course, bring them back in when departmental overhead rates are calculated for product costing purposes.

Lest the above description should seem oversimple, let us look at a borderline case or two. There are occasional situations in which normally noncontrollable items ought to be regarded and discussed as controllable. The reverse is also sometimes true. Usually depreciation on departmental equipment is held to be a noncontrollable item, whose amount is determined by company policy and therefore in no sense the department foreman's responsibility. However, we may have a special circumstance: The foreman has for a long time argued that the purchase of a costly special machine would cut labor and certain other costs in his department. The company bought this machine on the strength of his insistence. This month his other costs decreased a few dollars. What should be the attitude toward the substantial increase of depreciation on departmental equipment under these circumstances?

Take another illustration in the area of insurance. Most insurance is a matter of company-wide control and therefore usually not considered controllable at the departmental level. This is certainly true of insurance on the plant as included in rent factor. However, there may be special kinds of insurance necessary for protection against the hazards encountered only in certain departments, as, for instance, boiler explosion in the power department. Workmen's liability insurance rates depend in part on the observance or failure to observe certain safety precautions. What would we say about the increase in insurance cost caused by a foreman's negligence in enforcing safety precautions? What if he had been specifically warned that conditions in his department threatened to bring about a rate increase?

On the other hand, it is just as possible under certain circumstances for items which are normally controllable to react as noncontrollable. The amount and proportion of overtime used by a foreman are generally watched very closely as evidence of how well he is running his department. But what about a change in the terms of the union contract which forces him to give overtime work to laborers with the highest seniority—and the highest pay rates? What about overtime forced on his department by the breakdown of work schedules in some other department? The overtime under these conditions may still be controllable, but responsibility for its control has shifted for the time being to someone other than the foreman in whose department it happens to occur. Careless interpretation at this time could do real injustice and cause a dangerous loss of respect for the fairness of the accounting analysis.

The purpose of these illustrations is merely to point out that the problem of controllability of expenses is not an easy one. There is a temptation to keep things simple by drawing a clear, single line which will separate the controllable expense from the noncontrollable in all departments, but to do so may create a dangerous illusion. Regardless of any formal drawing of "the line" which may serve for most cases within a business, the final safeguard must be intelligent and imaginative interpretation and use of the figures as reported to management. The cutting edge of control will lie in discussions between the foreman and his line superior. The controller's responsibility is to be sure that the line personnel using the figures are aware of the possible misinterpretations, and sensitive to the effect of special and changing circumstances.

Measuring unit performance

Still another aspect of the control problem is the fact that behind all judgments of the propriety of expense increases or decreases lies the achievement, production, service, or performance of the unit. This concept reaches fullest maturity in standard cost accounting and budgeting. In the absence of these techniques, simpler measures must suffice. Some units, especially those directly engaged in production, can be measured directly in physical output units. In others the total of direct labor costs may suffice. Service units are likely to be harder to measure; the number of letters written during the month by the secretarial pool may be an adequate measure in some instances but quite unsatisfactory in others. The measurement of performance for the legal or public relations departments or for basic research practically defies solution. The controller may make his best contribution by warning against the use of oversimple concepts.

A final aspect of effective control through the accounting system is the humdrum matter of routine accuracy. All the fine theory would accomplish very little if the head of the department does not have faith that the charges to his expense accounts represent actual consumption of materials and services in his unit.

The controller's systems man has the initial responsibility for laying out the "bookkeeping" routines whatever mechanical or electronic devices are in use. The routines must recognize the several paths whereby charges enter the expense accounts: (1) Certain kinds of charges are unique and can be identified to specific departments at the invoice vouchering point. A purchase of welding rod is most certainly destined for the welding department; the purchase of 20,000 tons of coal is clearly intended for the power department; the bill for the annual audit, by our outside public accountants is chargeable somewhere in the controller's department, and so forth. (2) The second pattern of expense entries is that in which supplies commonly used in several or many departments are purchased, charged initially to general stockroom, and then issued to specific departments on the basis of requisitions signed by the department head. (3) Some services, such as water, gas, compressed air, can be metered to departments. (4) Electric power, produced by the company's own power plant can be simply metered, charged on a connected load estimate basis, or allocated on a formula recognizing maximum demand plus actual metered consumption. There may be still other patterns of expense entry recognizing special technological circumstances.

The simple theoretic concern of proper accrual accounting may be of considerable importance. Materials purchased directly for the department, or requisitioned from the storeroom, in sizable quantities and not consumed at the close of the reporting period might distort the reporting picture if not recognized either by formal adjustments or by informal allowance in the interpretation of results.

In every case it is important that the line unit head be informed of the techniques whereby his unit is charged and that he be fully convinced that the method used is adequate and fair. To back up his confidence in the adequacy of the system the line unit head should be allowed to ask for audit review of the results of any period which seems to him substantially out of line. It is, of course, to be hoped that such requests will not be frequent enough to constitute a burden. Probably the fact that he has the right to such review will go a long way to giving him confidence in routinely reported results.

Control action is not the controller's function

In one large organization the controller was commonly referred to as "The Hated Man," and he probably is a hated man in many organizations without having achieved this title in captial letters. Where this is the case it is almost certain that for one reason or another the controller has been given, or has assumed, line authority in the area of control. This is a clear case of violation of the controllership concept. If in addition to organizing and running the system of expense accounting, he has line responsibility to call in the line personnel for bawling out (or for praise), the organization of duties is clearly at fault.

A somewhat different situation, sometimes encountered in small businesses, is that in which the controller is given specific veto power over the making of certain expenditures. If he has the responsibility of saying "no" to traveling salesmen's expense reimbursement requests, he is unlikely to be popular with the salesmen. Somewhat parallel to this is the responsibility for approving specific capital expenditures. Perhaps this is less objectionable than control over salesmen's swindle sheets, but it is still the exercise of line authority and not within the basic controller function. Such authority should be assumed by the controller only as a clearly understood special extension of line authority and must be exercised with great care lest it jeopardize the controller's normal functioning. Again closely related and *not* improper is the controller's responsibility to sign his approval of the presentation of disbursement reports as to reasonableness of classification, valuation and so forth.

As the control function matures it eventually results in full scale budgeting. This topic is fully dealt with in later chapters. At this point it should begin to be clear that the controller will have substantial responsibility for the budget, but it should also be clear that his responsibility therein is limited by the concept of the controllership function.

The technical design of the budget, the periodic supply of historical background figures, the periodic collection of estimates from various sources, the setting up periodically of the proposed budget, the production of routine budget performance reports are all aspects of the information marshalling function and, therefore, properly the controller's function. It should be noted, however, that this list does *not* include the adoption, or willing-into-effect, of the budget or the subsequent budget *actions* (the praise, the blame, the allowance of exceptions, etc.). Such actions are line responsibilities under budget practice just as actions in the control of expenses would be without the budget formality. These fine distinctions are well worth careful attention just because they are so often missed in practice.

THE PROBLEM OF VENTURE MEASUREMENT

Items 2 (b) in the Chapter 1 outline of controllership purposes is venture measurement. This purpose is simple in concept but becomes difficult in the actual doing. The observed fact is that most businesses do not have a single activity source of revenue but multiple sources. The local shoe store has men's, women's and children's shoes for sale. The practical proprietor recognizes that the three divisions may have different rates of profitability and in many cases his informal judgment may be quite correct. This simply means that he is doing some pretty shrewd venture accounting in his head. It is also possible that he may be misleading himself by substituting his prejudice against the fussy job of fitting children's shoes for cold business judgment as to their profitability. Very few small businesses do an adequate job of venture analysis and it is quite probable that their failure to do so results in carrying lines unprofitably year after year. Note that the argument is not simply that the less profitable or even the unprofitable lines should be dropped, but that the manager should know what he is facing and then take any possible steps to rectify the situation. On the positive side of the argument, it is just as necessary to know which lines are most profitable in order to be able to maximize their profitability. What is to be *done*, it should be noted, is not controllership, but management and may involve many other important considerations than those presented by even a very effective accounting analysis.

Setting up an accounting system to provide venture analysis for the shoe store would begin with the segregation of inventories, sales and purchases of the three ventures. Sales and purchases returns and discounts on purchases should also be broken down. So far, all that is needed is routine and careful bookkeeping. To go beyond this begins to need more careful analysis. Breaking expenses down runs all the way from easy to impossible, and even in this simple business to do the job right would involve the same kind of thinking which would be needed in much larger businesses. For instance, a study of advertising expense would very likely show that certain ads had been directed specifically to one division (kids new shoes for the opening of school!). Other ads would have been for the business as a whole and could possibly be prorated to the three divisions on some significant basis. This problem parallels exactly the advertising cost analysis of the largest department stores. We would find innumerable similarities between the accounting for very small and very large businesses, and the critical study of what to do about it in each case could be very instructive. Frequently, the real problem lies in deciding how far to go in the attempted analysis. The answer to this query lies in possible use that management would get from the further analysis. If allocation is on such far-fetched bases that the accountant would feel apologetic when presenting it, or if the resulting dollar amounts are too small to be material, the expense should be left as general administrative or "unallocated." There is usually plenty of work to be done where there is "paydirt." In the large business the complications of intrenched organization interests and the difficulties of reporting techniques sometimes obscure relatively simple relationship—this is the reason for our frequently drawing the parallel to the humbler and more clearly visible situation of small business.

The kinds of interrelationships of the revenue segments of a business vary greatly and a study of the different pattern possibilities is the necessary background for accounting treatments which will be useful to management. The simplest pattern is that in which the ventures are basically similar or parallel. The clearest example of this is the department store whose many merchandising departments all involve buying, pricing, selling activities and whose expenses—wages, advertising, supplies, delivery, insurance, etc.—are much the same in all departments. Contrast the department store with the public utility which provides electric service, gas service, and steam heating to the public, plus having an extensive appliance merchandising activity. The production techniques of electricity, gas, and steam are very different (the gas may be purchased from Texas by pipeline); the merchandising of appliances resembles the department store operation and is entirely dissimilar in revenues, costs and expenses from the three service departments. Electricity and gas ventures are, however, quite similar in their important customer relations and customer accounting aspects. The steam business may be huge but sell to only a few hundred large customers in the metropolitan area.

A manufacturing business may resemble a department store superficially in that it has a great many related products whose manufacturing costs are parallel as are the costs of sales departments in a store. However closer examination would show that in manufacturing there are large elements of joint costs not paralleled in merchandising. A raw material common to all or many of the manufactured products, and depreciation of machinery used jointly are elements not found in merchandising though such common costs as housing and top administration are again quite similar in the manufacturing and merchandising. The large manufacturing business may also have nationwide or worldwide distribution of its products, and this introduces the concept of geographic areas as ventures which must be studied.

The suggestion of geographic areas as venture units again raises the question as to how far it is proper to go in any analysis. Visualize an optical instruments manufacturing company with one hundred products. It divides the country into seven regions each with from three to fifteen branches and with ten to fifty salesmen in each branch, with every salesman calling on two to three hundred customers. Theoretically, the sales, cost of sales, and selling costs could be broken down all the way to each customer's purchase of each of the 100 products. As a matter of fact, such analyses have been made and have been found useful. This degree of detail may come as a shock in contrast with the shoe store situation. It is important to see that both are legitimate illustrations of venture analysis and that they are basically similar. The shoe store, incidentally might have gone further in its analysis. The chances are that the store carries two or more brands of men's shoes, and beyond this there is a question whether the special order activity for extremely large or extremely small, or whether special orthopedic adjustment shoes, etc., should be investigated as to profitability. We would be inclined to guess that for the typical small town shoe store these final detailed possibilities had best be left to the proprietor's own cerebral treatment, but if we are talking about a big city shoe store which has established a reputation for handling all special shoe problems, the answer might favor clear cut accounting for the "specials" department. Maybe there should be three separate departments in this case: "men's extra large," "women's extra small," and "children's orthopedic."

For the optical company and for the shoe store, the answer as to how far to go in the venture analysis lies in the same kind of thinking. Does management, after carefully pondering the question, really need the refined information for specific, concrete decision making? For the optical company the question of individual customer profitability is a commonplace question in sales administration. This company would surely not continue to send a salesman to customer Jones at a continuing salary and travel cost of hundreds of dollars per year to produce a ten dollar gross sales profit. This customer might be completely abandoned or he might be put on a mail contact only basis at a cost of fifty cents per year.

Alternatively, a detailed analysis might reveal the real difficulty—that the sales to some customer were concentrated in short-margin products. Action by the district sales manager could then pressure the salesman to push longer-margined products on to this customer possibly converting him to actual profitable status.

Good sales administration applies the same techniques to sales regions, districts, offices. The product composition of sales in each area is studied against its potential in terms of attained margins and the pressures of reprimand, bonus, or promotion are effectively used for the sales administrations concerned.

Venture accounting and the "conglomerates"

The present-day glamour aspect of venture analysis is its sudden, tremendously increased importance in connection with the reporting for multidivision businesses. This problem, whose legal aspects have already been discussed in Chapter 3, is worthy of additional study now from the viewpoint of the very top management—the stockholders' interest and equity. Later in this chapter, it will also serve to demonstrate our thinking in the area of forensics. The problem takes its unique tone from the fact that in the typical conglomerate we are dealing with a business that got into its multiventure position by take-overs of and mergers with previously independent concerns, rather than by growth from within. Management needs and is presumably getting the same kinds of information as to venture profitability which is normally provided by good accounting. The controversy in this area arises from the fact that stockholders and their friends the financial analysts feel cheated because they are now not getting the facts as to venture profitability. This point will be treated more fully in the following section on forensics.

If anyone doubts the importance of venture measurement, he should read thoroughly ten or fifteen successive issues of The Wall Street Journal. It is safe to guarantee that such a reading would uncover a dozen or more news stories about corporations reporting words to the effect that the low net income of the past year or two was due to losses incurred in the operations of blank division and that this situation (a) has now been cured or (b) that the profitless division has been sloughed off by sale to so and so, which should improve the earnings, etc. There never seems to be any doubt in these stories about the fact that the managements know the truth about the profitability of the particular venture involved. We can only hope that such confidence is fully justified.

Another not unrelated angle is the proper functioning of the controller in the forward planning efforts of the management team. This should certainly not mean that the controller is making the decisions as to what to do about the future. It must however mean that he is taking a very large responsibility in providing information to management which is especially needed in the making of forward decisions. A clear picture regarding every present segment of the business is the take-off point in those decisions. A business may occasionally face a project so unique that there are no clues to its possible success in the records of past ventures. This, however, is rare compared to the usual forward planning situation which involves expansion or contraction of present ventures, or extension into more or less related fields in which the experience of the past may be assumed to be significant. When information needed for the forward planning must by its nature come from sources outside the company, the controller may still be the best equipped to obtain it, though it is also possible that at this point the determining information may be technical, nonquantitative, and entirely out of the controller's realm.

The full analysis of the controller's function in forward planning is presented in Chapter 19.

THE PROBLEM OF FORENSICS

By and large corporate accountants have neglected to give proper attention to this newest and very important aspect of management accounting. This is a strong statement and it needs careful framing. It does not mean that we have ignored controversial issues, but it does mean that our attention has generally taken the form of specific approaches and devices aimed at immediate issues. What has been neglected is the routine organization and collection of basic information needed to face up to future controversies as and when they may arise.

The older purposes—routine operations, control, and venture measurement—are generally serviced by the formal chart of accounts and by other records closely tied thereto. The marshaling of information for forensic purposes, however, has been largely an ad hoc in-the-presence-of-an-emergency procedure. A careful reading of discussions of forensic matters, especially court procedures, shows pretty clearly that the information used had to be dug out from a system designed for other purposes.

Acquiring information in such a manner involves two distinct disadvantages. First, essential information is likely to be unavailable or inadequate. Second, it does not take a particularly brilliant opponent to recognize and to make use of the fact that information resulting from special digging takes on the aroma of special rigging. Whatever the form of the contest involved, this makes the presentation less convincing than it would be if the same information were presented "from sources routinely available under our normal accounting procedures."

This, then, becomes the problem: How can the availability of adequate information for forensic purposes be assured?

Recognizing forensics

The clue has been suggested earlier, it lies in the recognition of forensics as a coordinate purpose of management. This purpose must be provided for in the routine processes tied to the chart of accounts, rather than by making hurried special studies after the fact when particular controversial emergencies arise.

Against the background of an established chart of accounts which is already doing an otherwise adequate job, it may be difficult to visualize the changes needed to incorporate information necessary for the growing forensic needs of the business. A degree of detachment is necessary to get away from the rigidity of things as they are. Insisting on forensic needs as a coordinate major aspect of the overall management information problem will be a good beginning. Beyond this the clue lies in certain delicate interpersonal relationships between the controller and the line executives.

The controller, or the systems man under his direction, generally has an adequate concept of the pattern of management information needs for most other normal management purposes. Even so, it makes good sense for him to consult with management at all levels whenever there is an opportunity for revision of any facet of the management information system. This is good accounting and good psychology. The "consumer" of information on the corporate management scene must be satisfied just as must the consumer of merchandise. This should mean that the controller constantly keeps open to management the question, "Does our present system of information reports take care of your management needs?"

While this attitude may seem to lay the systems man open to frequent requests for nuisance changes, it is a necessary price to pay for true flexibility in recognizing bona fide requests for information based on changing circumstances or on previously neglected needs. Judging the reasonableness of requests is the heart of systems work and requires real familiarity with conditions of line management and a full understanding of the possibilities and limitations of accounting technique. Furthermore, what seemed an unreasonable request a few years ago may be feasible with today's computer techniques. To fulfill his function, the systems man should get deeply into the matter of basic information needs rather than concern himself solely with the smooth running of yesterday's routine.

How shall this concept of full flexibility be applied specifically to the growing forensic needs of business? The form of the problem is the same—the controller must approach the concerned line and staff personnel with the same questioning attitude. He should not, however, ask, "Is the present system adequate?" Rather, he should ask the front-line executives to look ahead to any probable controversies and to analyze the situation in terms of information which would then be of maximum usefulness.

Underlying information

At this stage, executives untrained in accounting and unaware of its inherent limitations may ask for information in categories impossible to get by means of statistical or accounting techniques. They will have a tendency to ask for the *solution* to the problems which are foreseen rather than for *information which underlies the solution*. Great patience may be required in hewing to the line of this very real difference. It is the controller's function to supply the information. To decide just how that information is to be used in controversy is a line function.

With his growing top-management involvement, the controller will sit in on many strategy sessions in which he can hardly avoid getting into the decision area. To be of maximum aid to management, however, he will be well advised to recognize his change of hats so that he will not confuse his two responsibilities. The more clearly he visualizes the forces at play in coming controversies, the more surely will he be able to supply the needed information—ammunition for those on the front line.

It must be apparent that there will be great variety in the forensic situations which will face business managements in the future. Some of the problems will arise in any typical business. Income tax and labor contracts are practically universal sources of argument. Many businesses are in danger of running into trouble under the Robinson-Patman Act. Minimum wage statutes, sales taxes, cost inspection under government contracts, loss settlements under various forms of insurance, and SEC filing requirements—these all are common possibilities for forensic involvement.

Beyond such common problems lie great areas which are incidental to particular lines of business. The apartment landlord has rent control regulations, the agricultural enterprise has crop acreage limitations, the oil company has quotas, the stockbroker has the rules of the exchange, the race track has betting laws. The list could be extended considerably.

Brainstorming sessions

One effective mechanism to get at these elusive requirements would seem to be a series of brainstorming sessions in which the controller sits down with representatives from public relations, labor relations, legal counsel, and top management with the express purpose of letting imaginations run riot on all possible foreseeable controversial situations. Such brainstorming sessions have proven very valuable in other areas. They should be equally effective in this area. Many of the difficulties proposed in such sessions may on analysis turn out to be thin air, but the spirit of the game is to allow discussions to run rampant.

When the list of problems has been simmered down to those that have serious probabilities, the controller must move the discussion to the business of outlining the hard factual information needed to serve the company's interest in each controversy predicted. "Here's the situation we will be in"; "This is what we've got to face"; "What we will have to prove is—." These are the statements that lead to the basic information requirements. To be avoided at all costs is the future sad refrain, "If we had only seen this thing coming, we could have collected the dope so easily!"

Beyond this point, the problem becomes a technical one for the controller or his systems man. It is possible, of course, that the new information requirement might be something entirely unique and unrelated to existing categories and techniques. Such a situation would be a delightful challenge. Possibly it would turn out to be a problem for the statistician or the actuary with no tie whatsoever to the debit and credit system. Possibly it will be a statistical breakdown of totals which themselves fall into the formal ledger control at some point.

We would like to hazard a judgment at this point. If the original accounting layout was broadly intelligent, a substantial part of the "new" information required will turn out to call for rearranging data already being collected, and very often different only in degree of detail, further breakdown, closer identification of elements, and so forth. For instance, new property will have to be identified as to whether it is eligible for the off again–on again investment credit; the fringe benefit costs of labor will have to be broken down by new contract categories; the distribution of marketing costs to the product lines will have to be on recorded and logically justifiable bases. These and similar requirements involve no new principles. It is just that now they have to be utilized with a new purpose in mind—their possible forensic use.

Conglomerates and forensics

It may be useful to try out this concept against the great modern problem of conglomerate reporting. In its present stage this problem of conglomerate reporting is broadly controversial. We are debating the general pattern of portraying effectively the complicated situation of many ventures under one management. In one sense, this is not a new problem. As discussed earlier, proper analysis and presentation of multiple ventures has always been a basic requirement. However, this old familiar problem has now been blown up into huge new importance by two factors.

The first new factor in the picture is that the modern conglomerate characteristically results from the combination of previously independent units. Even this is not entirely new. We have had combination, vertical and horizontal, for a long time. We are fairly familiar with these "right angle" combinations, and with how to report them for internal management. The new combinations, however, are not at "right angles"; they are at any angle, often purposely with no operational relationship to other units in the combination. The effect of this on our accounting mechanics is to throw previously accepted relationships (expense allocations, interunit pricing, and so forth) into new kinds of tangles.

The second new factor in the modern conglomerate problem is the vastly increased interest of outsiders in the resulting picture. Present and prospective stockholders and investment analysts have become aware that equity interests are suddenly in a highly fluid state and that they may be greatly enhanced or harmed by complicated and illusive moves of acquisition and investment. As new moves are proposed, the stockholder may try to protect himself by his "yes" or "no" vote on the proxy, relying on proxy information which, he fears, is strongly colored by its sources. After the combination is completed, the stockholder finds himself holding new stocks. He watches the market price as the most available criterion of his investment's fate. Then he seeks solid evidence in the quarterly and annual statements of his new holdings. He would like to be able to trace the impact of his previously independent business upon the showing of the new conglomerate.

The investment analyst making his industry studies also wants to follow the fate of a previously independent unit which has become a segment of the conglomerate. He is exerting and will continue to exert considerable pressure for the kind of segmented reporting which he thinks he needs. The pressure is coming through public opinion, the SEC, and possibly direct congressional action. The whole concept of proper disclosure is highly involved and at the moment is in a very fluid state.

The companies have at least two good grounds for hesitating to put out the asked for information. There are undoubtedly many instances in which such disclosures would reveal information to competitors which should remain confidential. The second and probably more serious objection lies in the danger of reporting information which will be more confusing than revealing to the public.

The degrees of integration of previously separate operations are greatly varied. In some cases old managements disappear and the operations become practically departments thoroughly merged with other operations. In other cases the companies taken over maintain their identities virtually intact. Here the reported profitability of the unit might be closely comparable to the previous independently reported net. The completely merged operation would result in substantially different conditions, and the accounting net might reflect in addition to bona fide operating differences substantial relief from previous overhead, or, on the contrary, the possible allocation of new general company overhead—so that any comparison of present and past profitability would be definitely misleading.

Influenced by the concepts of direct costing, many controllers will be cautious about allocating general overhead to newly acquired units. If, however, the parent company (or home office) does render substantial services (engineering, marketing, financial) to the sub without accounting charges there is another form of misleading in the profitability picture. There are also the problems of nonrecurring costs and revenues often especially significant at or soon after the takeover, and they are by no means easy to identify for separate reporting.

Considerable debate concerns the definition of what shall be considered a segment for purposes of reporting. Certainly, no one is going to ask for public profitability reporting down to the point of customer or salesman as the unit. The practical solution is apparently going to be in terms of the percentage of the segment to the total business. The indicated compromise is in the area of 10 to 15 percent. Any segment (venture) showing less than such a percentage of the total gross revenue (or of the total net revenue, or of the contribution to overhead and profit) will not need to be reported separately. Such a percentage measure can be broadly applied—that is its advantage. It is however unfortunately crude. Some businesses could easily report segments much lower percentagewise and still significant, others will find that segments of 20 or 30 percent may be difficult to report significantly. If all analysts, stockholders and prospective investors had *CPA* equivalent training—and lots of time and energy to devote to studying the reports—the problem wouldn't be too bad. We are, however, trying to formulate rules for reporting immensely complicated situations so simply that even the untrained will not be misinformed.

Conglomerate reporting patterns

Financial executives have been working on this problem on a profession-wide basis, and some corporations have adjusted their own reporting to more clearly reflect significant segments. Very soon many more corporate conglomerates will be tight up against the problem and will have to come up with their own answers. While every situation will have its own unique aspects, we can begin to see the general pattern of the thinking which will be safe and acceptable. Two propositions stand out quite clearly.

First, if the report to the public can be tied to the accounting which is set up for normal management purposes, it will be easier to defend from attack than if it results from a special structure thrown together for public reporting purposes only.

Second, if the report can be clearly within the general principles which have been hammered out by the profession as sound and adequate, we will have a strong friend in court, whether it be the "court" of public opinion or a specific legal involvement.

The most important study on conglomerate reporting made to date, *Financial Reporting by Diversified Companies*,[2] by R. K. Mautz deserves intensive study by every financial executive. Even though it may be just the beginning of a long struggle to pattern the responsibilities of financial reporting, this study and its future amendments will provide needed support and comfort. To fight out each problem of disclosure on an entirely unique basis would not only be intolerably complicated but would lay each report open to separate attack.

The need for the brainstorming session in each corporation to implement use of the recommendations made in the Mautz study is apparent. The leading question for such a session should be, "Facing the coming pressures for new standards of reporting, what can we do to avoid criticism in the first place, or to meet it when and if it does come?"

The prevailing danger will be the accusation of inadequate segment reporting. What reporting is adequate will vary enormously from company to company. The possibility of unwise disclosure of competitive information also varies. Against this background, guided by the Mautz recommendations, each corporate management must analyze its particular situation and attempt to foresee its particular forensic involvements. To leave no stone unturned will require intense and conscientious attention of top financial management and public relations and legal counsel working closely with the controller.

Going back again to the first proposition, it should be obvious that while the new conglomerate problem will be discussed by managements in terms of reporting, we cannot properly report information which we have not properly accumulated in the accounting records. It is our contention that the controller will be well advised to take every possible precaution now to assure the availability of solid, organized information for his future reports—information that will support his conclusions even under the most unfriendly legal scrutiny.

In summary, there is a natural temptation to pay our greatest attention to the newest and most complicated forensic problem—conglomerate reporting. This is merely one of the forensic problems faced by management, and even it will probably be best handled by recognizing that it falls into the pattern of all forensic problems. The unique difficulty of forensic problems, as contrasted to other general management prob-

---

[2] Financial Executives Research Foundation, New York, N.Y., 1968.

lems, is the greater difficulty of foreseeing the information content which must be planned for. The difference is only one of degree, however, and the solution lies again in the full recognition and implementation of the basic controllership function—the provision of all necessary information for management use.

SUMMARY

The intriguing problem of business management can be most clearly visualized and provided for in terms of decision making. Analysis of this process reveals that it relies heavily upon the availability of pertinent information. While some problem situations are unique and impossible to foresee, they are the exceptions. By far the greater number of business problems are variations on three great general themes, control, venture accounting, and forensics. An appreciation of these three themes—the three purposes of management as outlined in this chapter—is the basis for the organization of the information plan which is the primary responsibility of the controller and, with care and imaginative adjustment to special circumstances, will have the best chance to come up with the most useful information when it is required for the almost infinite needs of management.

5 ORGANIZATION OF THE CONTROLLER'S DEPARTMENT

The principles involved in the organization of the controller's department are the same as those involved in business in general. The units of organizations, major and sub, to any degree necessary should follow the analysis of the function, first with regard to its relationship to other major functions and second with regard to its own subfunctional breakdown. While many other departments are involved in cross-functional relationships, the controllership function has certain unique cross-function involvements which are very important to its organizational problem. One purpose of this chapter is to develop a sensitivity to these special ramifications.

For anyone who is already familiar with the present form of organization of a particular controller's department, it may be difficult to assume a sufficiently detached attitude with reference to his own organization to think in general terms. As an aid to the attainment of such detachment, we will take a historical detour into the early stages of functional-organizational development to watch the growth that must have taken place in virtually every growing firm.

The striking basic similarities in the organizations of typical business are not explained by genetic inheritance but by the fact that the tensions of growth and management needs are similar. These tensions and needs are an expression of the differing functions which make up the totality of business management. The single owner-manager of a small new business must provide all of the functions of management. He may take great pride in this fact, but it is unlikely that he will be truly able in the functions of production, sales, finance, personnel, and all of their subfunctions.

The growth of the business organization can be visualized as the successive divesting of the special functions by the original entrepreneur and their assumption by individuals who are hopefully expert in their specialties. Even the initial hiring of workers to take on the muscle work is a breaking of the single total business responsibility into the two major functions of brain and brawn or more properly into management and labor. Our interest begins with the function of management and seeks to study out its necessary subfunctional specialization.

Early functional differentiation

The sole manager of a small business combines an immense variety of specialized functions in himself. Visualize owner-manager Jack Showalter who with ten employees was well established in the manufacture of wooden tables. In deciding to expand his shop to manufacture chairs as well as tables, he must do some market research to determine the sales potential; he must do some engineering to determine the design of the chairs, some personnel management to determine the availability of labor for the expanded venture, some public relations in deciding to announce his expanded job opportunities at some auspicious date. As he goes into production, his purchasing function expands; he takes on additional personnel functions as he instructs his new employees; and he performs some delicate financial management as he secures a loan from the local banker to finance the expanded payroll and raw material buying. Possibly, he must make legal decisions as he contemplates the fact that the technical design of the new chair closely approximates some patented features of his competitors' products. If Showalter makes a mistake in any one of these functions, his business will suffer.

The nature of the one-man management enterprise and the handicap under which it operates give clues to the principal tensions which control its growth pattern. If he has any imagination at all Showalter will take advantage of the growth of his business by hiring assistants with the special capabilities most needed. Probably, he thinks in terms of the jobs which he most dislikes doing himself, and these are quite likely the ones in which he has the least natural ability. The sales function is likely to be the first to be delegated, and Showalter will be lucky indeed if he finds a smart sales-minded young man to take this job off his hands.

As the business prospers and grows, Showalter needs and can afford more help. Possibly a factory foreman would be the next best development. This development might be thought of as relieving the general management of the production function. Actually, it is the delegation of several elements—engineering, personnel, and certain aspects of record keeping such as payroll. If Showalter does not wish to release the design aspect of engineering or the actual selection of new employees, he should be very specific to restrict the foreman in these respects. Note that their discussions along these lines are an effort to see clearly the functional and subfunctional lines. Business, being a part of humanity, is very complicated, and at this simple stage of development the functional organization will be far from perfect.

An attempt to visualize a growth and organization pattern on other than functional lines strains the imagination but may be useful in throwing light on to the nature and inevitability of normal functional development. Could Showalter have relieved himself of part of the total management task by bringing in an assistant to run the whole business on Mondays, Wednesdays, and Fridays while he retained the Tuesday, Thursday, Saturday responsibility? Or should he perhaps give the assistant responsibility for the work and problems of all female employees while he continues to boss all the males? Or should Showalter delegate all outdoor problems to the assistant while he retains all indoor problems? By contrast to these far-fetched suggestions, even the imperfect functional breakdown which is the usual pattern is far more likely to be workable.

At this stage, the principle that function is the basis of organization seems so obvious as to hardly need discussion. At the same time, its finer nuances are so elusive as to be often missed. Many business failures, and much of the controversy, squabbling, and in-fighting in business are caused by failure to recognize and utilize true functional breakdowns in organization. The larger the business the finer become the necessary distinctions between sub- and sub-subfunctional lines. The working edge of the problem, especially at the lower levels, gets right down to the matter of writing proper job descriptions.

Breaking out the controllership function

Identification of and provision for the controllership function in growing business is simply a part of this whole functional analysis problem. It does, however, have certain peculiarities which make it harder to set up properly than many of the other functions.

In the early days of his business, Showalter is probably not conscious of the fine point that the collection, marshaling, reporting, and interpreting of information are separable from the use which he as a manager is constantly making of that same information. Actually, the first recognition of the information function will almost certainly be the highly routine record keeping that is forced upon the business when it begins to sell on account, and purchase on account, to have a bank account, and to keep payroll records. Initially, Showalter keeps the records himself, but it is a task that he dislikes, so he is quite certain at an early stage to hire a bookkeeper, a graduate of the local business college or high school commercial course.

The management use that is made of the information at this stage will embrace such simple things as not writing checks when the bank balance is too low, proving to factory hand Joe Doke that his biweekly paycheck really is correct—he had forgotten about his social security deduction, etc. Somewhat more complicated use of information will be the refusal to extend more credit to the Jones Furniture Company on the basis of the poor collections shown by the account receivable. Since the credit function has not been specifically recognized and provided for, we may get a squabble at this point. Who cuts off the credit? The bookkeeper may be the first to see the facts. Showalter may take the action much to the disgust of his salesman who values Jones Furniture as one of his biggest customers and who happens to know that Jones's recent slow payments have been caused by some clearly temporary difficulties and that "Jones is as good as gold." This altercation may appear to be typically interpersonal, but actually it is caused by the failure to provide clearly for the credit function responsibility.

Undoubtedly, the bookkeeper, in the simple situation illustrated by the Showalter business, is the authentic ancestor of the controller; the line of descent through the accountant is clear. Just as any individual can learn much about himself by studying the weaknesses and strengths of his biological forebears, so can the controller of today become more aware of his own position and function by a critical appraisal of his humble professional antecedents.

Early management accounting effort—The expense accounts

The original books set up by the typical small business bookkeeper probably embrace 10 or 20 expense accounts of the mixed basis type commonly sneered at as "grocery store" accounts. The expense accounts would probably show: Salaries, Wages, Supplies, Insurance, Heat and Light, Office, Delivery, Advertising, Taxes, Power, Depreciation, Bad Debts, Commissions, Miscellaneous. If these categories are consistently adhered to, they might give Showalter some very slight management aid. For instance, a really radical increase in supplies expense in one year might alert him to some theft or wastage; a drop in insurance might alert him to the fact that he forgot to renew the public liability insurance, etc. Practically, the *if* in "if consistently adhered to" touches an important cause of uselessness in these accounts. A change of bookkeepers would be almost certain to cause shifts in classification. The increase in supplies expense, for instance, might have been caused by charging office supplies to "Supplies" in one year whereas it had been charged to "Office" the previous year. The driver's wages may be charged to "Wages" one year and to "Delivery" the next.

Even more important than the hazard of inconsistency is the issue that the typical small business expense accounts are virtually useless in fixing responsibility. The supplies expense is the clearest demonstration of this point. Since the use of supplies is in the hands of the factory work force, the office help, the sales manager, and the delivery man, an increase in the total for a particular period cannot be tied on to anyone. If Showalter becomes aware of this and asks the bookkeeper henceforth to use four supplies expense accounts, he will be thereby moving in the right direction to begin to make the expense accounts useful.

This material is "old hat" to any accountant. It is inserted here to demonstrate that the *function* of controllership is manifest in even a rudimentary stage of organization development. Recognition of the usefulness of classifying expenses by functional-organization-unit (delivery, office, sales) instead of by object of expenditure (wages, supplies, insurance) takes on management significance even at this early stage. It is controllership thinking though exercised by a $35-a-week bookkeeper for a humble businessman-boss.

Patterns of functional interrelationships

The simple situations discussed hereinbefore serve to introduce the concept of functional organization. The examination of the same phenomena but against the background of a larger more mature business should now prove useful. Again we will look at some of the functional-organizational problems in other departments preparatory to, and for the light that they will shed upon, our major task of organizing the controllership function.

The organizer and, of course, the controller always hope for the clean situation in which a function or subfunction is completely identifiable so that it can be organized without complications involving other organization units. Sadly, such situations are seldom found. The practical problem becomes one of ascertaining the nature of the involvements, and of setting up clear rules to govern the interunit activities and responsibilities in order to get as near to effective and frictionless cooperation as possible.

The personnel function is a good example calling for careful interdepartmental organization. The primary responsibility for handling workers must be in the hands of their immediate superiors—the working foremen. Yet common experience is such that the recruitment and hiring of workers cannot be left in the foreman's hands but must be taken over by a company-wide or plant-wide personnel department. The division of the function is obviously necessary as far as these two subfunctions, day-to-day supervision and original hiring, are concerned. But what about some of the other subfunctions of personnel? Who decides the initial wage rates? Where should responsibility for training the new employee lie? Who decides promotions to higher rate classifications? Who handles discipline problems? Who is responsible for the company's baseball team, for employees' family social service and home nursing? Some of the answers may clear up after a look at particular conditions in the business; some will have no obviously satisfactory answers and must be decided rather arbitrarily. In a manufacturing firm the personnel department is usually placed under production since its major concern is with production employees. If, however, personnel also hires and trains salesmen and general office employees, we would have a case of cross-function service.

There may still be further ramifications in the personnel situation. The legal department may have to be called in to determine the impact of minimum wage laws. The public relations department may bring strong pressure for the hiring of persons from minority groups.

Organization of the research function presents problems of a different pattern. In the first place is research an independent function coordinate with the grand functions of production, sales, finance? Or is it a subfunction of sales or of production? The answer to these questions is very much a matter of differences in different businesses. In some concerns, it would be found that research is almost purely sales-oriented, that research means new product research, market testing, etc. In others, research may be "pure" research looking far into the future. In still another company research may concern itself with improvements in the immediate production techniques. Investigation of the particular situation may thus give a fairly clean answer to the placing of research in the organization. Research may serve two or more purposes. In this case the research division may be placed for line organization purposes under one of the major units but its costs shared by the other affected functional unit on some agreed upon basis.

The credit and collections department provides an interesting problem of functional analysis. The on-going work of this department is fairly simply stated. The department decides whether to grant or refuse credit or to fix its limit for new customers. It watches the performance of each customer as evidenced in sales and collections; it follows up on slow accounts with a series of collection letters; it may transfer the responsibility for certain accounts to the legal department for collection; it has responsibility for recommending write-offs of uncollectible accounts. The traditional difficulty is whether the credit and collections department shall be considered subfunctional to the sales department or to the treasury department. The sales manager would like to be able to control credit granting—he has much at stake when under pressure to expand sales. The routine of passing on credit for normal sales to customers must articulate with the processing of the flow of orders from his salesmen. The Credit and Collections Department may rely on the salesmen for up-to-date data on customers. These considerations make credit and collection work sound like a subfunction of the sales function. Do these arguments justify putting Credit and Collection under the sales department?

A sticky practical consideration lies in the statement that "the sales manager would like to control credit granting." This fact is so true and so potent that the sales manager might be far from objective in making credit decisions. The stake is the safety of the company's funds and that is a competing function—the treasurer's. So the outcome often is that the credit and collection function is placed under the treasurer, with, of course, orders to cooperate closely -with the sales department in routine matters.

Finally, let us look at one more functional-organization problem. Where shall the maintenance function be organized? In the typical manufacturing business maintenance is normally under production. The actual maintenance work may be divided between the operating departments which do small routine repair jobs for themselves and a maintenance department which gets called in on major jobs. This division of duties seems to parallel the division of personnel duties which was noted earlier. There could be a real difference, however, in that the performance of the respective duties in personnel would be much the same, period after period, whereas the maintenance department might be called into a production department on a very irregular schedule—an occasional big job of damage repair or thorough department overhaul and then perhaps nothing for months. Such a difference becomes quite significant for setting up the cost accounts to do justice to all departments. If the maintenance department also runs a garage which services salesmen's cars, we have cross-function service completely outside of production and into the sales division. Frequently, too, the maintenance department will get involved in fairly significant new construction which is to be capitalized instead of being charged to any one's expense.

In each of these cases, personnel, research, credit and collections, and maintenance, the functional analysis is not simple but involved in one way or another with other functional units. The pattern of the involvement varies: It may be the necessary splitting up of rather routine duties, as in our personnel function illustration; it may be potential conflict over basic management authority, as in the credit and collection placement problem; it may involve technological relationships, as in the research placement problem; or it may have to recognize substantial period-to-period change, as in the maintenance situation. A recurring common theme is the *service support* given by one department to others, most clearly demonstrated by the company-owned power department. In organizing the departmental structure and in setting up the accounting system the general management and the controller must be aware of these complications and must study the various causes or types of involvements, i.e., the patterns of functional interrelationships.

All of the foregoing is background to the following consideration of the unique pattern of involvements between the controller's department and other departments.

The controllership function and the pattern of organization

The relationship of controllership to other major functions has already been discussed in our effort to get a working definition of the controllership function. Those same delicate differences and overlappings which were matters of defintion now become practical problems of organization. In chapters 1 and 2 we neatly divided the function of safeguarding the assets between the treasurer and the controller by saying that it was the controller's responsibility insofar as it could be achieved through the design and operation of paper work and the treasurer's responsibility insofar as physical and legal custody were involved. Now we are faced with the practical organizational aspect of the problem, for instance, the placing of the cashier organizationally under the treasurer or under the controller. The solution of this dilemma is usually to place the cashier under the treasurer in the formal organization chart, with the understanding that this expresses his *line responsibility* but that he also has certain *functional responsibility* to the controller. This arrangement of serving two masters, of "wearing two hats," is found in many other places in typical organizations. It is perfectly workable if correctly understood, and it is often the only feasible answer to many functional-organizational problems.

In the graphic representation of organization (boxes and lines) it is customary to show the formal line-authority responsibility by solid lines with broken lines (dotted, dashed) to indicate some of the particularly important functional authority-responsibility relationships.

The secretarial function can be briefly characterized as that of official correspondence. This includes notices of all kinds to stockholders (meetings, stock splits, proxies, etc.), reports to governmental units (census, tax returns, SEC reports, prospectuses), formal legal reports of many other kinds. Most of these documents require factual information which comes largely from the accounting system which is the controller's domain. Clearly the secretary and the controller must cooperate very closely both in terms of organizing their functions in the first place and then time after time in producing specific correspondence and reports. On many of these occasions the legal department also has a vital part to play. The annual federal income tax return is the prize example of interfunctional cooperation between three departments. In these cases the reports section will generally be organized under the controller responsibility to do the detail work of compiling the reports but, in respect to specific functional matters, it will be guided by the secretary (in proxy statements for instance) and by the legal department in others (controversial elements in the tax return, for instance).

Another example of necessary cooperation is the proper handling of payroll. In this task, the personnel department must take the responsibility for basic employment records, correct classifications for tax and social security deductions, pay rate changes, etc., yet routine payroll preparation and the correct accounting for the labor charges are controllership functions.

These illustrations of the involvements with treasurer, secretary, legal, and personnel functions are of the type in which the job itself is split among the functions and, therefore, requires cooperation in performance. Recognition of the basic fact that there are two kinds of responsibility, line and functional is the key to avoidance of conflict which would seem so likely under any "two masters" situation.

The unique controllership cross-function contacts

In addition to these pattern involvements, the controller function has some really unique contacts with other functional departments which flow directly from the nature of its basic information responsibility. Management needs information about every organization unit at all echelons. The controller cannot get this information by sitting in his own office but must make arrangements for capturing much of it at its original source. Theoretically, he could have one of his own employees at every spot in the whole business where events to be reported occur. Since this is obviously impractical, the controller must arrange to have the line employees who are themselves engaged in the events report those events. This is generally accomplished by requiring the employees to write tickets, punch buttons, make check marks, or still other devices to make the record of the event when it is observed. The filling out of the sales slip by the sales clerk is a typical example of this arrangement. The clerk is the line employee of the sales department but is performing a controllership function when she fills out the ticket. The correctness of the whole resulting accounting process depends upon the correctness with which the sales ticket is originally made out. The controller is vitally interested that every detail thereon should be complete and correct, yet he has to rely on the training processes in the sales department (or perhaps in personnel!), and on the continuing supervision of sales management for this discipline of accuracy.

Similar problems of organizing for the reporting of hundreds of other events throughout the business must be recognized and arranged through the line organization of all operating departments. Every nickel of cash sales must be properly punched into the cash register, every hour of the factory laborer's time must be recorded, every purchase invoice must go through many steps of checking, with a record of each step. Notice that in these examples the information with regard to each event had to pass through the eyes and ears of an employee, down to the fingers which press the button or push the pencil. This is a hazardous course involving the weak human link in great error probabilities.

Aware of these human weaknesses the controller, working through his systems department, tries to surround the process with safeguards which tie the record making as closely to the event itself as possible. For instance, when a check is written, that is the *event*, a carbon copy or a machined duplicate becomes the *record of the event*. To make change for the cash sale customer the clerk must open the cash drawer, and this will not open until an amount for the sale is rung up. This forces a record to be made. Further, the customer is encouraged to watch the pop-up tabs on the cash register to see that the *correct* amount is rung up.

With modern technology, it sometimes is possible to avoid entirely the weak human link in the recording chain and to make the event record itself automatically. Long distance dialing phone calls record themselves without human intervention. The electricity meter and gas meter record the event of service consumed, but unfortunately in most jurisdictions the meters still have to be read by fallible human beings making pencil mark records which can again be misinterpreted when the meter book is read in the office. At this point, the mark-sensing meter card can be used to eliminate one of the human error hazards. It is just a matter of time and investment until this whole chain of information will be mechanized.

It is hard to leave this fascinating topic of further mechanization. The point of concern for us is that the controllership function must reach down into virtually every facet of the business for the basic collection of information. This is a far wider cross-function contact than any other function experiences, and it is truly unique in its requirements.

The controller has still another unique cross-function contact. His information reporting and interpreting function requires him to report accumulated information in various degrees of summarization on every unit of the operation. These reports go down to the management of the units themselves and to all the higher organization above them. The important purpose of this detailed reporting is to measure the performance and costs of each unit. This means, or at least should mean, that every unit head has an intense personal interest in what the controller reports about his unit. It can make all the difference between firing and promotion. Again the controller is involved company-wide in a unique and delicate interunit relationship.

A few words are necessary to avoid what might appear a serious omission. The previous paragraph mentioned the measurement of performance as well as costs for each unit. The "measurement of performance" is a fine broad term which needs analysis. Some units in a business are actually revenue producing units. Their performance is significantly measured by the revenues they bring in and these can usually be determined quite accurately by simple accounting processes. This is the ideal way to measure performance. The sales departments in a retail establishment are the obvious illustration. A manufacturing business may have product lines which are clearly the responsibility of organization units. Olds, Chevy, Pontiac, and Buick are G.M. products whose revenues can be credited quite simply to the production units involved. Many other organization units do not produce their own revenues, but their processes may be simple enough so that certain physical measurements significantly represent their performance. The total kilowatt hours of electricity put out by the power plant during the month is a singificant measure of the department's performance. Units of product processed through a production department are often a significant measure. The number of service calls made by a public utility service department may be a fair measure. Such measures of performance must be very cautiously used as they may be subject to subtle changes from one period to the next which might make an incautious use dangerous. Service calls of our utility in a month of winter storms are quite different from those made in the balmy months.

Still other organization units are of such a nature that their real performance virtually defies significant measure. Research is one of the functions whose performance is difficult to appraise, especially by relatively short calendar periods. The performance of the controller's own systems department defies measurement except in the most general terms.

This is one of the controller's big jobs in every business—to measure each unit as significantly as possible in terms of its performance on one hand and its costs in the other. In terms of functional analysis it is still another of the controller's unique crosss functional contacts.

Controllership organization in practice

Rare indeed will be the complete carte blanche opportunity for any controller to organize a department as he thinks it should be. Yet the ideal of how his department ought to be organized will be a valuable guide whenever the opportunity for even a partial reorganization presents itself. Each such occasion will enable him to move closer to his concept of the most effective organization. For this purpose the controlling general principle will be the division if the total controllership function into its natural, inherent, subfunctions.

Here, again, we are faced with an easy-to-state but difficult-to-implement principle. The study of actual organization charts of controller's departments shows such a bewildering array of differences that it is difficult to trace the existence of any generally proper scheme.

In order to read any semblance of uniformity into these organization charts, it is necessary to recognize and appraise the effect of certain necessary differences in organization. The major cause of difference lies in the great variations in the businesses themselves. For instance, a public utility, with the pattern of its operations virtually fixed, its legally controlled revenue rate structure, its highly routinized customer accounting, and its gradual expansion largely dictated by population increase, is so very different from a large automobile producer, with its sharp price competition, the preponderant importance of its annual model change, its complicated dealer-customer accounting relationship. Contrast further the natural business pattern of an insurance company, a chain of banks, a railroad, and contrast these large businesses with small manufacturing, trading, and service businesses. Within these categories, individual businesses may have entirely unique circumstances which must be provided for by the controller. Even those elements which are standard to every business, such as systems, auditing, general accounting, taxes, forward planning, etc., will vary in relative importance from business to business.

Appraisal of the probable effect of these differences cautions us to expect uniformity of organization at only the major or top-level subdivisions of the controller's organization and to expect great variation at the lower echelons.

The second big reason for variation is the fact that most controller departments are not the result of any systematic overall planning but a patchwork of successive additions, shifts, and changes. Under this method of growth, it is inevitable that the pattern of organization should reflect the strengths, abilities, and relative aggressiveness of employees who were on the scene and available for new or expanded responsibilities as past changes were made. Though far from ideal, such an organization may prove quite effective as long as the unique conditions of the reorganization period prevail. Looking at the organization chart today, one can often only guess at the conditions which originally brought about its peculiarities.

A third and related cause of variation in organization lies in the differing interpretations of the limits of the controller's function. The whole group of service responsibilities generally thought of as office management are sometimes put under the controller, and at other times they are under an office manager who does not report to the controller at all. In studying this particular aspect of the problem, it is well to recognize that some of the office-management functions, such as stenographic, filing, telephones, etc., are services to many sections of the business, whereas other functions, such as order writing, billing, customer accounts, and data processing, are basically accounting in nature and come under office management only because they require relatively large amounts of clerical help, performing for the most part repetitive operations. The supervision of work of this kind requires very little knowledge of accounting theory or practice, but it does require a high degree of skill in organizing the flow of work and in managing personnel, and these are the presumed qualities of the office manager. Since it is but a small step from filing to office maintenance and housekeeping, we sometimes find these subfunctions added to the office-management group. If we use such a broad interpretation of the office-management function and put the office manager under the controller, we are indeed stretching the basic definition of controllership. And yet this may turn out to be the best arrangement that can be worked out for a particular case. On the other hand, even though the office-management function may not be under the controller in the formal organization, it may still include some of the routine accounting functions and operate them effectively for the controller on a service basis. Some controllers prefer to be relieved of the line responsibility for such routine work.

We have already discussed the overlapping of certain top-level functions. The abstract functional analysis has its obvious parallel in the organization chart, where the combination jobs are given specific recognition. Such a combination of top jobs simplifies the organization problem. If Jones is both the controller and the treasurer, for instance, we need not puzzle about where to organize the cashiering subfunction; we just put it under Jones. If the controller is also the secretary, we are relieved of the difficult task of splitting the reporting function between the two offices. If the controller also holds a vice presidency, he thereby attains prestige, which may ease the solution of other organization problems.

Whether such easy-solution combinations lose more than they gain is the pertinent question. Such obscuring of functional lines is tantamount to a refusal to accept the advantage of full functional specialization and may involve slight obvious gains at the cost of less obvious, but more important, disadvantages.

The final, perhaps the most significant, and certainly the most elusive, factor in accounting for differences in the organization of controllers' departments is the degree or stage of maturity reached in the long, slow evolution of the controller's function from relatively simple figure gathering through the significant-figure marshaling stage and into the conscious manipulation and use-of-figures-for-forward-planning stage. We cannot, of course, recognize any cutoff point between these stages or be sure from the named subdivisions or sections of the organization how far this march toward maturity has gone. Especially in smaller businesses, the subfunction of forward planning may be highly developed in the person and immediate staff of the controller himself without any specific mention thereof in the formal organization chart. It should be recognized that, in any controller organization, any subfunction not specifically delegated still resides in the controller himself. In larger businesses the forward-planning function has more chance of specific recognition in terms of organization units and titles. Even here we cannot be certain of the actual degree of development. The existence of a separate "budget" section, for instance, might mean anything from a quite routine expenditure-control process to a very enlightened planning for the long distant future. The appearance of a separate "analysis" section in the organization chart would seem to mean the recognition of the growing importance of the use and planning subfunction, but, again, a full investigation into the duties and actual performance of such units would be necessary to determine the actual degree of maturity.

The computer and the controller's organization

The computer and its peripheral equipment deal in information, largely quantitative, and therefore, in theory at least, belong in the controller's organization. In practice, however, the computer will be found in many different organization slots. In many concerns, the initial use of computers was in engineering where the trained mathematicians were more ready to use the new techniques than the generally "math-shy" accountants.

As understanding of the computer's capabilities have matured, we have found it serving many functions throughout the business, not the least of which are accounting applications from the highly routine to the highly sophisticated. It has become obvious that the computer cannot be considered the private facility of any organization unit and that wherever it is placed in the line organization it must be recognized as a service function to which anyone with a proper application must have access. Ideally, it would still seem that this service unit belongs in the controller's department. Practically, the line responsibility for the computer will usually remain in the unit which got there first, and which still has the most use for the computer. To assure a reasonably fair access to computer time to other units may necessitate some form of control by a committee representing all units which have substantial computer problems. This is just one more complication in the cross-function organization problem. This factor, maturity, though obscured and hard to identify, will be for the foreseeable future the most interesting and significant feature of any controller's chart.

Organization of the "ideal" controller's department

If we allow ourselves, unhindered by any consideration of vested interest, to bring together the reasoned analysis of the controller's function with the best elements of many observed systems, for a large business with a centralized management, what kind of organization for the controller's office would we produce? Not without considerable trepidation, the authors suggest that such an ideal controller's department may be visualized as shown on Figure 5–1. Knowing full well that very few practical organizers would accept this attempted ideal chart without

Figure 5–1
AN ATTEMPTED "IDEAL" CONTROLLER'S DEPARTMENT ORGANIZATION

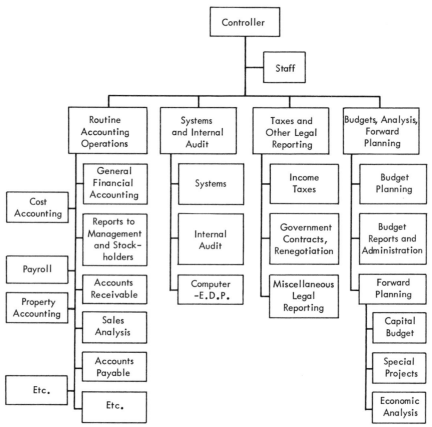

suggested changes, we offer it as at least a good starting point for further discussion. Consider the merits of a few alternatives. For instance, it is readily apparent that the suggested subdivisions under routine operations are likely to become too numerous and the task too heavy for a single responsible management head. If we visualize a larger concern, we would very likely wish to split the task of routine operations into two major subdivision—possibly financial accounting and cost accounting. We would probably divide the other routine functions as separated to the left and right of the stem in the chart. However, the weight of responsibility of each of the major divisions is not measured by the number of subsections under each, nor should the total number of employees be taken too seriously in appraising the importance of any unit. While we have argued in this chapter for the growing importance of the budgeting-forward-planning function, it should be clear that the importance of this function will vary enormously from business to business. The breakdown within the forward-planning function shown in the organization chart should be taken as purely suggestive.

The organization chart shows the entire management reporting function in one subsection. Though this may be proper in a rather simple and highly stabilized business, this subfunction might very properly be broken into separate sections for financial information reports, on the one hand, and control reports on the other, or these might be provided for as subgroups under the section as shown. Cost accounting, shown as a single section, might well be broken down to recognize the separation between the routine cost collection and cost or variance analysis.

In earlier chapters, we analyzed the controllership function in terms of its objectives as being primarily service to management, with protection of property and legal reporting as very important subfunctions. It might have been expected that the organization chart would follow these major functional divisions, and in a sense it does. The third and fourth subdivisions of the chart are clearly related to the legal-reporting and management functions. Protection of property lies largely in the second subdivision. However, the large first section, which makes provision for all routine accounting operations, is recognition of the fact that one basic set of accounting records must serve the three major functions and that the organization of the work of *keeping* these records must center around the records themselves, rather than around the objectives for which they are to be used.

The placing of the systems function with the internal audit function is in recognition of the practical circumstances of operations. In practice, most of the systems organization work actually becomes systems *reorganization*, and a great deal of this is in answer to the shortcomings of the existing system uncovered by the internal auditors. This close relationship between systems and internal audit is in line with the thinking of the Institute of Internal Auditors, which visualizes the function as a constant review of the system not merely for effectiveness of mechanical accuracy and protection of property but for effectiveness in the support of management usefulness and company policy. These are certainly purposes which the controller not only approves but which are of the essence of his own continuing effectiveness.

Many professional internal auditors argue that this purpose might be better served if the systems-internal audit function were taken out of the controller's jurisdiction to give them greater independence of criticism. This argument might be valid if the controller's own ability or dedication were in question, but otherwise it lacks force.

The chart shows Computer–EDP as a subdivision of the Systems and Internal Audit section. The present developmental stage of computer application is clearly a matter of systems development, and with this in mind the computer function seems properly located. However, as it matures and expands it might well be raised to the higher echelon as one of five sections reporting directly to the controller. Many computer men would argue for a position independent of the controller with direct reporting to the secretary, the treasurer, or elsewhere up the line. It will be interesting to reexamine this problem fifty years from now to see what becomes of the argument.

After the insistence in earlier chapters on the significance of seeing the services of the controller to management broken down as control, venture measurement, and forensics, there might be some expectation of seeing these terms displayed in the controller's organization chart.

Control—measuring the costs and trying to measure the performance of every organization unit—will apply just as well to the subunits of the controller's department as to production, marketing or any other units.

Venture measurement is very much a matter of tailoring to the particular business. Its implementation would lie in the sales analysis and cost accounting sections primarily.

Forensic problems would arise most obviously in the taxes and other legal reporting sections. However the full service of this function might concern any of the sections in the chart. Detail payroll records are germaine to the collective bargaining process. General financial accounting and reports to management and stockholders carry the burden of multi-product, conglomerate, reporting to the financial analysts. Forward planning when it includes acquisitions, risks the threat of monopoly actions by the Federal Trade Commission. Accounts receivable may carry a provision for interest on unpaid balances and risk running into laws controlling the rates and the proper disclosure thereof to the customer. Systems is directly concerned, every time a change is made, with the question of whether or not the resulting information pattern protects the company in any conceivable controversies concerning the area. It might be interesting to try to pick some detailed section which is entirely safe from any forensic involvement! It may be useful to raise the question whether a section devoted specifically to forensic planning should be created or given recognition somewhere on the controller's chart. Perhaps that function may best be assumed at present by the as yet undescribed *staff* section adjunct to the controller's own office.

Controllership organization in decentralized industry

Most large businesses are necessarily decentralized geographically as to operations. Probably the consideration of service to customers is the leading reason for this, though transportation costs, raw-material sources, availability of labor, and many other factors play important parts also. With the wide dispersion of operations, large elements of line management must also be dispersed, because many problems are local and immediately related to the scene of operations. Discussions and controversy relating to decentralization become much clearer when we realize that there is a wide area of authority and responsibility which lies between such necessarily decentralized management and the ultimate management controls which cannot be decentralized. The reasoned judgment of top management must determine how far each business is to go in decentralizing these elements of management. The advantages and disadvantages would depend on hosts of special circumstances in each case. Probably no good purpose is served by arguing the problem of centralization versus decentralization in general. It would be far more useful to try to discover what kinds of factors in a situation point toward the advisability of decentralization and what kinds indicate that centralization may be better. Our interest in this book is not directly in the problem of management decentralization, but an understanding of the reasons for or against management decentralization in general might cast a light on the more or less parallel problem within the controller's own organization. Whatever the form or degree of management decentralization, the controller must organize his accounts and reports to reflect the management performance clearly, but this does not mean that his own office need be decentralized.

The organization chart of the controller's office shown earlier in this chapter is a good starting point for discussion of decentralization. Visualize a business which has its major manufacturing operations divided into five plants, all at some distance from the main office. Even though the controller wishes to keep his organization centralized, he cannot escape the fact that certain important information elements originate at those scattered plants and that he must design a system which will collect and report that information. As was pointed out earlier, it is possible and often necessary to delegate the responsibility for the collection of many basic source data to operating employees. This same delegation is possible for our widely spread plants, but it is unlikely that the controller would feel it advisable to delegate the entire information system at the plants to persons not under his own control. In general, it is feasible to delegate to operating employees the collection of information which is entirely or almost entirely routine. When information, either at its source or at some later summarizing stage, becomes nonroutine, varied, or technical, so that its handling requires judgment, then the delegation to nonaccounting personnel becomes more and more questionable. At this stage the controller will want one of his own employees on the scene, and he is, therefore, faced with dispersion of part of his own working force.

Cost accounting and payroll are the sections most likely to reach the stage at which the controller will want his own men at the plants. If their purpose is still merely to collect information for transmittal to the home office, where all the essential processing will take place, we would hardly regard the arrangement as decentralization. Other elements which our organization chart classifies as the routine accounting operations follow the cost and payroll elements out to the plants. In these developments, there is little of theoretical or controversial importance. These routine tasks must be done, and it is often more economical to do them near the actual site of the operations. Each of these tasks could remain the direct responsibility of its counterpart section at the home office, but such a plan would become unwieldy. Sooner or later, all the accounting work at the plant is made the responsibility of one man. This is the earliest stage which should be recognized as true decentralization of the controllership function. The decentralization of authority and responsibility, rather than the decentralization of actual work and actual manpower, is the essential fact.

Generally, decentralization of controller's functions concerns the elements that we have included in our chart as routine accounting operations. There is much less reason in the typical instance to decentralize the remaining three organization elements except perhaps in very large businesses.

In systems work, the overall point of view, the reporting of all the business elements in proper perspective, is one of the top considerations. Other elements of systems work—the organization and reorganization of detailed routines and the subsequent policing thereof—benefit by a certain amount of detachment. Therefore, we would expect the systems-internal audit unit to remain centralized until a comparatively late stage in the growth and evolution of the controller's function.

The subfunction of tax and other legal reporting is, by its nature, a corporate responsibility and would therefore tend to remain at the corporate level. Even if the business in the process of its growth keeps its divisions alive as subsidiary corporate entities, the tax problem is usually so involved with the interunit transactions that it is necessarily administered centrally.

In the budgets-analysis-forward-planning area it is somewhat more difficult to visualize what is happening and what should happen in regard to decentralization. Much would depend on the degree of decentralization of actual operations and line management. Where these are quite decentralized and especially if the several decentralized units are quite varied as to the nature of their operations, the routine aspects of budgeting for control should be correspondingly decentralized. Probably even in this case, however, the basic analysis and planning functions—the fundamental judgments as to the degree of success of the several operations and the long-time pattern of expansion of capital facilities—should remain a centralized, top-level function. Further analysis of planning in a decentralized business must await our direct attack on the nature of planning in later chapters.

Problems of decentralization in controller's department—
The internal audit function

The decentralization of parts of the controller's function to follow and service the decentralized operations and management entails certain problems which must be clearly recognized for what they are if they are to be properly dealt with. These problems may be most effectively studied in terms of a concrete illustration.

Let us assume that the Acme Company has a parts-manufacturing division at some distance from the main office. The parts division does its own buying and its own hiring of production personnel. It carries its own accounts payable and receivable and payroll, does its own cost accounting, runs its own budget, and is otherwise quite independent of the home office except for matters that are clearly of a general policy nature. Parts division controller Smith will generally function as would the controller of an independent business. He bears essentially the same line relationship toward the general manager of the division as does any controller toward the president of the corporation. His primary responsibility is to service all levels of the divisional management with information which they need to run their business. A part of his day-to-day activity will comprise the responsibility for the running of the routine accounting operations of the division.

Theoretically, Smith will also have the responsibility for the other three elements of the typical functional breakdown of the total controller's function. Here, however, we begin to get into the differences between the divisional controller and his independent counterpart. With regard to the systems-internal audit function, for instance, considering home office and five branches altogether, it might be simply inefficient use of manpower to delegate this function in full. This aspect of controllership may very well be handled entirely or largely out of the home office, with, it is to be hoped, the sincere cooperation of divisional controllers and their staffs.

Obviously, this situation contains the seeds of possible friction and controversy. If controller Smith, in the parts division, has knowingly allowed inaccuracies, inefficiencies, or disregard of company practice and policy to creep into the accounting routines under his jurisdiction, the auditors from the home office, discovering these deviations, will be in the position to criticize him, and this, though painful, is necessary from the company-wide viewpoint. On the other hand, if the divisional controller, as would normally be true, is properly discharging his responsibility, he will regard the internal auditors as performing the audit function *for him*, helping *him* to police the work for which he is responsible, just as though they were his own audit force organized under his own control. If he can take this proper attitude, there should be no friction arising out of normal audit procedures.

The really delicate situation is that in which the divisional controller has deviated in some respect from general company policy at the specific request of his line boss, the manager of the division. Perhaps the word "deviated" is too strong in this context. It must be apparent that the complications of business are such that certain flexibilities should be allowed in the administering of company policies to adjust them to special circumstances at the local operating level. Suppose, now, that the divisional manager and controller Smith have made some adjustment in accounting or reporting which they believe is a reasonable adaptation of (instead of deviation from) regular company policy. The auditor from the home office, discovering this adaptation (deviation) should discuss it with the divisional controller. If the explanation satisfies the auditor, he may (a) completely disregard the matter in his report or (b) report it with his approval.

If, however, the auditor remains convinced that Smith and the local manager are significantly in violation of company policy, he must report the facts to his own boss, the company controller. This puts Smith on the spot—and illustrates the principal problem of decentralized organization, that is, that he serves two masters.

Resolution of this difficulty should lie in the recognition of the difference between the two kinds of authority represented in his two bosses. The local manager has line authority over Smith; the company controller has functional authority over him. If the matter at issue is functional, Smith should abide by the company controller's orders; if it is a line matter, the local manager's wishes should control. This is the principle which should govern, but, unfortunately, when we get down to actual working circumstances, it is not always easy to say what is "functional" and what is "line." If the matter in dispute has to do with the form and content of the monthly report on plant activities to be made to the home office, it is quite safely functional. If the dispute concerns whether Smith shall have his vacation in August or in January, it is safely line. If, however, the dispute is about the form, content, and frequency of a spoiled-materials report to be made to the head of a certain department at the parts plant, it involves considerations that have both functional and line significance. If this difference cannot be settled by discussion between the auditor, the local controller, and the local manager, the problem must be carried to higher authority for a ruling.

Even this process should still be entirely amicable. Recognizing that there is plenty of room for honest differences of opinion, the immediate parties to the argument decide to "toss it up the line and see what happens." The auditor reports his findings to his line boss, the corporate controller, and the plant manager tells his side of the story to the vice president in charge of production at the home office. The general controller and the production vice president can generally assess the dispute on its merits and come to a decision which will, of course, be binding on their subordinates. In the rare instances in which even these two highly placed officers cannot agree, there is a perfectly clear technique for obtaining a firm ruling by appeal to their joint superior, the president of the corporation. It obviously would be poor practice to let very many differences be carried up to higher levels for settlement. However, the fact that this possibility is always available is the built-in safety factor in every good organization.

It should be recognized that similar possibilities for controversy and similar techniques of settlement exist throughout the other divisions of any decentralized business. The functions of personnel, public relations, engineering, and others are subject to the same questions of whether to decentralize or not; and, whatever the decision, whatever the degree of decentralization of any of these functions, there will be plenty of opportunities for differences between the home office and the plant. The fact is that in all these relationships, as well as in the controller's area, the technique of up-the-line appeal for adjudication of disputes is always available, and its mere existence is the best possible guarantee that differences of opinion will in the vast majority of cases be settled at the lower echelons.

The philosophy of decentralized control

There would presumably be substantial agreement among controllers with the foregoing analysis of the general pattern of decentralization of the controller's function, including the fact that it is the more routine accounting operations which most obviously need decentralization. Most would agree that the legal-reporting function normally should remain centralized, that the routine aspects of budgeting may be decentralized, but that the more basic analysis and planning should remain centralized except in the very largest business.

Within this general framework of agreement, however, there seem to be two opposing attitudes toward the real position of the divisional controller which may be very interesting to watch in future years. The one attitude is that the function of the divisional or plant controller is *primarily* to service the division, plant, or other local unit to which he is attached and that his relation to the home office is purely functional. The other attitude visualizes the divisional controller more as the representative of the home office. While this controller does service the local management needs, his primary function is to see that, at least in financial and accounting matters, the division or branch follows home-office policies and practices. The differences of the two viewpoints are a matter of degree, and we do not wish to overemphasize the significance of the contrasting attitudes. Possibly a full understanding of the physical and technological nature of one business and its pattern of line decentralization might indicate clearly that it would be best served by the strong central controller concept, while in another business actual conditions might argue for the more independent divisional controller concept. There certainly is little probability that either school of thought on the subject will win a decisive victory in the foreseeable future. The observation of these two alternate philosophies is offered here merely as background against which many specific discussions and controversies will be easier to understand.

Further problems of decentralization— Reports and consolidations

Within the decentralized division the problem of reporting to management is closely parallel to the reporting problem in any nondecentralized business. In addition to such routine reporting, the controller of the decentralized business must give careful though to the designing and scheduling of the reports that must flow to the central office, both to support the legal-reporting obligations of the corporation to outside authorities and for the purposes of top management.

The actual requirements in different cases will be as varied as business itself. The best that we can do here is to visualize the outlines of any reporting system in most general terms. It is probably fair to assume that most of the detailed reports on budgets, operations, attainment of standards, and so forth, which are aimed at control at the department, section, and cost-center level, need not go beyond the divisional level. In general, the reports from the division to the corporate level will be those concerned with earnings, financial status, and top-level planning and control. The design of these reports must recognize that most of them will be involved in consolidation procedures necessary to reflect the overall success of operations and the attained status of the corporation. Proper original design facilitates consolidation greatly, whereas improper design can make the task of consolidation a nightmare. Actual implementation of these principles goes all the way back to the planning of the basic chart of accounts with a unified nomenclature and numbering-identification scheme. If the entire business is the result of growth from a central source and if the controller originally on the job had foresight enough to plan for the expanding future, this task is not particularly difficult. However, where the present large, decentralized business is the result of successive acquisitions of previously independent concerns, each with its own perhaps effective but probably unique chart of accounts, the problem of bringing about sufficient uniformity to facilitate consolidation of reports is a far more difficult problem. Chapter 7 "The Accounting Plan" will go into greater detail with regard to the problem of attaining an effective perspective of the business through the accounts and reports.

Closely related to the design of reports is the matter of scheduling of reports. The most perfectly designed system would fall flat on its face if careful provisions were not set up as to the timing of every element in the reporting system. Even in the relatively small centralized business, the publishing of periodic reports is often a slow process. Each person in the chain of reporting excuses his own tardiness by claiming that some piece of information which he needs has been held up by some other person in the chain, and too often such claims are justified. Not so very long ago it was fairly common for monthly reports to get out near the end of the succeeding month. Obviously, such timing robs the reports of a considerable part of their potential management impact. Today most businesses have improved this situation materially.

There was and is no magic formula for improved scheduling. The only way to make progress is by patient, arduous hammering on details. Every step of the information-marshaling system, from the original document down through all office routines, through the journals to general and subsidiary ledgers, and into the reports themselves, must be flow-charted and scrutinized. Mechanical accounting devices—"standard" bookkeeping machines, punch cards, and electronic equipment—are directly involved and, properly used, can materially facilitate the flow of information. The mere spending of money for machines and machine rentals is not the answer, however, for even these can be bottlenecked unless the overall flow is originally properly planned and subsequently properly policed.

At each stage in the process the systems man must look for opportunities for speed-up. Probably the most common obstacle he must learn to overcome is the old argument which says, "We've always done it this way," and "there isn't any way to speed it up without wrecking our accuracy and control." The systems man must expect to be somewhat unpopular with the office force while he is in this phase of his activities. The fact that most businesses have made very great strides in scheduling the information flow into really prompt reports all along the line shows that it can be done.

This is not the place to get into the details of systems engineering, but one or two suggestions may be useful. Sometimes the reason for a holdup of information is a too rigid insistence on perfectionism. There are instances where details of information for the last day or two of a reporting period may well be estimated rather than wait for actual final figures. The systems man should appraise every such situation, and where a report can be advanced materially by an estimate which will be so close to the actual that no management significance could be attached to the difference, he may well authorize the use of such estimate.

Such a legitimate use of estimates to speed the statement process should not be confused with another and entirely illegitimate process occasionally indulged in. This improper process is the use of an advanced cutoff date for all data. Some firms, for instance, cut off the monthly transaction stream on the 26th, 27th, or 28th days of the month, "in order to get the closing process rolling." This enables them to get out their "monthly report" a few days earlier. If, by this process, they put out a "January" report on February 5 instead of the 8th or 9th, they are actually misrepresenting the facts. If they identify such a statement honestly as for the 31 days ending January 28, they are getting nowhere at all and possibly ruining their report for purposes of comparison with industry statements for January. It should be apparent that this discussion applies to management operating reports and has nothing to do with the process of getting out monthly statements to customers which may be properly cycled to various dates throughout the month.

Most of what has been said above applies to getting out any periodic reports (monthly, quarterly, or annual) to the management of any concern. To get out the reports from a decentralized division is the same problem, with its difficulties accentuated and its importance increased. We are interested in it here primarily because of its bearing on the decentralization of the controller's function. The controller of a certain medium-sized manufacturing company recently reported that by decentralizing his function to the divisions he had reduced his own home-office force from some 200 persons to 21 key individuals. It is interesting to try to visualize the care with which this controller must have laid out the schedule of reports from his decentralized force, to get the same adequacy of top-management reporting that he had presumably built up under his previously closely controlled system. As a matter of fact, it is quite likely that one big reason behind the controller's move was the hope to get better and prompter reporting by moving adequately trained personnel out closer to the original source of information.

The study of actual organization charts

Most readers of this book will have access to the charts of organization of actual controllers' departments. It is suggested that the way to study such charts most usefully is to begin by comparing the major divisions with the "ideal" controller's chart in this chapter. After becoming familiar with the major functional breakdowns, follow each major division down to its subsections observing the degree to which each section is truly a sub to the major functional heading. At this stage reference back to the "ideal" chart may be more difficult but it should be tried.

As differences are found, at either level, avoid any hasty judgment that the actual chart is wrong because it disagrees with the book. Try, rather, within your knowledge of the actual conditions of the business (and with *great* charity) to figure out *why* the pattern is different.

The early part of this chapter analyzed some reasons for differences—you may discover many more. Bring to bear any knowledge you may have regarding the growth and development of the business and anything you can ascertain about the persons in charge of various sections and subsections.

It is important, especially in studying the organization charts of smaller businesses, to keep in mind that any subfunctions not specifically delegated in the chart must still reside in the controller. An elusive corollary of this principle is the fact that many functions are comprised of both routine, pencil-pushing, investigating, arranging, compiling, elements *and* of policy elements. It may be hard to draw the line between these two elements, but it is important to recognize that the intended delegation often extends only to the more routine aspects of the functions, while the officer who made the delegation still retains control of the policy. Practically this is accomplished by requiring the delegatee to *report to* his immediate superior with the understanding that the "boss" retains the right to approve or disapprove of any action taken by the subdepartments.

The steps in the delegation may be many or few, depending principally on the size of the business, but the same mode of functional division applies at all echelons whether it is specifically provided for in position descriptions or merely implied by the organization chart and confirmed by repeated practice. This is the essential principle which makes the organization viable, workable, even though it may be far from perfect in its formal design.

6 THE CONTROLLER IN ACTION

After the rather exhaustive generalized treatment of the controllership concept in the preceding chapters, the purpose of this chapter is to take a more concrete view of the typical controller visualizing him in action as a member of the management team. We may think of this action as a formal presentation by the controller to a meeting of the board of directors called to consider some very basic move, as a less formal meeting of the executive committee, as an impromptu call into the president's office on some immediate problem, or even as a completely informal discussion over the luncheon table. These are all management team situations and the controller should in each case respect his primary function as the provider of organized pertinent information.

We are under no illusion that it will be easy in these practical circumstances to separate the information function from the decision function. In the give-and-take of informal discussion the controller may often find himself making statements which in themselves sound like arguments for a decision in a certain direction. This will often be inevitable in his effort to be sure that the impact of certain facets of information are being properly interpreted. If the controller goes beyond this to actually "take sides," he will run the risk of losing the essential part of his impact. Those opposed to his argument would tend to lose confidence in the fairness and adequacy of the information picture which it is his duty to supply.

In the more difficult situation in which the controller bears additional executive authority as treasurer, vice president–finance, etc., his performance as a member of the management team is complicated but should be guided by the same general principle—the clear recognition of the limitation of the controller function as information and frank awareness of his acting in two capacities.

Practical strategies of information

We know, of course, that much management involvement is with broad, continuing problems of high costs, low volume, employee morale, long-range forward planning, and so forth. Many individual problems are essentially fragments of these broader problems and must be considered against the general background. For our present purpose, a realistic demonstration of the controller's function can best be made against the background of specific situations assumed to be more-or-less isolated and requiring clear-cut action decisions by management. Such action decisions would for instance be—to fire or not to fire an employee, to raise or not to raise the price of a product, to expand the selling effort into the Panhandle of Texas or not to do so, to make or buy a subassembly of the final product, to continue to use the old method of production, or to buy the new, expensive, automatic machine, etc. In general, the strategies developed here for these limited problems are also effective for problems of much larger scope, but sound pedagogy as well as the dictates of space limitation indicate the use of the short, sharp problems at this time. The apparent simplicity of these problems is often illusory, they may in fact call for as varied approaches as the broader more pervasive problems. The remainder of this chapter is devoted to the typical major strategies any or all of which might apply to any practical decision situation.

Identification of the problem

Some problems present themselves suddenly and sharply, others mature through vaguely felt stages of "something wrong" in some general area of the business followed eventually by a growing identification of the nature of the difficulty. In any case the identification of the essential nature of the problem is a very important part of the whole problem-solving process.

Business is replete with illustrations of improper identification of the true nature of the conflict, and such failure to identify properly is a severe hindrance to the finding of a solution. It cannot be emphasized too strongly that the exact identification of the difficulty is the first and necessary step toward solution of any problem.

For instance, in one situation, the inability of new employees in a certain department to come up to standard production within the expected time was blamed on the foreman until it was discovered that the personnel department was misinterpreting the specifications as to training which had been laid down for this class of employees. Identification of the real nature of the difficulty was tantamount to the solution of the problem. In another instance, a district sales manager had failed to come up to quota for several years. He blamed severe competition and kept pressuring the home office for special discounts, which, when granted, seemed to do no good. It was later discovered that this district sales manager had made his company very unpopular by refusing to make adjustments for small amounts of goods damaged in delivery which was a more or less normal occurrence with goods of this nature. The real nature of the difficulty was discovered when the controller called the general sales manager's attention to the fact that this district showed adjustment costs far lower proportionately than any other district. Again, identification of the real nature of the difficulty clarified the problem and clearly showed the way to its solution.

Often the controller can be of substantial aid in reducing the broader problems to sharper focus, thus bringing solution techniques to bear. A frequently recurring example of this situation is the difficulty of high product cost. There is no action that can be taken against the total high cost of any particular product, but if the cost accounting is effective, it will break this cost down into its elements to such a fineness that the particular element or elements of cost that are out of line can be spotted. Comparisons with the details of prior periods' costs, trade association standards, or more probably with the company's own engineered standard costs are the plausible techniques. These various approaches rely upon a considerable breakdown of total costs to details, and that process is clearly an aspect of the controller's marshaling of information. Just what shall be done to cure the specific high cost situation after it is identified is a matter for line management's decision.

It will strengthen our understanding of the controller's problem identification responsibility if we recognize that the same responsibility is found to be equally significant in other areas. If the morale of the labor force is declining, it is the primary duty of the personnel man to figure out the cause. Is it simply low wages, poor fringe benefits, uncomfortable physical surroundings, unfortunate foreman attitudes, or what? If the real nature of the problem is not identified, it will not be solved. Poor public relations is another area in which identification of real causes is difficult but of the very essence of the problem. If the company has been polluting the public waters, the cause is clear though the solution may be difficult. If, on the other hand, the company is vaguely regarded as a "poor citizen," the cause may be far more difficult to identify. It may lie in the personalities and actions of a few highly placed officers, refusal to cooperate in the community Red Feather drive, in poorly conceived and poorly timed publicity releases, or in still other elusive matters. These matters are clearly not the controller's responsibility but they do make the point that the controller is not alone in assuming one of the basic responsibilities of all management, that is the identification of the true nature of the problem.

Setting up the alternative solutions

When the difficulty or problem is identified, the next step is the search for possible solutions. Sometimes, especially if the problem is still somewhat vague, a considerable number of alternatives may present themselves, and there will be a stage of batting down some that are obviously bad after even slight consideration. Generally, two or three solutions stand out as being the best bets. In the process there is always the danger of entirely overlooking valid solutions simply because of the high visibility of certain initial possibilities. This is the stage at which a high degree of imagination is important. The plodding type of mind will hammer away, comparing one or two rather obvious solutions, and fail entirely to recognize other better possibilities just because they initially seem "off beat."

For instance, Company X was perturbed because of the rising purchase costs of the corrugated box packaging for the product of its three plants which were located 75 and 118 and 160 highway miles apart. The production manager suggested that the company buy its own box-folding machinery to be located at plant A. The controller collected cost figures and found that, even with the costs of trucking the bulky boxes from plant A to the other plants, a considerable saving could be made as against the present plan of purchasing the finished boxes. The president objected to the plan because of the dangerous situation the company would be in if the box machine were ever to break down. Because of their great bulk, production of boxes would have to be closely scheduled to production of the main product, with no possibility of storing more than a few days' supply. It was quite certain that the several outside suppliers of boxes would not step in to rescue the company if it had a breakdown after dropping them as suppliers. The president claimed that he knew their tactics very well and that this was not an idle threat.

Just when it seemed that the project would be dropped, the controller recast the estimated costs on the basis of the purchase of two box-folding machines, one to be placed at the most distant plant and the other to serve the two plants which were only 75 miles apart. Since the machines were not very costly, the saving of the long hauls originally contemplated approximately balanced the additional depreciation, insurance, and interest costs of the second machine. Space was available at both plants at no incremental cost. The danger of being cut off in event of a breakdown was virtually eliminated with two machines available. Either machine could be put on double shift if necessary at a few hours' notice. High hauling costs for a few days or weeks in the event of a breakdown of one machine would be unfortunate but not out of reason. The plan of buying two machines was approved.

In this case the final satisfactory solution was almost overlooked. The initial question, "Could *one* machine pay its way?" seemed to estop the thought of the purchase of *two* machines. Recognition of the possibility of using two machines was actually a fine example of the use of imagination.

Properly understood, imagination is simply the ability to recognize significant relationships between known facts. The differences between persons in the degree in which they have this ability is striking. It may actually be the most important mental trait possessed by the business leader, yet it is seldom studied or appreciated. Whether it is a purely inherited ability or whether it can be developed by training is not known. There may at least be some advantage in understanding the imaginative act and in watching for and analyzing significant instances of it in action.

For instance, the sales manager of a large bakery was trying to decide the best way to introduce a promising new cookie to a state-wide customer list. Rather high volume was necessary to secure low production costs. He contemplated a series of radio and television announcements, but the cost thereof was high and the area covered by the available stations did not correspond with his company's trade area. He contemplated a free-sample campaign, but the baker's trade association frowned upon such a plan. He contemplated the offer of a special stackup carton exhibit to all regular customers, but this device had been so often used that it had lost much of its punch, and there was danger that many customers might not adopt it. He contemplated a cut-price introductory offer to customers, but this had the disadvantage that it would be difficult to get prices up to normal later. Just before he had to make a decision between these rather unattractive propositions, he happened to overhear a neighbor's wife say that she was "on the state board of the Girl Scouts and that they were looking for some plan to involve all the scouts in raising funds. . . ." At this point the sales manager's imagination clicked, and he had solved his problem. This may well have been the origin of the ubiquitous Girl Scout Cookie Sales Plan. If Mr. Sales Manager's imagination had not been working, he would have seen no connection between the chatter of his neighbor and his own serious management worries.

The direct responsibility for suggesting alternatives is normally on the line executive in whose department the problem arises, but the controller may occasionally be of real service to management at this stage, if he has the requisite imagination. He certainly is in most cases possessed of a vast supply of information regarding all activities of the business. His knowledge of the various facets of the business will generally be broader and more detailed than that of any one else in management. Insofar as problems arising in one division may have their solutions in another division, the controller is often the best situated to suggest possible solutions. His mind should always be particularly alert to his special advantage as the "information partner on the management team." In the presence of every specific problem he should ask himself, "Is there any piece of information anywhere in our whole information system from inside or outside the business which conceivably bears upon this point?" Any scheme which can help him to canvass the situation more thoroughly will be especially useful. The following section is intended as such an outline.

Information system for specific problems

Wherever the completeness of the information canvass is in question, the controller can get some aid by visualizing his information system in terms of four phases (levels, sources) as follows. This is basic procedure to assure that he is not overlooking any useful angle.

Phase I. Facts from sources under routine debit and credit or routine statistical control. The better the organization of the normal information system, the more often will the routine accounting and statistical reports serve the practical purposes of management. If, on particular occasions, persons in management do not realize that the information needed is already available, the controller will gently call such information to their attention, with, of course, any interpretation that may be needed for the special circumstances involved. The vast amount of information necessary for judging the progress of the several ventures within the business and for maintaining efficient control should be available in routine reports, and such sources should always be canvassed first in the search for information pertinent to any particular problem.

Phase II. Special presentations which require the reorganizing, rearranging, reinterpreting of facts which are available from routine, controlled sources. Special studies presenting direct costs if the formal system is on total costing (or a special study demonstrating total costs if routine costing is direct only), studies of incremental costs of proposed projects, breakeven point analyses, studies of the profitability of product groups not routinely reported, capital budgeting, or engineering economy studies, and so forth, are illustrations of this phase.

Phase III. Facts brought in from outside sources. Sometimes facts from outside sources (government, competitors, trade association, statistical services, and so forth) are directly useful; sometimes they are useful in comparison with facts from the company's own sources to throw more intense light on some situation which is being studied.

The three levels of facts are, of course, not entirely distinct. The interpretation of routinely collected facts may involve their restatement; facts from outside sources may be brought in and combined with or substituted for facts from company origins. The purpose of this somewhat obvious three-way grouping of facts is rather to give the controller one more technique to assure himself that he is not overlooking any possible information that he should present. He may well put this three-level classification in terms of questions when building up his presentation for management's consideration in the face of a particular problem. He can ask himself:

What information is available in our routine system which bears on this problem?

How can I reorganize this routinely available information to make it more pertinent, more meaningful, for the particular problem in hand?

Is there any information available from outside sources which I could bring in to shed further light on the question before us?

It is suggested that it may on some occasions be appropriate for the controller in making his presentation to line executives to be quite explicit as to this severalty of the sources of information.

Phase IV. There is a fourth level of information which should be canvassed for every practical decision situation before management. This fourth level may be thought of as nonfigure information. Basically, this might not seem to be the controller's function but rather the function of the company's legal counsel, its public relations, industrial relations, engineering, research, and other technical units. The controller's first duty toward such nonfigure facts, as he sits with the top-management group, is to be in the frame of mind to acknowledge the importance of such facts. Figures do not, and should not, always rule the decisions of management.

Second, the controller's duty is to watch for every opportunity to reduce such supposedly nonfigure facts to quantitative terms whenever and to whatever extent is possible. The combination of facts of differing orders can be successfully effected if they can be reduced to terms of dollars. If the personnel man objects to a move on the ground that it would mean the loss of ten trained programers, the controller may be able to quantify this fact by pointing out that a recent study showed that the cost of recruiting trained programers was $1,700 apiece. If the industrial relations superintendent urges a concession to the union of triple pay for holiday work, the controller should be able to come up with a figure of $32,000 for the coming year as the real price of that concession. This process is limited, there will always be some purely nonfigure considerations, and frequently these nonfigure considerations will be determining. If the chairman of the board considers a proposed move as simply unethical it might be very unwise to attempt a dollar measure of his objection! The controller can perhaps contribute a few nonfigure considerations himself on occasion, such as the inestimable value of maintaining a tight debit and credit control over the large area of financial operations, the moral responsibility of the company in establishing an internal check system, and so forth.

An incidental advantage of studying information in terms of phases will be the light that it may throw on certain inadequacies of the routine information system. It reinforces the assertions, especially of Chapter 7, "The Accounting Plan," that the routine system should forsee to the greatest extent possible the kinds of data that will be needed by management. The analytical process here outlined will often indicate that needed information could easily have been obtained by normal routine techniques but that digging it out retrospectively is a far more difficult and less reliable method.

The range of estimates technique

One of the sticky little difficulties in setting up realistic appraisals of proposals is the fact that even knowledgeable and well-intentioned individuals often vary widely in their estimates of forecasted revenues and costs. The controller himself cannot be fully cognizant of many technical details; therefore, as a perfectly normal aspect of management team play, he seeks the opinions of persons in production, engineering, purchasing, and other divisions. When these vary widely on specific points, he is always in danger of offending one person by taking someone else's estimate into his presentation. Taking the average of two estimates may please neither and is also not particularly likely to be correct.

A frequently satisfactory way out of this difficulty is to set up two parallel sets of estimates for the proposal, one of which can be thought of as the most favorable and the other as the least favorable. Such use of both estimates will mollify the contestants by allowing their varying points of view to be incorporated in the showing. Specific estimates which are solid are entered at the same amount in both columns. In any fairly complicated situation where several or many varying estimates are handled in this way, the resulting totals of the two columns will probably be too favorable, on the one hand, and too unfavorable, on the other, since it is not very likely that all the most favorable estimates or all the most unfavorable would turn out to be correct. In effect, then, we may have narrowed the range of the probable outcome to such an extent that the decision may be quite clear. If the most unfavorable results are still satisfactory or if the most favorable are unsatisfactory, the decision will be in no doubt, and all parties will concede. If, on the other hand, the most favorable showed a wide margin of profit and the least favorable were almost tolerable, management would again be in a pretty fair position to decide. There will still be cases in which the decision is not so clear, and in which more work will have to be done to derive decisive figures, but even here the areas of disagreement will be highlighted so that the analyst will know where to put his efforts.

The systematic presentation under this range of estimates technique will have two distinct advantages where the initial attempt still leaves the problem unsolved. The first advantage is that this overall look at the problem should highlight those factors which it is feasible to further analyse and which are likely to be of significant consequence. Small-amount items may obviously be of no further interest even though the estimates are wide apart. The fact that some of the large items may be at best subjective will be clearly brought out in the discussion of the wide-ranging estimates. Certain other items, however, may be large enough to be significant and also susceptible to further investigation and more reliable quantification. A critical sorting out of the items along these lines will economize time and effort and move closer to a safe decision.

The second advantage of the systematic range presentation is that it should help materially to determine the point at which, even though the information is still quite inconclusive, the responsible executive must make his pit-of-the-stomach decision: "And that, gentlemen, right or wrong is what we are going to do." This will help to avoid the danger of indecision which is often worse than the wrong decision.

In certain very large scale decisions, the range of estimates method may be extended to the technique of simulation, as discussed in Chapter 25. The computer-dependent technique enables various combinations of the uncertain estimates to be brought together, and may also permit the relative likelihoods of the values estimated to be taken into account. Using simulation, the controller may present managers with a tabulation of the results which would be obtained if all the optimistic values arose and if all the pessimistic values arose, as in the range method; however, he will also be able to display the consequences of as many of the "in-between" values as seem likely to be helpful.

The recognition of problem categories

Substantial help can be secured in the discovery of possible alternatives, as well as in determining the form of the eventual solution, by recognition of the fact that business problems, in spite of their extreme variety, do fall into certain categories. The attempt to set up a complete "classification of all business problems" would be a rather hopeless task, but the description and identification of a few of the commoner varieties is feasible.

The relationship of a problem to the part or parts of the organization structure is a useful element in categorizing it. If a problem can be identified as "purely a matter of personnel" or "purely production," it is quite different than if it is evident that "this problem falls somewhere between cashiering and accounts receivable—concerns them both" or "this is more a matter of finance than it is of sales, but it does touch sales and personnel too, for that matter."

Whether a problem is a matter of venture accounting involving the segregation of revenues and the breaking-down of costs, whether it is in the great area of control, or whether it is in the routine services area of accounting is often a useful question to ask in coming to grips with some evasive difficulty.

Controllership and management writings give us a vast number of specific problem discussions, and it is extremely useful to recognize that these fall into loosely organized families or categories, each of which succumbs to a more or less standard pattern of approach. Among the more specific categories of problems which are commonly recognized as types are the "make or buy" situations which arise frequently in manufacturing businesses. These may involve the self-production or outside purchase of production parts, or they may concern the acquisition of capital assets—a piece of specialized machinery or even a plant extension. Assuming that the item needed is clearly specified, these problems reduce to comparisons of the costs of the two possible methods. The danger of error lies largely in the omission of some of the more elusive costs. When a business undertakes to produce a piece of equipment for itself, the propriety of allocating any of the fixed overhead may be a puzzle. While it would be wrong to charge such a project for normal fixed overhead, the use of facilities or services in connection with the project, in such a manner as to interfere with normal production or to cause an appreciable increase in the overhead item is certainly a properly chargeable cost. In estimating costs as the basis for the making of the decision, the overriding considerations are to get *all* costs in on both sides of the picture. The best guarantee of such completeness is to ask various persons who may have any knowledge of the problem to take a critical look at the estimated figures. This will be especially effective where, for any reason, the interested parties take sides for and against the suggested alternatives. This process can be very time-consuming, and the intensity of its use must be gauged to the seriousness of the particular problem in hand.

Another "pattern" problem is the timing of replacements of substantial pieces of equipment. Industrial engineers have given this problem a great deal of attention, and it has been extensively written up in books and current literature, often characterized as an "engineering economy study." The basic text by Grant has long been the "bible" in this area.[1]

A third common problem is the "incremental cost and revenue" problem which can take on many aspects and can be set up in many ways.

---

[1] Eugene Lodewick Grant and W. Grant Ireson, *Principles of Engineering Economy* (5th ed.; New York: Ronald Press Co., 1970).

The typical situation is that in which a business debates the advisability of going after a special chunk of revenue at less than its normal rate, on the argument that the costs thereof will be only the direct or incremental costs, so that the special venture will pay off at least in the sense of making a contribution to the general overhead. The immediate problem is the recognition of the true incremental costs and revenues. The final decision, however, may rest on considerations quite beyond the immediate figure representations.

The same form of "incremental thinking" is often involved in problems concerning only costs, that is, where the revenue is not affected. The delicate issue involved is again whether the total costs, including an appropriate share of fixed overhead, should be shown in the presentation and considered in the decision or whether only incremental costs are significant. It is not our purpose here to get into the substance of these problems but to argue that the recognition of the type or category of problem one is faced with is itself considerable help in its solution.

An important though easily missed aspect of the thinking about these incremental situations was identified by Professor Robert L. Dixon 20 years ago in the July 1953 number of the *Journal of Accountancy*, pp. 48–55 under the intriguing title of "Creep." Professor Dixon points out that a series of incremental thinking decisions, each of which appears separately wise and desirable, may have a combined cumulative result which is indeed not wise and desirable. This is a special application of the short-run–long-run conflict which calls for delicate consideration.

Analysis of weighting and probability in many factored problems

Many actual problems of business involve such varied considerations that the task of finally summarizing the pros and cons is quite formidable. If all the factors could be reduced to dollar evaluations, plus or minus, their summarization would be simple. The predicament lies in the fact that a single decision may have to take into account dollar facts of revenue and cost of different degrees of certainty, plus nonfigure facts of sales policy, industrial relations, public relations, legal consequences, and perhaps moral and ethical factors.

While the mental process of the person responsible for the final judgment may be very intricate indeed, we can at least point out two salient aspects that must be a part of that process. Assume that the alternatives have been narrowed down to two, A and B. Assume further that the arguments, have been reduced to a systematic list of ten quite distinct factors. The first aspect of the final bringing together requires the visualizing of the factors in terms of their *directional pull*. This can be set up graphically as follows: the significance of the signs being merely that a plus sign means that the factor favors the alternative under which it is shown, while the minus sign indicates the opposite directional pull.

Factor number	Alternative A	Alternative B
1	+	−
2	−	+
3	+	−
4	+	−
5	+	−
6	−	+
7	+	−
8	+	−
9	−	+
10	+	−

If we dared to make the naïve assumption that each factor bears an equal weight, a mere tally of the pluses and minuses would constitute a decision, and alternative A would win a 7 to 3 decision. At this point the accountant finds himself longing for the simple situation in which the weights of factors could be measured in dollars. We are trying here for a conceptual approach which may be helpful where dollar measures do not apply at all or where they may measure some but not all of the factors. Expressing the concept of varying weights of the factors graphically, we amend our chart, as shown immediately below.

Factor number	Alternative A	Alternative B
1	+	−
2	−	+
3	**+**	**−**
4	+	−
5	+	−
6	−	+
7	+	−
8	+	−
9	**—**	**+**
10	+	−

In any actual argument it is not likely that many of the factors would be thought of as having equal weights. The above representation indicates that factor 3 was somewhat more weighty than most of the others but that factor 9 outweighed all the others by a very heavy margin. Possibly factor 9 was the fact that alternative A was simply against the law and might result in the revocation of the corporation's charter if adopted. In the light of this consideration, all the other arguments would be of little consequence, and the decision would have to be for alternative B.

Even more elusive than the specific weight to be given to a factor is the difficulty of judging the *probability* of the impact of certain factors. For instance, the steel company is setting up its production schedules must judge the probability that there will be a strike in its largest customer, an auto manufacturer. In timing the purchase of a modern machine, a company must judge the probability that a still more modern replacement may become available in a year or two. The unhappy buyer for the women's wear department must judge the probability that the "midi" or "maxi, with or without the high split," will "really catch on." The necessity for such probability judgments is actually very common and must be brought into the decision process—sometimes as its most important factor.

We refer back to our attempt at graphic portrayal of the alternate A and B decision problem. Add to the assumed illegality of factor 9 the fact that a relevant case is now on its way to the Supreme Court testing the law which makes factor 9 illegal. Possibly, this would merely argue for a postponement of the decision, but some decisions cannot be postponed, and the probabilities for good or bad must be embraced in the decision process.

Putting together our discussion of the range technique for quantitative differences of opinion, our understanding of the directional and weighting pull of nonquantity factors and finally elusive probability for one or many of the factors, we have a complete pattern for the decision process. The controller in action should pose his specific problem against the full complications of the pattern. If he can fortunately rule out some or all of the difficulties of weighting and probabilities, his presentation will be simplified, but he at least will not rule out significant factors by sheer neglect.

Inevitably, the question must arise: Can the computer help us in this complicated situation, and the answer lies somewhere between "obviously not" and "it is our only hope." Actually, the attempt to computerize the decision process has been a great spur behind the effort to think the process through in basic terms. A leader in this effort has been Professor Robert O. Schlaifer of the Harvard Business School. His book *Analysis of Decisions under Uncertainty* is the leading exposition of thinking in the area.[2]

The principal idea which underlies the work of the decision theorists is that of quantification. As we have seen, many factors in a decision are easy to quantify; the real contribution of decision theory is in dealing with the others. In order to use mathematical methods to study a problem, it is necessary to persuade managers to express their intuitive judgments on the likelihood of future events in terms of probability. In the example above, the manager would be asked to assign a subjective

[2] Robert O. Schlaifer, *Analysis of Decisions under Uncertainty* (New York: McGraw-Hill, 1969).

probability judgment to the future action of the Supreme Court. If he is able to say, for instance, that he believes there is a probability of two thirds that the Court will nullify the law which makes factor 9 illegal, then perhaps the logically correct decision is to move ahead with the new idea. If he assesses the probability only at one quarter, the right decision may be to adopt alternative B. In some instances, it is possible to arrive at a "break-even probability" which is the probability level which would cause the manager to be exactly indifferent between the two alternatives. The manager who is supplied with this break-even probability may then make his decision depending on whether he believes the real probability to lie above or below the break-even level.

The decision theory technique is a very promising one and is slowly gaining popularity in some larger companies. It is nonetheless true that the method is difficult to use and will probably always be limited to the largest decisions and to those with a relatively small number of important qualitative elements. An alternative approach is the technique of simulation. This method is less precise than the decision theory approach, but it is easier to use in a practical situation. Even the simulation method is sufficiently expensive in use, however, that it tends to be used only for large scale decisions.

The controller may make a most useful contribution to the decision-making procedures of his company by making himself familiar with the basic ideas underlying the decision theory approach and the concept of simulation. A sound understanding of the methods and of their limitations will enable him to advise managers when these methods should be used.

It should be noted that the analysis of *directional* pull of factors can be reasonably accomplished even in the classroom but that the final steps in analysis—the *weighting* of the factors and judging their probabilities can be done in a realistic sense only by the businessman with his own hard cash at stake or by the corporation executive whose reputation, chances of promotion, and possibly job are at stake. The real pressures of real business are a necessary element in the decision. The classroom procedure should try to judge these factors in any problem by honest discussion which visualizes the practical conditions of business as well as possible. Sometimes role-playing, the taking of sides in the argument, can help attain a higher degree of verisimilitude.

Postdecision follow-up

After the die has been cast—the decision made—there is a natural tendency to wish to forget the agonizing details of the preceding arguments. To do so, is however, to miss one of the principal advantages of the careful decision process. It is unfortunate that so little attention has been given in discussions of the management process to the importance of following through on the pro and con involvements in the postdecision period.

Though the decision in our foregoing illustration, may have been made wisely for alternative B, that balanced wisdom does not automatically eliminate the reality of factors 1, 3, 4, 5, 7, 8, and 10 which were the disadvantages of this course of action. To now proceed blindly on course B might allow these adverse factors to have more impact than necessary. This is the business application of the old truism "Forewarned is forearmed." The point is easily illustrated.

Assume, for instance, that factor 1 objection to course B was that course B would come dangerously close to violation of a provision of the union contract. Would it not be wise to sit down with the union heads to discuss the point, to show that the general course of action was necessary, and to work out satisfactory administrative details. Would this not be far better than to wait for some hot-head to discover the move and to yell for grievance action?

Assume that the factor 3 argument against course B was that it would be interpreted unfavorably by the public. Would it not be wise to alert the company's public relations department to get ready some countermeasure? Perhaps public relations has up its sleeve a news release on some other topic which is highly favorable to the company. Perhaps the mere fact of the proper timing of the favorable release might go a long way toward overcoming the adverse effect of the announcement of action B. Similarly, every disadvantage that was foreseen for course B should be closely examined to head off as far as possible its adverse effects. The timing of this process may require immediate action or watchful waiting and subsequent action.

Postdecision follow-up concerns the taking of full advantage of the plus factors as well as the avoidance of the negative. If plus factor 2 had been the argument that course B would enable us to strengthen our Texas sales branch by buying some raw material from a Texas customer, let us be sure to make the purchase there, and let us be sure to tell our Texas sales manager about it, too, so that he can really cash in on the advantage.

If course B provides a new product which our salesmen have been crying for—to round out our product line—let us be sure to announce it to them in the most effective way and at the most effective time to get its full beneficial impact.

At the risk of rubbing in the point too hard, it is worthwhile repeating that the final success or failure of many action decisions may depend as much on such effective follow-up as upon the rightness of the decision itself.

Is there possibly a question as to whether or not this follow-up situation is the controller's business? Certainly, the taking of the suggested actions is the primary responsibility of the line executives—personnel, public relatives, sales management properly prodded by the general manager himself. We are undoubtedly close to the dangerous line. However, if the controller is really regarded as a member of the management team, he should be able to use his information needle gently. He can put himself into a strategic position if at the time of the decision he gets into the record the idea that "these factors are going to need some careful watching when we go ahead on this move." With this concept formally accepted he can safely later throw in an occasional "I hope you fellows aren't forgetting all the pro-ing and con-ing that we did in working up on this proposition." At this point it would be nice to be a *vice president*–controller!

An illustrative case

Some of the important problem-solving techniques outlined in this chapter can be demonstrated by the use of a concrete case. This illustration comprises the statement of the case, the solution as it might have been drawn up by a student or by a controller, and a few comments pointing out the application of principles.

GAIL INVESTMENT CORPORATION

Auto Washing Unit #4

The Gail Investment Corporation owned and operated 47 gasoline stations and 16 automobile-washing units in northeastern Illinois. Mr. John F. Gail, president and major shareholder in the firm, believed that each unit should be operated as a separate entity. In this way, he felt, unprofitable units would be detected more readily, and steps could be taken to make them profitable or to dispose of them. Each unit, therefore, was operated as a branch and was expected to show a reasonable return on invested capital.

Each unit was operated by a manager who received a guaranteed salary and a bonus for earnings in excess of a stipulated amount.

Car-wash Unit #4 had been one of the most profitable activities in the chain. It was located in a light manufacturing section of a moderate-sized suburb of Chicago. From 1959 through 1966, this unit regularly earned from $5,000 to $8,000 *after* payment of the manager's bonus that ranged from $2,500 to $4,000.

In 1967 the highway on which the property faced was elevated in order to pass over a series of railroad tracks. Traffic passing the location after elevation of the highway was 45 feet above ground level. It was not considered practicable to erect signs to attract customers because there was no means of exit from the highway for more than a mile in each direction.

The unit lost heavily in 1967 and 1968. In 1969 and 1970, the manager,

Tom Wells, suggested that the lower summer prices be maintained throughout the winter in order to attract marginal trade. As a result, only small losses were incurred in 1969 and 1970. Operating figures for 1970 are as follows:

Revenues:
22,880 washes at $1.75	$40,040	
5,496 washes at 2.00 (white sidewall tires).	10,992	
Total revenue		$51,032

Expenses:
Wages:
22,880 washes at $0.85	$19,448	
5,496 washes at 1.00	5,496	
Manager's salary.	7,000	
Cashier's salary	3,360	
Total wages		$35,304

Other expenses:
Heat	$ 2,512	
R. E. Taxes and licenses.	2,626	
Insurance	1,326	
Depreciation	6,125	
Maintenance	752	
Advertising	900	
Telephone.	157	
Electricity.	729	
Water.	991	
Soap	294	
Miscellaneous	566	
Total other expense		$16,978
Total expenses		$52,282

Net loss. . . . . $ 1,250

Figures regarding the properties which might be significant were as follows:

	Cost	Annual depreci- ation	Depreci- ation to date	Remain- ing book value	Estimated replace- ment cost—new
Land.	$ 7,000	. . . . .	. . . .	$ 7,000	. . . .
Building.	40,000	$2,000	$24,000	16,000	$ 65,000
Equipment.	28,875	4,125	20,625	8,250	35,000
Total	$75,875	$6,125	$44,625	$31,250	$100,000

In 1971, Mr. Gail made several attempts to sell the unit but was unable to get an offer of more than $20,000 for the entire property.

Tom Wells tried several times to convince Mr. Gail that they should seek more marginal business. Specifically, he had been approached by a representative of a local cab company whose service garage was directly across the alley with a proposition to wash each of their 300 cabs twice a week at $1.05 per wash. Wells had investigated the matter and concluded that, by operating all night for two nights a week, they could handle the 600 extra washes. He further learned that a package-delivery service in the vicinity, as well as another cab company, was interested in some similar arrangement, but no commitments had, as yet, been made.

Mr. Gail pointed out that wages could not be cut (they were set by a union) and that a 20-cent margin would not cover all the costs involved. To support this contention, he brought out the 1970 operating figures. He advocated raising prices, restoring the summer-winter differential, and sale of the unit as soon as practicable.

Evaluate the several feasible alternatives and recommend the most profitable action. Give special attention to Wells's suggestion of a marginal venture.

DISCUSSION

Available alternatives

The two leading or most obvious alternatives are virtually stated in the case:

(a) Mr. Gail's plan: Raise prices, restore summer-winter differentials, sell unit as soon as possible.

(b) Tom Wells's plan: Continue operations as at present plus the taking on of the marginal businesses of 31,200 cab washes at the proffered price of $1.05 each.

There is little likelihood that Mr. Gail's plan of raising prices would show better operating results in the near future, since it might very well cut the total volume. His plan, therefore, must be thought of essentially as the sale of the unit for the $20,000 price, which was the best offer that he had been able to get.

The judgment of Wells's plan involves a careful study of the probable incremental revenues and costs as developed later in this discussion.

Actually, there are several subalternatives which must be evaluated before an intelligent decision can be made. The possibility of adding still more marginal business—that of the package-delivery service and a second cab company—may offer very attractive opportunities, though the necessary facts are not given. This may be thought of as alternative (b_1). Another important possibility is to take on the marginal business for a long enough period to demonstrate its feasibility and then to sell out unit #4, presumably at a better price than the $20,000 now offered.

In deciding between these alternatives, the income tax impact cannot be disregarded. Assuming that the business in general (47 gasoline stations and 16 other car-washing units) is prospering, any loss on the sale of unit #4 will result in an immediate tax saving at the company's top rate.

If operations are continued, the "advantage of the tax loss" is not lost, because the excessive book values of the building and equipment will then be deductible as depreciation over the remaining life of the assets. It is also true, of course, that any profit made by operation or otherwise will be taxed at the same affective rate.

A more elusive bit of thinking is the fact that actually the major loss *has already been incurred* (though not taxwise). The "best offer" of only $20,000 for the book values of $31,250 is some evidence of this fact. Further evidence is the fact that replacement costs of the buildings and equipment, if depreciated proportionately to the original costs, would leave asset values of $26,000 and $10,000. For *these* values plus the land, the prospective buyer is willing to pay only $20,000. This indicates that a very substantial loss has already occurred. If we assume that the $20,000 is a realistic appraisal of the value of the property and then ask whether the property written down to this value could be operated profitably, we get a different perspective on the situation. We have no objective basis for assigning the $20,000 value to land, building, and equipment, but an allocation of land $5,000, building $10,000, and equipment $5,000 is probably close enough for our purposes. Depreciating these figures for building and equipment and using the original life estimates as evidenced in the book values given, we would have annual depreciation amounts of $1,250 for the building (i.e., 8 years left to go) and $2,500 for the equipment (i.e., 2 years left to go) for a total annual depreciation of $3,750 in place of the $6,125 used in the 1970 income statement. The saving of $2,375 of depreciation would change the 1970 net loss of $1,250 to a net profit of $1,125. It is more reasonable to use this figure in our thinking than the $1,250 loss, though, of course, the $1,250 loss would still be the taxable basis for unit #4 and would be a further real saving of taxes against income from other sources. Use of the $6,125 depreciation figure in the 1970 statement masks the loss caused by the elevation of the highway and shows it as depreciation.

This bit of analysis becomes even more important in the light of the showing of possible profit on the marginal business shown below. If there is, realistically, a profit on the regular business plus a profit on the marginal business, the continued operation of the unit may be an even better alternative than that shown in the formal presentation.

Analysis of the marginal business possibility

The safest approach to the study of a marginal business opportunity related as closely to the already existing business as in the present case is to set the actual and incremental revenues and expenses up in parallel columns as in Figure 6–1. This form is especially useful as a background for the discussion of the estimates, which are best seen as extensions of the known actual figures.

Figure 6–1

GAIL INVESTMENT CORPORATION
Analysis of "Marginal" Business Opportunity
on Car Wash Unit #4

Incremental opportunity
31,200 cab washes

Revenues:	1970 "actual" results	Most favorable estimates	Least favorable estimates
22,880 washes at $1.75	$ 40,040	$32,760	$32,760
5,496 washes at 2.00 (w.w.)	10,992	. . . .	. . . .
Total revenues.	$ 51,032	$32,760	$32,760
Expenses:			
Wages:			
22,880 washes at $0.85	$ 19,448	$26,520	$26,520
5,496 washes at 1.00	5,496	. . . .	. . . .
Manager's salary.	7,000	. . . .	1,000
Cashier's salary.	3,360	. . . .	. . . .
Total wages	$ 35,304	$26,520	$27,520
Other expenses:			
Heat.	$ 2,512	$ 250	$ 2,237
R. E. Taxes and licenses	2,626	. . . .	. . . .
Insurance	1,326	. . . .	265
Depreciations.	6,125	. . . .	. . . .
Maintenance	752	50	650
Advertising	900	. . . .	. . . .
Telephone	157	. . . .	. . . .
Electricity	729	50	243
Water	991	1,097	1,097
Soap	294	326	326
Miscellaneous.	566	. . . .	189
Total other expenses	$ 16,978	$ 1,773	$ 5,007
Total all expenses	$ 52,282	$28,293	$32,527
Net loss—regular business	$(−)1,250		
Net profit—marginal business.		$ 4,467	$ 233

It is assumed in this case that the forecasted figures for the marginal business of 31,200 cab washes are subject to wide ranges of interpretation and that therefore the range technique shown in the two right-hand columns headed "most favorable" and "least favorable" is necessary. It should be noted that this range technique is necessary because of various *kinds* of uncertainty. In this case for instance *interpretation* of certain items is quite uncertain. For instance, we are not sure whether "Heat" includes the cost of heating the water or not. If not, then the modest $250 of expense charged to the marginal operation may be sufficient. If $2,000 of the $2,512 heat expense is assumed to have been for heating water, this would justify a charge of something over $2,000 to the marginal business for water heating plus some additional amount for space heating for two nights of operation. This is presumably where the "least favorable" figure of $2,237 for heat came from. In actual business, this type of information difficulty would not arise in making estimates. Substantial differences would still have to be dealt with, however. For instance, there might be a real question as to whether any space-heating cost would be necessary when the washing line is in constant action. The intermittent operation of normal daytime business does not give good evidence on this point, and even persons in full possession of available facts would still have significant differences of opinion. This is an uncertainty caused by an essential judgmental difference rather than a difficulty of interpretation of given data.

The illustration assumes no real estate taxes and license expense chargeable to the marginal business. There is no difference of opinion on this item. The item of insurance shows a difference of $265. If insurance is interpreted as fire insurance only, there would probably be no increase for the two extra nights of operation. If it includes workmen's compensation insurance, that element would probably go up in proportion to wages. The $265 is 1 percent on the increased wages with this reasoning in mind.

There is no difference of opinion on depreciation, both columns showing zero. Maintenance shows a $600 difference in least and most favorable. This is probably largely a matter of interpretation of the meaning and content of the maintenance expense account. If this account includes the cost of replacement of brushes and other items of equipment, as seems probable because there is no supplies expense account, this item may well nearly double with the doubling of actual volume of work. On the other hand, if the replacement of brushes is included in the depreciation accounting, the remaining content of the maintenance expense may not increase more than the nominal $50 entered in the most-favorable column.

Advertising and telephone quite clearly show no prospect of increase because of the marginal business. Electricity expense again comprises an information puzzle. If the $729 of electricity is largely the cost of lighting a huge display sign, none of that cost should be charged to the marginal venture. Insofar as electric power is used for the chain that pulls the cars, for the revolving brushes, and so forth, the charge should be in proportion to volume. If cost of heating water is in electricity expense, the $243 would be too modest.

Costs of water and soap have been charged to the marginal business in simple proportion (31/28) to the expected increase in volume. "Miscellaneous" must be virtually a pure guess in handling this as a textbook case. In practice, inquiry into the actual kinds of expenses charged to this account would give a pretty good indication as to how it should be handled.

The usual vagueness of a case presentation, as here exemplified, is by no means a loss. The constant attention forced to the question of the weakness of the information system is itself healthy evidence of the kinds of information and the degree of breakdown of information needed in the practical decision process. Even in actual business there is seldom a decision situation in which the businessman is perfectly satisfied with the information available to him. Yet decisions must be made even in the absence of fully adequate data. As pointed out earlier in this chapter a feeling for the critical point at which it becomes necessary to "cast the die" is an essential element in business decision making. To hold up action too long may be a worse error than to decide on somewhat unsatisfactory grounds.

In textbook case discussions, it is, therefore, proper and desirable to be constantly open to the question of "what additional information we ought to have." Yet the absence of full information must not be used as an excuse for an unwillingness to come to a decision. This quandary parallels the business situation realistically and is one of the strengths of education by the case method.

Going back now to the problem of unit #4: Under the range technique we show extremes of net profit of $4,467 under the most favorable assumptions to a very small profit of $233 for the least favorable assumptions. The larger net profit figure would convert the $1,250 loss on the regular business into a total net profit of $3,217; the small net profit of $233 on the marginal business would leave the total net still in the red.

If the analysis earlier in this chapter, which recast the regular business results into a profit of $1,125 were accepted, the optimum interpretation of the whole situation would give us a net profit of $5,592 (before taxes), which on a real investment of $20,000 is not too bad. In the final analysis, of course, it is Mr. Gail who must make the decision, but the presentation made above should be of considerable aid to him.

Very important additional light could be thrown on the cost figures if the statements of other units of the firm or the operating figures from trade sources could be introduced.

Other considerations

Earlier in this chapter we pointed out that there is always a danger of overlooking significant alternatives and factors because of the higher visibility of foreground facts. The present case has one or two such other factors which should not be neglected.

So far we have blithely accepted Mr. Gail's statement that "the wages could not be cut (they were set by a union!)" as though it meant an airtight adherence to the 85 cents per car wage rate. Actually, the laborers and union are satisfied with this rate for the kind of intermittent operation which is characteristic of daytime operation which includes many very slow rainy mornings with only an occasional car going through. If the laborers and their union are at all realistic, they should recognize that a rate of 50 cents per car under conditions of steady work all night long would result in far higher take-home pay than the present conditions. If (and it is a *big* if!) the union could be persuaded to accept 50 cents or 60 cents or 70 cents per car, or some reasonable rate per hour, the total cost of operation would be very materially reduced—$3,120 for each dime that could be knocked off the rate—and this saving would go directly into the net profit. There is much more at stake in this possibility than in the small arguments regarding the other expenses. While unions are understandably stubborn in matters of rates, they are also realistic enough to talk in terms of take-home pay.

Another fine possibility is that the $1.05 price offered by the cab company might be an opening offer and subject to negotiation. If this could be upped a nickel per cab it would put another $1,575 into the net profit.

However, there may also be costs necessary to the marginal business to which the normal operating statement failed to give a clue. The statement is made that the cab company's service garage was directly across the alley. We have assumed that this made the cabs available when we were ready to wash them. But cabs do not run even across an alley on their own. Probably Tom Wells would have to hire two or three or more men just to drive the cabs from the garage to and from the wash unit. The cost of this little additional item might ruin the whole plan.

Might there be other costs of the marginal venture to which we are still entirely blind? Are there other nonfigure facts to which we have presently no clue? Perhaps the cabs are now being washed largely by our other units at the full rate as part of their regular operations!

These latter considerations stress the two leading points made earlier: (1) The relative weighting of the several factors is difficult and important, and (2) this difficulty makes necessary the machinery of the range technique.

To be fully realistic there is another aspect of information marshaling which was oversimplified heretofore, that is the fact that the valuation of some of the factors may be interdependent. We have a simple illustration of this in the manager's bonus agreement which provides for a slice of earnings in excess of a stipulated amount. Whether the old bonus rate would be carried over to earnings on the incremental business would be a matter for negotiation. Whatever plan was determined upon would have to be worked into the calculations more exactingly than the $0 or $1000 used in the illustration. Other cross-relations between revenues and expenses lie in such illusive areas as the company's bargaining for a lower wage rate per car wash while also bargaining for a higher charge per car for the service. These two factors may be interdependent in several delicate ways.

We have touched the probability angle in considering the question of obtaining wage rates and revenue rates other than those proposed in the opening statements. In practice these matters would be investigated and reduced to certainty before coming to decision. There would however remain certain factors which demonstrate the probability difficulty fully. For instance there is the probability of technological improvement—the fully automated car wash—which would throw all previously considered costs out of the picture. There is the probability that the cab company would build its own car wash facility. Smaller but significant probabilities that would have to be considered are the dangers of increases in electric rates, water rates, and insurance. Going back a few years: Gale sure missed out in not getting out of location #4 at the first rumor of the road elevation plan!

SUMMARY

The preceding case demonstrates the range technique, the nature of the incremental revenue and cost study, the danger of omitting very real factors simply because of the obviousness of certain given facts, and the need to be critical of the meaning of information produced by the routine accounting system. It illustrates clearly the four phases of information: (1) the routine data; (2) the data reworked, extrapolated in this case to the marginal business; (3) the possible use of data from other sources; (4) the possible nonfigure considerations—the possible loss of revenue in other units, the fine points of dickering with the union, the threat of technological change, etc.

The suggestions of this chapter backed up by the concrete case analysis will be most useful to the student and practitioner alike insofar as they serve to establish a working pattern of approach to real life problems. In the marshaling of information for management a very high premium must always be placed upon completeness of concept or the nonomission of significant factors. The great danger is the traditional one of being so close to a few of the trees that the view of other trees—and of the whole forest is obscured. The safeguard is the ability to refer back to a pattern which has been calmly and objectively established prior to the specific engagement.

The possibility that such a multifactored problem represents an opportunity for an advanced mathematical approach and/or computerization should not be overlooked.

Part II

Basic techniques

7 THE ACCOUNTING PLAN

Structurally, Part I of this book has set up the goal—what controllership is and what it is supposed to accomplish. In a very real sense, it is the function of the remaining sections of this book to make good on the implied promisses of Part I.

The purpose of this chapter, "The Accounting Plan," is to map out the general terrain over which the strategic battles will be fought in the rest of the book. Fortunately, there is much in business which is basically similar from one concern to another. A clear appreciation of the nature of the similarities is a great aid in the recognition and treatment of the differences, the occasional and very important unique factors which are certain to be encountered in actual business.

The central structural element in every accounting system is its chart of general ledger accounts. If the chart is well designed for the particular business, the rest of the accounting system can be visualized as a series of devices created to service the central account requirements.

A very practical observation is that the best possible way to become acquainted with any system, whether as a new employee or as a public accountant preparing for a first audit, is to make an intensive study of the general ledger chart. If it is well designed, the chart will give a clear picture of the overall nature of the business and will also show up those features which are unique and which may require special study and questioning.

The rest of this chapter constitutes an approach to business and the management thereof through the general ledger chart. The feasible approach to this very considerable task is to set up a general ledger chart which will be as serviceable as possible for the "typical" business even though we know of course that there is no typical business. This chart will be in the true sense a *stereotype* and, having developed it, we will then use it as a stereotype should be used—by knowing more or less what to expect, we will be able more quickly to recognize and appraise what we do run into whether it be the regular and expected

159

or the deviation. This is simply the application, at a high level in a very technical area of the old saying that you've got to know what you are looking for if you expect to find it.

THE FORMAL CHART OF ACCOUNTS

The basic structure of every chart of accounts goes back to the categories of accounting principles. Recognition of this simple fact is of practical value when approaching the complicated charts of even the largest and most diverse corporate situations. The constant insistence on reconciling what is found in the actual situation with what is standard, expected, and fully understood way back to principles is the effective approach. The systematic assignment of numbers to the five basic categories (assets, liabilities, capital, revenues and expenses), and to their breakdowns is a practical necessity for routine operating purposes and, if well done, it is of considerable aid to everyone concerned in visualizing the intent, the extent, and the limitations of the entire information system. In actual practice there are innumerable interesting variations in numbering schemes which usually reflect the growing pains of individual systems. We suggest here, as the basis of our further discussion, the following stereotype.

A typical classification and numbering system

The five major categories will be identified as follows:

```
1000   Assets
2000   Liabilities
3000   Proprietorship (Net Worth, Capital, Stockholders' Equity)
4000   Revenues
5000   Expenses
```

Each of these series will be broken down in such a way as to make the successive digits meaningful both by position and by value. For instance, in the 1000 series the hundred's position will identify the major position statement breakdowns as follows:

Classification of assets

```
1100   Current Assets
1200   Noncurrent Assets
1300   Nonoperating Assets, Investments
```

This leaves the tens' and units' digits for identification of finer categories and specific asset accounts, for instance:

1110   Cash
    1111   Cash—Petty Cash
    1112   Cash—Commercial Deposit, Ann Arbor Bank
    1113   Cash—Certificates of Deposit, Ann Arbor Bank
    1114   Cash—Commercial Deposit, Chase National Bank, etc.

Naturally, the pattern of development in the finer categories will be tailored specifically to the needs of each business. Further development of the typical system follows:

    1120   Accounts Receivable
    1130   Notes and Acceptances Receivable
    1140   Inventories
    1150   Prepaid Expenses

Detailed development of these categories might show accounts receivable broken down into wholesale, retail, installment, due from employees, and so forth. In another business, the breakdown of accounts receivable by geographic areas or by lines of commodities might be more useful. The common breakdown for inventories in a manufacturing business would be: raw materials, goods in process, finished goods. The full development of the inventory classification involves the entire materials-control system to thousands of separate raw materials; and the whole cost-accounting system whatever its ramifications may be.

Noncurrent assets break normally by physical characteristics into the following:

    1210   Land
    1220   Buildings and Other Structures
    1230   Machinery
    1240   Automotive Equipment
    1250   Patents, Franchises, Leaseholds
    1260   Others—as needed

The 1300 category suggested earlier as nonoperating assets will, in the relatively simple situation, carry investments in stocks and bonds owned for various reasons not involved with immediate operations, such as for future expansion, to provide official contact with a supplier of raw materials, and other reasons. The intent of this 1300 category is to enable the other two major categories to portray a clean picture of assets actually used in operations, possibly with a balance sheet total of the 1100 and 1200 labelled "assets used in primary operations" which is necessary if we are to get a clear report on the profitability of operations for purposes of comparison with prior years, trade-association standards, and so forth. The usefulness of this 1300 category becomes especially apparent when a business, while continuing its original operations, expands into conglomerate status. The 1300 category would be expanded to pick up the successive acquisitions while still maintaining clear reporting of original operating divisions in the 1100 and 1200 series.

Obviously, we incur the possibility of controversy by not immediately suggesting another primary category for intangibles which is still commonly found. The 1400 spot is, of course, open if this category is desired. Our stand here is that the drawing of a line between assets used in operations and those not used in operations is more significant to management than the facts of "intangibility" and "difficulty to evaluate," which are the apparent grounds, under the impact of the credit point of view, for setting up the category "Intangibles." Certainly, the amortization of patents and leaseholds bears a significance to operations comparable with that of depreciation on plant assets.

The more detailed classification of the noncurrent operating assets must be designed so that the depreciation and amortization thereon may be routed properly into the cost and expense classifications in accordance with the venture accounting of the business. Practically, this means that plants, machinery, automotive equipment, and intangibles subject to depreciation and amortization must be classified in accordance with their use by the separate ventures within the business rather than with sole regard to their physical characteristics. If such a classification is not provided in the formal chart of accounts, it will necessitate statistical reclassifications to make the reports meaningful. As business develops into decentralized profit centers, this aspect of classification becomes more and more important, since each division is expected to yield a profit on the assets which it has been given to operate. Under these conditions a division which has the benefit of a patent or leasehold ought to be charged with the amortization thereof and ought to be expected to return a profit on the cost or value basis of these assets. It should be observed that this discussion, in a very mild way demonstrates the fact that the basic accounting system must accommodate the several purposes—here venture accounting, and so far as profit centers are concerned an important aspect of control.

Classification of liabilities

If the 2000 numbers are to identify liabilities and if we are to use the hundred's position consistently with its use among the assets, the liability section of our typical chart will appear as follows:

```
2000  Liabilities
      2100  Current Liabilities
            2110 Accounts Payable
            2120 Notes Payable
            2130 Accrued Liabilities
      2200  Long-Term Liabilities
            2210  Long-Term Notes Payable
            2220  Bonds Payable
```

In the small and medium-sized concern the liabilities classification serves only routine purposes. It is only when business becomes so large that financing becomes the responsibility of divisional managements that we need more detailed classifications to implement control and venture purposes.

Classification of proprietorship

This part of our chart of accounts is of considerable interest to the beginning student of accounting. Here is where we demonstrate the real difference between single proprietorship, partnership, and corporate forms of organization. For the professional accountant this section of the chart is pretty much a cut-and-dried portrayal of the particular corporate structure. For the record, let us consider the following:

```
3000  Proprietorship (Net Worth, Capital, Stockholders' Equity)
3100   Preferred Stock, $100 Par, 7% cumulative
3200   Common Stock, No Par
3300   Retained Earnings (Surplus)
  3310   Retained Earnings Reserved for Expansion
  3320   Retained Earnings Reserved for Retirement of Bonded
          Indebtedness
  3330   Retained Earnings—Unrestricted
```

Obviously, these are not the commonest traditional titles for these categories, or do they even approach an exhaustion of the possible special situations. They are intended merely to suggest the necessary flexibility of description and the systematic use of identifying members.

The problem of contra and adjunct accounts

The proper numbering of contra and adjunct accounts is one of the "bugs" in the charting problem which has no one perfect solution. Every textbook tells us that "the Allowance for Bad Debts is a contra to the Accounts Receivable Account," but this might mean various different things against our more elaborate classification of accounts. If our accounts receivable are set up by geographic areas, we might want an allowance account for each such area. If we recognize a breakdown of our accounts into retail, wholesale, and installment, it would be very appropriate to have separate allowances for each of these groups. In certain cases we might be willing to use a single Allowance for Bad Debts for all the groups together. The point at issue here is that the numbering of the allowance or allowances accounts can be made to express the intended relation to the asset accounts. For instance, we may find:

```
1120  Accounts Receivable
1121   Accounts Receivable—New England
1122   Accounts Receivable—Midwest
1123   Accounts Receivable—Southeast (and so forth)
1129   Accounts Receivable—Allowance for Bad Debts
```

This numbering scheme would certainly indicate that 1129 was the joint allowance for all the regional control accounts. If we wished to set up the allowances separately for the several sections, the account numbers could express the relationship as follows:

    1120   Accounts Receivable
           1121   Accounts Receivable—New England
           1121.1   Accounts Receivable—New England—Allowance for Bad
                    Debts
           1122   Accounts Receivable—Midwest
           1122.1   Accounts Receivable—Midwest—Allowance for Bad Debts
           (and so forth)

A parallel problem of fragmentation of the contra account will appear in connection with the Allowance for Depreciation in the Noncurrent Asset sections of the chart.

Contra and adjunct accounts among the liability and proprietary accounts should follow the same practice as implied above, that is, the numbers should express the relationships of the accounts. For instance, if bonds have been issued at a discount, the accounts involved might be numbered as follows:

    2220   Bonds Payable
    2229   Bonds Payable—Unamortized Discount

If preferred stock was issued at a premium, the accounts might be numbered as follows:

    3100   Preferred Stock
    3109   Preferred Stock—Premium

The fact that the process of setting up the numbers forces us to consider the real relationships of the accounts is all to the good. The old procedure, still occasionally encountered, of showing the discount on bonds on the left side of the balance sheet becomes a little harder to swallow if one is called upon actually to assign an asset number to the discount. It is also quite likely that we will get a more critical consideration of the real nature of certain "reserves" if we are required to set up a definite 2000 or 3000 number for the account. Against the background of a good numbering system we can no longer set up weasel-worded titles for accounts which can mean different things to different persons.

The problems of complete detail

Up to this point we have pretended that a system of four digits would have the capacity to identify most of the necessary differences in categories. This, of course, will not be true of large and complicated businesses, nor will it be true for even modest businesses if we try to express the full necessary detail of certain accounts as part of the formal system. Two measures can be taken to get these expansions into the system.

The first method is the obvious one of setting up the system initially on a basis of five, six, or more digits, providing for the full expansion needs of any sector in the general framework of the system. This technique is uneconomical, however, since far more development is needed in some sectors than in others. For instance, even a fairly large business may have need for no more than the ten cash accounts which our four-digit framework provided, whereas the same business may need to differentiate thousands of kinds of raw materials.

The second method of providing expansibility is to provide an additional block of digits for accounts needing expansion beyond the basic number of digits. For instance, in our stereotype which uses the number 1141 for Raw Materials Inventory, we will provide an additional block of as many digits as may be necessary to identify every raw material handled. These detail or subclass digits are separated from the general account number by a decimal point (hyphen, slash, asterisk) to give us the full number of the specific item. This is an illustration of this development:

```
1141  Inventories—Raw Material
      1141.1000  Inv. Raw. Mat.—Lumber and Wood Products
      1141.2000  Inv. Raw. Mat.—Ferrous Metals
      1141.3000  Inv. Raw. Mat.—Nonferrous Metals
      1141.4000  Inv. Raw. Mat.—Plastics
                 (and so forth)
```

Obviously, the three final digits of the .1000 series are available for the fine sorting of lumber and wood products, the capacity of the system can be multiplied by ten or one hundred if necessary by the addition of one or two more digit positions. It might seem that our complete identifying number threatens to become unwieldy. However, for practical use within an accounting system, many routines may be laid out so that only the detail (right-of-the-decimal) part of the number need be handled. Many documents, processes, and reports concern only raw materials, and for these it is entirely unnecessary to express the left-of-the-decimal portion of the full number.

In a similar manner, individual customers may be assigned numbers which may identify them by sales districts, states, branches, and final unique identification. Such a customer number might run to eight or ten places. In the overall numbering-identification scheme it should be thought of as a right-of-the-decimal component of the basic category 1120 Accounts Receivable, but for most routine purposes it will be unnecessary to keep repeating the 1120 portion of the number, and no harm is done if, for most purposes, the customer number series is thought of as an independent system.

Many other places in the accounting system will need similar development of detail identification series tied to the major system closely or loosely as the situation demands. In a large plant every machine should bear a number, which may be a straight serial number by date of acquisition or which may identify the unit with its division, department, and cost center. Sales revenues from many products, and expenses by multiple classifications will need most careful development, as will be seen in ensuing paragraphs.

In a straight punched card system or in punched cards feeding into EDP, a color stripe may be employed to identify cards used for voluminous detail systems. For instance red-striped cards will be used for all raw material detail information, green-striped for accounts receivable, and so forth.

Classification of revenues

The significant things to be said regarding this section of the chart of accounts are simply implementations of the venture pattern of the business. Probably, the first and most general requirement of revenue classification is to recognize the difference between operating and nonoperating revenues. This would give us for the small traditional business:

```
4000  Revenues
      4100  Sales
      4200  Interest
      4300  Rent
      4400  Miscellaneous
```

As this type of classification works out, the sales would in most cases be the significant source of operating revenues, with interest, rent, and miscellaneous following as nonoperating drops in the bucket.

As this small business matures and recognizes the complication of its sales ventures, the classification expands:

```
4000  Revenues
      4100  Sales
            4110  Sales—Grocery Department
            4120  Sales—Meats Department
            4130  Sales—Produce
      4200  Interest
      4300  and so forth—
```

At the level of the full-fledged department store the sales revenue account would be broken down to the full list of commodity departments. This might mean a serial numbering using the ten's and unit's digits in a single series from 1 to 99, or the digit positions may be given more specific meaning. The number 4100 might identify typical owned merchandise departments. The number 4200 might be revenue from Leased Departments, with 4210, 4220, 4230, and so forth for Florist, Furs, Theater Tickets, and other departments commonly on a leased basis. The 4300 series might be revenue from service departments, such as 4310 Revenue—Shoe Repair Department, 4320 Revenue—Cafeterias, 4330 Revenue—Women's Apparel Alterations, and so forth. Interest, Rent, and Miscellaneous would be pushed into the 4400 and higher area. Revenues which are essentially "net," often characterized as "nonoperating income," might well be segregated in the 4900 group, or the nonoperating incomes and expenses could be further set out in the 7000 and 8000 series.

In the manufacturing business the major breakdown of revenues would be by sales of the various products. This might be a full-fledged divisional revenue breakdown, or it might be more simply the splitting of the sales revenue into a dozen or a hundred products, all produced by the single plant. Actually, a complete survey of the business in terms of its venture pattern must be the first step in setting up the revenue accounting plan. For a very extensive product sales analysis, it may be necessary to go to another right-of-the-decimal series which ties formally to the 4100 number but which for many operating purposes is regarded as an independent series.

Whatever the revenue analysis, it must be matched by the analysis of costs. This means product cost accounting and, to the extent possible, the parallel breakdown of distribution costs.

Basic classification of expenses

The systematic classification and numbering of assets, liability, and capital accounts are sensible facilitating devices and the classification of revenues as seen above is an obvious necessity in venture analysis. In the classification of expenses we finally come most directly to grips with the problems of management accounting—control, venture measurement, and forensics. All three of these purposes must be served by one basic classification, though the final details may be determined by the needs of the several purposes. The function of the rest of this chapter is to demonstrate how this can be done.

The general pattern of expense classification has already been touched upon several places where it was indicated that the expenses must follow the organization plan. This is still the formally controlling principle. Our task now is to see how it can be put into practice in a business of any size, and how it can be made to serve not only its obvious purpose of control but also any venture and forensic needs which the particular business faces.

The mechanics of routing the raw expense transactions in great volume and diversity into the organized expense accounts are a practical challenge to the systems man. Fortunately the outlines of this problem can be seen fairly clearly in terms of the systematic numbering scheme for expenses. Some expenses are incurred directly and solely for specific organization units. These may be charged at their first accounting recognition, i.e., from the purchase invoice, directly to the expense accounts of the identified, numbered units. Other expenses by their very nature, are incurred for the benefit of several or many units and must be booked initially into accounts describing the nature of the thing purchased, such as insurance, electricity, supplies. The term "natural expense accounts" is quite commonly applied to expense accounts of this kind. Sometimes the term "primary" is used to describe them but this is susceptible to confusion since "primary" may mean either initial as here intended or it may mean "most important." Probably the safest terminology would be to describe these accounts as "undistributed object of expenditure" accounts. This title has the advantage of implying the subsequent need to distribute the expenses, which goes right to the heart of proper expense accounting.

Applying the ideas of systematic numbering-identification to the expense area our stereotype grows as follows:

```
5000   Expenses
       5100   Expenses—Undistributed Object of Expenditures
       5200   Expenses—General Administrative Division
       5300   Expenses—Sales Division
       5400   Expenses—Manufacturing Division
```

The use of a number in the 5000 series, for instance 5101 for Insurance clearly identifies the content of that account as the value of the insurance expiration for a period. Unexpired insurance, an asset, would have a number in the 1000 series, for instance 1151 Prepaid Expenses–Insurance. Similarly, Rent Expense might be 5102, Rent Prepaid 1152, Rent Accrued–Payable 2132.

The development of the 5100 series in a straight forward manner would use the numbers 01 to 99 serially in the tens and units position to identify as many of the natural expenses as needed. Our stereotype expense classification proceeds as follows:

```
       (5000 All Expenses)
5100   Expenses—Undistributed Object of Expenditure (natural expenses)
       5101—Insurance
       5102—Rent
       5103—Electricity
       5104—Water
       5105—Gas
              (and so forth to 5199)
```

The numbers 5200, 5300, 5400 identify the major organization units and the tens' and units' digits further identify the sub and sub-sub-organization units thereunder.

    5200 Expenses—General Administrative Division
          5210—President's Office
          5220—Controller's Department
          5230—Legal Department
          5240—Public Relations Department
               (and so forth)
    5300 Expenses—Selling Division
          5310—Advertising Department
          5320—Traffic Department
          5330—Field Sales Administration Department
               (and so forth)
    5400 Expenses—Manufacturing Division
          5410—Manufacturing Service Departments
                    5411—Power Department
                    5412—Maintenance Department
                    5413—Personnel Department
                         (and so forth)
          5420—Manufacturing Production Departments
                    5421—Foundry Department
                    5422—Sand Blasting Department
                    5423—Finishing Department
                    5424—Assembly Department
                         (and so forth)

The use of the tens' digit to differentiate between the service and production departments within the manufacturing division is a nice use of numbers but would restrict the numbers of departments to 9 (or 10 if the 0 is used as an identifying number). To avoid this restriction, the numbers within the 5400 series can be set up as follows:

    5400 Expenses—Manufacturing Division
          5401-5420 Manufacturing Service Departments
          5421-5499 Manufacturing Production Departments

If even this is too restrictive, the system can be stretched out to five digits, giving ten times the capacity. Within the general administration and selling divisions, the units' digit is still available in the above scheme for sections within departments. Since this illustration is intended merely as a stereotype, we need go no further than this.

In theory, it might seem that the top-level breakdown into the three operating divisions used above would suffice for any manufacturing business. The study of actual charts of accounts, however, shows that deviations from this simple pattern are the rule rather than the exception. The common tendency is to show four, five, or more organization units at the top level. It should be remembered that the right or wrong of this question is a matter of organization and that the accounts must follow whatever the organization happens to be. The matter of firing vice presidents to change the organization to simplify the account numbering chart is beyond our present authority. The use of the 5700 series is suggested where nonoperating expenses become significant, and finally the 5900 series can serve as the greatest of all the expense breakdowns, the cost of sales, with tens' and units' places consistent with the sales breakdown to portray the essential venture analysis.

Detailed object of expenditure accounts

A simplified but valid approach to the relationship of the organization unit and the object of expenditure classifications of expense accounts visualizes the expense totals by organization units as the technique of holding the heads of the units responsible for their performance. Then, in order to help these heads improve their performance, the accounting system provides them with considerable additional detail regarding the composition of expenses within their units, so that they may figure out exactly which expenses have caused the trouble.

A little reflection along these lines will bring out the point that most organization units will be substantially similar with respect to the kinds of expenses they incur. Supervision, wages, and supplies will be elements in virtually every organization unit's expense list. Cost of utilities, insurance, and depreciation of equipment will commonly be significant. Beyond these expenses, the units will in many cases have expenses which are more or less unique.

Every good chart of accounts recognizes and takes advantage of this uniformity in setting up the accounts and numbering scheme for the detailed data within the units. To as great an extent as feasible, the accounts are set up on a uniform basis which will fit all organization units within the business. This facilitates memorization of the pattern for all who must know it, improves the accuracy of detailed accounting work, and makes possible certain interunit comparisons and summarizations that may be very useful to management.

The head of each department should be consulted in the determination of the expense accounts for his unit. In addition to the entirely unique expense items in many units, the degree of detail needed with respect to standard accounts will vary from unit to unit. For instance, in many units a single account for supplies consumed might be entirely adequate, while in others it might be necessary to subdivide supplies into several accounts. Generally speaking, only the operating head of a unit is familiar enough with his own management problems to know what kind of information to ask for. In other cases the problem of what detail is necessary may be of special interest to some executive farther up the line. This would be especially true where it is desired to have available data with which to compare the performances of parallel units.

The sophistication of managements with respect to the usefulness of detailed expense accounting such as is here suggested will be found to vary enormously. It is certainly the controller's responsibility to assay this point carefully and take all necessary steps to educate management on the matter. Such an education effort might, in some cases, go all the way to setting up demonstrations or seminars for groups of managers, but the chances are that the best education will be accomplished in informal personal discussions in which the managers are asked to examine presently available information and to suggest what else, or what greater detail, they would find useful. Gentle prodding by the controller on these occasions can be very effective in "spreading the word" as to the real usefulness of expense accounting.

To identify the necessary amount of detail, the typical system again makes use of the to-the-right-of-the-decimal device. The typical system might be set up with three such digits available to give ample room for flexibility as follows:

5421 **Foundry Department**
    5421.100 Supervision
    5421.200 Wages
    5421.300 Supplies
    5421.400 Utilities
    5421.500 Insurance
    5421.600 Depreciation of Departmental Equipment
    5421.700 Metallurgical Analysis—Contract Basis
    5421.800 Open
    5421.900 Prorated Rent and Service Departments

In this system it is presumed that accounts numbered 100 through 600 are standard in most departments. Account 700 seems to be an item which would be unique to this department. Account 800 is not used here but might be necessary for further unique items in other departments. Account 900 is probably found in every department which occupies appreciable space, it represents this department's share of providing housing or work space, including depreciation, taxes, and maintenance on the building.

If the practical problems of foundry management needed a further analysis of supplies, as seems likely, the 300 account could be subdivided as follows:

300 **Supplies**
    310 Core Boxes
    320 Sand
    330 Oil
    340 Small Tools
    350 Cleaning Materials
    390 Miscellaneous Supplies

The wages account is one which is often given considerable development especially for manufacturing departments. Our stereotype suggests the following:

```
200  Wages
     *210  Regular per Diem
     *220  Piece Work
      230  Overtime
            *231   Overtime—Time and One Half
            *232   Overtime—Double Time
      240  Premium Compensation
            *241   Shift Premium—Evening Rate
            *242   Shift Premium—Night Rate
            *243   Dirty Work Premium
            *244   Instruction Responsibility Premium
     *250  Sick Leave Pay
     *260  Vacation Pay
```

The reason for collecting such detail will be clear enough if we visualize the tensions and strategies involved in the periodic bargaining with a tough, aggressive union.

Mechanics of the account classification

The foregoing stereotype should not be interpreted to mean that the ledgers would actually contain an account for each number and title shown. Generally, it would be necessary only to have an account for the most detailed of the breakdowns shown in the stereotype, the other numbers being only "structural." This means two things: (a) that those numbers and titles are useful in explaining the classification plan as they were used above and (b) that they are available as steps in the summarizing process for statement purposes. For instance, in the wages classification shown above only those items marked with asterisks would actually exist as accounts. If, for some statement purpose the total of premium compensation is needed, it will be available as the total of the four accounts in the 240 series.

For the record, it should also be said, though perhaps hardly necessary, that the "accounts" provided for need not exist in the debit and credit ledger form of accounting theory, but may be carried in single-column statistical form on spread sheets, as holes in tabulating cards, as bits in a magnetized surface, or otherwise as long as they are in reliable form and available for "hard copy" reporting as needed by management and for reports to Internal Revenue Service, and so forth.

ADJUSTING TO THE IMPERFECT

We are not so naïve as to expect that, having set up an ideal stereotype, the chart of most businesses will immediately improve to near perfection. The incubus of the past together with the very real difficulties of matching accounting to the actual business situation will postpone this ideal indefinitely in most businesses. In the meantime, the concept of the stereotype—what accounting ought to do for management—can be used powerfully to protect management from overreliance on the imperfect accounting representations with which it must struggle.

If the revenue accounting system fails to produce an airtight breakdown, management had better be aware of the fact. If the revenue breakdown is tight but the corresponding costs are less than accurate, because of the intricacies of joint raw material costing, because of joint processing of some products, because product costing is on the basis of direct costs only, because no attempt is made to break distribution costs down to product lines, or for any other reason, the controller must carefully guard management from taking too seriously any showing of product profitability.

If the expenses of operating departments do not recognize the delicate nuances of controllability–noncontrollability at "the line," especially when circumstances change from one period to another, the controller must be aware of the situation and counsel fully with the concerned line officers lest they do an injustice to the department heads or fail to properly place deserved blame.

If the accounting evidence is less than conclusive in some dispute with outside parties, it is highly important to know of the weakness before exposing the corporation to real danger in the courts or other tribunals.

All of these imperfections in accounting information can be most clearly understood in terms of what the really mature accounting classification would have shown. With such knowledge, much can be done in specific cases by special ad hoc studies to adjust the formal accounting representations to full usefulness. If this is not feasible, the final safeguard is the controller's warning to management of the range of reliability–unreliability of the available figures. If he can say "this figure is possibly high or low by 5 percent," he will be aiding management greatly; the picture is quite different than if he had to estimate a possible 20 percent error. Obviously, the practice of being frank and specific about the shortcomings of the accounting system will give strong support when it becomes feasible to suggest improvements in the situation. It must not be supposed that basic improvements come easily—there is always support for inertia—letting sleeping dogs lie!

Legitimate deviations

To the newcomer on any corporate accounting scene, it is inevitable that certain accounting practices in use will seem out of line with the expected, in our terminology, out of line with the stereotype. Whether the "newcomer" is a public accountant in his first audit of the company, a college recruit being initiated to the system, or even an experienced controller shifting to a new job, there is danger in a too-ready condemnation of the actual practice. A far safer attitude is a questioning one which assumes at least a fair possibility that the deviation is only apparent and that fuller acquaintance with actual conditions will reveal the practice to be a reasonable adaptation. Incidentally, such a tentative, questioning stance is far better human relations for any newcomer than the alternative of too-ready criticism.

It is quite safe to say that *every business* would manifest at least a few peculiarities that would justify deviations from the stereotype accounting system. Our purpose in the remainder of this chapter will be to inspect a few situations and factors causing such differences and to tie them back to the chart so that the reader may begin to see the usefulness of the simple stereotype in handling necessary variations. Some of the illustrations will go back to situations already touched on in our earlier basic discussions, some will break rather new ground. We have no illusions that these efforts will fully cover the ground.

Application to nonprivate sectors

Some careful forethought as to the possible reasons for real or apparent deviations will be of help in recognizing them as they appear. The first and most obvious reasons for deviation from the norm are those caused by the nature of the unit whose accounting is being approached. A municipality, for instance, exists for service to the public. The concept of accounting for net income is absent, and with it a very large part of accounting theory which is aimed at the net income concept. However, the great problem of control is still very important though the units through which it is enforced are very differently organized, politically motivated, under complicated and cumbersome civil service regulations. The technique of control is the budget and appropriation system with legal force imposed upon the expenditure system. The annual struggle for adequate appropriations for each unit in the budget fight is a special variety of forensic engagement of paramount importance to the heads of the several functional divisions. Anyone who would try to apply accounting techniques to a municipality or any other government unit without recognizing these differences in situation would have a very rough time. Yet the basics are all there: routines of property accounting, payroll, receivables (taxes), and so forth; reporting of a highly specialized variety; venture accounting—the costs of the typical functions of education, police and fire protection, recreation, and so forth; control, and forensics, as already discussed.

Other governmental units would similarly deviate from the commercial industrial norm. The accounting problems of the United States government and of its subdivisions present a kaleidoscope of variations.

Somewhat parallel thinking would have to be applied to a vast range of nonprofit though privately owned organizations such as hospitals, fraternal organizations, athletic clubs, philanthropic foundations, and so forth. To approach and understand the accounting for any of these situations the most feasible technique is to screen them against the general pattern of purposes which we have been setting up with critical appraisal of the very real differences in actual situation.

Within the private sector with which we are here specifically concerned, there are still great differences in the actual situations which must be recognized and reconciled to the stereotype if we are to set up an accounting system effectively to serve management.

Venture pattern variations

As background, it is well to recognize again that even small businesses have venture-measurement problems. The local shoe store ought to recognize men's, women's, and children's shoes, and possibly the different brands of each as separable ventures which might manifest quite different profitability pictures. Actually, business of this size seldom attempts formal accounting measurement of ventures. Such analysis as is done by the informal appraisal of the owner is sometimes pretty shrewd and effective, sometimes wide of any realistic or useful results. The corner grocery store is a department store; the local garage clearly has three ventures, new car sales, used car sales, and service, with possibly sales of gas and oil as a fourth venture. At one time it was common for garages to apply the entire business overhead to the service departments, charging the sales departments only for direct costs. This procedure was certainly a deviation from expected good accounting. Was it justified by any sound reasoning? Try to figure that out!

It is unrealistic to recommend formal accounting recognition of the venture pattern with actual accounting distribution of general overhead items in these small businesses. However, if the knowledgeable accountant is ever in an advisory position to the small business man, his own understanding of what the full accounting would be, would help him greatly in making effective, simplified, suggestions regarding the real profitability of the several ventures.

Proceeding to the larger business scene, we find that the need for venture measurement is generally recognized, though the techniques of measurement are often far from perfect. Again the variations in the patterns are well worth looking into.

In some businesses we will find the ventures to be essentially parallel, in the sense that each will have similar revenues, expenses, and problems of management. The leading example would be the department store whose 25 or 125 departments, while selling different types of merchandise, nevertheless involve similar revenues (sales for cash and on account), similar expenses (supervision, wages, supplies, advertising, rent factor, etc.), and similar problems (personnel, price setting, turnover, etc.). The manufacturer of an extensive product line may also illustrate the parallel venture situation, though we may find that the problems of the several lines are not so closely parallel as are those of the departments in a department store. The *degree* of parallelism or similarity of its various ventures is itself an important aspect of the investigation into any business. By and large, the accounting for each department in the department store can be closely conformable to that for other departments. In the manufacturing business we might find that, while the accounting for the sales and distribution costs can be closely similar, the accounting for the manufacture of the several products may have to vary significantly.

To illustrate the venture analysis of the nonparallel type, consider the case of a large public utility. Detroit Edison, for instance, produces electric power for the southeast section of Michigan. It runs the second largest steamheating utility in the world, burning some 500,000 tons of coal each year in three plants to heat practically all the large commercial buildings in the city of Detroit. It also has a chain of electrical appliance stores which extends throughout its territory. These three major ventures have very different types of revenues, expenses, and problems of management. Within the electric utility venture, the business breaks down on its revenue side into industrial, commercial, residence, and special contract, sales subventures, each of which has distinctly different problems of revenue accounting, rate structure, public relations, and so forth, though the production of the electricity is joint for the three subventures.

The venture analysis of a large bank shows interesting nonparallel ventures, though all its activities are related by some aspect of money use. The bank's savings and commercial deposit departments are in some respects parallel, but its trust department, safety deposit, foreign exchange, mortgage loans, commercial loans, and other departments present quite different revenues, expenses, and management problems.

Not all businesses will fall clearly into parallel or nonparallel venture categories. Many will have certain ventures which are parallel and others which are unique. Even the department store will often have certain activities, such as its cafeterias, lending libraries, shoe repair, and what not, which are not typical sales departments but which must still be recognized and fitted into the scheme of revenue and expense accounting.

Major ventures and sidelines

Related to the main problem of venture analysis is the recognition of sideline ventures. Though the line cannot always be drawn between major ventures and sideline ventures in any particular business, the general distinguishing difference is that the sideline venture is usually entered into under some kind of pressure and not because of the attractiveness of its profit possibilities. For instance, the manufacturing firm which sets up cafeterias for its employees does not do so to make a profit out of selling food but as an accommodation to the employees—to save them carrying lunches—and in the hope that a hot lunch will result in better work. Other employee-pressure sideline ventures are the sale of protective clothing, a food or general merchandise commissary (company store), employee housing, and so forth. Another type of pressure comes from customers—for instance, the need to service the company's product after it has been sold, which may result in a service department of considerable size, or a finance division to facilitate sales to customers. A very common pressure into sideline results from the purchase of a complicated raw material which separates into the major wanted product and one or more byproducts which must be processed and sold to avoid waste. The meat packers are the familiar case in point, since they have been forced into bone meal fertilizers, glue production from hooves and horns, and clarinet factories to utilize the squeals. Utilization of excess manufacturing capacity has led many businesses into sideline ventures.

Whatever the reason for taking on the sideline, it must be recognized as a venture with revenues, expenses, and management problems of its own. If the sideline venture can be made to show a profit, that is all to the good. If it can be continued only at a net loss, management should do so with its eyes open to the fact. The sideline may be so simple or so small that it is hardly recognized as a management problem, or it may be complicated enough and large enough to have a complete management structure with many of the reporting needs of an independent business.

Ideally, the accounts for the sideline should be set up to show clearly its revenues and all its expenses. When this is not feasible, the systems man and the controller should be fully aware of the partial nature of the showing to be made for the sideline, so that management determinations regarding it may recognize the incompleteness of available facts and allow for them as well as may be possible.

Venture pattern—Accounting and management

Whatever pattern of coordinate major ventures and sidelines is discovered, it should be apparent that a primary requisite of the accounting plan will be to *portray and measure* the operations of those ventures as clearly as possible. Such measurement falls into two parts—the measurement of the revenue and the measurement of the expense of each venture. The study of the profit picture of the several ventures each period is the take-off point for much management thinking and planning.

At its very simplest, the problem is to push forward in those ventures that are able to produce a net profit and to play down or to eliminate those that show low profits or actual losses. More realistically, the profit picture is management's incentive to further inquiry into the "why" of the present status and on into the possibility of steps to improve further the success picture or to correct the unsuccessful results. Obviously, we are again upon the frontier between the proper area of the controller and the line management. The controller's function is to present the clearest possible picture as to what has happened to each venture, major or side line, at which point the function of management takes over and decides what to do about it.

Venture measurement and the chart of accounts

Having analysed the business as to its operating venture pattern—major parallel, major nonparallel, and sidelines—the implementation in terms of the chart of accounts is rather obvious as far as the revenues are concerned. The 4000 series of accounts can be directly broken down to exhibit the inflow of the revenues in whatever pattern is appropriate.

Adjusting the chart of expenses, the 5000 series, is not so easy since its general form is aimed at control. To convert this structure of expenses by divisions, departments, sections (i.e., by organization units) to the cost of ventures analysis is the whole problem of product cost accounting. Within the manufacturing segment of the business, whether we are using the most rudimentary "actual costs," the most enlightened standard costs or something in between, what we are trying to do is to recombine the expenses of the organization units with the costs of material and direct labor into a pattern of cost of goods produced which can be matched significantly with the revenue segments represented in the 4000 series.

Ideally, the same treatment should be given the expenses in the selling division and the general administration division—that is they should be analysed and recombined into a pattern that can be matched against the revenue segments. Some businesses have made extensive progress in the difficult area of "accounting for distribution costs," as it is usually characterized, others have done very little. Breaking down general administrative expenses by ventures would be still more difficult though still desirable in those circumstances in which it can be done meaningfully.

Even among the distribution costs there are great differences as between various expenses in the degree to which they can be meaningfully broken down by ventures, and the problem for specific expenses would manifest wide ranges of difficulty and resulting significance as between different businesses. How far to try to go in this effort in any particular business will again call for a high grade of judgment on the controller's part. Possible allocations may range from the sensible, obvious bases, clearly expressing the way in which revenue units have caused or have benefited from the particular expense, to far-fetched specious but hollow relationships which cannot be "sold" to the practical line executive as significant. Somewhere along this line is the intelligent cutoff, and to find it is the controller's responsibility. A very practical corollary is the fact that the *dollar amount* involved in the expense under scrutiny may in many cases be so small that its allocation to ventures under even the most rigorous analysis would be meaningless. This in itself gets the controller "off the hook," in many difficult situations and is just one more evidence that the controller must think in terms of practical management—must have the management point of view in many decisions as to right or wrong accounting.

The formal recognition of this difficulty in the accounts and statements is highly desirable. An account, Undistributed Costs (or a series of accounts breaking down the undistributable total to manufacturing, distributing, and administrative costs) should appear in the ledger and in the income statement in the Cost of Goods Sold section.

It should be noted that the allocations discussed above are often made merely as "off-the-books" analysis rather than by full debit and credit procedures.

Cost accounting and the chart of accounts

The accounts in which we accomplish the analysis and recombinations of the expenses of the manufacturing divisions into the venture pattern are simply expansions of the current asset account Inventory—Goods in Process, account 1142 in our stereotype. Under conditions properly using job costing, this account will be broken down to individual job orders using as many to-the-right-of-the-decimal places as necessary. Under sequential processing conditions, account 1142 will be broken down by manufacturing departments, with the to-the-right-of-the decimal digits tying to the organization chart numbers of the departments. Debits to these 1142 accounts will bring together the three elements of cost: materials, direct labor, and factory expenses. A fundamental aspect of accounting theory is manifested in the entries debiting the 1142 accounts and crediting the 5000 series as this is clear acknowledgement that these 5000 elements which have been called expenses are not really expenses after all but additions to the asset 1142 Inventory—Goods in Process. The essence of this relationship is not altered by the fact that the entries for burden application may be made on a variety of estimated bases, may be run through intermediate applied burden accounts, and may leave fragments temporarily in several kinds of variance accounts. Close attention to the numbering of all of the accounts involved in accordance with a systematic chart such as our stereotype forces an intelligent appraisal of the real nature of the fancy processes which are often only vaguely understood by student and practitioner. The numbers of the burden applied and the several variance accounts will indicate their nature as adjunct or contra accounts to the basic accounts in the chart. There may be argument as to exactly how they fit the stereotype, but that argument will certainly be sharp and incisive against this background.

Corporate structure and venture analysis

In the very large business, the major venture structure may be related to the history of the business in terms of the consolidation of originally separate businesses. In many of these cases the separate corporate structures of the previously independent units are maintained and their former accounting structures continued with little change. If the corporate lines truly correspond to the venture lines, this may result in proper venture accounting with virtually no special effort. However, as actual operations are consolidated, the old accounting classifications may need rather basic revision to tie in to the general business accounting while still reflecting proper analysis of the ventures.

The decentralization movement and venture analysis

Interesting, also, are the efforts of many large businesses to decentralize their operations on a profit-center basis. This move is simply the recognition of venture pattern all the way into authority and responsibility. Decentralization would be meaningless without the full development of the underlying accounting to reflect the success with which the decentralized units operate. Some of the most interesting problems in controllership are involved in this movement; it is successful where it follows venture lines and its insoluble difficulties are the result of creating decentralization segments which do not correspond to true venture lines.

Relation of venture and control accounting

In businesses where the organization is such that each of several ventures may be put in charge of a vice president or other high official, accounting for the venture coincides with control accounting at that level. The accurate measurement of venture success is at the same time an accurate measure of the responsibility of the vice president in charge. In these fortunate circumstances, the accounts should be given this double interpretation. The same revenue and cost figures which measure the venture for purposes of top-management planning also measure the effectiveness with which the man in charge has performed his function.

Beyond a one-to-one relationship of venture and control units, there may be special articulations. In department stores for instance an individual may be the "buyer" for a group of more-or-less related departments. Each department is accounted for as a venture and the total of the group becomes the control for the effectiveness of the buyer in charge. Similarly, the concept of product managers is found in many businesses where related products are grouped as to management responsibility. The extent of the authority of such a product manager must be carefully defined. He may be a product *sales* manager only, or his authority may extend back to the production phase, the purchasing of the basic raw materials, and so forth. To make the chart of accounts and the resulting statements reflect such varying responsibilities calls for a high degree of imagination on the part of the systems man. The focus of judgment must be on the product or venture profit margin, but the interpretation of results must respect random factors bearing on the particular period. This in effect recognizes the need for a very special definition of profit for the purpose of judging the product manager—a profit which measures all, and only those, factors over which he has real control.

Within such a venture-control unit, or down the line in any business not so organized, there will be successive echelons of authority and responsibility which cannot be identified with specific increments of revenue, but whose performance can and must be measured and compared with appropriate standards. Many things need to be said about the efforts to secure control. The matter of the proper units into which the business is to be divided for control purposes is the whole problem of organization over again. The measurement of the performance or production of each unit is in part the problem of budgeting and in part the difficult area of "work measurement."

Special project ventures

A special instance of venture and control involvement arises when a new project or product is approved on an experimental basis. It is important to watch the costs of such a project closely. This could be done by issuing instructions that all expenses incurred for the project be charged to a special account.

If the project is entirely separated from the normal operations of the business, under the supervision of a single responsible executive, this procedure would be entirely feasible, but this is rarely the actual situation; it is much more likely that several of the regular operating departments of the business will be contributing in various ways to the project. Chemical or mechanical research may be conducted in the regular laboratories, which may be occupied simultaneously with other projects as well; the factory may be making test runs and time studies on the proposed manufacturing operations; the purchasing agent may devote a large share of his time to unearthing sources of supply for the materials required; the sales department may be called on to make special test sales campaigns, and the advertising department to plan the promotion for these campaigns; and it may be necessary to consult the company's legal staff for advice on patent problems.

The normal method of recording all these expenses is to charge each to the account of the department head directly responsible for the expenditure, so that each account may present a complete record of the activities under the supervision of the responsible executive. If, in an effort to obtain information as to the cost of developing a particular product, expenditures that would normally be charged to these departmental accounts are diverted to some special account, the inevitable result will be that the departmental accounts lose their value as a medium of control because they present only a partial picture of departmental activities. Furthermore, from even a brief consideration of the nature and variety of the activities which may be involved in a project of this kind, it will be clear that it would be extremely difficult to segregate the cost of these activities with any accuracy at the time of recording the expenditure on the books; if the attempt is made, it is likely to result in incomplete and misleading information. The preferable solution in practically all situations of this kind is to adhere to the regular primary classification by responsibility in recording expenditures in the accounts and to answer any questions as to the results or costs of the special activity by secondary distributions of the primary accounts, either in regularly maintained supplementary records or in special ad hoc investigations and studies.

A fuller treatment of this topic will be found in Chapter 13 under Program Budgeting and Control.

Ventures, the chart, and statements

Everything that has been said above about venture analysis and the chart of accounts comes to its practical focus in the resulting reports and statements. While the quarterly and annual statements issued to the stockholders and public may well consolidate all revenues and costs into single figures, reports to management will exhibit the success of the several ventures in full detail. For situations of any serious degree of complexity this will require a system of statements consisting of a highly summarized general statement showing major venture totals, supported by a succession of more and more detailed statements which finally exhibit the ultimate available detail. The general statement may be essentially the traditional income statement with multiple columns for the major ventures. Final detailed statements will probably be computer printouts. In between, the form of reporting can obviously vary all over the place. In each business the controller should determine the pattern of statements in consultation with management, the right and wrong of things at this point will be what management needs and wants.

One caution which should be carefully observed in the design of statements is to be sure that the terminology does not go beyond the actual truth. Since the controller knows that not all costs have been broken down to ventures, he should avoid terms like "net income" or "net profit on" as the designations for final venture figures. The significant final figure may be labelled "venture operating revenue" or "venture contribution to company revenue," or some variant thereof more intimately reflecting the specific nature of the venture breakdown. Even at this point there will be great differences in different businesses. The final figures for some venture breakdowns will be so nearly "net" that management may well regard them as net in its decision process, while in other business this assumption might be far enough from the truth to constitute a real danger. It is the responsibility of the controller, in his interpretive function, to watch this point.

FORENSICS AND THE CHART OF ACCOUNTS

We must accept the controller's responsibility to produce information necessary for forensic involvement. Accomplishing this through the chart of accounts is, however, not as simple a matter as providing for control and venture purposes. Careful consideration reveals that controversial issues may arise from almost any facet of the business picture.

For instance, even among the usually cut-and-dried liabilities we run into the problem of how to reflect contingencies—damage suits in process, liabilities under product warranties which have not yet reached the legal action stage, and so forth. There is always a haunting fear that to recognize the contingency is to acknowledge the debt; yet to ignore the contingency may be quite misleading to readers of the statement. Many arrangements with major creditors involve the maintenance of certain ratios of debt to assets, current assets to current liabilities, minimum amounts of free surplus, and so forth. Interpretation of these agreements and the proper reflection of the concerned data in the balance sheet could be dangerous sources of disagreement with creditors unless properly handled.

Note that the above items are close to basic principles and category definitions which may become involved in controversy. There are many other possible situations in which the risk is any apparent deviation from "accepted accounting principles." It should be mentioned in this connection, that what had been a rather loose concept "accepted accounting principles" is becoming a much more definitive guide under the efforts of the Financial Accounting Standards Board. While this board's work is intended principally for the guidance of the CPA, most controllers will not wish to be caught out in left field at the time of the audit. Therefore, the study of the F.A.S.B. releases will henceforth be a very important screening device for the controller's thinking. "Do we measure up?" should be a constant test as questions arise which are concerned in any way with the releases. In event of serious controversy or actual litigation, the company whose practice does not follow the presently "accepted principles" would have to have a very convincing argument to support its nonaligned position.

The wide-ranging, varied nature of forensic problems carries with it the fact that specific chart of account provisions servicing these problems will need exceptional individual tailoring. Furthermore, such tailoring will have to be applied over or fitted into the chart which is designed primarily to service the needs of venture measurement and control. Many forensic problems are aspects of the other purposes.

For instance the defense of pricing policy attacked under the Robinson-Patman Law is purely venture accounting. The company is accused of selling one of its products to a certain large customer or to a segment of its trade at a price which discriminates against other customers. The company must prove that the prices in question do indeed reflect all of the differential costs of producing and selling to this customer or group of customers. This argument is generally referred to as "cost justification." The group of sales in question are a subventure and if the revenues and costs are properly matched they will be a legal defense as well as the measure of venture profitability for management use. If the area of sales in dispute does not coincide with the segment normally accounted for as a venture, the cost justification will require a special study of cost breakdown. If this special study can be honestly presented as applying the same principles as are used in the normal venture accounting, the argument will be on strong ground. If there is no routine, normal venture accounting by sales breakdowns, it will be much harder to make a convincing case for the particular sales in controversy. Forewarned is forearmed!

The detailed breakdown of labor costs has been discussed as a facet of control. Whether the same detailed breakdowns will be useful in the debates with the union is a moot question. In the recurring arguments on the extensions of the union contract the direct question will be how much each suggested change in the contract would cost. A significant criterion in judging this question will be exact information on what the costs of similar items have been in past periods. Here again, if this information is available from routinely recorded sources, it will be more effective in the argument than if it were specially assembled for the occasion.

On a far lower key there are many situations within the business itself that should be recognized as potentially controversial. For instance, there is real need to set up accounting routines to satisfy the individual worker that his weekly paycheck has been correctly calculated. This matter has been largely routinized through computer or other machine methods, but every time there is any change in the pay rate, or the pattern of deductions for any reason the systems man must incorporate the information into the payroll routine. The record must be clear not only for management's own use, but clear enough to satisfy the union steward and the worker himself.

Another low level controversial situation—this one tied directly to control—may in the long run be more important than some of the glamorous conflicts with outside parties. The necessity of measuring the routine economy and efficiency of every organization unit is an ever present source of strife. It is bad enough to be "bawled out" where the "bawling out" is deserved. Far worse in its effect on morale is to be blamed where blame is not deserved. The accounting classifications and routines must be so wisely designed and so carefully administered that even the person found at fault will acknowledge the measure to be accurate. This is a tough stricture. Not only must the system produce information that is accurate, but it must be so obviously accurate that it will stand up under conditions of attack—and that attack often under emotion-laden circumstances.

This small situation, properly understood, provides a basic and useful clue to the elusive forensic problem at various levels. Our usual assumption in setting up any accounting procedure is that of normal operating conditions. Forensic accounting goes further and looks in each instance for the possible hitches in the situation, for the troubles that might develop, for any source of dispute or misunderstanding with individuals or with the law. Not only must the information presented by clear enough to be understood but it must be so clear that it *cannot be misunderstood*. The fact that this must be accomplished without overloading the system with complications puts a high premium on imagination and foresight.

To exhaust the discussion of accounting preparation for forensic management is impossible. The range of problem situations extends from the homely types discussed above, up through myriad practical and legal contacts with outsiders to the most formal forensic situations represented by regulated public utilities in which control has gone all the way to prescribing the uniform account classifications to be used. The basic idea of such uniform accounting is to develop information which makes public control possible. Thus we have the forensic motivation at the very core of these accounting systems in contrast to private industry where provision for forensics is a come-lately consideration. As might be expected, however, a system aimed primarily at the controversial problem of rate regulation may be less effective than desired in the performance of other normal functions. This has long been the favorite gripe of accountants for the public utilities and has resulted in many cases in overlaid layers of accounting for normal management purposes.

The case of the railroads presents an interesting forensic pattern. The principal, long-time problem is their overall profitability. The rates they are allowed to charge are fixed to allow them a reasonable return on investment. What constitutes "investment" for this purpose involves rules as to what may be included and the valuation base for these included assets. Practically, the argument must proceed on the basis of specific rates to be increased or decreased (passenger, freight, and the subclassifications of each). Another recurring problem for the railroads is the pressure to abandon particular branch lines which because of auto and truck competition seem to be losing money. All of these problems are essentially venture-measurement problems and the issue in each case is the proper matching of revenues with expenses. The railroads must make their representations to convince slow-acting and cautious public authorities. The authorities in turn must consider the general public welfare and weigh it against justice or injustice to the roads. Here is forensic accounting with many millions of dollars at stake.

SUMMARY

This chapter has attempted the practical task of moving into the "how-to-do-it" phase of accounting. We know full well that implementation of accounting purposes will come fully alive only in the face of actual on-the-job conditions. This implementation can best proceed in terms of the chart of accounts, because the chart is the formal expression of basic accounting relationships, tying back on the one hand to the principles of accounting and on the other to the most practical conditions under which the controller must function.

8 MANUFACTURING COSTS

Objectives and techniques

Strictly speaking, the term "manufacturing cost" may be said to include only the expenses and losses incurred in converting raw material into the finished product. Manufacturing cost as thus defined would break down into three elements: direct labor, other manufacturing expenses, and material wastage or spoilage. The accounting for these elements of manufacturing cost, however, is, of necessity, closely tied in with accounting for the cost of the raw material itself, and the discussions in this chapter will cover the entire field of factory accounting for material, labor, and other expenses or "overhead."

Objectives of manufacturing-cost accounting

The objectives of manufacturing-cost accounting have been explained so often and so thoroughly that a definition of them here may seem to be a repetition of the obvious. But accounting techniques of any kind are useful and practical only to the extent that they are consciously and continuously directed at clearly defined basic objectives, and a statement of such objectives is necessary as a starting point for any discussion of the development of practical manufacturing-cost procedures.

The primary uses of manufacturing costs are the typing-in of the details of manufacturing operations with the overall accounting for ventures and control. At this intimate level, venture accounting becomes "product costing," and the uses of product costs are thought of as factory and sales "planning." Control becomes the provision of information as to the nature and purpose of expenditures for material, labor, and overhead and the measurement of such expenditures against some kind of formal or informal standards or yardsticks. This same information, analyzed, reorganized, and recast into different forms according to the particular problems involved, can be used in the planning of manufacturing operations; in overall planning and particularly in the formulation of intelligent sales and pricing policies, it is necessary to know the cost of each of the various products in the line. At this point, the actual techniques of control and product costing are very close together. For cost control and factory planning, costs are classified by manufacturing operations, while for sales planning they are classified by products.

In addition to their use for planning purposes, product costs are also necessary in determining the value of inventories so that costs may be charged against the sales to which they are properly applicable and correct statements of earnings and financial condition may be prepared. This may be considered a third important objective of cost accounting; however, the techniques necessary to meet this requirement alone are usually much simpler than those which must be developed for cost control and for planning purposes, and in that sense this can be considered a secondary objective. Still another consideration, closely related to that of cost control is the protection of the business from loss through error, wastage, or fraud in factory activities; for this purpose, there is no better tool than a comprehensive system of factory accounting, tied in with the general books.

Relationship between factory cost accounts and general accounts

The question of the relationship between the factory cost accounts and the general accounts warrants more than passing attention because it has a direct bearing on the attainment of the several parallel and somewhat overlapping objectives enumerated above and because it is too frequently an area of misunderstanding between the controller's department and the factory operating executives.

Most managements today demand monthly profit and loss statements and balance sheets and expect such statements to give a reasonably correct picture of operating results cumulatively through the year, so that under normal conditions there will be no unforeseen losses to be absorbed when the accounts are closed at the end of the fiscal year. In some companies which do not have complete factory cost-accounting systems tied in with the general books, the information required for current financial statements is obtained by charging the cost of all materials used and all expenditures for labor and manufacturing expenses to a Work in Process account and crediting that account and charging cost of sales each month with the estimated cost of shipments, determined by applying to the units of each product shipped an estimated product cost compiled from current data on material costs and factory operations. This procedure leaves the value of the Work in Process account unverified until a physical inventory is taken and priced, but if the procedure is carefully and intelligently executed by someone familiar with the company's operations, the overages and shortages in this inventory account can usually be kept within reasonable limits. An alternative procedure, which may be satisfactory where the product is uniform and where an analysis of cost of sales by items is not required, is to determine the amount credited to Work in Process and charged to Cost of Sales by taking a physical inventory each month, pricing it at estimated current costs, and adjusting the balance of the book inventory account accordingly.

There are many situations where one of these methods, or some modification of one of them, as crude as it may seem to the accountant accustomed to think in precise terms, may provide an effective and economical solution to the problem of preparing monthly financial statements. To insure the smooth functioning of these simplified methods, the cost estimates used in valuing inventories and costing sales must be prepared by someone with a good overall knowledge of actual operating conditions in the factory, and the methods are therefore more likely to work out well in small or medium-sized companies. In such companies, if a procedure of this kind is coupled with intelligent analysis of current cost figures and suitable controls of expense and waste at source, it may be adequate for all the management's needs and be less expensive to operate than a complete tie-in of the cost and general accounts. Certainly where such a setup is operating to the apparent satisfaction of the management, radical changes should not be undertaken without definite evidence of advantages to be gained.

The larger the scope and the more varied the products and the operations of a business, the more opportunities there are for waste and inefficiency in factory operation, the more complex are the management's selling and pricing problems, and the less assurance there is that a system of "memorandum" cost controls and product costs, not tied in with the general books, will furnish adequate and accurate information. Integration of the cost and general accounts, with the step-by-step recording of the flow of work through the factory, is not in itself a guarantee of the accuracy of reported results, but it does provide a foundation for complete cost control and accurate information as to product costs by insuring that every dollar spent in the factory is accounted for either in the cost of the finished product or as a loss incurred in manufacture. For the same reason, an integrated cost and accounting structure also provides more accurate data on which to base monthly financial statements; and if predetermined or standard costs are used, it makes it possible to summarize in the general accounts and in the profit and loss statements the information furnished by the cost accounts, showing the total amounts of variances between standard and actual costs arising from different causes and thus presenting a condensed overall picture of factory performance which may be very helpful to the management.

Many companies, especially larger ones, have computerized most or all of their factory cost accounting. In conjunction with a standard cost system (to be discussed shortly), a computer can be used to handle all the details of the factory accounts and may also be programmed to prepare the associated entries for the general ledgers. The inputs required for such a system include the daily outputs of each department, daily material and labor usage records such as requisitions and time cards, and a catalog of the current cost standards. The program can then be devised to compute departmental work in process inventory and to advise managers of the cost flows that have occurred. Variances from standard can also be prepared as a by product. It is very important, if a computer is in use, to pay close attention to the data collection step. Procedures for reporting inputs and outputs by department must be devised, and controls imposed to ensure their accuracy. These controls will normally include both prelist batch totals of each days records and physical inspection and suspension to emphasize the importance that managers attach to complete and accurate reporting of the data. A more complete discussion of this topic is offered in Chapter 23.

Some companies with computerized cost systems have found it possible to extend the system to include inventory control and/or production scheduling procedures. Others have devised outputs from the factory cost system so that the computer-based inventory control and accounting process is facilitated. For instance, the materials consumption records of one company known to the authors are reproduced on magnetic tape by the factory cost program for later use in an inventory recording model. In any event, the relationship between the factory, as consumer of materials, and the storeroom, as supplier, is sufficiently close and clear that the interface between the accounting systems sensing each must always be a completely free frontier.

The controller's task in the field of manufacturing costs

With these objectives of manufacturing-cost accounting in mind, we may say that the task of the controller in this field is twofold. First, he must see to it that the procedures for accounting for factory expenditures, supplemented by the nonaccounting controls established by the factory management, are adequate to meet the current needs of the business for cost control, product-cost information, and financial accounting entries and that they are simple enough that the expense of their operation will be reasonable in relation to the size of the business and the results achieved. And, second, he must see that the procedures are properly carried out and the results interpreted for the management with judgment and intelligence.

In performing the first part of this job—the development of the factory accounting procedure—the controller should be governed by the practical needs of the factory, sales, and general management and should keep his techniques as simple as possible, refining them step by step only as the operating executives themselves request additional information or are educated to its value and its use. To do this successfully, there must be complete and sympathetic cooperation between the controller's department and the operating departments, particularly the factory. This may seem to be a statement of the obvious, but it is an unfortunate fact that the relations between accounting personnel and factory personnel are often strained by misunderstanding and friction, and it must be said in all honesty that when such a situation exists, it is, as often as not, due to the failure on the part of the controller or those working under his direction to appreciate fully the viewpoint of the operating men. The controller should study the information needs of all departments of the business and should work to develop an integrated accounting structure which will meet those needs and will, at the 'same time, conform to a basically sound and consistent cost and accounting philosophy. If he can "sell" the operating executives on the advantages of such a long-term program and show himself ready to compromise when necessary between the ideal and the practical, most of the causes of possible friction will be eliminated at the source.

In carrying out the second part of his job in the field of manufacturing-cost accounting—the execution of the procedure and the interpretation of results—the first essential step that the controller must take is to educate himself and the management he serves in a sound cost philosophy, bearing in mind the limitation on the accuracy of the operating data on which all cost calculations are based and the limitations inherent in the methods used to compile and arrange the data in the form of cost information and cost reports. Controllers and public accountants alike have recently become increasingly aware of the layman's too ready acceptance of accounting and financial reports as statements of exact and definite fact, and they are attempting to educate the public to the realization that there are many factors of judgment and opinion which have an important effect on the results shown by any financial statement and that, even with reasonableness and consistency in applying these judgments, the financial condition and operating results of any business can be defined only within fairly broad limits of accuracy. Similarly, in the field of manufacturing costs the term "cost" is often invested with an implication of exactness which does not in fact exist, and this error in thinking has in the past been the cause of much confusion in the interpretation of cost data, particularly as they affect sales and general policy decisions.

Most of this confusion in the use of cost data arises from the failure to recognize one or more of the following facts about the nature and characteristics of costs and of the methods used in cost calculations.

1. There are many costs which are not directly chargeable to any particular job in the factory or to any particular product but must be allocated to jobs or products on some more or less arbitrary basis; and

different methods of allocation, all reasonably justifiable, may produce different "costs" for the same job or product.

2. (a) There are some costs, such as depreciation on plant and equipment owned, which represent allocations of past expenditures over the time period during which it is estimated that the benefit of the expenditures will be realized. The length of this period for any expenditure and the method of allocating the total expenditure over the period are matters of judgment, and variations in these factors often have a significant effect on total operating costs and on individual job and product costs.

(b) In most cases, past expenditures of this kind are to a large extent "sunk" costs—that is, the money is spent, and only a relatively small part of it can be recovered, no matter what action is taken by the management. Hence in using cost data as a basis for choosing between alternative courses of action in the planning of manufacturing operations, the "sunk" portion of these costs should be eliminated from consideration.

3. Almost all direct costs and some indirect or allocated costs are variable—that is, they vary in dollar amount as production volume varies and hence remain unchanged per unit of production. But other indirect costs (and occasionally some direct costs) are nonvariable in dollar amount and are therefore, different per unit of production at different activity levels; this means, of course, that the total cost of any individual job or the total unit cost of any individual product will depend in part on the activity level, actual or assumed, on which the cost calculation is based.

These fundamental facts about costs are familiar enough to factory operating men and cost accountants and are recognized in principle by most sales and general executives, but their effect on the meaning of the figures produced by the cost department is usually far from clear to those not mathematically inclined and not familiar with cost techniques. Every controller knows of the misconceptions that arise from the unthinking use of cost data or the use of cost data unthinkingly prepared, such as a complaint of one sales department that its costs have gone up in spite of increased sales because the sales of another department have fallen off, or a hasty conclusion by a sales executive that some product or sales territory which is "in the red" on the basis of a territorial analysis of net profits is necessarily a drain on the business and should be eliminated. It is important, therefore, that a clear understanding exist in the minds of all executives using regularly prepared cost reports as to the meaning and limitations of the figures involved and that cost information submitted in response to special requests be accompanied by an interpretation of the significance of the figures in relation to the particular problem under consideration. Only by such continuous education and interpretation can the best results be obtained from any cost-accounting procedure, whether it be a simple thumbnail system based on estimates and approximations or a comprehensive and highly refined structure completely integrated with the general accounts.

The purport of these observations summarizes into the statement that, for management, costs must be tailor-made, and there is no such thing as cost except in terms of intended use.

Types of cost-accounting techniques

In an "actual job-order" system, work is put through the plant in separate lots or jobs, the material and manufacturing cost applicable to each lot being accumulated on an individual job-order record and the actual cost[1] of the lot, as shown by this record, being carried into the finished-goods inventory. The manufacturing costs not directly chargeable to any individual job are first accumulated in primary departmental accounts, and the total for each department is then allocated to the various jobs on the basis of the work performed in the department. This basic procedure is the same for all types of cost systems, though various short cuts are possible in the interest of simplification, as already noted above in the discussion of the relationship between the factory accounts and the general accounts.

A radical simplification of the job-order procedure is possible when the product manufactured is uniform in character and the flow of production is continuous. In such cases, job orders for the collection of individual-lot costs may be dispensed with, and what is known as a "process" system may be used. In its simplest form, where only one product is involved and the plant operates as a unit, such a system may eliminate entirely the departmentalization of expenses except as necessary for current control, and the cost of any month's production may be determined simply by dividing the total dollars expended by the total units produced. Aside from errors in recording materials and expenses, such a single-product cost will be accurate in the sense that it is factual for the period covered, subject only to the correctness of the allocations of certain costs between time periods. But as the number of processes in a plant increases and especially as the product becomes more diversified, departmentalization becomes necessary to get a proper allocation of joint costs, and without job orders it becomes more difficult to place a correct valuation on work remaining in process and work completed and to determine the correct costs of the different items produced.

---

[1] The term "actual cost" is used here to denote a cost built up from direct or allocated charges of actual expenditures, as distinct from estimated or standard expenditures. In a very narrow sense, there is no such thing as an actual cost, since all costs involve allocations of expenses between products or between time periods, or both.

Many of these difficulties are minimized if, instead of transferring the product from one department to another and finally to finished stores at actual costs, a system of standard or predetermined costs is used and differences between actual and standard cost at each process are cleared to variance accounts. Such a standard cost procedure may also be helpful in simplifying clerical work under a job-order cost system; and under either the job-order or the process system this procedure has the advantage of fitting in with the whole concept of management control through the checking of actual results against predetermined assignments. There are certain situations, where most or all of the product is made to special specifications, in which the use of predetermined standard costs may not be feasible or economical; but in the great majority of business, where production is for stock and not for special order, the use of some form of standard cost procedure will be found to be the simplest and most effective method of achieving the objectives of manufacturing-cost accounting.

Standard cost technique

In a complete application of the standard cost technique, standards are set for each element of factory cost—i.e., material, direct labor, and manufacturing overhead. This involves fundamentally the determination of the following:

1. The standard quantity of each raw material in a given quantity of each product manufactured.

2. The standard price of each raw material.

3. The standard piece rate, or the standard labor hours and standard hourly wage, for each direct labor operation.

4. The standard burden rate, or overhead cost, of each factory activity, expressed in terms of dollars per unit of production, per labor hour or labor dollar, or per machine hour.

5. The standard processing routine for a given quantity of each product manufactured—i.e.:

   a) The standard hours of each direct labor operation.

   b) The standard units of production, labor hours or dollars, or machine hours required in each center of factory activity.

With these standards once established and tabulated, the actual costs of manufacture can be compared with them at various stages of processing and the differences written off in the books to "variance" accounts, while the standard costs are carried through the process accounts and into finished-goods inventories and cost of sales. The variance accounts, which reflect the overall efficiency of factory performance as compared with the standards, are usually broken down in five ways, corresponding to the five types of standards tabulated above:

1. Material-usage variance; also called "waste variance."

2. Material-price variance.

3. Direct labor variance (sometimes subdivided into labor-hour variance and wage-rate variance).

4. Burden variances, often called "over- or underearned burden." This is the difference between the total actual factory burden and the total burden earned in all of the factory centers. The burden earned in each center is determined by multiplying the actual activity in the center by the standard burden rate, i.e., the standard overhead expense for the center per activity unit.[2]

5. Production variance or time variance, i.e., the variance due to actual production being greater or less than standard production for the actual hours of activity. This variance arises from:

a) Differences between the actual and standard rates of production per labor hour or per machine hour at each of the various centers.[3]

b) Differences between actual and standard waste in processing, which result in differences in processing time per unit of finished product.

The effectiveness of the standard cost technique as a control tool for factory management depends on two things: first, the degree of care exercised in setting the standards in the first place and, second, the provision of adequate detailed information as to the nature and points of occurrence of the individual variances making up the totals, so that prompt corrective action can be taken. On both these points there are, in practice, wide differences in the degree of refinement to which the technique is developed in different companies. Many so-called "standard cost systems" are in operation with standards that are based merely on records of past experience or even, if such records are lacking, on the shrewd guesses of the factory manager or his foremen. Such standards are by no means entirely useless—they do provide a yardstick of a sort, and frequently they are a necessary first step in arousing interest in the possibilities of control through more scientific methods. At the other extreme, there will be found some systems in which great care is exercised in setting every element of the standards, the labor standards being based on detailed time and motion studies, material standards on a painstaking analysis of material utilization at each process, and overhead standards on a careful review of past experience and savings possibilities with respect to every type of expense.

The great majority of practical applications of the standard cost tech-

---

[2] If standard expenses are classified according to variable and nonvariable expenses, this burden variance can be further broken down into volume variance and controllable variance.

[3] In some centers, activity is measured by production rather than by labor-hours or machine-hours, and there is, of course, no production variance at these centers. Even in machine-hour and labor-hour centers, burden earned is sometimes calculated on the basis of actual units of production rather than actual hours of activity; when this procedure is followed, that portion of the production variance due to variations from standard processing time at each center is automatically included in the burden variance.

nique fall somewhere between these two extremes. This is sometimes due to inertia or a lack of understanding of the possibilities of more thorough methods, but it is often because, in the considered judgment of the controller, further refinements would not pay their way. Frequently, standards are used in accounting for the overhead element of cost only or for the labor and overhead elements, with material carried through the accounts at actual cost. In some of the short-cut methods of factory accounting previously described, the estimated product costs used in the preparation of the monthly financial statements also serve as standards of a crude sort for pricing and planning purposes; these product-cost standards may be supplemented by informal operating standards for the control of material and labor at a few key points, with reports showing variations from standard in units of material or hours of labor rather than in dollars. Where the standards are more comprehensive and more carefully set, there will usually be reports covering every phase of factory operations, with variations from standard stated in terms of dollars and tied in with the general accounts. One of the controller's major problems is to determine how far it is worthwhile to go in the refinements of standards and controls and the elaboration of the report structure.

Standards for raw-material prices

It should be pointed out in any discussion of standard cost technique that the application of the standard cost principle to accounting for raw-material prices is in a somewhat different category from the other applications mentioned in the preceding paragraphs. In most businesses, fluctuations in the prices paid for raw materials are affected more by external factors than by the efficiency of the purchasing department, and it is, therefore, impossible to set price standards in the same sense that standards can be determined for material usage, labor operations, or overhead expenses. But, in spite of their inadequacy as a measure of purchasing effectiveness, raw-material price standards do in many cases have a certain value as an overall control tool. If the standards are set at the beginning of each year at the estimated average prices for the year and are used in the preparation of the annual budget, the variances recorded in the accounts and shown in the profit and loss statements are helpful in presenting for the benefit of the top management a broad picture of trends in material costs. If properly analyzed by types of material, by departments, or by product classes, these variances may be the warning sign that some action is required to modify purchasing or sales pricing policies; however, if material is a large proportion of the total cost, it is necessary to set up some procedure that will bring price fluctuations to the attention of the management as they occur rather than after the materials have been purchased and consumed.

Another very important advantage derived from the use of standard material prices is the resulting simplification of the entries recording the movement of materials and product through the factory and to the customer. By carrying the difference between actual and standard costs of materials to a variance account at the time the materials are received or as they are put into process, it is possible to value the entire quantity of each material in process and finished stock and in cost of sales at the same standard unit cost, so that the clerical work involved in keeping the process accounts and finished-stock records and in costing shipments is greatly reduced and a fruitful source of accounting errors and dollar shortages in inventories is eliminated. There is, of course, a problem in determining how much of the price variance at the end of each month is applicable to the material content of the inventories and how much to the material content of production already sold and shipped. This is relatively easy if the materials are few in number and the product is reasonably uniform, and even when there are many materials and a diversified line of products, it is usually possible to make a satisfactory allocation of variances between inventories and cost of sales by grouping materials into classes and developing monthly ratios of actual to standard cost for each class as the variances are recorded.[4]

Standards for manufacturing-supply prices

Manufacturing supplies which are not a component of the finished product but are consumed in the process of manufacture are included in costs as part of the factory overhead. In setting standard overhead costs, it is necessary to assume some definite prices for these supplies, and any differences between these assumed prices and the actual prices paid are reflected in the burden variance accounts for the factory departments involved. These price fluctuations have nothing to do with the efficiency of factory operations, and, if they are significant, it may be desirable to segregate them by charging supplies into departmental costs at the prices assumed in the standards and carrying the price differences to a special variance account. There is no advantage of saving in clerical time in this procedure, as there is in the use of standard raw-material prices, because supply costs are not, as a rule, significant enough in relation to total costs to require an adjustment from standard to actual in valuing inventories. Hence the use of standard prices for supplies is usually limited to the few cases where price fluctuations are a seriously distorting factor in departmental statements.

Revisions of standards

The question as to how often standard costs should be revised depends on the cost philosophy adopted by the management, the use of

---

[4] See the Appendix to Chapter 11, "Inventory Valuation Policy and Procedure," paragraph II-B-2, "Group Material Pooling."

the cost figures, and the amount of money which the business can afford to spend on the operation of the cost system, and upon the practical circumstances, especially the actual and expected variations in volume. From the standpoint of the factory executives, it is desirable to have standards up to date at all times, so that variances due to accepted changes can be eliminated from reports used for control purposes. On the other hand, if the variances are used by the factory management as a measurement of the foremen's success in improving operating efficiency and if they are used by the top management as a similar measurement of the overall results achieved by the factory management, it is desirable to have the standards fixed for some period of time, so that cumulative variances will show what progress is being made from month to month. From the standpoint of the use of costs for sales pricing, it is perhaps not important that minor changes in costs should be reflected in the current cost figures used for costing the sales of regular products; but where quotations are being made on special products or on special bids for regular products, it may be highly desirable to have cost information completely up to date.

Perhaps the best way to reconcile these viewpoints is to allow the standard costs used in the accounts to remain unchanged during the fiscal year unless there are major changes in operating conditions, such as wage increases or decreases, important revision of machinery layouts, etc., but at the same time to keep a separate set of operating or current standards which will be up to date in all respects. If it is possible without too much detailed clerical work to use both sets of standards in the accounts, recording variances from the current standard as operating variances and differences between the current standards and the annual standards as a measurement of progress in cost reduction during the year, this would be an ideal setup. However, if it is felt that this involves too much detail, it is still possible for the factory executives, in interpreting the variances shown in their departmental statements, to make mental adjustments for cost changes which they know have been approved as permanent increases or decreases in cost.

An extension of the idea of using a fixed standard for a fiscal year is found in the so-called "basic standard cost" procedure, under which a "standard" is conceived of as a permanent base from which to measure cost variations over a long period of time, rather than as a yardstick for judging the effectiveness of current performance. Under this procedure a basic standard is set for each manufacturing operation and is changed only when there is a change in the nature of the operation or in the method of performing it; no other changes are made, even for such major factors as wage adjustments or variations in the level of supply costs. Obviously, variations from these standards do furnish valuable and interesting information on long-term cost trends, and the standards themselves provide a basis for setting up index figures which will show long-term trends in sales and factory activity without distortions due to changes in price or wage levels. However, if this type of basic standard is used, it is necessary for operating control purposes to inject into the cost procedure a second set of standards, which may be called "operating standards" or "budget costs," to distinguish them from the "basic standards." Without attempting to discuss in detail the advantages and disadvantages of this basic standard cost procedure, it is fair to say that in most situations it is difficult to justify the additional work involved in maintaining two sets of standards and keeping the "basic" standards adjusted for actual changes in the pattern of operations so that variances can be properly interpreted.

COST POLICY PROBLEMS; THE USE OF COST INFORMATION

Cost policy problems

There are many problems of policy and procedure which arise in attempting to build a cost structure in any particular business; it is clearly beyond the scope of this book to cover these problems in detail or even to enumerate all of them. A few of them, however, are fundamental in nature and are common to almost all situations, and a brief discussion of these will be helpful in rounding out this presentation of the subject. These questions are:

1. What level of activity should be assumed as a basis for the calculation of standard product costs?

2. What principles should be followed in determining the breakdown of the factory into departments and burden centers for the calculation of standard costs and the accumulation of actual costs?

3. What basis or bases should be used for allocating to productive departments the expenses of the various auxiliary departments, such as power house, mechanical department, general factory management, etc.

4. To what extent is it necessary or desirable to make entries in the accounts recording the allocation of auxiliary department costs to the productive departments?

5. Is it better policy to compute standards as closely as possible to expected actual costs, or should some margin of safety be injected?

Determination of standard activity levels

In determining the standard overhead cost of each operation to be used in building up product costs, it is necessary to decide what level of activity shall be assumed in the calculation. If the costs are broken down between variable and nonvariable elements and if the variable items are assumed to fluctuate in direct proportion to activity, the differences in unit costs at different activity levels will be in the nonvariable elements only, while if "step" standards are used for variable costs, as suggested in the previous chapter, the level of activity assumed will affect all cost elements. In any event, total product costs are usually significantly affected by the decision on this point, and the problem is a perennial topic of discussion among cost accountants.

Broadly speaking, there are three alternative bases on which to proceed: (1) expected sales volume for the period during which the standards are to be in effect, (2) normal or average sales volume (also termed "normal capacity"), and (3) practical plant capacity. Each of these alternatives has certain advantages and disadvantages. If the cost structure has not been developed to the point of making an adequate breakdown of expenses between variable and nonvariable, at least for factory control purposes, expected current sales volume may be the most convenient basis, and even where the expenses are so broken down, the use of this basis should reduce the range of variation between standard and actual activity and so minimize the inaccuracies inherent in adjusting the standard variable-expense allowances. As a practical matter, however, unless sales forecasting is unusually accurate, the estimated plant activity on this basis may be no nearer to actual than if the normal or average sales volume is used. The method has the decided disadvantage of producing costs that may fluctuate significantly from year to year as estimated sales volume varies, increasing in time of low volume when lower sales prices are needed to get more business and decreasing when business is good and higher prices presumably might be obtained for the product.

By using either of the other two bases—normal capacity or practical plant capacity—the effect of year-to-year fluctuations in sales volume is largely eliminated, and costs are at least partially stabilized. If practical plant capacity is the basis, the stabilization is complete except as expense levels vary or new manufacturing processes are developed or new facilities acquired. The normal capacity base is not quite so rigid, since it recognizes long-term trends in volume, either up or down, and permits of the gradual reflection of the effect of such trends in the standards.

It would be unwise to assert a too general preference for any one method, since their advantages and disadvantages vary with the circumstances of each business. For instance, of the three possible bases, estimated current sales volume may be satisfactory where the products are of a specialty nature and there are rapid changes in the variety of the plant's output or where plant investment is relatively small and fixed charges are a minor factor in costs. The practical plant capacity basis obviously tends to give minimum costs, since it assumes a volume which keeps the plant as near to full operation as is physically possible. Where the problem of overcapacity is acute or where there is danger of unwise expansion which might tend to such overcapacity, this method may be indicated. Otherwise, such costs are likely to be misleading, and the method will, of course, result in unabsorbed plant expense unless actual volume is stabilized at a very high level—and in that case practical capacity is not very different from estimated current sales volume.

Under more typical conditions, the use of normal capacity as a basis for standard product-cost calculations seems to avoid the disadvantages of the other methods and to permit relative stabilization of costs without the sacrifice of flexibility. It should be emphasized that the adoption of this basis does not imply the exclusive use of mathematical averages in determining the normal production or so-called "normal capacity" of the various plant departments. In the Accountants Cost Handbook,[5] various definitions are offered of "normal capacity" including the following: ". . . that capacity of a plant at which it produces a physical volume of goods sufficient to meet the average sales demand over a period of time long enough to level out the peaks and valleys resulting from seasonal and cyclical causes."

It is obvious that the average sales demand over such a period of time cannot be predicted with absolute accuracy but can only be estimated and that considerable judgment enters into the estimate. Historical averages of hours or production units in each department or burden center can be used as a guide, but consideration must also be given to the effect on future volume of known changes in manufacturing processes and of definitely established upward or downward trends in the sales of the various products. Also it may be desirable to modify the normal base for costs in some departments—as, for example, where, because of changes in sales trends of manufacturing processes or simply unwise plant investments, a machine or group of machines operates on a very low percentage of capacity, with the result that costs based on average estimated normal volume are too high to be competitive. In such a case some arbitrary production factor may produce a more useful cost than would be obtained by conforming strictly to the normal base. This amounts to the recognition of conditions making the practical capacity basis proper for this particular department. The aim in all these adjustments to historical averages should be to keep the base in line with the current trends in the business and at the same time avoid violent changes from year to year due to conditions that may be only temporary.

Departmental and burden-center breakdown

It has already been brought out in the discussion in a previous chapter that the primary classification of all expense accounts, including those

---

[5] R. I. Dickey (ed.) *The Accountants Cost Handbook* (New York: Ronald Press, 2d ed., 1960), p. 103.

covering factory expenses, should be by individual responsibility. As a general rule, the factory organization lends itself very readily to such a classification; usually there is an overseer or foreman in charge of each factory department, and these departments provide a natural basis for the accumulation of expenses preparatory to distributing them to the costs of the various products. However, it is frequently necessary to go somewhat further and break down some of these major departments into finer subdivisions, either for the purpose of securing better control of expense or in order to obtain a better distribution of the costs of the department to the various products. Even in such a relatively simple operation as a textile mill, there are usually several different kinds of machines under the supervision of some of the individual overseers, and the same machines may be used for different products, with significant differences in the amount of expense per hour of machine operation.

To decide on the proper burden-center setup in any particular case, it is necessary to make a careful analysis of the work performed in each department and to determine how detailed a breakdown of its activities is justified to secure better expense control or more accurate product costs. Theoretical accuracy should be balanced by consideration of the effort involved and the usefulness of results. Obviously, the finer the breakdown, the more clerical work is involved in keeping the cost accounts and the more difficult it is to achieve accuracy in breaking down actual expenses. The real test is "Does the proposed breakdown result in either (a) better expense control or (b) a significant improvement in the accuracy of the product costs?"

The purpose of cost allocation

In the next subsections, we shall consider overhead allocation principles and methods. Before that, however, it is appropriate to consider the circumstances in which overhead cost allocations should be made. As is so often the case, the use to which the cost will be put is the determining factor. If the cost of department output is to be used to assess the performance of the department foreman, allocations of cost from other departments may be misleading. Such costs will be misleading to the extent that they cannot be controlled by the foreman being evaluated. Fixed costs would fall into this category, and variable costs incurred by other departments may be in it also, because, while the foreman may influence these costs by his demands for services, he cannot (normally) control their level. It may be equitable to charge a foreman with the standard cost of a service his employees consume, but not with variances from that standard.

If the company is operating below capacity, so that its managers are anxious to obtain any work which will make a positive contribution in the short run, overhead allocations will usually be unhelpful. Such allocations may, if taken into account in price computation, cause managers to refuse work which they ought to accept, or to set a higher price than their customers will tolerate for a job the company needs badly.

On the other hand, a company which is fully occupied, and whose managers seek a cost foundation for a longer term pricing decision, may legitimately employ allocations. The overhead costs must all be recovered from somewhere if the company is to show a profit, and the main source is usually sales revenue. In the absence of a market controlled price, the full cost, including allocations of overhead, is as good a basis for price determination as any.

The typical company will find itself in both the situations mentioned in the two previous paragraphs at different times in its history. As it is not practical to make frequent changes from a full cost system to a direct cost system or vice versa, the best solution may be to prepare product costs on both bases. Of course, it is essential, if this is done, to ensure that the company's managers fully understand when each of the cost figures should be employed.

An especially important use of overhead allocations lies in the field of government business. Many governmental units purchase goods and services from companies. In many instances, the contract governing the transaction calls for the reimbursement of the vendor on the basis of cost. This may involve a "cost plus percentage" formula, or a "cost plus fixed fee" calculation. In either case, the cost referred to is normally the full cost of the product or service, including all "properly chargeable" overhead elements. The question of what is properly chargeable and what is not can be complicated, but the general principle of overhead allocation is well established in government business contracting. Evidently, if overhead were left out of the formula, the commercial business of the company would have to pay for the entire overhead and would thus be effectively subsidizing the government. The reverse situation would be equally unfair. The only fair distribution of the total cost is some means of allocation which recognizes the various overhead service demands of the various contracts or products.

Basis of allocation of indirect expenses

Behind everything that has been said about the allocation of indirect expenses, there lies a searching for some general principle. Actually, this general principle is not particularly mysterious or hard to find. The allocation of indirect expense to departments should be in the proportion in which those departments cause the expense to be incurred or the proportion by which they benefit from its incurrence. Some expenses seem easier to analyze in terms of cause, some in terms of benefit. Actually, the two approaches are in obverse–reverse relationship. They will never be found in contradiction to each other. Both terms are mentioned here because sometimes one and sometimes the other seems to be the easier approach for analysis and discussion.

The trouble with much that has been said and done regarding allocations is the hope for some simple, easy, overall method which makes specific thinking unnecessary. In every allocation problem, it is necessary to observe or inquire into the technological relationship of the incurrence and consumption of the asset value involved.

For instance, in a mature accounting system, it is not necessary to make any allocation of supplies consumed. Each item is charged to the using department (section, center, etc.) on the basis of specific requisition. If, for any reason, this detailed record keeping were not feasible, the proper allocation of supplies expense would be that which would most nearly approximate the specific issue pattern.

The best possible technique for charging machine depreciation to departments is to identify the machines by departments using them and to calculate depreciation directly for each department. If, for any reason, the machine depreciation is calculated in toto for the plant, it should be allocated to departments in as close an approximation as feasible to its incidence under the direct calculation method. This might be in proportion to the total book values of the machines in each department, or it might need more delicate adjustment if, for instance, the machines in some departments had longer average lives than those in others.

One of the most common indirect expenses needing allocation is the so-called rent factor, or cost of providing space. If quarters are rented, the case is fairly clear. If quarters are owned, the factors of depreciation, taxes, insurance, and maintenance on buildings are collected into one total and allocated as the rent factor. The obvious basis for this allocation is floor space, but this would not be proper if certain departments occupied space of much higher-than-average ceiling or space involving significantly more expensive structural features or if, by the nature of their operations (heavy vibrations, etc.), certain departments caused higher maintenance and depreciation. This sort of analysis could, of course, be driven to ridiculous extremes. In every case it should be followed as far as it involves significant amounts and not beyond. Rent-factor allocation demonstrates very well what is meant by examining the technological factors involved in causing the expense.

The allocation of insurance expense (other than on buildings) involves some interesting observations. Certain kinds of insurance are specific as to departments. Boiler explosion insurance should be charged to the only department—power—which operates a boiler. Plate glass insurance should be charged directly to whatever department—merchandising outlet, for instance—has plate glass in its operations. Employee liability insurance should be charged to all departments whose employees are covered in proportion to the number of employees or the payroll of each department, depending on the exact terms of the policy. If the risks vary substantially in different departments, the insurance premium may reflect those differences with a proportion to payroll four or five times as high in the high-risk as in the low-risk departments. This technological relationship must be respected in making the allocation of liability insurance.

Allocation of purchased utility costs—telephone, water, gas, electricity—should be in each case in accordance with the merits of the case. The number of telephones used by each department may be a good enough basis; but if purchasing and sales incur a lot of toll charges, whereas production departments use their telephones largely for interdepartment and local calls, this fact should be reflected in the allocation. If water is used merely for drinking fountains and sanitary purposes, distribution of water expense to departments in proportion to number of employees would be proper; but if certain departments use water, perhaps in huge quantities, in their productive processes, that changes the picture again. The cost of purchased gas may be a direct charge to some one department which is the sole user, or it may need to be allocated to several or many departments which use gas, on a metered or estimated basis. Purchased electricity may likewise be a rather simple or a very complicated problem of allocation. All these illustrations should serve to clarify what is meant by examining the technological relationships to determine the real causal-beneficial basis for allocation of the expense.

Allocation of expenses of auxiliary or service departments

The principle behind the allocation of expenses of service departments is the same as that behind general expenses. If, for instance, maintenance is recognized as a department with a responsible head, it is necessary, first, to collect all the costs under his functional control in order to hold him responsible. The total of such costs should then be allocated to the using departments periodically. The allocation should be made in proportion to the benefits received or the maintenance costs caused. The best way to accomplish this is to put actual maintenance work on a service-order basis, to set up a job cost on each maintenance order to which can be charged materials and direct labor actually used on the jobs. General maintenance costs can be prorated to departments on a monthly basis in proportion to their direct service-job costs, or the same thing can be accomplished by setting up a maintenance overhead rate which can be charged as each service job is completed. This system would automatically spread maintenance costs to departments in accordance with our general principle. Where formal job orders are considered too complicated, a proper basis for allocation might be approximated by having the maintenance boss keep an informal record of the hours of labor his crews spend in each department and allocating total maintenance costs on this basis.

Consideration of the problem of allocating personnel department costs is next. Here again we can begin with the simple possibility of allocating the total personnel department costs to departments in proportion to the numbers of their employees. This might be quite satisfactory under simple conditions, but it might be very inadequate under others. If department A has a higher turnover of employees, who must be processed by the personnel department, and department B has a very low turnover, it would be manifestly not in accordance with the causation principle to allocate on the simple number of employees. If employees in department C have to be put through a considerable training program by personnel, which employees of other departments do not need, that fact should be recognized in the allocation technique. If the activities of the personnel department embrace a home-nursing service for families of employees, perhaps the allocation formula should reflect the fact that in department D the employees average five kids each, whereas the company-wide average is only one and one third! Certainly, the benefits received and the expenses caused would run in this proportion.

Consideration of the proper technique of allocating costs of power generated in the company's own plant involves some especially basic elements. Again there is a too simple answer: Simply meter the electricity used by each department and then spread the total cost of the power department in proportion to the meter readings. This may be good enough in some cases, but it misses a refinement which may be important dollarwise. The design of a power plant must take into consideration the peak load to which it will ever be subjected. The use of electric power in some departments is quite erratic, running much higher at some times than at others. Such departments necessitate the building of much larger power plants than do other departments whose total consumption of electricity may be no greater on a period basis. Depreciation, taxes, insurance, maintenance, and some operating costs are a function of the size of the power plant. To recognize this situation in the allocation of power costs, it is necessary to break the problem into two parts: the fixed costs, which are a function of plant size, must be totaled and allocated to departments in proportion to connected power load (or demand factor); the variable costs, which are a function of power consumed, must be totaled and allocated to departments in proportion to the electricity consumed.

This analysis is quite clear for power plants, and in some concerns it might make a very substantial difference in the allocation of power costs as against a simpler system. Ideally, the same sort of thinking can be applied to other service departments. Certainly, maintenance and personnel have considerable elements of stand-by costs which could be differentiated from costs which are a function of operation volumes. Practically, it is unlikely that a full analysis in these cases would have as significant an impact as it does in the case of power, so it is generally and sensibly disregarded.

The whole problem of allocation is another good illustration of the relations of theory and practice. Good practice is simply that which follows the theory to the point at which resulting figures are significant, but it does not complicate the process by going beyond that point. Anyone who cannot visualize the theory is unlikely to reach and stop at the critical point.

The actual allocations may be made formally by debit and credit entry in the accounts or may be reflected only on worksheets and in statements. This option would not affect the principles involved, as discussed above.

Cost allocations—the mutual service problem

In some industries, especially those requiring significant technological and educational inputs, there are many auxiliary and service departments. Besides serving the main or production segments, these may also serve each other. For instance, the personnel department may find staff for the power plant, which in turn supplies heat to the personnel offices. It has been found that the hospital, steelmaking, banking and insurance industries, and many educational systems have numerous "mutual service" situations of the above general type, while many other industries have at least a few cases.

The cost determination process is considerably complicated by mutual service relationships. If the personnel and plant departments are related as mentioned above, and if the cost of personnel is the first to be allocated to other departments, one cost finding "answer" will be obtained. If the cost of plant is allocated first, however, another, perhaps significantly different, answer will be reached. The reason for the difference, of course, is that the first answer includes some personnel costs in the allocation of plant cost to other segments and no plant costs in the allocations from personnel, while the second answer includes exactly the reverse. It does not seem reasonable that two quite different answers for the cost of a product or service should be derived merely because of the sequence in which service departments are allocated, but that is very likely to happen.

One approach which can be used to eliminate this problem is algebra. Instead of allocating costs one by one, the analyst may express the relationships among the costs of the departments in equations. These may then be solved simultaneously, by standard algebraic methods, to give an answer which fully recognizes all mutual service aspects of the situation. While more complex in use than the standard allocation methods, this algebraic approach can be expressed in a computer program so that the mathematical steps need not be calculated by the analyst or accountant by hand.

The expression of the cost relationships in equations may be explained by example. Let us suppose a three-department organization, composed of personnel, plant, and production. The cost of personnel, let us say, may be chargeable 20 percent to plant, 80 percent to production, on some reasonable basis. Plant is chargeable 10% to personnel, 90 percent to production. In such a simple instance, of course, the cost of production can be found just by adding the three together; in a problem of normal complexity this simplistic solution will not work and a method like the following must be used.

The analyst (or his computer program, more probably) might express the cost relationships as follows, where P_1, P_2, and P_3 represent respectively the total costs of personnel, plant, and production, and where C_1, C_2, and C_3 represent the directly incurred costs (including direct overhead) of each.

$$P_1 = C_1 + 0.10P_2$$

$$P_2 = C_2 + 0.20P_1$$

$$P_3 = C_3 + 0.8P_1 + 0.9P_2$$

In words, the first equation states that the total cost of personnel (P_1) is made up of the original or direct cost (C_1) augmented by the allocated portion of the total cost of plant ($0.1 \times P_2$). This set of three simultaneous linear equations can then be solved for the three unknowns, P_1, P_2, and P_3.

Conservatism in costs

In many companies, particularly those which have been in existence during the period when modern cost techniques have been in process of development, there is a tendency to want to "load" any costs which are furnished for the use of the sales department by injecting "safety factors." Sometimes the loading is accomplished by using, for sales purposes, a separate set of costs which are frankly higher than those used for factory control purposes and for costing sales in the accounts. This is obviously less harmful than if the loading is accomplished by deliberate overstatement of standard factory expenses or understatement of standard production, but it is a serious question whether under present-day business conditions the cost-loading practice is really sound management at all.

Supposedly, the purpose of secret loading of costs is to gear the effort of the sales department using these inflated costs to a higher average attainment as to price than would have been the case if the costs had been placed somewhere near the proper amount. Undoubtedly, this is one way to keep the sales department from throwing goods overboard without due consideration of the profit requirements of the situation. Broadly speaking, however, the practice seems to be an attempt to make up for deficient management by the systematic presentation of essentially misleading information, in somewhat the same sense that many accountants, in the past at least, have characteristically tended to understate the results of operations so as to furnish a counterweight to the possible demands of stockholders for an unsound dividend policy. Both these practices may be of help in one direction but are likely to be seriously harmful in others. It is rarely possible to conceal the existence of such a practice from the sales executives who use the cost figures, and, unless the data as to the nature and extent of the loading are in the hands of the proper person, where these can be used when pricing problems are under consideration, there is great danger of all cost figures being discounted, perhaps to an unreasonable degree, so that the practice defeats its own ends.

Logically too, this process is bad, in that it contradicts the underlying major premise that clear portrayal of the facts is desirable. In this discussion we are going one step further and examining the possible management impact of an unclear portrayal of the facts.

The question of the content of the cost figure is not unrelated to the question of the reporting of the costs, which will be discussed more fully in a later chapter.

It is not, of course, desirable to have cost figures distributed indiscriminately to the entire sales organization, but if the sales executives are to take any responsibility for profit as well as for volume, they should be furnished with accurate information as to true costs. Sometimes the cost-price relationship can be satisfactorily worked out by cooperation between the sales executives and the factory executives, but usually it is necessary to have this function supervised by some central department or administrative executive whose primary concern is obtaining the maximum profit for the business as a whole. The presence of this central coordinating review is a matter not of theory but of hardheaded practical necessity. Some point of view is needed to resist the salesman's psychology when he forgets profits for business and to resist factory psychology when it forgets profits for some formal conception of cost.

Cost reports

Cost reports may be said to fall into two broad classifications, according to their purpose: first, what might be called "current control" reports and, second, "summary" reports. Current control reports are intended to point the way to losses or inefficiencies as they occur, so that prompt corrective action can be taken. Reports of this kind, to be effective, should show variances from standard at the point of occurrence, should be issued at frequent intervals (weekly or even daily), and should be designed primarily to meet the practical needs of the factory management. Summary reports, as implied by the term itself, are intended to summarize the gains or losses from standard over a long period of time—usually a month—as a check on the "current control" reports and as an overall measurement of operating efficiency. These reports are also used by the factory management and should, so far as practicable, be based on and tied in with the current control reports, so that overall variances from standard may be readily analyzed in detail. They also serve the additional purpose of keeping the general executives informed as to factory performance, and they must be designed with this added function in mind.

Current control cost reports may or may not be in terms of dollars. Strictly speaking, the term "cost report" should perhaps be limited to those in which the dollar is the basis of measurement, but, by whatever name they may be called, there are many reports useful to factory executives for control which show data in terms of physical units such as pounds, yards, hours, kilowatt-hours, etc. Summary reports, on the other hand, are almost always in terms of dollars and are tied in with the financial accounts in such a way that they support the overall dollar variances shown in the profit and loss statement. Most of the data for both types come from the same original sources in the factory, and a factory executive who has and uses a well-developed set of current control reports, either in dollars or in physical units, can tell in advance what trends the monthly summary report will show. If extended "post mortems" are necessary when the summary reports are issued, it is a clear indication that something is wrong with the current control information.

Illustrative report forms

There is a large body of literature available on the subject of cost reporting in many different fields, and it is clearly beyond the scope or intention of this volume to do more than illustrate fundamental principles and their practical application. It may be helpful, however, to illustrate a different type of monthly summary report which is widely used in situations in which production is functionalized, that is, where processing is not continuous but there are many different departments, all working on a wide variety of products. In this type of report, illustrated by the statement in Figure 8–1, the total monthly expenses of each department or "center" are compared with standard expenses, and the actual activity, in terms of units of product, labor hours, or machine hours, is compared with standard activity. The statement may, as in

Figure 8-1
RELIANCE MANUFACTURING COMPANY
Departmental cost statement

Unit of measure: Machine-hours

Actual:	1,118
Normal:	980
% of normal:	114.1

Dept.: 942
Period: 3-19XX

Expense	Normal standard	Percentage Vari-ability	Percentage Revision	Revised standard	Actual expense	Controllable	Variance—Gain or (loss) Volume Percent of normal standard	Volume Amount	Controllable year to date
.01 Direct labor—applied	$3,575	100	114.1	$4,079	$ 4,296	($217)	....	....	($605)
.02 Direct labor—unapplied	160	100	114.1	183	150	33	....	....	(4)
.03 Indirect labor	1,642	60	108.5	1,782	1,805	(23)	5.6	$ 92	(97)
.04 Supervision and clerical	735	20	102.8	756	740	16	11.3	83	90
Total wages and salaries	$6,112	....	....	$6,800	$ 6,991	($191)	....	$175	($616)
.11 Belting	133	90	112.7	150	158	(8)	1.4	2	(28)
.12 Machine parts	445	90	112.7	502	453	49	1.4	5	(10)
.13 Chemicals	496	90	112.7	559	516	43	1.4	7	159
.14 Miscellaneous supplies	164	75	110.6	181	205	(24)	3.5	6	(5)
.21 Maintenance department charges	265	70	109.9	291	405	(114)	4.2	11	33
.22 Power and light	470	60	108.5	510	530	(20)	5.6	26	19
.31 Spoiled work	530	100	114.1	605	502	103	....	....	196
Total direct costs	$8,615	....	....	$9,598	$ 9,760	($162)	....	$232	($252)
.61 Fixed charges	646	....	....	....	.. 646	....	....	....	....
Total expense	$9,261	....	....	....	$10,406	....	....	....	....

Proof

Direct expense absorbed:
3,615 × 114.1% = 9,830
Actual direct expense 9,760
 70

Variance above:
Volume 232
Controllable.... (162)
 Total 70

this illustration, be limited to the expenses directly under the control of the foreman of the department, or it may include all expenses, both direct and allocated; the pros and cons of this question were discussed earlier in this chapter. As indicated in that discussion, it is important, if prorated expenses are included, to segregate them from those under the foremen's control so that responsibility may be clearly defined.

In the statement in Figure 8–1, the standard expenses with which actual expenses are compared have been adjusted to reflect the actual rate of activity, and the overearned burden is broken down into two parts: that due to volume and that due to good or bad factory performance, which is called in this illustration the "controllable" variance. This implies, of course, that all elements of the standard costs have been broken down between variable and nonvariable, but, even where such a breakdown is not available and actual costs are compared with the standard for the standard rate of activity, the factory manager and foreman can often make good use of the report by noting the percentage of difference between actual and standard activity and making mental calculations to determine whether the variance in expense is reasonable in view of the variance in activity. Some factory executives prefer to operate on this basis, believing that any breakdown of expense between variable and nonvariable can be only an estimate at best and that they can exercise better control by working with a fixed standard and interpreting variances, as they occur, from their own knowledge of operating conditions. This, of course, requires close personal supervision by the factory manager, which is possible in a small or moderate-sized plant, but the procedure is inadequate for a large plant, where the chief factory executive cannot be in such intimate touch with all departments and must rely more on the accuracy of his cost reports to follow operations. It must be admitted, however, that there is a definite danger in relying on standards adjusted for activity unless the adjustments are based on careful studies of the actual effect of changes in activity on the various types of expenses.

Cost information for sales department use

Although factory executives, with a good deal of justice, are inclined to the view that their needs should be given first consideration in the development of any cost structure, it is probably safe to say that in most businesses there is more real danger of loss from misunderstanding and misuse of cost information by the sales department than from lack of adequate data for factory control. Some sales departments have a naive faith in the infallibility of a given cost for all purposes, while others are suspicious of all cost figures and are convinced that the factory is constantly conspiring to make it impossible to sell any goods at all.

Management policies as to the amount of cost information furnished to the sales department vary widely, but, with the increasing emphasis in recent years on the importance of making the sales organization profit-conscious rather than merely volume-conscious, the tendency has been to give the sales executives—at least at the top level—much more complete cost information. Competitive pressure has also forced a revision of pricing policies, requiring a better understanding of the true nature of the concept of cost and particularly of the relationship between cost and volume. As stated before, it is highly important that all executives using cost data clearly understand that there is no one true mathematical cost for any product and that any request for cost information should be accompanied by a clear statement of the use to which the information is to be put.

In spite of this emphasis on the caution required in interpreting cost data, the situation is not so confusing as it may sound. Although there will be special times and special circumstances in which the general rule will not apply, there can be little doubt that the product costs used by the sales department as a primary guide in price setting should be the same costs that are used in determining cost of sales in the financial statements; that is, they should be based on the actual or current replacement cost of material, depending on company policy, plus a manufacturing cost which includes not only factory expenses directly chargeable to the various products but also a fair share of all indirect or allocated costs. In other words, these product costs should be total costs in the sense that they absorb all manufacturing expenses at the standard level of activity.

The form in which this product-cost information is tabulated and the organization which is set up for keeping it up to date will vary according to the conditions in each case. In many branches of the textile industry, where fluctuations in selling prices are closely related to fluctuations in raw-material costs, the responsibility for keeping cost information current is often assigned to the sales department itself, while in other situations, where selling-price changes are less frequent, this may be a function of a special section of the cost department. In either case, the essential requirements are that some form of specification sheet, be available for each product and that there be a definite assignment of the responsibilities for the following:

1. Keeping watch on the trend of material costs.

2. Keeping manufacturing costs up to date, to reflect important changes in processing methods, wage rates, supply costs, etc.

3. Revising product costs to reflect these changes in material and manufacturing costs.

4. Reviewing constantly the relationship between changing product costs and selling prices.

These product costs computed to absorb a full share of factory overhead are the basic cost information for sales purposes. Over the long pull the business must recover all costs, plus a profit, in its selling prices, and the sales department is normally expected to aim at recovering such a full cost, plus a reasonable markup, for every product.

Other uses of cost data

The use of manufacturing cost data in the forecasting of cost of goods sold for budgetary control will be covered in Chapter 13, on "The Budget—Policies and Procedures." In addition to this use for budgetary purposes, information about the cost of the various operations in the factory is required for manufacturing planning, for example, in the determination of the most economical processing routine, where alternatives are possible, and, even more important, in the planning of expenditures for plant replacements or additions. This latter problem, which is one of the most interesting and most complex with which the controller has to deal, is discussed Chapter 15 on "Planning and Control of Capital Expenditures."

9 OPERATING COSTS IN MARKETING AND ADMINISTRATION

Conventional accounting for marketing and administrative expenses

The concept of marketing and administrative cost accounting is a relatively new development in the evolution of accounting science. In a manufacturing business the term "cost control" if used without qualification, usually refers to factory costs, and the "cost" of a product means, in common parlance, the sum of the costs of the materials used and the labor directly expended on the product plus an allocated share of other factory expenses incurred up to the time the product is placed in finished stock ready for shipment. As shipments are made, the "cost of goods sold" is determined, as a rule, by applying these unit product costs to the quantities of the various items shipped, so that in the profit and loss statement there is a direct correlation of manufacturing costs with the sales to which those costs are applicable. Marketing and administrative expenses, on the other hand, are usually charged to profit and loss as incurred, without any attempt to relate them to specific products or specific sales, but with the obvious implication that they are related to the production of current income.

This implication in the profit and loss statement that all marketing and administrative expenses are related to current income does not always stand up under close analysis. In a business where any significant portion of the sales order is booked for future delivery, some part of the expenses of field selling and related activities is clearly a cost of future, rather than of current, income. Even in a business which sells entirely on a "spot" basis, there are many expenses, such as advertising, promotion, research, etc., which are incurred at least partially for the

215

production of future income. But forward orders are in many cases subject to cancellation, as a matter of policy, if not legally, and the benefits to be derived from advertising and research are never certain until they are actually realized. Hence it is reasonable and "conservative" to write off advertising, selling, and research and administrative expenses as incurred—furthermore, it is convenient, as such expenses are seldom related to inventories on hand in any determinable way.

It is always possible to conjure up the special case which would justify a nonstandard treatment. As a matter of fact, the clear recognition and acknowledgment of such cases strengthen the propriety of the usual treatment of the usual conditions. Business A has been building up its inventory of a radically new product which it will release to the public on January 1. During the last three months business A has spent $100,000 on special advertising announcing the new product and advising the public to wait for its appearance. Salesmen report a tremendous interest and say that they will be able to sell far more than the company can produce. The actual manufacturing cost of the new product on hand on December 31 is $500 thousand. Under these conditions there is not much question that the situation presents an asset value of $600 thousand. Whether this be shown as finished-goods inventory, $600 thousand, or as finished-goods inventory, $500 thousand, and deferred advertising cost, $100 thousand, is hardly more than a matter of taste. If the facts are accepted as stated, it would be a misstatement of fact to expense the $100 thousand.

Business B has virtually no sales problems because its entire product is taken by one customer. The president of the company is an engineer, and he and his staff spend virtually all their time on the development of products and the study of production problems. Can there be any doubt that the "administrative expense" of business B is, in fact, largely manufacturing cost and that a large part of it should be so shown in the accounts and statements? Is there any less reason for including in inventory a part of this cost than a part of the production superintendent's salary.

However, special conditions such as outlined for business A and B are seldom encountered in practice. For the typical situation, the convention method of accounting, therefore, has a firm practical basis, and for the determination of overall earnings in accordance with "sound accounting practice" no marketing or administrative "cost accounting" is required.

Need for marketing and administrative costs

Although there is no need for marketing and administrative cost accounting in the preparation of financial statements, it is certainly inadequate for management purposes to consider marketing and administrative expenses as a lump-sum overhead to be covered out of total gross profits or to allocate them to products or customers on the basis of some overall factor, such as dollars of sales or dollars of factory costs. Marketing and administrative expenses are just as truly costs of operation as are manufacturing costs, and there is just as much need for information about them for control purposes and for use in the planning of operations. As a matter of fact, in practically every business a certain degree of control of marketing and administrative expenses is obtained by the use of classified expense accounts and the comparison of current expenses with budget or with the similar expenses of some previous period; even though this information is not usually thought of as cost data, it serves exactly the same control purpose as does departmental cost accounting in the factory. But in many businesses there is no attempt to relate these marketing and administrative costs to the results obtained or to reclassify them so that they will have significance for management planning purposes, and this is the field which has been relatively little explored until recent years and is still far from being fully developed.

Complexity of the marketing and administrative cost problem

The relatively slow development of marketing and administrative cost accounting has sometimes been attributed to inertia and to the absence of any need for such accounting in the determination of overall profit results. These factors undoubtedly tended to delay the recognition of the importance of analyzing and understanding marketing and administrative costs, but they cannot account entirely for the slowness in developing a more complete and exact science of marketing and administrative cost accounting when some of the best minds in the accounting and management fields have labored on the problem. Broadly speaking, there are two basic reasons for the apparently unsatisfactory results of these efforts. In the first place, marketing and administrative activities are fundamentally different in character from manufacturing activities and are carried on under conditions which make costing for control and planning purposes much more difficult; and, in the second place, the problem of indirect and joint costs is much more acute in marketing and administration than in manufacturing.

Control of manufacturing activities is simplified by the fact that the activities are carried on in one or a few locations. In most industries actual productive operations can be analyzed, standardized, and closely supervised, and output can be accurately measured, and if this management job is done effectively, the individual worker has little to do but follow instructions, with the knowledge that any deviation from standard performance will almost certainly be noticed and investigated. The reclassification of manufacturing costs for planning purposes is strictly a product-cost problem; the costs of material and direct labor applicable to any given product can be ascertained within very narrow limits, and a larger part of manufacturing overhead can be allocated to products on some reasonable and logical basis. For certain overhead costs, such as management, it is necessary to use somewhat arbitrary bases of allocation, but the total of these items is usually a relatively small part of the total of all factory costs.

For a few of the activities in the marketing and administrative classification, such as warehousing, packing, and shipping, these same general conditions apply, and these activities usually present relatively few serious costing problems. But in field selling activities, for example, the conditions are entirely different; such activities are spread over a wide area, and salesmen necessarily work most of the time without direct supervision. The ultimate objective of all field selling is to secure orders, but at any particular time the efforts of the salesmen may, as a matter of management policy, be directed in whole or in part to promotion or the building of good will, rather than to securing the maximum amount of immediate business. Even if the job is limited to securing orders, the "working conditions," which in manufacturing can be effectively standardized, are, in selling, largely out of control; customers are located to suit their own convenience, they have different temperaments, whims, and prejudices, their requirements vary with conditions over which they themselves have only partial control, and there are always competitors' activities to be reckoned with. Because of its diversity and complexity, the individual salesman's job demands initiative, adaptability, and judgment; the personal equation enters into it to a very high degree, and this equation cannot be reduced to a mathematical formula.

All these factors make it difficult to standardize the field selling job and measure its effectiveness, and they also complicate the problem of reclassifying costs and interpreting them for planning purposes. Furthermore, the organization of selling activities in many businesses is, of necessity, quite complex; a wide variety of products may be sold by a single field organization through several different outlets, which means that the problem of joint costs previously referred to becomes very troublesome, and it is difficult to determine the net effect of changes in sales policy with respect to any particular products, classes of customers, or methods of sale.

Other marketing and administrative activities are carried on in the office rather than in the field, and for some of them it is possible to standardize working conditions to a degree and even to measure results. These costs, however, may be affected by variations in any one of a number of factors—type of product, type of customer, method of sale, etc.—and it is often difficult to determine the real significance of costs reclassified on any one of these bases. Many office activities of marketing and administration are focused on such general functions as coordination, policy planning, finance, etc., and their cost can be allocated to products or customers only on an arbitrary basis; in most businesses these and other joint costs are a very large proportion of total marketing and administrative costs.

These complications in marketing and administrative cost accounting are brought out in more detail in the discussion in the remainder of this chapter, but, from what has been said so far, it will be apparent that, except in the very simplest types of organizations, it is not possible, in marketing and administrative cost accounting, to approach even the limited degree of uniformity, completeness, and accuracy that has been attained in manufacturing cost-accounting practice. It follows, also, that, while the principles underlying accepted manufacturing cost techniques are equally valid in the field of marketing and administrative costs, the techniques themselves cannot be applied in their entirety.

In the discussion of manufacturing costs in the chapters immediately preceding, emphasis was laid on the importance of adapting the techniques used, first, to the limitations inherent in the available data and, second, to the ability of the management, and indeed of the controller himself, to understand and use the information furnished. This is important enough and difficult enough in factory cost accounting, but it is even more important and more difficult in developing marketing and administrative costs. Even a poorly conceived factory cost structure will often yield some information which can be used to advantage, but any attempt to develop marketing and administrative cost information without a complete and clear understanding of the limitations of the data and the problem to which they are to be applied will result only in wasted clerical and executive time and hopeless confusion of thinking.

In spite of the complexities and difficulties involved, there is a great deal that can be done, by careful analysis and interpretation, to control marketing and administrative costs and to provide information about them which will be extremely useful in formulating policies and planning operations. Much of this information can be obtained by occasional special investigations and compilations, repeated from time to time as necessary, rather than by continuous routine accounting, and, except for the primary recording of expenses by responsibilities, as suggested in Chapter 7, "The Accounting Plan," marketing and administrative cost data can be recorded in supplementary records or work sheets rather than in the general books of account.

Classification of marketing and administrative costs

So far in this discussion the term "marketing and administrative costs" has been used to cover the costs of all activities not directly related to production. Clearly there are many different kinds of activities included in this broad grouping, and the first step in developing a costing program is to break down and classify these different activities. The most logical primary breakdown might seem to be between "marketing" and "administrative," but these terms do not carry clearly defined meanings. The classification shown in Figure 9–1, adapted in part from an article by E. Stewart Freeman, is based on definite functions and hence useful as a foundation for cost analysis. With this kind of general picture of the nature of marketing and administrative activities in mind, the cost analyst has to ask himself two questions: first, "How can the cost of these activities be controlled?" and, second, "What additional informa-

Figure 9–1

SUGGESTED FUNCTIONAL CLASSIFICATION OF
MARKETING AND ADMINISTRATIVE COSTS

Order-getting costs:

Advertising and sales promotion
Field selling
    Selection and training of personnel
    Solicitation of orders
Branch sales office expenses
General sales management, policy and planning

Research and product development costs:

Order-filling costs:

Warehousing
Shipping
Delivery (including transportation out)
Order and invoice handling

Money-collecting costs:

Customers' accounts
Credit and collection

Financing costs:

Treasurer's department

General administrative costs:

General policy, planning, and coordination
    (Chief executive's office)
Corporate and legal functions
    (Secretary's office)
Control functions   ⎫ Some of these functions
    Accounting and cost   ⎪ represent services rendered
    Statistical   ⎪ to other functions and
    Budget   ⎬ should be related to such
Centralized service functions   ⎪ other functions in cost
    Stenographic   ⎪ analysis.
    Filing, mailing, etc.   ⎪
    Paymaster   ⎭

tion about these activities does management need in order to do an effective job of planning and coordination?"

Cost control

Some of the control aspects of the problem have been partially covered in Chapter 7, "The Accounting Plan," and other aspects will be taken up in Chapter 13 "The Budget: Policies and Procedures." The rule that the primary accounts should be set up on the basis of individual responsibility is fundamental, and, as in the case of factory activities, any sound organization of marketing and administrative activities usually lends itself readily to such a classification. Marketing and administrative organization is by nature much less rigid than factory organization; in the plant there are definite processes or operations which necessarily follow in a logical sequence, and factory departmentalization and assignment of responsibilities are very nearly predetermined by this manufacturing pattern. An assignment of marketing and administrative responsibilities in accordance with the classification in Figure 9–1 would be entirely logical, but within any particular business there are often practical historical and personal reasons why it is not feasible to make quite such a clean-cut segregation of functions as this. In setting up a branch office, for example, it may be economical to combine some selling and some warehousing functions under one branch manager, or in the home office the controller may have supervision, through an office manager, over all clerical activities, including order writing and billing, credits and collections, and accounting, cost, and statistical work. Whatever the organization form may be, the primary accounts on the books should reflect it, and, if necessary, a regrouping of the accounts by functions should be made up in supplementary records as a first step in cost analysis.

Expense standards for control

With the accounts set up to show actual expenses of marketing and administration by individual responsibility, it remains to determine how the effectiveness of performance is to be judged—that is, against what standards actual expenses are to be measured. In the discussion of manufacturing costs, it was pointed out that, to measure factory performance, effectively, it is necessary to determine what expenses remain unchanged irrespective of activity and what expenses fluctuate with activity; the same problem presents itself in the measurement of marketing and administrative performance, with an added complication. In the factory, output can be definitely measured and quality controlled against fixed specifications, but for much of the work involved in marketing and administration no exact measurement of output is possible. This applies to all the order-getting costs, to most of the financing and general administrative costs, and, to a lesser degree, to some of the order-filling and money-collecting costs.

The performance of those engaged in order-getting activities is reflected in the sales obtained, but there are many other factors which have a bearing on sales results, and no one would say that sales per salesman's hour can be predicted with the same degree of accuracy as production per machine hour. A salesman's activities can be planned by a careful analysis of sales potentials and cost of coverage in his territory, his expenses can be budgeted when his routing is once determined, and a fair estimate can be made of what sales can be expected to result under certain assumed general business and competitive conditions; the part which cost analysis plays in problems of this type is discussed in the next chapter. For purposes of comparison with actual expenses, however, the expense budget, without any adjustment for variation in sales activity, is clearly the only sound standard. The same is true of other expenses of the order-getting function, such as advertising, branch expense, sales planning, etc.

In the order-filling group of activities, there are some operations which are not very different in nature from factory operations, and, in fact, warehousing and shipping are often included under factory supervision. Very often it is possible to develop standards for these activities in much the same way as for the productive departments, breaking the standards down between nonvariable and variable and adjusting the "variable" standard for any period to reflect actual activity. Activity may be measurable in some cases in terms of simple units such as pounds or yards, but more often, when there are different products of unlike nature, special studies are necessary to arrive at some arbitrary activity unit, perhaps combining the factors of bulk and weight, and to determine the number of activity units "earned" by the handling of one shipping unit of each product.

Included in the functional classification of marketing and administrative activities are a number of clerical activities which are routine and repetitive in nature and for which output can be measured with some degree of accuracy. Such operations as order writing and billing in the order-filling group, the posting of customers' accounts and the writing of collection letters in the money-collecting group, and certain parts of the statistical and stenographic work in the general administrative group can be standardized and time-studied in much the same way factory operations are. The control of expenses of this type can be considerably improved if unit standards are worked out for the variable elements of expense and the standards used for comparison with actual dollars of expense are adjusted to the basis of actual activity. In some large offices where there is a great deal of clerical work of a highly standardized nature it has been found possible to pay operators on a piecework basis or by some incentive plan, but this should not be attempted without a really scientific study of the operations involved, since even routine clerical operations are likely to be much less uniform in degree of difficulty than most factory operations.

It is often impracticable to expand and contract the clerical organization with short-term fluctuations in activity, and this must be recognized in any piecework or incentive plan and in the use of adjusted standards for control purposes. But even where scientific standards and close regulation of actual expenses for variations in activity are not feasible, it should be possible to develop some rough measurement of clerical volume which can be used to advantage in improving office efficiency. Such data will frequently stimulate department heads to watch for opportunities to transfer clerks to other jobs or make them available for special work of some kind when activity declines, and the measurement and publication of individual operators' performance, even though the measurement is not scientific enough to use as a basis for compensation, will often bring about a marked improvement in output.

With the exceptions already noted, the expenses classified in Figure 9–1 as "research and product development costs," "financing costs," and "general administrative costs" are not, as a rule, directly affected by the volume of business or by other activity factors, and, unlike many of the order-getting costs, they do not produce any definite results in the form of sales income which can be used as even an approximate indication of their effectiveness. Some few of these expenses, such as certain corporate taxes and filing fees, stock registrar's fees, etc., are wholly or partly beyond the control of the management, but most of them are determined solely by management policy. The standards for the control of such expenses, therefore, are the amounts budgeted and approved by the management.

Cost information for policy making and planning

The problem of determining what information about the costs of marketing and administrative activities will be helpful to management in policy making, and planning can perhaps be best approached by considering, first, the possible lines of action that the management of a business may take to improve its profit situation and, second, how marketing and administrative cost data can be developed to point the way to such action.

Broadly speaking, there are only two ways to increase the profits of a business, i.e., by increasing gross income without an equivalent increase in costs or by reducing costs without an equivalent reduction in gross income. The only mathematically certain way to more profit is by reducing the cost of performing specific operations in the factory, the field, or the office, without affecting the quality of the product or the effectiveness of performance. Management is constantly searching for operating economies of this kind, and the tools of cost control already described are often aids to this end, in that they stimulate the search for means of bettering standard or budget or at least fix a yardstick for the measurement of performance. But the increasing of operating efficiency is only one part of management's job, and perhaps the smaller part; in a well-run business, management's policy decisions and planning activities usually have an even more decisive effect on profits. And these problems of policy and planning almost always involve either the weighing of an increase or decrease in costs against a possible increase or decrease in income or the weighing of a certain decrease in some costs against a possible increase in other costs. Reducing an advertising appropriation or eliminating a salesman carries with it the definite possibility of loss of sales income; even discharging the controller, while it effects an immediate cost saving, may over the long term result in decreased income or increased total costs because of lack of information about the business.

What are the policy moves which management can make with the aim of increasing the profits of the business? To answer this question completely would obviously involve a treatise on management, which this volume is not, but it may be said that most of the possible moves of this kind fall into the following general classes:

1. Increasing or decreasing selling prices.
2. Changing product specifications (quality or size).
3. Adding new products to the line or eliminating unprofitable products now in the line.
4. Directing sales effort to more profitable products and/or customers.
5. Increasing or decreasing direct order-getting effort and costs:
   a) Advertising and sales promotion.
   b) Field selling.
6. Closely related to 5: changing sales outlets or methods of sale.
7. Increasing the efficiency of service to customers by increasing warehousing and delivery facilities, improving the servicing of products after they are sold, etc., or reducing costs by curtailing such facilities or services.
8. Increasing or reducing indirect costs, that is, costs not directly related to the production or marketing of the product—such as supervision and planning, coordination, information service, research, etc.,

In arriving at decisions on any of the foregoing types of management action, two kinds of information are needed: information about the sales market and marketing methods and information about costs of operation. Market research is a subject which has had a great deal of attention from sales and advertising executives in recent years, and in some industries there is a considerable amount of reliable data available, but even in such cases the job of estimating the effect of any of the above policy moves on sales income involves a high degree of judgment. Information about costs of operation can be made much more definite and factual, but in this field, too, judgment is required in interpreting the meaning and understanding the limitations of the cost data that may be developed. The controller is not usually primarily responsible for the Market-research functions, but to do an effective job in the field of marketing and administrative costs he must be familiar with the market-research program and work closely with those who are directing it.

From a brief analysis of the different kinds of management action listed above, it is possible to develop some definite ideas as to what marketing and administrative cost information will be useful in this field of planning and policy making.

1. *Changes in selling prices.* When selling prices are increased, there is a risk of losing unit volume to competitors, and even if competitors take similar action, there is a risk of a volume loss to the industry as a whole. The expectation is, of course, that even if volume does drop, the resulting loss in gross income will be more than offset by the added income due to increased selling prices plus the decrease in total expenditures which can be expected with the volume reduction. Conversely, if selling prices are reduced, the expectation is that the gain in gross income due to increased volume will offset both the loss due to lower unit prices and the increased expenditures required in connection with the added volume.

To make an intelligent decision on this sort of problem, the management needs to know how much all costs, including marketing and administrative costs, will increase or decrease as volume goes up and down. So far as marketing and administrative costs are concerned, if the plan is to raise or lower the prices of all products in the same ratio and the percentage reduction or increase in the unit sales of all products and to all classes of customers is expected to be the same, an average variable cost per dollar of total sales may be sufficient. But, more often, price changes will affect different products or different customer classes in different degrees; even where the rate of price change is uniform for all items, the new price schedule may result in a shift to lower-priced products or different outlets, and in such cases it may be necessary to develop a variable cost for each product or each customer class.

Included under this heading also are the problems of quantity discounts and small orders. The reason usually advanced in justification of quantity discounts is that it costs less to manufacture for and sell to a customer who buys in large quantities; in many cases, however, this is simply a rationalization, and the real reason for the discounts is the inability to obtain marginal business in any other way. Certain federal and state laws make the granting of such discounts under some conditions illegal unless actual cost justification can be shown; but, entirely apart from the question of legality, if such discounts run into significant figures, their reasonableness in relation to cost differentials should be known. Similarly, the cost of handling small orders should be known, so as to determine the limit below which orders cost more to handle than they yield in gross profit. The sales department may take the position that information of this kind is of little practical value because competition prevents any steps being taken to bring quantity discounts more in line with actual cost differentials or to refuse small orders or add a service charge for their handling. But even if this is true, the controller should see to it that the management has the facts in mind in fixing sales policies, so that an attempt may be made to work toward the correction of unprofitable situations as the opportunity offers.

2. *Changes in product specifications.* The cost information needed in deciding on changes in product specifications lies largely in the field of manufacturing costs, except possibly where changes in weight or methods of packing may result in changes in costs of warehousing, shipping, and delivery. Here again the management is interested in costs which will actually be affected by the changes under consideration, rather than in total costs, which include many indirect and joint expenses which will continue unchanged irrespective of what may be done about product specifications.

3. *Addition of new products or elimination of unprofitable products.* The addition of a new product to the line, as distinct from a change in the specifications of an existing product, results, if the product is successful, in an increase in overall unit volume. Conversely, the elimination of an existing product, if not replaced by a similar item, results in a decrease in unit volume. The problem here is, again, to determine the effect of these additions or reductions in volume on total costs of marketing and administration. In addition, in order to initiate the elimination of unprofitable products, it is necessary to know the variable costs of all the different products in the line, or at least of those products which show a less-than-normal margin over factory cost. If any large-scale additions or eliminations are contemplated, consideration must be given to a number of intangible factors, such as the value of a complete line of products in selling certain customers, the possible effect of the proposed move on the sale of other products, the possibility of increases or reductions in expenses not ordinarily considered as "variable," the extent to which the product line can be expanded without increasing the time spent by the salesman with each customer, and, conversely, the use to be made of the time devoted by the field and executive sales force to products schedule for elimination.

4. *Direction of sales effort to more profitable products and/or customers.* The direction of sales effort to the most profitable products obviously requires a knowledge of the costs of the different products

in the line. If these are known, advertising and sales promotion can be concentrated on selected items, and salesmen can be educated to push these items or encouraged to do so by higher commission rates, special bonuses, or other forms of incentive. However, many sales executives question the wisdom of carrying this policy with salesmen too far, feeling that there is a definite limit to any salesman's productive power and that too much emphasis on a few profitable items may result in neglect of the ordinary run of products which may make up the backbone of the company's business. This leads directly to one of the questions discussed in the next paragraph, viz., determining how much money it pays to spend on field sales coverage. The selection of the most profitable customers is even more closely related to the determination of the optimum expenditure for field coverage and is considered in the discussion of that problem.

5. *Changes in direct order-getting effort and costs.* Direct order-getting costs are broken down for purposes of this discussion between "advertising and sales promotion" and "field selling." Strictly speaking, field selling activities usually include a large element of promotion, but "advertising and sales promotion," as here used, refers to expenditures for other than field activities, such as magazine and newspaper space, radio and television programs, display material, direct-mail circulars, etc. The regulation of such advertising and promotion expenditures to yield the maximum net profit result is one of the major marketing problems in most businesses manufacturing products which reach the mass consumer market, and in its solution a great deal of information is needed as to the effect on sales of various campaigns or display "deals" that may be tested out in limited districts or extended on a national basis. In addition to information of this kind, which is not "cost information" within the meaning of the term as it is being considered here, it is necessary to know, in planning advertising and promotional effort, how much other costs will increase or decrease with variations in sales volume. This cost problem is exactly the same as that involved in estimating the effect on costs of volume changes due to the addition of new products—in fact, most of the analyses required in connection with any of the policy decisions thus far considered have to do with the effect on costs of changes either in volume as a whole or in the volume of some particular product or group of products.

In considering the effect of increasing or decreasing the money spent for field selling, the problem is entirely different. The objectives of cost information in this field are, first, to facilitate the planning of field sales coverage so as to obtain the maximum possible profit and, second, to provide the operating executives with a check on the actual results of this planning, so that the plans may be modified when they do not work out as expected. To accomplish the first of these objectives—the efficient planning of field coverage—it is desirable to know, if possible, the potential profit that might be realized from each customer, the cost of calling on the customer, and the cost of filling his orders—and again, as in other types of marketing and administrative cost information, we are concerned with variable costs of calling and order filling rather than with total costs. Now it is obvious that the direct cost of a call will be different for different customers and may depend on whether other customers in the same town are being called on, and it is clearly impracticable ever to attain exactness in this kind of cost calculation. A practical approach to the problem, suitable for at least some types of situations, will be discussed in the next chapter.

If territorial assignments can be planned on the basis of sales potentials, built up by a careful analysis of customers in each territory, or from general data as to purchasing power or some similar factor related to possible sales, the checking of the actual results of the sales planning is merely a matter of comparing actual and potential sales and actual and planned field coverage costs. Clearly there is a large element of judgment involved in interpreting comparisons of actual and potential sales, particularly as to the effect of past or present competitive activity. This is one of the factors in the control of marketing costs that can never be reduced to mathematical terms.

6. *Changes in sales methods or sales outlets.* In the foregoing brief discussion of the problem of adjustment of field selling costs to the most profitable level, it was assumed that the policy of the business as to what types of customer outlets would be covered had already been determined. But it is also possible to increase or decrease the cost of selling a given product in a given market by changing the outlets through which marketing is effected. A simple illustration of such a change is shifting from a policy of selling direct to retail stores to a policy of selling through wholesalers, or vice versa, and in the highly competitive and complex organization of the marketing structure today there are many other alternatives not so simple or clean-cut as this choice of wholesaler or retailer selling. To make an intelligent determination of marketing policy, it is often necessary to know, at least approximately, the relative cost of selling through these different outlets. The other side of the problem, the long-term effectiveness of various possible policies in producing sales income, which is often of even more importance, is not a cost problem at all, but one of judgment. The importance of cost studies by marketing outlets, therefore, depends on whether there is some real possibility of policies being modified; but even where fundamental policies are not readily subject to change, studies of this kind may point the way to sizable savings through minor policy modifications.

7. *Expansion or curtailment of customer service.* The improvement of service to customers by expanding warehousing and delivery facilities or other types of customer services is usually the result of pressure from the sales department to meet competitive practices or go competi-

tors one better. Curtailment of such facilities or services rarely occurs except in connection with a major change in sales policies or when the management is committed to a policy of expense economy. The costs or savings involved in expanding or curtailing these services are usually not difficult to estimate; the effect on sales income, on the other hand, is extremely difficult to judge.

8.. *Expansion or curtailment of "indirect" overhead.* The results of this kind of management action are the most difficult of all to measure, because the benefits derived from the supervisory and planning organization and from coordination and information activities, etc., are to a large extent intangible and often make themselves felt only over a relatively long period of time. The costs of a few of these activities, such as sales statistical analysis, stenographic, filing, and mailing services, etc., will tend to vary to some extent as the number of orders received or items sold goes up and down, and this must be taken into consideration in some of the cost calculations discussed in the preceding paragraphs. But in determining a policy governing expenditures of this kind there is no real "cost" problem involved—it is simply a matter of weighing the expense of various activities against benefits which are none the less real because they cannot be measured, keeping in mind always the income available to cover expenses of this type and the net profit objective of the business.

General types of information needed in planning

Reviewing the foregoing analysis of the various moves that management can make to increase profits and the nature of the marketing and administrative cost information needed to make decisions of this kind, it is apparent that there is a fundamental difference between the type of information needed on what we have called "order-getting" costs and the kind required on the other types of marketing and administrative costs, that is, the cost of research and product development, order filling, money collecting, financing, and general administration. Order-getting costs are incurred to produce the sales income from which all net profits are derived, and the important question to be answered about them is what level of expenditures and what method of making the expenditures will produce the maximum net income for the business. Other marketing and administrative costs are incurred either in connection with the execution of sales orders and the collection of the proceeds of such orders or for the financing, future development, and general administration and coordination of the business's activities; as to these costs, the basic problem is to relate them, if possible, to some activity factor and then to determine how the activity factor is affected by changes in volume, method of sale, product distribution, etc. For such of these costs as cannot be related to any activity factor, the problem is largely one of regulating expenditure to available income and securing the most effective services for the expenditure made; with respect to research and development costs, it is desirable to have some information as to the nature of the projects on which the funds appropriated are spent, but, with this exception, the classification of expenses for control purposes, as discussed in a preceding section, is the only cost information required.

Techniques of cost calculations

The usual techniques of marketing and administrative cost accounting are not basically different from the techniques used in factory overhead cost accounting. The first steps in each case are the assembling of costs by operations or functions and the calculation of a unit cost of performing each operation or function. In manufacturing cost calculations, the next step is the combining of these unit operation or functional costs to build up a cost for each product manufactured, while in marketing and administrative cost applications the functional costs are used not only to build up product costs but to make comparisons of the costs of different methods of selling, the costs of selling and servicing different types of customers etc. There is considerable literature available on the theory and practice of these techniques, and it is the purpose of this discussion not to review this ground already so well covered but rather to examine the more practical aspects of the problem and to stick closely to the question: "How can marketing and administrative costs be used effectively in the management of the business?"

Earlier in this chapter emphasis was laid on the fundamental differences between manufacturing activities and marketing and administrative activities, and some of the limitations of the usual factory cost techniques in the field of marketing and administrative costs were pointed out. These limitations are due principally to several inconvenient, but incontrovertible, facts, viz:

1. Many marketing and administrative functions cannot be related, even indirectly, to any definite factor of activity, and hence for these functions it is impossible to obtain unit costs that have any real significance. And many functional units of activity which are rather widely used are of very doubtful validity except for the very broadest kind of thinking; a good example is the salesman's call, which is often useless as a basis for cost information on specific problems. Activity factors used in marketing and administrative costing need to be much more carefully examined and tested than is generally necessary in setting up a manufacturing cost structure.

2. Certain costs of marketing—the group that has been referred to previously as "order-getting" costs—are entirely different in nature from all other costs, in that they do not depend on sales but are investments

for the purpose of obtaining sales—to some extent, at least, they are the cause of sales. The relating of these expenditures to definite products or definite customers is extremely difficult because the effort expended on various products or customers has no direct relation to results, which are the usual basis of allocation, and measurement of effort, particularly for activities as widely dispersed as field selling, is a real problem.

3. Even in the case of those marketing and administrative costs which are, broadly speaking, the result of sales and can be related to a definite unit of activity, it is frequently difficult to relate units of activity with any certainty to particular products or to particular classes of trade or customers. It is always necessary to bear in mind that the number of units of each functional activity which is applicable to any given product, or any customer, or any method of sale, is a variable, dependent not alone on the product, the customer, or the method of sale, but on all three and possibly on other factors as well.

To illustrate concretely: Product line A is sold very successfully in all territories and has a nationwide consumer acceptance, while product line B sells well in the northern territories but not in the South or Southwest. Because of the greater accessibility of the company's plants and warehouses in the north, average units of sale of all products are smaller than in other territories, and hence average order-filling costs per unit or per dollar of sales are higher. Clearly, under these conditions a cost analysis will show that product line B has a higher order-filling cost than product line A. If the restriction of product line B to the northern territories is due to qualities inherent in the product or in the market (as, for example, if product line B is woolen underwear and product line A is shirts), the cost differential has one meaning; but if it is due simply to competitive conditions or to a localization of advertising, the interpretation of the cost differential and the conclusions drawn from the cost figures will be quite different.

In view of these limitations, the usual techniques of marketing and administrative costing need to be modified if they are to be applied to practical problems, as follows.

1. In cost calculations and studies for use in planning and policy formulation, no attempt should be made to allocate any costs which cannot be related either directly to one or more of the cost factors under study (e.g. products, customers classes, etc., depending on the study) or to some unit of activity. Allocations on an arbitrary basis, such as dollar sales or total direct costs, simply distort real cost differentials and make interpretation more difficult.

2. Order-getting costs should be excluded from any calculations of unit product costs or individual customer costs and should be given separate consideration according to the specific problem understudy. In studies of the cost of marketing through different outlets, or classes of trade, order-getting costs are usually considered in total, rather than

in relation to particular products or customers, and hence can be included without distorting the results, and the same may be true in other special studies.

3. In interpreting and comparing marketing and administrative cost of different products, customers, or classes of trade, it is necessary to ask the question: Is it certain that differences in cost are significant in the problem under consideration—for example, if the study is one of product costs, is it clear that cost differences are inherent in the nature of the products and are not due to chance differences in customer or class of trade distribution?"

Mossman[1] identifies seven factors which tend to cause differences between product costs. It is appropriate for the controller to have these in mind in deciding whether a cost difference is pertinent to the problem he is studying. The factors are (1) marketing knowledge, the degree of knowledge of the product possessed by the customers in a given defined market; (2) density, the number of customers within the market area; (3) the average order size; (4) the time the product will remain fashionable or before it will perish; (5) the number of service calls the product generates; (6) the distance the goods are to be shipped; and (7) the volume sold.

4. The use of average costs for unstandardized operations should be avoided. As an example, costs per salesman's call will differ widely for different customers; some averaging is necessary to get answers to problems of policy, but an effort must be made to classify customers for averaging, so that variations within the averaged group will be relatively small, and even then the limitations of such an average cost must be consistently borne in mind.

Variable costs versus total costs in the marketing and administrative area

In the discussion in this chapter of the kind of marketing and administrative cost information which is useful for policy making and planning, the emphasis throughout has been on variable cost rather than on total cost, and it has been stressed that the principal concern of management is to know the amount of expense that will be incurred or saved as the result of various possible policy moves. It may be questioned why the emphasis on variable cost is so much stronger in the field of marketing and administration than in the field of manufacturing, where "cost" still, as a rule, means total cost.

There are at least two reasons why, in spite of this trend, total costs

---

[1] F. M. Mossman, *Differential Distribution Cost and Revenue Analysis* (East Lansing, Mich.: Michigan State University, Marketing and Transportation), Paper Number 10, 1962.

are nevertheless useful. One of these reasons is the accepted convention of valuing inventories of finished goods on the basis of total manufacturing cost; this, of course, does not apply in the case of marketing and administrative costs. The other reasons is the natural desire of management to know what the selling price of any particular product should be to recover its fair share of all costs. This desire is due to a recognition of the very real danger that an overemphasis on variable cost alone may result in discounting completely the nonvariable elements of cost. These nonvariable costs must, of course, be recovered out of overall sales income if the business is to operate at a profit, and, furthermore, they are nonvariable only up to the practical capacity of the existing manufacturing facilities and the existing organization.

The necessity of recovering nonvariable costs out of sales income must also be borne in mind in using marketing and administrative costs, but, as previously pointed out, it is usually much more difficult to make any reasonable allocation of nonvariable costs of marketing and administration to functional operations and to products than in the case of manufacturing costs, and hence total costs of marketing and administration have much less real significance. Furthermore, most of the so-called nonvariable costs of marketing and administration can be varied within certain limits by management policy, while a large part of fixed factory costs is determined by past investment in plant and equipment. Under these conditions, more can be accomplished in the use of marketing and administrative costs in product pricing by weighing total profits over variable costs against total nonvariable costs and attempting to bring the two in line than by the onesided process of allocating nonvariable costs to products and considering the resulting total unit costs as objectives to be recovered in selling prices. In problems dealing with selection of outlets and customers, the profitable order size, etc., total costs are of still less practical value, even as objectives; in fact, they are more often than not misleading and confusing in weighing alternative courses of action.

Variable costs necessarily approximations

Like a great deal of accounting phraseology, the terms "variable cost" and "nonvariable cost" have an unfortunate implication of exactness. In practice it is not possible to divide all costs neatly into these two classifications; there are, of course, certain costs which can be definitely classified as fixed by past or present management policies, but the remainder may vary to a greater or lesser degree with fluctuations in the activities to which they are related. In the factory it is often possible to get a fair idea of the extent to which costs vary with activity by studying historical records or "time studying" the various operations; but this technique is useful for only a very limited portion of marketing and administrative costs, largely because, as pointed out previously, most marketing and administrative activities are not standardized.

A simple example will serve to illustrate the problems involved in determining the degree of variability of marketing and administrative costs. In estimating the cost of adding salesmen to the field force, the only directly variable cost will be the salesmen's salaries and travel expenses, which can be predicted with reasonable accuracy, but there are other variable costs involved which are more elusive. What about branch—or home-office expenses of controlling the salesmen's activities—correspondence, routing, record keeping, etc.? Even such a nonvariable cost as branch-office rent may turn out to be variable—not, to be sure, as a result of adding one salesman, but if the expansion continues, however gradually. Actually, there is a need for two kinds of variable costs of selling and administrative activities: a short-term variable cost, reflecting the immediate and obvious effect of volume variations, and a long-term variable cost, reflecting the best judgment of the cost analyst as to the longer-range changes in costs resulting from fluctuations in activity. For policy-making and long-range planning purposes, the latter are more valuable, but they must be recognized as approximations and used accordingly.

Two other points should be borne in mind in using and interpreting the terms "variable" and "nonvariable." In the first place, while a variable cost is usually thought of as a cost which fluctuates in direct proportion to the unit volume of production or sales, there are, actually, many variable costs, particularly in marketing and administration, which vary with activity factors which do not necessarily change in proportion to volume, although they are affected by volume variations. In the second place, there are very few costs which are, strictly speaking, nonvariable in the sense that they cannot be changed by management action. It is only for lack of better concise terms that "variable" and "nonvariable" are used in the discussions in this chapter and elsewhere in this book to distinguish between those costs which vary automatically with volume or with some activity factor related to volume and those which are not automatically affected by variations in such activity factors.

Management science and the control of marketing costs

Practitioners of operations research and management science have long been interested in the possibility of using their various tools to improve marketing decisions. An admirable collection of recent models and applications has been prepared by Montgomery and Urban,[2] in which a selection of models for pricing, advertising, personal selling, and other decisions is presented. As might be expected, the greatest

---

[2] D. B. Montgomery and G. L. Urban, *Management Science in Marketing* (Englewood Cliffs, N.J.: Prentice Hall, 1969).

success has been achieved in those areas in which the variables are most completely understood, such as transportation and logistics. Efforts at model building in the analysis of consumer behavior and other fields in which psychological factors are critical have not worked out quite so well so far. However, considerable work has been done, and great progress has been made to such an extent that a few companies are able to report use of models on competitive bidding situations and in price analysis.

The selection of optimal transportation procedures has been a successful application of the technique of linear programming to marketing. The general type of the problem is as follows. A number of factories produces a certain product. In addition, there are a number of warehouses or retail outlets which sell the product and must be stocked from the factories. The cost of moving a unit from each factory to each warehouse is known with sufficient accuracy. Which factory should ship to which warehouse? The "transportation method," a special case of the linear program, is usable in such a situation. A general introduction to linear programming is offered in chapter 24, but readers interested in a more thorough exposition of the concept are referred to more specialized works.

10 DISCRETIONARY COSTS IN MARKETING, RESEARCH, AND ADMINISTRATION

PRACTICAL APPLICATIONS

A practical program

In the light of all that was said in the last chapter about the objectives, techniques, and limitations of marketing and administrative costs, what is a practical approach to the problem of developing and using such costs in the typical business?

If the organization of marketing and administrative departments is already substantially correct for these functions as outlined in the previous chapter, the practical program will obviously be greatly facilitated. Insofar as this fortunate circumstance does not obtain, the controller will be faced, first, with the very basic problem of whether or not to recommend changes in the organization structure to bring it into line. This may not be immediately feasible. As was brought out earlier, organization changes must often wait for auspicious occasions, but the controller should at least have his recommendations with regard to the more effective structure "up his sleeve" and ready for the opportunity. In the meantime, his awareness of the shortcomings of the present actual organization and his concept of the changes he would like to see made should enable him by informal rearrangements of reported results to avoid any serious misinterpretations on the part of management.

If we may assume that the available chart of expenses does at least measure the individual responsibilities of the present organization for control purposes, the first step in a costing program is to get an overall picture of the purpose and nature of these expenses by regrouping them for some period—preferably the most recent fiscal year or the current year, if a budget is available—on the basis of the classification suggested in Figure 9–1, or some adaptation of it. This will not necessarily be the final classification for the determination of the unit costs of the various functions, for the reasons explained earlier, but it will give a clear idea of the expense structure and the amounts spent on the various basic types of activity outside the factory.

Routine marketing and administration costs—A program for planning and control

The order-getting and research and development classifications of expense present special cost problems which will be discussed in separate sections later in this chapter; for the other types of expenses—that is, the expenses of order filling, money collecting, financing, and general administration—the following nine-point cost program is suggested. Effective application of each step against the background of varying conditions will be facilitated by careful attention to the purpose to be served, rather than to the routine following of the outlined procedure Used in this way, these nine steps should be found to be a powerful mechanism in coming to grips with the problems of planning and control in this difficult and elusive area.

1. *Preliminary analysis of expenses.* Examine the expenses in each classification and break them down into three groups:

a) Expenses which can be expected to vary directly with some unit of activity which is affected by sales volume, as, for example, with the number of orders written, the dollars of sales, the weight of shipments, etc.

b) Expenses which will tend to vary to some extent with one or more of these activity factors, at least over the long term.

c) Expenses which are fixed by management policy or by factors more or less beyond the control of management. These expenses are often referred to as discretionary or committed expenses, respectively.

Some difficulty may be experienced in determining whether certain types of expenses belong in group b or in group c; the general rule is that group c should be limited to those expenses which are not automatically affected by changes in sales volume, but change only as the result of management decisions or factors outside management's control. Examples of group c expenses are the salaries of the president and other general executives, expenditures for research and development, depreciation and taxes on office buildings, etc. The definition is not, of course, exact, and some judgment is necessary in making the classification, but this suggested program does not call for extreme accuracy, particularly in its initial phases.

2. *Estimate of range of variable costs.* *a*) Analyze the expenses classified in group b—those that vary to some extent but not in direct proportion, as the activity factors related to sales volume vary—and set down some rough estimates of what would happen to these expenses in the event of increases or decreases in sales volume amounting to 10 percent, 25 percent, 33⅓ percent, and 50 percent. In making this preliminary analysis it can be assumed tentatively that all classes of sales vary uniformly—that is, that there are no changes in the percentage of sales of each product to the total, the percentage of the total sold to each type of customer, the average size of orders, etc.

b) From these estimates determine the range of variability in the expenses in question, i.e. the maximum and minimum amounts of each expense which can be considered as varying directly with sales volume. The total of these maximum and minimum variable expense estimates, plus directly variable expenses in the a group, will give the estimated range of variable costs, and this range of costs, considered in relation to total dollar sales, will give a reasonably correct idea of the size and importance of the problem involved in cost analysis of marketing and administrative activities other than those connected with order getting. In developing the range, we are seeking to answer the following question: What is the greatest amount by which this semivariable cost element could be expected to change when a unit change in sales volume occurs, and what is the least such amount? The range will be greatest for those costs that are the least predictable and for those whose dependence on volume is the most tenuous.

3. *Review of nonvariable costs.* With the approximate range of variable marketing and administrative costs established, the approximate upper and lower limits of nonvariable costs are also known. The full significance of these nonvariable costs can be understood only by a complete analysis of the cost and expense structure of the business, including factory as well as marketing and administrative activities; but, in the absence of such complete analysis, a simple comparison of the nonvariable expenses of marketing and administration with sales and gross-profit possibilities will often indicate quite clearly whether the business is soundly organized for profit. A heavy nonvariable expense load obviously calls for management review and may point to the need for a basic reorganization of personnel and operating methods.

4. *Development of functional unit costs.* In a business which manufactures a single uniform product or a few very similar products and sells only through one type of outlet, these overall figures for variable marketing and administrative expenses, with suitable refinement by more careful studies of the degree of variability of each of the different expenses, will give most of the information that management needs to control these activities and to plan sales operations; in other words, the figures will provide a basis for anticipating the effect of changes

in sales volume on these expenses. In a more complex business with several product lines or several classes of customers, these figures will represent only averages for the business as a whole and will be of no value in deciding what to do in any particular situation. To obtain useful tools for solving specific problems in such a business, it is necessary to develop a variable cost per unit of activity for each operation or function. With these unit costs and an estimate of how the conditions of any problem will affect the activity of each function, the dollars of variable expenses under the assumed conditions can be computed.

As a simple illustration, assume that it is proposed to reduce the price of a certain line of products in order to obtain more volume and that information is desired as to the effect of the increased volume on the expenses of order filling, money collecting, financing, and general administration. To obtain this information the following steps are required:

a)   Determine the variable cost of each operation per unit of activity: the order-writing and billing cost per order or per line, the statistical cost per order item, etc.

b)   Estimate the additional activity units (i.e., the additional number of orders, lines, items, etc.) which will result from the proposed added volume.

c)   From a and b compute the dollars of additional expense for these operations.

Usually the estimates of additional activity units will be made on the basis of past actual records of activity per dollar or unit volume in the particular product line, but consideration must be given to possible changes in conditions, such as a switch of business to new outlets, larger- or smaller-sized orders, etc.

5. *Application of functional costs for control.* The variable costs of the different operations, in addition to furnishing the basis for building up data for policy decisions, will also provide the means for controlling the cost of these functions, within the limitations pointed out in the discussion of "Expense Standards for Control" in Chapter 9.

6. *Study of costs and cost differentials for different-sized orders.* Make a study of the variable costs of orders of different types and sizes, for the purpose of determining the following:

a)   The minimum-size order of each type which can be handled profitably, that is, with an excess of sales income over the total costs (factory, marketing, and administrative) which could be saved by refusing the order.

b)   The extent to which profits might be increased by placing a minimum limit on the size of orders accepted or by inducing customers to order in quantities above the minimum profitable order size.

c)   The cost differentials per dollar of sales for different-sized orders in each class of trade or customer class.

An analysis of the small-order problem usually requires special studies of warehousing and delivery costs, which may be considerably higher per order for small orders because of the necessity of breaking packaging or shipping units. The office costs of handling an order—that is, the costs of order censoring and order writing, invoicing, and money collecting—will usually be about the same, irrespective of its size, unless there are variations in the number of items per order. In many situations it will be difficult to find any differences at all in costs per order above a certain size, and differentials per dollar of sales will be entirely a reflection of differences in dollars per order.

While small orders may be a cause of losses in many businesses, the problem of quantity discounts or special prices on large orders is often even more troublesome. To secure the business of very large buyers, it may be necessary to bid against competitors who concentrate on this type of business and operate with very low overhead costs, eliminating many of the marketing and administrative functions which are essential in the management of a business which sells through normal trade channels. Orders of this kind may fail to cover even those costs of marketing and administration which would be saved by their elimination, and if they are a substantial part of the business, it may be desirable to set up special procedures for handling them. The large orders may, in effect, become a special venture—a large-order department. By actual reorganization of distribution techniques, management may be able really to reduce the costs involved in these orders. The accounting and reporting analysis aimed to show such a substantive difference is entirely valid and quite different from a juggling of figures intended merely to make a bad situation look a little better.

Care must be taken to avoid violation of the Robinson-Patmen Act which prohibits price discrimination among customers unless the differing costs of servicing them "justifies" the price difference. Although only a small number of cases have been brought to court under the cost justification provisions of the act, these have covered a considerable number of types of price discrimination. In most instances, the presence of the law, rather than its enforcement, has been sufficient to ensure that relatively few severe and unjustifiable price-discrimination practices are followed. A further discussion of the act and its cost consequences is to be found in Professor Herbert F. Taggart's "Cost Justification" (University of Michigan, Bureau of Business Research, 1959).

7. *Analysis of possibilities of selective sales effort.* Make a study of the possibility of increasing profits by emphasizing sales effort on the more profitable products or product lines. Sometimes the marketing and adminstrative cost aspect of this problem is relatively minor, as differences in the margins of selling prices over variable factory costs may be much greater than differences in variable marketing and administrative costs. This is not always the case, however, and before any deci-

sions are made on the basis of margins over factory cost, the variable marketing and administrative costs should be reviewed and compared. These marketing and administrative costs for the products or product lines would be built up from the costs of the various functions; but, as previously pointed out, any cost differences based on past experience as to functional activity per unit or dollar of sales should be carefully analyzed to be sure that they are inherent in the differences in the products and not due to fortuitous differences in type of outlet, geographical distribution of sales, or other factors.

The procedures involved in such product profitability reports will not be discussed in this chapter as such, because the topic is explored in Chapter 14 on Profit Planning.

8. *Studies of alternative sales outlets and methods.* Study the distribution of sales to the various types of outlets (retailer, wholesaler, mail order, etc.) the method by which the marketing organization reaches each outlet, and the selling-price differentials. If the same products are sold (or can be sold) through more than one outlet, calculate the comparative variable costs of order filling, money collecting, and general administration for the various outlets, based on the unit cost of the different functions and the number of activity units required for handling a given volume through each outlet. If the organization of the sales department is such that the order-getting costs for each outlet can be definitely segregated, it will be possible to present a reasonably complete picture of the relative profitability of the various outlets. In many cases such a sharp segregation of order-getting costs by outlets is not feasible without extensive and detailed studies of salesmen's activities to determine the differences in time and effort involved in selling the different types of customers. It may be possible, however, to work out some rough estimates of these time differences as a basis for a tentative cost calculation which will indicate whether more careful studies would be justified. Any analysis of existing costs is of little value in itself unless it points the way to possible savings by changes in marketing methods.

In planning and carrying out studies of this kind, it is necessary for the controller to work in close cooperation with the marketing executives who alone are in a position to pass on the feasibility of policy changes and to estimate what effect changes will have on order-getting costs. Such estimates involve many factors which even those in closest touch with marketing conditions may have difficulty in evaluating. As a simple example, if it is proposed to shift from a policy of direct selling to retailers to one of selling through wholesalers, it is necessary to consider to what extent the customs of the trade or competitive conditions will make it necessary to support the wholesaler by "missionary" selling to retailers. Basic changes in marketing policy are a serious matter, involving the risk of substantial loss of competitive position, and it cannot be too strongly emphasized that cost figures by type of outlet can be interpreted and applied only in cooperation with those who have a thorough knowledge of the marketing problems of the business. The decision to make a change of this order will inevitably be based largely on nonfigure considerations. The controller's awareness of this fact will protect him against any unwise pushing of figure considerations while at the same time enabling him to present most effectively such figure facts as are actually pertinent.

9. *Analysis of warehousing and delivery costs.* Study warehousing and delivery methods and costs and the costs of various possible alternatives, such as curtailment or extension of branch warehousing facilities or changes in terms of sale (f.o.b. points, freight allowances, etc.) routings, or types of carriers (railroad versus truck, etc.). In such studies the factors of service to customers and competitive practices must be weighed against the more calculable factor of cost, and any study will probably be a waste of time unless it has the sympathetic cooperation of the marketing executives.

Planning and control of order-getting activities

The nine-point procedure suggested above deals for the most part with the order-filling, money-collecting, financing, and general administrative costs; order-getting costs are excluded from consideration, except in the case of studies of costs by type of outlet in which the order-getting function is the primary subject of study. Exceptions may be taken to this principle of omitting order-getting costs from the other studies suggested; for example, in studying the small-order problem, it may be contended that the cost of getting a small order is just as great or nearly as great as that of getting a large order. In certain cases this may be clearly true, and the suggested procedure should be modified accordingly; but in many cases the customer, if he is once "sold" and kept sold by a reasonable number of sales calls, will place the same volume of business over a period of time whether his individual orders are large or small, and their will be no difference in order-getting cost per dollar of sales.

The omission of order-getting costs from product-cost studies may also be questioned on the theory that some products are harder or easier to sell than others and hence should be charged with a greater or smaller share of order-getting costs. Various efforts have been made to evaluate this and reflect it in product costs, but the application of selling effort is so difficult to measure and subject to so many arbitrary variations as a matter of policy or as the result of individual temperament that it is doubtful whether any method of allocation will produce costs which will have a great deal of value as a basis for management action. Because of the basic differences between order-getting costs and other types of marketing and administrative costs, which were discussed in the preceding chapter, an entirely different method of approach is required in the application of costs for management planning of order-getting activities.

The fundamental objectives of the use of costs in planning order-getting activities are to determine how much money can profitably be spent on these activities and to point the way to securing the greatest amount of income for the money expended. Analyzed into its elements, this means:

1. Determining who the company's customers are to be—that is, who are the ultimate consumers of the company's products—and whether they are to be reached by direct contact or through wholesalers or other intermediaries in the distribution process.

2. Determining what customers or potential customers, of all those who can be served within the limits of productive capacity, offer the greatest sales and gross-profit possibilities. In many businesses, productive capacity is more than adequate to serve all customers who can be secured under existing competitive conditions, and here the problem is to determine the minimum sales and profit potential at which coverage is profitable. In other cases a company may be able to choose only the more profitable customers; but, even when this is true, sales policy will often dictate a somewhat wider coverage to provide insurance against the inevitable loss of some customers to competitiors and to avoid making the success of the business too completely dependent on a few outlets.

3. Determining in what territories and for what customers coverage is to be by field salesmen and where other methods, such as direct-mail or telephone solicitation, are to be used.

4. Arranging salesmen's territories and routings to secure the required field coverage at a minimum of expense. This involves determining how often each customer is to be called on and how many salesmen are required, giving consideration to such factors as trade custom, competitive practices, strength of consumer demand for the company's products, etc.

5. Planning direct-mail and telephone solicitation, with due regard to the costs of solicitation and potential profits from customers to be contacted.

It will be clear on a little reflection that every executive responsible for field sales operations has to follow the steps outlined above in some fashion, however hit-or-miss, and many companies devote a great deal of study and effort to the solution of the problems involved. The first two steps—determination of method of sale and selection of potential customers, which fall in the field of market research—are obviously the key to the whole process, and elaborate cost calculations are of little value unless this part of the job is well done. In fact, the cost calculations required are in any event relatively simple, as the margin of error present in any estimate of sales potentials and the effect on costs of policy decisions which involve questions of judgment (such as, for example, the proper number of calls to be made on any customer) create a situation where highly refined cost calculations are superfluous.

In view of the emphasis above on market research, it may well be asked whether the average business, which has, at best, an imperfect knowledge of its market potentials, can hope to use costs effectively in planning and controlling its order-getting activities. The answer is that, except in businesses which are staffed and equipped to make extensive market surveys, the practical and sensible approach is to start with the situation as it exists, analyze it, and study it for major weaknesses, and point out facts which will stimulate thinking and lead the way to further investigation. This approach is sound because it enables the controller to test each step of his program by actual use of the results and to avoid the danger of getting too far ahead of the marketing management's ability to understand, digest, and use the information provided.

Naturally, in the preceding arguments, as well as those following in the remainder of this chapter, the position of the controller will be quite different if the marketing division of the business is adequately staffed to assume the primary responsibility for such market research. In this case the controller offers the market-research group the unstinting aid and cooperation of his own staff for the collection and analysis of figure facts, while leaving the basic planning of the research and the resulting decision making strictly in the hands of the marketing specialists. On the other hand, the controller must be able to "think along with management" in this area as well as in any other. He would not be able to give effective aid in the fact-gathering area if he could not visualize quite clearly the significance of the facts to be gathered.

Approximation of profit yield by territories

Assuming that order solicitation is to be by field coverage, the most logical first step in a program of this kind is to compare the gross profit on each salesman's volume, less the cost of filling his orders and collecting the proceeds with the cost of keeping him on the road. Here, as in other studies, the analyst is concerned primarily with variable costs, and, as this study is simply a first step in the analysis of the problem, he is willing to treat as variable the costs which would be saved if the territory were entirely eliminated, without considering other alternatives, and to deal with a range of variable costs rather than attempt too great a refinement in his calculations. Probably, the only completely savable costs in a territory are the salesman's salary and travel expense, and, bearing in mind what was said, the preceding chapter about the difficulty of drawing a sharp line between variable and nonvariable costs, the analyst may be content for the moment to set down his estimates of such costs in terms of approximations.

For simplicity of illustration, the salesman's day is used in this specimen statement, Figure 10–1 as the activity factor for all branch-office expenses, and the order written as the activity factor for all costs of order filling and money collection. If branch-office activities are confined to the supervision and servicing of salesmen and all order and invoice handling is done at the home office, these factors will usually be ade-

Figure 10–1

COST DATA SHEET FOR STUDY OF PROFIT YIELD BY TERRITORIES
(overhead cost of maintaining a salesman on the road)

	Total expense (annual rate)	Percentage variable		Amount variable	
		Min.	Max.	Min.	Max.
Branch expenses					
Managers' salary and travel	$ 28,240	50	100	$14,120	$28,240
Clerical salaries	28,000				
Supplies	6,020	25	50	10,762	21,524
Telephone and telegraph	5,256				
Postage	3,772				
Social security taxes	6,484	75	75	4,863	4,863
Office rent	7,064	10	25	706	1,766
Samples	7,328	10	25	733	1,832
City taxes	1,212	...	...	....	....
Fixed charges and miscellaneous	3,132	...	...	....	....
Home-office selling expenses:					
Field supervision salaries and travel	7,620				
Supplies, postage, etc.	1,530	0	20	....	1,830
Total	$105,658	...	...	$31,184	$60,055
Per salesman's day (2,750 days)	....	...	...	$11.34	$21.84

Cost of order fitting and money collection

	Total expense (annual rate)	Percentage variable		Amount variable	
		Min.	Max.	Min.	Max.
Home-office selling:					
General supervision salaries and travel	$ 11,500	10	20	$ 1,150	$ 2,300
Clerical salaries	30,000	25	50	7,500	15,000
Administrative:					
Credit (salaries, travel, and collection fees)	8,000	20	40	1,600	3,200
Stenographic and files (salaries, supplies, and postage)	41,400	25	50	10,350	20,700
Statistical (salaries and supplies)	14,800	50	75	7,400	11,100
Order and billing (salaries and supplies)	18,600	50	75	9,300	13,950
Sales records (salaries and supplies)	7,200	50	75	3,600	5,400
Total	$131,500	...	...	$40,900	$71,650
Per order (30,000 orders)	....	...	...	$1.36	$2.39

quate for an approximate study of this kind, although there may be some kinds of expenses which are more closely related to other factors—for example, credit department expense may tend to vary with dollar sales rather than with the number of orders. As the studies progress to the point where definite decisions are being based on these cost data, a more careful choice of activity factors should be made. It is also assumed in this example that the overhead cost of main-

taining a salesman is the same at all branches and that orders are sufficiently uniform in type that an average cost range can be used without
danger of distorting conclusions. In actual practice each situation should
be studied separately and different ranges of variable costs developed
for different branches or different types of orders if necessary. Also,
further studies may make it possible to narrow the range of variable
costs, but this is something than can be done as the need becomes
apparent.

With relatively simple cost data of this kind and an analysis of sales
and gross profits by salesmen, it is not a difficult job to set up reports
that will bring out at least the more glaring weakness in the field
organization:

Figure 10–2

TERRITORIAL PROFIT

(before fixed overhead)

Salesman: J. F. Robinson		Period: Year 19XX	
Sales		$80,000	
Gross profit		$18,000	
Variable costs of order filling and collection (1,850 orders)	$ 2,516	to	$ 4,421
Balance available for order-getting costs.	$15,484		$13,579
Variable order-getting costs:			
Direct—Selling	$ 7,500		$ 7,500
Travel	5,500		5,500
Overhead cost of maintenance (275 days)	3,118		6,006
Total	$16,118		$19,006
Profit (or loss) before fixed overhead	($634)		($5,427)

From this report it appears that this salesman is quite definitely failing
to pay his way, at least as a long-term proposition, since he is not
covering variable costs even on the minimum side of the estimated range.
If in the foregoing computation the manufacturing cost on which the
"gross-profit" figure is based includes fixed plant overhead and if the
plant is running at less than capacity, the salesman may be making
some contribution by carrying a part of the plant overhead; as a rule,
however, the management will not want to maintain a salesman permanently on this basis.

In preparing the above type of report, care must be taken to include
only the sales and gross profits for which the salesman is directly responsible. A frequent error is to include all acounts in the salesman's territory,
many of which may be long established and perhaps handled by the
principal sales executives, so that the field man's contacts are essentially
routine. It is difficult to determine in some cases which accounts in
the territory should be included, and judgment must be exercised by

the management in evaluating the salesman's performance on the basis of profit reports of this kind. With the exercise of such management judgment, a comparison of these reports for different territories will often disclose reasons for variations in profit results—for example, a low average gross-profit ratio may indicate too few sales of the more profitable products; high travel expense in relation to sales may indicate spread-out territory, poor routing, or an extravagant salesman. By using supplementary comparative data on number of calls, miles traveled, etc., an even more complete picture of the conditions and the problems in each territory can be obtained.

Obviously, the reports suggested above do not even approach a complete answer to the control of field coverage—a salesman who shows a very handsome net profit may be merely skimming the cream off his territory, which may be much too large (in terms of good potential customers) for one man, while another salesman may be struggling with a very low-potential territory which is not worth his time and effort. The most that these reports can do, therefore, is to provide a picture of the situation in the field organization as it exists, to show up the most obvious weaknesses, and to indicate where further investigations may prove most fruitful.

If desired, reports of the type described may be extended by making allocations of nonvariable expenses as well as variable, thereby showing which salesmen are carrying not only the variable overhead but also their share of total overhead. Such reports may have the virtue—if it is a virtue—of tying in with the actual overall earnings statements; but they can be grossly misleading if an attempt is made to use them as a basis for management action. The danger of such misuse can be minimized by setting up the reports to show profits both before and after the allocation of nonvariable costs.

Analysis of existing territories

The most natural second step in a program of analyzing and planning field sales effort would be to select those territories which are yielding the poorest return, or perhaps incurring losses even on a variable-cost basis, and see what can be done to improve their showing. Unless territories have been laid out in an entirely hit-or-miss fashion, the management must have some reason to believe that each one has possibilities of yielding a reasonable profit, and, since the cost analyst does not want to suggest changes until he has some tangible facts to back up his recommendation, he will deal first with the territories as they exist. It is possible, if desired, to make more or less elaborate calculations of the cost of calling on different towns or different customers in a territory, but a different and simpler approach will be found more productive of definite results.

The real problem in any territory as it exists is one of selection of customers to be called on. The number of hours of the salesman's time is fixed, and the cost of maintaining him on the road is practically fixed, except for the actual mileage cost of travel, i.e., rail or bus fare or automobile mileage allowance. In determining what calls should be made, a logical procedure would be as follows:

1. List all customers or potential customers, starting with those which have the greatest profit possibilities (and, in the absence of evidence to the contrary, this can be assumed tentatively to be the greatest potential sales volume) and working down to those which are less profitable, until there are as many customers on the call list as can be covered in the salesman's available time.

2. Work out on the map, by trial and error, the most economically possible routing to cover these customers and then examine it to see whether there is any particular town or series of towns which appears to offer, in total, low volume possibilities for the time required for coverage. Sometimes such cases will be fairly obvious, as when a single town is off the beaten track and hence requires time and extra mileage costs to cover; sometimes a less obvious situation may exist where the same thing is true of a particular section of the route, including several towns.

3. If such situations are disclosed, consider the possibility of eliminating these low-profit calls and substituting calls on other customers not individually as profitable but more accessible—in other words, increasing total potential profit by increasing the number of calls so as to more than offset the loss in potential profit per call. If no such substitute calls can be found, it then becomes a question of weighing the possible saving in actual mileage cost by eliminating low-profit calls against the loss in potential profit. The saving in mileage cost should be determined by comparing the costs of covering the routes before and after the elimination of the marginal calls.

Of course, the above steps may not be taken in exactly the order outlined, but the effect should be the same. Intangibles and judgment will weigh heavily in the process—for example, the management may have to decide the relative amount of time it wishes the salesman to devote to accounts which are regular customers, as compared with accounts which regularly buy from competitors; this will depend on what policy it believes will produce the greatest profit in the territory in the long run. But these judgments involve a weighing of immediate or ultimate comparative sales and profit potentials for a definite amount of time spent; the cost of the time, except for actual mileage cost, is predetermined for the limits of the problem, which is the analysis of an existing territory.

The procedure as suggested assumes a knowledge of the market—that is, of customers and potential customers—and, as previously emphasized there is no cost substitute for this knowledge in field sales planning and control. If it is impractical to evaluate potential customers individually, either because there are too many of them or for other reasons, an effort can be made to list at least the more important ones, and this can be supplemented by data as to purchasing power or other appropriate market statistics by counties or towns. Such statistics are available from several different sources, including government and industry surveys, and analyses of magazine circulation, etc.

Determination of optimum level of sales force

The foregoing discussion covers only the analysis of existing individual territories, the assumption being that the division of the market into territories has been well studied and carefully executed. This assumption can be roughly checked by a comparison of the potentials of the lowest-potential customers in each territory. In general, the potentials of these "marginal" customers in the various territories should be about equal, except where there is a wide variation in the cost of coverage per customer, owing to differences in density of population, types of customers, etc. If the comparison of territories where coverage costs per customer do not vary greatly shows a significant difference in the potentials of the marginal customers, it is an indication that the total time of the field men is not being efficiently used. This may call either for rearrangement of territories or, if there is unsold plant capacity, for the addition of one or more salesmen. If the plant is sold to capacity and if there are enough potential customers not being covered and their business is sufficiently attractive, a study may show that it will pay to enlarge the plant and add more salesmen. Plant expansion, of course, involves the permanent commitment of capital, with its accompanying risks and hence requires a more thorough evaluation of the market than a simple expansion of the field sales force.

Even where there are no significant inequalities between territories and it can be assumed that the most efficient use is being made of the existing force, it may be, if there is unsold plant capacity, that the addition of more salesmen would be profitable; or it may be, on the other hand, that enough unprofitable customers are being covered in all territories to warrant a reduction in the sales force. This leads naturally to the question: "What potential business is necessary to justify calling on a customer?"

An answer to this question could be developed in terms of averages by determining the average total variable cost per salesman for salary, travel, maintenance overhead, and order filling, and dividing by the average number of customers covered by a salesman to determine the average cost of covering and serving a customer. Such averages might be interesting, but their usefulness would be limited, and they would be of little help in indicating what definite moves could profitably be made. To be practical, we have to determine, on the one hand, what customers not being covered have the greatest potential, where they are located, and how and at what cost they could be covered and, on the other hand, where the lowest-potential customers now being called on are located, how enough of them might be dropped to enable us to eliminate one or more salesmen, and the effect of such elimination on income and costs.

Seven[1] has suggested that some companies will discover, upon careful analysis, that a large part of their profits can be traced to a small proportion of their product lines and a similarly small segment of their customer group. In the case of the unprofitable customers, he offers the following remedies to managers faced with the problem. First, shifting some selling effort from the unprofitable customers. Second, changing the discount structure to increase the prices to unprofitable customers. Third, changing the channels of distribution to serve the unprofitable customers by mail or through wholesalers. The fourth possibility, of course, was that of discontinuing service to the unprofitable customers altogether.

Let us assume that the analysis of customer potentials has disclosed that, of the highest-potential customers not being called on, the largest group is in a metropolitan area, where it is estimated that 100 additional customers could be covered by adding a salesman and rearranging existing territories. It is estimated that, considering competitive conditions, the company should be able to sell these 100 customers an average of 30 percent of their requirements and that, because of hand-to-mouth buying habits in this territory, this will involve handling about 50 orders a week or 2,600 orders in a year. The variable cost of maintaining the new man on the road and filling the orders taken, assuming that the cost figures in the tabulations on page 245 are applicable, is estimated as follows:

	Minimum	Maximum
Salary	$ 7,500	$ 7,500
Travel	950	950
Overhead cost of maintenance (250 days)	2,835	5,460
Cost of order filling, etc (2,600 orders)	3,536	6,214
Total variable costs	$14,821	$20,124

Assuming an average gross profit of 20 percent over variable factory cost, the total volume required to justify adding this salesman, assuming that there is unsold plant capacity, would be between $75,000 and $100,000. Since we are estimating that we can get only 30 percent of the total potential business, this means that the total sales potential of the 100 customers covered must be from $250,000 to $330,000, or

---

[1] C. H. Seven, *Marketing Productivity Analysis* (St. Louis: McGraw-Hill, 1965), p. 72ff.

an average of $1,000–$1,330 per customer. A considerable higher potential volume would be required to justify the added costs and risks of plant expansion. It is obvious that in this type of problem a great deal depends on the estimate of the percentage of the total potential business that can be obtained, and this is frequently determinable only by trial over a period of time.

As an example of a situation which may warrant a reduction in the field force, let us assume that the territory of J. F. Robinson, which was shown in the report reproduced in Figure 10–2 to be unprofitable, is adjoined by two or three other territories, of approximately the same market density, which are also clearly unprofitable, or at least in the doubtful column. The report on Robinson's territory shows direct variable costs (salary and travel) of $13,000 per year and indirect costs of $5,634–$10,427 per year, or a total of about $18,600–$23,400. Before accepting this as the amount which would be saved by the elimination of one field man in this particular situation, it would be necessary to select the customers who would be dropped from the call list if the move were made, determine the new routings of the rearranged territories, and compare the travel expense required to cover these routings with the present travel expense; this reduction in travel expense might or might not be approximately the same as the $5,500 of expense incurred by Robinson. Similarly, the reduction in the number of orders resulting from the expected loss of the business of the customers to be dropped might be more or less than the 1,850 orders received from Robinson's customers during the year. Assume, however, that the reduction in expenses, after considering the exact territorial changes to be made, is still estimated at $18,600–$23,400 and assume, further, that the rearrangement of territories results in dropping 125 customers whose total potential business would yield a gross profit (over variable factory costs) of $64,000, of which we are obtaining only 25 percent, or $16,000. Unless there is reason to believe that we can increase our share of the total business, the reduction in the field force appears to be a sound move.

Some companies have found it helpful to use standards in deciding on the distribution of the sales force by region. By historical study and by judgment, the number and duration of desired calls per year for each customer class is obtained and expressed in days per year. A study of the territory is next performed to find out how many of each type of customer it contains. By extension, the total number of salesman/days needed in the territory is calculated, and, with an allowance for lost time and office time, the sales force for the region can be assessed. Although this evaluation can be no better than the standards on which it is based, the thoughtful use of a system for work load measurement can prevent inequities between regions. The possibility that the total number of salesmen in all regions may be "wrong" remains, of course. The company may improve profits by increasing the number of calls made or may find that a cut in calls makes no difference to sales volume. Most authorities recommend experiments at regular intervals as the best if not the only way to discover the effects of a change in the total sales force size.

From these examples it is evident that the chief contributions that the cost analyst can make in problems of this kind are, first, to direct thinking along the right lines—which, paradoxically, means away from elaborate cost calculations and toward an emphasis on the study of market potentials—and, second, to supply relatively simple figures on the costs that will vary in particular situations as salesmen are added or dropped and as the number of orders increases or decreases. The range of variable costs in the examples given is rather wide, but no wider, perhaps, than the actual spread between short-term variations, which are immediately apparent with even minor changes in activity, and the total long-term variations, including those which appear more slowly as the cumulative effect of gradual changes in organization. The range can be narrowed by a careful study of the different functions and by a definite understanding with the marketing executives by whom the figures are to be used as to the basis on which variability is estimated, i.e., whether short term or long term.

Research and development costs

"Research" and "development" are terms which are used to describe a number of different types of activity, including basic or pure research in chemistry or physics, the application of basic discoveries to the development of new products or the improvement of existing products, studies in the improvement of machine methods, and experiments with new machinery or new processes. Sometimes, even routine testing and inspection, if performed in the laboratory, is improperly dignified with the title of "research." A definition of exactly what is meant by research and development and who is responsible for each type of activity is clearly a prerequisite to effective accounting control; in this field, as elsewhere in the business, the accounting plan must conform to the organization plan. If such a definition of functions and responsibilities is available, the current control of expenditures presents no particular difficulties; it is necessary only to apply the usual procedure of setting up primary accounts by individual responsibilities, budgeting the expense allowances for each responsible executive, and measuring actual expenditures against the budget.

The determination of what information about research and development costs is needed for planning and policy formulation would also appear to be a simple matter. Since these costs are not directly affected by the volume or type of production, the class of sales outlet, or other operating factors, there is no purpose in including them in studies of the type discussed earlier in this chapter. Research activities bear some resemblance to order-getting activities in that their cost is an investment, or a speculation, for the purpose of increasing income; but, in the case of research, the relation between expenditure and results is much less direct and is usually apparent only over a long period of time. Furthermore, although rough measurements of results over a period of years may be helpful in planning the general direction of future effort, it must be borne in mind that past results may have little relation to future possibilities. The controller may very well conclude, therefore, that all that is required for planning purposes is to allocate budgeted time and expense to specific projects, with some follow-up to see that the time and money are spent at least approximately as planned. But, in attempting to establish even this relatively simple type of cost accounting, he may encounter unexpected resistance from the research organization unless there is a satisfactory working agreement between the management and the executives in charge of research as to the method of planning and conducting research activities.

The reluctance of research personnel in some companies to accept controls of this kind is often due in part to impatience with accounting methods which have the appearance, but not the substance, of meticulous accuracy; this obstacle, however, can be overcome by rationalizing procedures so that they will be adapted to the needs of the research department and will not involve useless and irritating refinements in record keeping. Of more fundamental importance is the fear of the research organization—a fear which is sometimes well grounded—that, on the basis of the information provided by project–cost accounting, the management will interfere unduly in the research program by attempting to dictate the selection of projects and the amount of time spent on each. On first thought, this may seem to be a management prerogative; it is logical to ask the question "Why shouldn't the research department be subject to the same management control as other departments of the business?" The research man's answer to this is that he recognizes the right of management to determine how much money is available for research and development activities, and he expects to keep management advised as to the nature of the various projects which are being carried on. He expects to be guided somewhat by management's advice in determining the relative amount of effort that should be devoted to near-term developments, which have a prospect of paying a fairly prompt return, and long-term projects, on which any return will be some distance in the future. However, he is firmly convinced that management is not in a position to make sound judgments as to the relative merits and future possibilities of different projects and that no research program can be carried on successfully over the long term unless the management has sufficient confidence in the research director to defer to his judgment in this respect.

It is obvious that this is a question not of accounting but of the proper management use of accounting data. There are activities which are sometimes included under the heading of "research and development" but which are really in the nature of engineering projects and over which management can properly expect to exercise close control and direction; examples of such projects might be the designing of a special-purpose machine, the engineering of a new product to be made from familiar materials and to serve a definite purpose, or the development of a new chemical formula to produce a specific reaction in a manufacturing process. On the other hand, research which involves pioneering in unexplored fields or in the application of new discoveries to practical commercial use may be severely handicapped by management interference. It is impossible, therefore, to generalize on the question, and there is little that the controller can do, in any event, to help resolve the issue where it exists. When the issue is satisfactorily resolved, there should be little difficulty in convincing the management and the research organization of the advantages of having project-cost information available.

The accumulation of research project costs is essentially a rather simple job-order cost problem; provision must be made for direct charges to each project for salaries, special supplies, and other directly applicable expenses, and if the project costs are to be tied in, in total, with the total research department expense, the indirect or general expenses must be prorated over the various projects. Sometimes the project costs are not tied in with the total departmental costs but include only direct time and other direct charges; or a provision for indirect costs may be added by applying a predetermined rate per man-hour or per dollar of direct salaries and wages. Either of these procedures makes it easier for the responsible executive to interpret the results, since variances from budget on individual projects due to factors beyond his control are eliminated.

In establishing cost accounting for a research project, some difficulty may be experienced in securing information on which to base the distribution of the time of research personnel who may be working on several projects concurrently. Accurate timekeeping is not feasible; however, it is common practice for each research worker to keep a diary of his daily activities for the information of the research director and as a record for reference in the filing and prosecution of patent applications. Where such diaries are available, they can be used as a basis for time distributions which will be sufficiently accurate for all practical purposes. Time spent in activities not directly related to a specific project, such as general conferences and lectures, can be charged to a separate order and included in the overhead allocation or the predetermined overhead rate. Some companies charge all time at an overall average hourly rate or classify personnel into two or three groups and use an average rate for each group; this simplifies the procedure and eliminates any tendency for those in charge of particular projects to be influenced in their selection of personnel by differences in individual salary rates. Since extreme accuracy in the determination of project costs is unnecessary, procedures can be streamlined to a degree which would not be acceptable in the control of factory operations.

In a business where sales activities are subdivided into distinct departments by commodities or by classes of customers and where control is exercised by special departmental profit and loss statements, the accumulation of project costs makes it possible to charge the cost of research and development against the particular departments or sections of the business for the benefit of which the activities are conducted. Charges of this kind should be made only with the consent of the responsible departmental executive, or at least after thorough discussion with him.

Following is a summary of the procedure in effect in a company where basic research and product research are conducted in a separate research department under the supervision of a research director, and research on manufacturing methods and processes is conducted in a plant development department under the supervision of the plant manager:

1. All expenses of the research department are charged to a research department expense account in the "Selling, Administrative, and General Expense" group, with subaccounts by types of expenses. Expenses of the plant development department are charged to a separate burden center in factory overhead.

2. Any time spent by either the research department or the plant development department on routine testing, inspection, or control is charged to the factory burden center for which the work is performed and is excluded from the totals of research and development expenses.

3. If the research department performs work on specific factory projects at the request of the plant management, a charge is made for such services, based on the project cost. The amount of this charge is a credit to research department expense and a charge to factory overhead.

4. In general, expenses of the plant development department and charges to factory overhead by the research department are treated as general factory overhead and allocated to productive departments on the same basis as plant management expense. Direct charges to productive departments, based on project costs, may be made in special cases.

5. If the general management authorizes the development department to perform work on product development (as distinct from manufacturing research and development), a charge is made for such services, based on the project cost. The amount of this charge is a credit to

the development department burden center and a charge to a development expense account in the "Selling, Administrative, and General Expense" group.

6. Research department expense and development expense in the "Selling, Administrative, and General Expense" group are charged in part to sales departments (commodities) in internal statements (not on the books) at the budgeted cost of projects applicable to the several departments; these budgeted charges may be adjusted during the year, as changes are made in the research program, after discussion with the departmental managers concerned. The total of these charges to the sales departments does not agree exactly with the total research and development expense in the profit and loss statement, owing to (a) variations between actual and budgeted project costs and (b) a substantial number of projects which are not considered to be currently chargeable against the sales departments.

7. A statement is prepared quarterly for the general management, summarizing the cost of all research and development activities and indicating where these costs are charged in the accounts and statements.

A final point must be made before leaving the matter of research and development costs. In theory, these expenditures should be expensed or capitalized in accordance with the incidence of the resulting benefits upon the succession of accounting periods. It is entirely possible that substantial amounts of a company's expenditure, especially for "pure" research, will result in discoveries whose benefits will be felt for many years to come. In theory, such expenditures should be capitalized initially and then amortized to expense in the benefiting periods. The vast amounts being spent for research in modern business is clear evidence of faith that the future will in fact so benefit. Yet we find that virtually all expenditures for research and development are being charged to expense in the period of the outlay.

The decision for immediate charge-off is obviously a violation of major premise No. 1—the clear portrayal of observed fact—to the extent of untold millions. Yet we are not here arguing that this decision should be materially changed. The truth, of course, is that in practice there can virtually never be any assurance that any particular expenditure for research will, in fact result, in future benefits. The objectively observed facts which are quite clear for industry as a whole are actually rather hazy at the point of the practical accounting decision. Here the decision is made on the basis of major premise No. 2—the management-impact premise. There can be little doubt that in the majority of instances the better management impact is obtained by the more conservative method of expensing rather than by capitalizing.

A clear awareness of this pattern of thinking should enable the controller to be on the watch for the possible unusual situation in which the facts are clear enough to justify the alternative method. He should be hardy enough in his thinking to insist on the correct accounting when the facts are clear.

Incidentally, there is no doubt that income tax considerations play a part in the minds of many persons in making the decision to expense research costs immediately, and this is legitimate within the wide range of judgment allowed by the tax regulations. Even for tax purposes, however, there are circumstances under which the capitalization rather than the expensing of research costs may be the advantageous course of action. Our caveat is, then, against the oversimplification of thinking on the situation rather than a campaign for any substantial revision of present practices.

11 INVENTORY VALUATION

The problem of inventory valuation

The valuation of inventories is the most important single factor in any statement of the earnings of many industrial enterprises for a given period and its financial condition at a particular date. To the layman, who is accustomed to reading in corporate balance sheets that the inventories are stated at "cost" or at "lower of cost or market," the problem of valuation may seem to be no problem at all. The "cost" of anything is what you paid for it, and "market" is what you can get for it now, and what is there to be said? Even the "last-in–first-out" method of valuation can be explained, in principle, in relatively simple terms and would hardly seem to warrant the learned discussions and the sometimes acrimonious controversies that rage about it. But the controller, who is charged with the responsibility for the practical application of these simple concepts, knows that there is indeed, a problem of inventory valuation which must be carefully analyzed and for which a satisfactory and consistent answer must be found, if the financial statements which he prepares are to reflect the real facts about the business.

There are two phases of this inventory-valuation problem: first, the selection of the method of valuation; second, the definition of the terms to be used and the procedures to be followed in applying the method selected. These two phases are, of course, related to each other, since a definition of terms and some familiarity with what is involved in the practical application of each of the various methods are essential to an intelligent choice of the most suitable method in any particular situation.

The logic behind the valuation problem

In Chapter 1 some of the simpler aspects of the inventory valuation problem were discussed to demonstrate the use of the accountant's major premise number one "clear portrayal" and major premise number two "management impact." In this chapter we take on the full complications of inventory valuation with little attention to the formal steps of logic but with a maximum effort to get acceptable solutions. The careful reader will note, however, that the entire argument of this chapter is an application of our major premise number two—the effort to find in the maze of complications the method or methods which will be of greatest aid to management with due regard to all of its responsibilities; stockholder reporting and tax reporting as well as immediate management decisions.

The balance-sheet and the profit-and-loss viewpoints in valuation

The selection of the method of valuation which will give the clearest portrayal is a twofold problem involving the measurement of both earnings and financial condition. There is a natural tendency to view the asset side of the balance sheet as a statement of actual money values, absolute in itself; but this concept, which might be called the "balance-sheet viewpoint," can properly be applied in a going business only to cash, marketable securities, and accounts receivable. The actual money "value" of the other assets—inventories, prepaid expenses, and plant and equipment—depends on what can be realized on them in the normal course of future operations; this is the "earnings" viewpoint. So far as inventories are concerned, there may or may not be a serious conflict between these two viewpoints, depending on the circumstances. If such a conflict exists, the best modern practice demands that the earnings viewpoint govern—in other words, that the inventories be regarded as a deferred charge against future operations rather than as an accumulation of property with an inherent value.

The increasing acceptance of the earnings viewpoint has led to an intensive reexamination of the whole inventory-valuation problem. Over the years, accountants have come to realize that, in the broader sense, there is no such thing as absolute accuracy in financial statements, and they have long been struggling, with only indifferent success, to convey this realization to the general public. Over a period of time long enough to cover a business cycle, a reasonable approximation of true earnings is possible, though even for such a period there may be a large element of judgment involved, particularly in cases where there is a heavy investment in plant or other fixed assets.

The fully definitive determination of net earnings of any business would require complete liquidation—the conversion of all assets to cash and the payment of all liabilities. Even this state would still leave us faced with the very large problem of the change in the value of money between the origin and the dissolution of the business. An earnings statement for any short period of time is necessarily incomplete, not only in the sense that a single year's profits do not truly reflect the average earnings that can be expected from the business as a continuing entity, but incomplete in itself because of the difficulty of determining at any given date the real going-concern value of nonliquid assets, particularly of inventories. Experience has shown that the conventional methods of inventory valuation which have been in general use for many years are often unsatisfactory in this respect, and hence efforts have been made to develop new methods which will convey to the reader of financial statements a more useful impression of the true short-term earnings of business enterprises.

Conventional methods of valuation

The weight of usage and convention is still on the side of "the lower of cost or market" as the preferred basis of inventory valuation. Further "cost" in the above phrase is most commonly taken to mean cost as determined by the first-in–first-out method. It is, therefore, appropriate to begin this discussion with a consideration of the FIFO cost method and its variants and then to consider the possible interpretations of the words "market value." Thereafter, we shall consider a most significant alternative valuation method, last-in–first-out (or LIFO) cost, which is fundamentally different from FIFO and its variants in conception, and for which the market value of the inventory is not an acceptable substitute.

Identified costs versus assigned costs

The layman's definition of the cost of anything as "the amount paid for it" is simple and eminently sensible as a statement of the principle of the cost basis of valuation. A literal application of this definition would require the physical segregation and earmarking of each lot of goods purchased and the accumulation of actual costs of labor and other factory expenses on each such lot processed and converted into semifinished or finished products. The total cost of each lot divided by the number of units in the lot would give a figure which is, strictly speaking, the average unit cost of the lot, though this would generally be acceptable as the actual unit cost of each unit. It is so used in the following discussion. This procedure, which permits the determination of "identified costs" for all items in the inventories, is followed in some businesses, especially those in which purchasing and production are for specific customer's orders rather than for stock. But in a business which manufactures a product or a variety of products for general sale and is compelled to order raw materials and to schedule processing in advance of the receipt of actual sales orders, the procedure is cumbersome and impracticable.

Furthermore, unless some consistent rule is followed as to the sequence in which the various lots are taken out of the inventories, the identified costs of different lots of the same material or product in the inventories at any time may be quite different, particularly in a period of rising or falling material prices, and the profits or losses shown by the books would depend on the deliberate or accidental choice of the lots to be processed or shipped. Thus, although the valuation of inventories on the basis of the identified costs of individual lots is the most "accurate" possible method of valuation, there are relatively few businesses in which it can be applied in such a way as to give a useful picture of earnings and financial condition, and its use in actual practice is very limited. This method might actually make the determination of a period's profit depend on the whim of a stock clerk if he cared to notice the marked costs on the items available for issue.

The only practical alternative to the use of identified costs of individual lots in valuing inventories is the adoption of some consistent method of assigning costs. A point frequently overlooked in discussions of the relative merits of different methods of inventory valuation is that the identified lot cost is the only "actual" cost and that all other costs are determined by arbitrary rules, that is, by assignment. The accounting for each of these different methods is a clear portrayal of the results under the particular scheme of assignment of costs. The decision to be made is not between different methods of accounting but between different assumptions with respect to assignments of cost. Which particular items move first physically is of no consequence if they are all identical; hence the fact of physical movement may be disregarded. Thus the assumption with regard to assignment of cost becomes the significant fact to be recorded.

A very strict functional analysis might regard the selection of the assignment basis a management prerogative rather than the responsibility of the controller, with the controller then responsible merely for the accounting procedures necessary clearly to reflect management's choice. However, management would seldom be able to make such a choice intelligently without the advice of the controller, so the strict analysis of the situation is largely academic, and we may as well think of selection of methods as an accounting problem.

One of the most convenient methods of assigning costs to an inventory is to use predetermined standard costs of the items included in it. This method is probably more widely used than any other in valuing the labor and overhead elements of inventories. It has the virtue of eliminating from cost, and hence from the inventory valuation, the effect of variations due to unusual efficiency or inefficiency or to irregular timing of expenditures, and, if the standards are computed on the basis of a normal volume, it also eliminates the effect of seasonal and cyclical variations in volume of production. Such variations have, as a rule, no significant bearing on the value of any inventory, either from the balance-sheet or the profit-and-loss viewpoint, and their elimination, therefore, results in a more useful statement of earnings and financial condition. Standard cost methods have been given fuller consideration in Chapter 8.

Assignment of costs on a first-in–first-out basis

In most businesses which manufacture for stock, material must be purchased and perhaps wholly or partly converted into finished form before the receipt of the customer's order for which it is to be used. Under these conditions, the manufacturer, even though he does not attempt to segregate physically each lot of each material or product and identify its cost, is likely, nevertheless, to think in terms of the turnover of successive lots; that is, he looks on his operations as the purchase and conversion of a continuous series of lots in anticipation of sales, and he thinks of these lots as being used or sold in the sequence of their purchase or conversion. This very natural concept leads to the assignment of costs on the first-in–first-out basis, and it is this basis, or some modification of it, which is usually implied when the term "cost" is used in connection with inventory valuation. Complementary to the concept of *using* materials on the first-in–first-out basis is the method of value ending.

Variations of first-in–first-out

The most common modification on the first-in–first-out basis of assigning costs is what is usually referred to as the "average-cost method" of valuation. Under this method the units and dollar cost of each lot acquired, are added to the units and dollar value already appearing in the account, and the resulting average unit value is used to cost withdrawals until the next lot is added and a new moving average value determined. It is interesting to note that this concept of assigning costs is parallel to the physical conditions if the material is a miscible liquid stored in a large tank into which each new acquisition is poured and from which the issues are drawn through a spigot. Solid materials would virtually never follow physically the moving-average cost assumptions. In some cases the averaging may be done on a monthly or even quarterly basis rather than as each lot is received. It should be noted that even this slight change breaks down the parallel between the physical movement and the cost assignment. In a typical inventory, a study of the physical movements of different items would probably show first-in–first-out by management dictum for any perishable items, moving average for liquids in storage tanks, something approaching last-in–first-out for standard items like brass nuts stored in a deep bin, and all conceivable combinations of these movements for other items. Obviously, these physical movements cannot be followed in any literal sense by accounting.

The practical result of the averaging methods of assigning costs is to cushion the effect of changes in cost on the value of the inventory and to accelerate the effect on the cost of goods produced and sold; that is, when costs are rising, inventory values will be lower and the cost of production and shipments higher than on the first-in–first-out basis, and in a falling market the reverse will be true. Such a tracing of the effects of the several methods upon resulting figures is the kind of thinking that should lie behind the choice of methods.

A practical incidental consideration favoring the moving-average method is the fact that it works more smoothly with machine methods of detailed record keeping than does the first-in–first-out, though, of course, standard cost is a still more economical method. Actual detailed stock records on last-in–first-out would simply not be feasible.

Classification of inventories for determination of cost

An extremely important problem in applying the first-in–first-out principle of valuation is the definition of the classification of the inventories for costing purposes. If we adhere to the concept that a manufacturing business consists of the purchase, conversion, and sale of a series of lots, then a strict application of the first-in–first-out principle requires that a separate account be kept at each location with each item of raw material, each job in process, and each finished product and that the first-in–first-out procedure be applied to each such account. This may be feasible in a business which uses a limited number of raw materials and makes a limited number of finished products, but in a business of any complexity it is unnecessarily cumbersome, and in a very large business it may become completely impracticable. It is accepted practice, therefore, to short-cut the procedure by broadening the inventory classifications for costing purposes—that is, by pooling items or elements of the inventory that are alike or similar in nature or in end use, and considering each "pool" as a unit in applying the first-in–first-out rule.

Although the extent and method of application of the pooling principle for inventory-valuation purposes varies greatly in different companies, it is possible to distinguish at least four different basic applications.

1. The pooling of like items in the same stage of processing at different locations. A simple illustration of this would be an oil-distributing company considering all No. 1 fuel oil in all its tanks, wherever located, as one pool. The net results of this procedure is to eliminate from the

inventory valuation the effect of different rates of turnover at the different locations.

2.   The pooling of all quantities of a given material in all stages of processing at one or more locations; for example, in a company operating several cotton mills, the cotton in the raw state, in process, and in the finished product at each mill may be considered as a pool, or there may be a single pool for all the mills. This application obviously requires the conversion of material in process and in finished product to the raw-material equivalent by adjusting for waste in processing; also, it implies a separate determination of the labor and overhead elements of cost. It eliminates the effect, so far as material cost is concerned, of different rates of turnover of the various items of work in process and finished goods at the location or locations covered by the pool.

3.   The pooling of similar, but not identical, items for the application of average unit material or converting (labor and overhead) costs. A steel company, having in its inventories thousands of different sizes and grades of bars, plates, etc., at many different locations, may classify the inventories into a number of broad groups and use an average tonnage cost for each group, as the only practical answer to the costing problem.

4.   The classification of all the materials in an inventory into several pools based on the character of the material or the finished product, and the use of standard material costs and current variations from standard to determine the actual cost of each pool as a whole. Usually, each such pool will include materials in all stages of processing, though raw materials may be separated from the material content of work in process and finished stock if more convenient. This procedure is described in detail in paragraph II-B-2 of the specimen standard procedure reproduced in the Appendix to this chapter. It is especially appropriate where the inventory is made up of a large number of materials and finished products, none of which is in itself of major significance in relation to the total inventory value.

There are many variations and combinations of these basic applications of the pooling principle, and it is obvious that there may be considerable differences between the total valuations of the same inventory, depending on which procedure is followed. To the extent that the management tends to look on the operations of the business as a series of identified purchases, conversions, and sales and tries to explain profits or losses in detail in such terms, any departure from the strict first-in–first-out valuation by individual items will be disturbing. As a practical matter, such an analysis of profits and losses is not possible, except in the simplest kinds of businesses, and there is no real loss of accuracy in adopting pooling procedures which are suited to the character of the business. Such distortions as are caused by the use of averages tend to cancel out in a large inventory and no inventory valuation can be said to be accurate within a range of 2 to 3 percent. It is, of course, important that, whatever the pooling procedures adopted, they be carefully defined and consistently followed.

Lower of cost or market

So long as there is no substantial reason to question whether inventory costs, however determined, will be recovered when the inventory is sold, the cost basis of valuation is entirely adequate. This is the situation in some businesses, particularly those which manufacture on order or in which there is a high degree of stability in selling prices, irrespective of cost fluctuations. In the great majority of manufacturing enterprises, however, selling prices are sensitive to cost changes and also to changes in the balance between supply and demand, and there are frequent occasions when it is obvious that inventory costs cannot be recovered under conditions prevailing at the inventory date; in such cases both the balance-sheet viewpoint and the profit-and-loss view-point call for a valuation based on market rather than on cost. On the other hand, it is an established principle that profits are realized only on completed transactions, and hence any appreciation in inventory values due to rising costs or selling prices cannot properly be reflected in the accounts until the inventories are actually disposed of. This all adds up to the well-known lower-of-cost-or-market rule, which has for many years been the most widely used basis of inventory valuation. The use of market value is prohibited, it should be mentioned, in the case of LIFO cost which will be discussed later in this chapter.

Definition of market

The layman's definition of the "market" value of an item as "what you can get for it now" is just as fundamentally sound as his definition of the "cost" of anything as "what you paid for it." Furthermore, in defining "market," we are not involved, as we are in defining "cost," with the problem of identifying or assigning past expenditures—the only thing that concerns us is present value, which (it would appear) has nothing to do with historical records or accounting procedures. Yet it will be found that in practice there are a number of possible interpretations of the term "market" and that further clarification is necessary to avoid misunderstanding and confusion.

There are really two different concepts of market: (1) realization value and (2) replacement cost. "Realization value" is, of course, a paraphrase of the layman's definition "what you can get for it"; "replacement cost," on the other hand, is something quite different, and, indeed, one may question why it needs to be considered at all in the determination of market. To this question there are two answers, viz., conservatism and expediency. The extreme of conservatism is to consider market as the lower or realization value or replacement cost; even when there is no conscious effort at such conservatism, it is often easier to determine replacement cost and to demonstrate that it is below realization value than it is to determine an exact or even an approximate realization value. In taking the inventory of merchandising establishments, replacement cost is commonly accepted as market. In this case the concept of realization value is used only for merchandise which is clearly obsolete or shelf-worn. Since prices of finished goods generally vary much less than those of raw materials, realization value of typical merchandise inventories would be less likely than those of manufacturers' inventories to fall to or below replacement.

Realization value

The difficulty in determining realization value is that additional costs must usually be incurred to realize any item in the inventories, and such costs must be deducted from the selling price of the item to determine the true net amount that can be realized from its sale. In the case of finished goods for which there are firm sales orders outstanding at the inventory date, the only additional costs which need be deducted from the sales value are costs of shipping, billing, and collecting. With respect to unsold finished goods, costs of selling must also be considered, and in the case of work in process and unprocessed materials there are, in addition, the costs to complete processing into salable form. These various costs will be computed in accordance with the company's regular procedures, if there are no established procedures for computing selling costs, it is customary to use an average per unit or percent of sales for each class of product.

In a business which uses one or a very few raw materials, such a calculation of net realization value can be made quite readily if there is a common unit of physical measurement and if the pooling principle is applied by classifying finished products into a few groups and using an average selling price and average manufacturing, selling, and shipping costs for each group. If the inventory consists of a large number of items of raw material and finished and semifinished products and there is no common unit of measurement, the problem is much more difficult. As a rule, it is entirely impractical to compute a realization value for each item of unprocessed raw materials which may be used in many different products, and even for work in process and finished goods such a computation in detail may be very cumbersome. In such cases test calculations of realization value can be made for a number of major finished products and their raw-material components; if the realization value of any of the items tested proves to be lower than cost, additional tests can be made on related items and enough information accumulated to provide the basis for calculating an overall adjustment to reduce that particular portion of the inventories to approximate realization value. Obviously, the calculation of adjustments by this method is not entirely a mathematical process, and the results are not exact; but by selecting carefully the items tested, to be sure that they represent a fair cross-section of the inventories, and by applying consistent procedures in the determination of realization values, it is possible in most cases to arrive at a sound and reasonable overall valuation. It should be noted that the realization value of unprocessed raw materials is sometimes interpreted to mean the amount that could be realized by resale in the unprocessed state; this is something less than even replacement cost, since the cost of reselling, freight, and handling must be deducted. Unless the inventories are obsolete or excessive or the company is operating regularly at a loss, this is an unnecessarily conservative basis of valuation, since the materials are purchased not for resale but for conversion into finished goods in the normal course of operations.

Replacement cost

The computation of the replacement cost of an inventory is usually much simpler than the computation of realization value. If the inventory is taken by items, without pooling of material or converting costs, the unit replacement cost of each item can be built up from the specification sheets, which are basic records in any well-run cost system. Furthermore, if standard converting costs are used in valuing the inventories at cost, they will, except in unusual circumstances, be the practical equivalent of replacement costs and can be used without change, so that only the material element of each item needs to be refigured.

If one of the pooling procedures previously described is used in the valuation of material on a cost basis, it is a relatively easy matter to compute the replacement cost of the material element. If a separate pool is maintained for each material, the total quantity in the inventory can be valued at replacement cost by a single extension. If the procedure followed calls for group pooling of materials (as described in detail in paragraph 11-B-2 of the standard inventory-valuation procedure reproduced in the appendix to this chapter), it is, theoretically, necessary to make a complete recomputation of the price variances for each group by recosting all the purchases involved at replacement costs at the date of the inventory. However, a test comparison of replacement costs and actual purchase costs of the major items in each group will often show that any overall adjustment for the group would be relatively minor, and the complete recomputation should be necessary only when there has been a general downward trend in material prices within a few weeks prior to the inventory date.

Choosing a definition of market

The realization value method for assessing inventory market value is usually much harder to use than replacement cost, because the realizable value is hard to measure. As both methods are acceptable under the current list of generally accepted accounting principles, a company may choose either without risk of incurring an exception at the time of audit. The company should study its own special circumstances carefully and then use the definition of its choice consistently. This consistency is more important than the initial choice of a method. It will be much easier to achieve consistency if a written statement of inventory valuation policy is prepared, in which the principles to be followed are described in detail. An example of such a policy statement forms the appendix to this chapter.

The business cycle—The rationale for LIFO

As long as material costs, wages, and selling prices remain reasonably stable, adjustments to market under the "lower of cost or market" basis of inventory valuation will be relatively unimportant. In most businesses, however, there are cyclical fluctuations in costs and selling prices which necessitate market write-downs of substantial amounts from time to time. The pattern of events leading up to such losses is all too familiar. It begins with a period of rising raw-material prices, with activity increasing as the uptrend in prices becomes apparent. During this period even the manufacturer who wishes to follow a nonspeculative policy is forced to extend his inventory position somewhat in order to service the increased volume and maintain his competitive position, and this, of course, gives further impetus to the price rise. Although selling price increases usually lag behind increases in the cost of material purchases, nevertheless, the assignment of material costs on a first-in–first-out basis results for a time in wider-than-normal margins, and these unusual profits are further augumented by the low unit converting costs resulting from increased plant activity.

In this atmosphere of apparent prosperity and increased demand for labor, wage rates naturally tend to rise, and after a time other costs begin to creep up. There is a psychological pressure to loosen up on spending in all fields, and commitments may be made for increased sales promotion, plant expansion, etc. Then, at some point, the market for the finished product becomes saturated or something happens to break the price of one or more important raw materials, and the boom ends—often very suddenly. Buying dries up, it is discovered that there are excessive inventories at all points in the manufacturing and distributing process, and orders are canceled and shipments deferred all down the line. There is a period of hesitation until the downtrend is established, and then the downward spiral starts and quickly gathers momentum. There is a sharp break or a series of breaks in selling prices, raw-material markets continue their decline, plant activity drops to below-normal levels, and wages may be reduced and commitments of all kinds canceled or curtailed. Eventually, when excess inventories are worked off or other economic factors check the deflationary trend, there is a leveling-off of prices, a modest recovery in activity, and then usually a period of readjustment at near-normal levels of volume, until something happens to touch off the cycle again.

It is, of course, in the deflationary phase of this cycle that the largest write-downs to market occur under the lower of cost or market rule. The cyclical swings are widest and the inventory losses most severe in the industries using basic raw materials, such as metals, textile fibers, leather, plastics, and rubber, which are subject to wide price fluctuations. In these industries, earnings reports, showing alternate periods of extreme prosperity and heavy market losses, have sometimes approached the ludicrous; and these are only aggravated instances of a situation which exists in some degree in almost all businesses and which is inevitably disturbing to management, to stockholders, and to employees.

The natural reaction of the businessman to a succession of experiences with inventory profits followed by market losses is to question the good sense of the accounting rule which requires inventories to be alternately written up and written down as prices fluctuate. At this point the businessman, probably without realizing it, breaks completely with the concept of his operations as the movement of a series of lots purchased and converted in anticipation of sales and passing through the various stages, from the purchase of raw material to the sale of the finished products, in the sequence of their purchase or conversion. In place of this first-in–first-out concept he begins to look on his inventories, or some part of them, as a permanent reservoir of goods, with a stream of shipments flowing out at one end and a practically equivalent stream of replacements flowing in at the other, so that the level of the reservoir remains relatively constant. Hence he says why not assign to the outgoing stream of shipments the actual costs incurred for the incoming stream of replacements and let the assigned cost of the reservoir goods remain unchanged? This, in essence, is the underlying principle of the normal-stock method of valuation and of its derivative, the last-in–first-out method, popularly referred to as "LIFO."

The last-in–first-out method of valuation

The governing definition of LIFO is found in Section 472 (b) of the Internal Revenue Code, which provides that, in inventorying goods under this method, the taxpayer shall:

1. Inventory them at cost.
2. Treat those remaining on hand at the close of the taxable year as

being: First, those included in the opening inventory of the taxable year (in the order of acquisition) to the extent thereof, and, second, those acquired in the taxable year.

3. Treat those included in the opening inventory of the taxable year in which such method is first used as having been acquired at the same time and determine their cost by the average cost method.

The law also provides that the method may be used only in inventorying goods "specified in an application . . . filed at such time and in such manner as the secretary or his delegate may prescribe" and that the procedures followed "shall be in accordance with such regulations as the secretary or his delegate may prescribe as necessary in order that the use of the method may clearly reflect income." The regulations issued by the commissioner amplify the definition in paragraph (2) above by specifying that goods acquired during any taxable year may be valued either (a) at the cost of the most recent purchases or production, (b) at the cost of the earliest purchases or production during the year, (c) at the average cost of all purchases or production during the year, or (d) "pursuant to any other proper method which, in the opinion of the Commissioner, clearly reflects income." Whichever of these procedures is adopted must be followed consistently from year to year. (Regulation 1,472-2-d-1)

The LIFO method effectively creates a reservoir of inventory. The most recent acquisitions are added to the "upper layer" of stock, and the items consumed are regarded as having been taken from the upper layer also. The effect is that the lower layers of the inventory are not normally touched. This reservoir idea is considered to apply only to the costs of the goods, of course; the actual flow of the goods will more commonly follow the FIFO concept. The LIFO cost of the basic inventory reservoir is likely given stable consumption rates, to remain the same for a long time. On the other hand, if there should be a year of unusually heavy consumption of the material, some of the reservoir inventory will be consumed and will be charged out against the year's revenues. This charging out will be at the original reservoir stock valuation, at the cost which prevailed many years ago when the goods were obtained. This would lead to a very serious failure to match cost with revenue. Advocates of the LIFO method point out that companies do not normally eat into their basic inventory reservoirs, and that the benefits of LIFO in normal situations far outweigh the disadvantages in the unusual case of base stock consumption.

LIFO does, broadly speaking, accomplish the objectives of charging current costs against current sales and minimizing book profits and losses on normal inventories. If it is adopted at a time when costs and inventory valuations are not too far above what may reasonably be expected to be a minimum level and if the reservoir inventories are maintained at the end of each year at not less than normal working requirements, there should be no difficulty in administering the method and interpreting its results. If there are, at any time, losses due to the market value of the reservoir inventories dropping below the cost as computed on the LIFO basis, or gains due to the unavoidable liquidation of reservoir inventories, they can, if desired, be segregated in the internal operating statements as extraordinary inventory losses or profits.

Income tax considerations in inventory valuation

Except for the discussion of the statutory basis of the LIFO method, very little has been said thus far in this chapter about the income tax aspects of inventory valuation. This is not an oversight or an accident; it has seemed desirable to consider the subject first entirely from the standpoint of sound business practice, uninfluenced by tax laws and regulations, particularly as the acceptance of new ideas and procedures for tax purposes quite naturally lags somewhat behind their acceptance as sound business practice. But with tax rates around the 50 percent level, the relationship of income taxes to reported earnings before taxes may be seriously distorted if inventory-valuation policies deviate too greatly from established income tax procedure. This may be the determining factor in the selection of a policy in many cases, and in no case can it be entirely ignored.

General provision of the federal tax law and regulations

The provisions of the federal tax law with respect to inventories, other than those dealing with the "elective" (LIFO) method, are extremely simple. They are found in Section 471 of the Internal Revenue Code:

Inventories—Whenever in the opinion of the Secretary or his delegate the use of inventories is necessary in order clearly to determine the income of any taxpayer, inventories shall be taken by such taxpayer upon basis as the Secretary or his delegate may prescribe as conforming as nearly as may be to the best accounting practice in the trade or business and as most clearly reflecting the income.

The regulations issued by the commissioner under this broad authority say that "inventory rules cannot be uniform but must give effect to trade customs which come within the scope of the best accounting practice in the particular trade or business," and that "greater weight is to be given to consistency than to any particular method of inventorying or basis of valuation so long as the method or basis used is substantially in accord with these regulations." But they also say that "the bases of valuation most commonly used by business concerns and which meet the requirements of Section 471 are (a) cost and (b) cost or market, whichever is lower," and they go on to define "cost" as, essentially, cost on the first-in–first-out basis, and "market" as replacement cost.

Within the limits laid down in the regulations, the Bureau of Internal Revenue in general follows a liberal policy in interpreting what is meant by the "best accounting practice in the particular trade or business." Perhaps the most unsatisfactory feature of the regulations is their failure to recognize realization value as a basis for determining market, except in the case of obsolete or otherwise unsalable or unusable items. This point might prove troublesome in a situation where the use of "replacement cost" instead of "realization value" shifted taxable income to a year of higher tax rates, but it is hardly important enough to affect a decision as to the policy to be followed in determining reported earnings.

Implementing LIFO for tax

The implementation of LIFO in most businesses requires that pooling be used, for practical reasons. The computations involved in using LIFO directly to evaluate each inventory item separately are quite unrealistic. The basic idea of pooling has already been discussed in the section of this chapter on "Classification of Inventories for Determination of Costs." In many businesses, it is easier to employ a method known as dollar pooling instead of the unit costing systems already discussed. The dollar pooling method was originally used in the retail industries, in which the measurement of inventories in terms of value instead of in units has long been the practice. However, the concept has been found applicable in many other industries as well since 1947, when the legality of the idea for tax purposes was first established.

The method of dollar pooling requires the controller to assess the cost of each of the inventory pools at three cost levels; the base year cost, the beginning of year costs, and the end of year costs. This assessment may be performed by the use of a substantial sample instead of considering the entire inventory. The base year cost is the cost of the physical inventory at the end of the current year measured in terms of the material, labor, and overhead costs at the date of adoption of the dollar pooling LIFO system. The ratio of the costs of the inventory at the end of the year to the cost of the same inventory at the beginning of year prices is termed the index of cost change for the year. The index is applied to the ratio of the current costs to base year costs as it was at the end of the previous year, and the result is deemed to be the ratio of current costs to base year costs at the end of the current year. The base year inventory figures can then be derived from the ratio. An example will help to clarify the procedure.

Figure 11–2 presents a method of determining the Base-Year Cost valuation of the inventory. For each succeeding year, an index of cost change for the year is computed as shown in STEP TWO. The ratio of current costs to base year costs at the end of each year is then deemed to be the product of the same ratio at the start of the year and the index of cost change just computed. The ratio of the current costs to base year costs provides a basis for reducing the current valuation of inventory ($2,230,250 in the example) to its base year valuation (of $811,000).

Figure 11-1
THE COMPUTATION OF LIFO INVENTORY UNDER DOLLAR POOLING
(figures in thousands of dollars)

Year	Inventory at beginning of 1969			Inventory at end of 1969			Inventory at end of 1970		
	Base cost	LIFO cost	Ratio	Base cost	LIFO cost	Ratio	Base cost	LIFO cost	Ratio
951....	254	254	1.00	254	254	1.00	254	254	1.00
952....	130	136.5	1.05	130	136.5	1.05	130	136.5	1.05
953....	38	40.7	1.07	38	40.7	1.07	38	40.7	1.07
954....	88	96.8	1.10	88	96.8	1.10	88	96.8	1.10
960....	110	187	1.70	110	187	1.70	110	187	1.70
967....	125	287.5	2.3	11	25.3	2.30	11	25.3	2.30
968....	96	240	2.5	...	.....	....	...	.....	....
ub.....	841	1242.5		631	740.3		631	740.3	
970.....							180	495	2.75
							811	1235.3	

Figure 11-1 shows how the base year valuation of the inventory may be used to compute the LIFO total. The figures in the three right hand columns present the inventory at the end of 1970. At base cost, there was a total of $631,000 brought forward from 1969. Since the end of year inventory has been computed at $811,000 in base year terms, there must have been an increase of $180,000. As we know (Table 5, step 3) that the ratio of current to base year cost for 1970 is 2.75, the LIFO valuation of that $180,000 increment is 2.75 × 180,000 = 495,000. The resulting total LIFO valuation for the pool, being the sum of several years increments computed in the same manner, is $1,235,300.

The six left hand columns of Figure 11-1 illustrate the procedure when a reduction in the inventory level occurs. The inventory fell, in base year dollars, from $841,000 to $631,000 during 1969. This leads to a Lifo cost change of $502,200, computed as follows.

	Base decrease	Ratio	Lifo cost
1967.......	$114,000	2.3	$262.2
1968.......	96,000	2.5	240
	$210,000		$502.2

Figure 11-2
DETERMINATION OF A DOLLAR LIFO INVENTORY POOL COST
(at base-year costs using the "link chain" method)

Basic facts	Inventory at End 1969 at Base Year Costs	$ 631,000
	Inventory at End 1969 at 1969 costs	1,640,600
	Inventory at End 1970 at 1969 costs	2,108,600
	Inventory at End 1970 at 1970 costs	2,230,250

Step one   Ratio of current costs to base year costs as at the end of 1969

$$= \frac{1,640,600}{631,000} = 2.60$$

Step two   Index of cost change for 1970

$$= \frac{2,230,250}{2,108,600} = 1.0577$$

Step three   Ratio of current costs to base year costs as at the end of 1970

$$= 2.60 \times 1.0577 = 2.75$$

Step four   Base year valuation of inventory as at the end of 1970

$$= \frac{2,230,250}{2.75} = \$811,000$$

APPENDIX

THE XYZ COMPANY
Inventory Valuation Policy and Procedure

I. General policy

A. It is the policy of the company to carry its inventories at cost, with adjustment at the end of each fiscal year to the basis of cost or market, whichever is the lower. If market conditions warrant, such an adjustment may also be made during the year, with the approval of the Executive Committee.

B. Obsolete materials and merchandise should be valued at the end of each fiscal year at not more than net realization value, as defined in paragraph III-A-1 below. The procedure for determining obsolescence is covered by a separate statement of company policy.

C. Provision may be made on the books during the year for year-end adjustments in inventory valuations due to market write-down, obsolescence, or other factors. Such provisions will be reflected in the budgets or forecasts to the extent anticipated at the time the budgets or forecasts are prepared. When a budget or forecast has been approved by the Executive Committee, the provisions will be entered on the books in accordance with the budget unless changes are approved by the Committee.

D. In sections II and III following, the terms "cost" and "market" are defined, and detailed procedures are outlined for the valuation of the company's inventories in conformity with these definitions. These procedures have been developed by experience as being practicable and adequate for the purpose, and they should be followed consistently unless exceptions are specifically authorized by the Controller's Office. It should be borne in mind, however, that it is the basic definitions of "cost" and "market" which are governing in all cases; and if it appears at any time that, owing to unusual circumstances, the valuations obtained by the use of the standard procedures do not conform to these definitions, or if the procedures appear for any reason to be inadequate, the matter should be referred promptly to the Controller's Office, with a full statement of the facts.

E. Under the pooling methods used by the company in the valuation of inventories, it is possible to prepare condensed reports which will show in summary form the classifications of the inventories and the application of the valuation procedures. Forms for such summaries will be developed for the various plants, and the summaries will be submitted to the audit section of the Controller's Office for review before the inventories are recorded on the books.

II. Definition and determination of cost

A. Separation of material and converting costs. In the valuation of inventories at cost, the material and converting (labor and overhead) elements of cost will be separated.

B. Material cost. In general, the cost of material in the inventory at any date will be the actual cost of the most recent purchases prior to the inventory date. It will be determined by one of the two following methods:

1. *Individual material pooling.*—Under this method the total quantity of each item of material in all stages of processing will be determined, and the total cost of the item in the inventories will be the invoice value of the most recent purchases equivalent to this total quantity. Inbound freight will be added to the cost of certain designated major raw materials in accordance with established accounting procedures; other inbound freight will be charged to raw material stores burden accounts.

In determining the quantity of any material included in the inventory of work in process and finished goods under this method, allowance must be made for waste and shrinkage in processing.

2. *Group material pooling.*—Under this method raw materials will be classified into groups on the basis of character of material or character of finished product, and separate ledger control accounts will be maintained for each group. Materials will be charged into the raw stores accounts at standard cost, and the ratio of actual to standard cost of

each month's purchases in each group will be determined. The total material cost of the inventory of each group at any date will be determined as follows:

(a) The total standard material value of the inventories will be determined by multiplying the quantity of each item by the standard material cost per unit and totaling the resulting dollar amounts.

(b) The ratio of actual to standard cost of purchases in the last month preceding the inventory date will be applied to such portion of the total standard material value as is not in excess of the standard cost of the month's purchases, to determine the total actual cost of such portion.

(c) The similar ratio for the next preceding month will be applied to such portion of the remaining standard material value as is not in excess of the standard cost of that month's purchases, to determine the total actual cost of such portion, and so on, using the ratios for preceding months in inverse chronological order, until the total standard material value of the group has been covered.

Example: Total standard material value of inventory group, $500,000. Most recent purchases in the group:

Month	Standard cost	Actual cost	Ratio of actual to standard cost
December	$160,000	$120,000	75.0
November	250,000	200,000	80.0
October.	200,000	165,000	82.5

Determination of cost of inventory:

Month of purchase	Standard cost	Ratio of standard to actual cost	Actual cost
December.	$160,000	75.0	$120,000
November	250,000	80.0	200,000
October.	90,000	82.5	74,250
Total inventory . . .	$500,000	. . . .	$394,250

Where this method is used, inbound freight on certain designated major raw materials will be classified each month by inventory groups and added to the invoice value of the purchases for the month in the respective groups; inbound freight not so classified will be charged to the raw material stores burden account.

C. *Converting* (*labor and overhead*) *cost.* In general, the converting cost of work in process and finished goods will be the current actual cost at a normal volume of production, without loading due to idle time or excess plant capacity. Current actual costs will be determined by one of two methods:

1. *Item standards.*—Under this method each item in the inventory at each process will be valued at the current standard cost of converting from raw material to the state of completion at the inventory date, and each item of finished goods will be valued at the current standard converting cost of such item.

2. *Average group standards.*—Under this method the total inventory at each point of processing will be valued at the current standard cost of converting from raw material to such processing point; finished goods will be classified into groups, according to the character of the product, and the total quantity in each group will be valued at the current average standard converting cost for the group.

Under either of the above methods, if current standard converting costs have been recently revised, they should be approximately equal to current actual costs and should be acceptable without adjustment for purposes of inventory valuation. If standards have not been recently revised and recent experience indicates that actual costs are substantially different from the standards, owing to factors other than variations in volume, or if actual volume has varied substantially from standard volume over a long period of time, some adjustment to reflect differences between standard and actual cost may be necessary. In most cases the amount of such adjustment can be determined by an over-all estimate of the approximate difference between total standard cost and total actual cost.

The cost department at each plant will submit to the Controller's Office a brief statement concerning the standard converting costs to be used in inventory valuation, the relationship to current actual cost, and recommendations as to what adjustments, if any, should be made in the inventory valuation as standard to reflect actual cost.

D. Manufacturing supplies. In general, the cost of manufacturing supplies will be the actual cost of the most recent purchases prior to the inventory date. It will be determined by one of the two following methods:

1. *Item accounts.*—Under this method a separate account will be maintained with each supply item, and the actual cost of purchases and withdrawals (on a first-in, first-out basis) will be recorded in the account.

2. *Group pooling.*—This method is similar to the group material pooling method of determining material cost, described in paragraph B-2, above.

E. Consistency in classification and procedure. The procedure followed in determining the cost of each section of the inventories at each plant or warehouse shall be consistent from year to year, and no change shall be made in the classification or grouping of inventory items for cost determination without the approval of the Controller's Office, after discussion with the company's auditors.

III. Definition and determination of market

A. Definition of market. 1. In general, "market" for normal quantities in the inventory is defined as net realization value, i.e., average selling price less the current cost of any *uncompleted* operations of converting and selling.

(a) "Average selling price" means the weighted average of net selling prices, at the inventory date, to various classes of customers. "Net selling prices" shall mean those arrived at after deduction of trade and cash discounts and outfreight; the weighting of prices to determine the average shall be on the basis of the normal proportions of sales to the various customer classes, as evidenced by current sales records.

Exceptions shall be made to this rule in the following special cases:

(aa) If there are outstanding at the inventory date sales commitments which are firm as to quantity and price, the average selling price of such commitments shall be used in determining the market valuation of an equivalent quantity of inventory.

(bb) If selling prices are reduced between the inventory date and the date of closing the accounts, or if a reduction is in prospect at the date of closing the accounts, the reduction may be reflected in the average selling prices, to the extent that it is applicable to the quantities included in the inventories. Decision as to the course to be followed under these conditions will be made by the Controller's Office, after discussion with the company's auditors.

(b) "Cost of selling" for the purpose of this procedure includes cost of advertising, field selling, shipping, billing, and collecting, but does not include administrative expenses other than billing and collecting.

2. If the quantities of any material included in the inventories are in excess of normal requirements, the market for such excess quantities shall be current replacement cost, i.e., the current market quotations for the particular material, in the quantities in which usually purchased, plus inbound freight and handling if the regular accounting procedures provide for the addition of these items to the cost of the specific material in question.

B. Determination of market value. 1. Except for excess or obsolete stock or items which are regularly sold at a loss, market or realization value as above defined will be lower than cost only when, for a period prior to the inventory date, selling prices have declined more rapidly than book costs, or book costs have risen more rapidly than selling prices, and the change in the cost-selling price relationship has been sufficient to eliminate the profit margin. The accountant responsible for the valuation of the inventories shall make an examination of the trends in selling prices and margins in major products or product groups, the book costs of major raw materials, and actual costs of labor and overhead during the three or four months immediately preceding the inventory date, and shall submit to the Controller's Office a written report outlining the scope of the examination, the facts disclosed, and his opinion as to whether the market value of all portions of the inventories is clearly above cost or whether a detailed determination of market value should be made for any portion. The decision as to the extent of the detailed determination of market value required will be made by the Controller's Office after consultation with the company's auditors.

If a detailed determination of market value is required for any portion of the inventories, the determination shall be made by one of the methods outlined in paragraphs 2 and 3 below, depending on the method used in the determination of cost.

2. In those portions of the inventories where material cost is determined by individual material pooling (as described in paragraph II-B-1 above), it is possible to classify the finished product into a few broad groups and to determine an average selling price and average costs of various converting and selling operations for each group. In such cases the difference between the cost and the market value of the inventory of each group shall be computed by assuming the complete conversion and sale of all items in the inventories in finished form and comparing the total cost on this basis with the total sales value. A more complete description of this procedure is as follows:

(a) The total pounds of finished product which will be manufactured from the raw materials and work in process in the inventories of each group shall be computed, allowing for waste factors based on standards or on current experience, and this poundage shall be added to the poundage of finished goods in the inventories of the group to determine the total "finished pounds equivalent" of the group.

(aa) If any item of raw material or work in process is used in more than one finished product group, the quantity of such material in the inventories shall be allocated between the finished product groups on the basis of current processing schedules at the inventory date.

(bb) If more than one raw material is used in the manufacture of any finished product group, the computation of finished pounds equivalent for the group shall be based on the inventory poundage of the major raw material (or the normal poundage, if the inventory poundage is in excess of normal, as provided in paragraph III-A-2, above).

(cc) When subparagraph (bb) is applicable, the inventory quantity of any material other than the major raw material may be more or less than the quantity required for the finished pounds equivalent. If more than required, the excess over requirements shall be excluded from the calculation and valued at replacement cost, as per paragraph

III-A-2; if less than required, the cost of the additional amount required shall be considered as a cost of completing the conversion of raw material and work in process into finished goods, as provided in paragraph (b) immediately following.

(b) The total cost of completing the conversion of raw materials and work in process in the inventories of each group into finished product and the total cost of selling the finished pounds equivalent of the inventories of the group shall be computed. This total cost of completing the conversion and sale of the inventories of the group shall be added to the inventory cost of the group (excluding inventories in excess of normal quantities not included in the calculation of finished pounds equivalent) to determine the total final cost (material, converting, and selling) of the finished pounds equivalent.

(aa) In determining the cost of additional materials required to complete conversion (see subparagraph (cc) of paragraph (a), above) the unit purchase cost of the additional quantities required shall be assumed to be, first, for quantities covered by outstanding purchase commitments, the average cost of such commitments, and, second, for quantities in excess of such commitments, the replacement cost at date of inventory, as defined in paragraph III-A-2, above.

(c) The total net sales value of the finished pounds equivalent of each group shall be computed by multiplying the equivalent pounds by the average net selling price of the group.

(d) If the total net sales value of the finished pounds equivalent computed as per paragraph (c), above, is higher than the total final cost, computed as per paragraph (b), no adjustment to market is necessary; if it is lower, the difference between the two amounts shall be deducted from the total cost of the inventories of the group (excluding quantities in excess of normal not included in the calculation of finished pounds equivalent); the result will be the market (realization) value of such inventories.

The calculation of market value under the foregoing procedure is illustrated by the accompanying example.

3. In those portions of the inventories where material cost is determined by the group pooling method, market value shall be determined on an over-all basis for each group. In general, a number of typical major finished products in each group shall be selected, the ratio of total realization value to total cost shall be computed for the material content of these products, and it shall be assumed that this same ratio applies to the material content of the entire group. A more complete description of this procedure is as follows:

(a) The selection of typical products to be used in the computation for each inventory group should be made so as to give a fair cross section of the different products in the group. Enough items should be selected to make up a substantial proportion of the total value of

INVENTORY VALUATION POLICY AND PROCEDURE
Example of determination of market value
(when cost determination is based on individual material pooling)

	Raw materials				Work in process		Finished goods		Total	
	A		B							
	Lb.	Dollars	Lb.	Dollars	Lb.	Dollars	Lb.	Dollars	Lb.	Dollars
A Inventory at cost	500,000	75,000	25,000	5,000	100,000	33,000	150,000	78,000	.....	191,000
B Deduct excess of inventory of material A over normal quantity	(200,000)	(30,000)	.....	.....	.....	.....	.....	.....	.....	(30,000)
C Add: additional quantities of material B required for finished pounds equivalent	.....	.....	25,000	4,000	.....	.....	.....	.....	.....	4,000
D Adjusted inventory at cost (A − B + C)	300,000	45,000	50,000	9,000	100,000	33,000	150,000	78,000	.....	165,000
E Waste factor	20 pct.	.....	16 pct.	.....	10 pct.	.....	.....	.....	.....	.....
F Finished pounds equivalent (D × [100 − E])	240,000	45,000	42,000	9,000	90,000	33,000	150,000	78,000	522,000	165,000
G Labor and overhead cost to complete conversion of raw material and work in process									.....	92,000
H Cost to sell finished pounds equivalent									.....	15,000
J Total final cost, finished pounds equivalent (F + G + H)									522,000	272,000
K Net sales value (av. selling price, $0.49 per lb.)									522,000	255,780
L Adjustment to market value (J − K)									.....	16,220
M Market value (excluding excess inventories of material A) (A − B − L)									.....	144,780
N Market value excess inventories material A—at replacement cost ($0.1350 per lb.)									200,000	27,000
O Total market value (M + N)									.....	171,780
P Reserve required to adjust cost to market (A − O)									.....	19,220

the group; in most cases it should be possible to cover 60 per cent or more of the total value of the group by selecting 15 to 20 per cent of the items.

(b) The total cost of the material content of the inventories of the selected products shall be computed as follows:

(aa) The total quantity of each material shall be computed, using the standard specification sheets for the various products to determine material content per unit of product.

(bb) The unit cost of each material shall be the average cost of the purchases of such material included in the computation of the actual cost of the group (as provided in paragraph II-B-2).

(cc) The total cost of each material shall be computed by multiplying the quantity determined as per subparagraph (aa) by the unit price determined as per subparagraph (bb); the sum of these amounts will be the total cost of the material content of the inventories of the selected products.

(c) The net realization value of the material content of the inventories of the selected products shall be computed in accordance with the definition in paragraph III-A-1, above. The converting costs used in the computation shall be the same as those used in the valuation of the inventories at cost; cost to sell shall be based on standards if available, otherwise on current percentages of actual selling cost to sales value. In some cases it may be possible to combine similar products or different sizes of the same product into subgroups, and use average converting and/or selling costs for each subgroup.

(d) If the total net realization value computed as per paragraph (c), above, is higher than the total cost, computed as per paragraph (b), no adjustment to market is necessary; if it is lower, the ratio of realization value to cost shall be computed and applied to the total material cost of the inventories of the entire group. The result will be the market (realization) value of the material element of such inventories.

IV. Entries for inventory adjustments

In order to reflect clearly in the accounts the nature of the various adjustments which are made as the result of the physical count and valuation of the inventories at the end of the fiscal year (or other inventory date), the inventory adjustments shall be shown on the books in four accounts, as follows:

Inventory adjustment—Quantity
Inventory adjustment—Converting costs
Inventory adjustment—Write-down to market
Inventory adjustment—Obsolescence

The final inventory summaries at the several plants shall be prepared so as to show in tabular form for each major inventory classification the book inventories in dollars before adjustment, the adjustments as detailed above, and the final adjusted inventories in dollars. Copies of these summaries shall be filed with the adjusting entries and in the permanent inventory file in the Controller's Office.

12 DEPRECIATION POLICIES AND METHODS

The depreciation problem is a perfect illustration of an expense—the using-up or consumption of an asset in the normal course of business. The apparent difficulty of the subject and the controversies which have raged around it are caused by the fact that the basically simple facts of depreciation must be handled under such a variety of situations. What seems correct for one situation looks improper for another; that which is good from the balance-sheet point of view seems unsatisfactory from the income-statement angle; the method that is right for management may not fit the income tax regulations; the technique which is eminently sensible for a large business does not fit the small one; the depreciation accounting pattern for a single asset becomes something else when that asset is one of a large group; what works under "normal" conditions is misleading when we run into price changes or inflation.

Under these varied and multiplex conditions it has been difficult to write a single definition or to visualize a simple illustration which would satisfactorily serve all cases. The authors feel that a frank recognition of the complexity (not difficulty, but complexity) of the problem is the most important step in its solution. If this recognition is combined with a sound general statement of the purpose or purposes of depreciation accounting, it should be possible to work out a fairly satisfactory series of solutions for the more typical situations encountered in business.

Valuation or cost distribution

Probably the greatest single step which accountants have taken in learning how to handle the depreciation problem has been the recognition that depreciation should not be thought of in terms of asset valuation but rather in terms of the assignment of the cost of the asset to the periods of its life. Under ideal conditions—that is, where all the facts are clear, the estimates correct, and the price level stays put—the two results would, of course, be complementary—the correct assignment of costs to periods would ideally leave significant values at the intervening balance-sheet dates. The trouble is that the practical conditions are far from ideal. The attempt to accomplish both results becomes impossible in many cases and leads only to complete confusion. The better thinking, which agrees virtually to ignore the valuation aspect and to concentrate on a satisfactory distribution of the cost, has a fair chance of accomplishing its purpose.

This approach to depreciation received the official sanction of the Committee on Terminology of the American Institute of Certified Public Accountants in its *Accounting Terminology Bulletin*, No. 1 of 1953 which approved the following definition:

Depreciation accounting is a system of accounting which aims to distribute the cost or other basic value of tangible capital assets, less salvage (if any), over the estimated useful life of the unit (which may be a group of assets) in a systematic and rational manner. It is a process of allocation, not of valuation.

Depreciation for the year is the portion of the total charge under such a system that is allocated to the year. Although the allocation may properly take into account occurrences during the year, it is not intended to be a measurement of the effect of all such occurrences.

This definition was a step forward, but it leaves a great deal of thinking still to do when it says that the cost is to be distributed in a *systematic* and *rational* manner. "Systematic" is fairly clear. It means not haphazard, not random, but following some consistent pattern in successive years. The word *rational* is less helpful, in that it gives no clue as to what the criterion of rationality is to be, though it may be very useful if it gives a steer in the direction of the basic logic of accounting, which has been used at various places previously in this book.

The logic of accounting for depreciation

An attempt to apply the first major premise—clear portrayal of the objective facts—to the depreciation situation does not give much help. The original cost of the asset is an objective fact which can be shown, but, beyond this, it is precisely because the objective facts are so hazy that we are in trouble. What is the value of the asset at the end of each period? What is its total life, its scrap value, its replacement cost, its pattern of productivity, its maintenance history? If someone could give the accountant all these data as objective facts, he would have no trouble in setting up a clear debit and credit portrayal of the asset's life history. Actually, the only real fact available when the accountant establishes his accounting plan for the asset is its cost; everything else he would like to know is in the realm of estimates whose degree varies from solid to extremely shaky.

As a pedagogic device in an elementary course in accounting, we can say to the students, "Here are all the facts with regard to an asset's life history. Your problem is to set up the accounts and to make entries therein to reflect these facts clearly." This may be a useful teaching method, also useful in focusing attention on certain factors for discussion purposes, but it is not the approach which will yield results under practical accounting conditions.

Does major premise No. 2. give any more hope in determining what is rational in the depreciation area: " . . . that method is correct which will be most useful to management—which will lead to the wisest management decision—which will guide management most effectively and safely"? This thinking has more promise. It should be noted that, while the valuation aspect is associated with the motive of clear portrayal, the distribution of cost aspect is aimed at the management use of the figures and thus falls within the second major premise. If we can trace the impact of the various methods of depreciation accounting to the point of resulting management action, we may get some real light on the propriety of the methods. For instance (though these may be oversimplifications), a depreciation method which would lead to unwise dividends, distributing cash which was later sorely needed to replace the asset, would be a poor method. A depreciation method which matched the asset costs distributed period by period against the revenues produced by the asset, thus aiding management to make correct judgments regarding operating efficiency, would be a good method. The assertions behind these statements, as to what the management impact of the method would be, are minor-premise assertions and might, of course, be challenged in the actual arguments. The point made here is the fact that in each case it is the effect upon management action, good or bad, that is the important criterion upon which the method is to be judged.

The cost to be depreciated

Generally speaking, the cost of any capital asset is the amount paid to the previous owner in consideration of the transfer of title, plus such further expenditures (transportation, setting up, etc.) as may be needed to prepare the asset for service. In some cases, the identification of the asset itself may be quite a complex task. If a special concrete foundation has to be built to allow a heavy machine to be accommodated, the foundation may properly be regarded as a part of the machine. On the other hand, the rebuilding of an entire section of the factory, even if occasioned by the purchase of the machine, may better be regarded as an improvement in the building. Similarly, special power connections for a single machine may be regarded as part of that machine, but a total rewiring of the plant which precedes the installation of the machine would be a separate asset.

The practical clue in these questions lies in the depreciation treatment to be given the incremental cost element. If its service life is effectively bound to the machine so that it will have no further use when this machine is discarded, then it should be added to the cost of the machine. If, on the other hand, the new floor or renovated wiring will still be of service to future machines when this one is gone, then its treatment as a separate asset or as an increment to the building will give a clearer portrayal of the facts. Depreciation on the wiring and floor could then be shown consistent with the accounting for the charge as an independent asset or spread over the remaining life of the building.

The acquisition of a new plant is a simple case if purchased outright or constructed on a lump-sum contract. If the business does its own construction, possibly with certain special elements on contract with outsiders but by the use of its own men and facilities for substantial parts of the job, the situation involves more careful attention to details, that is, it is more complicated; but the general rule that all necessary and normal expenditures are proper inclusions in cost is still a reliable guide for each item that must be judged. Consider, for instance, the architect's fee and related items, such as special consultants' fees regarding the underlying geologic structure, legal consultation with respect to zoning angles, etc. As long as these items are considered necessary by the management, they are properly included in cost. Special insurance premiums to protect the company during the construction period are perfectly normal and should be included as a cost. If no such insurance is carried, the payment of a few minor doctor and hospital bills for such injuries as might be expected in the job would be legitimate inclusions as necessary and normal. If the company failed to insure against some really serious hazard and got caught for a loss of a million dollars, the payment might be necessary, but it would not be normal for a construction job whose total cost had been estimated at only two or three million. This million-dollar payment is a loss and should be shown as such. It might be normal and even wise for the company to spend $10,000 on a grand opening party for the public when the plant is complete, but this expenditure is not necessary to the construction and, therefore, should not be added to the plant cost.

These illustrations are simple and rather obvious, but they should set the pattern for the interpretation of the meaning of "necessary and normal" for more difficult situations. In many instances, the practical answer to the disposition of minor, borderline items will be made on the basis of income tax impact. If the item is legally deductible as a current year's expense, there is no serious objection to treating it in that way. This is again a management choice regarding the assignment of a cost as between periods. The controller is in the position of advising management as to the immediate advantage of a few tax dollars saved against the possible disadvantage of distorted depreciation costs over the ensuing years. It is not always clear that the tax advantage lies in immediate deduction. During the years of periodically increasing tax rates, many millions were lost by business by exercising the options of taking deductions too soon. Very commonly, the management prerogative of making the decisions will be delegated to the controller, so that he is acting in his management capacity in making the decision rather than in his pure controller function.

Supplies, small tools, minor improvements

These topics present a range of borderline problems in the depreciable cost versus immediate expense area. Many small items which are commonly and sensibly treated as expense when purchased would be clear cases of long-lived assets if we were to follow the objective facts closely. The financial vice president may clip coupons for twenty years with a pair of scissors which were charged to office expense when acquired.

Small tools out in the plant range from the hand file, which is used a dozen times and discarded, up to electrically powered tools, costing hundreds of times as much as the hand file and sometimes lasting for years. The vast majority of such items are charged to expense when acquired. In the medium-sized or large business, this results in a reasonably smooth stream of expense. If the resulting undervaluation of assets is considered material, a compromise can be made by carrying an asset account for Small Tools at an amount which approximates half the original cost of small tools typically on hand at any one time. Current purchases would be charged to expense, and the Small Tools account would be kept at a fixed amount unless expansion of the plant clearly indicated an increasing quantity of tools actually on hand.

The expenditure of money on an asset in such a way that it becomes longer-lived or more efficient is a clear case of adding to its value. The increase in efficiency may take various forms—greater speed, better product, lower power cost, more nearly automatic operation (less attendant labor), less upkeep. Often the physical change made is either the addition of a new part or the substitution of a better part for an original element, but the concept of improvement is not limited to expenditure on physical parts; the overall effect is the important consideration. It is clear that an improvement should be accounted for as an addition to the book value of the asset and depreciated henceforth as a part thereof over the remaining life of the asset. Actually, this discussion of improvements could well have been included under the heading of cost of assets.

On the other hand, a great many improvements are made in connection with current repairs, and it is very difficult to break the total cost of the job into that part which is improvement and that part which is current expense, Under these conditions considerable expenditure which is actually improvement is never recognized as such but is blanketed into current repairs expense. While this process might be regarded as a violation of the true-portrayal premise, it is justified for actual borderline cases on the grounds of the difficulty of full portrayal. Beyond the borderline cases it must be regarded as a management option, concerning the assignment of cost to the present period rather than to spread it.

The three issues raised here—supplies, small tools, and minor improvements—are difficult to handle if we try to stick to the principle of clear portrayal of the objective fact. The reasoning behind these illustrations is not directly under major premise No. 2. but under an essential corollary premise which arbitrates between the first and second major premises and can be phrased as follows: "If two methods of accounting give substantially the same results in terms of management effectiveness, the simpler method is the better."

Supplies, small tools, and improvements could all be accounted for under an exact interpretation of the clear-portrayal major premise. But what a nuisance it would be to set up depreciation accounting for scissors, files, and every small improvement. The accountant who did so could take great pride in his correctness under major premise No. 1. but he should be fired for wasting company time.

Certain safeguards can be built into specific accounting situations to head off the dangers of misrepresentation without the complications of full portrayal. The use of the Small Tools account has already been mentioned. The period adjustment for deferred expenses can be used to embrace the undepreciated value of the vice president's scissors as well as the measure of unconsumed coal in the bins and prepaid insurance. In all these measures, the controller will be guided by his knowledge that, in general, there is greater danger in overstating asset and income figures than in understating them. This conservative principle itself comes from following through to the management action point a host of possible differences. We do not accept the proposition that the more conservative of two methods is *always* correct, but experience certainly indicates a clear presumption in favor of the more conservative answer in the truly borderline cases.

The depreciation model

The discussion of the several methods of depreciation accounting and of the adjustments of any method to varying circumstances can be carried on most clearly against a hypothetical case or model of depreciation under simple or ideal conditions.

Assume the conditions as follows: Machine #62, which cost $24,700 on January 1, XX01, has a known salvage value of $700 and a known life of 12 years. The company owning this machine has numerous other machines of substantial value of various ages. The company manufactures a successful competitive product, has no pronounced seasonal fluctuation, is under no particular financial pressure, and expects to stay in the same business indefinitely. The years XX01 to XX12 were distinctly free of inflation or the threat thereof. Under these conditions, the accountant figures depreciation on a straight-line basis as $2,000 per year [(24700 — 700) ÷ 12]. The books are closed annually, the depreciation being debited to Manufacturing Expense–Depreciation on Machinery and credited to Machinery–Allowance for Depreciation, which account is shown in the chart of accounts and in all balance sheets as a contra to the asset account Machinery Cost. Since machine #62 was purchased and put into operation on January 1, there is no problem of fractional years' depreciation. A card record is set up for machine #62 as for every other machine. The detail on the cards reconciles with the general ledger control accounts. The annual depreciation entry is made on 12 consecutive December thirty-firsts. The Allowance for Depreciation stands at $24,000 on December 31, XX12, when the machine is scrapped and immediately sold for $700 cash. The entry for the scrapping and selling would be:

```
Cash . . . . . . . . . . . . . . . . . . . . . . . . . . . . .    $   700
Machinery-allowance for depreciation . . . . .     24,000
    Machinery-cost. . . . . . . . . . . . . . . . . . . . . . . . . . . . . . . . . .    $24,700
```

The placid, uneventful life of this machine allowed straightforward depreciation accounting. Variations from this accounting pattern can be visualized as brought about by the force of circumstances which deviate from the ideal ones set up for the model. Each variation should be seen as an attempt by the accountant to interpret the changed circumstances to management so that management will make the necessary adjustments in its thinking. The aim must be to produce such figures and reports that any decisions conceivably affected will be wise in light of the changed circumstances.

Adjusting for missed estimates

Estimating the life and residual values of assets is a necessity in the calculation of depreciation. The controller cannot possibly have the sometimes extremely technical knowledge necessary to make these estimates for the wide variety of assets of modern business. He should be entirely frank about going to any and all informed sources for this information. The company's own experience with similar assets is a basic source for standardized types of equipment but is of obviously limited value in the light of rapidly changing technology. The company's own engineers are the best-qualified source for many estimates, but the controller must learn to watch for their individual slants toward overoptimism or overconservatism.

The search for the proper life estimate must consider both the physical factors of structure, maintenance, and degree of expected use of the asset and the more elusive economic factors of obsolescence and inadequacy. The relation of the two sets of factors is a delicate one. In the past it has been common to assume that the physical factors could be estimated more certainly than the economic factors. This assumption was usually carried to the point of setting up the life estimate of the asset on the basis of the physical factors only, with obsolescence treated as a special situation when it actually caused the discarding of the asset. A variant of this attitude was to set up a general reserve for obsolescence not related to particular assets and intended to smooth out the impact of the actual charges for obsolescence as they became necessary.

Actually, few assets live out their full physical lives under modern conditions. In fact, the impact of obsolescence can be estimated and the depreciation can be computed on the basis of the probable life of the unit, whatever the expected cause for its termination. If specific assets must be scrapped before even these conservative life estimates have run, there will be the familiar adjustment of "Loss on Retirement of Plant Assets" which, when it becomes more than nominal, is actually the loss caused by unforeseen obsolescence.

On some types of assets—automotive equipment, for instance—the scrap or residual or turn-in value can be estimated with some degree of assurance. For many other types, the scrap estimate is even more of a guess than the life. Add the fact that there is frequently a cost of removal, which would also be difficult to estimate some years in advance, and it becomes evident that the tendency to use a zero scrap estimate is quite realistic.

As the life of an asset progresses, an occasional restudy of the estimates should be made. When it becomes evident that the original estimates were significantly wrong, some adjustment is in order. The most common adjustment is to disregard the errors of the past and to write off the remaining depreciable value over the new estimate of the remaining life. If the reestimated asset life is shorter than the original, this will result in a stepped-up depreciation for the remaining life of the asset. If the reestimate is longer than the original, the depreciation will be less than previously. Any significant change in the estimate of residual value can be considered in the recalculation. Under reasonably stable conditions, the increases and decreases in depreciation caused by these adjustments will tend to balance, and, insofar as this is the case, the question may well be asked whether there is any point in making the adjustments at all. The answer will depend on the circumstances.

If, for instance, the increases happened to be largely in certain departments and the decreases in others, the proper adjustments, while leaving the company-wide costs the same, might make a difference in departmental costs which would be significant. To rule on this intelligently, the controller would have to visualize the influence of the changed depreciation all the way through to its allocation to product costs. If the final effects on product costs were really insignificant, there would be no argument for making the changes under major premise No. 2. Making changes under these conditions would be no more than a harmless and pleasant exercise under major premise No. 1, but it would be a violation of the corollary premise, which favors keeping things simple.

If, however, the reestimates tended to run heavily in one direction, whether concentrated in certain departments or not, there would be a net effect on company-wide costs of production on the net income, and on the income tax position. In this case there is real pressure to make the adjustments.

In recent years, many businesses have been using life estimates prepared by the Internal Revenue Service (IRS) in Revenue Proceeding 62–61. These "guideline lives" were, of course, prepared mainly for tax purposes; many firms have found them good for book depreciation calculations as well. They are generally realistic, and may enable a manager to assess with some accuracy the life of an asset type which the company has not previously owned.

The guidelines are divided into four groups: general, nonmanufacturing, manufacturing, and a specialized group for assets used in transportaiton, communication, and utilities. Within each group there are between five and thirty classes, and the life expectancy of each is provided. For example, Group I Class 4 assets happen to be buildings, with lives ranging from forty years for hotels to sixty years for grain elevators.

The tax rules provide, however, that the lives used in computing depreciation deductions must be in line with the economic facts. The IRS does not permit a concern to continue to use a five year life for a particular asset type if in fact the assets are being used for ten years, for instance. The approach taken to justify the life estimates is called the reserve ratio test. A table of values is provided against which the company may compare its own reserve ratio for a given asset class. The reserve ratio is the allowance for depreciation divided by the cost of the assets. Various tables are provided to take account of differences in growth rate, different methods of depreciation accounting, and the different life estimates. The reserve ratio test will show if the company has actually replaced its assets after the life estimated, on the average. If it has not, the IRS may insist on longer lives being used for the tax depreciation purposes.

A tax regulation to supersede the above rules will take effect for assets placed in service after 1970. The "Asset Depreciation Range" (ADR) system permits the businessman to choose any life for an asset between 80 and 120 percent of the guideline life. Once the election has been made for a given year, neither the taxpayer nor the Internal Revenue Service may alter that election. This means that differences of opinion between the taxpayer and the IRS will have no effect on the result. An additional provision of the proposed system is that the reserve ratio test as described in the preceding paragraph cease to apply for tax year 1971 and beyond. It is to the advantage of the majority of businesses to make use of the ADR system, as the system permits the shortening of the asset life for tax purposes. An effective interest-free loan to the company from the Treasury arises if the election is made. The proposed regulation does not affect in any way the right of the businessman to use the accelerated methods of depreciation which will be discussed later in this chapter.

Depreciation by the production method

The charging of depreciation as a function of its effect in producing revenue is the ideal behind all depreciation accounting. Under most circumstances this relationship is so tenuous as to be practically not ascertainable. However, conditions here and there exist which enable the accountant to charge depreciation in proportion to the physical measurements of production of specific assets. Generally, it may be assumed that the influence on revenue is in proportion to physical production, so that the "production method" of depreciation accounting becomes a very good method indeed.

The conditions needed for this method are two: the physical production of the asset must be readily measurable within each accounting period, and the total expected physical production during the asset's life must be reasonably estimable. These conditions will be more or less true of assets used in connection with the production of certain natural resources. A mine tipple may have a useful life strictly conditioned by the known body of ore which it is built to extract. If the tipple cost $100,000 and will be used to extract 2,000,000 tons of ore, it is entirely reasonable to distribute its cost to the years of its life on the basis of 5 cents per ton of ore produced each year. This is not, it should be noted, an attempt to write off depreciation in proportion to net income, which will be affected by many other influences also, or in proportion to gross revenue as such, but in proportion to the effect of the tipple upon gross revenue produced, which is probably closely in proportion to the physical production.

A lumber mill might evidence conditions appropriate for use of the production method. Its annual production will be known in terms of board feet of lumber produced, and its lifetime production may be determined by the accessible standing timber owned or controlled by the company.

The tipple, the lumber mill, and other assets used in the production of natural resources have their lives determined by the amount of the natural resource available. Certain other assets may have lives determined by and measurable in terms of their own physical capacities. For instance, a trucking company may have had enough experience with its heavy trucks, which haul earth, sand, and gravel in construction projects, to know that they should be traded in after a life of 2,500,000 ton-miles of service in order to keep overall costs at a minimum. If it has become the established policy to trade in trucks after this amount of service, the trucking company can depreciate its trucks on the basis of ton-miles hauled each period more reasonably than on any other basis. Since the heavy hauling business is related to the construction business, it will probably have a highly variable volume of hauling in successive periods. The straight-line basis or any other time-measured basis would result in extreme variations in unit costs, which would be misleading if taken seriously by management.

Airplane motors are commonly depreciated in proportion to "hours in the air." Again the necessary data are easily available, so that this constitutes an ideal depreciation base for this asset.

While the circumstances permitting the use of the production method are not very common in a typical business, there is little doubt that the alert controller may find instances where this method is applicable which would be unlikely ever to occur to an outsider. The results of the method are so near to ideal that it ought to be used wherever feasible—probably much more than it is actually currently used.

Depreciation and deferred maintenance

Generally, the degree of adequacy of expected maintenance is one of the factors to be considered when estimating the life of an asset. Where obsolescence is expected to terminate the asset's useful life, this is much less important, and maintenance becomes a matter merely of keeping the asset in going condition rather than a factor in its total life span. Maintenance in the great majority of cases is considered merely a current expense to be charged to the account of the period in which the repair is made. This in itself is a concession to simplicity. Actually, the expense occurs when the wear and tear takes place and not when the repair is made. Since it would be extremely difficult to gauge normal wear and tear except as a function of the repair and since "current repairs" follow current wear and tear quite closely, the usual method is justified under the keep-it-simple corollary premise.

Out of this simple repairs accounting there grows a problem which has interesting theoretical overtones; that is the problem of "deferred maintenance." Assume that a business which normally spends $100,000 per year in maintenance is prevented by exceptional business activity from spending the usual amount during the last half of a fiscal year so that the total spent is $30,000 short of the usual $100,000. If nothing is done about this, the net income of the year will show a $30,000 fictitious increment, and the following year, in which $130,000 will have to be spent, will show a corresponding decrease. How could this situation be handled to get a full portrayal of the facts within the limits of the accounting language? A debit to Repairs Expense and a credit to Allowance for Deferred maintenance with the Allowance regarded as a special contra to the asset account involved is the obvious answer. A fairly convincing demonstration of this interpretation can be made graphically. Any book-value line drawn to show the facts of depreciation is so drawn on the assumption that maintenance is proceeding normally. If this is true, then very minor fluctuations in asset value (or remaining asset cost, if you will) occasioned by wear or small damage which will presently be made good need not be shown on the chart. In other words, the depreciation curve shows merely that loss in value which is *not* made good by current repairs. If, now, we violate these conditions by neglecting current repairs appreciably, the smooth depreciation line no longer tells the truth and should be shown to take a slightly greater drop during the period of neglected maintenance as in Figure 12–1. This drop would be cancelled and the line brought back to its regular position when the deferred maintenance was finally made up in the next period.

Notice that Figure 12–1 tries to show the objective facts as lines in a chart. The use of the special allowance for deferred maintenance shown as a contra to the asset shows exactly the same relationship in debit and credit terms. Both these devices are aimed at "clear portrayal of the objective facts," simply the application of the first major premise. The argument might also be made that the setting-up of the allowance before closing the books is desirable because the debit to expense will keep $30,000 out of surplus, thus restrict dividends, and thus make the cash available when it is needed in January and February for the extra slug of maintenance costs. This argument, under major premise No. 2., is a case in which clear portrayal and management usefulness coincide perfectly. If the debit to maintenance expense on the estimated basis were deductible for tax purposes, there would be perfect agreement all around!

Depreciation and extraordinary maintenance

In certain instances, it may be reasonable, from a managerial point of view, to account for maintenance costs other than by simple expensing

Figure 12-1
GRAPHIC PORTRAYAL OF DEFERRED MAINTENANCE IN RELATION
TO THE DEPRECIATION LINE

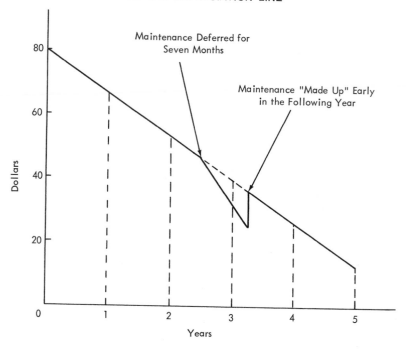

of the annual amount. If a company has a dominant asset or group of assets, and if it is known in advance that a large sum will have to be spent to refurbish that asset at some time in the middle of its normal operating life, a special accounting approach may give more meaningful measurements of success.

The method involves the annual transference of an appropriate credit to a reserve account, with a corresponding charge to current operations. In due course, the expenditure may be charged against the reserve, and any expenditure excess charged to the asset account for depreciation in subsequent periods.

Effectively, this method will reduce earnings in the years prior to the major repair and increase the earnings of the year of the repair, relative to the earnings which would be reported under the more conventional method of expensing upon incurrence. The method suggested would also diminish the earnings of the years following the major repair because of the higher depreciation charge. This smoothing of income would present the results of operations more clearly and in a manner more likely to lead to sound decisions than the conventional method. However, it should only be used in cases when the need for the major refurbishment is definitely known in advance, and when the amount of the expenditure can be assessed with reasonable accuracy at the date of acquisition.

Depreciation "methods" compared

Except for the special excursion into the advantages of the production method, the discussions of depreciation to this point have assumed the use of the basic straight-line method. Other methods which have been proposed and are in use can best be examined by comparing them with the straight-line method. As implied earlier in this chapter, th merits of the several methods should not be argued on the basis of correct portrayal of the objective facts but must, in general, be argued in terms of their various managerial effects. Most of these effects must be traced through product costs, the assumption being that the cost of the depreciating asset is recovered as cash through the sales of the product and that the sales price, and therefore, the total sales revenue are, at least in a general way, influenced by the dollars of depreciation cost which the accountant allows to flow into product. For any one product or any one period, this relationship is extremely tenuous, but the general assumption is presumably valid, and much discussion of depreciation policy is based on its essential reality.

Many discussions of depreciation and its financing effect take the less basic but still realistic approach that, regardless of any effect which depreciation may have upon the total revenue stream, the recognition of depreciation, either through the cost of product or as an element in administration and marketing expense, does cut down the showing of net income available for dividends and thus restricts the outflow of cash.

A still more immediate financial effect lies through the tax impact. Every dollar that can be justified as a deduction saves the corporation about 50 cents in tax money. In other than corporation business, the tax effect varies with the top tax bracket to which the taxpayer is subject. Since the total tax deduction is limited to the total cost of the asset, the different depreciation methods merely shift the years in which the deduction is made. Insofar as the deduction is made in earlier years rather than later, this "saves interest," but, more than that, it "puts the taxpayer into possession of funds" at an earlier date and thus increases his flexibility of financial management. The actual tax-saving argument is sometimes shortsighted, but the saving of interest and the increased financial flexibility are actual and constitute the real pressures behind depreciation accounting. The management-minded controller goes along with management on these points, but he does have the added responsibility, which he alone can fully take, of protecting management against the possible distortions of reported costs and misleading incomes which these pressures might engender.

Curved-line methods

Several of the curved-line methods have been respectable in accounting literature for a long time. The grandfather of these methods is the fixed percentage of diminishing value method, in which a percentage is calculated which, successively applied to the diminishing book value, will bring that book value down to the estimated scrap or residual value by the end of the estimated life. This method suffers the disadvantage of having to be calculated by a formula

$$(r = 1 - \sqrt[n]{\text{Scrap/Cost}})$$

requiring the taking of a root equal to the expected years of the asset's life. This computation is perfectly simple to perform on a calculator or a computer, of course, but went out of fashion in the precomputer era because of the cumbersome manual calculations it entailed. It has never come back into general use.

A method which gives closely similar results and which is easy to calculate is the "sum of expected life periods" (or sum of years' digits) method. The digits enumerating the expected years of the asset's life are added to produce a denominator. The years' digits taken in reverse order are used as numerators for a series of fractions which are applied to the depreciable value (cost minus estimated scrap value) to produce a series of dollar amounts which are the respective years' depreciations.[1]

A method specifically eligible for federal income tax returns is the use of an arbitrary percentage, not more than twice the straight-line rate, applied to the diminishing book value in successive years. Since most taxpayers want a large deduction, this method is virtually always used with twice the straight-line rate. Since this method would never write the asset down to zero, the additional option is allowed of shifting over to straight-line depreciation for the latter years of an asset's life.

The so-called annuity and sinking fund methods, which involve compound interest in the depreciation calculation, also produce curved-line book values, but they are of little interest outside certain regulated fields and are therefore omitted from the present discussion.

The three curved-line methods outlined above have in common the phenomenon of heavy early-year charges to depreciation, counter-balanced by lower charges in the later years. All three are effective in terms of income tax deferment and fund accumulation though in varying degrees. An additional, independent argument is often made for

---

[1] This method is easier to illustrate than to describe. For an asset costing $10,000 with a ten-year life and a $300 scrap value, the calculations would proceed as follows: $1 + 2 + 3 + 4 + 5 + 6 + 7 + 8 + 9 + 10 = 55$. The first year's depreciation would be $10/55 \times \$9,700$, or $1,763; the second year's depreciation would be $9/55 \times \$9,700$, or $1,587; the tenth year's depreciation would be $1/55 \times \$9,700$, or $176. After booking the tenth year's depreciation the book value would equal the estimated scrap value.

these methods as follows: Since, on any specific asset, maintenance costs tend to increase as the asset ages, it may be well to take heavier depreciation in the earlier years while maintenance is light, in order to even out the total costs of using the asset over the years of its life. The parallel between this thinking and the argument for the spreading of specific heavy maintenance items is clear. Practical judgment rendered on this argument for the curved-line methods is also similar to that for the maintenance allowance. For the relatively small business, with few but costly assets, the argument for balancing depreciation against maintenance might be significant, whereas for the somewhat larger business, whose depreciating equipment is of well-distributed age groups, it is rather unlikely that this balancing will change overall results appreciably. A practical consideration in favor of the curved-line methods is to get the book value down early, so that the shock of unexpected obsolescence will not be so great if it does happen where it was not taken into consideration in determining the estimated life of the asset. Again it is the controller's responsibility to visualize the effects of the several methods in terms of their materiality to management.

There is no right and wrong as between these methods and between them and the straight-line method which can be judged under major premise No. 1. The curved-line methods approach the objective fact of the resale value in the case of many assets, but that can hardly be considered an argument in their favor, since the whole background of depreciation accounting is the normal, going-concern concept under which the resale value of plant assets is of no significance. Another objective fact which can be ascertained for some assets and is sometimes brought into the discussion is the curve of technical or engineering efficiency. Especially in discussions of appraised value, the technical ability of an asset to perform its function is often brought up. For some assets, the input–output relationship can be measured at different points in the asset lifetime. Kilowatts per ton of coal for a power plant or miles per gallon of gas for a truck may be a measure of the technical condition, but the attempt to follow such physical measures as depreciation is obviously beside the point. Where the portrayal of objective facts is not a guide, the controller falls back on the management effect as the criterion of good accounting.

Composite method

The methods described and discussed were all in terms of application to single assets, and that is highly desirable in getting at the important relationships involved. Ideally, it would follow that the actual accounting record should be set for each significant unit, so that its complete life history to date and its present status would be shown. This, in fact, is exactly what is done by many firms.

There are, however, circumstances in which such complete item accounting would be unnecessarily detailed and in which great savings can be made by certain composite records for similar items. For instance, it would be obviously silly for a telephone company to set up a detailed record for each one of its many thousands of line poles. The first degree of concession to practicality would be a batch accounting system in which an account would be set up for all the poles installed at one time on a certain line. Further extension of the batching idea would be to set up an account for all the poles installed in one year in each accounting area, and still further extension would be to group all the poles of all ages in one account. At this point the accountant would have to do some careful planning to reflect the depreciation properly. The company's experience with respect to the useful life of poles of each description would give the basic information. While the lives of individual units may vary considerably, it has been found that averages can be worked out which are a reliable guide. It should be noted that the retirement of a unit under such composite accounting does not result in an accounting loss or profit, the assumption being made that the retired unit was fully depreciated in each case. For units retired at an actual age less than the estimated average upon which the group depreciation rate was set, this means that a real loss is unrecognized, that the allowance for depreciation is debited for too high an amount, the undistributed cost of the asset group is understated, the net income for the period is too high. The assumption is made that these errors will be balanced by corresponding errors in the opposite direction when other units of the same group attain lives beyond the group average before they are retired. This assumption is justified only if the original estimates for the group were carefully made. Since actual physical experience and company policy with respect to retirements may change with the years, the controller using such group methods should make an occasional critical examination of assumptions behind the process and the actual results produced to assure himself that the figures reported are still reasonably in line with the facts.

Depreciation and the changing price level

The subject of changing price levels is much broader than that of its impact on depreciation, though this narrower phase is the one which most commonly forces its attention on the controller.

The most difficult aspect of depreciation policy has been left as the final topic of this chapter in the hope that the treatment given the less difficult topics might build up the necessary rationale to facilitate its consideration.

A thorough discussion of price-level change inevitably gets into the question of the nature of the measuring stick to be used. For the overall problem, the consensus is to use some general index, such as the United States Bureau of Labor Cost of Living Index. For the more specific problems involved in depreciation of plant assets, the use of a construction cost index or even, where available, the specified replacement cost of particular plant units may be indicated. In any case the controller should be cognizant of the possible different results under the use of different indexes and should adjust his interpretation of results accordingly.

The attack on the depreciation and price-level problem under major premise No. 1 is interesting. It is undoubtedly still an appealing approach to try to portray the "objective facts" of the situation as clearly as possible, even under the very difficult conditions of changing price levels. To bring the problem into sharp focus, let us try to see it as it applies in the case of our model machine #362 (with $24,700 cost, 12-year life, $700 scrap, purchase January 1, XX01). Assume a nice round 100 percent price increase during the 12 years of this asset's life. Even this apparently simple condition has a great number of variations, each of which we must consider in our study. The inflation might come in one or two of the first years of the twelve, it might all occur in the last year or two, it might come suddenly in the middle of the machine's life, it might occur as a gradual increase throughout the twelve years, or it might come in erratic spurts.

It should be called to attention that the clear-portrayal principle does not necessarily mean an attempt to follow the changes in the price level. The original cost is still a fact, and management might exercise its prerogative to ask for, or the controller might decide in favor of, the clear portrayal of the distribution of this cost fact. If this seems an arbitrary interpretation, reflect that, in any case, someone must select which facts to show in the accounts. The choice of the original cost as the significant fact rather than some aspect of the replacement cost at the end of each year is simply one of many possible choices.

Once the selection has been made, we can think in terms of clear portrayal of the chosen fact or set of facts, but the real problem before us is the making of the choice, and that can be done intelligently only in terms of the management usefulness of the resulting representations.

The full list of the impacts of this decision on management would be too long and varied to be cataloged. We can, however, select two or three of the most obvious and most important, as we have done in earlier discussions, and phrase our arguments in terms of these. The most basic concern is probably the effect on reported product costs. Second—and this effect is in part operative *through* the product costs—is the effect on financing. Third is the bearing that the decision may have on the judgment of top management as to the efficiency or success of lower echelons of management or of decentralized units.

To attack the easiest situation first, assume that a 100 percent increase in replacement cost as measured by a reliable index has occurred within the first year of life of our model machine and that the best judgment is that prices will remain stable henceforth. If product costs are to be used at all in setting selling prices or in determining sales policy, it would seem that they should reflect the inclusion of depreciation on the increased replacement cost. The setting of prices intelligently competitive with those of other producers who enter the scene after the costs of machinery have gone up, supports this view. Necessary judgements regarding alternative used of machine #62—the shift to a different product, for instance—should also be made on the basis of the replacement costs.

Possibly, some light can be thrown on this question even under major premise No. 3 (the social consequences criterion). What would be the picture from the social point of view if all producers of the competing product of machine #62 took their accounting costs seriously, and if half of them, or any substantial number of them, were pricing products on the basis of their low historical cost while the rest, who had purchased their machines after the price increase, priced their products on the basis of the 100 percent increased recent costs? This might conceivably drive those with the high costs out of the market, put all sales, at lower prices, into the hands of those with the older, "cheaper" machines at prices which recovered only the original costs. Would this be a desirable status of competition from an economic-social point of view? The ramifications are enormous, but the alternative situation of having all competitors on a reasonably similar and up-to-date basis with respect to capital costs seems to merit at least initial approval. The idea that this would make competition depend on the *essential* differences in costs rather than on the accident of the date of machinery purchases is the important consideration.

The more restricted viewpoint of the probable direct effects on finance over the period of the machine's life also seems to favor the recognition of the increased cost of the machine. Under the simple assumption that the increased cost came in the first year of its life and assuming further that competitive conditions permit the increase in the selling price of the products of machine #62 in response to its higher annual depreciation, it would be possible during the twelve years of its life to recover the total replacement cost out of increased sales, or, if selling prices cannot be increased, it might be possible to recover the increased replacement cost by the restriction of dividends out of income from other sources. These outcomes seem more desirable than the obvious alternative of finding the firm at the end of twelve years with only $24,700 of funds with which to replace the machine at a cost of $49,400.

Any argument such as the above is under the suspicion that its simple assumptions are all too simple. Actually, this high degree of abstraction is necessary to focus attention on the influence of the particular factor at issue. It is true that the bringing to bear of other elements which will be found in the full concrete situation may alter the findings, but, if the simple assumptions have been fairly made, the probability that added factors would alter the answer in one way is no greater than that they would alter it in another. Putting the same thought differently: An argument of this kind does not pretend to be conclusive for all concrete cases; it merely aims to ascertain the *directional pull* of the particular factors isolated for attention. This is the philosophy of abstraction against the background of accounting, controllership, and management. Whether the particular conclusion apparently approved by the writers is valid is not as important as that the technique of approach shall be well demonstrated.

Probably the top-management judgment is that of the stockholders regarding the general success of the operating management. What is the conceivable importance of the alternative showings of depreciation for machine #62 to this decision? If the firm is one of a lucky few who have bought major equipment just before a 100 percent price increase and if market conditions are such as to raise selling prices on the product to cover the higher depreciation for the majority of the competing firms, then, if our firm accounts for depreciation on the original-cost basis, its showing of profit will be higher than under previous normal conditions. This would lead stockholders to an unwarranted favorable conclusion regarding operating management success during the time when such conditions remained effective. If, on the other hand, selling prices did not go up to cover depreciation on the higher replacement costs, our firm with its depreciation on original cost would show normal profits at a time when it is really heading into the difficulty of not providing for replacements. Therefore, it seems that, for both the possible price-competitive situations, the stockholder judgment based on net income would be wrong. If depreciation were put on the higher replacement basis, the stockholder's judgment would be right for either price situation, i.e., "normal profits" if prices did increase to absorb the higher depreciation, or "poor profits," with the reason obvious, if prices did not increase to absorb the higher costs.

The second way in which inflation may strike into the life history of machine #62 is to occur very late in the period of its lifetime. After eleven years of stable prices, during which depreciation has been accounted for on the original-cost basis, the replacement cost suddenly goes up by 100 percent. It might be desirable to recognize this increase during the twelfth year for product-costing purposes, but it is quite evident that the overall effect on finance will be relatively small, since the recovery of the increased price will be confined to one year. To finance the increased replacement cost in this case, management will have to seek new investment funds or fall back on earnings which have been retained as a matter of general policy.

If the inflation comes suddenly at midpoint of the twelve-year period, recognition of the fact in production costs and resulting sales prices would succeed in recovering half of the increased replacement cost during the remaining six years but would still leave management the problem of finding $12,350 elsewhere than in depreciation funds. Recognizing the difficulty of this situation, management might *want* to raise selling prices high enough during the remaining six years to recover the entire increased cost of replacement, but the assumption of normal competition would presumably make this impossible. The remaining two cases—gradual or erratic appreciation during the lifetime of the asset—may be visualized as more complicated variations of the single sudden increase at the mid-point.

In all cases, if management *foresees* the increased replacement costs before the actual increase has happened, it may be well advised to increase the selling price of the product to the extent allowed by competition or to restrict dividends from any source of earnings to build up funds for the foreseen higher costs. These tactics, however, must remain in the area of general management or finance. Few controllers would care to recommend an actual accounting allowance for depreciation on *expected* appreciation of plant assets!

The American Institute of Certified Public Accountants has given considerable thought to the inflation question. Accounting Research Study No. 6, "Reporting the Financial Effects of Price Level Changes," was prepared by the Accounting Research Staff of the Institute in 1963. In that study, general adjustment of the accounts (including, of course, depreciation and asset accounts) by means of a general price index was recommended in preference to the piecemeal adjustment of specific assets. Disclosure of the adjusted accounts as supplements to the conventional annual statements was recommended. The study does not have any official force but was well received as a theoretical statement at the time it was issued. In 1969, however, the Accounting Principles Board (A.P.B.) of the Institute gave material impetus to the concept of price level adjusted accounting statements when it issued Statement No. 3, "Financial Statements Restated for General Price Level Changes." The statement does not have the force of an opinion of the Board, contravention of which would place a heavy burden of proof on the auditor. However, the statement does signify greater official recognition of the problem than has existed previously.

The statement expressed the A.P.B.'s belief that general price level financial statements were useful additions to the conventional statements but should not replace them. The Board recommended the GNP Deflator as a suitable index of price level change and went on to illustrate in detail how an adjustment would be computed.

SUMMARY

This chapter has dealt with depreciation policy and methods and with problems closely related thereto. Almost every facet of these problems must be considered in terms of Major Premise No. 2, that is, in terms of the management impact. The general discovery is that few questions can be dealt with as categorical rights and wrongs. The circumstances of the size and complexity of the business must always be considered in deciding what treatment will be proper for any event in the life of any asset. Behind everything that can be said on all the specific problems lies the great problem of changing prices and the unreliable dollar yardstick. All the topics in the chapter were treated both for their substantive values and for the opportunity they present for practice in the use of logical analysis.

Part III

Operational planning
and control

13 THE BUDGET: POLICIES AND PROCEDURES

What is a budget?

In common usage and even in professional usage, the word "budget" has various meanings and connotations to different persons. To the man in the street (or the woman in the home), budgeting generally means not spending, saving for some future purpose, sometimes specific and well defined, sometimes as vague as the traditional "rainy day" or as inevitable as the coming of old age. The core idea of planning for prudent financial management is present in even this simple concept, as it is in the more sophisticated concepts of budgeting. Most individual budgeters discover the two principles of choice: first, between alternative present choices and, second, choices on the time scale—now or later. Most commonly these choices must be considered by the individual against a fairly rigid total of income.

In the governmental budget, whether the unit is municipal, state, or federal, the basic emphasis is still on planning for prudent financial management, but the element of binding force of a legally adopted budget changes the pattern of thinking. The total of prudent expenditures in the government unit is limited by the erratically flexible taxing power of the unit—in the end, how much the taxpayer will stand for. Once adopted, the governmental budget becomes a matter of limiting expenditures in sometimes broad and sometimes very narrow appropriation categories, with the choice within the categories determined by administrators and with an intricate machinery of debits and credits to prevent overexpenditure.

In the business budget the fundamental purpose is still planning for prudent management, but here the rigidities of the fixed revenue total and of the legal restrictions on expenditures disappear, and both revenues and expenses can be planned with greater flexibility. Another new element which enters the picture is the causative relationship between expenditures and revenues, both as a whole and as between particular expenditures or groups of expenditures and particular revenues. The basic purpose is still prudential, now clearly visualized as the production of the highest long-run net income consistent with the broad constraints imposed by law and by company policies.

In the broadest sense no business has ever been without a budget. The old-fashioned "captains of industry," who would have nothing to do with such new fandangles as budgets, actually did a great deal of budgeting, some of it quite effective, in their heads. The need for budgeting is not something new; it is just that the growth and complication of modern business demand an ever more conscious and formal attention to the details of budgeting. It is also true, of course, that in the great majority of cases the careful study of purposes and the searching attention to detail are paying off in far more effective results.

In some companies budgeting is limited to one or more specific areas of operations to meet some particular need of the business. Perhaps the most common budgets of this limited type are those covering cash receipts and disbursements, operating expense control, and major plant and equipment expenditures. These limited budgets can serve useful purposes and often prove to be initial steps in the development of a complete budget procedure for all phases of the business. With the rapid advances in management techniques during the last twenty years, there are, today, probably few businesses of substantial size (say, over $25 million in sales) which do not operate with some form of overall budget.

How, then, can we define the complete business budget? Since the heart of the budgeting process is planning for profit, and since planning implies setting objectives, we can describe the budget as "a summary in financial terms of the performance objectives and plans established for all departments of the business." Perhaps a better definition, to emphasize the necessity for the coordination of departmental plans, is "a coordinated plan for the operation of the business, expressed in financial terms." The term "budgetary control" also implies a continuous follow-up after the budget is adopted, to check actual results against the plan. This is necessary so that management can take prompt action, either to correct deficiencies if results are falling short of the plans, or—sometimes of even greater importance—to take advantage of some profit opportunity not envisioned when the budget was prepared.

The controller and the budget

A great deal of the work of preparation as well as of administration of the budget necessarily involves dollar facts, records, the marshaling of figures, all of which are part of the controller's historic function.

In addition, the controller is often given specific responsibility for the budget leadership by law, board of directors' resolution, or administrative order. In most companies the actual budget work is organized in a section under the controller; but in other cases his responsibility may take the form of the chairmanship of a budget committee or still other forms.

Whatever the particular set-up for formulation of the budget, the adoption of the budget, in the sense of willing it into effect, is not the controller's responsibility but that of the line command. This may mean its formal approval by the board of directors, the executive committee, or the president. This is one of the fine lines of distinction helping to establish a clear concept of the controller's function.

General budget procedure

The technique of budgeting for modern business was first described in detail in J. O. MacKinsey's pioneer work, *Budgeting Control,* which was published in the early 1920s. The fundamental principles of this technique are the same today, although many modifications and improvements in detail have been developed as a result of practice and experience.

The steps in the development of the budget and its use as a tool for operational control and the part the controller plays in each of these steps are summarized briefly in the following paragraphs.

1. A fundamental requirement for effective budgetary control is the definition of individual responsibilities in the organization and the setting up of the accounting records to reflect the results of the activities of each responsible individual. This principle of "responsibility accounting" is the first axiom of formalized control.

    The definition of organizational responsibilities is, of course, the function of top management; the preparation of the accounting plan to reflect these responsibilities is the function of the controller. Very often the process of setting up an accounting plan on the responsibility principle will point up ambiguities in organization that need to be clarified if operating control is to be effective.

2. The first step in budgetary control, once responsibilities are defined, is to set performance objectives for each executive. This usually begins with a budget of sales revenue, broken down by product lines and/or by sales territories, to pinpoint the objective for each product line manager and field sales manager. This sales budget, when approved by top management, becomes the basis for a plan of production. Such a production plan involves planning the quantities and values of raw material purchases and inventories to be carried and the direct and indirect labor and other expenses in each

factory department. From this production plan the budgeted cost of goods sold is developed, with a breakdown by product lines, to conform with the breakdown on the sales budget.

In an integrated control structure, the objectives set for the various responsible executives, which are, in effect, the definition of management's near-term plans for operating the business, are converted into dollars, following the responsibility accounting set-up, and are summarized into the financial budget—that is, the budgeted profit-and-loss account and budgeted balance sheet for the period covered by the plans, which is usually the calendar or fiscal year.

The responsibilities of the controller in this initial budgeting process are:

a) To provide financial, statistical, and cost information on which to base operating standards and budgets;

b) To advise and counsel with the operating executives in the preparation of their plans and in the coordination of the plans of all departments; and

c) To establish procedures for the translation of the many elements of the operating plan into an integrated financial budget.

3. The next step is for management to review and analyze the budget, as a whole and in detail, to determine (i) whether it represents a sound operational plan—that is whether it yields an adequate profit and at the same time provides for future progress in conformity with long-range plans and objectives—and (ii) whether the individual assignments in the budget are reasonable and attainable. This analysis and review may lead to changes in details of operating plans or even to changes in basic operating policies for the period. The design of the product may be altered to make it more attractive or to reduce its cost; more efficient methods of manufacturing may be devised; research and development programs accelerated or retarded; allowances for selling expenses reduced or increased as part of a program to secure additional sales; or administrative functions rearranged on a more economical basis. This process of revamping the operating plan continues until the estimated profit is at the optimum level for the existing conditions, i.e., until it reflects the best obtainable balance between the need for immediate earnings and the necessity for development and expansion to insure the future progress of the business. The relative weight to be given in the plan to current earnings and future development is a matter for decision by the top management.

At this point in the budgetary process the controller's role is to evaluate, objectively and dispassionately, the soundness of the budget as an operating plan and the realism of the objectives and projected results, and to make constructive suggestions for modifications of the plan.

4. When the budget is finally accepted as a satisfactory operating plan,

each responsible executive knows what his assignment is, and management has a yardstick against which to measure actual results is guiding the business toward the attainment of its profit objective.

Here the responsibility of the controller is to provide all levels of management, from the president to the foremen, with prompt reports of variances from planned performance, and to assist the operating people by pinpointing problem areas and determining the causes of the variances.

5. A final and important element in effective budgetary control is provision for the continual appraisal of changing conditions, both within and without the organization, and the continual updating of operating plans, with the purpose always in mind of attaining the original objectives—adequate profit and progress toward long-range goals.

It should be understood that, as far as operating details are concerned—for example, the amount of a specific product to be manufactured in a given period of time—the budget serves only as a general guide, and operating decisions are made on the basis of reports on day-to-day changes in internal or external conditions which cannot be anticipated in the formal budget. When the cumulative effect of those day-to-day changes has a significant impact on budgeted profits, or on profit opportunities, a review and revision of basic operating plans are necessary.

In this phase of budgetary control, it is the responsibility of the controller (i) to recommend to management the ways and means of building this flexibility into the control structure, (ii) to act, as he does in the preparation of the original budget, as an advisor to the operating executives in the revision of their plans, and (iii) to coordinate and summarize the revised plans into financial forecasts in a form that will be practical and useful as a control tool.

One point that should be clear from this very condensed summary of the control process is that the accountant, in the discharge of his control functions, operates as a staff executive, without line authority. He does *not* formulate operating plans, he does *not* set standards, and he is *not* responsible for initiating corrective action—his role is that of reporter, analyst, and advisor.

Theory and practice in budgeting

In addition to his activities in the execution of the budgeting process, as outlined in the preceding section, the controller usually has the responsibility for developing, or at least recommending, many of the procedures that are followed in building up the plans of the operating executives and summarizing them into the final budgeted profit and loss statement and balance sheet. It is not the purpose of this discussion to describe all phases of budgetary procedures in detail, but simply to outline briefly the broad method of their application and to consider some of the practical problems involved. Most of these problems revolve around the question "How far does it pay to go in applying the logical, detailed, theoretical technique of budgeting in this particular situation?" Here the experience and judgment of the controller come into play. There is real justification for suspecting detailed forecasts which make a great show of thoroughness but are simply extrapolations of past performance and not supported by definite operating plans, with specifically assigned responsibilities. The controller should constantly be striving to extend the scope of the information—about both internal operations and the external environment—which is available to management as a basis for intelligent budgeting. He should also exert every effort to convince the line managers of the value of planning their activities in reasonable detail and using their plans to construct a budget that will be meaningful as a control tool. At any point in time, however, the form of budget and the procedures followed in preparing it should be geared to the ability and willingness of the organization to plan realistically and effectively.

Problems in practical budgeting

The following are some of the key points for consideration in this problem of practical budgeting:

1. How much time does it pay to spend in attempting to develop accuracy in sales forecasting? In how much detail should the forecast be prepared? Should it be in dollars only or in dollars and units? Broken down by a few major groups or in complete detail, by individual products?
2. Who should prepare the sales forecast—the controller or other inside budget officer, the general sales manager, or the field salesmen?
3. How shall the manufacturing cost of goods sold be budgeted? Shall the cost of individual products or groups of products be built up by units, or shall the estimate be based on overall ratios to sales or on costs per unit by product groups? Shall actual costs be budgeted, or shall standard costs be used, with the amounts of variances from standards budgeted? If the latter, how shall these variances be estimated?
4. What provision shall be made in the budget for losses due to obsolescence or shrinkage in the market value of inventories?
5. In estimating selling and administrative expenses, what allowances, if any, shall be made for fluctuations in expense as volume fluctuates?
6. In how much detail shall the cash budget be prepared? The balance sheet budget?
7. What period shall the budget cover, and how frequently and in how much detail shall it be revised?

8. Under what circumstances should the master budget, based on lines of functional responsibility, be supplemented by project or program budgets for the control of activities which cut across normal functional lines?

9. What can be done to secure the maximum cooperation of all levels of management in the execution of the budget?

Accuracy of the sales forecast

Some companies hesitate to attempt the preparation of a formal budget because they do not know how to go about making an accurate forecast of sales. Since the entire budget structure is usually based on the sales forecast, these companies feel that their inability to make such a forecast within a reasonable margin of error means that somehow their businesses are different and that the budget, however valuable in other situations, is not practical for them. Other companies refuse to be intimidated by this problem and spend a great deal of time and money in an effort to increase the accuracy of their sales forecasts. Economic services and charts, market studies, Washington letters, and various other sources of information are read and digested, and detailed studies are made of general economic indices, the volume of business and the cycles in the particular industry, and the trends in the company's own operations. In recent years, increasing use has been made of more refined statistical methods to organize available external economic data, project them into the future, and develop correlations with industry and internal company trends.

The degree of success attainable by these more advanced forecasting techniques will vary considerably, depending on the type of business and on competitive conditions within the industry. In a stable industry, where technological and product changes occur relatively slowly, a company which has a substantial share of the total market and has developed good sources of external intelligence can often, under normal conditions, forecast its sales, at least for a year or so ahead, within a range of 2 to 3 percent. At the other extreme, in a business in which there is a large element of fashion or fad in consumer acceptance, sales forecasts must necessarily be tentative estimates, subject to more frequent revision. The majority of businesses will fall between these two extremes, and there will be periods of uncertainty about general economic prospects when any sales forecast must be considered tentative, and operations must be planned accordingly.[1]

---

[1] For an excellent example of the successful use of statistical methods as an aid in sales forecasting in a medium-sized company, see *Statistical Sales Forecasting*, by Vernon G. Lippitt (New York, Financial Executives Research Foundation, 1969) Appendix A (pp. 255–262). The description of the organization required to develop the forecasts (page 261) illustrates the importance of balancing the cost of the forecasting effort against the benefits realized.

The inability to overcome the obstacles to accurate sales forecasting does not by any means nullify the value of the budget as a management tool. It simply means that in most cases the budget cannot be a rigidly predetermined plan but must be made flexible enough that it can be adapted to meet changing conditions. If a business can develop an apparent correlation between its own volume trends and the fluctuations of some external index, it has an extremely valuable aid in planning its operations; but even in such a case the management would be wise not to rely too completely on the accuracy of its forecasts, for some of these apparent correlations have been known to go suddenly very far astray as new and unforeseen factors appeared in the situation. The soundest policy is to determine what is a reasonable range of possibilities as to sales volume and to be prepared to operate anywhere within that range.

The required flexibility in the detailed planning of operations can be obtained by various controls collateral to the budget and not necessarily tied in with it—as, for example, the use of maximum and minimum limits on finished stock as an aid in production planning. Flexibility in the financial budget can be obtained by frequent revisions or by the preparation of two or more complete alternative budgets at different levels of volume; and for some departments of the business, it may be possible to construct a complete flexible budget, with expense allowances predetermined for every probable level of volume. Thus the budget, without pretensions to accuracy, serves as a base to which executive planning and thinking can be related and from which variations can be measured as conditions change. In making long-term commitments for new plant and equipment or for the development and marketing of new products, the possibility of variations in sales income must be recognized, and the decision as to how far to extend such commitments must be governed by the management's estimates of the risks involved and the strength of the company's financial position.

Responsibility for the sales forecast

Who should prepare the sales forecast? Many controllers or budget executives feel that from their knowledge of past sales trends and current plans they can prepare more accurate forecasts than anyone else in the management, and some companies operate on this basis. Psychologically, however, it is far better for the preparation of the forecasts to be the responsibility of the general sales manager; naturally, the advice and suggestions of the controller, based on studies of past operations, will be most valuable, but the more direct responsibility the sales manager assumes for the final figures, the more seriously will he be inclined to regard them as an actual plan of operation and the more earnest will be his efforts to attain or better the estimates.

Where an intimate knowledge of individual customers is an important factor in the sales forecast, as, for example, in a specialty business where sales are relatively few in number and large in amount, it may be desirable to extend participation in the preparation of the forecast farther down the line to the district manager or even to the individual men in the field. In a business serving a large number of relatively small outlets, such as the retail drug or grocery trade, for example, the participation of the field men is of doubtful value, since the general sales executive can usually form a much better opinion of broad trends from market information available to him and from the complete operating picture taken from the company's records. However, it is undoubtedly helpful psychologically to give the field men an opportunity to review their individual quotas and to discuss with them any suggestions or comments which they may offer.

Form of the sales forecast

The form of the sales forecast is a real problem in companies having a diversified line of several hundred or several thousand different items. In such a situation the only practicable forecast is often one based on broad product groupings, with subgroupings as required either for intelligent analysis of operations by the sales department or for factory planning. The groupings should be the same as those used in recording sales in the accounts or supplementary statistical records; the principles on which such groupings can best be determined have already been discussed in the chapter on "The Accounting Plan." If some overall unit of measurement, such as yards or tons, is available for each product group, even though the product is not strictly uniform, the budgeting of sales and the recording of actual sales in such units as well as in dollars will be very helpful in interpreting results by showing clearly the approximate effect of changes in selling-price levels as distinct from variations in volume. In interpreting such figures, however, it is necessary to be on the lookout for changes in the character of the yardage or tonnage within each of the various product groups.

In addition to the breakdown of the sales forecast into these product groupings, it is highly desirable to have some form of budget or quota for each individual field territory. These quotas may or may not agree in total with the forecast sales included in the operating budget; obviously, it will be helpful in keeping all executive thinking on sales and operating plans on a uniform basis if the quotas represent a breakdown of the operating budget, but there may be psychological or other reasons which make it desirable to use a lower or higher figure in the quotas for individual performance. Sales performance records or incentive plans are frequently based on such specially calculated quotas; sometimes a point system is used which gives greater credit to the salesmen for products which the management is anxious to push, so that the sales quotas may not even be expressed in terms of dollars.

Budgeting cost of goods sold

The technically correct procedure for budgeting cost of goods sold is to break down the sales forecast in detail into individual items to be produced and sold and to build up the estimated cost of these items on the basis of anticipated expenditures for material, labor, and overhead. Theoretically, the detail of production requirements which is obtained by breaking down a sales forecast can be used in actually planning factory operations and raw-material purchasing; but in most types of businesses the sales estimates which are included in the financial budget can be used for these purposes for only a very short period of time following the preparation of the estimates. The sales demand for individual items may fluctuate greatly, even if the overall sales forecast is reasonably accurate, and usually the budget estimate must be supplemented by frequent revisions at short intervals, or actual production scheduling and week-to-week purchasing must be done on the basis of collateral controls, such as maximum and minimum limits placed on stocks of finished goods and raw materials.[2]

The task of estimating the cost of goods sold for the financial budget can often be simplified without any real sacrifice of accuracy by basing the estimate on a budgeted ratio of dollar cost to dollar sales or, if overall unit measures are available and are used in the sales forecast, on a dollar cost per unit of sales. These ratios or unit costs are ordinarily based on past experience, modified by a knowledge of current changes in material or manufacturing costs and the competitive relationship of such costs to selling prices.

Use of standard costs in budgeting

In a business which has an extensive and varied line of products, the budgeting of cost of goods sold by these short-cut methods and the analysis of variances between actual and budgeted results are greatly facilitated if a system of predetermined or standard manufacturing costs is in use. Under such a system, standard costs of labor and factory overhead are used in the determination of cost of production and of cost of goods sold for the monthly entries on the books, and the differences between standard and actual costs are segregated in one or more variance accounts.[3] This makes it possible to budget the cost ratio or unit cost of each product or major product group on the basis of a

---

[2] See the discussion in Chapter 18 on "Inventory Control."

[3] This procedure is described more fully in Chapter 8, in the section on "Standard Cost Technique."

stabilized labor and overhead cost, without regard to the variances, and to budget the variances separately.

In budgeting cost of goods sold by this method, the budgeted cost ratios or unit costs can be based on the current actual ratios or costs, as shown by the monthly statements, with adjustments to reflect anticipated changes in material costs and, in the case of cost ratios, anticipated changes in selling prices. In budgeting variances, it is necessary to consider (1) the difference between budgeted production volume and the volume on which the standard costs are based; (2) differences between anticipated and standard wage rates, supply costs, etc.; and (3) anticipated variances from standard costs due to factory efficiency, management policy, or other factors. If the standard labor and overhead costs are broken down between variable and nonvariable elements—i.e., between those costs which vary with volume and those which remain relatively constant, irrespective of volume—there will be information available as to the nature and causes of actual variances during the months immediately preceding the budget period; with this information and a knowledge of any expected changes in operating plans and operating conditions, it is a relatively simple matter for the factory management to do an intelligent job of forecasting variances for the budget. If the breakdown of standard costs between variable and nonvariable elements is not available, the problem is somewhat more difficult; in such cases the variances can be budgeted by making a detailed estimate of the expenses which will be incurred for labor and factory overhead at the budgeted production level and then comparing the total of such expenses with the total standard labor and overhead cost of budgeted production.

In some cases it may be advantageous to extend the use of predetermined standards in budgeting to material costs as well as manufacturing costs. In a business where selling prices are slow to respond to changes in material costs, the ratios of standard material costs to selling prices for various product groups can be projected on the basis of current actual ratios, with adjustment for anticipated selling-price changes, and anticipated changes from standard material prices can be budgeted as a variance. This method is not suitable, however, if selling prices tend to follow material-cost fluctuations closely; in such cases moderate fluctuations in the level of selling prices and material costs may have little effect on gross or net profits, and the best procedure may be to budget material costs first and then use the current actual ratios of selling prices to material costs as a basis for budgeting selling prices. If radical changes in material costs, either up or down, are anticipated, the effect of inventory appreciation and depreciation must be considered in preparing the budget; this is discussed in the section immediately following.

The foregoing discussion does not attempt to cover all the problems involved in budgeting costs of goods sold; it is intended simply to illustrate how the procedures followed in this rather difficult phase of budgeting can be simplified and adapted to the conditions in each particular business.

Inventory adjustments

In many businesses one of the most troublesome operating factors to control and to budget is inventory depreciation. Every management, of course, tries to hold losses due to shrinkage in inventory values to a minimum, but, in industries where the market prices of basic raw materials fluctuate within wide limits, or where style is an important factor in the sale of the finished product, some losses of this kind are unavoidable. The problem of losses due to raw material price declines has been less acute in the inflationary economy of the last few years than it was prior to World War II, when wide price fluctuations were a common occurrence. The problem still exists, however, in a few industries, and it is an unfortunate fact that in such cases the losses due to shrinkage in a declining market are nearly always greater than the appreciation realized in a rising market. Business is usually good when prices are rising, making it necessary to increase inventories and purchase commitments in order to cover material requirements for the increased volume; and, unless the management is unusually fortunate in forecasting the exact peak of the price cycle, it is quite likely to find itself with inventories that are larger than normal when prices turn down. When the decline in material prices once gets under way, it is likely to be much more precipitous than the preceding rise and to be followed more closely by a similar trend in selling prices, so that the usual result is a net inventory loss over the cycle. In budgeting operations in a period of market inflation, therefore, it is certainly sound practice to make a careful estimate of the possible inventory shrinkage if material costs and selling prices recede from the budgeted levels to normal or even subnormal levels and to include such a provision in the budget.

The LIFO method of inventory valuation, which has been firmly established in accounting and (in the United States) in tax practice for the past twenty years, provides a technique for eliminating from stated earnings all or a part of the "paper profits" due to inventory inflation in periods of rising prices and the offsetting losses in periods when market prices decline. The industries most affected by raw material price fluctuations were among the first to adopt the LIFO method, but with the acceptance of "dollar pooling" techniques, described in Chapter 11, the use of the method is now available to almost all types of businesses. Where the LIFO method of inventory accounting is incorporated in budgetary procedures, any anticipated changes in material prices, wage rates, and overhead rates are reflected promptly in the budgeted cost of sales. This tends to exert pressure on the operating managers

(1) to move promptly to adjust selling prices, and (2) to give close attention to inventory management as costs rise above normal levels. In many cases the result is an improvement in aggregate profits over the cost-price cycle.

Losses due to style obsolescence, as distinguished from those due to fluctuations in raw-material prices, can often be predicted with a reasonable degree of accuracy on the basis of past experience. In a business where such losses are or may be a major factor, it is desirable to have responsibility for the inventories of each department or product line assigned to a merchandising executive. If this executive has complete responsibility for both the purchase of raw material and the sale of finished goods in his department, obsolescence losses can be budgeted as his direct responsibility, the amount allowed being an indication to him of the extent to which he can afford to take risks on style merchandise or new and untried products. Whatever the organization plan, the responsibility for losses of this type should be definitely fixed and allowances budgeted for each line in relation to its gross profit possibilities.

Other adjustments in inventory values may be necessary for various reasons. If inventories are carried at a standard or predetermined manufacturing cost, a significant reduction in costs because of changes in manufacturing processes, or simply because of increased volume, may necessitate a write-down. Experience may indicate that, even with the best possible physical and accounting control of stocks, some shrinkage in quantities takes place because of loss or theft. To the extent that such contingencies can be anticipated on the basis of past experience or future plans, they should, of course, be provided for in the budget.

Marketing, administrative, and general expenses

The budgeting of marketing expenses and of general and administrative expenses usually presents very few problems, provided that the accounting plan has been set up to correspond to the actual organization of sales and administrative activities. Sometimes it is desirable to introduce some degree of flexibility into these budgets by making certain expenditures contingent on the attainment of certain definite objectives in sales or earnings—for example, an advertising campaign may be budgeted for a new product based on a reasonable estimate of probable sales, with the provision that only one half or one quarter of the advertising expenditure is definitely authorized and that the authorization of the remainder will not be released until it is apparent that the initial expenditure is justified by the sales results. Or, similarly, the actual authorization of a portion of a budgeted research program may be deferred until it appears that operating plans are working out successfully and that earnings will be available to finance the program. This really amounts to making two or more alternative budgets with respect to the expenses in question, one being incorporated into the operating plan and the estimated financial statements and the others being supplementary or contingent budgets to be substituted if the operating plan does not produce the overall earnings anticipated, or if some particular phase of the plan does not work out as expected.

In addition to this partial flexibility in the budgeting of specific expenditures, it is theoretically possible to plan for different levels of certain types of selling and administrative expenses for different sales volumes, so that expense is automatically expanded or contracted as sales rise and fall. Such complete flexible budgeting is not unusual in the control of manufacturing costs, but in practice its application to selling and administrative expenses, except to a very limited degree, is extremely difficult. In the great majority of companies, flexible budgeting of selling and administrative expenses is limited to the preparation of plans for accelerating or retarding research or development expenses of various kinds or for reorganizing certain departments where changes can be made, if necessary, with the least harm to the business. In some routine departments, such as order writing, typing, data processing, etc., it is possible to measure production on certain operations and to compare actual expenses with standards adjusted for variations in activity. Even in these departments, however, it is usually necessary to maintain reasonable regularity of employment in order to keep intact the organization necessary to handle a normal volume of work; and the regulation of actual expenses to conform to such adjusted standards is really practical only where temporary help is readily available to absorb the peaks of the volume curve, or where the office organization is so large and the operations so completely routinized that training of new employees is not a serious problem.

Short-term cash budgets

One phase of the development of financial management concepts over the past twenty years is the increasing emphasis on the utilization of all of the firm's financial resources. In the past, many companies considered that they had no cash problem as long as they had ample funds available to meet their obligations, and substantial cash balances frequently were carried with little or no return. With the increasing pressures on management, at least in publicly-owned companies, for rapid growth in sales and profits, the most conservative companies are now making use of debt to obtain earnings leverage; and when cash is available which is not being used in the business, company treasurers are cutting every corner to put it to work at the best possible return. The recent sharp rise in interest rates, which seems unlikely to be significantly reversed in the near future, has added to this pressure. As a result of these trends, cash control and cash budgeting have assumed increased importance, even in well-financed companies.

In considering the techniques of cash budgeting, it is useful to distinguish between short-term budgets (one to six months) and budgets for a longer term. The short-term budget is a tool which the treasurer uses to keep bank loans at a practical minimum and to keep excess funds as fully invested as possible. A budget of this kind must be developed from detailed estimates of receipts and disbursements, with the timing of the inflow and outflow of funds pinpointed as closely as possible. In a multidivision company, where collections and disbursements are made at many different locations, this close budgeting and control of cash can be a formidable task. The problem can be somewhat simplified if the cash "float" is reduced by having customers mail remittances direct to one or more "lock boxes" at banks which act as collecting agents and forward to the depositor details of the amounts collected, together with remittance data received from the customers. Arrangements may also be made for automatic transfer of funds between divisional or branch depositaries and headquarters bank accounts, and for prompt increases or decreases in short-term borrowings and/or investment to maintain cash balances at an acceptable minimum level.

Even with these devices for close cash control, minimum balances must be maintained as a cushion against errors in timing in the cash budget, and also to meet the requirements of the banks extending credit to the business and performing the collection function. Part of this cushion can, of course, be supplied by delaying payments to vendors when collections from customers are behind budget; during the credit squeeze of 1969–70 even some large companies adopted this practice and at the same time put pressure on their suppliers to allow the usual cash discounts in spite of the delays in payments.

As with any other control procedure, the cost of the time and effort spent to perfect cash budgeting must be weighed against the benefits received. In periods of tight credit it may be necessary for top management to make basic decisions as to the policy to be followed in dealing with customers who delay their payments and suppliers who resist extending their credit terms.

Long-term cash budgets and balance-sheet budgets

Unlike the short-term cash budget, which in many companies has become almost a day-to-day control tool, the purpose of the longer-term cash budget and the balance-sheet budget is to enable management to look ahead for periods of six months to a year or two, or even five years, to anticipate the funds that will be needed to finance planned operations and, in many cases, to adjust plans to conform to the funds that can be made available within the limitations of the company's financial policies. Cash requirements are, of course, a key figure in this longer view, but the budgeted balance sheet adds an important further dimension to planning in that it gives a comprehensive overview of the anticipated use of the company's financial resources during the budget period. With this overview, steps can be taken to change objectives for the turnover of inventories and receivables or to speed up or defer investments in plant and equipment, and other changes can be made in the planned sources and uses of funds.

It is possible to construct a long-term cash and balance-sheet budget by the same detailed procedures followed in building up the short-term cash budget. In most cases, however, the longer-term budget can be prepared more easily, and with just as much accuracy, from a knowledge of the major elements of the profit and loss budget and the planned capital expenditures, without working back, step by step, to the budgeted sales, manufacturing and purchasing programs.

In this simplified approach to the preparation of a budgeted balance sheet, the budgeted amounts of the principal classes of assets and liabilities are determined as follows:

1. *Cash.* Cash is tentatively budgeted as equal to the minimum required working balance; this amount may be adjusted as the last step in the preparation of the balance sheet, after it is determined from the other estimates whether there will be an excess of cash or whether current borrowings will be required.

2. *Accounts Receivable.* Accounts receivable are budgeted as equal in amount to the budgeted sales for the period immediately preceding the balance-sheet date equal to the average anticipated collection period. If there are several classes of customers with different average collection periods, the receivables for each class are budgeted separately.

3. *Inventories.* Inventories are roundly estimated, based on operating plans or on past experience with respect to inventory turnover at various levels of sales, with adjustment for any known significant changes in purchasing policy.

4. *Plant and Accumulated Depreciation.* Capital expenditures are usually under top-management control, and even if no formal budget is prepared, the management will have some kind of informal plan covering proposed expenditures for plant additions, replacements, and removals. With a knowledge of these plans and of the annual depreciation charges included in the profit and loss budget, the budgeted plant values and accumulated depreciation can readily be determined.

5. *Current Trade Liabilities.* Current trade liabilities are estimated in round figures on the basis of past experience, giving consideration to the budgeted sales and production volume during the months immediately preceding the balance-sheet date.

6. *Changes in Capital Structure.* Sinking-fund payments for the retirement of long-term debt or senior stock issues are either fixed in

amount by the terms of the issues or, if dependent on earnings, can be calculated on the basis of budgeted earnings; similarly, the effect of other proposed changes in the capital structure can be reflected in the balance sheet without difficulty.

7. *Retained Earnings.* Retained earnings is budgeted to reflect the balance at the beginning of the budgeted period, adjusted for budgeted earnings and dividends for the period and for any contemplated direct charges or credits.

In the foregoing estimate of assets and liabilities, the balancing item is either cash or short-term borrowings. If the total of the budgeted assets is less than the total of the budgeted liabilities, capital, and surplus, the difference is added to the budgeted cash balance; on the other hand, if the total of the assets exceeds the total of the liabilities, capital, and surplus, it is evident that short-term borrowings will be required to finance the business, and the two sides of the balance sheet are brought into agreement by budgeting such borrowings in the necessary amount.

In most companies a complete balance-sheet budget at six-month intervals will be adequate for the purpose of medium-term and long-term financial planning. However, the relative simplicity of the procedure makes it possible to construct such budgets at shorter intervals with a minimum of extra effort. This may be worthwhile as a check on the detailed cash budgets; and it also has the advantage of permitting a more meaningful analysis of the reasons for variations between actual and budgeted cash balances.

The budget period

Most companies which operate on a budget make the fiscal year the budget period. The reasons for this are obvious—management planning and thinking are almost necessarily geared to the annual cycle, which covers the usual seasonal variations which affect sales volume, and is long enough to give time for the results of planned effort to become apparent and short enough to permit of continuity of such effort. Also, the annual financial statements are the generally accepted measurement of the success or failure of the management in the eyes of the owners of the business, and it is natural that plans should be made accordingly. Broad policies are properly developed for the long term—five to ten years ahead, or even longer—but for detailed planning based on such policies the fiscal year is the most satisfactory period.

Some companies believe it preferable to limit their budget to three months or six months ahead rather than operate it on a fiscal-year basis, while a few budget continuously for a full year ahead, adding a month or a quarter as each current month or quarter elapses. The principal argument advanced in favor of the short-term budget is its greater accuracy; the principal disadvantage is, of course, the absence of the continuous and coordinated planning which a longer view makes possible. The plan of keeping the budget projected continually for a year ahead seems logical on first thought and may be advantageous in stimulating forward thinking in general terms, but it will usually be found that any definite operating plans can better be limited to a fiscal-year period, particularly if the fiscal year corresponds with a well-defined natural business year.

Budget revisions

One of the attributes of good business management is the ability to move quickly to meet changing conditions. This does not mean veering from a charted course every time there is a momentary shift in the wind. It does mean constantly evaluating the significance of any shifts in the wind and not waiting until the storm breaks before taking countermeasures. Flexibility in operational control is important in good times as well as in period of declining business—more money may be lost, in the long run, by being out of stock in an expanding market than by being too slow to curtail operations when sales fall off. And flexibility is necessary in the details of operational planning and control, as well as in the overall rate of operation and spending—for example, if there is an unforeseen delay in bringing a new product to market, some steps must be taken to offset the resulting loss in protfit.

In the earlier sections of this chapter, considerable emphasis has been laid on the importance of this element of flexibility in budgeting, and various methods of achieving this end, in whole or in part, have been mentioned. A completely flexible budget, with every expense budgeted in advance for every probable level of volume, is the theoretically correct answer, but rarely the practical one. Such a plan can be an extremely useful management tool when applied to well-standardized operations, particularly in the factory, but, in spite of its name, it is too rigid to be practical in planning operations as a whole. Sales volume is not always a good measure of the need for changes in the plan—margins may be narrowed by increases in costs without compensating increases in selling prices, sales may shift from profitable to unprofitable items, new products may show such unexpected possibilities as to warrant increasing development expenditures—the range of possible changes in conditions that might call for revamping the operating plan is almost unlimited. No matter how much flexibility is introduced into the budget by relating routine expenses to volume, earmarking specific appropriations as contingent, etc., it is essential that there should be at least partial revisions of the plan at fairly frequent intervals.

This need to obtain practical flexibility in short term planning and control presents a real opportunity to the controller who is management-minded. It has already been suggested that the controller should see to it that the best available information about the present and projected business environment is communicated to management in an orderly and useable form. And as to internal trends, there is no one else in the organization who has direct access to all of the facts about the current status of product development programs, sales promotion campaigns, profit improvement projects, and other factors that have a vital effect on profits. With this knowledge, the controller should be constantly looking into the future, appraising the effect of all these trends on the operating plan for the budget period, and seeing to it that operating management is alert to the need for changes in planning to achieve the budgeted profit—and alert, too, to any opportunity to raise its sights and plan for a higher profit than called for in the budget.

In a small business, or in a business with a limited product line and a relatively simple manufacturing operation, this flexibility in control and planning may be achieved on an informal basis, by direct oral communication between the controller and the operating executives. In larger companies, with a diversified product line and a more complex organization of responsibilities, it is necessary to have some formal procedure for evaluating the effect of changing conditions on the profit plan. Some companies do this by preparing quarterly or even monthly profit-and-loss forecasts, broken down in considerable detail for one to three months ahead and in less detail for the remainder of the budget period. Usually, these forecasts can be prepared by starting with the budget and adjusting it for known trends and changes in plans, but if external or internal conditions change radically, it may be necessary to do a complete job of recasting the entire operating plan. In this, as in every phase of operational control, the procedures must be adapted to the particular situation. The important thing is that management get a clear picture, at frequent intervals, of where it stands in relation to its budget goals, not only for the year to date, but for the entire budget period.

Budgeting for nonfunctional profit responsibilities

All of the discussions in this chapter, up to this point, have dealt with budgeting and control based on the normal functional lines of organizational responsibility. In a business which consists of a number of well-defined major ventures—often called operating divisions—each of which is treated as a profit center, the functional responsibilities are almost always grouped by such profit centers, and the budgets based on functional responsibilities are, therefore, profit-center budgets. Sometimes there will be, within a profit center, one or more "profit responsibilities" which cut across functional lines, and for which budgets are prepared supplementing the overall profit-center budget. Perhaps the most common example of this type of responsibility is the product-line or commodity manager, who may be held accountable, at least in theory, for the profit of a particular commodity or group of commodities, although he has no direct control over the manufacturing processes, or, in many cases, over the field organization that sells the product. If the profit responsibility of such a commodity manager is to have any real validity, there must be a careful definition and control of the services that are to be rendered to him by the functional departments and the cost of those services. An example of a profit-and-loss statement in an actual situation of this type is shown in Figure 13–1. In this particular business the commodity executives are responsible for purchasing and inventory control and to some extent for control of customers' accounts receivable; hence, in determining the Sales Department Profit (or Loss), cost of goods sold includes the actual cost of raw material, and deductions are made for inventory losses due to market write-downs and obsolescence and for interest on the capital invested in inventories and accounts receivable.

Although every effort is made to have these statements for the commodity executives reflect results which are under their direct control, this purpose is not entirely achieved, since the greater part of the selling and administrative expenses included are general or joint expenses which are spread over the several commodities on various appropriate bases of allocation. This is recognized as a defect in the statements, but in practice these joint expenses are kept under close control by careful budgeting, and the allocation of the total budget to the commodities is reviewed in detail with each sales executive. For example, the charge to each commodity for field sales expense, which is the major allocated item, is determined by planning the amount of each salesman's time to be spent on the commodity, and the field sales manager works closely with the commodity executives and the branch managers to see that the field men's time is actually applied as planned. Under these conditions, actual charges of allocated expenses to the various commodities run very close to budget, and the commodity executives understand the charges and are satisfied as to their fairness, so that there is little disposition to question the net results shown by the commodity statements.

In a business where this type of control of allocated expenses is impractical, commodity profits which reflect allocated expenses are usually given little real weight by responsible sales executives, who rightly feel that the results are influenced by too many factors over which they have no jurisdiction. This presents something of a problem, as it is certainly desirable to have some reflection of these indirect expenses in the control statements, in order to prevent the development of an exaggerated idea of the profits being earned and to give the executives

Figure 13–1

SPEEDWELL MANUFACTURING COMPANY—WESTERN DIVISION
Sales Department Profit and Loss Statement—Commodity B
Quarter Ended March 31, 19XX
(all amounts in thousands)

	Amounts		Percentage of sales		Per pound	
	Actual	*Budget*	*Actual*	*Budget*	*Actual*	*Budget*
Net Sales—Pounds	622.8	593.3	. . . . . .	. . . . . .	. . . . . .	. . . . . .
Dollars	$473.3	$458.7	100.0	100.0	$0.7600	$0.7731
Cost of Goods Sold (material at actual; labor and overhead at standard)	329.7	323.4	69.7	70.5	0.5294	0.5451
Gross Profit (material at actual, labor and overhead at standard)	$143.6	$135.3	30.3	29.5	$0.2306	$0.2280
Direct Departmental Expenses:						
Advertising	$ 27.1	$ 27.5	5.7	6.0	$0.0435	$0.0463
Selling	10.8	10.7	2.3	2.3	0.0174	0.0180
Total	$ 37.9	$ 38.2	8.0	8.3	$0.0609	$0.0643
Profit before General Expenses	$105.7	$ 97.1	22.3	21.2	$0.1697	$0.1637
General Expenses:						
Selling—Field	$ 51.9	$ 51.2	11.0	11.2	$0.0833	$0.0863
Home Office	13.3	13.5	2.8	2.9	0.0214	0.0228
Administrative	19.4	19.0	4.1	4.2	0.0311	0.0320
Total	$ 84.6	$ 83.7	17.9	18.3	$0.1358	$0.1411
Merchandising Profit or (Loss)	$ 21.1	$ 13.4	4.4	2.9	$0.0339	$0.0226
Sales Department Profit Adjustments—(Charges) or Credits:						
Interest on Inventories and Receivables	($ 12.9)	($ 10.6)	(2.7)	(2.3)	($0.0207)	($0.0179)
Inventory Adjustments:						
Market Write Down	(1.6)	(1.6)	(0.3)	(0.3)	(0.0026)	(0.0027)
Obsolescence	(3.7)	(3.0)	(0.8)	(0.7)	(0.0059)	(0.0050)
Total	($ 18.2)	($ 15.2)	(3.8)	(3.3)	($0.0292)	($0.0256)
Sales Department Profit or (Loss)	$ 2.9	($ 1.8)	0.6	(0.4)	$0.0047	($0.0030)

concerned a correct impression of the approximate contribution of the commodity to the net earnings of the business. A satisfactory solution to this problem in some cases may be to charge each of the commodity sales executives with a fixed budgeted amount for the indirect expenses or with a fixed amount plus or minus an adjustment based on the difference between actual and budgeted dollar sales or actual and budgeted number of orders written, the adjustment being calculated at a predetermined rate approximately equal to the variable indirect expenses per dollar of sales or per order.

Usually a sales department profit and loss statement, that is, a control statement for sales executives, will include gross profits based on standard labor and overhead costs and will not reflect the effect of variations in sales volume on factory burden absorption. This is a sound basis for such statements in the majority of cases if the standard factory costs are calculated on the basis of normal capacity, since fluctuations in volume will approximately wash out over a period of years. In some businesses, however, it may be difficult to arrive at a satisfactory determination of normal capacity, and if there are rather wide fluctuations in sales volume or if fixed charges are a high percentage of factory cost, it may be desirable to bring home to the sales executives the effect of volume on factory costs by including some adjustment for it in their control statements.

The best method of reflecting the effect of volume variations in factory costs in the control statements for the commodity executives is not by allocating the actual over- or underearned factory burden, which is affected by the sales activity in other commodities and by variations in factory efficiency, but by charging or crediting each commodity with a predetermined or budgeted amount per dollar or per unit on the difference between its actual sales and the sales volume on which the standard manufacturing costs are based. This predetermined charge per dollar or per unit can be calculated to approximate the amount of fixed factory burden earned; possibly, if there is considerable variation in the fixed burden earned by different products, different rates may be computed for several subclassifications of the commodity, but the number of rates used should be kept at a minimum, so that the calculations will be simple and easily followed by the sales executives. A calculation of this kind, based on the commodity statement in Figure 13–1, is shown in Figure 13–2; the actual and budgeted overearned burden of $12,400 and $9,800, respectively, could be included in Figure 13–1, if desired, as an additional item under Sales Department Profit Adjustments.

The procedure suggested in the preceding paragraph and some of the procedures previously suggested for the allocation of joint expenses will produce commodity profit and loss figures which will not agree exactly in total with the overall results shown by the master profit and loss statements. This is not a serious matter, since in this case we are

Figure 13–2

SPEEDWELL MANUFACTURING COMPANY—WESTERN DIVISION

Factory Burden Absorption at Standard Product Rates—Commodity B

Quarter Ended March 31, 19XX

	Poundage			Fixed burden per pound	Actual		Budget	
Product class	Standard	Actual	Budget		Pounds over or (under) standard	Over or (under) earned burden	Pounds over or (under) standard	Over or (under) earned burden
B-A	200.0	246.8	205.4	$0.1725	46.8	$ 8.1	5.4	$0.9
B-B	100.0	115.0	103.3	0.2150	15.0	3.2	3.3	0.7
B-C	125.0	109.3	150.5	0.2535	(15.7)	(4.0)	25.5	6.4
B-D	125.0	151.7	134.1	0.1925	26.7	5.1	9.1	1.8
Total	550.0	622.8	593.3	. . . .	72.8	$12.4	43.3	$9.8

concerned not with a neat accounting allocation of all book charges and credits but rather with the development of a tool which will be useful and practical for the control and measurement of the sales executives' performance.

Program budgeting and control

In addition to the permanent profit-center responsibilities which cut across functional lines within a major profit center, there may be important special programs or projects, each headed up by a project manager who is charged with accomplishing a specific objective, utilizing the services of a number of the functional departments. Examples of such programs, which may be either within a major profit center or at the corporate level, divorced from profit-center operations, are the development and launching of distinctive new product lines, extensive basic changes in processing methods, plant relocations or major changes in plant layout, test marketing programs, development and computerization of a management information system, etc. The budgeting of costs for such programs and the accumulation of actual costs require special accounting procedures, usually involving setting up one or more program cost orders and the supplemental coding of all expenses chargeable to those orders. Special attention is necessary to be sure that all costs applicable to the program are identified as incurred and are properly handled in the accounts. There will be more assurance of correct handling if the project costing is carried through the accounts by means of service credits to the functional departments, with offsetting charges to one or more primary accounts set up for the project. It is almost inevitable that there will be disputes between the project manager and the functional managers about the validity of these charges, but the resolution of these disputes serves the purpose of keeping the spotlight on the project costs.

Program budgets are, of course, useful in keeping actual expenditures within authorized limits, but for certain types of projects, which contribute nothing to current income but are essential for the future progress of the business, it is equally important to be sure that costs are not curtailed below authorized limits, without top management approval, in order to effect an apparent improvement in near-term operating profits. And periodic progress reports on costs incurred and results achieved are essential so that, where an option exists, unsuccessful programs can be cut off early in the game and successful ones "beefed up," if necessary, by the authorization of additional funds. The efficient budgeting of time for results to be achieved, the measurement and reporting of actual achievement in relation to budget, and the time correlation of reports on results with reports of costs incurred are often difficult planning and control problems. A partial answer to these problems may be found in the use of one of the several variations of the "network analysis" technique, such as CPM (Critical Path Method), PERT (Program Evaluation and Review Technique), PERT/COST, etc. These techniques provide, in general, for (a) breaking the program down into its component tasks and each task into its component steps, (b) preparing a network flow chart showing the chronological sequence of the steps in each task, the time budgeted for each step, and the interrelationship of the component tasks, and (c) reporting periodically the actual time for each step and revising the budgeted time (and the flow chart) when necessary. For simpler projects this can be done manually, but for large and complex projects the use of a computer is necessary.[4]

When substantial sums are involved in a program or project budget, it is customary to require a detailed projection of the effect of the program on profits and the rate of return that will be earned on the total investment in the program as the result either of increased sales and income, or lower costs, or both. The principles and procedures to be followed in making such projections and rate-of-return calculations are basically the same as in the planning and budgeting of plant expenditures, as discussed in Chapter 15. Program budgets, like plant expenditure budgets, frequently include both capital charges and expense charges and consideration must be given to the impact of income taxes on the required investment and on the net income or savings resulting from the investment. An authorized program usually involves a much larger element of expense charges than the ordinary plant expenditure authorization; and both elements—expense and capital—must be reported and monitored if control of the program is to be effective.

Securing cooperation of management in the budget effort

The most elusive and in some respects the most important problem connected with the budget is attention to the interpersonal relationships which the budget brings into sharp focus. No matter how carefully the technical aspects of the budget are handled, it will not be an effective instrument if it is not properly sold to the line management. Bringing in an outsider to set up the budget procedures, attempting to put even a well-considered budget into effect too rapidly, imposing a too detailed expenditure control upon department heads who are accustomed to considerable freedom of action, stirring up the common prejudice against "red tape," failure to recognize the sometimes delicate line between controllable and noncontrollable expenditures—any of these errors of

---

[4] For a good simplified description of CPM and PERT see *The Executive Strategist*, by R. C. Weisselberg and J. G. Cowley (New York: N.Y. McGraw-Hill, 1969), pp. 92–107. A more recently developed technique is described in the article "Accomplishment/Cost: Better Project Control," by E. B. Block, in the May-June 1971 issue of the *Harvard Business Review*.

judgment can get the budget into bad repute with executives down the line. And, once an unfavorable attitude has been aroused, it often becomes extremely difficult to reverse the image and to secure the co-operation without which it is almost impossible to get results.

With this caution as to the importance of good judgment in developing budgetary procedures, it must be said, realistically, that there are situations in which some operating executives will not readily accept even the minimum requirements for effective budgetary control. To avoid this obstacle, or to overcome it when it arises, it is essential that the budget, whatever its form, have the approval and active support of top management. The slightest evidence that those at the highest echelon are not in full sympathy with the budget effort is taken as a signal down the line that it is not necessary to give more than lip service to it. Probably, the second most necessary factor is that the persons primarily responsible for the budget must have the personal qualities which enable them to get along well with other people in any relationship. There are some people who rub their fellow men in the wrong way in all kinds of contacts. Budget administration requires the very opposite type of person, because it so often sets up situations of implied or real criticism. Estimates must be challenged, requests turned down, failure to meet quotas pointed out, excess expenditures called to attention, and so forth. To operate within this area and still retain the respect and liking of all levels of management requires a person with a great deal of natural tact. Such tact is in large part an inherent characteristic, but in some degree at least it can be attained by a person who is conscious of its importance, who is imaginative, and who is willing to observe his own performance critically so as to learn by his own mistakes.

The authors of this book do not presume to be psychologists, but there is one piece of advice on interpersonal relationships that is commonly enough accepted that we may properly inject it into this discussion. The basic rule in getting along with one's fellows within the business, which certainly applies to this budget context, is to have real respect for the other person's point of view, and this is important at all phases of the budget process. It has already been mentioned that it is often psychologically good to solicit salesmen's and branch sales managers' estimates of sales possibilities. It would be very unwise, however, to ask for such estimates and then to disregard them as of no value. If they cannot actually be accepted at face value, care should be taken to explain the need for revision. If production superintendents are asked for suggestions for capital expenditures for plant improvements, every suggestion made should be carefully appraised by those responsible. And the fact of this care should be communicated to those who have made the suggestions, with bona fide reasons for acceptance or rejection. Administrators at all levels should be consulted as to the kinds of expense information and the degree of detail that they believe useful to them in their close-to-the-scene-of-action efforts to control costs. The real job of running the business is, after all, in the hands of the line authorities. The budget should be a help to them, and they should be sincerely convinced that it is intended to be just that. The controller and his staff are facilitating agents in the budget picture; the real responsibility both for the creation of the budget and for its administration is in the line. The entire process is one of rather delicate interpersonal adjustment and cooperation, and it must be recognized as such.

Computer-assisted budgeting

The use of the computer in long-range planning is discussed in the section on "Computerized Financial Planning," at the end of Chapter 19. The conclusion stated there, that "computer projections, however developed, are not a substitute for detailed operational planning by the responsible line executives," applies to short-term (annual) budgeting as well as to long-range planning. In the relatively few businesses which have developed "financial models," the models may be used as an overall check on the reasonableness of the budget, but this use alone would not justify the time and effort required to develop the models. The computer can be very useful in the preparation of reports comparing actual operating results with budget, particularly in speeding up the computation of the budget figures adjusted to actual volume when a flexible budget is in use.

Other phases of budget procedure

The discussions in this chapter have been concerned with the practical problems of the sales and financial budgets and overall budget adminis- tration. Other problems, which overlap into the fields of manufacturing costs and marketing and administrative costs, have been touched on briefly and are discussed in more detail in the chapters on those subjects. There is also a more extended discussion of the use of the flexible budget technique as a management tool in the next chapter, which, to conform to popular terminology, has been given the title of "Profit Planning." Thus, the basic idea of the budget—coordinated planning in financial terms—enters into all phases of the controller's management function.

14 PROFIT PLANNING

Profit planning and budgeting

In the introduction to the discussion of budgeting in Chapter 13 the term "budget" was defined as follows:

Since the heart of the budgeting process is planning for profit, and since planning implies setting objectives, we can describe the budget as "a summary in financial terms of the performance objectives and plans established for all departments of the business." Perhaps a better definition, to emphasize the necessity for the coordination of departmental plans, is "a coordinated plan for the operation of the business, expressed in financial terms."

Thus budgeting is, by definition, planning for profit, and the discussion in this chapter on "Profit Planning" will simply deal in more detail with certain techniques which were mentioned briefly in the chapters on the budget, manufacturing costs, and marketing and administrative costs.

Although "profit planning" is in itself a very general term, it has come to be associated in practice with the use of the "flexible-budget" technique in the planning of operations. This technique has been described in more or less elaborate detail by many writers, from many different viewpoints, and under many different names, but the basic principle in all these expositions is the same and is extremely simple. This principle is the recognition of the fact that some costs and expenses tend to vary with the volume of sales or production, while others are not affected by volume but remain relatively fixed, either indefinitely or until changed by direct management action. If all costs and expenses can be broken down between variable and nonvariable and if this breakdown can be carried into the costs of individual products or product lines, it is possible to determine with relative ease the effect on profits of changes in total volume or shifts in volume from one product to another, to calculate the amount of business required to carry an additional salesman, and to answer many other questions that have a direct bearing on the planning of operations for maximum profit. The key to the technique is, of course, the use of variable costs instead of the conventional total costs which include an allocation of the nonvariable-cost elements. The various applications of the technique and its limitations, which become apparent in practice, are discussed in the following paragraphs.

Selection of product

Probably the simplest application of the profit-planning technique is the selection of the product to be run on available equipment when there is enough demand to keep the equipment operating at capacity. An illustration of this type of problem can be found in a textile-weaving mill which buys yarn and weaves it into cloth on looms that are adaptable to a variety of more or less staple fabrics. It is common practice for such mills to sell through commission agents at prices determined by open-market quotations, and under all but the most depressed conditions capacity sales at some price are assured. Under these conditions the selection of the fabrics to be sold can be made by calculating for each fabric the dollars of profit over variable cost which will be earned per hour of loom operation. Such a calculation is illustrated in Figure 14–1. It will be noted that although style A shows the greater profit

Figure 14–1
COMPARATIVE COSTS AND PROFITS OF TWO TEXTILE FABRICS

	Style A	Style B
Yards produced per loom hour	4.20	5.40
Variable costs:		
Cotton	$0.0678	$0.0695
Labor and overhead	0.0555	0.0509
Total	$0.1233	$0.1204
Nonvariable costs	0.0221	0.0195
Total costs	$0.1454	$0.1399
Selling price	0.1685	0.1595
Profit over total cost	$0.0231	$0.0196
Profit over variable cost:		
Per yard	$0.0452	$0.0391
Per loom hour	$0.1898	$0.2111

per yard, based on either total cost or variable cost, style B will yield the greater profit per operating hour. Any decision to switch looms from one fabric to another will take into consideration not only the profit return as thus calculated but also the cost of the loom changes and of any special loom equipment which may be required for the new fabric, the probability of the continuation of the existing differential between the fabrics, and the long-time effect of the switch on the company's relations with its customers.

This type of problem becomes somewhat more complicated if more than one process is involved, but if the processing is continuous and all products pass through all processes, the same method of calculation can be followed. Thus, in a textile mill which spins its own yarn instead of buying it outside, the profit per loom hour can be calculated for each fabric, using the total variable cost of the fabric, built up process by process. In this situation, however, it is necessary to be sure of two things: first, that the scheduled production is within the capacity of all departments and, second, that if a change in production schedule results in the reduction of machine hours in any department, the expected savings in variable costs can actually be effected without disrupting the organization or conflicting with the company's established labor policies. As a rule, it is better, if possible, to plan operations so as to secure a balanced mill, with maximum output in all departments; under these conditions the organization can be maintained, and, furthermore, the pressure for production will tend to keep up output per labor hour and thus keep actual variable costs in line with standard.

Passing from this relatively simple planning in a textile mill with continuous and uniform production to a more complex business with a varied line of products which do not all pass through the same processes, the problem becomes much more difficult, but the same principles apply if the conditions are the same—that is, if the entire plant capacity can be sold and the question is simply the selection of the most profitable products. It will usually be found that for each major line of products there is some one bottleneck department, or possibly two departments, either of which may be the bottleneck, depending on the production schedule, and that attention can be concentrated on the scheduling of these departments on products which yield the greatest return over total variable cost.

In scheduling the bottleneck departments it is necessary to be sure that the schedule selected is in accord with the long-term sales policies of the business and that it does not cause a serious imbalance in the plant or create other plant operating problems. If the schedule makes significant changes in the level of activity in any department, the variability of some cost elements in that department may change, and the breakdown of costs between variable and nonvariable may have to be revised. Furthermore, if the alternative schedules from which the selection is made involve radically different products or different levels of dollar sales, consideration must be given to possible differences in the capital required to finance inventories and customers' accounts and the resulting differences in interest costs.

It should be understood that the above discussion assumes a market in which management has complete freedom of action in the selection of products to be produced. In many multiproduct companies this assumption is not valid, as radical changes in an established product mix can usually be made only over a relatively long period of time. Even a decision to emphasize a high-profit item at the expense of a poorer profit contributor, within the framework of the existing product lines, may be difficult to implement because of customer preference or inertia on the part of the field sales organization. In cases like these the application of these principles of profit planning is usually effected as an element of the company's long-range plan, rather than through day-to-day or month-to-month changes in production scheduling.

Under some circumstances the technique of linear programming may be useful in optimizing profits when operations are at or close to full capacity. The technique is particularly appropriate when a limited stock must be apportioned among competing product groups. The manager of an oil refinery, for example, may use his given crude to make gasoline, kerosene, heavy fuels, and other products. Linear programs have proved effective in selecting the best mix of output from the process. A simplified description of how the technique is applied to a similar problem is given in Chapter 24. Here again, there is an assumption of flexibility of production, at least within certain specified constraints; and the technique is, in many cases, better adapted to longer-range planning than to the management of current operations.

Determination of most profitable level of operation

If a plant is not operating at capacity, the problem of profit planning is entirely different. Let us turn again to the cotton-textile industry for a simple illustration: assume a mill making a single specialty fabric sold in several different markets for different uses—both consumer and industrial—and assume, further, that in some of these markets this fabric is running into competition with substitutes which are sold at a lower price. The ideal solution to this problem of maintaining profits is, of course, to find new uses for the fabric or to improve it so that it will command a premium over the competitive fabrics; but if neither of these courses is possible, the management must make a major policy decision as to how it shall plan its operations. In general, it has three options: to cut prices; to increase its selling or promotion efforts, particularly in the consumer outlets; or, if some substantial part of the market is a monopoly (i.e., there are no usable substitutes), it is possible that profits might be increased by raising prices and abandoning the more competitive sections of the market. In other words, the problem is to find the right balance between selling price, volume, and selling cost.

In a situation as simple as the one outlined, where only one product is manufactured, the mathematics of the problem can be very effectively presented in a chart showing the relationship between volume, costs, and profits at a given selling price. This is the familiar break-even chart illustrated in Figure 14–2, in which dollar sales and total dollar costs

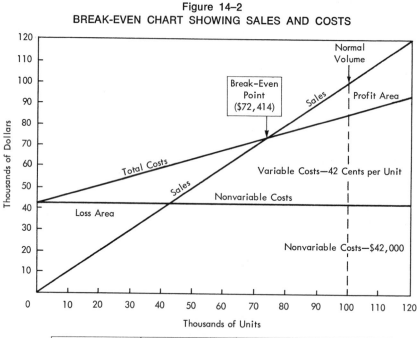

Figure 14–2
BREAK-EVEN CHART SHOWING SALES AND COSTS

Basic Data	Decrease		Normal	Increase	
	20 PCT	10 PCT	Volume	10 PCT	20 PCT
Sales............	$80,000	$90,000	$100,000	$110,000	$120,000
Variable Costs....	33,600	37,800	42,000	46,200	50,400
Margin over Variable Costs...	$46,400	52,200	58,000	63,800	69,600
Nonvariable Costs.	42,000	42,000	42,000	42,000	42,000
Profit............	$ 4,400	$10,200	$ 16,000	$ 21,800	$ 27,600

at various levels of unit volume are plotted as straight lines, total costs being broken down between nonvariable costs, which are shown as constant at all levels of volume, and variable costs, which are plotted as a function of unit volume. The volume point at which the dollar-sales and the total-costs lines cross is the point of no profit or loss, i.e., the break-even point; the vertical distance between the two lines at any point to the right or left of this break-even point represents the dollars of net profit or loss, respectively, at the indicated unit volume. The relationship between sales volume and net profits can be charted directly as in Figure 14–3 but this does not bring out the cost structure of the business quite so clearly.

In Figure 14–2 the break-even point is $72,414; and, at the designated normal volume of 100,000 units, sales are $100,000, nonvariable costs

Figure 14–3
BREAK-EVEN CHART SHOWING SALES AND PROFITS

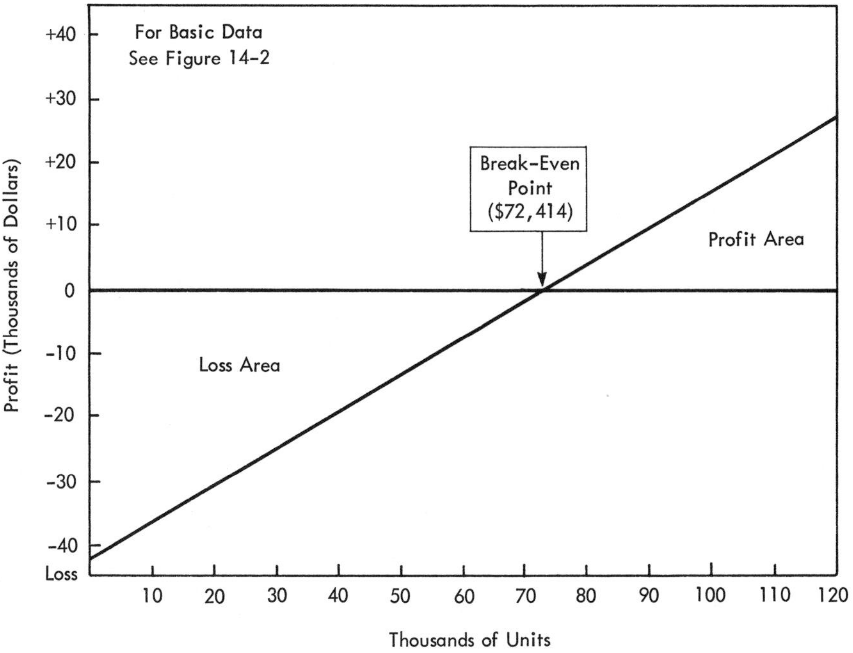

Thousands of Units

$42,000, variable costs $42,000 (42 cents per unit), and net profits $16,000. If sales can be increased by 20 percent or 20,000 units, at the same selling price, profits will increase from $16,000 to $27,600; in other words, if a 20,000-unit increase in volume can be secured by the expenditure of any amount less than $11,600, net profits will be increased by the difference between $11,600 and the amount spent. If this expenditure takes the form of increased sales effort, the nonvariable-costs and total-costs lines on the chart will be raised, while if the expenditure is made as a price cut, the slope of the dollar-sales line will be less steep; in either case, the break-even point will be raised. On the other hand, if prices are increased without changes in costs, the slope of the dollar-sales line will be steeper, the breakeven point will be lower, and the same or a greater net profit can be realized on a lower unit volume. Figure 14–4 shows the volume required to earn the normal profit of $16,000 at various selling-price levels.

Figure 14–4
VOLUME REQUIRED TO PRODUCE NORMAL PROFIT
AT VARIOUS SELLING PRICES

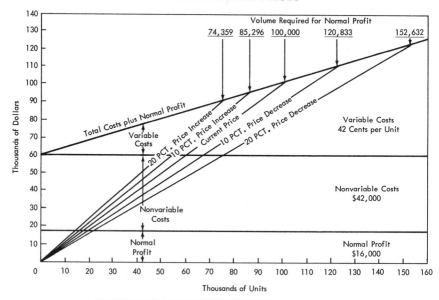

Basic Data	Price Decrease		Current	Price Increase	
	20 PCT.	10 PCT.	Price	10 PCT.	20 PCT.
Sales Units	152,632	120,833	100,000	85,296	74,359
Unit Price........	$ 0.80	$ 0.90	$ 1.00	$ 1.10	$ 1.20
Sales Dollars......	$122,106	$108,750	$100,000	$93,825	$89,231
Variable Costs	64,106	50,750	42,000	35,825	31,231
Margin over					
Variable Costs...	$ 58,000	$ 58,000	$ 58,000	$58,000	$58,000
Nonvariable Costs.	42,000	42,000	42,000	42,000	42,000
Profit............	$ 16,000	$ 16,000	$ 16,000	$16,000	$16,000

Pricing policy

The case discussed in the preceding paragraph is a very simple illustration of a problem in pricing policy. Even in this illustration the solution to the problem is far from being purely mathematical, since it requires the exercise of judgment as to the probable effect of changes in prices or in sales effort on unit volume; that is, it requires a knowledge of the market as well as of the facts about costs. And in all but a very few companies the problem of pricing policy is far more complicated than in the case of the single-product business illustrated in these charts. The limitation to one product implies continuity and departmental balance in manufacturing and relative simplicity in marketing operations, with a correspondingly simple cost and expense structure which can readily be broken down into nonvariable and variable elements. These ideal conditions are rarely found in practice in companies of any substantial size, and in most situations it is necessary to recognize the existence of a considerable margin of possible error in the breakdown of costs between nonvariable and variable and to interpret basic cost data in the light of the particular problem presented and the particular solution proposed.

The intelligent use of cost data in determining what to produce and at what price to sell is the essence of profit planning, as the term is used in this discussion. At this point the businessman or, more especially, the sales manager is up against one of the most complicated problems of economics—the function of price in the equating of supply and demand. Economists get a fairly clean set of rules by using the luxurious assumption of the perfect market in which the buyers and sellers are all intelligent economic men. We here propose to shift the basis of thinking by acknowledging a very imperfect market in which we shall study the operations of a very intelligent sales manager. The controller's interest in this situation is to furnish the sales manager with all the information regarding costs which the sales manager could reasonable ask for, and we should remember that it is the sales manager and not the controller who will make the decisions.

For the great majority of manufactured products it is unrealistic to assume either an automatically determined sales price which the company must meet or the simple alternative in which the company can always sell at its cost plus some desired markup. Either of these situations may obtain for certain products and for certain periods. The more standardized and competitive the product, the closer the situation will come to the automatic market price; the more unique the product, the closer will be the cost plus the desired profit situation. Many products while new (especially if under patent protection) approach the cost-plus pricing situation but later drift toward the automatically determined market price. The sales manager's job is to figure out where his product stands against this range of situations. In addition, the sales manager should be acutely aware that his reasoning may be quite different if the plant is operating at capacity from what it would be if the plant has substantial idle capacity, and this factor may, of course, change in a fairly short time. Add the complication of multiple products in different circumstances, and the stage is really set for the sales manager's pricing operation.

The most definite help that the controller can give the sales manager is a clear picture as to the breakdown of each product cost into variable manufacturing cost, total manufacturing cost, and, as far as feasible, the cost to sell and deliver. The sales manager will then set his price, if possible, to cover all costs and to yield a profit. If this cannot be done, he will back down from this ideal, surrendering successively the net profit and the fixed costs if necessary but hoping in each instance to get some margin over variable costs. If the plant is operating at full capacity, he will be in a much stronger position to resist these surrenders; his problem then is to get for each product not less of a margin than he could get for some other product which is competing for the limited plant capacity.

In making decisions of this kind, if major price changes are contemplated, or if a large special order is involved, it may be necessary to review the available cost data in detail, department by department, to determine whether reductions in any items of cost are feasible and, in the case of special orders or a planned increase in volume, whether capacity is available in all departments. These determinations should be made by the responsible operating executive, with the advice and assistance of the controller or the appropriate member of his staff. This process of cost review will be meaningful only if the cost information is up to date and well organized and the decision maker is familiar with the plant operations and is objective in his determinations. One of the controller's contributions to the process is to exert his influence on the side of reasonable conservatism in recasting the cost data.[1]

The reasoning applied above to the pricing of a product applies also to the narrower problem of the sales available by calling on an individual customer. It is to be hoped that the sales to each customer can be made to yield a net profit over all costs, but if such fully profitable sales cannot absorb the entire capacity, it will be good judgment to sell to those csutomers whose purchases will still show a margin over variable costs.

Corollary to all of this there are, of course, certain exceptional cases in which a business may make sales for less than even the total variable costs. The introduction of a new product very commonly involves such heavy distribution costs that no net profit is expected to be produced for a varying initial period. The ultimate is to sacrifice all costs by giving away free samples to introduce a new product, though, interestingly, this may save more in distribution costs than it sacrifices in variable production costs.

Another corollary to the simple principle of selling down to variable costs is consideration of the overall effect of such a procedure. There is always the danger that the acceptance of business below total cost by one firm may set in motion similar action by competitors, with eventual consequences far more serious than the loss of the profit on a sale or two. Thus action which may seem eminently intelligent from the individual point of view may turn out to be collective insanity. Judgments at this level must be based more upon market and business sense than upon cost accounting, and the controller's contribution when he sits in the top councils on these matters may well be to guard against a too serious use of his own figure analyses.

---

[1] The use of computer terminals to facilitate such a cost review process is described in an article "Terminal Costing for Better Decisions," by M. S. Morton and A. M. McCosh in the May-June 1968 issue of the *Harvard Business Review*.

Other uses of the break-even chart

In a business which manufactures a single product or a group of products so similar in nature that selling prices and costs can properly be expressed in terms of overall averages, the simple break-even chart shown in Figure 14–2 not only shows the effect of volume on profit but also tells a good deal about the strong and weak points of business. The percentage of capacity actually utilized, the level of non-variable expense, and the slope of the total-costs line, reflecting the ratio of variable costs to sales, are the important factors in the profit result, and, while the same information can be obtained from the figures from which the chart is constructed, the chart itself shows the interrelationship of these factors in such a way as to suggest the logical points of attack to effect improvement.

This analysis is particularly valuable if comparisons can be made with other businesses in the same industry, and in this relatively simple type of business it is sometimes possible to do this, even though detailed cost figures are not available. If a plotting of the actual profit results of a competitive business against sales volume over a period of years produces a reasonably straight profit line, the fixed costs of the business and the ratio of variable costs to sales can be computed, using the sales and profit figures at any two points on the line, and a chart similar to Figure 14–2 can be constructed. From a study of such charts for several competitive concerns it may be determined, for example, that the nonvariable costs of the business are too high in comparison with others in the industry, or perhaps that the ratio of variable costs to sales is low, with a low sales volume in relation to capacity, suggesting that sales prices may be out of line on the high side or that additional sales or advertising effort may be justified. Naturally, the chart does not provide the answer to any profit problem; it merely points up the facts and suggests one or more possible analytical approaches.

In a more complex business, where there are several product lines with different ratios of profit to sales, the simple single-line break-even chart is obviously inadequate to express the relationship of volume, costs, and profits for each of the different segments of the business. It is possible, of course, to construct a separate chart for each product line, but this requires the allocation of fixed costs which are not directly related to any one of the product lines if the sum of the break-even points for the individual lines is to agree with the break-even point for the entire business. Such allocations, no matter how carefully developed, are necessarily arbitrary to some degree, and are likely to change from year to year if they are to be kept at all realistic. Unless the allocated costs are very minor in relation to total fixed costs, the product-line break-even chart may well be more misleading than helpful. Better results can be obtained by constructing numerical tables showing the contribution of each product line (that is, the margin over variable costs) available to cover nonvariable costs and profit, in somewhat the following form:

| | Product lines | | | |
	A	B	C	Total
Sales, units.	10,000	15,000	20,000	
Selling price.	$3.00	$2.00	$1.00	
Dollars	$30,000	$30,000	$20,000	$80,000
Variable costs:				
Per unit	$0.75	$0.80	$1.00	
Dollars	$ 7,500	$12,000	$20,000	$39,500
Contribution:				
Per unit	$2.25	$1.20	0	
Dollars	$22,500	$18,000	0	$40,500
Nonvariable costs				22,500
Profit.				$18,000

It should be noted that even a contribution statement of this kind does not give a complete picture of the product-line cost structure, as some of the nonvariable costs may be directly chargeable against one particular product line and some may be general overhead costs which cannot be allocated to product lines except on a highly arbitrary basis.

Limitations of the break-even chart

Some of the limitations of the break-even chart were touched on in the preceding discussion. The single-line chart is constructed on the assumption that both sales income and variable costs will vary directly with unit volume, but this is rarely true, for selling price is an important factor in volume and sales income, and some costs are neither fixed nor a direct function of volume. The necessity of considering the effect of selling price on volume can be brought out in the chart by drawing profit lines for several different selling prices, as in Figure 14–4, but even then, as stated in the preceding section, the chart is valid only if changes in volume, selling price, and costs are uniform for all products.

As to costs, the assumption of direct variability with volume will often be found to be inaccurate, as pointed out in the chapters on manufacturing costs and marketing and administrative costs. Even in the factory, where so-called "variable" costs can usually be reasonably well controlled in relation to production, some significant items may remain fixed within fairly wide limits of volume and may increase by "steps" rather than in a straight line, while many nonvariable costs will be increased or reduced by management action if substantial changes in volume occur. In the case of many selling and administrative costs, the relation to volume is much less direct, and the dividing line between variable and nonvariable elements of cost is even more difficult to determine. Considering all these limitations, it is apparent that the greatest value of the break-even chart is that it presents clearly and dramatically the general principle underlying the relationship of volume to costs and profits; the practical application of that principle almost always requires the evaluation of many more interrelated factors that can be effectively condensed into chart form.

The "direct costing" controversy

Although the break-even chart and the basic profit-planning techniques described above have been used by some managements and some industrial engineers for more than fifty years, it was not until the late 1930's that there was a general recognition in business of the importance of distinguishing between variable and nonvariable costs in sales planning and pricing. As this recognition developed it led quite naturally to the suggestion that product costs computed in the conventional way, including an allocated share of nonvariable costs, have little practical usefulness and that variable product costs should be used for all financial and cost accounting purposes. This is the so-called "direct costing" technique, which, for a long time, was one of the most hotly debated issues among management accountants.

Under direct-costing procedures the conventional form of profit and loss statement is modified to show the sales and variable cost of sales for the period covered by the statement, the margin over variable cost available to meet nonvariable costs, and the actual nonvariable costs *incurred* during the period. The whole point of the procedure is that nonvariable costs of production are charged off as incurred, and only the variable costs are carried to the inventory account and thus deferred until the product is sold. It is contended that this handling not only gives management a clearer idea of the relationship between volume, costs, and profits, but also results in more accurate profit and loss statements, since earnings are not increased simply by producing in excess of sales requirements and thus increasing the nonvariable cost element of inventories, or reduced by the carryover of such nonvariable costs in the opening inventories in periods when production is less than sales.

The arguments pro and con direct costing have been so thoroughly aired in the literature that no attempt will be made here even to summarize them. The controversy has now simmered down, with the recognition that neither direct costing nor conventional full costing holds the perfect answer to all management problems. Certainly, there are real grounds for questioning the wisdom of overemphasizing variable cost as the primary basis of accounting and management thinking. The most intelligent approach to product pricing and sales planning is to consider both variable cost and total cost and use the information to obtain the best possible long-run profit result. Whether it is better to anchor management thinking to total cost and back off to variable cost as necessary, or to emphasize variable cost and build up toward the goal of total cost plus profit, is largely a question of psychology and habit. In either case it is necessary, in dealing with product costs, to recognize that both total cost and variable cost are approximations and that variable costs may change significantly with major changes in volume. The controller's objective should be to make certain that the executives responsible for sales policy and pricing have a clear understanding of the cost structure of the business and know how to interpret the cost figures they are given to use. It should be possible in most cases to accomplish this whether the accounts are kept on the direct-costing basis or the more conventional full-costing basis.

First steps in the development of profit planning

The logical procedure to follow in developing the profit-planning technique in a business where it has not previously been used is to make a careful study of the cost and expense structure, to determine which costs and expenses are variable with volume and which are fixed by external factors, by past management decisions, or by present management policy. As a preliminary to such a detailed study, it is sometimes possible to establish at least an approximate relationship between volume and profits or costs, either for the business as a whole or for one or more of its departments, by using figures taken from actual past experience. In the simpler types of businesses, if selling prices and costs have been reasonably stable over a period of time, a break-even chart of the kind illustrated in Figures 14–2 and 14–3 can often be constructed simply by plotting actual costs or net profits at various levels of unit or dollar sales volume, taking care to eliminate significant nonrecurring items of income and expense. If the points thus plotted do not form a pattern which indicates quite clearly a straight-line relationship between overall volume and costs or profits, it is evident that further analysis is required; and even if the straight-line relationship appears to be established from the overall figures, the assumption should be confirmed by a careful study of the facts and conditions during the period covered by the chart.

In a business manufacturing a single product or a group of homogeneous products, any deviation from a straight-line relationship between volume and profits is most likely to be due either to changes during the period in the relationship between selling prices and raw-material costs or to changes in the internal cost and expense structure. Under these conditions it should be possible to develop and chart a normal, or standard, cost and expense structure representing current conditions or a reasonable objective and to determine the relationship between volume and profits under this cost structure at various levels of selling prices, as illustrated in Figure 14-4.

In the more frequent cases where there are several or many different product lines, the simple break-even chart, as pointed out earlier in this discussion, does not reflect adequately the real facts and conditions, and it is necessary to approach the profit-planning problem by a more detailed analysis of costs in all departments of the factory and office. Here, again, it may be possible to use the empirical method, preparing a chart for each department by plotting total actual costs against departmental activity for each month over a reasonably long period. If this does not give a pattern indicating clearly the relationship of total departmental costs to activity, each element of departmental expense should be similarly charted. By adjusting the figures, where necessary, to put wage rates, supply costs, and other external factors on a current basis and by correcting for cost fluctuations due to changes in maintenance policy and other arbitrary management decisions during the period, it should be possible—in the factory departments at least—to make a reasonably accurate breakdown of the total current departmental costs between the variable and the nonvariable elements. In the office departments, since individual jobs are usually not so well standardized as in the factory and since employees' time and production are not so closely controlled, the relationship of costs to volume may not be so apparent.

In the initial stages of a program of this kind the controller's department may conduct the project as a research study, using factory and office records and consulting with the plant and office managements to secure the information necessary to interpret the figures and charts. At some point, however—and the earlier, the better—an effort should be made to draw in the plant and office managements as active participants in the study. This will serve a double purpose—it will bring to bear on the problem the practical working knowledge of those most closely in touch with actual operations, and it will serve to create interest in the possibilities of the technique for control purposes.

Profit planning and operating control

As the operating departments are drawn into the profit-planning study, it may be found that the technique is already being used for control, perhaps in a partially developed form; for example, the factory management may have worked out some approximate method of adjusting the standard amounts of various expenses set up in the foremen's monthly reports to reflect current variations from standard volume, without attempting to tie in these adjustments in any way with the books or summarize them for recording in the profit and loss statements. It may or may not be possible to integrate completely these working control mechanisms with the data compiled for profit-planning purposes and to make a complete tie in with the accounts—this is a step that can be considered as the program develops—but, in any event, the factory studies and the profit-planning studies should be checked against each other and correlated, and the factory should be encouraged to make the maximum practicable use of the technique. The more thorough the analysis of the variability of each of the different items of cost and the better the actual control of these variable costs in relation to volume, the more reliable will be the data developed by the profit-planning study as a tool in the formulation of sales and general management policy.

Variable product costs

When the costs of each factory department have been broken down into the variable and nonvariable elements, it is a simple matter to make a similar breakdown of the factory costs of individual products, provided that there is available for each product a manufacturing specification sheet showing the buildup of its total manufacturing cost by departments, based on the activity in each department per finished unit. Once the technique is fully developed, the specification sheets themselves may be set up to show the breakdown of total departmental costs between variable and nonvariable. Direct labor, which is usually, though not always, 100 percent variable, may be added separately as a total per unit of finished product or included in the departmental costs, depending on how it is handled in the accounts. Direct material is, under most conditions, entirely a variable cost; the amount per unit of finished product can be determined by extending a material specification sheet at current market material prices or at the standard or estimated prices to be used for planning purposes.[2]

Where there are a large number of products in the line, it will probably be found cumbersome and impracticable to use individual product costs for broad planning and forecasting. In such cases the products can be classified into groups, and an average ratio of variable manufacturing cost to total manufacturing cost developed for each group by weighting the ratios of all the individual products or of a number of selected products typical of the group. The grouping should, if possible,

---

[2] Under some conditions, direct labor costs or direct material costs may not be 100 percent variable—for example, minimum-wage guarantees may increase unit labor costs when volume declines, or material may be bought more advantageously in large volume. If such irregularities in variability exist, they must, of course, be considered in using and interpreting the variable-cost data.

be the same as that adopted for sales analysis and sales forecasting, so that the data developed can readily be used by the sales and general-management executives; but if the assortment of products sold in any group is likely to vary to any extent, some subdivision of these major groups may be necessary. It is important that these subdivisions be made so that there will not be too much variation in the ratios of variable cost to total cost for the different products in any group—in other words, so that any probable changes in the assortment of sales within the group will not result in a material change in the average ratio for the group. At the same time, it is desirable, in the interest of simplification, to keep the number of groups to a minimum; as in many other problems, some compromise must be struck between accuracy and practicability.

If the breakdown of product manufacturing costs between nonvariable and variable, as described in the preceding paragraphs, is based on and tied in with a system of variable standards for the control of factory operations, it should be possible to obtain a very good check on the accuracy of the variable costs of individual products or the group ratios of variable cost to total cost. This check can be made by using the product-cost data to compute the total variable cost of the goods produced for one or more months and comparing this with the total standard variable costs of all the factory departments during the same month, adjusting for changes in work in process. It should not be expected that the two figures will agree exactly, but over a period of several months the differences should tend to offset, and it should be possible to reconcile within 2 or 3 percent.

All the foregoing discussion of variable product costs is concerned with manufacturing costs only. The problems involved in determining variable costs of marketing and administration were treated in Chapters 9 and 10. As pointed out there, it is usually possible to determine with reasonable accuracy the variable cost of such activities as warehousing and shipping and perhaps of other routine order-filling and money-collecting functions, such as billing, accounts receivable posting, and the like, if they are actually under close control in relation to volume. However, many of these costs are, to all practical purposes, fixed by management policy—at least within a relatively wide range of volume changes—and the degree to which they will vary with major volume changes over the long pull can only be estimated. Order-getting costs, such as advertising, salaries, and expenses of field salesmen, etc., must be considered as variable only by management policy and have no place in the calculation of variable product costs.

As a practical matter, unless the order-filling and money-collecting costs are unusually high in relation to factory costs, it is satisfactory, in the early stages of development of the profit-planning technique, to make some rough approximations of variable marketing and adminis-trative costs, using the best information available, and to defer refinements in this phase of the study until the actual use of the data by the management points to a real need for greater accuracy.

Use of variable-cost data

When the controller has in his possession all the basic information about the cost and expense structure of the business, he still has the problem of conveying that information to the management so that it will be put to practical use. The uses that can be made of data of this kind in planning and policy making have been described at length earlier in this chapter and in the chapters on marketing and administrative costs, and various charts, forms, and reports have been suggested. If a budget procedure is in operation, it is theoretically possible, by the use of variable-cost data, to adjust each month's profit and loss budget for the effect of variances from budgeted sales volume—in other words, to make the budget completely "flexible." This may be desirable as an ultimate objective, but such a budget will be of only academic interest unless the management understands the basic relationships between volume and cost in the various sections of the business and has become accustomed to making practical use of the variable-costing technique in actual operations.

It is not possible to lay down any step-by-step procedure which the controller can follow to bring this technique into effective use throughout the business. He may be in a position to make what might be called a direct "frontal attack" on the problem—that is, to present to the management a complete analysis with specific recommendations for the practical steps to be taken. This is more likely to be effective in a business where the cost structure is relatively simple and the facts about the relationship of costs and volume can be easily and clearly demonstrated. More often the best results can be achieved by a more gradual approach, studying the practical application of the technique to each executive's operating problems, working with him in its development, and thus building up an understanding of the basic philosophy. Here, again, is an opportunity for the exercise of the real art of controllership.

15 PLANNING AND CONTROL OF CAPITAL EXPENDITURES

The term "capital expenditures" is commonly interpreted to mean expenditures for long-life assets purchased for use in the business, rather than for consumption (as material entering into the product or as operating supplies) or for resale. "Long life" is often arbitrarily defined as a useful life of more than one year; but the anticipated useful lives of most capital assets range from three years, as for motor vehicles and semipermanent tooling, through five to twenty-five years for machinery and equipment, up to forty years for the more permanent types of building construction and even longer periods for land and natural resources such as timber, mineral rights, etc. The discussions in this chapter will deal principally with the planning and control of expenditures for real estate plant and equipment in a manufacturing business. The same principles apply, however, to all other types of capital expenditures; and they also apply to expenditures for research and development projects, special marketing programs, etc., which are charged in the accounts against current earnings but are expected to yield a return over a longer period.[1]

The importance of proper planning and control of capital expenditures can hardly be overemphasized. The amounts of money involved are usually so substantial and the recovery of funds, once expended, is spread over such a long period of time that unwise commitments may lead to serious impairment of the financial position of the business, and even to insolvency. For this reason such expenditures in well-managed companies are carefully planned in advance and are usually subject to the approval of the top management or even of the directors. The controller should have an active part in the assembling and presentation of data needed for planning, and he will, of course, have complete

---

[1] See the section in Chapter 13 on "Program Budgeting and Control."

responsibility for the installation and operation of the necessary control procedures.

Long-range capital budgeting and financial policies

Long-range budgeting of capital expenditures is necessarily based on broad operating plans and policies which are subject to frequent revision to meet changing conditions. For this reason, many small and medium-sized businesses are inclined to neglect somewhat the long view and to concentrate on solving the more tangible and urgent problems of the present and the immediate future. But even though a long-range budget must be a loose and extremely flexible document, it is helpful to put down on paper the outlines of a definite plan, so that the financial requirements of the business may be foreseen and adequately provided for.

The long-range budget of capital expenditures, to be most useful, must be tied in with the profit and loss and financial budgets. What funds will be available over a period of years, from net earnings and from depreciation, for investment in plant replacements or additions, after paying dividends, meeting sinking-fund obligations, and providing for working capital needs? On the other side of the equation, what additional plant assets or replacements of existing assets will be required to carry out the sales policies and programs which the managers of the business have in mind? These questions obviously involve much more than the budgeting of any particular type of expenditures; they reach into the field of corporate strategic and tactical planning, which are discussed more fully in Chapters 19 and 20.

Preparing the long-range capital budget

Since the long-range capital budget must be fitted into the broad financial plan, the amounts actually budgeted will be limited by the availability of funds. But a tentative budget or "want list," including all the plant expenditures which management would consider if funds were available, will provide the necessary information for formulating an intelligent budget and keeping it up to date as conditions change. Such a want list will be more useful if the proposed expenditures are broken down into the following classes:

Necessary replacements of facilities which are physically exhausted through wear and tear.

Replacements, improvements, or additions to effect cost savings.

Additions needed to provide for normal growth.

Additions required in connection with contemplated development and expansion projects.

Desirable replacements, improvements, or additions not falling in any of the above categories, but important from the standpoint of quality, personnel relations, prestige, or for other intangible reasons.

The budgeting of replacements which will be necessary because of the exhaustion of existing assets through wear and tear is essentially an engineering problem. While there is considerable latitude as to the time at which any given replacement can be made, nevertheless a careful survey will in most cases yield a reasonably dependable forecast. But in most industries obsolescence of equipment or of manual methods due to advances in the art of manufacture is a much more important factor than exhaustion through wear and tear, and this is the source of most cost-saving replacement and addition proposals. The want list should include all known possible replacements and additions which would effect cost savings, plus a projection of a lump-sum total of unidentified cost-saving projects, based on past experience and a knowledge of pending developments in the industry. Frequent close contact with marketing, engineering, production and research personnel should help to alert the controller to at least the major developments which would cause any extraordinary obsolescence due to sudden changes in product acceptance or radical improvements in manufacturing methods.

In every established and healthy business there is a normal rate of growth and expansion, not only in the known outlets for existing products, but also in the addition of closely related products and the development of new outlets. This normal growth can usually be forecast with reasonable accuracy, and required plant expenditures can be planned accordingly. Besides this type of gradual expansion, there may be other and larger expansions contemplated by the management—for example, an effort to touch a large section of a still undeveloped market, to break in on competition with a new product, or perhaps as part of a process of vertical integration for the purpose of controlling sources of raw material or outlets for finished products. Major expansion plans of this kind will presumably be based on careful studies of existing capacity and of present and potential consumption in the industry and will include a projection of funds required for new plant and for additional working capital. Capital budgeting, in other words, is an important facet of general forward planning and must be dealt with as a part of the overall plans for the future.

The annual capital budget

While the long-range capital budget is a valuable tool for intelligent forward planning, actual commitments of funds to specific projects are usually made only once a year, when the annual capital budget is prepared. As in the case of the long-range budget, the preparation of this annual capital budget should be an integral part of the overall budgeting process. In companies which are so fortunate as to have unlimited funds at their disposal, the major question may be how far the organization is prepared to carry out the long-range plan; in the great majority of businesses, however, the problem is to make the best use of the funds that can be made available. The program finally adopted will be influenced by such factors as the physical condition of the plant assets scheduled for replacement, the imminence of major repairs, the possible direct cost savings from various proposed expenditures and the relative benefit possibilities and risks in contemplated new developments. The classification of proposals by the categories suggested earlier for the long-range "want list" will be useful in assisting management to maintain a balanced total program and to avoid committing too large a proportion of available funds to projects which do not have a tangible favorable effect on earnings.

Evaluation of capital expenditure proposals

In a well-organized annual capital budgeting program detailed information will be submitted for each proposed project, showing (a) the investment required, (b) the cost savings or additional profits, if any, anticipated from the project, and (c) some form of mathematical calculation relating the savings or additional profits to the investment, to assist management in ranking the projects for final selection. This brief statement is deceptively simple; actually there is an extensive and growing mass of literature on the subject of capital budgeting, most of it revolving around refinements in the mathematical calculations and the use of the calculations in selecting the projects to be carried out. Our approach to the subject in this chapter will be (a) to restate the fundamental principles which should govern the preparation of capital expenditure proposals, (b) to discuss briefly the types of mathematical calculations which are most frequently used, (c) to identify the major problems that arise in interpreting and applying the mathematical calculations to arrive at sound decisions, and (d) to refer the reader to some of the less esoteric literature suggesting solutions to these practical problems.

Summary of basic principles

Following is a condensed and admittedly oversimplified statement of basic principles in the evaluation of proposed capital expenditures:

1.   In studying any proposal all practical alternative courses of action should be considered.

2.   The investment required in connection with any proposal includes not only the cost of the capital assets to be acquired, but also design and development costs, installation costs, wiring and service facilities,

rearrangement and moving expenses, startup costs, and all other costs and expenses that will be incurred in connection with the project, less (a) the salvage value of any old equipment or facilities to be replaced, and (b) a credit for the income tax saving on the expenditures which are chargeable against current income, rather than to the fixed asset accounts.

3. Estimates of savings or increased income attainable by a proposed expenditure should be based on special studies of the cost and expense structures under the various possible alternatives.

4. If the proposal involves an increase over the current rate of annual production and salable output, then:

(a) the investment should include the increase in working capital (cash, accounts receivable, and inventories) necessary to finance the added volume of business; and

(b) the estimate of cost savings or additional income should take into consideration not only the additional manufacturing costs, but also the resulting increases in marketing, warehousing, and administrative expenses.

5. Consideration should be given to the varying degrees of risk involved in different projects.

6. Calculations of savings or additional profits should take into consideration a charge for the use of capital employed, giving recognition to the time value of money—i.e., the principle that a dollar received today is worth more than the same amount to be received at some future date. For convenience we will refer to this charge for the use of capital as an "interest" charge, although the term "interest" has connotations that are not strictly appropriate for our purpose.

7. In presenting the results of any study for management decision, the intangible factors for or against a proposed investment—i.e., those considerations which cannot be expressed in dollar terms—should be clearly stated.

Each of the above principles is discussed briefly in the paragraphs immediately following.

Study of alternatives

Before submitting a capital expenditure proposal, consideration should be given to any possible modifications or alternatives which might yield all or part of the estimated cost savings, or additional income, with a lower investment of funds. In studying any cost-saving problem (replacement or new equipment), emphasis should be placed on analysis of the job to be performed, rather than on the characteristics of the equipment itself. In many cases there will be several alternatives, such as different types of machines, combinations of machine and handwork, changes in processing methods, letting all or part of the work out on contract, etc. This type of imaginative analysis is properly the responsibility of the company's industrial engineering or methods engineering department, but the controller, or one of his staff, should collaborate with the engineering personnel in developing the cost estimates and should be in a position to suggest new alternatives for study.

Investment requirements

The principle that all costs associated with a project, whether capitalized or charged against current earnings, should be included in the required investment may seem self-evident, but it is surprising how often some of the noncapital factors are overlooked or underestimated. Again, this is the responsibility of the manufacturing engineering group, but again, the controller should have some opinion on the adequacy of the provisions included in the proposal.

When a proposal involves the removal and sale or scrapping of major elements of old equipment, special attention should be given to the income-tax effect of the removal. This is particularly important where there is a difference between income-tax and book accounting for depreciation or where it may be possible to claim an extraordinary obsolescence loss for income-tax purposes.

Estimating costs

In estimating manufacturing costs and other expenses under the various alternatives in any study, conventional overhead rates and unit costs should be disregarded and an engineering survey should be made to determine how the dollar amounts of each element of cost would vary under the different methods of operation. It should be particularly noted that book allocations of past expenditures have no bearing on the savings or profits that can be realized from future expenditures. This principle is now understood and accepted by most managements, but as recently as fifteen or even ten years ago it was frequently violated in one or both of two ways:

1. By adding to the investment required for a proposal the undepreciated book value of old assets to be replaced. This error, which obviously made the proposal less attractive, was often justified on the grounds of conservatism, on the theory that a business cannot afford to make reckless investments and must recover somehow the money it spends on plant assets.

2. By calculating depreciation on such old assets, for the purpose of cost comparisons and savings calculations, by applying regular depre-

ciation rates to their original cost or by spreading their undepreciated book value, rather than their current realizable value, over their remaining life. This fallacy, which almost always overstated the future cost of continuing to use the old assets and thus overstated the anticipated savings or profits, was most often advanced by production men, who were interested in having the most modern equipment and felt that the calculation of depreciation on current realizable value made it difficult to justify many improvements that were necessary for an efficient and competitive operation.

These fallacies represented attempts to influence capital expenditure decisions (in opposite directions) by injecting into the calculation of savings or profits considerations which, however valid, should properly be considered separately, on their own merits, as discussed later in the section "Intangible Factors."

Additional production

1. When a proposal provides for the replacement of existing equipment or the substitution of machine operations for manual operations, without any increase in annual production, the cost calculations should be based on forecast or actual average current sales volume, even though the particular new equipment to be purchased may have a greater capacity then the equipment to be replaced. The same annual rate of production should be used in estimating present costs and costs after the proposed investment.

2. If the estimated savings from a proposal result in whole or in part from a projected increase in the annual rate of production and salable output, the proposal should include details of plans for disposition of the added production and the effect of these plans on working capital requirements and on all elements of cost. In cases where the planned increase in sales is greater than demonstrated normal growth, an extensive market research study may be required. This is, of course, the responsibility of the sales or marketing department, but it is certainly the controller's duty, in his review of the proposal, to stress the market and competitive factors, so that the assumptions on which the estimated savings are based may be clearly understood.

Degree of risk

1. The longer the payback period on any project (i.e., the time required for the cash return from the project to equal the investment), the greater the degree of risk.

2. Risk varies considerably with the type of investment. This is sometimes recognized by assigning different target rates of return to different

types of investments. Thus one large oil company at one time established target rates of 10, 14, and 18 percent for investments in marketing and pipeline facilities, refining facilities, and development wells and petrochemical facilities, respectively. Another possibility is to set different target rates for different asset categories (e.g., land on contiguous site, land on special site, standard buildings, special buildings, standard machinery, special machinery, etc.) and to compute a weighted average target rate for each major project, according to its investment elements. Such predetermined target rates, adjusted for risk, can be useful as general guidelines, but other techniques for risk evaluation, discussed later in this chapter, afford more opportunity for the exercise of management judgment on each project at the time investment decisions are made.[2]

The "interest" factor

When a business firm makes a capital expenditure, it expects that over the life of the assets purchased it will recover its investment plus an adequate return on the capital employed. The firm is in the same position as a bank or savings and loan association investing in a mortgage which is to be repaid over a period of years. Many such mortgage loans provide for a level annual payment, part of which is applied to interest on the unamortized balance of the loan at the beginning of the year and the remainder to paying down the principal of the loan. As an example, it can be determined from interest tables that the level annual payment required to pay off a five-year mortage loan of $10,000 at a 10 percent interest rate is $2,638. An amortization table on such a loan would be as follows:

Unamortized balance beginning of year	Application of annual payment ($2,638)	
	Interest at 10%	Principal
$10,000	$1,000	$ 1.638
8,362	836	1.802
6,560	656	1.982
4,578	458	2.180
2,398	240	2.398
Total principal payments		$10,000

The procedures followed in applying this principle in capital expenditure evaluation studies are described in a later section on "Methods of Calculation and Presentation." In general, either (a) the calculations should reflect an "interest" charge for the use of capital employed or

---

[2] See the sections later in this chapter on "The Payback Period in Risk Evaluation" and "The Sensitivity Factor in Project Evaluation."

(b) the anticipated rate of return on the required investment should be considered.

It is sometimes argued that if the proposed investments are to be financed by special borrowings; the charge for capital employed should be computed at the actual interest rate on such borrowings. But in most situations, this is basically unsound, as the cost of borrowed money is almost always less than the firm's target rate of return on its total capital. A more equitable procedure is to establish a target rate of return for use in all projects, or, as suggested in the preceding section, a number of different target rates, depending on the type of investment. In the past, rates of return as low as six percent have been used, but this is unrealistic, as we are dealing here with *risk* capital, rather than with anything approaching pure investment capital. A realistic average rate of return in most industries should be much higher, possibly a minimum of twenty percent before taxes, to result in a net of ten percent after taxes. As noted earlier in this chapter, in the sections on "Preparing the Long-Range Capital Budget" and "The Annual Capital Budget," there will inevitably be some capital expenditures which do not have a tangible favorable effect on earnings; hence, to achieve an overall *average* after-tax return of 10 percent the target rate on profit-yielding projects must be set somewhat higher.[3]

The literature of capital expenditure planning

For many years the only published material (as far as the authors are aware) which completely and correctly set forth the principles discussed above and the presently accepted basic methods of calculation and presentation for capital expenditure proposals was the book *Principles of Engineering Economy* by Eugene L. Grant. Although this book, originally published in 1930, was widely used as a textbook by engineering students, it was almost unknown to business managers; and until the late 1950's and early 1960's there was a great deal of confusion and some positive misinformation on the subject in the literature of management accounting. The most recent edition of the book[4] is one of the most complete reference works on the subject available today; a more condensed and less technical general treatment will be found in *The Capital Budgeting Decision* by Harold Bierman, Jr., and Seymour Smidt[5] and *The Capital Expenditure Decision* by David Quirin.[6] In

---

[3] The determination of a target rate of return is a major element in the formulation of corporate strategy, as discussed in Chapter 19. See particularly the section in that chapter on "Investment Policy."

[4] *Principles of Engineering Economy* by Eugene L. Grant and W. Grant Ireson (New York: Ronald Press, 1970).

[5] New York: Macmillan, 1960.

[6] Homewood, Ill.: Richard D. Irwin Inc., 1967.

addition to these (and several other) books covering the subject as a whole there are now literally hundreds of articles on specialized aspects of the problem in accounting and management publications; some of these are referred to in later sections of this chapter.

Methods of calculation and presentation

The two basic methods in common use for the calculation of the relative merits of alternative capital expenditure proposals in accordance with the principles discussed above are:

1. Comparison of the total net present values of the required investments and the estimated earnings (i.e., net cost savings or additional profits) at a stipulated target rate of return.

2. Comparison of the "time-adjusted rates of return" on the required investments. The "time-adjusted rate of return" on any project is the discount rate at which the present value of the estimated earnings from the project is equal to the present value of the required investment—in other words, the rate at which the net present value of the project is zero.[7]

Since both of these methods of evaluation provide for the recovery of the required investment over the life of the project, the estimated earnings are stated *before* the deduction of depreciation on the investment. In other words, the earnings are stated on a cash basis; hence the use of the term "discounted cash flow" to describe any time-adjusted method of computation. It should be borne in mind, however, that in determining earnings the effect of income taxes on cash flow must be considered, and since depreciation is deductible in the computation of income taxes this is a complicating factor in cases where the useful lives of depreciable assets for income-tax purposes are different from the project lives, or where accelerated methods of computing depreciation are used in the determination of income taxes.

Figure 15–1 shows an illustration of the computation of (a) net present value at a target rate of return of 10 percent and (b) the time-adjusted rate of return on investment, in a very simple case where the original investment in the project is $10,000 and the estimated after-tax earnings are at a uniform annual rate of $3,400 for a four-year period. Following is an explanation of the calculations in this table:

1. Net-Present-Value Method. The first four columns in section A show the computation of the net present value of the project at a 10 percent target rate of return.

   a) The factors in the third column are taken from interest tables

---

[7] The time-adjusted rate of return is often referred to in the literature as the "internal rate of return."

Figure 15–1
EXAMPLE OF COMPUTATION OF NET PRESENT VALUE
AND TIME-ADJUSTED RATE OF RETURN
A—Computation of Net Present Value

			@ 10% discount rate (Present value)		@ 15% discount rate (Present value)	
	Year	Amount	Factor	P.V.	Factor	P.V.
Investment	0	$10,000	1.0000	$10,000	1.0000	$10,000
Earnings	1	$ 3,400	.9091	$ 3,091	.8696	$ 2,958
	2	3,400	.8264	2,809	.7561	2,571
	3	3,400	.7513	2,555	.6575	2,234
	4	3,400	.6830	2,323	.5718	1,944
Total		$13,600	3.1698	$10,778	2.8550	$ 9,707
Net present value				778		(293)

B—Interpolation for Time-Adjusted Rate of Return

Net present value	at 10%	+778
	at 15%	−293
Difference	5%	1,091

Time-adjusted rate of return $\qquad 10\% + \left(\dfrac{778}{1091} \times 5\%\right) = 13.6\%$

C—Proof of Time-Adjusted Rate of Return

Year	Unrecovered investment beginning of year	Application of annual earnings ($3,400) Interest at 13.6%	Application of annual earnings ($3,400) Recovery of investment
1	$10,000	$1,360	$2,040
2	7,960	1,083	2,317
3	5,643	767	2,633
4	3,010	409	2,991
Total			$9,981

showing the present value of a future single sum at a 10 percent discount rate (Appendix C). In this illustration, where after-tax earnings are at a uniform annual rate, the total present value of the earnings for the four years can be computed by applying to the $3,400 annual earnings rate the cumulative factor of 3.1698, which can be read directly from another interest table showing the present value of a future *annual* sum at the 10 percent discount rate (Appendix D). However, in cases where there is a year-to-year variation in earnings, the longer computation, using the factor for each year, is necessary.

b) The project has a positive net present value of $778, indicating that it will earn more than the 10 percent target rate and should, therefore, be accepted if funds are available for all projects meeting the target rate criterion.

c) In ranking projects for selection when limited funds are available, it might appear that the preferred projects would be those with the greatest positive net present values. However, a selection on this basis would not give weight to differences in the amounts of investment required and hence in the relative risks involved. The procedure usually recommended is to base the ranking on the "benefit/cost ratios" of the various projects,[8] computed by dividing the present value of the benefits (earnings) for each project by the present value of the required investment, as shown in the example in Figure 15–2.

Figure 15–2
COMPARISON OF BENEFIT/COST RATIOS FOR THREE
PROJECTS WITH IDENTICAL NET PRESENT VALUES
(thousands of dollars)

		Project I	Project II	Project III
	Present value of:			
(A)	Investment	50	200	200
(B)	Gross income from project	100	500	230
(C)	Operating costs and expenses of project	30	280	10
(D)	Net earnings of project (B–C)	70	220	220
(E)	Net present value of project (D–A)	20	20	20
(F)	Benefit/cost ratio—net basis (D/A)	1.40	1.10	1.10
(G)	Present value of investment plus present value of operating costs and expenses (A plus C)	80	480	210
(H)	Benefit/cost ratio—gross basis (B/G)	1.25	1.04	1.10

On the basis of the benefit/cost ratios shown on line F, Project I is obviously to be preferred and Projects II and III are of equal ranking. But the equal ranking of II and III ignores the much larger amount of money committed to Project II and the consequent risk of larger dollar errors in the estimates of income and expense on which the calculations are based. If the benefit/cost ratios are computed by dividing the present value of the *gross* income by the sum of the present values of the investment and the project operating costs, the result, as shown on line H, indicates a preference for Project III over Project II.

It is interesting to note that Bierman and Smidt, who are ardent

---

[8] The "benefit/cost ratio" is sometimes referred to as the "profitability index," but the latter term also has other meanings in the literature.

advocates of the present-value method of evaluation, do not recommend using the benefit/cost ratio procedure, on the grounds that it is impossible to distinguish between investment-type outlays and outlays of the expense type.[9] The computation of the ratio on the gross basis, as on line H above, would appear to meet this objection.

2. Time-Adjusted Rate-of-Return Method. Referring back to Figure 15–1, the last two columns in section A show that at a discount rate of 15 percent the project has a negative net present value of $293, compared to the *positive* net present value of $778 at 10 percent.

a) The present value factors in the fifth column are derived from interest tables, as explained in paragraph 1 (a) above, using a 15 percent discount rate instead of 10 percent.

b) To calculate the time-adjusted rate of return (by definition the rate at which the net present value of the project is zero), it is necessary to follow a trial and error procedure, interpolating between a rate resulting in a positive net present value and a rate resulting in a negative net present value. This interpolation calculation, shown in section B, gives a time-adjusted rate of return of 13.6 percent. If this rate is equal to or greater than the target rate of return established for the project, the proposal is considered acceptable, and in a capital-rationing situation preference is given to those projects yielding the highest rates of return.

c) Section C is a proof of the correctness of the 13.6 percent time-adjusted rate. The $3,400 earnings in each year are applied first to "interest" on the unrecovered investment at the beginning of the year, and the remainder is applied to the recovery of the initial investment of $10,000. This calculation is similar to the mortgage loan amortization table in the earlier section of this chapter on "The Interest Factor."[10]

Present value versus time-adjusted rate of return

There is a great deal of controversy over the relative merits of the two methods of evaluation described above. Most theoreticians appear to have a strong preference for the present-value method or its derivative, the benefit/cost ratio,[11] but most business managers, at least in

---

[9] Bierman and Smidt, *Capital Budgeting Decision*, p. 47, n7.

[10] For detailed procedures and forms for the calculation of the time-adjusted rate of return in cases where the assumption of a uniform annual rate of earnings from a project is not valid, refer to the article "Profitability Index for Investments," by R. I. Reul, in the July-August 1957 issue of *Harvard Business Review*. A discussion of this article, with copies of some of the forms, will be found in Grant and Ireson's *Principles of Engineering Economy*, pp. 519–25. (The term "Profitability Index," as used by Reul, refers to what we have called the time-adjusted rate of return.)

Standard computer programs are available which will perform the search for the time-adjusted rate of return; these programs must, of course, be supplied with the flows of cash and their respective timings.

[11] But see Grant and Ireson's comment on "The Cult of Present Value," *Principles*, pp. 560–61.

the authors' experience, prefer to deal with a rate of return that they can "latch on to," rather than a present-value figure or benefit/cost ratio that has no meaning to the layman who is not schooled in the theory of compound interest. There is no question that the use of a single discount rate—the target rate of return—for the calculation of the present value and the benefit/cost ratio of a project simplifies many of the calculations, and this is true even though computer programming has eliminated much of the manual work of the trial-and-error calculations necessary in the determination of the time-adjusted rate of return. But advocates of the present-value (benefit/cost ratio) method also point to other factors which, they contend, make the rate-of-return method difficult to use correctly or likely to lead to erroneous conclusions:

1. In choosing between two projects with different lives, the project with the lower rate of return but a longer life may (possibly) be the better choice, unless the funds released by the shorter-lived project can be reinvested at a rate higher than that earned by the longer-lived project. As a contra-argument, it may be pointed out that the present-value method arbitrarily assumes the reinvestment of funds at the stipulated target rate of return, which may be less realistic than the rate of return on the terminated project, particularly if the firm is unable to undertake all projects meeting the target rate criterion, due to lack of funds or because of management limitations. The reinvestment rate assumed in any situation should be the rate which it is forecast can be earned at the time the funds become available.[12]

2. Under certain conditions—specifically, where negative cash flows occur some years after the original investment in a project—the calculation of the time-adjusted rate of return may give two different rates which are equally valid on the basis of the assumptions on which the calculations are based.[13] Instances of this kind are relatively rare in practice; where they occur, the reasons should be carefully evaluated, and a supplemental present-value calculation (not necessarily using the target rate of return) may be helpful in arriving at a sound decision.

The payback method of evaluation

The method of evaluation of capital expenditure proposals most widely used by business managers before the presently accepted, more

---

[12] Techniques have been developed for computing an average rate of return over the life of a project on the assumption that the funds released from the project each year are reinvested at any selected "pool rate" for the remainder of the project life. See the article "Evaluating the Return on Capital Investment," by James C. Hetrick, in the August 1969 issue of *Financial Executive*, pp. 24–28.

[13] For an explanation of this phenomenon see Bierman and Smidt *Capital Budgeting Decision*, pp. 40–43. Bierman and Smidt assert that the present-value method avoids this problem, but Grant and Ireson *Principles of Engineering Economy*, pp. 560–61 do not agree.

scientific methods were generally understood was the so-called "payback method." Under this method, (a) the payback period—that is, the number of years required for the cash earnings from each project to equal the investment—is determined, (b) only projects with less than a specified payback period (often as short as two or three years) are accepted, and (c) preference is given (as far as mathematical factors are concerned) to those projects with the quickest payback. This method is still used by some business managers who feel that more refined techniques are a waste of time because of the inaccuracies inherent in any projections of future savings or additional income. The advantages claimed for the method are: (a) that for practical purposes it results in the most efficient use of cash resources when limited funds are available, and (b) that it insures against the danger of rapid obsolescence due to improvements in manufacturing methods or changes in market conditions.

The obvious weakness of the payback method is that it does not take into account variations in the lives of different projects and hence gives no clue as to differences in total project earnings or rates of return. This objection can be overcome, for many simpler projects, by using the table reproduced in Figure 15–3, which shows the time-adjusted rate of return for payback periods from 1½ to 10 years and useful lives up to 40 years. This table, which is easily constructed, by interpolation, from the interest table in Appendix D, gives a correct reading of the rate of return for any project which meets all of the following conditions:

1. the investment in the project is to be completed within one year;
2. the estimated after-tax earnings from the project are to be realized at a uniform annual rate over the project life; and
3. the project does not involve any increase in annual production or salable output, or other factors that would require additional working capital.

The payback period in risk evaluation

The disadvantages of the exclusive use of the payback method of evaluation in order to minimize risk were emphasized in the preceding section. But in view of the increasing range of possible error as estimates of costs and benefits are projected further into the future, some recognition should certainly be given to payback periods in choosing among competing capital expenditure projects. As a minimum the presentation of the mathematical calculations of every proposal should include a simple statement of the payback period, so that those responsible for investment decisions can at least make subjective judgments of the impact of the timing factor on the relative risks of the various projects. When a choice is to be made between major projects, it is helpful to dramatize the

Figure 15–3
TABLE SHOWING RATES OF RETURN ON INVESTMENT
FOR VARIOUS PAYBACK PERIODS AND USEFUL LIVES
(assuming uniform annual income)

Useful life (years)	Payback period (years)							
	1.50	1.75	2.00	2.25	2.50	2.75	3.00	3.25
2.	21.6	9.4	. . . . .	. . . . .	. . . . .	. . . . .	. . . . .	. . . . .
3.	44.7	32.8	23.4	15.9	9.7	4.5	. . . . .	. . . . .
4.	Over 50.0	43.9	34.9	27.8	21.9	16.9	12.6	8.9
5.	DO	49.6	41.1	34.3	28.7	23.9	19.9	16.3
6.	DO	Over 50.0	44.6	38.1	32.8	28.2	24.3	21.0
7.	DO	DO	46.7	40.3	35.2	30.9	27.1	23.9
8.	DO	DO	47.9	41.8	36.8	32.7	29.0	25.9
9.	DO	DO	48.7	42.8	37.9	33.8	30.3	27.3
10.	DO	DO	49.2	43.4	38.6	34.6	31.2	28.2
11.	DO	DO	49.5	43.7	39.0	35.0	31.9	28.9
12.	DO	DO	49.7	44.0	39.3	35.5	32.3	29.4
13.	DO	DO	49.8	44.2	39.5	35.8	32.7	29.7
14.	DO	DO	49.9	44.3	39.7	36.0	32.9	30.0
15.	DO	DO	49.9	44.4	39.8	36.1	33.0	30.2
20.	DO	DO	50.0	44.5	40.0	36.4	33.4	30.7
25.	DO	DO	50.0	44.5	40.0	36.5	33.5	30.9
30.	DO	DO	50.0	44.5	40.0	36.5	33.5	30.9
40.	DO	DO	50.0	44.5	40.0	36.5	33.5	30.9

payback figures by preparing a chart showing the year-by-year cumulative net cash flows of the competing projects.

A technique for taking into consideration the time value of money in comparing the cash flows of competing projects is described in an article "Capital Budgeting: A Modified Approach to Capital Allocation," by L. P. Anderson and V. V. Miller, in the March 1969 issue of *Management Accounting*. The procedure suggested calls for calculating and charting the year-by-year cumulative *net present values* of competing projects, computed at the target rate of return. In comparisons between projects with different lives, provision is made for using a range of reinvestment rates for funds released from the shorter-lived projects. The charts derived from these calculations show, at a glance, which proposal is superior, in terms of its net present value, at any given point in time. Thus they provide management with a clear visual picture on which to base a final subjective assessment of relative risks due to the decreasing reliability of earnings estimates in later years.

The sensitivity factor in project evaluation

As frequently mentioned in the preceding sections of this chapter, business managers are conscious of the limitations on the accuracy of projections of the costs and future benefits of capital expenditure proposals. For this reason, it is common practice to make at least three mathematical calculations for any important proposal—one based on

Payback period (years)									
4.00	4.25	4.50	4.75	5.00	6.00	7.00	8.00	9.00	10.00
.....	.....	.....	.....	.....	.....	.....	.....	.....	.....
.....	.....	.....	.....	.....	.....	.....	.....	.....	.....
7.9	5.7	3.6	1.7	.....	.....	.....	.....	.....	.....
13.0	10.9	8.9	7.1	5.5	.....	.....	.....	.....	.....
16.3	14.3	12.5	10.8	9.2	4.0	.....	.....	.....	.....
18.6	16.7	14.9	13.3	11.8	6.9	3.1	.....	.....	.....
20.3	18.4	16.7	15.1	13.7	9.0	5.4	2.4	.....	.....
21.4	19.6	18.0	16.5	15.2	10.6	7.1	4.3	2.0	.....
22.3	20.5	18.9	17.5	16.2	12.0	8.4	5.7	3.5	1.6
22.9	21.2	19.7	18.2	17.0	12.7	9.5	6.9	4.8	3.0
23.4	21.7	20.2	18.8	17.6	13.5	10.3	7.8	5.7	4.0
23.7	22.1	20.6	19.3	18.0	14.0	11.0	8.6	6.6	4.9
24.0	22.4	21.0	19.6	18.4	14.5	11.5	9.2	7.2	5.6
24.7	23.2	21.8	20.6	19.5	15.8	13.1	11.0	9.3	7.8
24.9	23.4	22.1	20.9	19.8	16.3	13.7	11.7	10.1	8.8
25.0	23.5	22.2	21.0	19.9	16.5	14.0	12.1	10.6	9.4
25.0	23.5	22.2	21.0	19.9	16.5	14.0	12.1	11.0	9.8

an optimistic (but reasonable) estimate of costs and benefits, one on a conservative estimate and one on a "middle-of-the-road" or "most likely" estimate. With the use of a computer to perform the mathematical calculations, it is possible to determine readily the results of any number of combinations of variations in the several elements of the projections.

A further refinement suggested in the literature, where major projects are involved, is to have the responsible operating executives assign probabilities to each of a range of values for each element in the projections. The simulation procedure described in Chapter 25 can then be followed to generate a report on the "risk distribution" for the project, showing the probability of each of a range of time-adjusted rates of return or net present values, from the most pessimistic to the most optimistic. With this risk distribution available, management is in a better position to make a decision on the proposed investment, considering not only the most probable outcome but also its willingness to incur the risk of a less favorable result.[14] The practical usefulness of this kind of calculation will obviously depend on the familiarity of the individuals assigning the probability values with the internal operations and competitive

---

[14] For a brief summary of the possible degrees of automation of the capital expenditure decision process, see the article "The Trend toward Automated Capital Investment Decisions" by J. C. Lampe in the April 1971 issue of *Management Accounting*. The article includes a description of techniques for substituting automation for management judgment even in the final step of risk evaluation, but concludes that these techniques are not sufficiently developed to be reliable in practice.

developments in their respective functional areas, and on their ability to be reasonable and objective in their judgments.

Discounted cash flow versus financial accounting

Both the present-value method and the time-adjusted rate-of-return method of evaluating capital expenditure proposals are, by definition, based on the discounting of the estimated flow of cash disbursements and receipts over the lives of the various projects. On the other hand, the financial accounts, which are the basis for earnings reported to shareholders and to the public and also for internal control and, in many companies, for management incentive plans, are kept on the accrual basis. Because of the difference between cash flows and accrual accounting results, total reliance on either of the discounted cash flow methods in the selection of projects to be carried out may result in some erratic variations in reported earnings. In cases where very large projects are involved, the variations may be significant enough to have a serious effect on the company's long-range plans for maximizing the market value of its stock by demonstrating a steady rate of growth in earnings per share.

In a company which has well-established budgeting and long-range planning procedures, the effect of approved capital expenditure projects—including expense elements such as design and start up costs and product and market development expenses—will be reflected in the budget and long-range plan profit and loss statements, so that the operating management will be made aware of any unusual impact on earnings. At this point in time, however, it may be difficult, or even impossible, to change the capital expenditure budget, and to forestall such a situation the controller should make it a rule to include in the presentation of any major capital expenditure proposal a supplemental statement showing the effect of the proposal on earnings as they will be reported in the financial statements.

Computerized procedures for modifying capital expenditure decisions based on discounted cash flow methods to recognize an earnings-growth restraint are outlined in the article "Limit D.C.F. in Capital Budgeting," by E. M. Lerner and Alfred Rappaport, in the September-October 1965 issue of *Harvard Business Review*. In another article, "Capital Budgeting: A Pragmatic Approach," by A. A. Robichek, D. G. Ogilvie and J. D. Roach, in the April 1969 issue of *Financial Executive*, more complex procedures are suggested for recognizing other constraints—i.e., current year's earnings, the total amount of the capital budget, and total required cash flows. So far as the authors are aware, these techniques (some of which involve the use of linear programming) are still in the experimental stage.

Intangible factors

In considering any plant expenditure proposal and its possible alternatives, weight must be given to the intangible factors which cannot readily be introduced into the formal estimates of costs and savings but which may be decisive, once all the facts are in. These intangibles are of special importance when the savings calculations show only a slight advantage in favor of any particular course of action or when there is a wide margin of possible error in the forecasts of useful life, costs, etc., on which the calculations are based. The controller can hardly expect to have a complete understanding of all the intangibles affecting any particular problem, but he should make an effort to see that they are all presented for consideration, either in a written report accompanying the savings estimates or in discussions of the report. All the interested operating executives should have an opportunity to express their views; the evaluation of all the factors involved and the final decision are, of course, the responsibility of the top management.

While it is impractical to enumerate all the intangibles which may be relevant to a choice between alternative proposals, a brief discussion of some of the more important of them will serve to illustrate the need for a broad approach in arriving at conclusions:

1. *Conservation of capital and timing.* Every investment in plant assets involves some degree of risk, and if the profit advantage to be derived from the investment is not definite and decisive, it may be assumed that the business will suffer little if the investment is at least postponed until there is clearer justification for it. This applies particularly to replacements of existing capacity or to choices between an immediate investment and a deferred investment and is most important in an industry where rapid progress is being made in developing new types of equipment, so that there is a real danger of obsolescence. To commit the business to a substantial investment in the newest and best equipment available may turn out to have been a serious error if something still better is just around the corner. Yet it is obvious that a chronic hesitation in fear of this error may be a still worse error.

2. *Competitive reaction.* It has already been pointed out that proposals which depend for their justification on expansion of capacity and increased volume involve the problem of disposing of the additional output and that competitive factors must be considered in such a situation. Even though these factors are given consideration in the savings calculations, there remains an element of risk which cannot be entirely ignored.

A somewhat similar situation exists when a proposal involves a vertical extension of manufacturing facilities—that is, expansion for the manufacture of parts or semifinished materials which are currently being purchased from outside vendors. Presumably, a proposal of this nature will not be considered until some experimental work has been done as a basis for material and manufacturing cost estimates. If the calculation of savings shows a large gain on the proposed installation, amounting to more than a normal return on the investment, there are obviously two possible explanations—either the estimated costs are lower than the outside vendor's costs, or the vendor's profit margins are unduly long.

In the absence of a known advantage due to improved processes or greater efficiency, the conservative course in a situation of this kind is to be skeptical of an estimated manufacturing cost lower than that of a vendor who certainly has had the benefit of experience in his particular field. Investigation may show that the estimated cost of purchasing the items from the vendor is based on prices and margins prevailing under unusually favorable conditions and that the average margin between the vendor's selling price and his raw-material cost over a period of years has been much lower than assumed in the savings calculation. Or, if the vendor has succeeded in maintaining high margins, an intimation to him of an intention to manufacture the parts or semifinished product (actually, a third alternative!) may be effective in securing a reduction in the purchase price. All these angles need to be carefully considered before reaching a conclusion that a proposed installation of this kind will actually prove profitable.

3. *Keeping abreast of progress—Pilot investments.* As against the somewhat conservative viewpoint expressed above, it may be urged that there is such a thing as overcaution. Estimates of savings should be carefully prepared and based on reasonable expectations; a slight conservative bias is proper, but this should not be carried to an extreme. Sometimes the possible savings on a new type of equipment may not be susceptible of proof except by actual trial on a factory scale; in such cases it may be desirable to invest in "pilot" facilities so that the manufacturing organization can become familiar with the new methods and be in a better position to evaluate their possibilities. Undercapacity may be equally as disastrous as overcapacity, if it results in loss of opportunity for growth and expansion when conditions are favorable. A business does not stand still—it moves either forward or backward— and the assumption of reasonable risks is necessary to progress.

4. *Quality of product.* In some situations an investment which does not show a particularly attractive return may be desirable for the purpose of improving or controlling the quality of the product. This is a factor which, in its very essence, is intangible; it may be impossible to reduce to dollar terms, but it may be very real indeed.

5. *Personnel relations.* The establishment and maintenance of good labor relations is a prime objective of every forward-looking management. Working conditions are, of course, an important factor in employee

good will, and this is recognized in the planning of plant expenditures. In some cases it may be the sole justification for a proposed investment; in others it may tip the scales as between two possible alternatives. To secure the maximum benefit from investments of this kind, it may be desirable to consult with the employees or their representatives before making the commitment, so that they will most surely feel that their interests or wishes are being considered in the matter.

At the executive level, there is an even more intangible factor, which might be called "company prestige." Competent executives take pride in being associated with a progressive organization; this, of course, means an organization which operates profitably, but it also means an organization which is guided by constructive and dynamic policies. Obviously, no management can afford to let company prestige dominate its plant investment policy, but it can see to it that the operating executives are given an opportunity to express their views and to acquire an understanding of the company's policy and the reasons for specific decisions.

6. *Social responsibilities.* Business managers have long been conscious of the importance of good "public relations"; and capital expenditure decisions are often influenced, if not determined, by their probable impact on the company's "image" in the communities in which it operates and in the eyes of the general public. An obvious example of such a situation arises when there is a choice between extensive rehabilitation of an existing plant to improve its profitability and building an all-new plant in a different location. This concern for its public image is a matter of enlightened self-interest, and with the drastic changes in our social climate during the past few years it has become even more of a factor in management thinking.

More specifically, management must now reckon with the public reaction against all types of "pollution"—chemical, sonic, visual and thermal. Government-set standards for antipollution measures, if applied uniformly and fairly throughout an industry, will tend, in one way, to minimize the problem as far as capital expenditure decisions are concerned; but they may also result in a conflict of social responsibilities— it, for example, they point up the desirability of moving an existing plant to a new and remote location. In any event, the ability of any firm to discharge its social obligations over the long term depends on its maintaining its viability by profitable operations and sound financial management.

In closing the discussion of this subject, it is well to emphasize again that the necessity of weighing these intangible factors in deciding on the course of action to be followed in any situation does not in the least minimize the importance of estimating as carefully as possible the financial results of proposed expenditures and their possible alternatives. A proper evaluation of the intangibles is impossible without a knowledge of the tangibles, so far as they can be predicted; and no business, however well supplied with funds, can afford to make investments in fixed assets without considering their probable effect on earnings.

Developing a practical program

In view of the many ramifications of this complex subject, how should the controller determine what procedures to recommend to his management for evaluating capital expenditure proposals and choosing from among competing projects? His job here is to find a reasonable compromise between the theoretical and the practical, considering (a) the inherent limitations on the accuracy of projections of the costs and benefits of proposed expenditures, (b) the time and effort that operating personnel are able and willing to devote to the problem, and (c) the degree of sophistication of the middle-level line executives ·who are responsible for originating most projects and their superiors who review and accept or reject them. If most managers in his company are accustomed to think in terms of rate of return on investment, there is a strong inducement for the controller to adopt that method, unless he has a firm conviction that the present-value method is greatly superior and is prepared to undertake an educational campaign to sell that conviction to all levels of the organization. Furthermore, he will be well advised to try to establish relatively simple procedures for the 80 to 85 percent of all projects that might be called "run-of-the-mill"—that is, conventional and straightforward replacement or cost-saving projects—but to insist on detailed and careful studies of the relatively small number of projects that involve substantial expenditures for development of new products, projections of increased sales of existing products, or a variety of possible alternative courses of action.

As an example of this approach, one large multidivisional company uses the table in Figure 15–3 to evaluate and compare all "conventional" projects, even though it is recognized that there are several theoretical imperfections in this procedure. But when a major project proposal—e.g., for a new plant or a substantial addition to an existing plant—is in preparation, representatives from the controller' staff work closely with the industrial engineers and the responsible line executives to be sure (a) that all reasonably feasible alternatives are considered, (b) that there is a sound basis for the projections of costs and benefits, (c) that the income-tax effect of each alternative is carefully analyzed, and (d) that the rate-of-return calculations are based on detailed estimates of the amounts and timing of all cash flows.

A major aim in the discussions in this chapter has been to identify the problems involved in the application of capital budgeting theory in the real world of business management; and several references have been made to the literature on advanced techniques which have been developed in the effort to cope with those problems. An understanding of the principles and possible uses of these techniques—though not necessarily of the mathematics involved—is essential to the controller in fulfilling his responsibility for the adequacy of the procedures by which his company's management arrives at its capital investment decisions. The extent to which the techniques can be put to actual use in any company depends largely on the attitude and interest of its top management. If there is skepticism or indifference at that level, the controller can attempt to overcome it by suggesting an experimental application of one or more of the techniques at an opportune time— perhaps to assist in reaching a decision on some particularly important capital expenditure project.

Postcheck on estimates of project costs and earnings

It is certainly desirable, in theory, to maintain regular procedures for making after-the-fact comparisons of the actual and estimated costs and benefits of significant capital expenditures, in order (a) to foster objectivity in the preparation of the original estimates, and (b) to provide information that will assist in improving the estimating process.

A postcheck on the estimated investment in a project is usually a relatively simple matter if there are adequate procedures for the control of plant expenditures, as outlined in the next section. But the scope of postchecks on estimated operating costs and earnings is limited, in practice, by the difficulty of obtaining relevant information on actual results. Even in the simplest case of a conventional cost-saving project it is necessary to make a special analysis to determine the actual effect of the project on operating costs; when such an analysis is undertaken, it is usually limited to the first year or two of the operation of the new equipment, as the identification of relevant costs becomes more difficult as time goes on. It is impractical, therefore, to determine the actual rate of return (or net present value) of a project for comparison with the estimate on which the decision was based. Furthermore, the soundness of a decision involving a choice between alternative investments cannot be verified, since it is not known what actual results would have been if the decision had been different. But even the limited postchecks which are feasible will very often give a clear indication as to whether the results of a project are substantially in line with the estimates.

A postcheck on profits derived from expenditures for expansion is a still more complicated matter. When the expansion is for the purpose of providing for normal growth in the existing business, it will usually be sufficient to supplement the cost comparisons by a comparison of actual and estimated annual volume and peak load, to determine whether the need for the facilities actually materialized, without attempting to calculate the profit on the added volume. For projects involving significant expenditures for major new facilities, the development of new product lines, etc., a post-audit in itself is ineffective; procedures of the type described in the section on "Program Budgeting and Control" in Chapter 13 should be applied in such cases.

The collection and interpretation of the information required for post-audits requires close cooperation between the controller's staff, the industrial engineers, and plant management, and, for certain types of projects, the marketing, product engineering, and sales executives. Responsibility for the actual preparation of the formal audit reports may be assigned either to the controller or to the appropriate operating department, but in either event it is important that the controller satisfy himself that the reports are objective and as factual as possible, considering the limitations discussed above. Emphasis should be on the use of post audits to point the way to improved accuracy in future planning, rather than as a tool for enforcing strict management control.

Control of plant expenditures

The details of the mechanism for the control of plant expenditures in any company will depend somewhat on its organization structure, but there are certain underlying principles which will apply in all cases:

1. A clear definition should be made of the basis for classifying expenditures as between capital charges and expense charges.

2. The extent to which plant and maintenance expenditures are to be subject to advance authorization by the top management should be defined.

3. Procedures should be established for collecting the actual costs of capital jobs and maintenance expenditures, and these actual costs should be compared at frequent intervals with the authorized amounts.

4. A reasonably detailed record of all plant and equipment should be maintained, and the record of identifiable equipment should be verified at regular intervals by a physical inventory.

Capital versus expense

Consistency in the classification of expenditures between capital and expense is important not only from the standpoint of control in the ordinary sense but also because it has a vital bearing on the correct statement of earnings from year to year. It is by no means easy to define the basis for such a classification; particularly troublesome are borderline cases involving remodeling, rehabilitation, partial replacement, etc. Usually a broad policy is laid down by the top management, and the details of its application are worked out by some compromise between the theoretical and the practical. A written statement of policy and procedure will be found most helpful in achieving consistency in practice, and it is advisable to have copies of all capital orders and all maintenance orders over a specified dollar amount clear through the controller's office for review. It is particularly important that any maintenance job which might be considered on the border line between capital and expense should be supported by adequate descriptions, so that the propriety of the expense charge can be established when the company's income tax returns are examined; obviously, the time to prepare such descriptions is when the work is done rather than three or four years later, when it may be difficult to recall the essential facts about the job.

Advance authorization

Because of the "twilight zone" between capital and maintenance charges, any control by advance authorization must, to be effective, be extended to both types of expenditures. As to capital expenditures, the safest course is to establish a rigid rule that plant assets shall be purchased or removed and that charges or credits to plant accounts shall be made only when authorized in advance by a designated representative of the top management. Minor plant expenditures can be covered by blanket authorizations which the operating management can use as it sees fit, subject to a maximum limit on the amount of any individual expenditure. Control of maintenance cannot, as a practical matter, be quite so rigid; it is probably best effected by establishing budget totals covering a year or a quarter and permitting the operating management a relatively free discretion as to the method of expending the total appropriation. Advance authorization may be required for jobs involving unusual nonroutine expenditures; as to other jobs, the post-check suggested in the following section should be sufficient.

Comparison of actual and authorized expenditures

In any business which has set up the usual mechanisms for the distribution of labor and supply charges, the accumulation of actual costs of capital and major maintenance jobs and actual maintenance totals will be a relatively simple matter. In most cases the plant management will desire for its own use monthly comparisons of actual and authorized expenditures on open jobs, and in the case of plant expenditures these monthly reports should be supplemented by a quarterly or semiannual analysis of additions and removals, tying in with the ledger accounts and showing overexpenditures or underexpenditures against authorizations and the unexpended balances of open authorizations. These reports should be audited in the controller's office, and any substantial variation between the amounts authorized and the amounts actually spent should be called to the attention of the top management.

Plant and equipment records

A record of plant and equipment in reasonable detail, with descriptions of the buildings and equipment and information as to date of acquisition, vendor, purchase price, etc., will prove extremely useful for both planning and control purposes. Some record of the kind is essential for intelligent long-range forecasting of plant expenditures; and if it is tied in with the accounts, showing book value for at least the major individually identifiable units, such as machines, motors, etc., it makes possible a much more consistent handling of plant and depreciation accounting. If historical data for setting up such a record are not available, a start can be made by allocating gross book values and reserves on the basis of appraisals made for insurance or other purposes; such allocations, however, should be carefully reviewed by the plant engineer and production executives, and adjustments should be made in cases where, because of obsolescence, the appraisals do not properly reflect actual value in use.

In addition to the detailed plant ledgers suggested above, it is desirable to compile and file for future reference complete annual analyses of plant additions and removals and charges and credits to depreciation reserves. The plant job orders, showing the details of charges to each capital job, should also be kept in a permanent file, together with vendors' invoices for major equipment units. Maintenance job orders and all supporting data, including labor tickets, stores issues, etc., should be preserved until all income tax audits for the year have been completed and there is no possibility of a redetermination of tax liability.

The maintenance of the records and the preparation of the reports described above are routine accounting functions which can readily be performed by the computer, with a significant saving in clerical costs and greater speed and flexibility in the output of the information needed for planning and control.

Standard procedures

In a preceding section it was suggested that a consistent classification of expenditures between capital and expense can be greatly facilitated by making available a written statement of policy and procedure. Such a statement will be even more useful if it is extended to cover all phases of the control and recording of plant expenditures and major maintenance expenditures. In Appendix A there will be found an index showing the topics which might be covered in a detailed "Capital Expenditure and Property Record Procedure," and Appendix B is a statement outlining the salient points in a "Maintenance Control and Accounting Procedure." It should be noted that these procedures are written for a company which has several manufacturing divisions, each of which maintains its own cost accounts and plant and equipment records; they can of course be modified to conform to any particular organization structure.

16 STATEMENTS AND REPORTS FOR MANAGEMENT

INTRODUCTION, CLASSIFICATION OF REPORTS, OPERATING CONTROL REPORTS

Importance of statements and reports

It would hardly seem to be necessary to dwell at any length on the importance of adequate statements and reports for management in the discharge of the controllership function. It is obvious that successful communication to management of the essential facts about the business is the real climax of all the effort that the controller puts into the management phase of his activities. And yet this is often where the controller falls down badly or succeeds only indifferently, not because he does not have the facts but because he does not take the necessary steps to get them across to those whom he is serving. To present the facts is not difficult, but it is not enough; they must be communicated before the controller can consider his job as done. The problem is worthy of his continuous attention and study, and he should organize his department so that he will be free to devote a major share of his time to it.

To achieve his objective of successfully communicating the essential facts about the business to the management, the controller must have a clear conception of the purposes, possibilities, and limitations of the many different types of statements and reports, and he must also understand the problems and viewpoints of the operating executives and make sure that they, in turn, understand the true meaning and the limitations of the reports he prepares for them. Most of the discussion which follows is necessarily devoted to an analysis of various types of reports and their uses, but it cannot be too strongly emphasized that such an analysis

380

is simply an explanation of the tools available and that the use of these tools is the real art of controllership.

Types of management reports

In the chapter on "Manufacturing Costs" it was suggested that reports on factory operations are of two kinds: current control reports, which are intended to assist in the immediate control of factory activities by pointing out deviations from standard performance at the source as promptly as possible after they occur, and summary reports, which summarize the effect on profits of all deviations from standard over a given period of time, thus serving as a check on the current control reports and also as an overall indication of the effectiveness of factory management. In extending our discussion to include statements and reports for management on all phases of business activity, it will be useful to fit this classification of factory reports into a more complete classification which will serve as a basis for working out a comprehensive and well-balanced report structure. Such a classification is offered in Figure 16–1; there is nothing rigid about it, and some reports may partake of the characteristics of more than one of the classifications named, but there are very real distinctions, either in objective or in approach,

Figure 16–1
CLASSIFICATION OF REPORTS FOR MANAGEMENT

Operating Reports
Control Reports—used for the direct control of operations.
 Current Control Reports—to spot deviations from planned performance as they occur, so that prompt action may be taken to stop losses.
 Summary Control Reports—to summarize deviations from planned performance over a period of time (usually a month), as a check on current control reports and as an indication of the overall effectiveness of the performance of responsible executives.
Information Reports—used for planning and policy determination.
 Trend Reports—based on vertical comparisons of the results of the same activity or group activities over a period of months or years.
 Analytical Reports—based on horizontal or cross-section comparisons of the results during a given period of different activities or of similar activities in different locations, or on comparisons of actual results with some formal or informal policy standard or objective.
Venture Measurement Reports:
 Individual-Activity Reports—venture and responsibility coinciding.
 Joint-Activity Reports—ventures under joint responsibility.

Financial Reports
Static Reports—limited to an analysis of financial strength and structure as of a given date.
Dynamic Reports
 Financial Control Reports—measuring actual financial condition against planned (budgeted) condition.
 Measurements of Effectiveness of the Use of Funds—based on the relationship between the investments in various classes of assets and the use made of them.
 Reports of Changes in Financial Condition—summarizing and analyzing changes in financial condition during a given period.

between the various types, and an understanding of these distinctions is important in avoiding confusion and duplication in reporting.

In this suggested classification, a fundamental distinction is made between operating reports and financial reports, the former dealing with the results of operations and the latter with the financial condition of the business or its various sections. The basic operating report is, of course, the profit and loss statement, and the basic financial report is the balance sheet, or statement of assets, liabilities, and capital. More will be said about the interdependence of these two kinds of reports, but for practical purposes this is a useful and well-recognized grouping.

Operating reports can be divided quite readily into two broad groups: control reports, which, as the name implies, are used primarily for direct control of operations, and information reports, which serve the broader purpose of presenting the facts which management needs to formulate intelligent plans and policies. As was brought out in Chapter 7, "The Accounting Plan," virtually every business of any considerable size embraces multiple ventures. The measurement of the degree of success of each of these ventures is basic to the determination of current policies, as well as future plans and policies, and must therefore be clearly reflected in the information reports to management. In recent years reports on the significant ventures of a business have been incorporated in the income statement itself, (see chapter 3) though usually only in a rather gross form. More explicit and detailed segment reports are commonly restricted to reports intended only for managers. The subclassification of control reports into current control reports and summary reports was illustrated in Chapter 8, "Manufacturing Costs"; the distinctions between the different types of information reports and between the different types of financial reports are summarized briefly in the outline in Figure 16–1 and will be explained in more detail in the discussions which follow.

Reports and statements

Another point of terminology that requires clarification is the distinction between the terms "report" and "statement," which are generally used rather loosely and often interchangeably. In these discussions the term "statement" will be applied to any tabulation of figures and the necessary accompanying footnotes, while the term "report" will be used in a more comprehensive sense, including a single statement without comment, a group of statements with extended explanatory comment, or any formal or informal comment on business activities, whether or not accompanied by statements.

Current control reports

The preparation of adequate current control reports is one of the major objectives of cost accounting for factory, marketing, and administration activities, and the important points to be considered in the development of such reports have been covered in the discussions in Chapters 8–12. This chapter will be devoted principally to the other types of reports enumerated in the outline in Figure 16–1, but a brief résumé and some amplification of the discussions of current control reports will be helpful as background for the discussion of the other types.

Current control reports of sales income

In most small businesses the owner or manager exercises personal current control of sales—so far as sales can be said to be subject to control—by a scrutiny of the orders received in each day's mail. In this scrutiny he has in mind at least two questions: first, "What are the sales of each product he manufactures?" and, second, "How is each salesman performing?" If the business is one in which orders are relatively few in number and large in amount, he may look further to see how much business individual customers are placing, checking their current orders against his knowledge of their normal requirements; a few extra-large orders from good customers may mean a comfortable volume for days or weeks ahead, while if the salesman's regular calls in a good territory have brought in only token orders, it may be a real storm signal for the business, calling for intensified efforts in other territories or for changes in tactics or policies.

This, of course, is a very elementary type of control, practical only where one individual has an intimate knowledge of salesmen, territories, customers, and sales policies. In all but the very smallest businesses, such control by personal contact must be supplemented by regular statements which will relate current results—product sales, salesmen's performance, and perhaps certain individual customers' orders—to the longer-term trends. The form, frequency, and amount of detail in these statements may vary widely, according to the nature of the business and the requirements of the executives who use them; generally they are most useful if kept relatively simple, showing units or dollars of orders received during the current week in each of the principal products or product groups for the entire business and for each salesman and corresponding figures for the year or season to date, compared with budget or quota or with actual results of some previous period. Information as to sales to individual customers is more likely to be kept in special customers' records, and where there are too many customers for an effective follow-up by a periodic review of the records, various "flagging" devices may be used to call attention to those who do not order within a normal time. In a large business, detailed follow-up records of this type are often located in branch sales offices, where they can be more conveniently used by the district managers and field sales force.

Current control reports for the factory

In order to be useful to operating managers at the foreman level, factory control reports must be prepared very quickly. A weekly report should be in the foreman's hands on the following Monday, and in some businesses a daily report may be prepared for submission to the foremen the following day. To permit this speed of response, factory control reports must normally be very simple, and must concentrate on variables which can be controlled day by day, such as labor and machine usage and materials consumption.

It does not matter whether the labor report is expressed in time or in dollars in most factories—promptness of reporting is much more important, as is consistency in method from one report to the next. At the foreman level, comparative numbers for the "same day last week" or "yesterday" are also of doubtful worth, as the foreman is very close to the operation and can be expected to know what is normal and what is not. Such comparative figures do no harm, of course, unless their addition to the report delays its presentation to the foreman.

In the case of materials, the nature of the business will dictate the type and content of the foreman's report. If it is feasible to weigh or measure materials as they are used, regular variance reports can be provided that will be most informative. If standard products are manufactured, so that a standard issue of materials for each batch can be provided, the variance reporting can be simple and rapid. The variance can be taken directly from extra requisition notes and from "goods returned to stores" documents. Of course, such a system presumes an effective physical control of goods to prevent hoarding at the foreman level. In other companies, it may be impractical to measure materials or to set specific job standards. If this is so, reliance must be placed on overall checks of total consumption of important materials against the standard content of actual total production. If necessary, temporary physical inspections and controls can be added when consumption becomes abnormal. In every case, the goal is to trace abnormalities to their source as soon as possible.

At the operating level immediately above the foremen, which may be that of the plant manager or assistant plant manager, the current control problem is slightly altered, and the reporting system must be adjusted to match. The manager is indirectly responsible for many activities, not directly reponsible for a single activity. Therefore, he should receive reports which permit him to identify quickly those segments of the plant which need action. Departments should be reported on to the manager with comparative data to aid evaluation. At this level, figures for "same day last week" or "standard" are appropriate, and variances from past performance or from the norm should be shown. Indirect expenses, often uncontrollable by the foremen, should be reported to the plant manager regularly, probably on a weekly or monthly basis. The lower frequency is made possible by the relative stability through time of most indirect expense items.

Current control reports for other expenses

Expenses of marketing and administration are even less subject to short-term fluctuations than the indirect factory costs discussed in the preceding paragraph. As pointed out in Chapter 9, there are some routine clerical activities which can be standardized and time-studied in much the same manner as factory operations, and in these cases control reports based on actual output should be prepared on at least a weekly basis, or even daily, if the management's policy and the circumstances permit day-to-day adjustment in the clerical personnel. Otherwise, it will usually be found that monthly statements are adequate and that all that is required is a comparison of the details of the actual expenses of each department with the budgeted or standard amounts for the month.

Summary control reports

The purpose of summary control reports is to summarize for executive review all the deviations from planned operations and to show their effect on budgeted profits. The master summary report of any business, therefore, is the monthly profit and loss statement with its accompanying comments, comparing actual results for the month with the most recent budget and cumulative actual results for the elapsed months of the year (or other budget period) with the budget originally set for those months. Supporting this master report, there should be more detailed summary reports on the various operating activities, following the setup of responsibilities as reflected in the accounting plan or classification of accounts. The master report gives the top management a condensed comparison of actual and planned operating results, while the supporting reports provide them with the added details necessary for a more complete understanding of the master report and also give each of the executives responsible for the different activities a complete record of his actual performance compared with budget or with standard.[1]

Most readers will have seen an example of the hierarchical structure of control reports, either in practice or in an earlier course in accounting.[2] As the upper levels of management are responsible for a wide range of activities, they are necessarily remote from the activities of the units

---

[1] "Budget" and "standard" are not necessarily synonymous, as the budget may provide for variances from standard performance, particularly in factory operations. Statements for the factory departmental executives are usually prepared to show comparisons of actual and budgeted variances from standard.

[2] For expositions on this topic, see a standard cost accounting textbook such as Shillinghaw G., *Cost Accounting, Analysis and Control* (Homewood, Ill.: Irwin, 1961) Chapters 2 and 21 or A. Matz, O. J. Curry, and G. W. Frank. *Cost Accounting*, 4th Edition (Cincinnati, O.: Southwestern 1967) pages 308–311 and 674–687.

they govern. They normally exercise control through the establishment and adjustment of procedures and occasionally of policies rather than by the issuance of direct operating commands. It follows that a control report for a senior manager must allow him to assess the success of current procedures, or, more precisely, to pinpoint whether, where, and why these procedures have failed. Variances from plans, budgets, or other targets become very critical at this level. The provision of some comparative numbers as a basis for judging current performance is highly desirable, and simplification of the reports by condensation of details is almost always helpful. Supporting documents may be offered in addition to the summary control report, as suggested earlier, but the senior manager should only be obliged to look at them if an abnormality is seen in the summary.

Control reports versus information reports

It is difficult for anyone with accounting training and background to realize how easy it is for executives whose primary interests are in other fields to draw incorrect or incomplete conclusions from even the most routine accounting statements. To avert this danger, the controller must, of course, be an interpreter as well as a reporter, and he will find his job of interpretation just so much simpler if he will take care to distinguish between the objectives of different kinds of reports and to limit the use of each kind to the specific purpose for which it is adapted.

As previously stated, current control reports and summary control reports may overlap and merge into each other; both are concerned, in different ways, with controlling operations in accordance with plans or budgets and hence must be set up by individual responsibilities. Information reports, however, are not intended for control of current operations but as an assistance in the formulation of long-term plans and policies; and, to be significant and fully informative, they must cover relatively long periods of time and must often depart from the primary classification of income and expense by responsibilities and show them distributed or allocated by classes of product, classes of trade, sales territories, or in such other manner as will give the management information as to the trends in sales and profits in various sections of the business. The difference between the purposes of the two types of reports is very clear, and it is rarely that one report will serve both purposes satisfactorily.

Summary control reports of sales and gross profits

The senior manager will depend for his control information on summaries which report on the performance of the various segments of the company he runs. These reports will of necessity be arranged according to the responsibility centers his subordinates control. In addition to these reports, which are summaries in the most literal sense, the senior manager may well ask for summary reports on sales and gross profits analysed on other bases. It is very common, for example, for the manager to seek sales analyses by product (or product group), by salesman or territory, by customer class, by sales branch, or by commodity.

If the sales budget is broken down for direct control purposes into one or more secondary classifications, as well as the one used for the primary analysis, the analyses by such secondary classifications may also be considered as summary control reports; but if the other classifications are for information only and not for control, i.e., if they do not follow actual lines of responsibility, the reports for them fall in the category of information reports. A common example of a report by a secondary classification serving as a summary control report is found where the responsibility for sales promotion rests with a group of commodity sales executives but where the actual selling of all commodities is done by a single field sales organization, headed up by several branch managers reporting to a field sales manager. The sales budget will often be broken down for control purposes both by commodities and by field territories, and summary control reports will be prepared for both classifications.

Where the sales organization is held responsible for profit as well as for volume, the summary control reports for each sales executive should, if possible, include not only the sales for which he is responsible but also the resulting gross profits. If the procedure followed in determining the cost of goods sold each month calls for the costing of each item on every sales invoice and if the unit costs used for this purpose correspond with the costs properly chargeable to the sales departments, the analysis of gross profits presents no serious problem. Frequently, however, the costing of sales for accounting entries is at standard cost, or on some other basis not suitable for reports reflecting the responsibility of the sales department, and in such cases the information required for gross-profit analysis can be obtained only by an additional costing, either of each item on every sales invoice or of the total unit shipments of each product for the period covered by the analysis.

In businesses where there are many hundreds or thousands of products, the expense of obtaining data for a complete analysis of gross profits may be prohibitive, and the analysis may be omitted altogether or prepared on some partial or estimated basis. The question of how far it pays to go in analyses of this kind is frequently a very troublesome one; the use of modern punched-card equipment or electronic data processing makes it possible to turn them out in almost any detail that is desired, and this very fact sometimes results in building up the reporting routine to a point where the organization is unable to digest or use the figures produced. This is simply another illustration of the general problem that the controller has always with him, namely, the weighing of the value of the various types of information that can be made available, the cost of producing them, and their probable actual usefulness to management.

By way of illustration, a summary control report in use in a textile company is presented in Figure 16–2, and a supporting schedule in

Figure 16–2
RELIANCE MANUFACTURING COMPANY
Statement of Sales and Gross Profits by Commodity Classes
Quarter ended March 31, 19XX
(all amounts in thousands)

| | Net sales | | Gross profits | | |
	Yards	Dollars	Dollars	Percentage of sales	Per yard
Commodity class a—actual	4,213	836.4	177.1	21.18	$0.0421
(budget)	(4,429)	(822.4)	(196.5)	(23.89)	(0.0444)
Commodity class b—actual	2,310	395.6	61.4	15.52	0.0266
(budget)	(2,177)	(344.8)	(60.5)	(17.55)	(0.0278)
Commodity class c—actual	6,243	1,367.2	194.2	14.20	0.0311
(budget)	(5,728)	(1,157.8)	(170.7)	(14.74)	(0.0298)
Commodity class d—actual	3,521	892.7	168.3	18.85	0.0478
(budget)	(3,220)	(753.5)	(156.2)	(20.73)	(0.0485)
Commodity class e—actual	1,190	420.1	99.8	23.76	0.0839
(budget)	(1,410)	(482.7)	(115.9)	(24.01)	(0.0822)
Commodity class f—actual	4,426	1,258.6	253.6	20.15	0.0573
(budget)	(3,998)	(1,069.4)	(233.9)	(21.87)	(0.0585)
Total—actual	21,903	5,170.6	954.4	18.46	$0.0436
(budget)	(20,962)	(4,630.6)	(933.7)	(20.16)	(0.0445)

Figure 16–3. In this company, it happens that presentation of the gross profit by commodity is a justified step; the executives responsible for the sales of the various commodities can also be held responsible for the gross profit achieved.

In these illustrations, both unit (yardage) and dollar sales are shown, and gross profits are expressed in terms of dollars, percentage of sales, and cents per yard. The overall statement is by major commodity classes, which correspond with executive responsibilities, while in the supplementary statement the figures for commodity class A are broken down into the five commodities which make up the class. If the commodities included in each commodity class are fairly uniform in character, selling price, and cost, it may be more useful to make this supplementary breakdown by classes of customers, particularly if there is a wide variation in profit margins as between such customer classes.

Figure 16–3
RELIANCE MANUFACTURING COMPANY
Statement of Sales and Gross Profits by Commodities—Commodity Class A

	Net sales		Gross profits		
	Yards	Dollars	Dollars	Percentage of sales	Per yard
mmodity A-1—actual	978	203.3	54.1	26.61	$0.0553
(budget).	(1,254)	(243.6)	(70.3)	(28.86)	(0.0561)
mmodity A-2—actual	733	151.9	35.3	23.34	0.0481
(budget).	(943)	(183.8)	(45.2)	(24.59)	(0.0480)
mmodity A-3—actual	401	90.4	15.3	16.92	0.0381
(budget).	(380)	(78.0)	(15.3)	(19.62)	(0.0402)
mmodity A-4—actual	1,160	195.2	43.9	22.49	0.0378
(budget).	(1,018)	(155.9)	(40.8)	(26.17)	(0.0401)
mmodity A-5—actual	941	195.6	28.5	14.57	0.0303
(budget).	(834)	(161.1)	(24.9)	(15.46)	(0.0298)
Total—actual	4,213	836.4	177.1	21.17	$0.0421
(budget).	(4,429)	(822.4)	(196.5)	(23.89)	(0.0444)

Analysis of gross-profit variations

In interpreting the analysis of sales and gross profits in Figures 16–2 and 16–3 for the information of the interested executives, the difference between actual and budgeted gross profits in each commodity class can be broken down between the amount due to volume variations (using yardage as a measurement of volume) and the amount due to margin variations, by the following calculations:

Volume variation = Gain or loss in yardage
$\qquad$ × Budgeted margin per yard

Margin variation = Actual yardage × Gain or loss in margin per yard

These calculations can be made on an overall basis for the business as a whole, by commodity classes, or by individual commodities; these three calculations, based on the statements in Figures 16–2 and 16–3, are illustrated in Figures 16–4, 16–5, and 16–6.

It will be noted from these calculations that the breakdown between volume variation and margin variations is quite different, depending on which approach is used. The overall calculation gives a total favorable volume variation of $41,900 and an unfavorable margin variation of $21,200, while in the calculation by commodity classes the favorable volume variation is $39,900, and the unfavorable margin variation is $10,200. For commodity Class A, which is the only class for which the detailed commodity calculation is worked out in the illustration, the

Figure 16–4
RELIANCE MANUFACTURING COMPANY
Analysis of Variations Between Actual and Budgeted Gross Profits
Quarter Ended March 31, 19XX
Analysis on Overall Basis

Volume variation:

Total yardage—actual   21,903
            budgeted   20,962

Gain in yardage   941

Budgeted average gross profits margin $0.04454

Volume gain—941 × 0.04454 . . . . $41.9

Margin variation:

Margin per yard—actual $0.04357
            budgeted 0.04454

(Loss) in margin . . . .   ($0.00097)

Margin (loss)—21,903 × (0.00097) . . . .   (21.2)

Net total variation $20.7

Figure 16–5
RELIANCE MANUFACTURING COMPANY
Analysis by Commodity Classes
(all amounts in thousands)

Commodity classes	Yardage gains (or losses)	Budgeted margins per yard	Volume variations gains (or losses)	Actual yardages	Gains or (losses) in margin per yard	Margin variations gains (or losses)	Total variatio gains (c losses)
Class A	(216)	$0.04437	($ 9.6)	4,213	($0.00233)	($ 9.8)	($19.4
Class B	133	0.02779	3.7	2,310	(0.00121)	(2.8)	0.9
Class C	515	0.02980	15.3	6,243	0.00131	8.2	23.5
Class D	301	0.04851	14.6	3,521	(0.00071)	(2.5)	12.1
Class E	(220)	0.08220	(18.1)	1,190	0.00167	2.0	(16.1
Class F	428	0.05850	25.0	4,426	(0.00120)	(5.3)	19.7
Total	941	. . . .	$30.9	21,903	. . . .	($10.2)	$20.7

Figure 16–6
RELIANCE MANUFACTURING COMPANY
Analysis of Commodity Class A by Commodities
(all amounts in thousands)

Commodities	Yardage gains (or losses)	Budgeted margins per yard	Volume variations gains (or losses)	Actual yardages	Gains or (losses) in margin per yard	Margin variations gains (or losses)	Total variatio gains (c losses)
A-1	(276)	$0.05606	($15.5)	978	($0.00074)	($0.7)	($16.2
A-2	(210)	0.04793	(10.1)	733	0.00023	0.2	(9.9
A-3	21	0.04026	0.8	401	(0.00211)	(0.8)	. . . . .
A-4	142	0.04008	5.7	1,160	(0.00224)	(2.6)	3.1
A-5	107	0.02986	3.2	941	0.00043	0.4	3.6
Total	(216)	. . . .	($15.9)	4,213	. . . .	($3.5)	($19.4

calculation by classes gives unfavorable variances of $9,600 due to volume variations and $9,800 due to margin variations, while in the detailed calculation by commodities the corresponding figures are $15,900 and $3,500, respectively. A little study will show that these differences in results are due to the differences in the groupings of yardage sales to determine average margins. This indicates the necessity of clarifying our thinking the meaning of the term "volume" as used in analyses of this kind.

In the statements discussed in the preceding paragraph, volume is measured in terms of a physical unit (i.e., yards), in order to eliminate from the analysis the distorting effect of fluctuations in selling prices. But the use of such a physical unit—yards, pounds, gallons, or the like—is strictly accurate only when sales are limited to one product; when more than one product is sold, the expression of total sales in units becomes a more or less arbitrary approximation, and the greater the diversity of products, the greater the possibility of distortion and inaccuracies in the impressions derived from the figures. By grouping together products of a similar nature and of approximately the same dollar sales value and dollar cost per unit, the distortions are minimized, but such a grouping does not always correspond with the grouping which is most suitable for management control or for sales analytical purposes. Thus, in the illustrations in Figures 16–2 and 16–3, there is clearly a significant difference between the various commodity classes and between different commodities in the same class, and this would point to the desirability of basing the analysis in this case on the detailed commodity breakdown for all classes. This is undoubtedly the correct answer as far as the individual commodity executives are concerned, but in analyses for the general sales management and top management it is preferable to retain a broader grouping if possible.

In order to meet this need for an overall summary control for the general executives, based on a broad sales grouping, the analysis can be presented on the basis of commodity classes (Figure 16–5), with a further breakdown of the margin variation in each commodity class between the amount due to differences between the actual and budgeted assortments of commodities within the class and the amount due to differences between actual and budgeted unit margins on each of the several commodities. This breakdown can be obtained by the calculation shown in Figure 16–7, or it can be determined by reference to the detailed analysis by commodities (Figure 16–6).[3]

In these illustrations the problem is admittedly simplified by the assumption that it is feasible to make an analysis of commodity classes

---

[3] The $6,300 unfavorable assortment variation is the difference between the unfavorable volume variations of $15,900.00, as determined by the detailed commodity calculation (Figure 16–6), and $9,600.00, as determined by the commodity class calculation (Figure 16–5).

Figure 16–7
RELIANCE MANUFACTURING COMPANY
Breakdown of Margin Variation—Commodity Class A
Quarter Ended March 31, 19XX

			Gross profits		
	Yards	Budgeted margins per yard	By com- modities	Totals	Varia- tions
(1) Actual yardage at budgeted margins: For commodity class over-all	4,213	$0.04437	. . . . .	$186.9	. . . . .
By commodities: Commodity A-1	978	0.05606	$54.8		
A-2	733	0.04793	35.1		
A-3	401	0.04026	16.1		
A-4	1,160	0.04008	46.5		
A-5	941	0.02986	28.1		
(2) Total by commodities	4,213	. . . .	. . . . .	180.6	. . . . .
(3) Assortment variation	. . . . .	. . . .	. . . . .	. . . .	($6.3)
(2) – (1)					
(4) Actual gross profit.	. . . . .	. . . .	. . . . .	177.1	. . . . .
(5) Unit margin variation	. . . . .	. . . .	. . . . .	. . . .	(3.5)
(4) – (2) Total margin variation	. . . . .	. . . .	. . . . .	. . . .	($9.8)

by individual commodities. In a business which markets a wide variety of items, it is often impractical to carry the analysis to this point, and the breakdown of each commodity class must be made by subclasses, which in themselves may present all the problems of lack of uniformity pointed out in the above discussion. Obviously, it is impossible to obtain absolute accuracy in analyzing gross-profit variations under such conditions, but with an intelligent product grouping, revised at intervals as new products with different characteristics are developed, the essential facts about volume and margin variations can be presented regularly in broad terms, and these regular presentations will indicate when supplementary special analyses in more detail are needed.

The controller, though never making the substantive decisions involved, can sharpen his reporting techniques by visualizing management's possible actions based thereon, in the continuing struggle for the more profitable combinations of commodities. Realistically, of course, the design of the report should be the result of extended consultation with management as to exactly the framework and content desired.

Dollars as a measurement of sales volume

There are many situations where there is no physical unit which can be applied, even within groups of products, and where it is necessary to fall back on dollar sales as a measurement of volume and to measure variations in costs and gross profits in terms of ratios to dollar sales. Measurement on this basis is a common practice, particularly with salesmen and sales executives, and it is just as satisfactory for many purposes as measurement on a unit basis, so long as selling prices do not fluctuate to any marked degree. Where there are frequent important changes in selling prices, it is obvious that dollar sales do not correctly reflect physical volume trends, and ratios of gross profit to costs or to sales become less satisfactory for the determination of markups or profit objectives since the expenses which must be met out of gross profits—i.e., expenses of selling and administration—do not usually follow trends in selling prices except on the relatively infrequent occasions when there is a major change in underlying economic conditions. Some companies meet this problem by measuring volume in terms of fixed or standard selling prices; and by computing actual prices in terms of percentage discounts from list. Where there is no such standard list, it is possible to construct a set of index prices which can be used for the same purpose; perhaps the simplest way to do this is to take the actual selling prices on all products as of some date when prices were at or near their peak, using in each case the price for the smallest quantity, so that all prices will be comparable, and adjusting, where necessary, if the prices of particular items were out of line because of unusual circumstances. Any such set of list or index prices cannot be absolutely fixed, since changes must be made from time to time to reflect the addition of new products and changes in product specifications and processing methods. If there are many changes of this kind or if the selling price relationships of the different products change to any marked degree, the index sales figures tend to lose their value as trend indicators.

The procedure for analyzing variations in sales and gross profits where sales at standard prices are adopted as a measurement of volume is essentially the same as where a physical unit of measurement is available, the gross profit per standard sales dollar being used as the measurement of margins in place of the gross profit per unit. To make the procedure completely effective, it is, of course, necessary to value all actual sales and all sales budgets and forecasts at the standard prices as well as at actual or budgeted prices, and, except where invoices are regularly priced and extended at list, this involves either an extra pricing and extension on each invoice or a pricing and extension of total periodic unit sales of each product. As a substitute for a permanent set of list or index prices, if it is desired simply to establish a basis for comparison between actual and budgeted results or between the results of two different periods, actual sales for the period analyzed can be extended at budgeted prices or at the prices of the earlier period; this eliminates some of the difficulties involved in maintaining an adequate index but does not, of course, provide data for permanent long-term comparisons. The remarks made earlier in this chapter as to the importance of maintaining a sense of proportion in setting up reporting and analysis procedures apply equally to this aspect of the problem.

Analysis of variations in selling prices and unit costs

In all the analysis procedures discussed above, gross-profit variations have been broken down into volume variations, unit margin variations, and assortment variations, and no attempt has been made to show how much of the unit margin variation is due to variations in selling prices and how much to variations in unit costs. This assumes that the sales executives are held responsible for profits, i.e., for the cost-selling price relationship, on the sales of their commodities, branches, or departments, following one of the plans outlined in Chapter 7 or some other logical plan which fits the actual methods of operations, and that the unit costs used in costing sales can be and are in fact determined with this in mind. Under these conditions, the analysis is considerably simplified and clarified by the direction of attention to unit margin variations as such; where a large unit margin variation exists, a glance at the comparative unit selling prices (or at the discounts from standard prices if the analysis is based on that method of volume measurement) will give a very clear idea of whether it is due principally to price variations or to unit-cost variations.

Carrying our thinking on this point a little further, in a comparison of actual results with a current year's budget or forecast, variations in selling prices may be due to (1) changes in price lists or quotations, (2) differences in the classes of customers sold, or (3) changes in assortment within the product group. Variations in unit cost, if the effect of manufacturing variances is eliminated, as it should be, by the use of standard labor and overhead costs, must be due either to (1) variations in raw-material prices or (2) changes in assortment. If the grouping of products is at all reasonable, the assortment variations in selling prices and costs should tend to wash out, and if differences in classes of customers are not important, the margin variation then boils down to a variation in the relationship between material costs and selling prices.[4] If differences in classes of customers are important, the job of complete analysis is considerably complicated, but it is doubtful whether the best solution of the problem is to attempt to break down the margin variation any further, since the introduction of too many factors into the analysis may tend to make the statement an exercise in mathematics rather than a useful executive tool. A more useful statement will generally be obtained by limiting the analysis of variations to the three factors of volume, unit margins, and assortment and by supplying supplementary data and explanations to bring out the reasons for the margin variations.

---

[4] If the comparison is with a previous year, the element of changes in standard labor and overhead costs must also be considered.

If the variations in margins in a commodity class due to differences in classes of customers are more important than those due to differences in products, it is possible to make the breakdown and analysis of each commodity class by customer classes instead of by products, so that the assortment variation will indicate changes in profits resulting from changes in the assortment of customers. Usually, however, the statement will be clearer to the reader and simpler to prepare if the entire analysis is based either on a product classification or on a customer classification, and the other factor is brought in by supplementary statements or explanatory comment.

Analysis of sales and gross profit by territories or customer classes

All the approaches to sales and gross-profit analysis thus far discussed have been based on a primary breakdown by commodity classes, on the assumption that the sales department is organized on that basis. Such an organization form is found in most cases where there are several different lines of products, since it is generally recognized that sales planning and promotion can be most effectively handled by concentrating the attention of one executive on each product line. Even where the business is small enough that one executive can span two or more of the lines, it may still be desirable to report the lines separately, if they are recognized in management thinking as essentially different ventures.

In business built around a single type of product, where there is no real commodity classification either in organization or in management approach, the primary division of sales responsibilities will usually be by sales territories or, less frequently, by classes of customers, and the venture analysis in the statements should, of course, follow the same pattern. In either case the summary control statements of sales and gross profits will be in the same form as Figures 16–2 and 16–3, substituting sales territories or customer classes for commodity classes, and the procedure illustrated in Figure 16–5 can be applied to the analysis of gross-profit variations in each territory or each class of trade. Whether the more detailed analysis of margin variations illustrated in Figure 16–6 is useful under such circumstances will depend on whether there are significant differences between the margins in the various subclassifications.

As pointed out earlier in this chapter, if the budget is used for direct control of field sales activities, the analysis of sales and gross profits by territories falls into the category of a summary control report, even though there may be a similar analysis by commodities for the commodity executives. Sometimes the control of sales and profits by territories may be based on sales quotas entirely dissociated from the master budget, but it is important that a statement be prepared for each territory comparing the actual sales and, if possible, the actual gross profits with some control figures.

Importance of adequate reports on sales and gross profits

Considerable space has been devoted to this discussion of reports and analyses of sales and gross profits, because in any but the simplest business it is the most difficult section of the profit and loss statement to understand, owing to the complexity of factors that may produce changes in gross-profit results. It should be emphasized again that the practical usefulness of this type of analysis depends on (1) a clear definition of organization responsibilities, not only for various classes of sales but also for the relationship of costs and selling prices, and (2) a clean-cut accounting plan which follows and reflects this organization of responsibilities.

Other summary control reports

In addition to the summary control reports on sales and gross profits, it is customary to prepare summary reports on other elements in the profit and loss statement. Normally these will include selling and administrative expenses, and various kinds of overhead expense. In every case, the principles outlined above are applicable, and are usually easier to apply than in the case of sales. The first basis for presentation should be responsibility to ensure that the executive who committed the expenditure is kept aware of its progress and results. Then it may be desirable to perform analyses by cause, so that managers are advised of the changes in overhead which could be anticipated if they were to change operations, either by increasing volume of a product, mechanizing a process, or selecting a new distribution channel.

Most of the expenses in these categories are less susceptible to rapid change than are sales and cost of goods sold. It is quite in order, therefore, to report these expenses less often. Monthly reports have been found sufficiently rapid in many companies, and reports prepared more often than weekly are not likely to be justified.

Considerable flexibility is often available to the manager in deciding exactly when to incur overhead costs, especially costs like maintenance. Accordingly, it is often instructive to prepare a report giving the cumulative total amount spent in each overhead category for the "year to date" as well as the amount for the current period. The year-to-date figures may be offered in comparison with the budgeted amount for the same period. In this way, a manager who seeks to conceal an indifferent performance at the gross profit level by judicious manipulation of the postponable expenses lower down the income statement would be prevented from doing so, or at least would run the risk of being spotted by his superiors.

Comments accompanying control reports

Current control reports, since they are primarily concerned with pointing our deviations from standard performance as promptly as possible, are usually limited to a statement of facts, and it is left to the responsible executives receiving the reports to determine the reasons for the variances and take corrective action. As to summary control reports, the situation is somewhat different; the purpose of such reports, as stated earlier, is "to summarize for executive review all the deviations from planned operations, and to show their effect on budgeted profits." Each summary control statement is prepared for the benefit of the executive whose area of responsibility it covers, to give him a picture in dollars of the combined effect of deviations from standard which he has already noted from his current control statements, if the latter are doing the job they are supposed to do. But, in addition to this use of summary control statements by the executives directly responsible for the operations covered, each such statement will, in a properly functioning organization, be reviewed by the immediate line superior of the responsible executive, and many of them will be reviewed by the top management as supplements to the master operating report, the overall profit and loss statement.

In view of this use of summary control statements by executives who are not personally familiar with the operations covered, there is an obvious need for some brief comments explaining the reported deviations from budget or standard; such comments should be prepared in each case by the executive responsible for the operations covered by the statement. The facts necessary to understand any such statement should already be in the possession of the responsible executive, either from his personal observation or from the current control statements which he has been receiving during the month. If additional facts are needed, they can be dug out by the cost or accounting departments insofar as they are contained in the records, but the interpretation of the facts is the responsible executive's job and should not be assumed by anyone else.

The responsibility for interpretation here declared to be that of the operating executive and the controller's general responsibility for interpretation should not be confused. Briefly, the controller's responsibility is to interpret the relationships between the figures of his report, while the executive responsibility is the interpretation of those figures in terms of the causative technological operating conditions with which he is directly familiar and for which he is assumed to be responsible.

Whether these interpretations by the responsible operating executives are incorporated into formally written comments will depend on the policy of the management and the circumstances in each case. With plant foremen and office department heads, the more effective procedure is usually to have these executives discuss the reports personally with the plant manager, either individually or in a group meeting, and to omit any formal written reports. The same procedure may be followed with respect to reports covering a wider area of responsibility, up to the top management itself, except that where the executive reporting is in a different location from his line superior, as in the case of the manager of a plant some distance from headquarters, some written comments are almost a necessity. It is important to have the discussions in these individual and group conferences supplemented by brief written comments submitted by the principal executives in charge of sales, manufacturing, and administration; these comments, prefaced by a condensed statement prepared by the controller setting forth the highlights of the variances from budget for the month, can be presented to the top management or the directors with the monthly profit and loss statement as the complete master summary control report.

17 STATEMENTS AND REPORTS FOR MANAGEMENT (continued)

INFORMATION REPORTS

Purpose of information reports

The purpose of information reports is to sift out of the records of operating results all the facts which have an important bearing on business plans and policies and to present them to the management as simply and clearly as possible. It is obvious that reports of this kind will cover a much wider field than control reports, which are concerned primarily with keeping the business running efficiently by the checking of actual results against plans and budgets. The framework of a proper control report structure is usually reasonably clear if the business is organized along functional lines and operations are budgeted and recorded by individual responsibilities; this framework provides a useful model for the construction of certain basic information reports, as will be brought out a little later in this discussion, but it does not begin to provide a complete outline for adequate information reporting. Some such outline is necessary, for in any business it is possible to present a great variety of facts in an almost infinite number of different ways, and sometimes the mistake is made of doing exactly that, with the result that each executive uses and emphasizes the report which happens to strike his fancy—perhaps the one which comes nearest to confirming his preconceived ideas or hopes—and fails to obtain a clear and complete understanding of the actual situation. This inevitably leads to confusion and lack of coordination in management thinking and planning and defeats the purpose for which the reports are prepared.

There is no doubt that a certain amount of variety and flexibility is desirable in information reporting, to meet changing conditions and to maintain interest and freshness of viewpoint, but there should be a foundation of regular reports, carefully worked out to meet the continuing needs of the business, and the special reports which add the element of variety and flexibility should conform to the same basic principles as those followed in the setup of the regular reports with which the management is familiar, even to the point of using the same terminology where possible. It is not necessary to be an expert in semantics to appreciate the great variety in the meanings attached to the same word by different people, and, since the whole purpose of reports is to inform the executives for whom they are prepared, it is highly important that such terms as "cost of goods sold," "operating profit," "merchandising profit," "direct expenses," etc., should be clearly defined by usage and should mean the same thing no matter where they appear in the report structure.

Types of information reports

Because of the great range covered by information reports, it is not possible to make any rigid classification of them, but there are certain recognizable types which serve somewhat different purposes, and an understanding of the differences between these types will be helpful in working out a sound reporting plan.

In the first place, no set of figures reflecting the results of business operations is particularly useful except in comparison with some base of reference. In control reports, the comparison, of course, is directly with the current operating plan, i.e., the budget. Information reports can be divided in this respect into two broad types, which we may call, for convenience, the "trend" types and the "analytical" type. In the trend type of report, the results of the same activity or group of activities are compared over a period of months or years, to bring out the facts as to growth or shrinkage in volume, changes in products or outlets, variations in the relationship of costs and expenses to sales, etc., while in the analytical type comparisons are made for the same period between different activities, between similar activities in different locations, or with some formal or informal policy standard or objective. In other words, trend reports are limited as to the area of activity covered, but with a wide range in time, while analytical reports derive their value from cross-section comparisons, limited to the current time period but covering a wider area of activity.

In addition to this distinction based on different methods of approach to the evaluation of facts, we can recognize another distinction, between "individual activity" reports, i.e., those which are limited to activities under the direction of a single responsible executive, and "joint-activity" reports, which cut across lines of individual responsibility and show the combined results of activities which are related but do not head up to one executive. Thus a report which compares sales in a given field territory or district over a period of years is an individual activity report, while a report which groups the results of related sales, factory, and administrative activities, is a joint-activity report.

In the paragraphs immediately following, the characteristics and uses of these various types of information reports are discussed, and consideration is then given to the principles involved in developing a balanced reporting program.

Basic trend reports

The most natural first step in the development of a plan of information reports is to supplement the control report structure with a similar set of trend reports comparing current results with the results of the corresponding period of a previous year or years. Just as the master summary control statement is the profit and loss statement comparing actual results with the current budget, so the master trend statement for any business is a profit and loss statement showing comparisons with the results of one or more previous years. Supplementary trend statements will also, up to a point, parallel the supplementary summary statements; thus, if there are summary statements comparing actual sales and gross profits by commodity groups and subgroups with the budget and comparing actual and budgeted expenses of the various sales and administrative departments, there will be trend statements giving comparisons with the corresponding items in previous years. For factory trend statements some modification of the summary statement forms may be necessary, since the standards by which factory results are measured are usually changed each year and, if the changes are significant, the variances shown on the summary statements are not comparable from year to year. In such cases trends in costs can be brought out by year-to-year comparisons of the various elements of cost and comparisons of labor hours or machine hours and productive output, either for the plant as a whole or for individual departments; if standard costs are figured on the basis of normal capacity, comparisons of typical important product costs will also be informative.

A comprehensive trend report for the entire business, embracing the statements mentioned in the preceding paragraph, should be prepared at least once each year, as an internal annual report for the top executives. This report should include comments summarizing the factors causing changes in earnings from the previous year and bringing out the more important longer-term trends shown by comparisons with earlier years. Each of the responsible operating executives can be given copies of the statements relating to his activities and asked to write his own comments, and these comments can either be incorporated as part of the report or used as the basis for more condensed comments prepared by the controller. A very effective procedure is to divide the internal annual report into two sections, one including the detailed reports of the several responsible operating executives, with the statements pertaining thereto, and the other containing the overall highlight analysis by the controller.

It may be found desirable to make an overall trend report of this type, or in some modified form, oftener than once a year, possibly semi-annually. If the business is subject to seasonal cycles, however, it is difficult to maintain the continuity of a complete trend analysis in report form, and the objective can often be achieved more easily by the use of "running comparisons" or tabulations of key figures, as described in the paragraph on "Other Trend Reports," several paragraphs below. If, on the other hand, the business is subject to a very long cycle—two or three years or more—the comparisons and comments in the internal annual report described above should obviously extend back far enough to include the cycle.

Combination of basic trend reports and summary control reports

In a business where no budgets or operating forecasts are prepared, prior-month or prior-year results are often shown in the regular monthly statements as a basis for comparison with current actual results. Such statements are, of course, trend reports, but they have to do service also as a control tool of a sort, though their shortcomings for that purpose are obvious. Even where the primary control is through comparisons with the budget, it is not unusual to find prior-year comparisons, both for the current month and for the year to date, in the same monthly statements with the budget comparisons. This rather common practice of using a single statement for a combined control and trend report has the advantage, of course, of compactness, in the sense that it provides more information on the same sheet of paper, but it is likely to have the collateral disadvantage of diverting attention from the principal purpose of the statement, which must be either to check actual results against budget or to bring out trends.

As a rule, detailed comparisons with the budget are useful only if they cover a relatively short period of time—not more than a quarter—because that is about as far ahead as it is usually possible to make detailed operating plans; on the other hand, genuine operating trends become apparent in most businesses only over a somewhat longer period of time, since month-to-month fluctuations are likely to be due to any one of a number of possible temporary abnormalities. Most executives can absorb just about so much in the way of operating data, and the best results will usually be achieved by making a separate report for each type of presentation. If prior-year comparisons are included in a statement accompanying a control report, they should be limited to the cumulative figures for the elapsed portion of the year, because only in rare instances does the comparison of any individual month with the same month of the previous year have any real value. Furthermore, the comments accompanying the statement should be directed to its control aspects, that is, to the comparisons with budget, and the cumulative comparison with the previous year should be regarded simply as supplementary data, intended to give some degree of orientation as to trends. Similarly, if budget figures are included in a statement accompanying a trend report, they should be used only incidentally to the trend comparisons; for example, in the internal annual report described above, the actual trend in certain sales or expenses might be compared with the expected trend shown by the budget, but too much of this type of double comparison is likely to be confusing.

Other trend reports

In addition to the basic trend reports paralleling the control reports and tying in logical sequence with the trend profit and loss statement, there may be numerous other regular or special reports showing year-to-year, quarter-to-quarter, or month-to-month trends in various departments or activities of the business. Thus the sales department may desire reports showing sales and possibly gross-profit trends in the various commodity groups in each field territory, and the plant management may be interested in reports showing maintenance trends in relation to activity in the various manufacturing departments. It will frequently be found convenient to set up departmental data of this kind in the form of permanent columnar tabulations, adding the figures for each successive month, quarter, or year as they become available; as a matter of fact, the controller will find it most helpful to have at his disposal similar tabulations of operating data covering all important activities of the business on at least a quarterly basis.

As pointed out in a preceding paragraph, comparisons of operating data on a month-to-month basis are subject to distortion because of temporary or chance fluctuations; they are of most significance when conditions are relatively stable, as in a plant manufacturing a uniform product and operating continuously at or near capacity. In quarter-to-quarter comparisons of manufacturing data many of the chance distortions are ironed out, and if such reports show comparisons of variances from standard and the standards are adjusted to reflect changes in activity, the trends shown may be a real index of progress or loss of ground. With sales, however, quarterly trends are subject to distortion by seasonal factors, which are often quite variable from year to year, and even annual trends in sales must be interpreted with an eye on the normal long-term cycle of the business.

Reports and tabulations of the type discussed above are useful in formulating or modifying policies or setting current objectives rather than as control tools in themselves, and there is always the danger of their diverting attention from the real control, which should be the current budget. A multiplicity of reports, including comparisons with several different bases, makes for confusion rather than clarification, and the controller, while making every effort to give the operating executives all the information which will be genuinely helpful to them, should try to keep the reporting routine as simple as is consistent with this objective and should emphasize the importance of the budget as the standard for current performance.

Consistent accounting essential as a basis for trend reports

It seems rather trite to say that consistency in accounting methods and account classification is essential to provide the proper basis for reports showing trends over a period of time, but the point is often overlooked and, even when recognized, is frequently a source of difficulty. All healthy businesses experience a certain amount of growth: New products are introduced to supplement or supplant old ones, manufacturing facilities are expanded or revamped, and the organization structure and executive responsibilities are modified to meet changing conditions. Such changes in the functioning of the organization must be reflected in the accounting plan, and every time a change is made in the accounting plan it is necessary to consider its effect on trend comparisons and in many cases to analyze and recast the figures for previous years to make them comparable with the new classification.

When a fundamental change is made in the method of operating a business, it is quite likely to be followed by a series of minor rearrangements and reclassifications as experience is gained on the new basis, and after a year or two it may be necessary to recognize that the organization of the business has changed so completely that the link with past experience is pretty well cut and that comparisons with previous years must be limited to overall total figures of sales, costs, and expenses. Sometimes the controller is asked to report on the effect on profits of such changes in organization or operation; all too often, this is a job which requires not only a very careful analysis of the accounting figures but also a considerable degree of judgment in evaluating the cause-and-effect relationships of various changes in income and expense.

Consistency in accounting principles and methods is just as necessary to the validity of trend reports as consistency in account classification. It is particularly important that a definite and consistent policy be followed in the compilation of the standard costs which are used as a basis for the costing of sales and for the overall measurement of factory performance as reflected in the summary figures in the profit and loss statements. For this purpose the normal-capacity basis of computation, as described in Chapter 8, "Manufacturing Costs," is usually most satisfactory, since revisions in the standards from year to year will be due not to fluctuations in volume but only to such factors as changes in manufacturing processes or methods or in wage rates, supply costs, etc., all of which, in a competitive business, will normally be reflected in selling prices.

Under the fairly common circumstance of considerable excess capacity incident to long-range expansion plans, the practical capacity basis for standard costs may be more useful for year-to-year comparisons. Whatever basis is used, the controller must see to it that management understands the impact of the method, so that trend changes shown are recognized for what they really are.

Analytical reports

In almost any business, it will be found desirable to supplement the trend reports by at least a limited number of analytical reports. As examples, let us consider the two illustrations used in the section above, on "Other Trend Reports," i.e., reports on field territorial activities and on plant maintenance expenses.

If the summary reports for field territorial activities show comparisons of actual and budgeted sales and gross profits by broad commodity groups, the sales department is quite likely to ask for supplementary information reports, giving for each field territory a breakdown of actual results in each commodity group by individual products or a breakdown of total actual results in the territory by classes of customers, or even by individual customers. Of course, if the budget is carried into these finer breakdowns, these supplementary reports are really a part of the primary control report structure, but in a business of any complexity it is rarely practical to budget in this detail, and the information disclosed by supplementary reports of this kind is usually used not for direct control but as an aid in determining policies and planning future performance—in this case, for example, as an aid in maintaining the proper balance of sales of individual products within each commodity group or of sales to different customer classes. The information may be used by comparing the sales and gross-profit breakdowns with some predetermined policy objective—that is, with a general pattern of product or customer distribution which the management considers desirable—or by making comparisons of product or customer distribution in the different territories.

Just as comparisons between field territories are often helpful in planning sales objectives, analytical reports comparing certain types of costs in similar plants may be of assistance to the chief manufacturing executive. Such reports need not necessarily be in dollar terms; for example, the general manager of a group of cotton mills may find it extremely useful to have a monthly or quarterly statement showing each mill's consumption of various types of machine parts, stated in units per machine hour.

Since the use of the analytical reports described above is based largely on comparisons of similar activities in different locations, it must be recognized in interpreting them that conditions may vary somewhat between the several locations. Thus the factors of custom, climate, or competitive strength will affect product distribution in different field territories, and differences in age or type of equipment will have a bearing on maintenance costs in different plants, even when the plants are superficially quite similar. As a matter of fact, important collateral benefits from the use of reports of this kind are the clues which they give to such fundamental differences in conditions and the effect of such conditions on potential sales or costs.

Another analytical report which is extremely important in many businesses is an analysis of research and development activities. It is quite common practice to have all research personnel account for their time by charges to various projects or job orders and to prepare a monthly, quarterly, or annual statement showing the cost of each project, based on the wages and salaries charged, with or without an allocation of the research department overhead. This is not a control statement, since obviously the expenditures of the department can be much better controlled in total by the normal budget procedure, and the distribution of time will be checked currently as the work proceeds, probably against some informal time budget or assignment schedule. The value of the statement of project costs is that it brings home to the management how the money allocated for research is being spent, so that the results achieved on each project, its cost, and its future possibilities can be evaluated as background for forward planning.

Ideally, the success of each project ought to be followed into subsequent operations, at least to the point of the sales volume of the resulting products, if not to the net profit therefrom, since such considerations must be the final justification for the expenditure. Whether this can be done in anything approaching a routine report or whether it can be done only on the basis of an occasional special study must be determined by the controller in each situation. At best, a vast amount of research must be undertaken with very little, if any, proof of its utility in terms of specific results. The history of recent years bears ample proof that money spent in research is often extremely productive. The danger that this may lead to research expenditures based on nothing but blind faith can be met to some degree by reports aimed at demonstrating the results obtained wherever this is in any sense feasible.

Venture-measurement reports

Earlier in this book, under consideration of the accounting plan and later in this book under forward planning, we are deeply concerned with the accounting recognition and management significance of venture measurement in business. At this point we are interested in the presenta- tion aspect of venture analysis. The stark fact is that, no matter how good the accountant's thinking on the subject may be, it is only through his skillful communication in the statements that his service to manage- ment can become effective. The numbers of forms and devices that can be effective in presenting venture analysis are as varied as the possi- ble combinations of ventures.

A review of the business situation and a reconsideration of what has already been said about statements and reports brings out the fact that under many conditions the measurement of individual responsibility for control and information purposes also fortunately measures a sig- nificant venture segment of the business. Where sales can be organized into product groups of such essential similarity that the group can be made the responsibility of an individual, the fortunes of the commodity group take on a venture significance which is in addition to the responsi- bility significance of the individual in charge. This coinciding of re- sponsibility and venture significance makes possible at least an apparent economy in statement presentation, since the single statement serves the purposes of high-level control, the reporting of information for cur- rent planning and product judgments, and the long-range planning of the future course of the venture. In very large multiple businesses, espe- cially those in which the several ventures are quite different from one another, the organization of management normally and easily follows venture lines. In smaller businesses and in the subventures of larger businesses, the several ventures become joint activities within the single structure of responsibility.

In such joint-activity situations it is still imperative to report upon the several ventures in whatever degree of separation and detail manage- ment deems useful. Obviously, the difficulties of proper reporting here became much greater; for here there is not only the inherent difficulty of allocating joint costs to the ventures but the superimposed difficulty of presentation in a manner that is not too complicated for serious ac- ceptance by the various echelons of management concerned. The alloca- tion of fixed expenses on the most reasonable basis is necessary; yet management must never be allowed to forget that fixed expenses are indeed fixed. The significance of fixed expenses and their allocation to separate ventures to which the business is committed is quite different from the significance of fixed expenses at the time that management is considering the commitment of the business to a new venture or at the time that management is considering the withdrawal from a ven- ture. It is entirely proper to expect the ongoing venture, which is a regular part of the business, to absorb its full share of fixed expenses, and if it does not do so, there is grave cause for management concern. This is quite a different problem from the recognition that under certain circumstances the contribution of a venture toward total fixed costs—that is, the excess of its revenue over its variable cost—is the important quantity to watch. It can even be granted that it may be intelligent for a business under some circumstances to continue more or less permanently to operate a venture which covers somewhat more than its variable costs but less than its total costs, but this does not contradict the need to show the total picture of what is happening venture by venture in the routinely prepared management reports. In this day of prosperous, expanding business every management should expect to make every venture yield a net return over all costs. Any segment which cannot do so should be carried on the contribution to fixed overhead theory only until a substitute venture can be found to use the capacity really profitably. It is the function of properly designed statements and reports to keep this situation unmistakably before the eyes of management. It is difficult for any management to avoid a certain amount of complacency if overall results are satisfactory, but as long as this means that certain profitable ventures are carrying others that do not make a net profit, there should be no complacency.

In getting at this problem of reporting on the multiple venture, it is always tempting to concern ourselves with the dramatic situation of the net-loss venture carried by the really profitable ones. However, the more mundane situation in which all ventures yield some net profit is probably by far the more common and, therefore, the more important case. Shall management be allowed the luxury of complacency in this situation? It should be clear that the real issue is the satisfactoriness of the rate of return of each venture, and that there is nothing particularly significant about the passing of the zero rate into the low plus figures. As long as there is any flexibility in the business situation, allowing room for improvement either by stepping up the efficiency of present ventures or by shifting to entirely new ventures, the pressure should be kept on management by a clear portrayal of the present results. More detailed analysis of this entire situation as it applies to the actual decision-making process will be presented in the chapter on forward planning. Here we are properly concerned with the statement presentation of the facts.

Either the trend or the analytical format may be used to bring out the essential developments of the venture segments of the business. Where the ventures are quite unlike each other, the trend comparison of each venture with its own showing in previous periods may be the more significant. Where the ventures are essentially parallel, as in the sales departments of a department store, the analytical form may be the more useful.

There is one very down-to-earth angle that should be noted with respect to the construction of statements which measure individual responsibilities, on the one hand, and the construction of statements measuring venture success within the joint activity, on the other hand. Both statements require allocations of certain general expenses. Where these are chargeable against the responsibility of an individual, there is an automatic safeguard against crude errors in that individual's intelligent self-interest. Such allocations must stand the test of the individual's knowledgeable scrutiny, whereas in the parallel situation of charges against a venture there is no personal interest to fight back against an unfair allocation. This puts greater responsibility upon the controller to see to it that the allocations are correct in the first place.

For instance, a report on the success of a venture may include deductions from gross profit for inventory adjustments, home-office and selling expenses, and manufacturing variances. In devising this report, the controller would do better to deduct the direct costs of the venture first, such as inventory adjustments, and arrive at an interim profit figure. After that, the overhead and variance items may be subtracted to arrive at the net profit for the venture. The advantage of this arrangement is that the manager in charge of the venture can see at once whether a change in the total contribution of his department is attributable to items he can control, or to overhead items outside his responsibility, or to a mixture of the two. His superior may make a similar evaluation.

Use of ratios and percentages in operating reports

It will be noted that in many of the operating statements used for illustrative purposes in the preceding discussion the various items of cost and expense are expressed in terms of percentages of sales as well as in dollar amounts. This breakdown of the sales dollar, showing how much goes for factory cost, how much for advertising, selling, and other types of expense, and how much is left for profit after all costs and expenses, is a natural and sound first step in the analysis of operations. Such a breakdown in itself tells a great deal about the nature of the business, and sometimes it discloses the more obvious points of strength and weakness, particularly if selling prices are relatively stable and if comparisons are made over a period of years or with other businesses in the same industry.

For internal management purposes, however, the sales-dollar breakdown is ordinarily useful only as a general indicator of trends and relationships and in the great majority of businesses its value for control, and even in information reports, is definitely limited. The reason for this lies in the variability of sales volume from month to month and year to year and the impossibility of adjusting costs and expenses in proportion to these fluctuations. Even if prices are stable, unit sales volume is usually subject to wide fluctuations over a period of time; and if prices also fluctuate, the instability of dollar volume is, of course, accentuated.

A very great deal has been done in the field of trade associations, university bureaus of business research, and similar groups in the analysis of business through the use of ratios. This type of effort largely involves smaller concerns, where the independent units are more or less uniform in their business activities. Independent jewelry stores, drugstores, laundries, and so forth are quite similar within their groups except for the factor of size, and this factor can be reduced by the analysis of the statements of each business on ratio and percentage bases. Some of these studies have gone so far as to establish sets of ratios for several size groups to attain standards still more closely applicable.

To be even approximately effective, such a study must require reporting members of the group to establish uniform classifications of accounts, which in itself usually constitutes an improvement over the haphazard systems often found in small businesses. Usually the businesses report annually on uniform forms, and from these the central authority makes up standards which may be the averages or medians or some more sophisticated measure, which can be reported back as a guide to the participants. In addition to setting up separate standards for size groups, some of these studies set up special standards by size of community in which the business operates and by other special criteria.

Where such standards are carefully compiled on the basis of reasonably uniform accounting systems and then intelligently studied by the individual businessman, they will identify the differences of each business from the common pattern. These differences may be caused by real variations in the local business situation from the norm, or they may be indicators of significant errors of the local management. Such uniform standards can be effective only through the use of ratios and percentages. They have undoubtedly been of very great service in many fields.

Just how far up the scale toward larger businesses similar devices may be useful is an interesting question. The larger the business, the more likely it is to be multiple-venture and the more certain it is to be unlike any other business. The Blue Cross–Blue Shield "industry" is one example of a rather large business which is attempting to aid its members by uniform reporting and ratio analysis techniques. Various studies of department store operating results have been made for the same purpose. The Machinery and Allied Products Industry (MAPI) has made extensive studies of operating ratios among its members.

The whole subject of uniform accounting and reporting for comparative purposes revolves around the statements and reports designed to bring out the greatest possible significance in compact, economical form. Though this is a specialty going beyond the scope of this book, it may not be a waste of time for the controller to contemplate its possible importance to his own business.

Perhaps the most significant operating ratios, from the long-term viewpoint, are those that show the relationship of profits to capital investment. A distinction must be made here between "operating profits," before the payment of interest charges and taxes on income, and "net profits," or the amount remaining for the stockholders after the payment of all charges. The ratio of operating profits to total capital employed in the business from all sources is, theoretically, the best universally applicable measure of strictly operating effectiveness, since it is not affected by differences in financial structure or by advantages or disadvantages in position with respect to taxes on income. The ratio of net profits to stockholders' equity indicates the earning power of the owners' investment; obviously, this may be more or less than the ratio of operating profit to total capital, depending on the amount and rate of interest charged on borrowed capital and the relationship of taxes on income to profits before such taxes. These two ratios are of prime importance to management in evaluating the overall effectiveness of its performance, and a table or chart showing their trend over a period of years should be included in the controller's general comments in his annual report to management. Where there are several classes of securities outstanding, it is also desirable to include year-to-year comparisons of "earnings coverage" on each class, i.e., the number of times bond interest and preferred dividends are earned and the earnings per share of common stock.

The relationship of profit to capital employed is important not only for a business as a whole but for each of its departments or activities. The advantages and limitations of reports breaking down the profits of a business by commodities or other broad activities were discussed at some length earlier in this chapter; where such reports are practical, it is highly desirable to go a step further and determine or estimate the capital employed in each activity, so that the return on the investment can be at least approximated. This return can be expressed in terms of the ratio of operating profit before interest and taxes to the capital employed, or, interest on the capital employed can be charged at a predetermined rate, and an average rate of income tax applied to get a net profit after interest and taxes.

In comparing ratios of profits to capital investment over a period of years it is important that both the profits and the investment used as a base for the calculation of the ratios should be on a consistent basis for all years. Changes in depreciation policy or reductions in the amount of depreciation charged because of fully depreciated assets being continued in use, changes in the basis of inventory valuation, and changes in the ratio of depreciation reserve to gross plant because of an accumulation of insufficient or conservative depreciation charges are all factors which may distort the trends and make them very misleading, and this effect should be eliminated by appropriate adjustments.

Miscellaneous nonaccounting reports

Almost all business executives have and use constantly at least a few statistical reports which are not a part of, or tied in with, the accounting records. Some of these have already been described in the discussions of current control reports in the chapters on "Manufacturing Costs" and earlier in this chapter; but others, such as unfilled order reports, reports on the current cost of important raw materials, and reports on the number of employees, average employee earnings, etc., are really outside any of the classifications applicable to the regular accounting reports. Sometimes, as in the case of a report on current raw-material prices, they anticipate trends which will show up later in the accounting records, and thus point the way to prompt management action, but in other cases they are simply for purposes of general information, rounding out and clarifying the picture of operations which every executive needs to keep in his mind. Ideally, all such reports should be considered a part of the information system within the controller's responsibility. Where they are already being satisfactorily prepared by employees in other functional areas, the controller need not disturb existing procedures, but he should be familiar with such reports so that he may integrate them effectively with his own reports.

Attaining balance in the information report structure

One of the most common continuing problems with which many controllers have to deal is the demand for new reports of all kinds and types. Once an organization becomes sold on the importance of a knowledge of facts as a basis for operating plans and decisions, it is quite likely to develop an insatiable appetite for more and more information. This demand can easily get out of hand. In some large companies the situation is handled by having one of the principal executives, or perhaps a committee of the top management, pass regularly on all requests, or at least on all requests for reports involving an additional clerical cost in excess of some specified amount. Whether or not such a formal procedure is followed, the controller or someone on his staff must take the responsibility for scrutinizing every such request to determine whether the need which inspired it cannot be met by one of the existing reports, perhaps with some slight modification or adaptation. This rather defensive approach to the problem, however, is not enough; the controller should himself take the initiative in developing an adequate and well-balanced information-reporting program. To accomplish this, four steps may be suggested:

1. A review with each responsible executive of the control reports which are issued to him, to determine whether there is any additional useful information about his activity that could be supplied in supplementary individual activity reports. Such supplementary reports may be of the analytical type, which derive their value from comparisons of similar activities in different locations or from comparisons with some general policy objective, or they may be of the trend type, which present a picture of performance over a longer period of time. In setting up trend information on individual activities, the use of running tabulations, as suggested in the discussion of trend reports in the preceding chapter, will often 'be found more economical than, and fully as satisfactory as, the preparation of formal statements.

2. The development of the necessary basic information for a comprehensive annual trend report of the kind described in the preceding pages. Most of this information will usually be available from the regular control reports and needs only to be tabulated for comparative purposes. Sometimes special analyses may be required to bring out the facts as to new developments or changes in the character of the business and these should be maintained currently so as to be readily available at the time of the annual review.

3. A study of the business to determine whether its operations can be divided into two or more groups of activities which represent essentially different ventures, with a view to the development of joint-activity reports for the various ventures. This, of course, is a job for which ·no standard blueprint can be prescribed, since each business has its own peculiarities.

4. A study of the information needs of the top-management executives to determine the extent to which they make use of the individual activity reports prepared for the various operating executives, and how such reports could be adapted, condensed, or summarized so as to be more easily assimilated by those whose primary responsibility is the supervision and coordination of a wide range of activities.

An important part of each of the foregoing steps is a process of mutual education—the education of the controller to the needs and viewpoints of the operating executives and the education of those executives in the proper use and interpretation of the information made available to them. And even when the report structure is once set up, the job is not done; the process of education must continue, and the structure itself must be regularly reviewed and brought up to date, to meet changing conditions.

The problem of communication

At the beginning of this discussion of statements and reports for management, it was emphasized that the controller's job is not complete until the facts which he has assembled about the business are not only presented but are also actually communicated to those who are in a position to act on them. In all that has been said about the classification of reports, the uses and limitations of different types, and the techniques of preparing and presenting them, the central aim has been to outline an approach to the selection and organization of the vast amount of information that can be made available by modern accounting and statistical methods. Selection is important to keep the volume of reports within the limits of usability and their cost within the means of the business; organization is necessary to put the information in a form that can be readily assimilated by the executives by whom it is to be used. Intelligent selection and organization are essential to the third and final step—communication—which is perhaps the most difficult of all.

Concerning this final step of communication, advice can be offered only in the most general terms. In the following paragraphs, a few basic principles are suggested for each controller to adapt and apply to his own particular situation.

1. *Unity of theme.* This simply means that each report should be aimed at one and only one objective; for example, if it is a control report for one department of the business, it should not be confused by bringing in a trend analysis or a comparison with other departments.

2. *Concentration on exceptions.* This is particularly applicable to control reports, and in the illustrations of such reports in the preceding discussions it will be noted that attention is uniformly directed to variations from planned or budgeted operations. It also applies to information reports of the analytical type; in the trend type of information report, all activities will be covered, though more attention will usually be devoted to trends disclosing weaknesses than to situations which are satisfactory.

3. *Adaptation of reports to personalities.* The recipients of reports are human beings with likes and dislikes, emotions, and greatly varied training backgrounds. The report that might be effective for Jones, who was trained in the best business schools in the country, might fall quite flat if presented to Smith, who is an entirely self-made man. The executive who has come to his present position by the sales department route or through engineering might require quite a different report than one who was himself an earlier controller of the company. There is a process of mutual education between the controller and the line operators which comes to a head in the reports of the controller, which are the principal point of formal contact. Sometimes the adjustments of reports to the needs of the persons to whom they are addressed are merely subtle differences in wording; at other times they will lie in the degree of detail to be shown; and, occasionally, they will be differences of principle.

4. *Balance between consistency and variety.* Clearly, it is essential that there be in every business a basic structure of reports which remains consistent from month to month and year to year changing only as necessary to reflect changes in the business itself. These are the "old reliables," to which management can turn with confidence, knowing the sequence that they will follow and the scope of the picture that they will unfold. But dependence on these reports alone carries with it the danger of thinking in a rut, and the controller should see to it that these old reliables are supplemented with just enough new and different material to preserve a sense of perspective and a freshness of viewpoint. This can often be done by reports on new or special activities which require management attention or on which management interest may be focused at the moment. The controller's annual report to the management offers an opportunity for new approaches and often suggests special analyses to follow up some points disclosed by the regular review of operations.

5. *Use of graphic and verbal presentations.* Variety in method of presentation is another aid in combatting the effect of repetitive reporting routine, and graphic and verbal presentations are often more effective than written reports in communicating facts to those who are not figure-minded. There are several volumes available on the fundamentals of graphic presentation, and with a little experimenting and the application of common sense any controller can develop charts which will express clearly the more fundamental facts about operations and financial condition. Simple line and block charts on an ordinary arithmetical scale are usually most effective, and it is wise to avoid attempting to crowd too many data into one chart.

Verbal presentation and discussions are a natural supplement to written reports and are used to some extent in practically all organizations. They may be conducted in formal meetings of the interested executives or informally and piecemeal, as special questions arise or as general developments are discussed over the luncheon table. These informal discussions are particularly valuable to the controller in keeping him in touch with the problems of various departments of the business and with the thinking of his associates in the management.

Reports an aid to management, not a substitute for it

Jerome Frank, former chairman of the Securities and Exchange Commission, pointed out, in an address before the Controllers Institute, the inherent tendency of every human being to view the world in the light of his own occupation and activities. He said, in part:

Every man is likely to overemphasize and treat as fundamental those aspects of life which are his peculiar daily concern. To most dentists, you and I are, basically, but teeth surrounded by bodies. To most undertakers we are incipient corpses; to most actors, parts of a potential audience; to most policemen, possible criminals; to most taxi-drivers, fares . . . . We make life in the image of our own activities.

Controllers are no less prone to this failing than dentists, undertakers, or taxi-drivers, and they cannot remind themselves too often that in the management phase of their activities their duty is to provide information to aid the people who make up the management, rather than to set up controls which will function automatically as a substitute for management.

The advent of electronic data processing, with its complicated programming of many reports, threatens to add to the rigidity and fixity of reports. There will be a dangerous tendency to consider such reports routine and to fail to adjust them to changing conditions and varying management requirements. The controller will have to exercise great judgment in knowing when to call for the scrapping of expensive programs in order to keep his reporting alive and vivid. The persons in management should not be regarded as creatures whose chief function is to consume reports. The controller will still do well to think of his relationship to management as that of one person reporting to other persons, with the formal battery of reports comprising the necessary impediments—aids to memory—the detail support of his written or verbal interpretation which is the real communication.

18 INVENTORY CONTROL

Definition of inventory control

The term "inventory control" is rather loosely used to cover two functions which are really quite different. These two functions, which might be called "accounting control" and "operating control," are related to each other only in that they both require the maintenance of adequate records of inventories, receipts, and issues. The purpose of each can be defined as follows:

Accounting control of inventories is concerned with (a) the safeguarding of the company's property in the form of raw materials, work in process, and semifinished and finished products and (b) the proper recording of the receipt and consumption of materials and the flow of goods through the plant into finished stock and eventually to customers.

Operating control of inventories is concerned with maintaining inventories at the optimum level, considering the operating requirements and financial resources of the business.

This distinction is important to the controller because there is a decided difference in the degree of his responsibility with respect to the two functions. Accounting control of inventories is generally recognized as an important part of the controller's property-control function, as that function was defined in Chapter 4, and he is expected to assume primary responsibility for it.

Operating control of inventories, on the other hand, is the primary responsibility of operating management, with the controller's responsibility ideally limited to the recordkeeping and data reporting to make such management possible. In discharging this responsibility, however, the controller must visualize the basic management problem involved, so that the two aspects can hardly be separated in discussion. Again, since the two aspects are so closely intertwined, it is not surprising to find many controllers assuming at least a part of the substantive responsibility for inventory management. If this delegation of management function is intended, it is unobjectionable; but if it is not specifically provided for in the bylaws or otherwise, it may constitute an area of overlapping responsibility which could become dangerous under certain conditions.

The subject of accounting control of inventories was covered in the earlier chapter on the property-control function, and the mechanisms used in controlling the consumption of raw materials and the flow of goods in process were discussed in Chapter 7 "The Accounting Plan" and Chapter 8 "Manufacturing Costs." The discussion of inventory control which follows will be limited to the operating control aspects.

Objectives of operating control of inventories

It was stated above that operating control of inventories is concerned with maintaining inventories at the optimum level, considering the operating requirements and financial resources of the business. When this statement is amplified somewhat, the objectives which must be kept in mind in developing and maintaining such control are as follows:

1. Service to customers. (Sufficient stocks of finished product must be maintained to meet the reasonable expectations of customers for prompt delivery of their orders.)
2. Effective use of the capital available to the business for the financing of the cycle of purchase, manufacture, sale, and collection.
3. Reduction to a minimum of the risk of loss through obsolescence or shrinkage in market value between the time of purchase or manufacture and the time of sale.
4. Manufacturing efficiency, as affected by
   a) availability of stocks of raw and semifinished material for processing as required, and
   b) The scheduling of processing in lots sufficiently large for economical production.
5. Economy in purchasing, as affected by
   a) Quantity buying, and
   b) Favorable raw-material markets.
6. Avoidance of "out-of-stock" danger.

While these objectives are stated in terms of application to a manufacturing business, it should be clear that, with slight amendment, they are also applicable to merchandising. It should be noted in this connection that No. 6 applies with quite different force to manufacturing than it does to merchandising. While the merchandise business might lose the profit on a sale by being out of stock in some item, the consequence to manufacturing might be the stopping of an assembly line, with its far greater loss. In manufacturing, furthermore, there must be an adjustment of the safety factor for the relative criticalness of the item. Some items can be replaced easily, with only a small price premium. Shortage of other items might be little short of a disaster.

It is sometimes assumed that "inventory control" means keeping inventories as low as possible, but this is a narrow conception of the function. It will be noted that the objective with respect to capital investment in inventories, as stated above, is "effective use of available capital." If there is a risk of shortages or if it appears that prices are likely to advance, it may be desirable to expand inventories beyond immediate operating requirements—in fact, this may be essential to the maintenance of the competitive position of the business. Such a move would be in line with two of the objectives named above—viz., keeping adequate stock of raw materials available and furthering economy in purchasing— but it would be in conflict with the objective of reducing market risks. Thus it is apparent that inventory control requires a balancing of these various objectives and that in this balancing process it is necessary to make certain basic policy decisions.

Basic policy decisions

The policy decisions necessary to the development of intelligent inventory control are so fundamental that they should be made at near top-management level. They should cover the following points:

1. What shall be the company's policy as to service to customers? Shall the attempt be made to ship all orders within 24 or 48 hours after receipt or is a longer time permissible?

2. What are the current limitations on the funds and physical space that can be used for inventory? Should these limits be changed?

3. Is the purchasing policy to be strictly nonspeculative (i.e., are purchases to be made only as required to meet processing schedules, with a reasonable safety factor), or is forward buying for price advantage to be permitted? The answer to this question can often be stated in terms of the number of weeks' requirements which it is permissible to have on hand and on order at any given time; such a limit can, of course, be varied as conditions indicate a valid change in policy.

4. What weight is to be given to the possibilities of cost savings by purchasing and processing in lots larger than are strictly necessary to meet manufacturing and shipping schedules?

The answers to the foregoing policy questions are interdependent and must be considered in relation to each other and in the light of the conditions under which the business is operating and the practical alternatives open to it. In the majority of businesses a certain minimum standard of service to customers is fixed by competition, and there are working limits to the minimum size of purchase orders and processing lots. The line between nonspeculative and speculative purchasing is not always clean-cut, particularly, if style is a factor in the business or if volume fluctuations make it difficult to forecast sales accurately. The amount of capital that is available for investment in inventories depends to a large degree on the company's overall financial policy, which must provide for flexibility to meet changing conditions. As a practical matter, therefore, these basic policy decisions should be stated as guiding principles rather than as iron-clad rules or detailed procedures, and the operating executives should be allowed considerable freedom of judgment in applying the policies and should be permitted and encouraged to question them when new or unforeseen situations arise. But the policies must be defined, within limits, before there can be any real inventory control—or, indeed, any understanding of what inventory control is expected to accomplish.

Nature of the inventory-control problem

The essence of inventory control in manufacturing business is the correlation of production with sales and the correlation of raw material and supply purchasing with production requirements. If all production could be initiated after receipt of the customer's order, if time of delivery were no consideration, and if materials and supplies could be obtained from vendors in exactly the required quantities and landed at the factory door just in time to be put into process, then the only inventory required would be the work actually in process of manufacture. This statement is so obvious as to be a platitude, but it is a good starting point for the consideration of the fundamentals of the inventory-control problem.

In normal times, when materials are in reasonably good supply, a manufacturer of products made to customers' specifications can do a fairly large volume of business with relatively little inventory investment—for example, a maker of custom-built furniture often gets his orders by showing drawings or photographs of the finished pieces and samples of woods and fabrics which he knows he can obtain on short notice from the suppliers. Even in a business of this type, however, it may be desirable to carry stocks of raw materials in order to speed up deliveries or to realize the cost savings which are often possible if materials are purchased in larger lots in anticipation of future sales; and with the decision to embark on such a policy, the real problem of inventory control begins.

In a business where production is for stock rather than on order, customers usually expect deliveries ranging from "prompt" to "immediate," and this necessitates the carrying of inventories of finished product. If production is limited to one item or a few similar items, this may not add greatly to the inventory-control problem, but, with an increase in the number and variety of the products manufactured and the number of materials used, it may become necessary to build up inventories at various points, in order to keep the flow of production properly correlated with sales. And, finally, the most difficult problem of all exists in the type of business in which there is a significant style factor in the finished product, especially if the business is highly seasonal or if a long period of time is required for the purchasing and manufacturing cycle.

Techniques of control

At the preplanning stage, there are two fundamental decisions which a manager may take with respect to any product or commodity in inventory. He may determine the number which should be ordered at any given time. And he may decide when the order should be placed. The techniques of control seek to assist the manager in reaching these decisions.

The simplest technique involves setting maximum and minimum stock limits for the item, and establishing a standard order quantity. Various attempts have been made to set the order quantity to its optimal value, by using mathematics to derive the lowest cost result. The mathematical procedure is commonly called the economic order quantity approach. There are certain situations which cannot be handled mathematically, however, and the technique of simulation has been employed successfully in controlling inventory in these cases. All of these methods involve laborious calculations, mainly because of the large number of items carried in inventory by modern businesses. For this reason, many companies maintain their inventory records on a computer.

The job of developing inventory control in any particular business can be broken down into four steps:

1. Deciding whether to use the limits method, an economic order quantity formula, or simulation for each of the various sections of inventory.
2. Devising the operating procedures and clerical work to make the system function. Writing the necessary computer programs, and preparing the needed files of data in computer-readable form.
3. Educating the personnel who are to operate the controls to the intelligent use of these mechanisms and to the exercise of judgment where judgment is required.
4. Planning internal audit steps to insure compliance.

The third and fourth steps, which are too often overlooked or slighted, are of particular importance, because no procedures, however carefully devised, will function automatically under practical operating conditions.

Maximum and minimum limits

In setting maximum and minimum stock limits and standard order quantities on any item of material or semifinished or finished product, the following factors must be taken into consideration:

1. The rate of consumption or shipment, determined from past experience or from current sales forecasts. (This means not only the average rate, but also the peak rate, which, in the case of semifinished and finished products, must be considered in relation to maximum machine capacity.)
2. The time required to purchase or manufacture the item, including a carefully considered "safety factor" for unavoidable delays.
3. Economical purchase quantities or manufacturing lot sizes.
4. Maintenance of full employment for at least a basic personnel organization. (This may require the building-up of stocks during seasonal slack periods.)
5. Storage capacity.

This method of control is most effective where the purchase or production time is short and where the products manufactured are well established and the rate of sale is steady, without large sporadic or seasonal fluctuations. Where these favorable conditions exist, it is often possible to schedule purchasing or manufacturing of the more important materials and products for a week or even a month in advance, with only secondary reference to the maximum and minimum limits. Where conditions deviate still more from the simple ideal, it may be necessary to set up formal accounting for materials reserved for production orders scheduled (or in sight) and for materials on order. Such a system shows currently not only the actual balance on hand for every item but also the "balance available," which is the total of the quantity on hand plus the quantity on order minus the quantity reserved. This type of system is rather cumbersome when attempted manually but is quite feasible to implement on a computer.

If the same semifinished parts or materials are used in a number of finished products, the processing time for such products can be reduced by carrying inventories in the semifinished state. This facilitates the use of maximum and minimum limits, but, if extended to other than the really active items, it may tend to increase, rather than reduce, total inventories.

Sales estimates

In developing a manufacturing and inventory program from sales estimates, consideration must be given to substantially the same factors as those that enter into the determination of maximum and minimum limits, and, even though no definite limits are fixed on individual inventory items, some overall "normal" or objective inventory must be established, in order to plan operations intelligently. As to the preparation and use of the sales estimates, the following basic questions have to be answered:

1. Who shall prepare them? This is usually, though not always, a responsibility of the sales department.

2. How often shall they be revised? The only answer to this question that fits all situations is "No oftener than is required to plan manufacturing intelligently." In rare cases regular weekly revisions may be necessary; usually once a month is sufficient, and in some businesses quarterly or even semiannual revisions may be adequate if provision is made for special revisions under unusual conditions.

3. In what form shall the sales estimates be prepared, and how shall they be converted to production and purchase requirements? Although this is a question of detail in procedure, it is fundamental in any control program.

4. What procedure shall be set up for top-management review of the estimates and their periodic revision? Top-management review of financial budgets and budget revisions is usually provided for by established budgeting procedure, but in many cases the actual planning of operations is based on interim sales estimates not tied in with the financial budget.

Economic order quantity

The classical inventory control model is a very simple equation, in which the total incremental cost of the inventory is computed from three components. Many of the more recently derived models now in use in businesses for the calculation of an economic order quantity are variations, refinements, and extensions of the basic idea. The classical model does not take account of stockout costs, which is rather a severe limitation; we shall return to this point in discussing simulation.

The model was developed by observing that the total inventory cost could be broken down into holding costs, ordering costs, and purchasing or manufacturing. If the consumption could be assumed even throughout the year, there would, on the average, be half of the quantity ordered on hand. The storage and interest costs would, therefore, be

$$C_1 = HQ/2$$

where H represents the cost of storing one unit for one year, and Q is the quantity ordered (the figure we want to know). The costs of placing an order (O) would be incurred every time such an order was placed. If we expect to consume U units per year, we will be placing U/Q orders, and the total ordering cost will be

$$C_2 = OU/Q$$

Obviously, the total cost of purchasing the inventory will be UP, where P is the unit price. The total cost of the inventory then, would be

$$C = HQ/2 + OU/Q + PU$$

By differential calculus, we can find the value of Q which causes this equation to attain its minimum value, and this is

$$Q = \sqrt{2OU/H}$$

In theory, therefore, the lowest overall cost of inventory would be attained by buying the amount Q every time. Unfortunately, the formula does not take account of a number of factors, such as the cost of stockouts, and the possibility of fluctuation in demand.

It is normal to combine the order quantity computation with a calculation designed to estimate the best order point. This is the cue which gives rise to the placing of an order; it will usually be indicated by the decline of the number on hand to a predetermined level, though, occasionally, the simple passage of time may be the basis. Obviously, when the reorder point is established in terms of physical quantities on hand, the smaller the level the lower will be the average investment inventory. This gain is offset by the higher probability of running out of the product which a small reorder level entails. It is a question of fact which can be stated mathematically what the level should be to minimize the total cost of investment plus stockouts. Unfortunately, some of the numbers needed in the equations are not as precise as one would wish.

Various attempts have been and are being made to adapt the classical inventory model to deal with the less precisely known factors. While many such mathematical models have been devised, the literature is not unanimous about the best approach to take and a generally applicable mathematical model for inventory control does not appear to be available as yet.

The simulation approach

The conceptual and mathematical difficulties that have caused the problems in the development of an algebraic solution have also led many business managers and their staff assistants to seek other approaches to the development of inventory models. The most promising technique is simulation. This technique is more fully discussed in Chapter 25 in general terms; its applicability to the inventory control problem deserves some consideration here.

The simulation technique is particularly well suited to the study of flows; whether the flows be of goods, money, people, or something else. In fact, the costs associated with inventory are very closely associated with the physical flows of the goods into, within, and out of the business.

If the flows can be studied in physical terms, therefore, it is a fairly straightforward step to obtain the cost figures.

There are six factors which enter into the calculations in a simulation model of inventory.

1. The rate of consumption of the item. This may be a fixed quantity in units per day, or may be described by a complex probability distribution as discussed in Chapter 25.
2. The cost of storing the item, per unit, per day.
3. The cost of placing an order for the item, or of setting up the production process for it.
4. The value of the item.
5. The delivery delay, or the time it will take to manufacture the item. This may also be fixed in days, or subject to a distribution.
6. The opportunity cost which will be incurred if the company runs out of the item. This may, of course, be a very large number indeed, if the absence of the item would hold up other work.

The management of the business has control over two further elements in the inventory process, the reorder quantity and the reorder point. The reorder quantity is the number of units which will be ordered at one time, (the quantity Q in our earlier discussion), while the reorder point is the level to which the present inventory must fall before an order will be placed.

The simulation model must be designed to test out a variety of possible repairs (reorder point and reorder quantity). The model must calculate the quantities which will be on hand and available over a lengthy period of simulated time under each assumed pair, and compute the cost total which would be incurred given this physical flow. The need to perform the calculation over a longish period, to permit the "law of averages" to operate, implies that this type of computation can only be done on a computer. Evidently, the result of this investigation will be the identification of a given reorder point and a given reorder quantity as being the least costly, given the input information.

Definition of responsibilities

Before a clean-cut working plan can be developed for the application of the techniques described above, it is necessary to determine who is to be responsible for the execution and coordination of the various steps in the required procedures and to specify, as far as possible, the policy limits within which each responsible executive must work. This is a fundamental organization question which must be settled by a clear and definite statement by top management if confusion and "buck-passing" are to be avoided.

In most manufacturing business where production is for stock rather than on customers' orders, it is obvious that the preplanning phase of inventory control is an integral part of the planning of day-to-day manufacturing operations. Under these conditions, the final responsibility for determining the time and size of purchase and production orders customarily rests with the factory management, subject, of course, to the general policies laid down by the top management. In a stable and well-established business, the factory management can lean heavily on past experience in working out the purchasing and production schedules, but this must be supplemented by a knowledge of current sales prospects, which can be provided only by the sales department. It is at this point of contact between the sales department and the factory that weaknesses in inventory control are most likely to develop, and it is here that the closest attention by some coordinating authority is essential to work out answers to the questions of procedure previously discussed and to keep the procedures functioning properly once they are established.

An effective method of accomplishing this coordination is to assign the responsibility to a committee which includes representatives of all the departments concerned. This may be the general management committee or executive committee or the committee charged with budgetary control functions, if one of these exists, or it may be a special committee set up for this particular purpose. The controller, because of his responsibilities in budgeting and financial planning, should be an active member of this committee, and, as such, he may be given specific authority to assist in making the policy decisions required in the day-to-day operation of the controls. If a new control procedure is to be developed or the existing one reviewed for weaknesses, he is quite likely to be delegated by the top management to supervise the job; in such cases he will, of necessity, work closely with the sales and factory managements, coordinating and sifting out their ideas, and, as far as practicable, tying in the mechanisms established with the financial budgeting procedure and the accounting controls. When satisfactory procedures are once established, the controller will have the responsibility for issuing the reports used in the operation of the controls or for postchecking purposes. He should not, however, attempt to assume responsibility for the actual operation of the detailed forecasting and planning routines; if he does so, he is clearly stepping out of his proper field to take on functions which, under a sound organization setup, would be assigned to other executives.

The usual practice of placing on the factory management the primary responsibility for the decisions required in inventory planning is not necessarily the best in all cases. The following are two types of situations in which exceptions to this practice are justified.

1. If the purchasing department is not under the supervision of the factory management, the final responsibility for the timing and size of purchase orders may be placed on the purchasing agent. This arrange-

ment is particularly suitable when market and supply factors are likely to be of more importance than production requirements in determining purchasing policy, as, for example, in the purchasing of cotton or cloth in a cotton-textile business. Purchasing will be a major function, often under the direct supervision of one of the principal officers of the company, and the responsibility of the factory management is limited to furnishing schedules of estimated production requirements at the proper intervals and cooperating with the purchasing agent in planning for material handling and storage.

2. In the comparatively rare cases where the business, or some department of it, is organized so that one executive assumes responsibility for sales, processing schedules, and raw-material purchases, the responsibility for inventory control clearly rests with that executive, except with respect to the maintenance and supply items merely incidental to the manufacturing processes.

Control by dollar or turnover limits

In situations where the control of inventories is a major problem, the search for ways and means to improve its effectiveness sometimes leads to the suggestion that definite limits be placed on the funds available for investment in inventories, either in terms of fixed dollar amounts or in terms of turnover rates, and that the responsible executives be required to keep the actual investment within these limits.

A plan of this kind can be made to function under the type of management organization described in the last paragraph of the preceding section, under which responsibility for all decisions affecting inventory quantities is centered in one individual, provided that the markets for raw materials and finished products are such that a quick turnover is possible at all times. Department stores sometimes operate on this basis, the buyer of each department being held rigidly to the limits set for his department, even to the point of being required to move excess stocks by mark-downs, if necessary. Certain departments of at least one large textile company are set up on a somewhat similar basis; here, the raw material is cloth, for which there is almost always a ready market, and the various department managers are authorized to dispose of surplus inventories by sales to other departments or to outside parties. Under this method of operation, the department manager is, of course, judged by his overall profit result and must take the penalty of any losses incurred if it is necessary to dispose of inventories at less than cost.

Even where conditions are favorable for rigid controls of this type, it is unwise to rely entirely on their automatic operation. Sound management procedure calls for a precheck by competent authority of the sales estimates on which the department manager proposes to base his purchase commitments and for a review by such authority of any proposed sales of excess stocks, at least where losses of more than a stated maximum are involved. If this review leads to the frequent deferment of sales of excess stocks, in order to avoid the losses resulting from hasty liquidation, then the element of judgment enters, the controls are no longer "automatic," and the "inventory limits" become merely "inventory objectives." This is a much more satisfactory method of operation in the great majority of cases, since no automatic controls can take the place of market judgment in handling inventory problems.

Under the usual type of management organization, where the responsibilities of the sales executives with respect to inventory control are limited to the furnishing of sales estimates and the planning of production is a function of the factory management, the control of inventories by rigidly enforced dollar or turnover limits is even less practical. The establishment of normal, or "objective," inventories is an essential step in the intelligent planning of operations, but the correction of deviations from these normals is a problem which cannot be satisfactorily solved by arbitrarily forced liquidation of excess stocks.

Postchecking the problem of surplus stocks

Generally and understandably the routines of stock control are aimed primarily at avoiding the dangers of shortage. Preplanning and postchecking, if intelligently conceived and executed, can do this successfully. Typical procedures are not, however, designed to handle the complementary problem of surplus stocks in the same automatic manner. The ever-present pressure for conservatism in purchasing and the obsolescence of specific items of raw materials as newer materials become available inevitably create surpluses of materials in any active business. The cost of the space tied up and the actual investment in such surplus materials become a serious problem unless specific steps are taken.

Close, critical scrutiny of periodic stock reports by management personnel who are really familiar with operating requirements is the fundamental means of identifying such surpluses. The problem of actual physical disposition is similar to that which confronts the housewife who tries to keep the attic in order; a constant series of decisions must be made as to what to throw away or sell to the junkman and what to keep, on the chance that it may have some future use. And it is so much easier to keep an item than to make the hard decision to dispose of it! The big difference is that the cluttered attic is merely a nuisance and a fire hazard, while the cluttered inventory costs real money.

In addition to the detailed item-by-item review by the responsible operating executive, it is customary for top management to require reports at least once a month showing the dollar amounts of the inventories, broken down by major classifications which correspond to the control accounts in the general ledger or cost ledger. These overall reports are most helpful if set up in the form of a comparative running tabulation, a column being added for each month's figures as they become available. The interpretation of the reports is greatly facilitated if the inventories are carried and reported at the standard cost of both material and manufacturing, with variances between standard and actual material cost shown in one overall total or by a few broad classifications; this permits the separation of fluctuations in quantity from fluctuations due to price changes.

The decisions to discard can be made intelligently only by those who are in close touch with actual operations; frequently, the responsibility is delegated to an "obsolescence committee," consisting of representatives of the factory, sales, and controller's departments, with the recommendations of this committee being reviewed by the chief operating executive before being made effective. The policy statement by the top management should be limited to defining the functions and authority of this committee and its method of operation and should not attempt to prescribe rules to govern its decisions.

As to the accounting treatment of surplus stocks, there are very tangible advantages in laying down definite rules for the writing-off of obsolete and slow-moving stocks, irrespective of whether or not a decision has been made as to their final disposition. Such a policy calls attention promptly to errors in sales estimating, manufacturing planning, or purchasing judgment and thus acts as a constant reminder to the operating executives of the importance of tempering optimism in planning with proper consideration of inventory risks. The statement of these losses in dollars before they have become ancient history also acts as a spur to prompt action in disposal and to the exertion of every effort to retrieve or reduce the losses where possible. And, finally, the policy prevents the building up in the balance sheet of what might become a significant overstatement of inventory values; whatever understatement results is relatively minor, since any recoveries on obsolete items will usually be made within a relatively short time, except under unusual circumstances, will be small in proportion to the amounts written off. A specimen statement of policy embodying these principles will be found in the Appendix at the end of this chapter.

APPENDIX

THE XYZ COMPANY
Inventory Obsolescence Policy and Procedure

I. General policy

It is the policy of the company to charge currently against earnings any losses due to obsolescence of raw materials, packages, supplies, finished products, or other inventories of any kind. Obsolescence is normally determined in one of two ways: (1) inactivity of stock movement or (2) elimination of a product from the line or changes in formula, style, or packaging.

II. Responsibility for execution of policy

The execution of this policy shall be the responsibility of the Obsolescence Committee, which shall consist of representatives of the Sales Management, the Works Management, and the Controller's Office. Decision of this committee involving the disposition or write-off of any item of more than $1,000 in value shall be subject to the approval of the General Manager.

III. Procedure

In order to insure the proper application of this policy, the Obsolescence Committee shall operate under a program which will provide for continually, through the year, writing off inventory items that for any reason have become obsolete. This program shall include the following provisions:

1. At least once every three months, or oftener in the discretion of the Committee, all stores balance cards and finished stock records shall be reviewed, and any item on which there has been no activity during the preceding twelve months shall be declared obsolete and charged off by requisition to the appropriate profit and loss account. The Committee will decide whether such obsolete items shall be disposed of or retained in stock for possible future use.

2. At least twice each year, all stores balance cards and finished stock records shall be reviewed and a list prepared of all items on which the stock on hand is equal to more than one year's supply. The Committee shall take such action as it may see fit with regard to disposition of the excess stock, and may at its option direct a part of the stock to be charged off.

3. Whenever a product is eliminated from the line, or changes are made in the formula, style, or packaging, any raw materials, packages, or supplies, the use of which is discontinued, and any finished stores which become obsolete as the result of such change shall be immediately written off by requisition charging the appropriate profit and loss account. Lists of all items charged off shall be prepared for the use of the Committee in directing disposition of the items, but the write-off shall be made irrespective of the possibility of use of the items.

4. If items of substantial value which have been charged off are retained in stock and are later reinstated or used in significant quantities, the value shall also be reinstated; where only a few units of small value are involved, they may be used without charge and without reinstating the value.

5. Every effort shall be made to allocate to a definite department the responsibility for every write-off of obsolete items, and in such cases the charge shall be made to the responsible department. Where responsibility cannot be so allocated, the charge shall be made to the account inventory Adjustment—Obsolescence, which will be considered the responsibility of the General Manager.

6. Provision shall be made for maintaining a record of all inactive and obsolete items until actually destroyed, used, or reinstated in active stock, and for requiring the authorization of a responsible executive for the actual destruction of any item and its elimination from this record.

Part IV

Long-range planning

19 CORPORATE STRATEGY

Evolution of long-range planning

The concept of formalized long-range planning in business is relatively new, and the recognition of the need for a definition of corporate strategy as the basis for long-range planning is an even more recent development. The earliest long-range planning efforts consisted principally of forecasting trends in sales, profits, and perhaps in capital requirements, in the existing operations of the business, using substantially the same procedures and techniques as in the preparation of the annual operating budget. If these long-range forecasts were carefully put together and well-documented, and if top management considered them credible, they sometimes provided the basis for a simple definition of sales and profit objectives, or for checking the reasonableness of objectives which management might already have defined, formally or informally.

In these earlier stages of the evolution of long-range planning, operating executives were often inclined to regard any planning beyond two years, at most, as a theoretical paper-work exercise, carried out to satisfy the whims of the president, or the controller, or the director of long-range planning if such a person existed in the organization. It is difficult to say with certainty what brought about a change in this attitude, but there were two developments during the 1960's, after the long post-war boom had spent itself, which undoubtedly influenced management's ideas about the usefulness of long-range planning and the way the planning job should be approached. One of these developments was the rapid acceleration of technological change, to the point where no business, however long-established and apparently secure, could afford to be complacent about the future of its products and markets. The other development was the increasing pressure on management from stockholders—and from the entire financial community—for "performance"—meaning, very simply, rapid growth in earnings per share, to stimulate appreciation in the market value of the company's stock. Under the influence of these twin pressures, an alert management could hardly fail to recognize the need for a dynamic concept of long-range planning, guided by a clear-cut but flexible overall corporate strategy.

What is "strategy?"

If we go to the dictionary, we find that "strategy" is primarily a military term, which has been borrowed and adapted for use in other connotations. A typical dictionary definition reads: "the science or art of military command as applied to the overall planning and conduct of large-scale military operations." In the same dictionary[1] the word "tactics" is defined as "the technique or science of securing the objectives designated by strategy." Without becoming involved in semantic hair-splitting, we can say that business strategy is the sum of management's basic decisions as to its long-term objectives and the directions it will follow in utilizing the resources of the business to attain those objectives.

This concept of directing the utilization of a company's resources to the attainment of clearly defined long-term objectives is implicit in the following definition of long-range planning, taken from an article by John T. Hickey, Vice President–Planning of Motorola, Inc.[2]

"Long-range business planning is an orderly process by which management rationally decides both the amount of profit growth it intends the business to achieve and the product and market directions in which it intends to achieve this growth. It is based on realistic appraisal of the prospects for the outside environment and a sound evaluation of the company's present strengths and weaknesses. It also includes specific plans for pursuing the intended growth in the intended directions."

The major difference between long-range planning as envisioned in this definition and as practiced in the earlier stages of its development lies in the concept of a purposeful strategy to utilize fully the company's resources. The first two sentences of the definition are concerned entirely with strategy; while the last sentence involves tactics—that is, detailed plans and their implementation.

Corporate objectives

The obvious first step in the development of a corporate strategy is a tentative definition of corporate objectives. In today's performance-oriented business environment the primary objective of a firm is often stated in terms of growth in earnings per share, or, perhaps more perceptively, growth in the market value of the stockholders' equity. But

---

[1] *American Heritage Dictionary.* (Boston: Houghton Mifflin), pp. 1273 and 1309.

[2] "Guidelines to Successful Future Planning," in *Financial Executive,* November 1966, p. 33.

neither of these criteria is sufficient in itself to provide a guide for strategy formulation. Other factors, such as financial structure, dividend policy, return on capital employed, and degree of diversification (to minimize risks due to cyclical characteristics and product or market obsolescence), also deserve to be thought of as "basic" objectives. Furthermore, other subobjectives are needed to define constraints on the pursuit of the basic objectives and to point up the steps to be taken to achieve them. Examples of such subobjectives are: share-of-market criteria; geographical limitations on markets; quality image; rate of new product development; inventory and receivables turnover; personnel policy, etc. And it is becoming increasingly important that business objectives give full weight to the social responsibilities of the firm—i.e., its responsibilities to its employees, its customers and the general public.[3]

The "planning gap"

With a tentative set of objectives established, the next step in the development of a strategy is to determine whether it can reasonably be expected that the existing business, operating according to the criteria laid down in the statement of constraints and subobjectives, will be able to attain the firm's primary objectives. This is essentially the process of elementary long-range planning described in the opening paragraph of this chapter; but the added stimulus of an understanding of top management's basic goals should result in a more aggressive approach to the search for growth opportunities. If this phase of long-range planning indicates that the business as it now exists is not likely to attain management's primary objectives, there is a "planning gap" which must be filled unless management is willing to lower its sights and accept more modest objectives than it originally envisioned. Conversely, if it appears that the existing business can meet the basic objectives, management has the choice of raising its objectives to *create* a planning gap, or resting content with the situation as it is. Decisions made at this point will affect fundamentally the whole future course of the business; and the plans of the operating managers should be carefully scrutinized and, if necessary, reworked several times to provide the greatest possible assurance that they are sufficiently ambitious and at the same time realistic.

The "strategy matrix"

If a "planning gap" exists after these studies and deliberations, the next step in strategy formulation is to determine how it is to be closed—

---

[3] An illuminating discussion of business objectives will be found in Chapters 3 and 4 of H. Igor Ansoff's *Corporate Strategy* (New York: McGraw-Hill, 1965), pp. 29–74.

that is, to decide on the "product and market directions" which the firm will follow in pursuit of a more rapid rate of growth. The "strategy matrix" shown in Figure 19–1 is a useful tool in visualizing the alternatives open to a business in determining its product-market strategy.[4]

Figure 19–1

	Existing Products	New Products
Existing Markets	Operations Improvement	Product Development
	*	Acquisitions
New Markets	Market Development	Internal Development
	Acquisitions	Acquisitions

The subdivision of each of the four boxes in this matrix may be taken as a rough guide to the relative attractiveness of the two alternatives—internal development or acquisition—in each area in an average situation. The asterisk* in the upper left-hand box indicates that the possibility of securing growth of existing products in existing markets by the route of acquisitions is severely limited, for many companies, by federal antitrust laws and Federal Trade Commission policies. In the lower right-hand box the larger area assigned to "acquisitions" reflects (a) the greater freedom from government restraints when complete diversification is the objective, and (b) the advantage of the shorter time required to achieve growth by acquisition rather than by internal development in an entirely new field. The allocation of space in the other two boxes gives weight to both of these factors—the probability of government restraints and the relative time required to achieve growth by each of the two alternative strategies.[5]

Choice of strategy

In approaching the problem of choice of strategy, management has to evaluate both its own resources and the risks of alternative courses

---

[4] This diagram is an adaptation of one included in J. T. Hickey's article, previously quoted. A somewhat similar diagram appears in Ansoff's *Corporate Strategy*, p. 128.

[5] This breakdown is intended only as a general guide. Special circumstances in an industry or in a particular company and varying estimates of the risks involved in each course of action may change the relative attractiveness of the two strategies.

of action. The evaluation of strengths and weaknesses, referred to in the definition previously quoted, should cover not only financial resources, but, just as importantly:

Knowledge of product design and manufacture
Manufacturing and distribution facilities
Marketing know-how
Skills of the work force
Administrative management talent

Management's rating of these resources will be a major factor in its decision as to what risks it can afford to take, particularly in its approach to an acquisition strategy. On this point, John Hickey, in the article previously referred to,[6] has these relevant comments:

One of the fallacies of many staff-oriented approaches to business planning is that premature emphasis is given to the sale of new products into new markets . . . [by] acquisitions, mergers, or other means of entering completely new businesses . . . [This possibility] involves the greatest risk of failure because it includes areas with which the firm has no experience. . . . Sale of existing products into new markets, "market development" on the chart, or sale of new products into existing markets, "product development," requires use of at least some skills, experience, reputation or franchise which the firm already has, and should, therefore, involve relatively less risk. . . . I don't believe that the managements of many companies are operating their existing business—the sale of *existing products into existing markets*—as well as they really know how. Certainly, attention to "operations improvement" . . . should involve less risk of failure than the other courses described above.

Strategy should be flexible

Lest the above discussion give the impression that the development of a strategy is pretty much a mechanical process, it should be stated that one element of any sound strategy is flexibility. Many of the judgements involved in determining whether a "planning gap" exists, and, if so, to what extent, are necessarily subjective, particularly in a multidivisional business, where evaluation of a wide range of product and market activities is involved. Furthermore, an aggressive strategy, to be successful, must have the enthusiastic support of the key members of the management group. Somewhere between the extremes of complacency with things as they are and a heedless refusal to recognize limitations on the firm's resources, the chief executive—who, in the last analysis, determines strategy—must set his course. In most situations he will instinctively keep his options open—that is, he will not shut out completely any of the avenues of growth illustrated in the strategy

[6] "Guidelines," p. 40.

matrix; and he may, from time to time, vary the emphasis on each of them as conditions change or new opportunities arise.

Organization for long-range planning

There is one point on which managements which have had experience in long-range planning are almost unanimous: that is, that the primary responsibility for planning should rest with the line organization. This does not mean, necessarily, the same line management which is responsible for existing operations—in some companies the planning and the early stages of the development and operation of new ventures are assigned to individuals who are wholly detached from day-to-day involvement in the problems of the established business. Furthermore, it is generally recognized that a staff function is necessary to achieve the best results from planning; but the majority belief is that "the proper staff role is to encourage, facilitate, support and coordinate adequate planning by line management."[7] This is quite similar to the basic philosophy of business budgeting, emphasized at several points in the discussions in Chapter 13, and similar to the delicate relationship of the controllership function to the line operating functions, as argued in the introductory chapters.

In the early stages of the development of business long-range planning, the responsibility for the staff phases of the function was often—perhaps in most cases—assigned to the controller. This is understandable, since, as previously noted, long-range plans were, at this point, conceived to be essentially an extension of the annual budgets. If the controller had established himself as a forward-looking member of the management team, and if he had demonstrated his ability to work harmoniously and effectively with the line management as budget director, it was only natural for him to assume this added responsibility. And when long-range planning came to be considered sufficiently important to be established as a separate staff function, a former controller, or a member of the controller's staff, was often chosen as the first director of the function.

As long as the operating managers simply tolerated long-range planning as a theoretical exercise, and top management had not reached the point of developing a strategic approach to planning, the job of the planning director often settled down into a largely technical and rather routine assignment. But as the concept of long-range planning developed, along the lines discussed earlier in this chapter, the job of the director became more exacting and much broader in scope. In most cases it became necessary for him to act for the chief executive in indoctrinating the operating managers in the evolving philosophy of planning, designing the procedures to implement the philosophy, and defining

---

[7] Hickey, "Guidelines," p. 36.

the duties of the line and staff personnel in the planning process. And when the line managers realized that the formulation and implementation of a corporate strategy involved decisions that would vitally affect the future direction of the business and the measurement of their own performance, the planning director became a focus of the conflicting ideas, interests, and pressures that exist in any organization. One author who made an extensive survey of long-range planning practices in a number of large companies came to the conclusion that "the ideal choice for such a post should be a man who is both philosopher and realist, theoretician and practical politician, soothsayer and salesman and, as one planner points out, he probably should be able to walk on water."[8]

It is small wonder that many planning officers with a controllership background had difficulty in meeting these specifications and that the reaction to this result was a conclusion, by some observers, that "the individual who at least historically was most successful as a controller achieved his success because he possessed talents and attitudes which are almost antithetical to those required in a director of long-range planning."[9] But one may wonder whether the great majority of specialists in marketing, engineering, or any other business function would, as a group, have been any more successful as planning officers than controllers if they had happened to be assigned to the function in its early stages of development. The really successful controller today must combine technical competence in his own field with a broad management viewpoint, an attitude of both objectivity and involvement, and the ability to establish cooperative working relationships with the line organization. If he has these capacities, and if he recognizes his limitations in technical fields other than his own, his experience as the information collector, organizer, analyst, and interpreter for the entire business should make him well qualified for the planning job.

Whatever the background of the planning officer, he will need the assistance of all of the staff specialists in the organization to help him in his efforts to "encourage, facilitate, support, and coordinate adequate long-range planning by line management." In the Appendix following this chapter there is a statement of a form of organization defining the line-staff relationships in the planning process in one multidivisional company where long-range planning is an accepted way of life. This statement reflects the general philosophy of the organization of planning responsibilities as developed in the preceding paragraphs. It presupposes that all line and staff executives have participated in the development of corporate objectives and strategy and understand the necessity for genuine long-range planning to implement the strategy and attain the objectives.

---

[8] E. Kirby Warren, *Long-Range Planning: The Executive Viewpoint* (Englewood Cliffs, N.J.: Prentice-Hall, 1966), p. 43.

[9] Ibid., p. 44.

An examination of this statement will disclose the usual areas of potential friction in line-staff relationships which cannot be resolved by a mere definition of responsibilities. For example, according to paragraph C-(3)-(e) the corporate staff department heads are responsible, in their respective functional areas, for "periodic formal or informal contacts with divisions to determine progress in the implementation of major phases of plans; and reporting of their observations to the group vice presidents and the director of corporate planning." Obviously, staff department heads must use judgement and tact in fulfilling this responsibility; and they should observe one of the fundamental rules of line-staff relationships—i.e., they should not report any observations about a line manager's performance without first discussing the observations with the manager himself, and, if possible, persuading the manager to make his own report on the problem area to his superior. As for the planning director, this definition of responsibilities makes it clear that Mr. Kirby's description of the ideal choice for the part, quoted above, is neither fanciful nor exaggerated.

Long-range financial planning

In one sense all long-range plans, like annual operating budgets, are financial plans, in that, to be meaningful, they must be summarized in financial terms, analyzed, evaluated, and if necessary reworked to meet management's established financial objectives. The responsibility for this summarization and analysis, and for coordinating the evaluations of the line and staff executives may rest with the director of long-range planning, but the controller or other financial officer will play a major role in the process. An intelligent evaluation of long-range plans requires information on the prospective business and economic environment and on the performance of other firms in the same industry; and again, the financial officer may be charged with all or part of this information-collecting function. But "financial planning," as the term is used in this discussion, goes beyond these limits—it comprises participation in the establishment of rational financial objectives and the determination of the steps to be taken to obtain the funds required to finance the planned growth called for by the objectives.

Variables determining earnings—growth rate

As noted earlier in this chapter, if a firm is guided by the concept of fully utilizing its resources to obtain optimum growth, its prime basic objective will usually be stated in terms of growth in earnings per share or in the market value of its stockholders' equity. It can be shown mathematically that the rate of earnings growth that can be attained with a given amount of equity as a base depends on four variables: (i) The rate of return on total capital employed, (ii) the percentage of earnings retained in the business (i.e., not paid out in dividends), (iii) the ratio of total debt to total equity, and (iv) the interest rate on debt. The simple formula for calculating the earnings-growth rate for any combination of these four variables is:

$G = RP + D/E(R - I)P$, where

G = annual growth rate

R = rate of return (after tax) on total capital employed

P = percentage of earnings retained in the business

D/E—debt equity ratio

I = interest rate on debt (net of tax).

The calculation in Table A in Figure 19–2 shows that for a company earning a 10 percent return on total capital, retaining 60 percent of

Figure 19–2
GROWTH-RATE COMPUTATION
(Table A)

$G = RP + D/E(R - I)P$

$G = 10(.6) + 1/3(10 - 3) \cdot 6 = 6 + 1.4 = 7.4\%$

	Total capital	Debt	Equity	Percent of Total capital	Equity
r 1					
lance beginning of year	100,000	25,000	75,000		
rnings before interest			10,000	10.0	
terest on debt (after taxes)—3%.			(750)		
t earnings			9,250		12.3
vidends—40% of earnings			3,700		
rease in equity	5,550		5,550		
crease in debt (1/3 of increase in equity)	1,850	1,850			
· 2					
lance beginning of year	107,400	26,850	80,550		
rnings before interest			10,740	10.0	
terest on debt (after taxes)—3%.			(805)		
t earnings			9,935		12.3
vidends—40% of net earnings			(3,974)		
crease in equity	5.961		5,961		
crease in debt (1/3 of increase in equity)	1,987	1,987			
· 3					
lance beginning of year	115,348	28,837	86,511		
Net earnings Year 1 as above			9,250		
Year 2			9,935		
Increase			685		
Percent increase			7.4		

its earnings, and maintaining a debt/equity ratio of 1/3, with an after-tax interest rate on debt of 3 percent, the annual rate of earnings growth will be 7.4 percent and the return on stockholders' equity will be 12.3 percent. Table B (Figure 19–3) shows that if the rate of return can

Figure 19–3
GROWTH-RATE COMPUTATION
(Table B)

$$G = RP + D/E(R - I)P$$

$$G = 12(.75) + 1/2(12 - 3) \cdot 75 = 9.00 + 3.4 = 12.4\%$$

	Total capital	Debt	Equity	Percent of Total capital	Equi
Year 1					
Balance beginning of year	100,000	33,333	66,667		
Earnings before interest			12,000	12.0	
Interest on debt (after taxes)—3%.			(1,000)		
Net earnings			11,000		16.
Dividends—25% of earnings			(2,750)		
Increase in equity.	8.250		8,250		
Increase in debt (1/2 of increase in equity)	4.125	4,125			
Year 2					
Balance beginning of year	112,375	37,458	74,917		
Earnings before interest			13,485	12.0	
Interests on debt (after taxes)—3%			(1,124)		
Net earnings.			12,361		16.
Dividends—25% of net earnings			(3,090)		
Increase in equity.	9,271		9,271		
Increase in debt (1/2 of increase in equity)	4,636	4,636			
Year 3					
Balance beginning of year	126,282	42,094	84,188		
Net earnings Year 1 as above			11,000		
Year 2			12,361		
Increase.			1,361		
Percent Increase			12.4		

be increased to 12 percent, and if the dividend payment is reduced to 25 percent and the debt/equity ratio set at 1/2 instead of 1/3, with the same interest rate, the earnings-growth rate can be raised to 12.4 percent and the return on equity to 16.5 percent. It should be noted that the achievement of these growth rates will depend on *all* of the capital available being used so as to produce an average return of 10 percent in the first case or 12 percent in the second case.

Of the four factors which determine the earnings-growth rate for any business, only one—the rate of return on capital employed—is directly affected by the firm's operating efficiency. The percentage of earnings retained in the business and the debt/equity ratio are matters of financial policy, subject to the constraints of stockholders' dividend expectations and the company's credit standing, respectively. The range of possible interest rates on debt (which, of the four variables, has the least effect of earnings growth) is determined largely by conditions in the money markets, but the rate actually paid by a firm is also affected by its credit standing and the timing of its long-term borrowings. And, to complete the interlocking circle of cause and effect, the firm's credit standing is affected by the financial community's evaluation of its operating efficiency (as evidenced by its return on total capital), the risk inherent in its debt/equity ratio, and its rate of earnings growth. The job of financial planning involves determining what balance of these interlocking factors is appropriate for the particular business, giving weight to the environment in which the business operates, the preference of its stockholders for dividend income or earnings growth, the firm's strengths and weaknesses in all areas of its operations, and the attitude of the key members of management toward the risk-taking usually necessary to achieve a rapid rate of growth.

Effect of leverage

The term "leverage," as used in financial planning, refers to the effect of the debt/equity ratio on a company's earnings and earnings growth. Obviously, if money can be borrowed at 3 to 4 percent (after tax) and put to work earning 10 percent, net earnings will be increased by 6 to 7 percent of the amount borrowed, with a resulting increase in the rate of return on equity and in the potential earnings-growth rate. During the 1960's, many companies which had historically operated almost entirely without borrowed capital were able to show substantial earnings growth simply by the utilization of leverage, without any improvement in operating efficiency. Eventually, of course, when the debt/equity ratio reached the point beyond which management, for whatever reason, was unwilling to go, any further effect of leverage was limited to the borrowing potential created by an increase in equity, either from retained earnings (as in Figures 19–2 and 19–3) or as the result of new equity financing.

The risk of a high debt/equity ratio lies in the obvious fact that leverage works both ways—that is, the more leverage, the more rapidly net earnings decline as earnings on total capital shrink, due to the fixed charges on debt, just as net earnings increase more rapidly as operating earnings increase. In the past there have been various rules-of-thumb as to a suitable debt/equity ratio, and some of these are still in vogue. But the most logical approach in any particular company is to forecast the effect on operating earnings and capital requirements of a possible decline in sales, or narrowing of margins, or both, down to a recession level, and decide what amount of fixed charges on debt (interest and principal payments) could be sustained without creating serious financial problems.[10] This decision, like all elements of financial planning, will be greatly affected by the nature of the growth objectives which management sets for itself and the degree of risk which it is willing to assume.

The P/E ratio

Although many companies have stated their primary financial objectives in terms of growth in earnings per share, it would appear more logical and more realistic to speak in terms of growth in the per-share market value of the company's common equity. It might appear that over a reasonable period of time the two rates of growth should tend to correspond; but there is no doubt that factors other than historical earnings and earnings growth enter into the determination of the price which the investing public is willing to pay for a company's shares. The evaluation of these other factors is reflected in the relationship between the company's P/E ratio—(that is, the ratio of the market price of its shares to its per-share earnings) and the average P/E ratio for a cross-section of companies with similar earnings-growth records.

The question of what determines this P/E relationship is a complex one, and there are no definitive answers. Probably, the major factor is the investor's estimate of *future* growth, tempered by his evaluation of the degree of risk in the particular industry and the particular company. The market price of a companys' stock may be affected, for a limited period of time, by overoptimism due to fads in types of industries, overselling of the corporate image, etc., or, conversely, by overpessimism when the tides of change appear, for a time, to be running against an industry or a company. Also, the supply-and-demand factor, due to the activities of funds, buying for takeover bids, etc., may result in temporary, or even prolonged price aberrations. Nevertheless, the foundation for maintaining a favorable P/E ratio lies in demonstrated consistent earnings growth, with a financial structure appropriate to the type of business, plus the development of sound and viable plans for future growth, and, very importantly, the communication of these plans to the investment community through a rational and temperate financial public-relations program.

At the conclusion of the discussion in the earlier section of this chapter "Variables determining earnings-growth rate," it was stated that "The job of financial planning involves determining what balance of these interlocking factors is appropriate for the particular business, giving weight to the environment in which the business operates, the preference of its stockholders for dividend income or earnings growth, the firm's strengths

---

[10] See *Corporate Debt Capacity* by Gordon Donaldson (Boston, Division of Research, Harvard Business School, 1961) for a comprehensive discussion of this problem.

and weaknesses in all areas of its operations, and the attitude of the key members of management toward the risk-taking usually necessary to achieve a rapid rate of growth." To these interlocking variables we should add the P/E ratio, not as an element in the mathematical formula, but as a factor which is difficult to predict, but which must, nevertheless, be considered in any determination of the "optimum" earnings-growth rate.[11]

Investment policy

From a practical management point of view, one of the chief benefits of an understanding of the earnings-growth formula discussed above is that it emphasizes rather dramatically the importance of operating efficiency—that is, the maintenance of a high rate of *operating* profit to *total capital* employed—as a basis for earnings growth. No one will argue with the theoretical proposition that firm's investments—whether in plant and equipment or in product or market development—must earn an average rate of return at least equal to its cost of capital if a gradual dilution in earnings per share is to be avoided. But, however obvious, this is a statement of a theory; and, furthermore, arguments about how the cost of capital should be computed tend to dull the impact of the principle in its theoretical form.

In most situations, it is much more effective to present several computations of possible earnings growth based on different combinations of the variables in the growth formula, using values for the variables that are within the range of near-term possibilities in the business as it is currently operating and currently financed. For example, if the aftertax return on total capital is currently 9 percent, the debt/equity ratio is 3/10, and one third of earnings are paid out in dividends, the possible earning growth with that structure might be compared with the growth possible with operating returns of 10 to 12 percent, debt/equity ratios of 4/10 to 6/10, and various percentages of dividend payout. The values assigned to the several variables should, of course, be realistic in the light of the firm's current position, with emphasis on the effect of possible improvement in operating efficiency, as evidenced by the overall rate of return.

A presentation of this kind can be used to convince even an unsophisticated management of the importance of fixing an average target rate of return to be achieved on its operating investments and then con-

---

[11] The recent literature of financial management is replete with theories and arguments about the evaluation of the various factors that enter into—or should enter into—financial planning and financial policy formulation. For a practical and nontechnical introduction to this controversial subject the reader is referred to two articles by Charles D. Ellis in the April 1969 and September 1969 issues of the magazine *Financial Executive*.

trolling its capital and development expenditures with the objective of achieving that rate of return. It should be understood that such a target rate of return is *not,* necessarily, a "cut-off point" in the selection of investments, as the nature of the industry or the particular business may require that some activities be carried on at a lower rate of return. If this is the case, it can be pointed out that other activities must earn a higher return to maintain the overall target rate. This is particularly pertinent when new ventures, outside the firm's area of demonstrated competence, are under consideration.

Computerized financial planning

The computer can be a useful tool in projecting the overall parameters of long-range operating plans, the capital required to finance such plans, and the results of various methods of obtaining the required capital. Many large banks in the major financial centers of the country now offer a service of this kind, using either their own computers or a time-sharing service. The usual procedure is to obtain, through the computer, an analysis of the historical results of the business over at least a five-year period, including the sales and earnings growth rates, the major operating and financial ratios, and, if possible, the trends in the total market and in the firm's share of each of the major markets which it serves. Projections are then made on the computer of the operating and financial results of various rates of growth, assuming either a continuation of the historical trends in growth and in the relationships of costs, expenses, and investment to sales, or one or more alternative relationships based on management's judgment as to how past trends might be modified. The results of these projections are summarized in a series of profit-and-loss statements and balance sheets, the latter showing the capital requirements for each projection; and by including in the input data the anticipated percentage of dividend payout and the limit on debt/equity ratio, it can be determined at what point in each growth projection there will be a need for new equity capital. The computer makes it possible to obtain very quickly the projected results of many different combinations of growth rates, operating ratios and financial policies, and thus provides management with information which can be helpful in establishing the overall financial objectives of the firm.

The practical usefulness of the projections obtained from this type of computerized planning depends, of course, on the validity of the projected trends in sales and in the operating and financial ratios. If these are projected on a linear basis, using historical relationships, the results are merely an extrapolation of past history, and will be of dubious value. The best results are probably obtained by having those most familiar with the business assign a value to each major variable relationship in each year covered by the projections. A much more sophisticated approach, which has been developed by a few large companies, is to construct a corporate financial model by the use of the simulation technique, described in Chapter 25, and use the model to make profit-and-loss and balance-sheet projections.[12] But computer projections, however developed, are not a substitute for detailed operational planning by the responsible line executives who must define the specific steps to be taken to achieve the projected results in each particular situation and then follow through to see that the plans are implemented.

APPENDIX

Organization for long-range planning

Note: The form of long-range planning organization outlined in this appendix is for a business with more than twenty divisions and subsidiaries, operating as separate ventures or profit centers, and a corporate staff spanning the full range of functional responsibilities. Obviously, the organization in any particular company must be adapted to the size, complexity, and management policies of the firm. The discussion in the section "Planning effort more important than 'the plan,'" in Chapter 20, is relevant to this point.

A. *Line and Staff Responsibilities*

Planning is a responsibility of line management, with staff advice and assistance in coordination, scheduling, evaluation, and monitoring.

B. *Divisional Organization*

1. Division general managers have the primary responsibility for the long-range plans of their respective divisions.
2. Divisional long-range planning procedures should provide for the active participation of all divisional executives in the planing of activities in their respective areas of responsibility.
3. Division controllers should be responsible for the summari-

---

[12] The most successful applications (reported in the literature) of computer methods to long-range planning seem to have been in utility companies, where market and share-of-market projections are less of a problem than in the average manufacturing business and operating and financial ratios are relatively stable and predictable. The Detroit Edison Company, for instance, makes regular use of a simulation model which projects the financial condition of the concern as far into the future as the manager may wish. This model was specially designed to fit the company, and the complex systems of equations in the model took several man-years to develop. The resulting model has proved sufficiently accurate that it can be used to test the probable effect of important decisions, such as the size and type of proposed new generating plants.

zation of departmental plans into the overall divisional financial plans and for evaluation of the reasonableness of the financial projections.

C. *Corporate Organization*

1. The ultimate responsibility for defining objectives and policies and approving plans rests with the president.
2. The group vice presidents are responsible for:
   a) Seeing that effective long-range planning procedures are maintained in the divisions reporting to them.
   b) Reviewing and approving the plans prepared by their divisions.
   c) Following-up on the implementation of their divisions' plans.
3. The several corporate staff department heads (i.e., the directors of marketing, market research, research and product engineering, manufacturing services, and organization development, and also the corporate controller) will be responsible, in their respective functional areas, for:
   a) Continuing review and analysis of changes in the economic environment, developments in technology, and competitive sales and profit trends; and communication of significant information to corporate and divisional managements.
   b) Advice and assistance to the divisions in the preparation of their plans and to corporate management in the development of plans for activities outside the scope of divisional responsibilities.
   c) Review and evaluation of divisional plans for realism, soundness, and consistency with corporate and divisional objectives.
   d) Review and evaluation of annual divisional budgets, with particular reference to their consistency with long-range plans.
   e) Periodic formal or informal contacts with divisions to determine progress in the implementation of major phases of plans; and reporting of their observations to the group vice presidents and the director of corporate planning.
   f) Preparation of long-range plans for the corporate activities for which they are responsible, based on the requirements for such activities as disclosed in the divisional plans and as necessary to adequately service corporate management.
   g) Recommendations to corporate management on company objectives, strategy, policies and plans.
4. The director of corporate planning will be responsible for:
   a) Coordinating the activities of the corporate staff depart-

ment heads related to long-range planning, as described in paragraph (3) above.

b) Developing and recommending corporate objectives and supporting policies.

c) Participation in the development of divisional objectives for sales, profits, inventory turnover, and other operating criteria.

d) Reporting to corporate management on his evaluation of divisional and corporate staff departments' long-range plans and annual budgets, and on progress in the implementation of plans, based on the evaluations of the corporate staff department heads and his own contacts with the divisions and the group vice presidents.

e) Consolidating financial summaries of divisional plans, projecting total capital requirements, and comparing consolidated totals to overall corporate objectives.

f) Participation in the development of plans and programs designed to:

(1) Modify or supplement divisional plans as necessary to attain corporate objectives.

(2) Utilize fully all available capital resources.

g) Developing and recommending methodology and format for planning.

h) Participation in acquisition and merger studies (identification, evaluation, and negotiations), as directed by corporate management.

20 LONG-RANGE PLANNING FOR EXISTING VENTURES

The anatomy of long-range planning

The first step in coming to grips with the actualities of long-range planning is to break down corporate objectives by the several ventures within the business. Such a breakdown is relatively easy in a multidivisional business if the divisions, as is usually the case, represent separate (though possibly related) ventures, manufacturing basically different product lines or serving different markets, or both. Where this type of divisional organization exists, the accounting plan normally follows divisional lines; and any company which is seriously considering long-range planning will probably be accustomed to using budgetary controls on a divisional basis. In a business which is not divisionalized, and in some divisions of multidivision companies, there may be a breakdown of product development and/or marketing responsibilities by product lines, or by the various types of markets served, while the entire manufacturing function may be under the jurisdiction of a single responsible executive. Even in such cases, however, there should be some form of venture analysis in existence which will provide a basis for long-range venture planning.[1] If the accounting plan and the operating control system do not provide for such analysis, the accounting and reporting procedures must be restructured if long-range planning is to be really effective.

If the overall corporate financial objectives have been worked out by the process outlined in the previous chapter, the divisional or venture objectives will have been developed, reviewed and approved, at least within reasonable limits, before the corporate objectives are finalized. This is preferable to an arbitrary breakdown of overall objectives by top management fiat, but it does require that top line management,

---

[1] See the section on "Program Budgeting and Control" in Chapter 13.

452

utilizing whatever staff assistance is available, do a thorough and pains-taking job of analyzing and evaluating divisional or venture plans, par-ticularly as to their balance between short-term and long-term results. Such analysis and evaluation is, in any event, one of top management's major responsibilities, and making it a part of the process of formulating overall objectives offers the opportunity to make the divisional and ven-ture managers participants in the development of corporate strategy.

The long-range planning period

In most companies which have formalized long-range planning proce-dures, the period covered by the plans is five years. Whatever the origin of the five-year period, the rationale for it is that the time span is long enough to permit planning for expected growth and for basic changes in strategy or tactics, and at the same time not too long for reasonably detailed plans to be meaningful. The general practice is to review long-range plans annually, and at least update them by a supplemental docu-ment, incorporating modifications for the last four years and adding projections for another year. By the time two years have passed, it is usually found desirable to prepare a complete new plan, though much of the basic data can be carried forward from one plan to the next.

In industries which are dependent on scarce natural resources—such as the petroleum industry—or where continuing heavy capital expendi-tures are required, as in the case of electric power companies, some elements of long-range planning may be extended to ten or twenty years, or even for a longer period.

Responsibility for the venture long-range plan

The assignment of responsibilities for the divisional or venture long-range plans in a multidivision business usually follows the pattern outlined in the statement on "Organization for Long-Range Planning" in the Appendix to Chapter 19. Basic assumptions as to general eco-nomic and technological trends over the planning period may be established by the central corporate management, and corporate staff assistance may be provided on any phase of the plans at the request of the venture managements, but the plan as finally produced is the venture manager's statement of what he expects the venture to accom-plish and how his projected results are to be achieved. Each venture plan is, of course, subject to review by the corporate staff and final approval by top corporate management.

Elements and structure of the venture long-range plan

Much of the detailed structure of the venture long-range plan follows the pattern of the venture operating budget, but there are important elements in the long-range plan that do not enter into the short-term budget. The basic approach to effective long-range venture planning is illustrated in the following outline of a comprehensive format in which the various elements of a long-range venture plan are coordinated and organized for logical development and presentation. The several sections of this detailed format can be condensed and adapted in accordance with the size of the venture, the degree of sophistication in management control, and the amount of management time that can be made available for the long-range planning activity.

1. Business charter
2. Evaluation of strengths and weaknesses
3. Summary of objectives
   a) Profits
   b) Financial resources
   c) Marketing and selling
   d) Products
   e) Manufacturing
   f) Organization and personnel
4. Basic assumptions
5. Plans (same breakdown as item 3 above)
6. Projected profit and loss statements

Each of these elements is discussed in the paragraphs which follow.

The business charter

This is, very simply, a brief definition of the business or businesses in which the venture is engaged or plans to be engaged. It should spell out, first, the broad area of the venture's operations and, second, the types of products to be sold and the markets to be served within that area. The charter should be reviewed annually and updated in the light of technological and market developments.

Evaluation of strengths and weaknesses

An objective evaluation of the strengths and weaknesses of an existing venture is an essential element in any long-range plan. It is essential, first, to the establishment of realistic objectives and, second, to pinpointing actions that must be taken if the objectives are to be achieved.

The first step in a comprehensive evaluation of this kind is the accumulation of statistical data about the industry and markets in which the business operates and about the past performance of the business itself in comparison with the performance of competitors and potential competitors. Such statistical data would include: industry sales over a period of five to ten years, broken down by market area if feasible;

demographic and economic trends affecting the industry; and internal and competitive trends in sales, earnings and key operating ratios (return on sales and on investment and turnover of receivables, inventories, plant assets and net worth). Less tangible, but equally important, are the facts as to industry and competitive channels of distribution and marketing policies and other management practices.

The second and most difficult step in this process of self-evaluation is the scrutiny and sifting out of the available data and the honest determination of the strengths that can be capitalized on, the weaknesses that impose limitations on the scope of the long-range plan, and the specific steps to be taken to remedy the weaknesses.[2]

Summary of objectives

This section of the plan format is a summary, partly statistical and partly narrative, of the objectives set forth in more detail in the functional plans in section 5. The first two pages in the section are summaries of sales, profits, and net worth for several past years, the latest budget or forecast for the current year, and the projections for the five years covered by the long-range plan (see Figures 20–1 and 20–2). A third summary (Figure 20–3) gives a comparison of the profit and return-on-investment objectives with the last previous long-range plan, and the format calls for a brief explanation of major changes in objectives and growth rate between the two plans.

The remaining subsections of this section are intended to be narrative in form, with a few statistical tabulations where appropriate, and with cross-references to the detailed plans in section 5. Some of the topics that might be covered under the various headings are as follows:

Financial Resources
a)   Turnover of receivables—credit terms and collection policies
b)   Turnover of inventories—improved inventory control
Marketing and Selling
a)   Definition of served markets
b)   Share of markets by broad product groups
c)   Channels of distribution
d)   Export markets
e)   New markets to be developed
Products
a)   New and improved products
    1)   Policy—innovation or imitation?

---

[2] For two excellent check lists of data useful in the self-evaluation process and key questions in such evaluation, refer to *How to Make a Profit Plan,* by Patrick H. Irwin (1964. The Society of Industrial and Cost Accountants of Canada), pp. 26–28 and 30–32.

2) Major improvements in existing lines
3) New lines
b) Unprofitable products or product lines
c) Engineering capability
Manufacturing
a) Maintenance policies and procedures
b) Plant utilization (shifts and percentage of capacity)
c) Disposition of excess capacity
d) Plant replacements and additions
e) Cost reduction programs (see Figure 20–5)

Figure 20–1

DIVISION LONG-RANGE PLAN 1971-75
SUMMARY OF FINANCIAL OBJECTIVES
PROFITS AND RETURN ON INVESTMENT (NET WORTH)
(000 DOLLARS)

| | Gross Sales | Net Sales | Divisional Pretax Profit | | | Net Worth | |
			Amount	% of Sales	% of Opening N. Worth	Beginning of Year	Increase (Decrease) for Year
Actual							
1964							
1965							
1966							
1967							
1968							
1969							
Forecast							
1970							
LRP							
1971							
1972							
1973							
1974							
1975							
1976							
Increase							
1969 vs. 1964							X
1970 vs. 1969							X
1972 vs. 1970							X
1975 vs. 1970							X

Figure 20-2

DIVISION LONG-RANGE PLAN 1971-75
SUMMARY OF FINANCIAL OBJECTIVES –
INVESTMENT (NET WORTH) AND TURNOVER RATIOS

NOTE – Turnover is computed on average balance at beginning and end of year. Assets, liabilities and net worth are at beginning of year.
(000 DOLLARS)

| | Quick Assets | | | Current Liabil-ities | Net Quick Assets | Inventory at Current Cost | Plant & Equipt. Net | Goodwill, etc. | Other Assets | Total Net Worth | Turnover into Sales | | | |
	Cash	Receiv-ables	Other								Total Net Worth	Receiv-ables	Inven-tories	Net Plant & Equipt.
Actual														
1964														
1965														
1966														
1967														
1968														
1969														
Forecast 1970														
LRP														
1971														
1972														
1973														
1974														
1975														
1976														
Increase														
1969 vs. 1964											X	X	X	X
1972 vs. 1970											X	X	X	X
1975 vs. 1972											X	X	X	X
1975 vs. 1970											X	X	X	X

Figure 20–3

DIVISION LONG-RANGE PLAN 1971-75
COMPARISON OF PROFIT AND RETURN-ON-INVESTMENT
OBJECTIVES WITH LAST PREVIOUS LONG-RANGE PLAN
(000 DOLLARS)

	Gross Sales	Net Sales	Divisional Pretax Profit			Net Worth	
			Amount	% of Sales	% of Opening N. Worth	Beginning of Year	Increase (Decrease) for Year
1969							
Actual							
LRP 1970-1974							
1970							
Forecast							
LRP 1970-1974							
1972							
This LRP							
LRP 1970-1974							
1974							
This LRP							
LRP 1970-1974							
Increase (Decrease) vs. LRP 1970-1974:							
Year 1970							X
Year 1972							X
Year 1974							X

Organization and personnel
a) Management organization and development
b) Organizational climate
c) Worker performance and training

Basic Assumptions

For a long-range plan to be meaningful and intelligible, it is necessary to make definite assumptions as to:

1. The economic growth factor in the industry, and, where relevant, in each product line.
2. Selling price levels.
3. Costs of raw materials, supplies, and services.
4. Wage and salary rates.

The last three of these basic assumptions are particularly important in the current inflationary environment. With the inflationary element in GNP running as high as 6 percent in recent years, and forecast by most authorities to continue at a rate of not less than 4 percent in the foreseeable future, any plan which does not recognize and provide for this factor is simply unrealistic. If feasible, the financial projections in the plan should be made in both current dollars and plan-year dollars, so that it will be clear how much of the planned sales and earnings growth is real and how much is simply the result of inflation. This segregation of the inflationary element is provided for in the sales and

Figure 20-4

DIVISION LONG-RANGE PLAN 1971-75

GROSS SALES PROJECTIONS
(000 DOLLARS)

	1970	LONG-RANGE PLAN				
	Forecast	1971	1972	1973	1974	1975
Total Gross Sales Orders of Preceding Year						
Economic Factor						
Sales Effort: National Accounts						
Field Sales Force						
Advertising						
Promotions: (Preceding Year Effect)						
Projected Year Effect						
Product Addition: Replacement						
Addition to Line						
Product Deletion						
Decreased Product Growth Rate						
Competition						
TOTAL GROSS SALES ORDERS						
(Increase) or Decrease in Backlog						
TOTAL GROSS SALES (SHIPMENTS)						
AT 1970 AVERAGE PRICES						
Price Increases over 1970 Level						
%						
Amount						
AT PLAN-YEAR PRICES						

profit and loss projections illustrated in Figure 20–4 and 20–6, and in several of the other supporting exhibits listed in Figure 20–7.[3]

Plans

This section of the plan format includes (a) a statement of the steps to be taken to effect the improved utilization of financial resources (as

Figure 20–5

Division Long-Range Plan 1971-75
Cost Reduction Program 1966-75

Annualized Savings on Cost Reduction Projects Shown by Year in Which Completed

(Thousands of Dollars)

	Actual				Forecast		Long-Range Plan			
	1966	1967	1968	1969	1970	1971	1972	1973	1974	1975
Identified										
Material										
Labor										
Overhead										
Shipping & Freight										
Subtotal										
Unidentified										
Total										

This statement shows annualized savings of cost reduction projects completed during the years 1966 through 1969 and estimates for 1970 through 1975.

It should be borne in mind that some projected savings will not be fully cumulative through the five-year period. As products on which savings have been made are modified or eliminated, or processes are changed, the savings may no longer apply. Therefore, in projecting the cumulative effect of these savings on profits over the five-year period, a slippage factor has been applied. Because of the slippage factor and because completion of projects is usually spread over a period of some months, the total savings as above tabulated do not agree with the figure for "Effect of Manufacturing Cost Reduction Projects" in the profit and loss statement and its supporting exhibits.

indicated by the net worth projections illustrated in Figure 20–2), and (b) the outlines of the plans and programs of each major function of the business to effect the accomplishment of the overall venture or divisional objectives. It is intended that plans and programs for at least the first two years of the five-year period should be specific and reasonably detailed, including timetables and assignments of responsibilities,

---

[3] The segregation of the effect of inflation on actual operating results would require that price indexes be maintained for selling prices and the major elements of cost. The salesprice index is particularly important to an understanding of sales trends and the relationship between actual and planned results. But even where such indexes are not maintained, the estimated effect of inflation can be identified in the long-range plan projections.

Figure 20–6

DIVISION LONG-RANGE PLAN 1971-75

PROFIT AND LOSS STATEMENT

Thousands of Dollars										% To Net Sales				
		Long-Range Plan										Long-Range Plan		
Actual	Fcst	In 1970 Dollars			In Plan-Year Dollars					Actual	Fcst	In Plan-Year Dollars		
1969	1970	1971	1972	1975	1971	1972	1975			1969	1970	1971	1972	1975
									Gross Sales					
									Net Sales					
									Gross Profit before Product Engineering Expense					
									Product Engineering Expense					
									Selling, Admin., & General Expenses					
									Advertising & Sales Promotion					
									Marketing					
									Selling					
									Field Engineering					
									Warehousing					
									Administrative					
									Divisional					
									Corporate Service Depts.					
									Corporate Staff Depts.					
									Total					
									Other Income & (Expense) - Net					
									Divisional Pretax Profit					
									Operating Net Worth					
									% Pretax Profit					
									To Net Sales					
									To Operating Net Worth					
									Profit Effect of Inflationary Factors:					
									Selling Prices	X	X	X	X	X
									(Material Prices)	X	X	X	X	X
									(Freight & Transp. Rates)	X	X	X	X	X
									(Wage & Salary Rates)	X	X	X	X	X
									(Other)	X	X	X	X	X
									Net Increase or (Decrease) in Profit	X	X	X	X	X
									Profit Effect of Cost Reduction Programs					
									Identified	X	X	X	X	X
									Unidentified	X	X	X	X	X
									Total					

with plans for the remaining three years stated in terms of major projects only, with tentative time schedules.

The amount of detail to be included in these outlines of the functional plans is a matter of judgment. Generally, the outlines should be in narrative form, with supporting exhibits where appropriate. A comprehensive list of suggested exhibits is shown in Figure 20–7, but a great deal of flexibility must be allowed the venture managers in determining which of these exhibits is useful and meaningful (and practical to prepare) in each particular situation. The narrative comments should make clear the steps to be taken to achieve the projections shown in the exhibits—for example, the sales projections in Figure 20–4 should be supported by a brief description of (a) any planned changes in distribution policies or channels, and (b) the advertising and promotional programs, field sales force expansion, and other actions which are expected to produce the planned increases in sales.

Figure 20–7

SUGGESTED EXHIBITS FOR LONG-RANGE PLAN FORMAT

Summary of Financial Objectives – Profits and
Return on Investment (Net Worth) (Figure 20–1)

Summary of Financial Objectives – Investment (Net Worth)
and Turnover Ratios (Figure 20–2)

Comparison of Profit and Return-on-Investment Objectives with
Last Previous Long-Range Plan (Figure 20–3)

Gross Sales Projections (Figure 20–4)

Gross Sales and Share of Market by Product Line

Gross Sales by Class of Customer

Gross Sales by Region by Product Line

Product-line Profit and Loss Statements

Plant and Equipment Accounts and Reserves for Depreciation

Summary of Capital Expenditures

Details of Major Identified Capital Expenditures

Summary of Cost Reduction Programs (Figure 20–5)

Summary of Manpower Projections

Projection of Exempt (Management) Manpower Needs

Profit and Loss Statement (Figure 20–6)

Sales and Manufacturing Costs

Manufacturing Overhead Summary

Profit and loss statement

The profit and loss statement illustrated in Figure 20–6 represents
the financial summarization of all of the functional plans of the venture.
The procedures followed in preparing this statement will be much the
same as in the preparation of an annual operating budget, except that
the long-range plan statement is shown both in current-year dollars and
in plan-year dollars. As indicated in the list of exhibits in Figure 20–7,
it is intended that this profit and loss statement be supported by somewhat more detailed statements of the elements of cost of sales and
manufacturing overhead.

Highlight summary and major check points

As an aid to top management and its staff in evaluating a detailed long-range plan of the kind contemplated in the format described above, and in following up on the implementation of such a plan, it will be found useful to prepare a "Highlight Summary" of the type illustrated in Figure 20–8, and also a list of "Major Check Points," setting forth the major action programs essential to the accomplishment of the plan and the check dates for completion or progress reporting on each step. Both of these exhibits should be keyed to the contents of the long-range plan by page references, as shown in Figure 20–8, so that supporting details can be quickly located when a follow-up is required.

The long-range plan and the annual budget

As stated at the beginning of this chapter, any company which undertakes formal long-range planning will usually be accustomed to the use of budgetary controls in the management of its current operations. In some companies which have progressed from budgetary control to long-range planning, the annual operating budget is made a part of the long-range plan—that is, the first year of the plan is the annual budget. Under this procedure there is automatically a tie-in of the budget with the long-range plan, with a follow-up each year on changes from the previous plan. Other companies have found that this consolidation of long-range planning and budgeting imposes too much of a burden on the line personnel, and have separated the two types of planning to spread the effort involved more evenly over the year. In such cases the review of the annual budget provides an opportunity for a check on progress in relation to the first year of the long-range plan, without waiting for a new plan. The list of major check points referred to in the preceding section will serve a useful purpose in this connection.

Planning effort more important than "the plan"

The foregoing discussion, perhaps inevitably, seems to place a great deal of emphasis on format, with the possible implication that the preparation of a long-range plan document is the ultimate goal of long-range planning. It should be understood that the format is simply a guide to the organization of the planning effort and to the presentation of the results of that effort in some kind of orderly sequence, and that a detailed plan, conforming in every way to a standard format, is of value only if it reflects careful and thoughtful step-by-step planning by the responsible operating executives. The job of the long-range planning officer, as it relates to these venture plans, is not to enforce adherence to a specified format, but to get a feeling for the amount of genuine

Figure 20–8

DIVISION LONG-RANGE PLAN 1971-75

HIGHLIGHT SUMMARY

(000 DOLLARS)

Pages		Actual 1969	Forecast 1970	Long-Range Plan		
				1971	1972	1975
	GROSS SALES AT 1970 PRICES					
	Products Existing in 1970					
	New Products					
	Total					
	Index (1970=100.0)					
	GROSS SALES AT CURRENT PRICES					
	Outside					
	Intercompany & Interdivisional					
	Total					
	NET SALES AT CURRENT PRICES					
	DIVISIONAL PRETAX PROFIT					
	% Net Sales					
	% Operating Net Worth					
	Incr./ (Decr.) Due to Inflation					
	Cost Reduction Programs:					
	Annualized Savings on Projects					
	Completed during Year					
	Cumulative P & L Effect					
	OPERATING NET WORTH (Beg. of Year)					
	TURNOVER INTO SALES					
	Total Operating Net Worth					
	Receivables					
	Inventories					
	% TO NET SALES					
	Product Engineering					
	Marketing					
	Advertising & Sales Promotion					
	TOTAL MANPOWER (END OF YEAR)					
	Direct					
	Indirect - Hourly					
	Salary Mfg.					
	Salary Other					
	Total					
		Actual 1969	Forecast 1970	Long-Range Plan		
				1971	1972	1973-75
	CAPITAL EXPENDITURES					
	Buildings					
	Machinery, Equipment, Tooling					
	Other					
	Total					
	DEPRECIATION PROVISION					

planning underlying the formal presentation, and to develop a judgment as to whether the plans as presented are realistic and attainable. As stated in Chapter 19, the planning officer in a large multidivisional company will need the assistance of all of the staff specialists in the organization to assist him in this phase of his responsibilities. In a smaller organization, or in a large organization where only limited staff assistance is available, the planner will have to spread his time more thinly, perhaps scheduling attention to the various ventures or functions on a rotating basis and establishing priorities in accordance with his best judgment.

Practicalities of the five-year plan

The development of long-range planning of the scope contemplated in the format described in this chapter is in itself a long-range project, requiring a firm commitment on the part of top management and the gradual education of the line operating executives to a realization of the value and importance of the planning effort. There will inevitably be a great difference between line managers in their degree of acceptance of long-range planning, the amount of time and effort they are willing to devote to it, and the thoroughness and realism of the plans which they produce.

The reservations of those managers who are slow to accept the philosophy of long-range planning are rooted in the very natural question as to whether there is any value in attempting to plan in detail for more than a year or two ahead, when experience has shown that the most careful forecasts and projections for longer periods are subject to a wide range of error. The answer to this question is simply that long-range venture planning requires the managers to think about their objectives for the future and to develop definite, if tentative, plans for the actions that must be taken to meet those objectives. For example, referring to Figure 20–4, no one would seriously contend that a sales manager can predict accurately for five years ahead the factors that will enable him to attain the sales growth that he has set as his objective. But the very act of attaching some numbers to the various factors that can produce the growth compels the manager to give some thought to the practical steps that must be taken to build for the future if he is to attain his objective. He may well change his thinking, from time to time, as to the relative weight to be given, for example, to advertising and field sales effort, or as to the effect of competitive actions on growth possibilities; but a buildup of this kind, if properly used, can be a valuable working tool in developing a flexible long-term sales and marketing strategy.

The financial summarizations of the long-range plan, as expressed in the projected profit and loss statement (Figure 20–6), operating capital requirements (Figure 20–2), and return on net worth (Figure 20–1), are developed, in this format, from detailed projections prepared by the functional departments. It sometimes happens that these financial projections, incorporating all of the departmental plans for product development, marketing and sales effort, manufacturing cost reductions, improved inventory control, etc., will indicate a growth in earnings and return on investment, particularly in the later years, that appears unrealistic in the light of industry and competitive conditions. When this occurs, good judgment dictates that all elements of the plan, particularly the projected gross profit margins and advertising and selling costs, be reviewed and adjusted to recognize that competitive pressures will, in all probability, limit to some degree the return that can be earned on capital employed. If divisional venture management does not agree that the plan is unrealistic, the best course for top management is to let the plan stand, in the belief that experience will result in more realism in future plans, and to provide for a contingency factor when the plans of the several ventures are consolidated, as described in the next section.

The large element of judgment that enters into the financial projections for the later years of any five-year plan is sometimes cited as another reason for questioning whether any benefit is derived from the work involved in building up the projections for those years from the details of the functional plans. Alternatives sometimes suggested are to state the projections for the last two or three years of the plan as broad targets or objectives or to construct them by applying historical or specially developed operating and financial ratios to the sales dollar projections, in somewhat the same manner as described in the discussion of "Computerized Financial Planning" in Chapter 19. Either of these procedures obviously divorces the financial projections from any direct connection with the functional plans, and may well lead to a de-emphasis of functional planning and a consequent dilution of the benefits of the whole long-range planning effort.

All this discussion of the practical considerations involved in developing a five-year business plan serves to reemphasize the point brought out earlier in this chapter, that the planning effort is more important than the document called "the plan." The benefits of long-range planning for existing ventures will be realized only if the line managers doing the planning are convinced that it will help them to do a better job of operating their ventures over the long term. The format and procedures outlined in this chapter are not ends in themselves—they are tools, developed from experience, which must be used by the line organization if they are to be of any practical value.

Summarization of venture plans

The final step in long-range planning for the existing operations of a business is to consolidate and summarize the financial projections of the several venture plans to obtain the overall projections for the total business. As a minimum, these summary projections will show, for each year of the planning period, (a) sales, pretax profits, income taxes, and net profits, and (b) a statement of (i) funds generated from earnings and depreciation, (ii) dividends to be paid out, (iii) additional capital requirements, (iv) stockholders' equity, and (v) additional borrowings required or funds available to reduce presently outstanding borrowings. The summaries can, if desired, be expanded to include more detailed profit and loss statements and complete condensed balance sheets; for these more detailed projections, it may be worthwhile to develop a computer program and prepare the necessary input data from the figures in the venture plans.

This process of summarization of the venture plans is one of the steps in the initial development of corporate strategy, as described in the discussion of "The Planning Gap" in Chapter 19, and its repetition every year or two is necessary to determine whether modifications in strategy are required to meet the established corporate objectives. A significant change in the projected results for one or more existing ventures may indicate for the first time the existence (or absence) of a planning gap, and lead to a reassessment of corporate strategy and objectives; and changing estimates of earnings and capital requirements will call for a review of financial plans and policies.

For a consolidated summarization of the projections of the venture plans to be meaningful, it is necessary, as previously pointed out, that the individual venture plans be carefully scrutinized and evaluated "to provide the greatest possible assurance that they are sufficiently ambitious and at the same time realistic." If some of the venture plans appear to be unrealistically optimistic or even if they all appear sound in themselves, it may be desirable to inject into the consolidated summaries a contingency provision, or safety factor, based on top management's best judgment of the risks in the venture plans and the possibility that not all of the ventures will be successful in attaining their objectives. As stated in the section, "Strategy should be flexible," in Chapter 19, "Many of the judgments involved in determining whether a 'planning gap' exists, and, if so, to what extent, are necessarily subjective, particularly in a multidivisional business, where evaluation of a wide range of product and market activities is involved."

Measurement of actual venture performance against long-range plans

The philosophy of venture long-range planning as expressed in this chapter may seem to some readers to be too flexible and permissive, because it allows the venture managers considerable freedom in the way they present their plans and recognizes the necessity of gradually educating the managers in the importance and value of long-range planning as an aid to their own performance and personal progress. But the procedures discussed do provide for continuous follow-up on actual performance compared to plan, and if the planning officer performs his job well and has adequate assistance from other corporate staff specialists as needed, top management will be able to form a judgment as to the degree of real planning and the realism of the action programs behind the formal written presentation.

This philosophy seems to the authors to be more realistic than one which regards the long-range plan as a "contract," or firm commitment, on the part of the venture manager and imposes penalties for failure to accomplish the planned results. During the five-year period covered by most plans, general and industry economic conditions and competitive factors may change drastically and new technological developments may occur, necessitating a more or less radical overhaul of plans and action programs. The success of the venture manager in meeting and overcoming such obstacles to the attainment of his planned financial objectives will certainly be a factor in top management's evaluation of his performance, but any attempt to pin the manager down to specific results for five years ahead is likely to discourage initiative in risk-taking for growth and to lead to unsound actions to improve short-term results at the expense of long-term development. Long-range planning does not and cannot provide definite answers to management problems; rather, it is a process which, if followed cooperatively at all levels of the organization, enables management to guide the future course of the business more intelligently and more effectively.

21 NEW-VENTURE PLANNING

Why new ventures?

Based on the discussion of corporate strategy in Chapter 19, it should be possible, in all logic, to say that new-venture planning is undertaken to close the "planning gap" between long-range corporate earnings-growth objectives and management's evaluation of the earnings-growth possibilities of the existing business. There is certainly nothing wrong with such a statement, but, in any particular situation the tone of new-venture planning and the whole approach to it depend on how ambitious and aggressive management is in setting its long-term objectives. If the objective is simply to maintain or effect a modest improvement in the historical earnings-growth rate of a well-established business, then new venture planning will tend to be defensive and cautious; if, on the other hand, the objective is to make maximum use of the firm's resources to accelerate earnings growth, the approach will be more positive and wide-ranging, and at least a reasonable degree of risk-taking will be encouraged. This is not, of course, a matter of black or white, but of degree; and in any new-venture planning program it is important to be in tune with top management's attitude toward innovation and risk-taking. The planning officer, by exercising good judgement and persuasion, may be able to bend management strategy slightly one way or the other, but he will rarely find it possible to change basic convictions rooted in the temperament and background of the responsible top management executives.

Selection of products and markets

The basic philosophy of any management with respect to new-venture planning will find tangible expression in the criteria it approves for the selection of products and/or markets for new ventures. In an established company with modest earnings-growth objectives, the criteria for new ventures will tend to be restrictive, including only products or markets closely related to the existing business. The emphasis will be on presenting to stockholders and to the investment community a clear picture of the kind of business the company is in, and digressions which might savor even remotely of "conglomeratism" will be discouraged. The difficulty with this approach, of course, is in finding enough new ventures that meet the restrictive criteria to fill any planning gap that may exist.

A step away from this restrictive approach is the so-called "vector" route of expansion—where a company in the abrasives business, for example, will expand into ceramics manufacture because of the related technology and, with that accomplished, find it logical and profitable to purchase or manufacture other unrelated products for sale in the markets in which it sells its ceramics products.

Where there is a large actual or potential planning gap, the search for new product and market directions can be systematically expanded by (a) a combing over of industries, using the SIC classification, to find those which have some link with the present business and appear to have growth possibilities, and (b) a careful analysis of the technology, market structure, and competition in the industries selected as possible avenues for expansion. At the extreme end of the scale is the conglomerate approach, where the product and the market are of little or no importance and the sole basic criterion is profitability or, more properly, investment opportunity.

Internal development or acquisition?

The considerations involved in deciding whether to expand by internal development or by acquisition were discussed briefly in the section on "The Strategy Matrix," in Chapter 19. Here again, a management that is conservatively inclined will often tend to lean toward internal development, simply because it seemingly represents less of a break with its traditional way of doing business. But a major program for the development of new products or new markets requires careful planning and a careful evaluation of the risks involved, either in developing an acceptable product at a competitive cost or in breaking into a market where there is established competition or both.[1] Two other negative aspects of internal development are (1) the necessity for charging development costs against current earnings and (2) the time required to acquire production capabilities and break into new markets. These con-

---

[1] A plan for a major program of this type should include (a) product design and engineering schedules, (b) market analysis and share-of-market projections, (c) forecasts of advertising and promotional expenses, (d) estimates of the costs of alternative production methods and facilities, and (e) return-on-investment projections. For adequate monitoring, a program budget should be established, along the lines discussed in the section on "Program Budgeting and Control," in Chapter 13.

siderations have led many companies, including even some that are conservatively inclined, to choose the route of expansion by acquisition, even when this results in some temporary dilution of earnings.

Criteria for acquisitions

A statement of specifications for acquisition prospects, similar to that illustrated in Figure 21–1, is essential as a starting point in the develop-

Figure 21–1
SPECIFICATIONS FOR ACQUISITION PROSPECTS

A. *Of major importance*
  1. Annual Sales 10 to 40 million dollars.
  2. Potential for:
     a) attainment of 25% pretax return on total investment (purchase price plus assumed debt) within 3 years.
     b) elimination of any dilution in per-share earnings within 3 years.
  3. A significant share of market (at least 10%) in an industry with a projected annual growth rate of not less than 12%.
  4. Customer acceptance based on product design and quality and/or a high standard of customer service.
  5. Low seasonal and cyclical factors.
  6. (Specification as to any limitations on the types of products and/or distribution channels.)
  7. Future capital requirements in keeping with our financial capabilities.
  8. Strong management organization, requiring only normal supervision by our present management.
  9. Compatibility of top management philosophy.
  10. Adaptability to operating as a profit center.
B. *Desirable*
  1. Products that are not subject to a short shelf life or high style factor (less important if the acquisition prospect has strong management experience with these problems).
  2. Opportunity for synergy through consolidation of expenses and/or exchange of know-how in engineering, manufacturing, marketing, or finance.
  3. Existing or potential international manufacture and/or distribution.

ment of an acquisition program. Such a statement fixes the initial parameters within which the planning officer should work; but it should be regarded as a set of guidelines, rather than a rigid directive—first, because it is rarely possible to find an acquisition prospect that meets *all* the criteria satisfactorily; and, second, because the degree to which some of the criteria are met by any particular prospect may be a matter of individual judgement. For example, the statement that future capital requirements should be "in keeping with our financial capabilities" may be subject to a wide degree of variation in interpretation, depending on the attractiveness of the prospect in other respects. Or, a situation may arise where the possibilities of synergy are so evident, or the opportunity to break into a new market is so attractive, that management may be willing to accept deficiencies in meeting some of the other criteria. The planning officer has the difficult job of maintaining an open-minded and imaginative approach in this phase of his work and, at the same time, keeping his proposals within at least the outer range of the limitations imposed by top-management philosophy.

Evaluation of acquisition prospects

The list of specifications for acquisition prospects serves as an outline for an initial qualitative screening process to eliminate companies that are clearly unsuitable in the light of top management's declared strategy and philosophy. Judgements made at this stage as to extent to which any prospect meets the established criteria are, of course, tentative, and may well be revised after later more detailed investigation. Assuming that a prospect appears attractive, the usual next step, even before any overt approach to the prospect's management to determine its availability, is to make a preliminary financial evaluation, based on the data that are available in published reports and financial services.

There is a literally overwhelming mass of literature now available on the financial evaluation of acquisition or merger candidates. But whatever the variations and ramifications in detailed techniques, the calculations of an acceptable purchase price of a possible acquisition are essentially of two types: (a) estimates of the present value of future cash flows, at one or more appropriate discount rates; and (b) projections of the effect of the acquisition on the acquiring company's earnings per share and financial position. Of these two approaches, the latter is the more useful; the present-value calculation can be helpful as supplemental information, but has certain limitations (discussed further below) which make it inadequate as a sole criterion. In the bibliography at the end of this chapter there is a list of articles describing the logic and techniques of these evaluation methods and the problems that arise in their practical application. The two articles by R. W. Ackerman and L. L. Fray and by G. E. MacDougal and F. V. Malek deal with the principles underlying two somewhat different techniques, while the three following articles describe in detail some more sophisticated techniques involving the use of a computer.[2]

The discussion which follows will be limited to a summarization of principles and techniques and some comment on the practicalities of the various methods.

Accounting treatment of acquisitions and mergers

The accounting rules for the treatment of acquisitions and mergers are set forth in detail in Opinions 16 and 17 of the Accounting Principles

---

[2] Since these articles were published, procedures for accounting for acquisitions and mergers have been modified by Accounting Principles Board *Opinions Nos. 16 and 17.* These modifications affect some of the detailed points covered in the articles, but the basic principles and techniques discussed therein remain unchanged.

Board, dealing with "Business Combinations" and "Intangible Assets," respectively. In general, two methods of accounting are recognized—the "purchase method" and the "pooling of interests method." An acquisition for cash or its equivalent is always considered a purchase, but an acquisition using common stock may be either a purchase or a pooling of interests, depending on the facts in each case, with quite different effects on the future reported earnings of the combined companies. While the statutes and accounting rules governing such business combinations are too complicated to be discussed in detail in this book, it is possible to make certain generalizations about both types of transactions and their effect on earnings projections and on the evaluation of proposed acquisitions.

When an acquisition is treated as a purchase the consideration given (cash or its equivalent or, if common stock is used for the acquisition, the fair value—usually market value—of such stock) must be allocated to the assets and liabilities of the acquired company on the basis of their fair value, irrespective of the amounts at which they are carried on the books of the acquired company. If the consideration given exceeds the fair value of the net assets acquired, the amount of the excess must be shown in the balance sheet of the combined companies as "goodwill," which is nondepreciable for income tax purposes but must be amortized in the accounts over a period of not more than forty years.

If an acquisition using common stock can qualify as a "pooling of interests" under the rulings of the Accounting Principles Board, the stock issued by the acquiring company is valued at the book value of the acquired company's stock (or net assets), and the assets and liabilities of the acquired company are carried into the balance sheet of the combined companies at their book value. This treatment eliminates the problem of allocating the purchase cost to the acquired company's assets and liabilities and eliminates any possibility of having to carry "goodwill" in the balance sheet of the combined companies. It simplifies considerably the process of estimating the future earnings of the combined companies as described in the following section on "Projection of Earnings and Capital Requirements."

Projection of earnings and capital requirements

The first step in either the present-value or earnings-per-share calculation is the projection of future earnings and capital requirements for a period of five to ten years ahead. These projections start with an estimate of the rate of sales growth, which is usually based on historical trends in the industry and in the candidate company itself, modified to reflect the acquiring company's plans for the injection of added capital for product and market development or for new plant facilities or both. Projected earnings will, in most cases, be based on ratios of operating costs to projected sales, as such costs would be after reflecting the following adjustments:

1. changes in accounting methods
   a) additional depreciation of assets that will be revalued upward in the event of acquisition
   b) changes in policy with respect to capitalization versus maintenance
   c) changes in method of inventory valuation
   d) amortization of goodwill if required
   e) elimination of nonoperating income and expenses (income from nonoperating investments, interest on debt, extraordinary gains and losses, etc.), net of the income tax effect of such items
2. synergetic effects (net increased income or reduced expenses made possible by the combination of the two companies)
3. reduced income due to possible negative effect of the proposed combination on competition or on present customers
4. reduced income due to additional selling and promotional expenses to attain projected sales volume
5. increased income or reduced expenses resulting from additional capital investments after acquisition.

The projection of the amount and timing of additional capital requirements (i.e., funds required for expenditures not charged against current earnings) should include;

1. Working capital to finance growth and inflation
2. Plant investments for:
   a) increased capacity (existing products or new products)
   b) cost reductions reflected in the earnings projections
   c) replacements and general purposes
3. funds provided by noncash charges to earnings, such as depreciation, amortization of goodwill, and deferred income taxes

It is obvious that the adjustments necessary to reliable projections of the earnings and capital requirements of an acquisition candidate can be made only after a detailed study of the company's records, its operating history, and the potential for operations improvement. In a preliminary financial evaluation for screening purposes it is necessary to make some broad assumptions, based on the best information available. As a first step, sales and earnings may be projected at a constant rate of growth based on the existing facilities and capitalization, and capital requirements may be estimated based on historical industry or company ratios of capital turnover. These projections provide a basis for computing the value of the business as it is currently operating, without the benefits that are expected to result from the combination with the acquiring company. If the candidate company passes the preliminary screening test, the projections can be revised and refined as additional data become available.

Present-value calculations

A simplified illustration of the calculation of the acceptable purchase price of a proposed acquisition, based on the present value of future cash flows, is shown in Figure 21–2. In this illustration it is assumed that sales and operating earnings (after taxes) will increase at the rate of 10 percent annually (compounded) over the next ten years, and that historically the business has turned over its total capital twice a year, indicating that additional capital requirements will be equal to 50 percent of the annual increments in sales.[3] The going-concern value of the business at the end of the ten-year forecast period is assumed to be between 12 and 15 times tenth-year earnings, and calculations are made for both ends of this range. It is further assumed that the acquiring company's target rate of return is 12 percent and that a 15 percent return will be reasonable in view of the risk factor in this particular acquisition situation.

From the mere enumeration of these assumptions and an inspection of the wide variation in the solutions (that is, in the acceptable purchase prices) determined under the various assumptions, it is clear that the results obtained by this method of calculation are anything but definitive. It will be noted particularly that the estimate of the going-concern value of the business at the end of the forecast period makes a significant difference in the acceptable purchase price.[4] Perhaps the principal value of the calculation is that it highlights the problems and risks involved in the projections of earnings and capital requirements and compels management to form a considered judgment as to the longer-term value of the proposed acquisition.

It should be noted that the acceptable purchase prices resulting from this type of computation represent the estimated present value of net *operating* earnings, eliminating all nonoperating income and expense elements, including interest on debt. To determine the acceptable purchase price of the total business as it exists, it is necessary to deduct from the present value of the operating earnings the amount of any existing debt and to add the amount of such items as excess cash, market-

---

[3] "Additional capital requirements," as the term is used in this chapter, includes the required increase in *net* fixed assets—that is, the excess of fixed asset expenditures over depreciation charges.

[4] In the article by Ackerman and Fray included in the references for supplemental reading, the issue of terminal going-concern value is avoided by continuing the projections beyond the tenth year on the assumption of a 4 percent annual growth rate for an additional forty years. This, in effect, pegs the tenth-year going-concern value at a conservative level.

Figure 21-2

CALCULATION OF PURCHASE PRICE OF PROPOSED ACQUISITION
AS PRESENT VALUE OF FUTURE CASH FLOWS
($000)

Assumptions:

Sales and earnings growth rate—10% per year
After-tax operating profit (before nonoperating income & expense and interest on debt, net of income taxes)—7% of sales
Additional capital requirements—50% of annual increase in sales (assuming 2 times capital turnover)
Going-concern value at end of tenth year
  A—12 × tenth year earnings
  B—15 × tenth year earnings

Year	Sales	Operating profit net of tax	Additional capital requirements	Net cash flow	PV Factor 12%	PV Factor 15%	PV Amounts 12%	PV Amounts 15%
0.	10,000	700						
1.	11,000	770	500	270	.893	.870	241	235
2.	12,100	847	550	297	.797	.756	237	225
3.	13,310	932	605	327	.712	.658	233	215
4.	14,640	1,025	665	360	.636	.572	229	206
5.	16,110	1,127	735	392	.567	.497	222	195
6.	17,720	1,240	805	435	.507	.432	221	188
7.	19,490	1,364	885	479	.452	.376	217	180
8.	21,440	1,500	975	525	.404	.327	212	172
9.	23,580	1,650	1,070	580	.361	.284	209	165
10.	25,940	1,816	1,180	636	.322	.247	205	157

Going-concern value, end of tenth year:

				Net cash flow	PV Factor 12%	PV Factor 15%	PV Amounts 12%	PV Amounts 15%
A—12 × tenth year earnings				21,792	.322	.247	7,017	5,383
B—15 × tenth year earnings				27,240	.322	.247	8,771	6,728
Present value—basis A							9,243	7,321
basis B							10,997	8,666

able securities, and the cash value of other assets which are unnecessary to the operation of the business.[5] This discussion so far has been in terms of an acquisition for cash. When an acquisition is made in whole or in part by an exchange of stock, there is the added problem of placing a fair valuation on the acquiring company's stock. Market value is the usual criterion for companies whose stock is actively traded, but this may not be a true measure of the real value of the company's future earning power. For this reason, the present-value calculation is of less importance in an exchange of stock transaction; and more attention will usually be directed at the effect of the proposed acquisition on future earnings per share.

Earnings-per-share projections—Acquisitions for cash

In projecting the effect of an acquisition for cash on future earnings, it is necessary to make assumptions as to (a) the annual earnings-growth rates of the acquiring company and the acquisition candidate, (b) the additional capital requirements of the acquisition candidate over the projection period, (c) the percentage of earnings to be paid out in dividends, and (d) the cost of the money invested in the acquired company. Figure 21–3A shows the calculation of dollar earnings and earnings per share over a ten-year period based on (a) the purchase of the company illustrated in Figure 21–2 for an effective purchase price (i.e., cash paid plus debt assumed,[6] less realizable cash value of non-operating assets) of $8.5 million and (b) assumptions with respect to the two companies as stated in the heading of Figure 21–3A.

The calculations in this figure show that this acquisition will require substantial additional capital after the initial investment, but that it will, nevertheless, have a favorable effect on earnings, which will be $10.37 in the tenth year, representing a 7.6 percent average annual growth rate, compared to the $8.95 per share and 6 percent growth rate projected without the acquisition. But a closer scrutiny shows that most of this improvement in earnings is not due to the faster growth rate of the acquisition candidate, but simply to the leverage factor—that is, to the use of 4 percent borrowed money in an investment yielding 9 percent ($770,000 profit on $8,500,000 investment) in the first year.

---

[5] An alternative procedure is to allow for leverage in the projected earnings on the basis of an acceptable debt/equity ratio (either the acquiring company's target ratio or a ratio considered normal in the industry of the candidate company) and to adjust the purchase price (either upward or downward) by the amount necessary to make the candidate company's balance sheet reflect this ratio. But when this procedure is followed the rate used in discounting future cash flows should be the acquiring company's target rate of return on its equity, rather than the target rate on total capital employed.

[6] It is assumed in this illustration that the acquisition candidate has no debt outstanding.

Figure 21-3A
PROJECTION OF EARNINGS PER SHARE—ACQUISITION FOR CASH
($000)

Assumptions

(1) *Effective purchase price (as defined in text)* – $8,500

(2) *Acquiring Company*

Sales—Year 0	85,000
Net income—Year 0	5,000
Annual sales & earnings growth rate	6%
Dividend payout (% of net income)	25%
After-tax interest rate on debt incurred to finance purchase	4%

(3) *Acquisition Candidate*

Sales—Year 0	10,000
Net income—Year 0	700
Annual sales & earnings growth rate	10%
Additional capital requirements (50% of sales increase)	
No debt outstanding	
Book value of equity (= purchase price)	8,500
Fair value of assets and liabilities same as book value	

Year	0	1	2	3	4	5	6	7	8	9	10
Acquiring company											
Net income	5,000	5,300	5,620	5,950	6,310	6,690	7,090	7,520	7,970	8,450	8,950
Per share (1,000,000 shares)	5.00	5.30	5.62	5.95	6.31	6.69	7.09	7.52	7.97	8.45	8.95
Acquisition candidate											
Investment—beginning of year	700	8,500	8,678	8,853	9,025	9,192	9,358	9,513	9,660	9,799	9,925
Net income before interest on investment		770	847	932	1,025	1,127	1,240	1,364	1,500	1,650	1,816
Less, interest on investment @4%		340	347	354	361	368	374	380	386	392	397
Net income after interest on investment		430	500	578	664	759	866	984	1,114	1,258	1,419
per share (1,000,000 shares)		.43	.50	.58	.66	.76	.87	.98	1.11	1.26	1.42
Dividend 25%		(108)	(125)	(145)	(166)	(190)	(216)	(246)	(278)	(314)	(355)
Additional capital requirements (Figure 21-2)		(500)	(550)	(605)	(665)	(735)	(805)	(885)	(975)	(1,070)	(1,180)
Net cash (deficit)		(178)	(175)	(172)	(167)	(166)	(155)	(147)	(139)	(126)	(116)
Investment end of year		8,678	8,853	9,025	9,192	9,358	9,513	9,660	9,799	9,925	10,041
Combined companies											
Net income		5,730	6,120	6,528	6,974	7,449	7,956	8,504	9,084	9,708	10,369
per share (1,000,000 shares)		5.73	6.12	6.53	6.97	7.45	7.96	8.50	9.08	9.71	10.37

Figure 21–3B

PROJECTION OF EARNINGS PER SHARE—ACQUISITION FOR CASH
($000)

Assumptions

As per Figure 21–3A, except:
(1) Annual sales and earnings growth rate of acquisition candidate 6% instead of 10%
(2) Additional capital requirements of acquisition candidate (50% of sales increments) reduced because of slower sales growth rate.

Year	0	1	2	3	4	5	6	7	8	9	10
Acquiring company											
Net income	5,000	5,300	5,620	5,950	6,310	6,690	7,090	7,520	7,970	8,450	8,950
Per share (1,000,000 shares)	5.00	5.30	5.62	5.95	6.31	6.69	7.09	7.52	7.97	8.45	8.95
Acquisition candidate											
Investment beginning of year	700	8,500	8,498	8,482	8,446	8,396	8,320	8,225	8,112	7,968	7,800
Net income before interest on investment		742	787	834	884	937	993	1,053	1,116	1,183	1,254
less: interest on investment @4%		340	340	339	338	336	333	329	324	319	312
Net income after interest on investment		402	447	495	546	601	660	724	792	864	942
per share		.40	.45	.50	.55	.60	.66	.72	.79	.86	.94
Dividend 25%		(100)	(112)	(124)	(136)	(150)	(165)	(181)	(198)	(216)	(235)
Additional capital requirements		(300)	(320)	(335)	(360)	(375)	(400)	(430)	(450)	(480)	(505)
Net cash surplus/(deficit)		2	15	36	50	76	95	113	144	168	202
Investment/end of year	8,498	8,483	8,446	8,396	8,320	8,225	8,112	7,968	7,800	7,598	
Combined companies											
Net income		5,702	6,067	6,445	6,856	7,291	7,750	8,244	8,762	9,314	9,892
per share (1,000,000 shares)		5.70	6.07	6.45	6.86	7.29	7.75	8.24	8.76	9.31	9.89

This leverage results in an increase in earnings in the first year of 73 cents or 14.6 percent, while the annual increase for the remainder of the ten-year period is only 6.8 percent. And the calculations in Figure 21–3B show that if the sales and earnings growth rate of the acquisition candidate were only 6 percent—equal to that of the acquiring company—earnings per share of the combined companies in the tenth year would be $9.89—in other words, of the $1.42 per share gain in Figure 21–3A, 94 cents is due to leverage and only 48 cents to the faster growth rate of the acquisition candidate. The tenth-year earnings of $9.89 represent an average annual growth rate of 7.1 percent (against 7.6 percent in Figure 21–3A); and this is achieved without having to put in any additional capital after the initial investment—in fact, the net investment is gradually reduced during the ten-year period.

Is this proposed acquisition attractive on the basis of the assumptions and calculations set forth above? The answer depends on the financial position of the acquiring company and the growth objectives established by its management. If the company has a large unused borrowing capacity which management is anxious to put to use at a relatively low risk, and if the indicated growth rate of 7.1 to 7.6 percent for the combined companies is in line with management's expectations, the acquisition might be satisfactory, if not exciting. Nonfinancial considerations might also play a large part in the evaluation—for example, if the business of the candidate company were an especially good "fit" with the business of the acquiring company, or if it had a strong management that could contribute to the further growth of the combined companies, these factors might well tip the balance in favor of the purchase.

Earnings per share projections—Acquisitions for common stock

Figure 21–5 illustrates the principles involved in projecting the effect on earnings per share of a proposed acquisition by the exchange of common stock at market value, based on the assumptions stated in Figure 21–4.

Comparing the assumptions with respect to the acquisition candidate in Figure 21–4 with those in Figure 21–3A, it will be noted that (a) year 0 sales and earnings are the same, (b) the sales and earnings growth rate is the same, and (c) there is the same assumption that no debt is outstanding, but (d) book value is assumed to be $5,000,000 instead of $8,500,000 and (e) no assumptions are stated as to dividend payout or additional capital requirements. In the absence of any statement as to dividend payout or capital requirements there is an implicit assumption that the amount of earnings retained in the business each year will be equal to the additional capital required.[7] In any situation

---

[7] If additional capital requirements in the situation represented in Figure 21–5 are assumed to be the same as in Figure 21–3A (50 percent of annual sales increases),

Figure 21-4

	Acquiring company	Acquisition candidate
Shares outstanding............................	1,000,000	200,000
Net sales, Year 0..............................	85,000,000	10,000,000
Net earnings, Year 0...........................	5,000,000	700,000
Per share....................................	5.00	3.50
Projected annual sales and earnings growth rate......	6%	10%
Price/earnings ratio...........................	12/1	15/1
Debt outstanding..............................	None	None
Market value of shares outstanding		
Per share..................................	60.00	52.50
Total in dollars.............................	60,000,000	10,500,000
Book value—dollars............................	50,000,000	5,000,000
Excess market over book value...................	10,000,000	5,500,000
Amortization of goodwill ($5,500,000 over		
40 years)—per year...........................		137,000*

Shares of acquiring company issued in exchange:

$$\frac{\$10,500,000}{60} = \qquad\qquad 175{,}000$$

Total shares outstanding after acquisition..........	1,175,000

* In this preliminary projection the entire 5½ million dollars excess of the market value of the shares to be issued for the acquisition over the book value of the net assets to be acquired is attributed to "goodwill."

where this assumption was not valid it would be necessary to decrease (or increase) the projected earnings of the acquisition candidate by the interest cost of the additional funds required (or the income from the excess of the funds generated over requirements).

The calculations in Figure 21-5 show that if the proposed acquisition can be treated as a "pooling of interests," so that there is no goodwill to be amortized, there will be a dilution of earnings that will not be eliminated until the sixth year, and tenth-year earnings of $9.16 per share will be only 2 percent better than the $8.95 per share projected for the acquiring company alone. If the acquisition is treated as a purchase, there will be an annual charge against reported earnings of about 12 cents per share for the amortization of goodwill, and dilution is not eliminated until the ninth year. The principal reason for this unattractive result is the higher P/E ratio of the acquisition candidate (15/1 against 12/1 for the acquiring company), which inflates the number of shares that must be issued if the exchange is based on market values. The

---

a dividend payout of approximately 35 percent would leave retained earnings equal to the capital requirements. For example, in year 5:
Retained earnings—65% of $1,127,000 $733,000
Additional capital requirements   735,000
(Figure 21-3A)

Figure 21-5

PROJECTIONS OF EARNINGS PER SHARE—ACQUISITION BY EXCHANGE
OF COMMON STOCK

(assumptions—see Figure 21-4 and following text)

Year	Acquiring company (1,000,000 shares)		Acquisition candidate (175,000 shares issued)		Combined companies (1,175,000 shares)			
					Before amortization of goodwill		After amortization of goodwill	
	$000	Per share	$000	Per share	$000	Per share	$000	Per share
0......	5,000	5.00	700	4.00	5,700	4.85	5,563	4.73
1......	5,300	5.30	770	4.40	6,070	5.17	5,933	5.05
2......	5,620	5.62	847	4.84	6,467	5.50	6,330	5.39
3......	5,950	5.95	932	5.32	6,882	5.86	6,745	5.74
4......	6,310	6.31	1,025	5.86	7,335	6.24	7,198	6.13
5......	6,690	6.69	1,127	6.44	7,817	6.65	7,680	6.54
6......	7,090	7.09	1,240	7.09	8,330	7.09	8,193	6.97
7......	7,520	7.52	1,364	7.79	8,884	7.56	8,747	7.45
8......	7,970	7.97	1,500	8.57	9,470	8.06	9,333	7.94
9......	8,450	8.45	1,650	9.43	10,100	8.60	9,963	8.48
10......	8,950	8.95	1,816	10.38	10,766	9.16	10,629	9.05

difference in P/E ratios presumably reflects the higher projected growth rate of the candidate company, but unless there are strongly favorable nonfinancial factors in the situation, the management of the acquiring company is unlikely to agree to the exchange on the market-value basis.

Negotiating an acquisition

It may seem to the reader that in these simplified illustrations of the evaluation of prospective acquisitions the assumptions have been deliberately established to produce rather unexciting results and generally negative or neutral conclusions. In a sense this is true, but it is fair to say that these results are not untypical of the majority of acquisition proposals. Unless the company seeking acquisitions has either (a) a large unused debt capacity which can be turned to good account simply by the leverage inherent in cash acquisitions, or (b) a high P/E ratio which gives it an advantage in making acquisitions for stock, it is likely to have difficulty in finding acquisition prospects which appear, on first inspection, to be of better than borderline attractiveness from a financial standpoint. But there are certainly situations where an acquisition which looks financially dubious in a preliminary evaluation may offer sufficient possibility of advantages to the buyer or seller, or both, to warrant further exploration. Some of these possible advantages are: new markets for existing products or new products for existing markets; increased availability of working capital for expansion; greater depth in research capabilities; strengthening of management in one or more functional areas—marketing, manufacturing, engineering, finance, or administration; entry into an industry with better growth prospects and a generally higher P/E ratio; and sometimes, in the case of privately held companies, diversification of the owners' estates. If an approach by the prospective buyer to the prospective seller discloses a mutual interest in the possibility of these benefits, there may be considerably more flexibility on both sides in the negotiation of financial terms. Furthermore, at this point the projections on which the preliminary evaluation was based can be refined in the light of the additional information that becomes available.

As the refinement of the evaluation calculations proceeds, both the buyer and the seller, recognizing the uncertainties inherent in long-term projections, will want to establish a *range* of values, at least to the extent of determining maximum, minimum, and median values based on optimistic, conservative, and middle-of-the-road estimates of future performance. The acquiring company will also want to project the effect of the proposed acquisition on its future financial position, perhaps under a number of different methods of payment and different financial structures, and the stockholders of the acquisition prospect will want to visualize the effect of the various methods of payment on their earnings per share, their dividend income, and the probable market value of their holdings. Depending on the size and relative importance of the acquisition, it may be worthwhile to go a step further and make a risk analysis, following the simulation procedure described in Chapter 25, to establish a "one best valuation." In all these calculations the development of a model for analysis through a computer makes it possible to obtain quick projections of the results of any number of combinations of basic assumptions, and for the more sophisticated approaches to valuation and determination of method of payment the computer is an absolute necessity.

When negotiations have progressed to the point where a meeting of the minds seems probable, the acquiring company will want to make, or have made for it, a comprehensive operating, financial, and management audit of the acquisition prospect, and in some cases, particularly where the two companies are of comparable size, the prospective seller may want to have a similar audit of the prospective buyer. Such audits, besides giving the parties reassurance as to the basic soundness of the deal, can be useful in identifying points of variation in policies, so that any necessary adjustments can be anticipated. Needless to say, this step should not be undertaken until a strong empathy has been established between the two managements. The scope of any audit should be agreed on in advance and the investigation should be conducted with the utmost consideration for the key personnel involved—and, indeed, for all personnel, including the shop operators. This is particularly important when a large, publicly held company is negotiating with a smaller, privately owned firm.

The responsibility for conducting acquisition negotiations, at least after the initial contacts have established some mutual interest, is properly assumed by the chief executives of the two companies. The financial officers of both the buyer and the seller are the logical persons to direct and interpret the analytical studies, and they will, in most cases, play an important part in the investigations and exchange of information as the negotiations develop. They should also be sufficiently familiar with the nonfinancial aspects of the proposed deal to be able to express an intelligent opinion on its desirability to their managements. Their opinions will carry weight to the extent that they have previously demonstrated the breadth of their knowledge of the operations of their respective businesses and their objectivity in dealing with internal management problems.

The judgment factor in acquisition evaluation

The procedures and techniques discussed in the preceding sections are essential to give both sides in a proposed acquisition adequate background on the possible financial consequences of the deal. The depth and sophistication of the financial studies will depend on the importance of the deal to the two companies, particularly the acquiring company, and, to some degree, on the temperaments and methods of operation of the two managements. In the last analysis, the valuation will be determined by management's judgment, which will almost always be heavily influenced by nonfinancial factors. To quote one planning officer with long experience in all phases of long-range planning:

The real task in valuing a potential acquisition is the same task encountered in setting your own objectives and goals, that of deciding what will determine its future market value . . . sophisticated formulae for determining worth based on some form of discounted cash flow usually serve only to confuse the issue. . . . Price then becomes largely a matter of management judgment. That judgment will consider, in addition to future earnings potential, what the acquisition will accomplish for the acquiring company and how those accomplishments are likely to be valued in the market place. A further consideration will be the method of payment and the consequent impact upon earnings per share. In the final analysis, the price may well be dictated by events of the marketplace or needs of the seller over which there is no control, and each management will have to arrive at its own personal estimate of value.[8]

Harmonizing of management policies

Of all of the nonfinancial factors included in the statement of "Specifications for Acquisition Prospects," in Figure 21–1, perhaps the most important to the success of an acquisition or merger is the item "compatibility of top management philosophy." If the acquiring company is accustomed to highly formalized operating and financial control procedures, for example, it will have difficulty in assimilating an acquisition with a free-wheeling, informal, and loosely structured management organization. Such differences in management attitudes should be thoroughly explored and frankly discussed in the course of the acquisition negotiations, and an understanding reached as to the degree of supervision which the acquiring company expects to exercise, and even the specific control procedures which will be adopted by the acquired company. Unless the acquiring company has enough organization depth and know-how to take over the direction of the acquired company, it must obviously rely on the existing management, and it should make every effort, both during negotiations and after the acquisition, to establish a working rapport between the functional executives of the two companies. This problem of the harmonization of management policies extends into every function of the business, including marketing, engineering, manufacturing, and organization and personnel but it is of particular concern to

---

[8] From the book *Effective Long-Range Business Planning* by James R. Collier, p. 143. © 1968 by Prentice-Hall, Inc., Englewood Cliffs, N.J. Reprinted with permission.

the controller (or other financial officer) who must establish, coordinate, and administer many of the control procedures.

REFERENCES FOR SUPPLEMENTAL READING

General

Ansoff, H. Igor. *Corporate Strategy* (New York: McGraw-Hill, 1965), Chapter 7, "Why Firms Diversity," pp. 122–38.
Rockwell, William F., Jr. "How to Acquire a Company," *Harvard Business Review* (September–October 1968).

Financial evaluation of acquisition prospects

Ackerman, R. W., and Fray, L. L. "Financial Evaluation of a Proposed Acquisition," *Financial Executive* (October 1967).
MacDougal, G. E., and Malek, F. V. "Master Plan for Merger Negotiations," Harvard Business Review (January–February 1970).
Glover, J. D., Hawkins, D. F., and McCosh, A. "The Use of Computers in Merger Analysis," *Mergers and Acquisitions* (Summer, 1967).
Kraber, R. W. "Acquisition Analysis: New Help from Your Computer," *Financial Executive* (March 1970).
Chambers, J. C., and Mullick, S. W. "Determining the Acquisition Value of a Company," *Management Accounting* (April 1970).

Part V

Advanced techniques

22 INTRODUCTION TO COMPUTERS

A sound awareness of what a computer can and cannot do is a very important factor in the successful management of a large business information system in the present era. A proper understanding of the effectiveness of a computer system in the solution of business problems will be of considerable competitive advantage to the manager. He need not, however, be aware of the technical details of how the machine works.

The computer is capable of doing many things which have a near miraculous appearance to the uninitiated and are indeed highly significant advances over the possibilities of twenty years ago. A computer, however, will do nothing unless it is instructed to take action. The previous sentence must be interpreted absolutely literally; the machine has no common sense whatever. It will print a million dollar paycheck just as rapidly as a correct one, unless some provision is made in the program to prevent it. It will continue to place orders for an obsolete part unless somebody remembers to tell it not to do so. The programs developed for the computer must be capable of supplying the "common sense" needed to carry out the task successfully. On the other hand, it would be just as much of an error to imagine that a computer can do nothing more than process the payroll and the accounts receivable. A general purpose computer can carry out any task which can be reduced to a permanent set of instructions. The payroll is an obvious case in which the instructions are permanent, of course, but a cash planning simulation model, an inventory control system, a linear program for production scheduling or a capital budgeting analysis model can also be reduced to a set of permanent instructions. These applications have all been made with considerable success in many business enterprises, and the controller should be aware that the possibility exists for performing some highly sophisticated and complex studies using the computer. This chapter will begin with a short discussion of the parts of the typical computer, followed by discussions of programming, file storage systems, and processing methods. Thereafter, the main focus will be on the management of a computer system, and on the general management problems associated with running the computer in a business setting.

The parts of a computer

A manager with overall responsibility for the supervision of a computerized information system is well advised to know the names and functions of the parts making up the machine under his control. In addition to the physical parts of the machine there are numerous, perhaps even more important, items called "software" which must exist if the computer is to serve management properly. In this section we shall be examining the physical devices and the associated software which collectively comprise the computer system of a company.

A generalized outline of a computer system of moderate to large size is shown in Figure 22–1. Many simpler configurations are possible

Figure 22–1

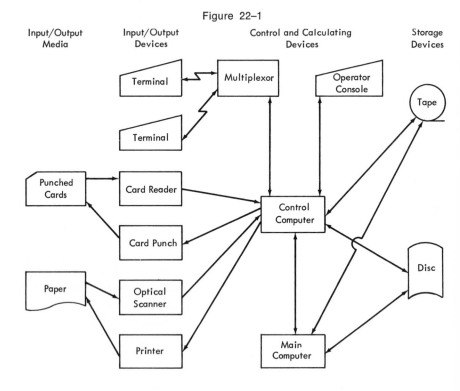

| Input/Output Media | Input/Output Devices | Control and Calculating Devices | Storage Devices |

and more complex configurations are also available. The figure, however, is reasonably typical of large, advanced computer systems operating in a business environment in the early 1970's.

The figure is divided vertically into four segments. These are input-output media, input-output devices, control and calculating devices, and storage. Only the most significant members of each segment have been shown, in the interests of clarity.

The most important input-output media are punched cards and paper. Almost everyone has seen a punched card in one form or another at this stage in the growth of the computer industry. The information on the card includes a series of holes which have been punched into it, either by a special keypunching machine which is manually operated or by the computer itself. There may also be printed information on the card, so that humans can read it. The use of printed material for input to a computer system is relatively new, because the necessary optical scanning equipment has only recently been perfected. The advantages of enabling the machine and the user to read the same document is that the expensive process of keypunching data from a humanly readable form to a computer sensible form can be avoided.

Although some useful partially mechanized input procedures are not included in the figure, they should be mentioned now. In certain businesses, data can be recorded in computer sensitive form at the outset. Many gasoline companies issue credit cards, and the forms which are used with these cards can be read by optical scanning machines. Labor time cards for use in a factory environment may also be partially prepunched with the employees name and number, leaving only the hours worked to be added. Some public utility concerns make use of mark-sensing in recording consumption; instead of writing the numbers in longhand, the inspector uses a special pencil to record its digits on a computer card. A special machine is then used to read these numbers. These methods of data recording save time, avoid the laborious keypunching process, and greatly reduce errors. They have so far been used mainly by companies with large numbers of detailed records to process.

The input-output devices in general use include card-handling machines, paper-handling machines, and terminals. The functions of the card reader and card punch are obvious from their names: they permit data to be transmitted from cards to the computer memory and from the computer memory to cards, respectively. The optical scanner reads from a printed document and transmits the data to computer memory. The optical scanner is a recent development, and the capabilities of such machines are changing very rapidly. Some of them can only read specially shaped characters, others can accept any normal typescript, and a few can read hand-printing. The printing machine is designed to take data from the computer memory and transcribe it on to paper. These machines work very rapidly, commonly with speeds up to 20 lines of 120 characters each per second.

In more modern machines, particularly those installed since 1967, it is common for a terminal or a series of terminals to be a part of the equipment of the computer. A terminal is a device which permits the user of the machine to interact with the computer in what has been called "conversational mode." The computer, which must be capable of "time sharing" if it is to support terminals, may operate in conjunction with several terminals at the same time, in addition to supporting the normal operation of the card reader, the card punch, the optical scanner and the printer.

The selection of the appropriate input-output device for a particular job is in the hands of the user. Punched card input is a faster method of loading data into the machine than that of a terminal but is slower than optical scanning. An optical scanning machine costs (at the time of writing) very much more than a card reader, and this differential is only compensated by the higher speed of the optical machine if the volume of transactions to be handled is great. One study suggests that the break-even volume of transactions is in the region of 400,000 transactions per month. The computer terminal is very slow, but since many of them can be connected to the computer at the same time, it has special advantages. For instance, the reservation of space in an airplane by several different booking clerks can be performed effectively by this type of input vehicle.

The control and calculating devices which form the heart of a computer system do not impinge directly on the user. Although the effectiveness of these devices is very important in determining the overall efficiency of the system, the user need not be concerned about them as long as they work. Two of the devices shown in the exhibit may be discussed here briefly. A multiplexor is capable of the complex message-directing task needed in a time-shared system. It causes telephone messages from the terminals to be correctly directed into the relevant area in the computer system and deals similarly with output messages from the computer.

The control computer is a relatively new approach to computer operations. It is a small machine, which is used for the management of the larger main computer. The control computer accepts input, loads data into disc files, operates upon output data, controls such peripheral machines as the input-output devices, and instructs the main computer which job to work on next. The main computer, freed of all these necessary housekeeping chores, is able to perform the main calculating job more efficiently.

Storage media

It is worthwhile for the controller to become familiar with the various types of storage media. The great majority of the effective storage media in the present era are magnetic. The differences between these devices can, however, be quite important to the user of the computer in determining how to implement a particular application. A *magnetic tape*, for example, can be purchased for about $30. On a single tape of 2400 feet in length it is possible with normal technology to store slightly more than five million characters of data. This data can be erased through demagnetization of the tape or alternatively, the data can be permitted to reside there for as long as desired. The relatively inexpensive storage provided by tapes is somewhat offset by the difficulty sometimes found in using them, because the magnetic tape must be read in a sequential order. Evidently, if you are interested in a piece of data which is stored at one end of the tape and the computer drive is currently set to read the other end, the entire length must be rewound or wound on before the desired piece of data can be located. This is a relatively slow business and can cause the performance, in terms of time, of a program to deteriorate quite substantially. On the other hand, for those applications for which a sequential ordering of data can be employed (and many accounting jobs are naturally sequential), a tape is a very fast means of storage and very effective. A *disc pack* is the most common alternative method of storing information in a computer system. Such a disc pack gives more effective access than the typical tape system but it is more expensive. A disc pack on which twenty-five million characters may be stored will vary in price, depending on the manufacturer, between $500 and $1,000—substantially more expensive than tape. However, a disc can be accessed on a random basis, that is, any piece of data stored on a disc pack can be pulled out from it very quickly and the delay in access is not dependent on the position of the record on the disc pack. Clearly, for such applications as accounts receivable debiting or payable crediting, in which accounts must be updated in order of transactions, it is highly preferable to have the data stored on the disc, so that access to the relevant account can be had with as little delay as possible. A controller responsible for the selection of such a device must weigh carefully the benefits to be obtained from direct access systems against the price. It will often be found in a commercial installation that several disc packs and a small number of tape drive mechanisms will be the optimal mix of storage units.

A *punched card* is also a storage device. Moreover, it is a storage device which is permanent, nonerasable and relatively cheap. As with the tape, access to a particular record from an extensive punched card file may be slow unless the reading is performed in a sequential order. Even if the reading is sequential in order it is much slower than magnetic tape.

Processing methods

The parts of a computer system are not solely physical. In addition, the maker of the machine must create and supply an "operating system," which is a special kind of computer program. This program instructs the machine which steps to take and the order in which they should be taken. There have been significant advances made in operating systems, and it is instructive to compare the capabilities of present day machines with their ancestors.

The earliest computers accepted jobs one at a time. The job, probably composed of a program and some data, would be fed in, probably on cards. The computer would perform whatever calculations were required, and produce output. When the first job was completed, and only then, the next job would be started. The method of processing then used was called unit processing, and it was very inefficient. The reason for its inefficiency was the relative speeds of the components of the machine. Even in the early machines, the central processing unit was very rapid, while the input and output devices were very slow. Therefore, the central processing unit was in use only for a very small proportion of the total time the computer was in operation; the central processor, of course, is a very expensive item, and cannot reasonably be left idle for long.

The first improvement on this system was called "over-lapping" and various other names. Under this revision of the unit processing method, the computer could be reading in one job, calculating a second, and printing the results of a third all at the same time. This was a great improvement, but was still relatively inefficient in keeping the central processor occupied. A refinement of this method was therefore developed, called "batch processing." Under this system, a large number of jobs, not necessarily related to one another, would be fed into the machine. The computer would work on each as rapidly as possible, and would thereby keep the input and output devices going at full speed. Even this method, did not fully utilize the central processor.

In an effort to increase the efficiency of core usage, the concept of multiprogramming was developed. This method permitted the computer to work on several jobs at the same time, by dividing the core memory into segments and allocating one segment to each job. This proved to be a complex undertaking from a technical standpoint, because it required the use of several input devices and several output machines to keep the central processor fed. In turn, these various devices made complex safeguards necessary, to ensure that the various jobs being operated on did not get mixed up during processing. The technical problems have been largely overcome, however, and multiprogramming is now in general use.

The processing method called time sharing was a logical outgrowth of multiprogramming. Instead of handling a number of small jobs at the same time, allocating a piece of the central core to each, time sharing systems perform a large number of jobs at once. Instead of dividing up the core among the users, however, each user is given the use of as much core as he needs for a very short period of time. After that time has elapsed, the computer moves on to service another customer.

Although the time slices are very short, the large scale computer systems now available can do enough work within that short time slice to satisfy the users demand for service.

A particular user at a terminal may type or have typed a message calling upon the computer to begin a certain calculation. The message is transmitted by telephone lines or otherwise to the multiplexor and thence to the control computer. The latter instructs the main computer to withdraw the relevant program from in the disk pack, and to commence to calculate in accordance with the program selected. The user may specify that the program operate on data residing in a particular location in the disk pack, or on data which is fed in, piece by piece, through the terminal at the time the calculation has to be performed. A program which is designed for such time-sharing use will typically be arranged so that the calculations will proceed until a point is reached where further information is required. At that time, the program will cause the control computer to transmit a message (through the multiplexor and back to the terminal) asking the user to specify the information now required. When the user has specified the amount of the variable, the information is transmitted back to the main computer and it proceeds with the calculation of the remainder of the problem. While the transmission back to the terminal is occurring, the control computer will arrange for the temporary deposit of all the user's activities, transactions, data and programs in a storage unit, and will arrange for the main computer to work on the problems of one of the other connected users, pending the response the first user was asked to provide.

Time-sharing activities through a terminal device are a valuable tool of management. It is possible, employing one of these programs, to make use of the manager's skill, judgment, and experience to estimate the values of variables which ought to be considered in a calculation, while at the same time permitting the computer to perform that part of the task which it does supremely well—rapid calculation.

A time-sharing system is automatically an "on-line" system. The words on-line mean that the original entry point of the data is connected directly to the computer system. This contrasts with the older batch system, in which data had to be gathered, keypunched, batched, and then submitted to the computer when suitably collected together. The advantages of on-line operations are that the machine can provide service much more rapidly than it could under the older approach. Also, the costly operations of keypunching and verifying the material are avoided under on-line operations. On-line systems are expensive, however, and should only be considered when there is a real need for rapid response.

Preliminary planning—Problem identification

The management of an installation involves careful advance planning. This planning and the subsequent installation procedure should follow a logical sequence. The first step in the analysis should be a careful study of the various operations of the information function in the company to find out which of these could be improved. In one concern, receivables might be causing a difficulty: the bills may not be going out quickly enough, there may be a problem of transactions getting lost, the follow-up procedure for slow payers may be imperfect. In another business, the problem area may be inventory. There are many types of inventory problems, including overordering, hoarding, excessive stockouts, delay in the recording of movements of materials, and shipping and receiving misplacements. Whatever the nature of the difficulty, it is essential to pin it down as accurately as possible first. The reader may wonder why this obvious step is being emphasized; the reason is simple. In many companies, the step was omitted; as a result, the computer installation was devoted to nonessential tasks, and a great opportunity to improve the business operation was lost.

When the problems have been identified, in general terms, the next step should be to look at each problem area, and to attempt to solve the problem by making adjustments to the manual or mechanical system presently in use. These adjustments are very important and must be done before the desirability of a computer installation is considered at all. If this step is not taken, the economic worth of the computer installation may be seriously overstated in the estimates to be prepared. It is certainly bad management to count a gain in system effectiveness as a benefit of computerization, if in fact that gain could be achieved without the machine.

When these preliminary steps have been undertaken, the manager should be left with a list of problem areas which have not been solved by adjusting the present system. Of course, if all the problems have been solved by minor adjustments to the present system, the feasibility of a computer installation could only be established if the benefits from total replacement outweighed the costs. In many companies, particularly larger companies, this benefit (in the form of cost savings) can be more than enough to make the installation worthwhile. Even though the present system works quite well, the computer system may be more efficient.

In most cases, however, some problem areas will remain unsolved after the review of the manual system has been completed. A computer systems study may be instituted at this point.

The system study

In order to perform a systems study effectively, the manager must concern himself with the identification of critical variables, study the time need for information, and have his staff perform data destination studies, data collection system reviews, transaction analyses, and data manipulation descriptions.

The identification of the critical variables has already been hinted at in the previous section. The company must devote its computer effort to solving the really difficult problems of managing the business. A study reported in 1963 showed that the companies which had had the greatest success with their computers were the ones which had devoted the machine to the critical variables. This identification must be made in explicit terms. It does little good to say that "we must have data on inventory." This is clearly true enough, but it does not pin down the importance of inventories to the business, nor does it indicate what sort of information is required and when it will be needed. Instead, the manager must be able to say "I need to know the level of all items in inventory regularly every month, and I must be told within five hours of any item in inventory which has fallen below its reorder level, and I must know within one week of any item which has exceeded its over-stocking level." This not only identifies the nature of the data the manager must have, it also tells when he must have it, and how frequently. The critical variable in this instance is exemplified by the rapidity with which the manager wishes to hear about potential shortages.

The time need for data is also exemplified in the statement above. There is no need to provide data to a manager instantaneously, just because the company has a fancy new machine which makes this possible. The emphasis must be on the time and frequency with which the data are needed. This may be called the presentation frequency of a report. There are four basic presentation frequencies: (1) instantaneous, (2) regular, (3) by-product, (4) cued. The meaning of the first presentation frequency, the instantaneous frequency, is fairly obvious. Data in this category cannot be provided too quickly. A credit manager should be able, if possible, to advise on the standing of a customer before a sale is consummated. A stockbroker must be able to quote the current price of a share. A commodity buyer must be aware of the current quoted price for his commodity. In general, there are relatively few pieces of data which must be provided with this sort of speed. It is in this area that time-shared real-time computer systems have the greatest promise because of the speed with which such a system can provide the answers sought.

The second presentation frequency is the regular rate. A piece of data will definitely be needed at a certain time, but there is no real advantage in having that data in advance. Clearly, the great majority of accounting applications fall into this group. There is little point in having payroll data much before the checks have to be prepared. There is usually little point in trying to prepare a customer's bill long before it is going to be mailed. These applications can be planned substantially in advance, and the general nature of the information need can be specified quite clearly.

The third, by-product rate, presentation frequency requires more explanation. In this instance, the demand for the information would call for its production at a certain frequency, but the cost of doing so would be relatively high. If the manager is prepared to wait a while, however, it may be very easy to produce the data as an offshoot of some other program. The labor breakdown, for instance, is often produced as a by-product of the payroll program. This may be the most practical method even though there may be some pressure for its being produced separately at a different time. The manager must ask himself whether the need for the data at a different point in time is enough to justify the cost of performing a special run in order to get it.

The fourth and last presentation frequency is the cued report. In this case, the report is only presented to the manager if some key indicator requires it. The stockout possibility mentioned earlier is an example. The manager only wishes to know when there is a real possibility of the stockout occurring, but in order to make this possible, it will be necessary to review all the stock balances at frequent intervals. In particular, if he is to be made aware of potential stockouts within five hours of the reorder level being passed, the system must review all inventory balances at least that often, in order to find which balances have passed the danger level. It may be possible, alternatively, to perform this review function every time a unit is requisitioned out of inventory. The stock shortage report would then be printed as a by-product of the inventory program. If no report is printed, the manager still has the assurance that the balances have been reviewed, and knows that he would have been told if there was anything needing his attention.

In selecting a presentation frequency for a given report, the analyst should consider the importance of the item being reported. In many companies, for example, a small number of products account for a large proportion of total sales volume. The manager may well choose to receive a regular report on the sales of all products and a cued report on the critical products if their sales level deviates significantly from expected levels.

The general problem of data management is also an important one when a systems study is being performed. This problem can be resolved into three parts, data destination plans, manipulation plans, and the data collection system. The *data destination plan* is the formal presentation of the information needs of the various individual managers making up the organization. The systems analyst must review the information the manager has asked for, and any other information he ought to receive, and set down on paper a formal list of each manager's requirements. The manager in charge of accounts payable, for instance, would probably include the following in his list of information requirements. He would want to receive a listing of all account balances at regular intervals and a daily list of accounts requiring immediate payment. He would need a list of new accounts added to the ledger. In many cases, of course, the manager would promptly delegate this material for the attention of his assistants, but the data would be classed as necessary for his department to use. On a more personal level, the accounts payable manager would need to know of any changes in payment terms required by suppliers and would also require data on any accounts in dispute. He would need to know which officer of the company had placed an order for goods or services in order to be able to verify the account. Similar lists of requirements would be prepared for each major manager in the firm, or at least in that part of the firm which is expected to be affected by the proposed computer system.

The *data manipulation process* may be examined in several ways, but the commonest and probably the most effective method in the system flowchart. The purpose of system flowcharts is to ensure that the information needs of the individual managers, as shown in the data destination map, are in fact filled as far as is economically possible. At this stage in the proceedings, a system flowchart is preferable to a detailed or program flowchart, as the broader field of application of the system flowchart enables the manager with overall systems responsibility to see the whole picture and ensure that the whole job is being performed.

An example of a system flowchart for accounts payable is given in Figure 22–2. The inputs to the system are shown above the higher dotted line, while the outputs from it are shown below the lower line. The system is concerned with the updating of a number of files and the production of a variety of data lists, checks and other records in the

Figure 22–2

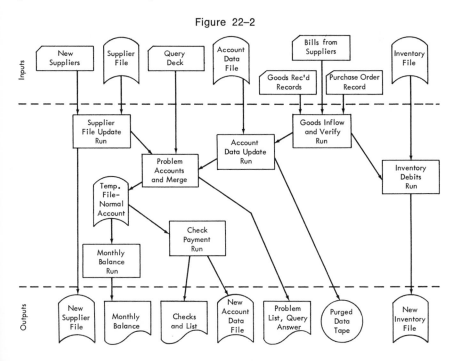

process. The system flowchart divides this process into seven separate computer programs, each with its own function. The "account data update run" for example, is intended to accept the month-to-date list of transactions for each account, and the new transactions which have occurred today, and merge these into a revised temporary file of transactions. At the same time, the run is expected to purge the file of transactions of any data no longer required, and to store these transactions on a special preservation tape; these records may be destroyed after a reasonable interval. The "check writing run" is obviously an important member of the series. This program would compare the due dates of each shipment record with the current payment date, and write a check for those which had come due. In addition, this program would update the record of the account to include the check, and would present a listing of the checks for the payment period. The function of the other runs in the accounts payable system is reasonably clear from the diagram.

A study of the revised *data collection* system may also be made during the feasibility study. The input elements consist, in the accounts payable example just reviewed, of both carryover and new data. The carryover data, of course, are the old balances and supplier descriptions. The new inputs consist of billings received, descriptions of new suppliers, revisions to the descriptions of existing suppliers, and query data. Query data are input by the accounts payable manager, asking the system to provide him with a detailed printout of the account of any supplier he wishes to study especially, such as one whose balance is in dispute. An alternative system, not explicitly defined in the chart, might include in the "Problem List" a statement of any accounts which have violated certain built-in constraints. For instance, the manager may wish to see any accounts which now exceed a certain balance or any accounts which have past due contents.

The data preparation and input process must be designed carefully. Descriptions of any new suppliers, giving names, addresses, credit terms, delivery methods, and other pertinent data must be provided to enable the system to function. The data must be transferred onto computer input media, such as cards, and there must be a system of verification to ensure that the data thus input are correct. This implies verification of the keypunching, of course, but must also include verification procedures within and around the computer to see that certain limits and constraints have been observed. In the accounts payable example, separate input cards for the purchase order, the supplier invoice, and the goods received are suggested. One of the programs compares these data and adjusts the payment accordingly.

While we are on the subject of data input, two points of general applicability should be made. In the first place, the operation of putting data into a machine-readable form is very expensive. This step usually takes the form of a keypunch operation. Once this has been done, the computer can manipulate the item with considerable dexterity, if suitably programmed. The incremental processing cost of an additional manipulation of data which is already in machine-sensible form is very much less than the cost of performing such an additional manipulation in a manual environment. It follows that as many different things should be done with data as may be useful to management, once the initial decision to put the data into the machine has been taken. For instance, if the decision is taken to put the payroll on the computer, it is a relatively minor step to adjust the program so that useful management data are also provided. Such things as departmental labor costs can be found, or perhaps job charges in a job-costing environment.

This brings us to the second point. The analysis mentioned in the previous paragraph can only be performed if the input data are suitably coded in the first place. There is no way the computer can provide a sales analysis by territory, for instance, unless the territory in which each sale took place is recorded on the transaction record at the time of input. This implies that considerable foresight is needed in the planning of the input records, so that as many as possible of the outputs which might be demanded are made available.

Once the entire system which may be affected by the computer installation has been studied through the flowcharts described above or otherwise, it is necessary to evaluate the overall profitability of the installation proposal. This evaluation is basically identical with any other capital investment decision, and must be treated as such. There has been an unfortunate tendency, in some instances, to evaluate a computer installation on some other basis than that applied to a machine purchase or other major business acquisition. This may have arisen because of the "mystique" of the computer, but cannot be excused on these grounds. It must be admitted that some of the gains which can be attributed to a computer are not easily measured, and to that extent the usual capital budgeting rules may be hard to employ. For example, a manager may find it hard to assess the value of receiving a given report on Tuesday when formerly he had to wait till Friday. A manager may also find it hard to assess the value of the built-in limit checking procedures which may prevent certain errors getting through the system. In this regard, however, the manager is not in any more difficult position than when he is trying to measure the qualitative features of a new machine tool. The evaluation process should be the same as that for any other major investment possibility.

The early history of an accounting application

When the machine has been installed and the operating system is working satisfactorily, the first of the production systems must be prepared for use on the machine. The selection of the first system will depend on the projected profitability of all the systems, of course, but will permit the staff of the installation to gather experience and confidence, prior to tackling some of the tougher problems. The steps involved in implementing a system include:

1. Preparing the program flow charts
2. Writing the computer programs
3. Converting the data files to computer-sensible form
4. Testing and debugging the system

We shall be concerned primarily with the first of these steps.

As an example of an accounting application, consider one of the runs taken from the system flowchart shown in Figure 22–2, an accounts payable system. We shall consider only the check-writing run. The reader will note that the supplier's names and addresses have already been merged with the accounting data file, both of which have previously been updated and purged of old material. The check-writing run is expected to prepare a check for the total amount payable and no more, and to ensure that discounts and credit periods are correctly handled.

It is at this level, the level of detailed run design, that the problem of staffing becomes most acute. Evidently, the program to be written must be capable of handling the various commercial concepts associated with check-writing and analysis of payments. In fact, the designer should have business training and/or experience as well as computer programming skills in order to implement this system. Such a combination of business and computer skills is very scarce.

The flowchart presented in Figure 22–3 is a program flowchart, which is quite different in purpose and scope from a systems flowchart like the one shown in Figure 22–2. The system flowchart is intended to give the broad outline of the design of an entire system, such as accounts payable, or may even seek to describe the entire information system of an enterprise. It is not the purpose of the system flowchart to show how each task will be performed, but rather to indicate which tasks will be performed. A program flowchart is intended to describe how a particular job will be done. The purpose of the program must be understood, of course, before it can be written at all. In the actual writing of the program flowchart, however, the details of "how" are much more important than the generalizations of "what," and "why."

The flowchart is, in fact, a diagram of the sequence of steps which the computer program itself will later be asked to follow. The program flowchart directs the computer to read in the data, account by account, checking each of the items on an account to see whether it must be paid at the present time. If it must, the program will cause the check total to be increased, and then look at the next account item. When all the items in an account have been processed, the check is printed

Figure 22–3

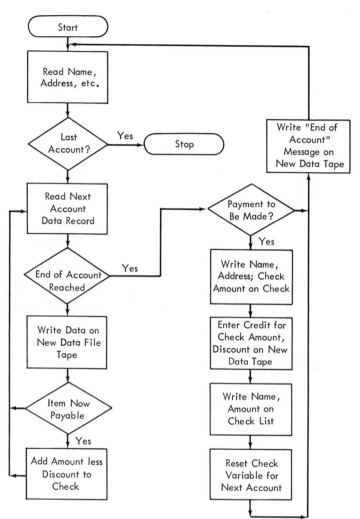

if required, the check data are written on the new accounts payable record file, and the next supplier's account is considered. The process is entirely straightforward, and the resulting program is very short indeed.

Once the flowchart had been prepared, the second step in the implementation process is coding and debugging. This is a mechanical step which is necessary to make the computer program useable, and in order to make sure that the answers it produces are correct. The third step is to run the program with some test data, to ensure that all the possible combinations of circumstances have been handled adequately. If the test data are thorough, it should be possible to verify the correctness of most if not all of the options in the program. The fourth step, once all the programs in a system have been prepared, is to convert the data from the prior system to the data bank for the new computer system, and to run the old and new systems in parallel for a time until the management can be certain the new one is able to handle the system adequately. After a reasonable test period, the old system can be discontinued, and the "cutover" is complete.

Staffing the computer function

Let us now examine the personnel which are called for in a typical business computer installation of moderate to large size. Naturally, the cost of adding these people to the staff would have to be taken into account when the overall desirability of the project is being reviewed. There are many different skills needed in order to get good results from a computer installation, and most of these skills are in short supply at the time of writing. The scarcity of skilled people in the computer field is likely to continue, because the number of installations is growing faster than the number of people who can be trained to staff them. The salaries which skilled computer personnel can command are also increasing at a noticeable rate.

The groups of people who must be available to assist in operating a medium to large computer installation are as follows:

1. Computer operators and hardware maintenance staff
2. Operators of peripheral equipment, including keypunch machines
3. Programmers
4. Systems analysts
5. Installation manager

The first group are those directly involved with the operation of the computer. These people are usually trained by the manufacturer, and the computer makers have set up schools for training them. The function of the operators of the machine is to load work into the machine, and to ensure that necessary supplies, such as cards, paper, tapes, and so on are loaded into it. The hardware maintenance staff are normally in the employ of the manufacturer, and are made available when needed to the using company. The customer engineer's job is to keep the machine is running order, and to carry out all necessary maintenance.

The operators of peripheral equipment constitute the second major group of personnel of the installation. Operators of keypunch machines and verification machines must be available to convert the basic raw data into computer sensitive form. In many accounting applications, this is a large scale task, and many employees must be available to perform it. More modern machinery is available, which enables data to be placed directly onto a magnetic tape from the keyboard. Even this process is limited, however, by the typewriting pace at which an operator can work. If cards are keypunched, it is desirable to employ verifier operators, whose task is to check that the data has been correctly punched into the cards by employing a machine called a verifier. In most installations, it is also useful to have card sorting machines, tabulators, and reproducers, which serve as useful peripheral aids to the main computer. There must, of couse, be a person or group in the organization who can use such devices.

A most important group of employees in a computer installation is the programming staff. These range in skill from people who can take a completely described flow diagram and convert it into a sequence of machine instructions to people who can also perform the complex analytical work leading to the program flow diagram. The actual computer coding process, involving the conversion of a flowchart into a program, is essentially a mechanical step. There is no innovative skill involved, and the people who perform this work need not understand the nature of the problem on which they are working. The program analysts and systems analysts must, of course, understand the system perfectly.

Systems analysts are also very important members of a computer department. The skills which a systems analyst must bring to bear on a problem are of a high order. It is the duty of the systems analyst to study the entire sequence of steps now involved in a procedure, with a view to improving the efficiency of that sequence, or recommending a change in the procedure, or adjusting the system so that its output is more closely aligned with the needs of the manager receiving the results. Clearly, a systems analyst must be of managerial calibre, and must be fully conversant with the needs of the operating managers in the enterprise. Because of regrettable shortage of systems analysts with this managerial point of view, many companies have found another position necessary. There is no fixed title for this person, but he might be referred to as a "liaison officer." The liaison officer is a member of the staff of a department which hopes to use or is using the computer. It is his function to ensure that the systems analysts are constantly aware of the needs of the using department, and the changing character of these needs. In the other direction, the liaison officer must keep his department advised of the progress that has been made on a new system, and must help the systems analyst explain his actions to managerial personnel in the using department.

From the point of view of the controller, as chief information officer of the company, the person in the computer installation who is most important is the installation manager. In most companies, the installation manager reports to the controller. Even if the computer is not under the controller's command, however, the installation manager is a person with whom the controller must deal frequently if the accounting system is even partially computerized.

The installation manager is expected to ensure that the machine is adequately staffed, that it is properly maintained, that the operating system is current and functioning well, and that reserve computing power is available in the event of a collapse of the principal machine. In many installations, the installation manager is also expected to set priorities for program running, priorities for selection of new systems to be implemented, and the assignment of scarce systems personnel. It is in this second set of functions that the installation manager will have the greatest impact on the company. If possible, the installation manager should be a person with considerable business training and experience. With such training, coupled with his knowledge of the technical aspects of the installation, he should be able to evaluate the competing claims of various departments which want to use the machine. In this evaluation, he can call on the advice and counsel of the controller, his immediate superior, so that the valuable resource under his control is allocated in the most profitable way.

Most companies using computers have found it helpful to appoint a management supervisory committee to oversee the computer's use. This committee seems to work best when chaired by the controller and composed of senior representatives from the major using departments. This type of top management support for a computer installation has been observed in the great majority of successful installations; top management support is a key factor if the installation is to produce the desired results.

23 INTERNAL CONTROL AND AUDIT IN A COMPUTERIZED SYSTEM

Many business enterprises, especially those of medium and large size, have converted significant portions of their information processing operations to computerized systems. Traditionally, the controller has been responsible for the smooth operation of the information systems of the business. The conversion to the computer does not, in most companies, change that responsibility; the conversion does, however, introduce an additional dimension to the problem. In this chapter, we shall be concerned with the new and unique control problems which arise when the system is computerized and with some of the procedures which have been found helpful in maintaining or increasing the degree of control which can be exercised over the system.

Much of the published work in this field has been prepared by practitioners of public accounting. The practitioner has often been confronted with a completely new environment for auditing when the computer is installed, which calls for significant changes in audit approach. The controller and the CPA have common interests in this area. The CPA seeks assurance that the systems are well-designed, and that they are functioning properly; the controller is evidently concerned about the same questions. In the present chapter, therefore, no distinction is drawn between the work of the internal audit team (under the controller) and the work of the public accountants. The topics are important and must be given due attention by both parties.

The chance of a modern computer making a mistake is very slight indeed. The manufacturers have been made aware of the great need for accuracy over the developmental years since the first commercial computer was installed in 1953. Numerous devices have now been installed in computers to ensure that errors are not permitted to pass undetected.[1] Unfortunately, the same precision cannot be ascribed to the people who supply data to the machine and write programs for it. Almost all the errors which are blamed on the computer in the popular press are really the fault of the operator, of the programmers, or of the data collection staff. In the present chapter, we shall be concerned with those control procedures designed to minimize the effects of the human errors associated with computer systems.

System changes often accompanying computerization

At the outset, a number of differences often observed between the traditional manual systems and computerized systems may be listed. These new features create the need for novel control and audit procedures.

An EDP installation is an expensive piece of equipment in almost any corporation. Naturally, the management of the company is interested in maximizing the efficiency of operation of that installation. In order to do this, it must pay close attention to the basic economics of a computer system. When data have been inserted into a computer, it is generally economic to do as much as possible with it internally, printing out results only when necessary. There is, in fact, an economic incentive for the proprietors of a computer system to leave no printed trace of a transaction, between the time of an event's entry into the system and the occasion when it appears in a final report.

A further aspect of efficiency in computer operations is the fact that a computer has calculating power and capacities roughly proportional to the cube of its cost. This implies, of course, that a corporation (which has not chosen to decentralize on purpose) should obtain the largest, single computer which it can use instead of several small ones. This economic fact has led, in many businesses, to considerable concentration of data processing and computing activity in a single centralized data processing center equipped with one substantial machine. This, in turn, tends to diminish the traditional separation of responsibilities which have formed a cornerstone of internal check procedures for many decades. If the computer and the associated peripheral equipment can process data quickly and efficiently without the assistance of outside personnel, there is a natural tendency for management to seek to make use of this power, perhaps at the cost of reducing the possible internal check procedures.

It is already possible for records to be entered directly onto computer files from the factory floor. Automatic time recording devices have been devised which permit direct data entry. A factory employee may load

---

[1] For a discussion of these devices, see G. Davis, *Auditing and EDP* (New York: AICPA, 1968), Chapter 4.

into a data entry device a card describing the job on which he is working and another card representing his own number. By pushing a button the employee can advise the computer that he is starting to work on that job, and later, by pushing another button can tell the computer when he has finished the work. There is no need for any physical document of original entry under such a system. There are obvious and complicated auditing and internal control problems associated with the use of such machines.

The computer has, however, brought with it certain advantages in terms of internal and external auditing. An EDP system is usually extremely complex if the computer is being used fully by the business. Because of this complexity, the corporation is forced, for its own protection, to maintain careful documentary records controlling the organization and administration of the EDP system. These records can be of immense value to auditors, both internal and external, if they review carefully the various documents supporting a particular computerized application. The auditor should be able to perceive readily what he needs to do to check if the system is working. In addition, the controller or external auditor may turn the computing power, speed, and accuracy of the machine to his own advantage by using it in his review procedures if he has the necessary skills at his command. The auditor would undoubtedly be very well advised to obtain such skills either by training himself or by adding people with the necessary skills to his staff.

Organizational and administrative controls

Four basic principles of internal control have long been recognized as essential to a smoothly operating and effectively governed accounting system. These same principles hold when the system is computer-based. First, there must be a sound organization design, in which reporting responsibilities are clearly explained to the staff, and in which there is no overlapping responsibility. Second, there must be a system of authorization for transactions and for the movement of assets within the concern, so that every event is brought to the attention of the person responsible. Naturally, there will be times when a responsible official will elect to delegate some parts of his authority to others; however, such delegation should be clearly and formally established in advance. Third, there must be a coherent set of operating rules and procedures governing the activities of the department so that all personnel know what to do in all circumstances. Last, the staff of the department must be sufficiently skilled and adequately trained to carry out the duties and responsibilities which have been assigned to them. In the present section, we shall examine the implications of the first three of these fundamental principles for the organization and administration of a computer and systems department.

With respect to *organization,* two distinct topics must be considered. First is the organizational location of the computer department as a unit within the company. Second, the duties and responsibilities of the various members of the staff of the computer department must be distinguished from each other.

It is strongly recommended that the EDP department be independent of user departments. In a business computer organization, a substantial part of computer usage will be concerned with inventory control, receivables, payables, and cash. The machine may, of course, also be employed to service production and engineering, but the former departments are the main business units using the machine in most companies. It has long been recognized as a principle of internal control that, for example, the accounts receivable and cash departments should be separated and that no person should have control over the entries on both sides of a customer's account. Clearly, if the receivables department or the cash department can exercise control over the activities of computer department, this basic principle of separation of duties will have been violated indirectly. A similar problem would arise if the payables department could control the computer department and the computer department was involved in the processing of cash transactions.

Practice has varied considerably among firms with respect to the organizational location of the computer department. In most companies, according to a recent survey, the computer department has been made an independent function within the controller's jurisdiction. In other companies, the chief of the computing center has been made to report directly to the vice president for finance or administration. Another, less common, location has been under the vice president for production or manufacturing. The benefits and problems associated with each of these will depend greatly on the specific nature of the business. As long as there is no control exercised over the computer department by the subsidiary sections of the accounting department, which are its primary "customers," no internal control problem seems likely.

Within the computer department itself, it is desirable to maintain a high level of separation of duties. If at all possible, an organization chart of the data processing department should be prepared. The duties of each individual or section should be defined clearly and the reporting line of authority drawn as carefully and as precisely as possible. A possible chart of organization for the various computer activities is provided in Figure 23–1. The operators of the computer are separated from the analysts, who are, in turn, separated from the data control function. The important thing is that there is a recognized hierarchy and that the responsibilities of each group are well established.

The subdepartment under the computer manager has the responsibility for keeping the machine in working order and for running it. This responsibility includes the actual operation of the machine: the loading

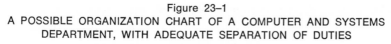

Figure 23-1
A POSSIBLE ORGANIZATION CHART OF A COMPUTER AND SYSTEMS
DEPARTMENT, WITH ADEQUATE SEPARATION OF DUTIES

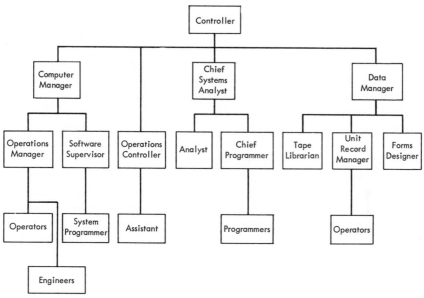

of tapes, supplying cards and paper, changing disc-packs, and operating the console. This subdepartment is also responsibile for repairing the machine if it should break down, or at least for getting in touch with the manufacturer's engineer. The software department is responsible for the maintenance and adjustment of the operating system of the machine, the main control program which governs the operation of the machine and assigns priorities to the jobs submitted by users. The software group is often also responsible for maintaining the programs in disc libraries, and for ensuring that the user is able to access the program he wants after following prescribed methods.

The operations controller frequently reports to the computer manager, but we have suggested that he report to the controller directly, as that would improve the internal check. The operations controller is responsible for monitoring the work of the computer and for reviewing the console printout and the program run books and logs. The exact nature of these documents will be discussed later. The purpose of the review is to ensure that the time taken by the machine for each assigned task is reasonable, and that no unscheduled interference with the work by the operators has occurred. As this review provides a control over the work of the operations manager and the software group, it is preferable that the operations controller and his assistant be organizationally divorced from the former sections.

The *systems department* is responsible for the development of applications programs. Systems analysts work with the staffs of departments who wish to put a task on the computer. They design the new computerized systems, and the programmers write the associated programs. Internal control at this juncture is normally quite weak. It is often difficult to check on the validity of the work done by the systems analysis group and to ensure that the programmers have done exactly what the analysts requested. Nonetheless, it is impossible to separate the analysts from the programmers in any effective way, if they are to be at all efficient in the work of preparing the programs. They must be permitted to consult each other, and to work together. Internal control over this area must be exerted by thorough review and test procedures before a program is brought into use on a regular basis.

The data control section is responsible for the preservation and integrity of those data which have been committed to computer media. This group can help improve internal control by ensuring that access to data tapes is confined to the staff who needs such access. Also, access to data should be limited to as short a period as feasible. There have been cases, for example, on which an accounts receivable tape was removed from the library and copied onto another tape minus a few records of interest to the person who "borrowed" it. The revised tape was then returned to the library. Proper issue control would limit such activities to a few people, who would be easy to identify if necessary.

It is also possible to exercise organizational control through other forms of control of access: For instance, there should be careful control over access to the computer room. If such access is confined to the operators of the machine only, so that systems analysts and representatives of using departments are not permitted to enter, this would help considerably in reducing the possibilities of fraud. A systems analyst is in a much better position than a computer operator to adjust the processing of a job directly through the control console because the systems analyst knows how the program works. Clearly, however, he would not be able to make any such alterations if he cannot get into the computer room. For essentially similar reasons, it is advisable to restrict access to the control data printed by the machine itself. These control data include program running time documents, internal billing procedures, documentation of adjustments to the operating system of the computer, and miscellaneous operating details. A system analyst, user, or operator with fraudulent intent could obtain much valuable data by studying this output and, therefore, should be prevented from studying it where possible. An *operations control* group should exist in the EDP department, as suggested in Figure 23–1, the group being held responsible for the study of system control data and the interpretation of such data including the decision to investigate particular aspects of the computer processing system which seem to have gone wrong or to be out of line.

The second major element in the system of internal control is the *authorization* procedure. This mechanism is intended to ensure that the assets of the company are not moved without the active consent of the responsible official. Usually, this consent is given by the official when he signs a document. A given official is normally allowed to sign for the movement of goods up to a preset dollar limit. In the great majority of cases, the authorization system in effect prior to computerization will continue to operate satisfactorily after the installation; the computer will not affect the authorization system at all. In a few instances, though, the need for normal authorization documents may cease to exist when the computer is put in.

Instead, the authorization process may take the form of establishing limits over expenditures, credit, or some other operational figure. When these limits are exceeded, appropriate error messages may be printed by the machine enabling the responsible official to take such action as appears appropriate. This authorization is just as effective as the procedure outlined in the last paragraph and has the advantage that the official need only be concerned with problem situations.

A third facet of internal control is the set of *operating procedures* and rules. The procedures must be complete, so that staff members know what to do in all circumstances. They must cover the topics of systems studies, machine operations control, and file management, among others; we shall look at each of these topics in the following.

While the general concepts associated with a system study have already been discussed in Chapter 22, it is important that a company establish a system for carrying out its surveys and resurveys on a regular basis. Once the machine has been installed, there will be numerous opportunities for new system studies and applications and a coherent process for reviewing the viability of each such application is essential.

Many concerns have found it possible to employ a company-wide systems and programming manual to effect this administrative control. The contents of such a manual are obviously at the discretion of management involved but should contain, as a minimum, a description of the procedures and approval arrangements needed before a new system or any substantial new subsystem can be put into use. Many data processing managers use the manual to standardize the content and specification of requests for adjusted systems by potential user departments throughout the corporation. In general, a requirement should be included that all systems be flowcharted prior to or concurrent with the development of the programs implementing the system. Also, all new systems should be subject to careful study by representatives of the using department, by the data processing manager or his staff, and preferably by a senior management group with competence in this area. In the case of a system which affects the assets and accounts normally subject to audit, a representative of the company's outside auditors should also be invited to comment on the proposed system.

It is particularly important that a procedure be instituted for controlling adjustments to already existing systems and programs. Such system changes should arise only at the request of a senior manager in the using department who must specify in detail the nature of the adjustment he wishes to install. When such authorization and requests have been prepared, a system analyst, or a team of systems analysts, must be set to work. The same basic sequence of documentary steps should be taken in controlling a change in a system, as was taken when the system was installed in the first place. The systems analyst must prepare all necessary documentation covering the change, including an updated edition of the flowchart of the program. His efforts must be reviewed by the data processing manager and by a person from the using department appointed for the purpose. The revision of the system flowchart is particularly important. If this updating is not performed, the program will very rapidly cease to resemble the flowchart from which it was originally created. As changes are plugged into the program but not inserted on the flowchart, the discrepancy between program and flowchart will expand rapidly and the usefulness of the flowchart as a guide to the program will diminish in proportion. The possible loss for any reason of the systems analyst who had been working on this program would lead to severe problems if a later change in the system seemed desirable. For example, in one large manufacturing concern, when a simple change in the social security law was instituted, changing the maximum taxable income, the program change cost *two thirds* of the original cost of the entire payroll program because the analyst who had been working on the program had left without documenting his earlier program changes.

Administrative control over the operation of the machine itself may be achieved through review procedures. The control group in the computer department should study the console printout at regular intervals to ensure that no unauthorized adjustments to the normal running of the programs has taken place. This review should establish that the operators of the machine have not interfered with normal program operations, except in specific emergency situations. The need for such review is less acute if the company machine is a third-generation computer than if it is an earlier model. In a third-generation machine, the typical mode of operation is called multiprogramming. This involves the simultaneous execution of many programs by the central processing unit, each job being located in a different part of the core of the machine. Concurrently with this multiple processing, the machine may be printing one or more additional jobs on which processing is complete and may be loading others into storage for processing when space becomes available. This type of nonstop multijob operation means that the operator would find it very difficult to intervene fraudulently during the processing of any individual program. However, in the case of the older, second-generation machines, which tended to process one job at a time, the possibility of operator intervention could not be excluded, and careful review of the console printout would be very important in such cases.

It is advisable to maintain a program run book to ensure that no unusual circumstances pass unnoticed. If a particular program which normally takes, say, one hour to run, is found to have taken four hours on an occasion, the program run book should reveal this fact, and responsible officials should find out the reason for the delay. In a recent case, the running time of a particular program doubled. Investigation revealed that the operator had accidentally updated the accounts receivable file twice. Effectively, this meant that customers were billed twice over for any transactions occurring during that period and received double credit for any checks received in that interval. Clearly, such a situation would be revealed promptly by the responses of the customers, but a similar error in an inventory program might not be revealed until too late. In addition to the administrative control provided by the program run book, such a book permits an analysis to be performed of the usage of the machine so that planning and loading can be more efficiently organized.

The management of the computer center should pay a considerable amount of attention to the procedures for protecting the computer files. In most companies, these files will be maintained on magnetic tape. There should be a library procedure for safeguarding these tapes, under which each user of a tape is required to sign a receipt for the tape when he draws it from the library and is also required to check it in when he returns the tape. We have already explored some of the problems that can arise if no such controls exist. The use of the tape librarian also has the merit of fixing clearly the responsibility for physical custody of the files.

Procedures to prevent the accidental destruction of tape files, or at least to diminish the effect of such a loss, must also be enforced. The commonest method of preservation is the so-called "grandfather" system. This is illustrated in Figure 23–2. The basic idea behind the system is that a copy of every file should be preserved, and should be stored in some other location other than where processing occurs. In the figure, for instance, a daily file updating procedure is illustrated. On Monday, the computer will process the current master file (B) with the transactions of the day to produce the new master file (C). The *grandfather* master file (A) is kept apart from the process in some safe place. On the following day, the new master file (C) is processed again. This

Figure 23-2
FILE RETENTION/RECONSTRUCTION SYSTEM
One file is preserved without processing in case an accident should befall
either of the files being processed. On Mondey, for example, tape file A is
preserved, while B and C are processed.

	Monday	Tuesday	Wednesday	Thursday	Friday
Stored Tape File— "Grandfather"	A	B	C	A	B
Input Master Tape —"Father"	B	C	A	B	C
Data	Monday Transactions	Tuesday Transactions	Wednesday Transactions	Thursday Transactions	Friday Transactions
Output Master Tape —"Son"	C	A	B	C	A

time file (B) is preserved and stored apart. Of course, many concerns
like to preserve several generations of important records, although only
one generation is shown being saved in the exhibit. If an accident occurred during processing on Tuesday, say, so that the current master
(C) was lost, the situation could be retrieved, after repairing the cause
of the accident, by running master file B with the two sets of transactions
for Monday and Tuesday.

It should be noted that the record preservation regulations of the
Internal Revenue Service may impose a more severe constraint on the
operations of the computer system than the needs of management or
the requirements of the system itself. In a 1964 revenue procedure,
the IRS required that the general ledger and any subsidiary ledgers
be written out in printed form at tax reporting periods, that vouchers
and transactions should be traceable through the system, and documentation for the behavior of the system must be preserved and available.
The procedure also pointed out that the record retention period rules
are not affected in any way through the computerization of the system.
The same duration of records is called for whether the system is computerized or conventional manually operated. It is to be hoped that
these severe constraints will be relaxed, as both IRS and taxpayers become better acquainted with computer techniques and capabilities.

Techniques of data control

The fundamental principles underlying the techniques of control do
not change with computerization, any more than the principles of internal control change. However, the procedures required to implement

these principles are changed, at least in appearance, when a computer is used. We shall first briefly examine the purposes of data control, and then look at some of the procedures.

It is desirable, in any accounting system, to ensure the following about the data being processed:

1) That each datum is correct and complete.
2) That all transactions or events have been recorded.
3) That nothing has been recorded which should not have been.
4) That the integrity of a set of data is preserved from the point of first recording onward.
5) That mistakes made at any point in the process are rectified as soon as possible after they happen.
6) That some form of backup systems and files should exist which ensure that no mistakes, however serious, can destroy or permanently damage the vital records of the business.

Notice that there is no mention of the computer in the above list, and that the goals and purposes are common to any system. In our discussion of the procedures, however, we shall be emphasizing those purposes which are achieved differently in a computer than in a manual system. For example, purpose (2), ensuring that all transactions have been recorded, must be achieved the same way with a computer as with a manual system, so we shall not discuss it in this chapter. Also, we have discussed purpose (6) earlier in this chapter. We must, therefore, consider procedures to ensure the correctness and validity of a record and the integrity of a data set or file.

In seeking to ensure that the original data are properly recorded, it is important to maintain control over the source documents themselves. Source documents should be prenumbered, preferably before their arrival in the company's premises. In addition, all such source documents should be preserved even if errors have been made in completing them. If these two precautions are taken, proper control over the source documents may be exercised by (1) periodic inspection of the rate of consumption of source document blanks to ensure that usage is reasonable and that no large-scale theft of documents has occurred, (2) verification that the actual user of the source document was the only person seeking to obtain copies of it, and (3) a periodic sort of the source documents into prenumbered order to ensure that there are no duplicates and that there are no missing copies which have not been processed within a reasonable time. By maintaining this sort of control over the source document and by careful surveillance over the personnel using it, the possibility of introducing inaccurate or unauthorized data into the system will be reduced.

In some instances, it may also be possible and desirable to control access to the point of data entry. This is clearly not a practical solution where the data are entered on the floor of a retail store to which access has to be unlimited. However, in cases where data are entered through a terminal (as in the automatic time recorder devices mentioned earlier) control over the physical availability of the terminal is desirable. This control need not take the form of physical policing but should involve limiting the number of legitimate user identification badges which can be accepted from a particular terminal device.

The next step in the recording of source data is the transference of information to a computer-sensitive medium. Normally, this would take the form of a keyboard operation either to punch cards or directly onto a computer tape. It is strongly recommended that once the cards have been punched they should be verified using a verification machine and another operator. Although verification is an expensive process, essentially doubling the cost of preparing the input medium, it effects a noticeable reduction in the number of errors. Various experiments have been performed to investigate the efficiency and effectiveness of key punching with verification versus key punching without verification. As key verification is essentially a complete repetition of the key punching process, it is not surprising that almost all these experiments showed that the cost of key punching plus verification was double the cost of key punching alone. However, addition of the verification step reduced the number of errors passed by factors ranging upward from fifty. Even the least impressive result, a fifty times increase in accuracy for a two times increase in cost will often be worthwhile.

Another method for verification of input data is to load the cards into a listing machine and obtain a printed list of what has been recorded by the key puncher. If the number of input media is substantial, it is not easy to obtain a clear measure of difficulties or errors simply by scanning such a list. However, if some of the cards have been mispunched so that a data field is out of its proper location, the listing may reveal that problem.

There are a number of shortcuts which may be taken to ensure the proper recording of source data on computer-sensitive media. The shortcuts usually involve the use of the computer to prepare its own input as far as possible. For example, in some applications it is possible to prepare input cards with most of the data prepunched, the variable data only being added. This will be possible, for example, in an hourly employee's time card system in which the only variable data is the number of hours worked at normal and at overtime rates. The name, social security number, and other data pertaining to the employee normally carries forward from one period to the next and can be prepunched by the machine. This would reduce the amount of key punching to two fields out of a complete card, with obvious savings in terms of error prevention. In other cases it is possible to record input to the system on an exceptional basis only, the assumption being that the remainder will carry forward unaltered. For instance, the updating of an accounts receivable name and address master file would not normally involve the repetitive input of the entire file but would only involve the addition of any new customers and the deletion of any with whom relations have terminated. The same basic concept may apply to the carry forward of salaried employees, accounts payable and a master file for slow-moving inventory. A third shortcut to the input process is the use of prepunched returnable documents. In this instance, the computer prepares a card with all necessary data on it. This is mailed to the customer as part of his bill for a period. He is expected to return the prepunched card with a check for the balance, and this card can be fed directly into the machine once the check has been compared with it. By this means, the cash receipts posting can be done with no key punching at all, provided customers send back only the amount billed to them.

The steps listed above seek to promote accurate recording of data. As such, they contribute toward purposes 1, 3, and 5 listed earlier in this section. We must next consider purpose 4, preserving the integrity of a data set or file. Once a group of transactions has been recorded and punched, we want to ensure that the group does not get changed in any way prior to processing.

When the data are supplied to the machine in batches, certain controls can be added to each batch. The first and most obvious of such controls is a record count. This simply involves adding up the number of transactions which are being fed to the machine and adding an extra record to the end of the list which has the total punched on it. The machine, of course, can be programmed to verify exactly that number of records is processed. For similar reasons batch totals and hash totals are frequently employed. A batch total might be used, for example, when a number of invoices are being fed into the machine. The batch total is simply the result of adding the dollar amounts of all the invoices together and appending a card with the total to the back. The machine, of course, will be programmed to add up the dollar amounts on the invoices. The total is compared with the total read in and a suitable error message is printed if any difference should arise. A hash total is essentially similar to a batch total, except that the numbers added together are not meaningfully related one to another. For example a hash total might be composed of the sum of the date of the transaction, a customer number, and the dollar amount. Clearly, the sum of these three numbers is meaningless on its own, but when compared with a similarly prepared hash total for all transaction records it may reveal an error in any one of the three fields listed. The best results are achieved if the hash or batch totals are added to the set of records by the originating department. If the batch totals are added at the source, the transmission of the batch to the keypunching department and from there to the computer room can be verified. If the batch total is not added until the keypunching step, the absence of records lost on the way to the keypunch department will not be spotted by batch total error.

The designer of the system should give considerable thought to the various error messages he wishes to print if a control total is violated. By careful design of the error messages, the system designer can help a great deal in speeding up the repair work. The messages should, if possible, identify the recipient (the person, or at least the department, who made the mistake) and the location and type of the mistake. Notification of the error should also be directed to supervisors, so that they are aware of problems within their jurisdiction.

Another elementary precaution in controlling a batch of source data is labelling, so that a computer-sensitive medium can be identified by inspection. Suppose, for example, no label has been attached to a file, such as a tape. The only way someone finding this tape can find out what is on it is by printing it out, a prolonged and quite costly process. It may even be risky in that during the printing some or all of the contents of the tape file may be damaged. It is common for files of data to be transmitted from one part of a business enterprise to another, especially now that large centralized computer systems are being installed in many businesses. It is highly important that suitable transmission documents be prepared advising the sender, the carrier, and the recipient what the various files are.

It is also important to see that the error correction procedures are *used*. There must be some individual whose responsibility includes a positive comparison of the totals, for instance, of all the source documents with the totals printed out by the computer later. Otherwise, the error printing procedure involving the machine itself will be completely wasted. Similarly, there is no purpose whatever at having a verification step in the keypunching process, if the operators, on discovering an error, simply shuffle the defective record in with the correct data for further processing, without doing anything to rectify the mistake. There will be natural tendency for the operators to do exactly this, unless some positive controls are maintained over their activities.

Transmission control in the case of an on-line data processing system is a much simpler though more expensive process. By definition, the input device is connected directly to the computer itself. The machine can then exercise suitable controls immediately as the data are fed in by the operator. In effect, the keypunch operator is connected directly to the computer which can be programmed to impose checks on her activities. The machine, for example, may ask the operator to retype a customer's account number if her first version had been compared with the list of legitimate numbers and found missing. Again, the machine may ask the operator to supply the number of pieces of merchandise which are to be sent to a customer and may itself supply the price and extend the total figures. The disadvantage of an on-line system, of course, is that if the operator tells the machine that 110 units have been supplied to a customer when the actual number is 1100, the machine will be unable to dispute this unless the shipping department also inputs data which can be used for comparative purposes. The need for accuracy and control in an on-line system is just as great as in a conventional batch process, although that control will take quite different forms.

In addition to the procedures listed above for data control and file preservation, there are a number of further steps which can be taken in furtherance of purpose number 1, that each datum be correct. These procedures can be applied to the contents of a single record, to find out if these contents are reasonable. The procedures are the combination check, existence checks, and limit checks.

A combination check is intended to verify that a relationship between the data in two fields is within the bounds of possibility. For example, if a customer is located in Georgia, the salesman servicing the account should not be in Seattle (in normal circumstances). Combination checks are unique to each application and to be devised to solve a particular problem in a particular program. A completeness check, on the other hand, is a much simpler concept involving a verification that all fields on the data input record are occupied. It may be impossible to process a sale record without the customer number, the date, the product number and the dollar amount. The completeness check would verify that each of the fields representing these items was occupied by a nonzero number. Obviously, these controls do not guarantee correct input—all they do is prevent the input of data which are certainly wrong.

It is particularly important that the user build existence checks into his program. An existence check verifies a customer number by comparing it with a table of complete and verified customer numbers. Similar existence checks can be applied to salesman number, product numbers, and territories. The same basic approach can be applied to dates. The day of the month, for example, must never exceed 31, while the month must be no more than 12.

The most powerful data control which can be built into a program is a reasonableness or limit check. In its grossest form, a limit check verifies that a number is possible and is, therefore, similar to an existence check. For example, the hours worked during a week by a particular employee must never be greater than 168 which is the actual number of hours in a week. In general, however, the employees will not have worked anything like this amount. The idea of a limit check is to cause different action to be taken if particular limit levels are exceeded. For instance, the processing of a payroll record might be suspended if the record suggested that an employee had worked more than, say, 90 hours in that particular week, a figure which would be unreasonable in most organizations. Similarly, a record might be printed out for the attention of management for any employee working more than 60 hours, but the processing of a check for such an employee might continue. Of course, all employees working more than a standard week are likely to be involved in overtime, so another limit check would have to be installed in the program at the standard working hour level. Management might also be interested in having a list of all employees who work less than, say, 30 hours in a particular pay period. The organization and the devising of such a limit check system is an important managerial function in a computerized environment.

If at all possible, the processing program should not cease to operate when an error is located in a data set. A special output file should be set up, connected directly to the output channels of the computer; toward which error messages, violations of limit checks, differences in batch totals, combination checks and the like should be directed as they are noted. The program may, therefore, continue processing the correct data pending management review of the wrong material. Of course, if the error which has been located makes it impossible for the job to run correctly, the entire run may be suspended after all data errors have been observed and printed out for correction.

Using the computer to audit

During the second half of the decade of the 1960s, auditors began to realize how useful computers could be to them. As more and more companies converted their records to computers, an everincreasing por-tion of the records subject to audit inspection came to be computer-sensi-tive. In turn, this implied that the auditor had to arrange for the repro-duction of these records on paper if he wanted to inspect them by conventional means. Gradually, auditors came to realize that it would be more efficient if they left the records on magnetic tapes or discs and changed their techniques of inspection. In seeking to verify that a computer program was handling data correctly, operators began using "test decks" of dummy transactions, and these are now standard tools. In attempting to test the quality of a file of records, auditors began to use computer programs of their own to retrieve information for inspec-tion. Some of these programs were written specially for a particular client organization, while others were written more generally so that the same set of audit functions could be used on the records of several clients. In the two remaining sections of this chapter, we shall consider how test decks and audit programs may be used to help both the internal and external auditor.

The purpose and use of test decks

The primary purpose of a test deck is to ensure that the programs developed for manipulating business data do in fact correctly process all data supplied to them. In addition, a test deck should be designed to check that adequate controls have been built into the program to prevent the processing of erroneous data and to avoid the misprocessing of correct data. The system reviewer will prepare and analyze a series of fictitious but typical transactions by hand, so that he knows what answers ought to be obtained when they are processed. He will then submit his test data in keypunch form for processing, preferably at the same time as, or immediately after, a routine run of the program. The resulting output can then be studied, and any difference between the system answers and those prepared manually by the reviewer can be reconciled. If no reconciliation is feasible, either the manual test or the processing routine is wrong, and appropriate steps to correct the errors must be taken. The designer of a test deck must establish that all probable errors are included in his test deck so that the error controls in the programs can be tested properly. It is also advisable to include some unlikely but possible transactions to find out whether appropriate notification of unusual items are provided for management review. The reviewer should also ensure that his deck includes as many combinations of errors as seem reasonable because a program which handles individual mistakes correctly may be unable to handle two or more at the same time.

If a program is able to deal accurately with the various errors and tests built into a carefully prepared test deck, it is likely to be a sound and correct program. The test deck method permits the reviewer to inspect each program more thoroughly than the alternative methods in common use.

The external reviewer should ensure that the program he is testing is the one which is used by the organization in day-to-day routine. Running the test data immediately after a routine job can be a good way of doing this, especially if the auditor brings his test data during an unscheduled and unannounced visit. Alternatively, the reviewer may insist upon a recompilation of the program and a mechanical comparison of the resulting machine code deck with the machine code deck being used by the company at the time of an unscheduled visit.

An additional problem can sometimes arise when the reviewer of the system wishes to run his test deck but cannot obtain a master file copy to run with it. The typical business computer application involves processing a data file against a master file of some sort, whether it be accounts receivable, accounts payable, inventory, or whatever. Such a master file will normally be available only if careful preparations are made in advance to have a copy made and preserved for audit use. The problem is not too severe in a batch operated system but can be very awkward when the system is on-line. In an on-line system, the master files are permanently stored in the disc packs of the system and are accessible at any time by any qualified user. Therefore, if the test data are provided by the reviewer to such an on-line system, and if they are realistic, they will be treated exactly as if they were live data and will be posted to the appropriate accounts. Obviously, it would be most unsatisfactory if such test data were permitted to remain in a customer account. Further, it can be a technically complex operation to remove them again. In general, the auditor would be well advised to set up a system of dummy accounts for testing such an on-line procedure so that the *real* accounts were not affected.

The computer as an audit tool

A computer can be used to perform three types of routine auditing work if the auditor is willing to write programs, namely to perform routine data verifications, to carry out special searches, and to retrieve appropriate samples for testing.

The routine checking aspect of the computer's contribution to auditing is extremely straight forward and involves writing a simple program or series of programs to verify data. The typical computer user has a substantial proportion of his data on tape files. In order to verify that all the items in this file have been included in a summation, the auditor must either insist on a printout which can be summed manually or he must write (or have written) a program to do the summation and cross-footing. It is clearly in the interest of the client as a matter of efficiency and in the interest of the auditor as a labor saving process to use the computer to check computer-sensitive records as far as possible.

The auditor may also employ the computer to perform numerous special investigations on his behalf. The extent of this type of application is limited only by the computer system of the client and the ingenuity of the auditor. As a couple of examples, which are certainly not intended to be exhaustive, the techniques of master comparison and accounting method change evaluation may be mentioned. The master comparison technique requires the auditor to obtain two copies of a given master file as at different dates. A special search program may be prepared to compare them and print differences. In an inventory application, for instance, net changes in particular items of inventory may be spotted by comparison of the inventory master at the beginning and at the end of the month. The listed changes could be subjected to further audit procedures as desired. The same procedure could be applied to any master file such as a payroll, customers, suppliers, or stockholder register file. Testing the materiality of a change in accounting methods may also be facilitated by use of the computer. A client, for example, may elect to change his depreciation method from straight-line to sum-of-the-years digits in a particular year. The external auditor is required to report on the significance of this switch and can only comment on its materiality if he knows what the old method would have produced in the way of depreciation charges. In the case of businesses with substantial capital investments, the comparative investigation could be an enormous task and a specially written computer program might prove to be the most economical way of performing this review.

Another valuable contribution which a computer can make as a tool of audit management is in selecting audit samples. Commonly, an auditor is involved in testing the validity of a set of data. In performing this validation, the auditor commonly has to test some of the actual records to find out whether the summaries or control totals are reliable. When the records are maintained in computer-sensitive form, the auditor has to choose a method of sampling appropriate to that environment. The computer can pull a sample according to any specifications devised by the auditor, printing only those parts of the sample which require visual inspection. This procedure is faster than manual sampling, cheaper to the client, and produces a valid sample if the auditor describes his requirement correctly. However, in order to achieve this cost saving, the auditor has to have programs which will perform these searches and sample selection procedures. It will not generally be worthwhile to create these fairly complex programs for a single application to a single client. But if an auditor has several such clients, or one client with many of its records maintained in computer sensitive form, the development of special purpose sampling programs may be economically feasible.

A sample can be drawn from a population according to an attribute or a selection procedure. Estimation sampling for attributes is a valuable part of the auditing process. If the data are stored in computer sensitive form, a computer program can search for any attribute efficiently and quickly. For example, an auditor may be interested in obtaining a list of all customers whose balances are in excess of their credit limit, or he may wish a list of customers who have balances in excess of a previously determined level. Once the auditor has specified his requirements, the computer can produce a list according to these requirements more carefully and more rapidly than a manual procedure could. With this information, the auditor is in a much stronger position to evaluate the quality of data upon which his opinion must be expressed. It is not appropriate here to discuss the techniques of statistical sampling. It is enough to observe that the techniques of statistical sampling have been widely accepted as powerful aids to the auditor and that a computer can assist in implementing these tools in a practical way in a computerized accounting system.

To use a computer in an audit, the outside auditor must have the analytical programs which will permit him to study the records in the client's computer file records. There are three ways in which such programs can be made available. The client's staff may have prepared a number of analytical routines for their own use. Certain inventory valuation problems, for example, may be solved by special purpose computer programs for inventory control which the company staff may have created. The auditor may be able to employ these in his own operation. Second, the auditor may create special purpose auditing programs for use with a particular company data file on a particular computer. Normally, he will not be able to use these programs elsewhere. This approach is a very expensive way of performing an audit, as the effectiveness of the audit program can only be weighed against the cost of a manual search through the same data set. Unless the data set is very large, it is probable that this method would not be economical. The procedure, therefore, is likely to be used only in connection with very major companies.

There are certain audit procedures which will differ from business to business only in format or layout of the file which is being sampled. A sampling program developed for one such business could be used in another with only minor adjustments. Obviously, if the auditor can do this he is much better off. Some auditors, notably the larger professional firms, have developed a series of general purpose auditing programs which can be applied to any client data set, permitting standard audit verification procedures on each set. The general design and outline of these general purpose audit programs varies, of course, from firm to firm. In general, however, the packages include a series of routines each of which performs a useful function from an audit standpoint. One routine might sum and cross-foot, another might select a sample, and so on. Further routines usually include summarization, abstraction, and arithmetic procedures. Several of the general purpose programs require a preliminary rearrangement of the records in the file. This rearrangement reshapes each record into a standard format, upon which all the other audit routines have been programmed to operate. Experience thus far suggests that these general purpose audit programs have considerably speeded and improved the routine audit work in computerized systems.

24 INTRODUCTION TO OPERATIONS RESEARCH

The use made of operations research (OR) varies widely from one company to another. Also, the use made of these concepts within the financial and accounting areas is independent of the level of acceptance of OR in other parts of the business. Some controllers, therefore, have had no exposure to OR at all, while others must supervise the OR group directly, and must therefore know a great deal, including technical details, about OR. In this chapter and the next, we shall examine OR from the viewpoint of one who has not yet been affected by it, but who wishes to learn what it is. We shall also examine, in more detail, two of the techniques which have proved useful in the finance and accounting fields, namely linear programming and simulation.

Operational research is the attack of modern science on complex problems arising in the direction and management of large systems of men, machines, materials, and money in industry, business, government, and defense. Its distinctive approach is to develop a scientific model of the system, incorporating measurements of factors such as chance and risk, with which to predict and compare the outcomes of alternative decisions, strategies or controls. The purpose is to help management determine its policy and actions scientifically.

The above definition was developed by the Operational Research Society of Great Britain as a description of the concept. Similar definitions have been put forward by other professional groups, including the Operations Research Society of America. The definition emphasizes the scientific aspects of OR work; the use of models is one aspect of this, but the scientific approach to defining the problem is also a most important characteristic of OR.

The basic idea of the scientific method is the hypothesis-testing experiment. A phenomenon is noticed. A speculation as to its cause is developed, after refinement, into a hypothesis. An experiment is devised to establish the validity of the hypothesis and then performed. On the basis of the experimental results, the hypothesis is rejected, accepted, or revised. If revised, it may be necessary to repeat the experiment. If accepted, the hypothesis graduates to the status of a theory and is used to explain the phenomenon.

It is very difficult to carry out an experiment, of the type common in the physical sciences, in the study of business management. The expedient of trying something out, which is basically what an experiment is, can only be used in business if the manager knows that the possible losses can be tolerated. The more critical a problem is, the greater the potential loss if something goes wrong, so the experimental approach can hardly be used in such circumstances. Instead, a mathematical model developed by an OR worker may be used as a substitute for the enterprise, and may be experimented upon as often as necessary.

It has been found useful in practice to approach the very complex problems of business management by means of a team of workers instead of a single person. By bringing to bear on the issue a team representing a number of different types of training and a number of different points of view, the chances of finding a solution increase. Traditionally, a problem has been identified first as a "marketing problem" or an "accounting problem" and then referred to the appropriate specialist. In many cases, particularly those large-scale problems which OR workers have tended to consider, the problem does not lend itself to this type of categorization. No one is sure what sort of skills are going to be needed in order to reach an answer. Evidently, the more people with different skills who examine the problem the more chance there will be of finding an answer.

There are two more characteristics of OR which must be discussed in this section before we consider the problems on which OR workers have been employed. First, there is the tendency of OR workers to improve the management decision process by bettering the problem definition step; this involves ensuring that the natural boundaries of the problem are used as constraints, instead of an artificial boundary imposed by an organization chart or an imperfect initial perception of the problem's nature. Second, OR workers tend to use models in searching for the answers to their employers problems; this has already been mentioned in the definition and needs some amplification.

A major contribution that operations research has made to the development of the science of management lies in the area of problem definition. Until operations research came along, there was a tendency, particularly in well-established industries, for managers to look at one side of a problem only. A production manager might emphasize engineering and manufacturing methods as the way to solve a problem, perhaps thereby losing sight of a marketing solution of greater efficacy. An accountant might tend to emphasize cost reduction where revenue expansion could have helped more. Concurrently with the growth of operations research, there has been an increasing tendency for managers to solve problems from a more general point of view. The best solution to a problem can usually be reached only after all aspects of the problem situation have been taken into consideration.

The general idea may be illustrated using a problem originally offered by Ackoff and Rivett.[1] The management of a high-rise office building had been receiving numerous complaints about the speed of the elevators. Tenants claimed to have very long waits for them and the company engineers had established that the delays were real. The management immediately identified three possible solutions to the problem: increase the speed of the elevators, increase the number of elevators, or convert some of them into express elevators with a limited number of stops. Each of these options was costly, and the company was concerned about the profitability of the building if any of them were adopted. At a "council of war," however, none of the accountants or engineers or other managers could come up with any better alternative. A psychologist in the group, however, noted that the office workers who had been complaining often spent at least a part of the day in nonproductive activity while at their desks. Why, he asked himself, should they be upset about the delay of the elevators? He reasoned that the time wasted at their desks by the office workers, although nonproductive, was being spent *pleasantly*. The wait for the elevators, however, was not a particularly pleasant way of passing the time. He, therefore, suggested that mirrors be installed at all the elevator lobbies; this gave the ladies something to do while waiting, and also permitted the men to look at the ladies without being obvious about it. The complaints stopped at once. The solution of the problem was inexpensive and came about because the psychologist was able to define the problem better than the other managers. Instead of simply stating that the delay was too long, he observed that the users were *perceiving* the delay as too long, and set about altering their perception instead of the delay.

The above, possibly apochryphal, illustration clearly illustrates the need to use natural problem boundaries. As long as the problem was seen from an engineering viewpoint, its boundaries were being artificially curtailed. When the full nature of the problem had been perceived, however, a rapid and cheap solution became possible. The use of teams of diverse skills is obviously helpful in these cases, because it is very hard to tell in advance how a problem solution is going to be reached.

It is very common for an operations research engagement to expand considerably beyond the original problem assigned by management for the team to solve. A common area for operations research study is inventory. Company management often will be concerned about the amount

---

[1] Ackoff, R. L., and Rivett, P., *A Manager's Guide to Operations Research* (New York: Wiley & Sons, 1963), p. 20.

of money invested in inventory and will request the operations research men to examine the purchasing procedures. In many cases, of course, this can be a very worthwhile project in its own right. However, it is sometimes impossible to solve the problem as originally posed without making changes in other related areas. Rational purchasing depends on forecasting the demand for parts, which in turn depends on production inventory and work flow. Production activity in turn depends on market demand for the final product or products. It is not common now for a company to start from a market projection and proceed directly to a system of purchase orders by an automatic process, but the interdependence of these elements is undeniable. The possibility of improving any single element of the whole sequence totally independently of the rest must always be limited.

This tendency, on the part of operations research specialists, to wish to solve the whole problem, has sometimes caused friction between them and operating management. The operations research team feels unable to contribute to the fullest extent unless it is permitted to tackle the issue in all its complexity, while the manager may feel that the researcher is empire building in the process of extending his coverage to fields not originally assigned for study. The OR group and its immediate supervisors must exercise considerable care and pay close attention to the rights and responsibilities of operating managers if they believe an extension of their area of study is needed. Evidently, if the problem can be defined using its natural boundaries in the first place, the potential conflict may be avoided. This situation is quite parallel to that of the controller in performing a staff function; as long as the decision-making responsibility remains unarguably in the hands of the line manager, and the analyst confines his attention to the marshaling and analysis of the information, the assignment of responsibilities should not be a problem.

The use of models in operations research

The great majority of the problems which have been referred to operations research groups, both in industry and in military circles, have been impossible to solve by experiment. If one were to try to find the best way of scheduling production in a factory by testing every possible schedule in turn until the best one was found, the business would surely go bankrupt long before the answer had been arrived at. Many business problems are sufficiently complicated so that hypothetical reasoning will not suffice, but at the same time no experiment can be attempted. In such situations, the use of a model of some sort is a very valuable substitute for the experimental approach. A model, of course, may mean literally a scaled-down physical replica of a structure, on which tests may be made in the hope that the real structure will behave the same way. Wind-tunnel tests of aircraft models are excellent examples of this variety. Most models of business enterprises must be mathematical in nature, because the scaling process cannot be implemented.

Some early examples of models, in the sense the word is used in operations research, are to be found in the traditional theory of basic economics. The demand curve for a product which demonstrates that the demand for the item will increase as the price is reduced is such a model. It seeks to describe in terms amenable to analysis how two quantities of interest are related. The human element in the demand function for most products is a very significant factor: we cannot tell in advance what the individual buyer is going to do. Instead, we look at buyers in the mass, and hope that they will collectively conform to the model of behavior implied by the demand function. Although it is usually shown as a graph in traditional basic economics texts, the demand function could readily be written as a mathematical equation. It is in the latter form that the function is most useful in operations research applications to the business world.

If a particular business phenomenon can be described with adequate precision by means of an equation or a system of equations, the business-man is in a much stronger position to plan his future activities. He can use the equations to test out certain possible courses of action and select the course which seems most beneficial. Obviously, the business-man will not be willing to trust such a system of equations unless it has been proved capable of handling all the relevant factors. The tradi-tional demand curve, for example, would be of little value on its own. That curve attempts to relate the price to the demand and takes no account of such variables as the competitor's price, the amount spent on advertising, the market's perception of the product's quality, and so on. Nonetheless, a good measure of the price elasticity of demand would be most helpful to the executive faced with a pricing decision.

In the majority of situations, operations research workers try to find a mathematical model which will be of use to management in planning their future actions. There are several types of general purpose models in use, and, in addition, a large number of special purpose models have been created to help a particular manager handle a unique problem. We shall take a closer look at some of the former type of models later in the present chapter.

Categories of problems on which operations research methods have worked

The scientific method can, obviously, be applied to any problem what-ever. The fact is, however, that the majority of the business problems which have been tackled successfully by operations research workers have fallen within three categories. Each of these categories cover a wide variety of business functional areas but only a small part of each area. The categories are:

1. Inventory problems[2]
2. Resource allocation problems
3. Facility or queueing problems

Normally, a business executive would regard a *cash flow problem* and an *undersupply of sales staff* as being totally different types of problem. In a sense, of course, they are different, because they apply to different parts of the business enterprise and are normally under the control of different executives. An OR worker, however, might be inclined to regard the two problems as examples of a single class of problem, perhaps amenable to treatment using the same basic approach. In both cases, the problem is one of inventory. In the first instance, the manager is trying to decide how much cash he must keep in the bank to cover the bills without losing interest unnecessarily, while in the second instance, he wants to know how many salesmen he must employ in order to bring in as many orders as he wishes without having some of the salesmen idle.

Although the subjects of the two problems are quite different, the basic form is the same: How much of item X should I keep on hand? There have been many successful applications of OR techniques to inventory problems of different sorts. Some of the traditional inventory control applications have already been discussed in the chapter on inventory control. The concept of an economic order quantity is now well established in the theory and practice of inventory management, particularly in manufacturing companies. Linear programming, which will be discussed later in more detail, has also been applied to the inventory problem, as well as simulation. The basic issue in inventory problems is one of trade-off; the larger the inventory, the more it costs to carry, but the less likelihood there is of shortages, the cheaper it will be to obtain, and the longer the production runs can be. There is often an optimum level of inventory, defined as the level of inventory investment which minimizes the total overall cost from all of these competing factors.

Some additional complications in inventory problems can arise when the inventory does not consist of a single quantity or store. Many companies have a number of different warehouses, and the number of these is itself an inventory problem. Once the number has been determined, the quantities which ought to be kept in each is also an inventory problem. Also, companies may be able to choose the form in which the inventory will be maintained. If they choose to keep the inventory in

---

[2] The word inventory as used here has a special meaning, which is analogous to but not quite identical with the normal use of the term in accounting. The reader will understand both the meaning and the analogy as the discussion proceeds.

the form of raw materials, the cost of that inventory is relatively low. It will take them quite a long time, however, to produce the goods ordered by a customer. A company electing to store its inventory in the form of finished goods would be able to serve customers quickly, but would pay heavily for the availability of those goods. It is evident that an infinite numer of intermediate inventory storage methods could also be investigated.

As a specific example of the inventory problem, let us consider the size of a sales force. Clearly, the larger the number of salesmen, the greater the total compensation will be. Offsetting the cost of the salesmen is the contribution from the sales they generate. This depends on the number of calls they make in a period (which can be controlled and preplanned), and the number of calls they have to make to achieve a sale. The latter factor is not easily managed, and depends in part on the quality of the salesmen. The quality of the salesman is in turn dependent on the compensation he receives. One can quickly find himself going round in circles in attempting to solve the problem. Various attempts have been made by operations research workers to evaluate the sales per call ratio, by historical analysis, by experiment, and by simulation. Montgomery and Urban[3] cite seven models of this type in their interesting analysis of the problem.

One of the commonest and most successful classes of applications of operations research has been to resource allocation problems. The typical business is constrained in its operations by a shortage of resources, whether these be cash, inventory, plant, or people. The manager has to decide what to do with the limited supplies available and usually will have a criterion for allocating the resources to possible uses. In certain cases, however, the allocation problem is a very complicated one, because of the number of types of resource and the number of possible uses, and because of the complexity of the relationships among these elements. Mathematical programming methods have proved quite successful in solving allocation problems, where the criterion for deciding can be specified precisely. We shall be looking at an application of linear programming to an allocation problem shortly. The other more complicated types of mathematical programming techniques are quadratic programming and dynamic programming; these more complex methods can handle more difficult situations than a linear program can, but serve a similar basic purpose. As we shall see, the linear program is confined to cases where a linear relationship between the variables can reasonably be assumed. The other methods permit this constraint to be relaxed in various ways.

One successful application of operations research to resource allocation problems has been in the management of an oil refinery. The man-

---

[3] David B. Montgomery and Glen L. Urban, *Management Science in Marketing* (Englewood Cliffs, N.J.: Prentice-Hall, 1969), p. 247ff.

ager of the refinery has certain crude oil products available to him. By setting the controls which govern the operation of the refinery, he has the choice of producing a wide range of mixtures of saleable oil products, ranging from heavy materials like asphalt through kerosene to light fuels such as gasoline. He is faced regularly with the problem of deciding on an optimal output mix. The technical character of an oil refinery happens to lend itself well to the use of a linear programming model. Such a model permits him to use the profit objective as a criterion to select that mix of outputs which will make the best possible use of the crude oil.

Another type of problem which OR methods have helped to solve is the facility problem. Sometimes, this class is known as the queueing problem. The company wishes to know how many of a particular kind of facility it should offer in order to conduct its business most profitably. The facility could be anything which serves "customers" in sequence. Examples would include the checkout desks in a supermarket, the pumps in a gas station, and the toll booths on a turnpike. Larger scale problems of the same basic type include the determination of the number of runways at an airport, deciding on the number of million-dollar printing presses to install at a newspaper office, or analyzing the effect of adding another lane to a turnpike. Other related problems may also be studied, such as estimating the length of time the typical customer is going to have to wait before being served. The technique used to solve this sort of problem is simulation; although we shall be looking at simulations in the next chapter, they will be of a different sort. The simulations most useful in the solution of queueing problems are physical simulations, in which the movements of people or cars or other objects are the entities within the model. Special computer languages have been developed to deal with this sort of situation, SIMSCRIPT and GPSS being examples of these languages. In the following chapter, we shall be looking at financial simulations, in which the flows are not physical but financial. The basic concept is not different, however.

A variation on the general type of queueing problem is the special case of sequencing. In many industries, particularly the construction and defense businesses, a single job consists of many different and substantial subsidiary operations. Each of these operations must dovetail with the others, so that the whole project is completed according to plan. Typically, there will be preliminary tasks that must be finished before another task can begin; the tasks must be performed by a certain time if they are not to interfere with progress on other segments of the whole project. Under these conditions, a technique called network analysis can be used. This method permits the particular circumstances of the entire project to be analyzed by a computer program and tells the manager which projects must receive the greatest attention, because they are the most likely to cause the whole project to fall behind plan.

The manager may elect to devote additional resources to those tasks which are critical, thereby improving the speed with which the whole project will be performed. In general, there is no point in devoting such extra resources to a task selected at random. If that task were not one of the critical group which determines the total time of the project then speeding that task up would not help. The most widely used methods of network analysis are PERT (program evaluation review technique) and CPM (the critical path method). The methods differ in their mode of operation but serve identical purposes. By permitting careful planning of the project at the outset, and by demonstrating to the manager where things have gone wrong at intervals throughout the life of the project, these methods assist materially in keeping large scale complicated projects under control.

There is no theoretical limit to the range of problems which can be 'tackled using the concepts of modern science; operations research, therefore, could in theory be applied anywhere in the business enterprise. As a practical matter, however, OR workers have tended to concentrate their attention on a narrower front. The earliest successful OR applications were in the field of inventory control and production management, and this remains the most heavily tilled field of operations research. In part, this is so because the mathematical tools first employed by OR workers were of particular effectiveness in this area. Also, managers have come to associate OR with the production management area, thereby losing sight of the opportunities to apply OR methods in other fields. The reason for the early concentration on inventory and production can hardly be specified in any simple manner; an important factor, however, is certainly the relative definability of the variables in this area, compared with such fields as market analysis, consumer behavior study, stock market analysis, and the like. There were, to be sure, a large number of variables in the production process; however, these variables could be studied in semicontrollable situations, and the behavior of each could be described with some accuracy. Even the less certain variables, such as delay between ordering a part and receiving delivery of it, can be analysed through repeated observation, and a distribution of the quantity derived. This can, of course, be done with market variables also, but the uncertainties are greater and the resulting models have tended to be less than perfect.

An operations research investigation is likely to be an expensive undertaking. This is certainly not to say that it will be unprofitable, but it is likely to involve a substantial investment of time and money before the benefits accrue. It is not at all uncommon for a team of four or five highly paid men to take a couple of years over a major problem, and many investigations are much larger than this. Accordingly, it is desirable that OR methods be attempted only in cases where the opportunities for cost saving are substantial. It is incumbent upon the management of the company to direct the OR team toward projects of high potential payoff, though the team itself may find that they must extend their investigation beyond the initial confines of their assignment in order to get results. A case has been recorded of a company which assigned its first operations research men to study costs of distribution. Distribution amounted to approximately one tenth of one percent of sales and consisted almost entirely of postage charges. The savings the OR man was able to suggest were not substantial, and the company management concluded that operations research was not a profitable activity and closed the department. In short, if a manager desires to cause the OR group to fail, he can do it very effectively by not letting them touch significant segments on the business.

Some operations research projects have been outstandingly successful, others have failed completely. The reasons for the failures can usually be traced to one of four causes. The operations research group, may, of course, be less than competent. The variables involved in the problem may be so little understood that a model cannot be created which will interrelate them on a realistic basis. The management of the company may confine the study within too narrow limits, so that the interface between the model and the environment surrounding it is both artificial and intractable. The payoff from the project may not be equal to the cost of it, despite predictions to the contrary at the outset. Of these four difficulties, the second is the technically limiting factor on the expansion of OR application. One cannot build an effective model when he does not know how to set up the equations. In practice, however, the most common reason for failure has been the third. If company management in its anxiety to prevent the cost of the project from rising thereby preventing the OR team from studying a crucial element, the entire study may be invalidated. It is often difficult indeed to tell when a manager is being cautious and when he is being overcautious in this regard. A strategy that has been used with some success in a number of companies is to set up a series of observation points throughout the life of the project, each of which may produce useable results. If the project can be terminated at any such stage, the manager may be able to reconcile himself to supporting a large project, which he would refuse to sponsor if the whole thing had to be taken as a single package.

A closer look at linear programming[4]

The remainder of this chapter is devoted to an introductory discussion of the technique called linear programming. The basic characteristics

---

[4] The following material on linear programming is based on an earlier work, "An Approach to the Solution of Allocation Problems," prepared at the Harvard University Graduate School of Business Administration for use in class discussion and not as a definitive report of research or conceptual statement. Copyright ©

of a linear programming solution to a problem will be demonstrated, without going any further into the technique than is essential. The reader should note that any practical application of linear programming in a business setting would almost certainly be done using a standard computer program; the solution of a linear program by manual methods is a most tedious business, but a computerized solution is fairly straightforward.

Sometimes in business, the opportunity to earn profits is restricted by a lack of resources, and nothing can be done in the short term to alter the amount of resources available. In these cases, the businessman will want to make the best possible use out of his limited resources. Usually, the criterion which he uses to guide him in the allocation of resources among alternative opportunities will be profit, which he wants to maximize, or costs which he wants to minimize. We shall give a number of examples of this type of problem and formulate them for solution in order to see more clearly what their general characteristics are.

Example 1: A product mix problem

Mr. Hennessy, a manufacturer of machine tools, is planning to exhibit a lathe and a milling machine in a forthcoming national trade exhibition. He has decided that these machines will be shown in operation, and that three giveaway products—an ash tray, a paperweight, and a metal ruler—will be produced throughout the exhibition. He is anxious to keep both of the machines in action for the full 100 hours of the exhibition. The machining times per unit for the various products are:

	Lathe time (hrs)	Milling time (hrs)
Ash tray	0.1	0.4
Paperweight	0.3	0.2
Rate	0.2	0.4

All the "giveaways" use an expensive form of brass stock, and Mr. Hennessy would prefer to minimize the amount of brass that he must use to keep the machines busy for the full 100 hours. The ash tray uses 0.2 pounds per unit of brass stock, the paperweight uses 0.3 pounds per unit, and the ruler uses 0.1 pounds per unit.

Mr. Hennessy has to make *choices;* he has to decide how many of each of the three products mo make. His actions are subject to the *constraint* that he wishes to keep both machines in operation for the whole of the exhibition. There is a *criterion* by which to judge the appropriateness of the decisions made; namely, the amount of brass consumed must be kept to a minimum.

1964 by the President and Fellows of Harvard College, whose specific permission to use it here is appreciated.

The problem can be set out in a table (see Figure 24–1). There is a column for each of the choices open to Mr. Hennessy. There is a row for each of the constraints on his choices, and a further row for data about the criterion by which the choices are to be judged.

Figure 24–1

	Ash tray	Paperweight	Ruler		Total time available (hr)
Constraints:					
Lathe time..........	0.1	0.3	0.2	=	100
Milling time	0.4	0.2	0.4	=	100
Criterion:					
Brass usage (lb.)	0.2	0.3	0.1		

The numbers in the rows are the *rates* at which the limited lathe time and milling time are used per unit of each choice. In the columns, all the information about the choices is shown: the amount of time a unit will use on each machine and, the amount of brass each unit will consume. It is important to note that the table can be made up only if *every* ash tray uses up 0.1 hour of lathe time, *every* paperweight uses up 0.2 hour of milling time, and so on. If the rates at which the products use up the constraints cannot be stated as an exact number or very reliable average, the linear programming approach will not apply. Also, the approach will not apply unless the criterion value can be stated exactly. In this case the criterion value is the brass usage of each of the finished products, and *each* ash tray must use 0.2 lb. of brass stock.

Example 2: A nutrition balancing problem

In the livestock business, feeding stock in the most economical manner possible is an important and continuous problem. The animals have to receive certain nutrients, which are available in varying quantities in the commodities used. The nutrient requirement per day per animal is as follows: protein required 2 lbs., roughage required 6 lbs., and carbohydrate required 8 lbs. The commodities available are *oats,* which contain 0.2 lb. of roughage and 0.1 lb. of carbohydrates per pound and costs 1½ cents a pound. *Corn,* which contains 0.2 lb. of protein, 0.1 lb. of roughage, and 0.3 lb. of carbohydrates per pound and costs 2 cents per pound. *Alfalfa* which contains 0.1 lb. of protein, 0.4 lb. of roughage, and 0.2 lb. of carbohydrate per pound and costs 1 cent per pound. And *linseed oil meal* which contains 0.5 lb. of protein and 0.1 lb. of roughage and costs 5 cents per pound. Once again, we can set up a table (see Figure 24–2). A column is allotted to each choice, namely, each of the foods to be purchased, and a row to each constraint, namely, each nutrient. The criterion, which is the cost of the mix, is represented by the row of unit costs.

Figure 24–2

	Choices				
	Oats	Linseed meal	Corn	Alfalfa	Requirement per animal per day
Constraints:					
Protein (lb.).	0	0.5	0.2	0.1	at least 2.0
Roughage (lb.).	0.2	0.1	0.1	0.4	at least 6.0
Carbohydrate (lb.). . . .	0.1	0	0.3	0.2	at least 8.0
Criterion:					
Cost per pound (in cents)	1 1/2	5	2	1	

As before, it has been possible in this case to specify the *choices* open to the decision maker as well as to specify the *constraints*, (in this case the requirement of each class of nutrient that must be fed to an animal in a day). It has been possible also to state that *every* pound of oats contains 0.2 pound of roughage, and so on, in such a way that the direct proportionality exists between the amount of oats and the amount of roughage obtained. Finally, we have also been able to specify the cost of each choice.

This situation differs from the previous one in that the total requirement of each nutrient may be exceeded, though it must not fall below the amount specified. The column at the right shows the smallest total that is permissible under the constraints.

Example 3: A warehouse supply problem

The H.J. Heinz Company manufactures ketchup in a number of plants scattered across the United States and distributes this ketchup from about 70 warehouses located in all parts of the country. In 1953, the company could sell all of the ketchup that it could produce, so ketchup was allocated to the warehouses proportionately to their demand. The total amount allocated amounted to the total capacity of the plants. Management wished to supply these requirements at the lowest possible cost of freight. However, as capacity of plants in the West exceeded demand of warehouses there, while the reverse was true in the East, a substantial amount had to be shipped eastward. The cost of supplying each warehouse from each plant was known.

The choice open to management is the selection of the routes of supply to be used. The constraints on the choices are the given demands of the warehouses and the given capacities of the plants. The criterion is that the cost of transportation be kept to a minimum.

While a table could be set up for the above example, it would be very large indeed; instead, suppose that there were only two plants called X and Y, both with capacities of 50 units, and two warehouses called A and B with demands of 80 units and 20 units, respectively. If the cost of moving one unit of ketchup, which would be a truckload, along each route is known, we can set up a table as shown in Figure 24-3, where route X-A denotes the route supplying warehouse A from plant X, and so on.

Figure 24–3

	Choices				Total required or available
	X-A	X-B	Y-A	Y-B	
Constraints:					
A............	1		1		≥ 80
B............		1		1	≥ 20
X............	1	1			≤ 50
Y............			1	1	≤ 50
Criterion: cost of moving one unit along the route	$45	$60	$50	$55	

The number 1 in the first row and the first column is the *rate* at which the requirement of warehouse A is satisfied per unit of choice on route X-A. Looking along the first row, we see that the total amount brought to warehouse A from plants X and Y must not be less than 80 units; the third row tells us that the total amount shipped from plant X must not exceed 50 units, which is the capacity of the plant.

In this situation, the sense is different between the first two and the last two constraints, in that the amount to be delivered to the warehouse must not be less than the amount specified, while the amount shipped from the plants cannot exceed their capacities.

General Characteristics of the Problem

When a problem is such that:

1. The decision maker has to decide among choices
2. The choices are subject to constraints
3. The selection among the choices is made according to some criterion.
   and
4. One can construct a table of the form we have shown in the examples, then the problem is soluble by linear programming.

The decision maker has to decide among choices. He has open to him a number of possible courses of action, a number of possible uses of the resources he has at his command, and he must decide which of them to adopt, or, more typically, which combination of the choices to adopt.

The choices are subject to constraints. There must be certain boundaries on available courses of action open to the decision maker. In the first example, the two machines had to be kept in operation for the full length of the exhibition. For linear programming to be applicable, the constraint must be specified exactly. The amount of the constraint must either be known with certainty or the decision maker must be willing to treat it as if it were known with certainty. The 100-hour constraint in example 1 is a specific and exact figure, and the decision maker was willing to use that number in the calculation.

The selection among the choices is made according to some criterion. It is necessary to specify two things about the criterion. First of all, it must be possible to assign a fixed proportion of the criterion to a unit of each of the choices; for example, *every* ash tray in example 1 used up 0.2 pounds of brass stock, and *every* unit of ketchup transported along route X-A in example 3 cost $45. Second, it must be possible to combine the criterion for each choice with those for other choices to arrive at an objective function. For example, the objective function in example 1, if A were the number of ash trays, P the number of paperweights, and R the number of rulers, would be

$$0.2A + 0.3P + 0.1R$$

which would be the amount Mr. Hennessy wishes to keep to a minimum.

One must be able to construct a table. This implies that it must be possible to put single fixed numbers in the table, which in turn implies that the usage of constraints must be directly proportional to the number of units of each choice. In example 2, it must be possible to state that there are 0.2 pound of roughage in *every* pound of oats. In Example 1, *every* ash tray must use up 0.1 hour of lathe time. If the problem was such that the first 100 ash trays took 0.1 hours each, the second 100 took 0.09 hours each, and so on, there is no longer a constant ratio between usage of constraint and number of units produced, and the methods of linear programming would not apply. There are certain other techniques which can be applied to such a situation, which are beyond the scope of this book.

How linear programming works: A simplified description

To illustrate an approach to solving linear programming problems, we shall take a simple example and follow it through towards a solution.

The tabular approach will be illustrated; although for reasons for clarity, the example is also considered graphically.

Consider a businessman, who is trying to decide how many of each of his two styles of ladies hats he should make in the coming period, before and during which no changes in capacity will be possible. The hats are identical in basic structure, but one of them has a feather in it, while the other has a large ribbon, which is made out of the same material as the rest of the hat.

He has enough material to make 250 feathered hats, or 200 ribboned hats, or any combination between the two. There are 200 feathers in stock, and one is used for each feathered hat. Because of the relative complexity of the process of tying the ribbon, the amount of labor time available will permit the creation of either 300 feathered hats or 150 ribboned hats. While feathered hats are in fashion and can be sold in unlimited quantities, the demand for ribboned hats will only amount to 125. The contribution per feathered hats amounts to $3, while that for ribboned hats is $4.50. The objective of the businessman is to maximize his total contribution.

We can set up a table (Figure 24–4) of the same form as that in the earlier examples.

Figure 24–4

	Feathered hats	Ribboned hats	Total capacity (percent)
Contribution	$3.00	$4.50	
Material	$\frac{100}{250}$	$\frac{100}{200}$	100
Feathers	$\frac{100}{200}$	0	100
Labor	$\frac{100}{300}$	$\frac{100}{150}$	100
Demand	0	$\frac{100}{125}$	100

The numbers enclosed in the rectangle represent the percentage of each total capacity used by one hat, e.g., one feathered hat uses up 100/250 percent of the total available material.

To assist you in visualizing the problem being considered, a graphical presentation of the problem is shown in Figure 24–5. The production of the feathered hats is plotted vertically, that of ribboned hats is plotted

Figure 24-5

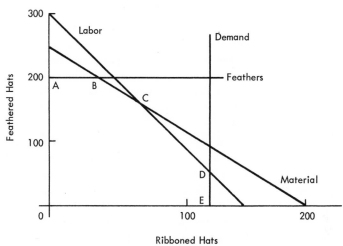

horizontally. It should be noted, however, that the great majority of problems for which linear programming is used in the real world are far too complicated to be formulated in a graph (or to be solved by hand). Most such problems are of a scale that will require an electronic computer before the computation can be attempted.

When an electronic computer is being programmed to solve linear programming problems, the tabular formulation which we have shown in all the examples is required so that the computer operator can feed the data to the computer in the correct form. From that point on, there are standard computer programs available which will produce the solutions and other relevant information. It is important that you understand what is happening "in the works," however, in order that the assumptions made are clearly understood.

We shall now follow the route that the computer program will take in arriving at the answers. First of all, a possible solution is postulated; the computer will start at the zero solution, that is, nothing being produced at all. A test is carried out, to see if the addition of one production unit results in a higher contribution total; this is seen to be the case, as both types of hat have a positive contribution per unit, and the machine will then select one possible change; let us assume that the decision is made to make feathered hats.

The largest number of feathered hats that can be made within the constraints will be considered, and then the next situation is examined. This situation is equivalent to point A on the graph. The most severe constraint here on the production of feathered hats is the availability of feathers. At this point, a further test is made; the question is asked "we are now making 200 feathered hats and no ribboned hats, can we do any better?" The computer will find that the production of a number of ribboned hats is possible, each of which will give a positive contribution, without reducing the number of feathered hats at all.

It will therefore examine the situation which arises when we produce the 200 feathered hats as before plus the greatest number of ribboned hats that are possible under the present constraints. The first constraint encountered in this case is the supply of material. We have now reached point B on the graph. It is now necessary to test for possible improvements once more.

From this situation, the analysis of the merits of an alteration is not trivial, as was the case in the first two situations. For the first time, trade-offs become necessary, in which every extra ribboned hat must be accompanied by a cut in the number of feathered hats produced. Graphically, as we move from point B towards point C, we have to give up feathered hats at a rate of 250 for every 200 ribboned hats we make, or 1.25 feathered hats per ribboned hat.

It is necessary to find out whether this trade-off is worthwhile, and the computer will do this automatically. The extra contribution received by making one extra ribboned hat would be: (a) the contribution of that ribboned hat, less (b) the contribution lost by not producing 1.25 feathered hats. This amounts to $4.50 − 1.25 × $3.00, or 0.75, a positive quantity. The computer would conclude that the move was profitable and would continue to make this substitution until the next constraint was reached. This corresponds to point C on the graph.

To arrive at the contribution total at point C, when the limiting constraints are those of labor and material, it is necessary to solve the equations for these constraints.

$$\frac{1}{2.50} F + \frac{1}{2.00} R = 100 \tag{1}$$

$$\frac{1}{3.00} F + \frac{1}{1.50} R = 100 \tag{2}$$

where F is the number of feathered hats and R the number of ribboned hats. This results in totals of $166\frac{2}{3}$ and $66\frac{2}{3}$ for the feathered hats and ribboned hats, respectively. The contribution total that results from this product mix is computed as follows:

$$\$3.00 × 166\tfrac{2}{3} + \$4.50 × 66\tfrac{2}{3} = \$800.$$

The next step in the process is to consider whether the addition of further ribboned hats to the mix would be a profitable course. This would be along the same lines as the previous analysis, but the rate of substitution is different. We now have to give up feathered hats at a rate of 300 for every 150 ribboned hats produced, or 2 feathered hats per ribboned hat; graphically, we are investigating the feasibility of moving from point C toward point D.

The additional contribution achieved by adding one ribboned hat to the mix is given by:

the contribution of the ribboned hat		$4.50
less the contribution of two feathered hats lost		
	2 × $3.00	$6.00
	Negative contribution	$1.50

As this figure is negative, it will be concluded that the addition of more ribboned hats would not be a profitable move. It can be shown that any mix of products near point C but "inside" the polygon provides a lower total contribution than the point C does, so that the ratio of production given by point C is the *optimum solution* to the problem.

If instead of making feathered hats as a first step in the computation, the decision had been taken to make ribboned hats, the same result would have been reached, but by a route corresponding to points E, D and C on the graph.

Additional information: The "shadow price"

While the decision maker is primarily interested in arriving at the optimal solution, he may also be interested in other information about the problem. In particular, he is often interested in discovering how much it is worth to him to be able to slacken the constraints on his choices; how much he should be prepared to pay for an additional unit of capacity for each of the constraints. For instance, in our last example, he might be interested in finding out the value of having available an extra unit of labor, an extra unit of material, an extra unit of demand for ribboned hats, and an extra unit of feather capacity. The value of such an extra unit is called the "shadow price" of that constraint.

It is evident that an additional unit of demand for ribboned hats or an additional unit of feather capacity would be worthless to the decision maker. These two constraints are not affecting his choices at present; they are not the limiting constraints. In fact, the shadow prices of the demand and feather constraints are zero.

In terms of the graph, we can see that the lines depicting the demand and feather constraints do not pass through the optimum solution point. On the other hand, both labor and material constraints are critical. They are the constraints which are presently imposing limits on the total contribution. Our problem now is to determine their "shadow price."

If 1 percent more material is made available, the optimal choice is still limited by the labor and material constraints. The new optimal choice is the solution of:

$$\frac{100}{250} F + \frac{100}{200} R = 101 \tag{1}$$

$$\frac{100}{300} F + \frac{100}{150} R = 100 \tag{2}$$

and is a production rate of 173⅓ feathered hats and 63⅓ ribboned hats. The new contribution is given by:

$$\$3.00 \times 173\tfrac{1}{3} + \$4.50 \times 63\tfrac{1}{3} = \$805.$$

As the previous contribution was $800, the shadow price of a 1 percent increase in material capacity amounts to $5. It should be noted that the $5 increase in contribution is made up of two separate parts, one an increase, the other a decrease. The production of feathered hats has increased from 166⅔ to 173⅓ and that of ribboned hats has gone down from 66⅔ to 63⅓. The contribution relating to this change is:

$$(173\tfrac{1}{3} - 166\tfrac{2}{3}) \times \$3 - (66\tfrac{2}{3} - 63\tfrac{1}{3}) \times \$4.50$$
$$= \$20 - \$15$$
$$= \$5$$

This emphasizes the trade-offs involved in the situation. The net gain from having the extra capacity was made up of a gain in contribution on one of the outputs together with a lesser loss in contribution on the other.[5] If a similar calculation were to be performed for the shadow price of the labor element, that would be found to be $3. This represents the gain when 161⅔ feathered and 70⅔ ribboned hats are made.

Linear programming is a technique for the optimization of the use of available capacity or other resources under certain conditions. It is an iterative method, in which the computations are repeated over and over until the best solution is finally reached.

Certain types of business problems lend themselves to solution by the methods of linear programming. The essential characteristics that make a problem soluble by linear programming techniques are linearity, (the constant ratio of a change in volume to the resulting change in capacity used), certainty, (absolute numbers being used instead of ranges), and the possibility of defining the quantity to be maximized or minimized.

Most problems of a business nature will be on a scale that will require the use of an electronic computer for their solution, as they will involve the interaction of too many variables to be solved by hand, either graphi-

---

[5] Of course, neither ⅔ or ⅓ of a hat is a feasible unit to produce; obviously, some adjustment to round off to the nearest unit would be made in the analysis of a real problem.

cally or by algebra. The essential processes of solution do not differ from those indicated, however, the sheer size of the problem being the main difference between the example and the typical real world application. In setting up a problem for solution by means of a computer program, the tabulation in the form of Figures 24-1 through 24-5 is all that need be done, the rest of the operations being carried out automatically.

Linear programming is a technique which, if applied wisely, can effect substantial savings in costs or notable increases in profits. If great care is not exercised, however, to see that its basic assumptions are valid, or very nearly so, in any given application, misleading and perhaps harmful consequences will follow from the use of its results.

25 SIMULATION IN FINANCIAL PLANNING

Ever since the beginning of the scientific age, man has tried to improve his understanding of his environment and himself by using, among other approaches, the general process of simulation. Simulation involves representing a real-world situation by some simple and easily manipulated model. Experiments can then be carried out on the model, so that the probable effects of similar actions in the real situation can be assessed in advance. In this way, plans can be tested and the effects of strategies explored before the commitment is made to take action in the real world. In this general sense, a map is a simulation. A military commander may study a map of the territory through which he wishes to move his troops; he may test several possible routes and choose the best after his examination is complete. Only then, need he commit himself to moving his men.

The business manager, concerned about the future welfare of his company, would also like to get as much help as possible in making his decisions. He is concerned about the future course of the economy, at least as it affects his own industry. He would like to know much more than he typically does about the demand for his products. He knows that there are many factors at work in the business, some external (such as government, labor unions, customer groups, and competitors) and some internal (such as prices, hiring policies, purchasing procedures, manufacturing techniques, and financial planning) but he does not always know which are the most important. If there were some way of telling which things mattered most, the business manager would be able to do a much better job of planning.

There are various ways in which the businessman may seek this information. He can hire consultants, read the business press and the trade journals, observe the fate of competitors when they carry out some innovation, take a guess, study what has happened to his own company in past periods, or employ a simulation. Most managers employ a selection of these approaches in their planning. In this chapter, we shall be concerned with the role of simulation in business planning, with the uncertain future, and the preplanning process; a simulation model is only useful if it permits the manager to make better evaluations of the consequences of his decisions before the decisions are taken.

Simulation is a method of approaching a problem. It is not a technique which depends on a particular mathematical procedure, such as linear programming. Instead, the simulation concept provides a framework within which the planner, working closely with the managers involved, can create a useful model. There are no practical limits to the range of problems which may be tackled using this approach, because there are no built-in assumptions. A linear programming model can only be used if the linearity assumption is approximately valid, that is, if the relationship between the variables can be expressed by means of straight lines. A simulation model, in contrast, must be designed anew with each new kind of problem, so that only those assumptions which are realistic in the circumstances need to be made.

Additional insight to the nature of simulation may be derived by comparing it with the scientific method of experimentation. A scientist, seeking to measure the effect of, say, heat on water, would approach the problem experimentally. Very simply, he would apply heat to the water, and by measuring the amount of heat applied and the temperature of the water he would obtain his results. In business, experiments can rarely be performed. The businessman might be interested in knowing the effect on sales of a 25 percent price increase but would be most unwilling to seek his answer by putting such an increase into effect, for obvious reasons. The risk is too great. Also, a test market of the price change might be invalid because of the unique character of the test city. However, if he had access to a model which simulated the market environment with reasonable accuracy, he might try the price increase on the model. In this way, he can obtain useful information for planning without taking the risk of effecting the actual price change. For this reason, the simulation approach has been called a "synthetic experiment." If the model is properly designed and validated, it can be used to supply data comparable to that which could be found experimentally.

In this field of business planning, especially in the financial area, a specialized type of simulation has been found useful. This is a Monte Carlo mathematical simulation model. In the present chapter, we shall explore the nature of this type of model, its advantages and disadvantages, when it can best be used, and how such a model may be created. The appendix to this chapter provides some definitions of the mathematical terms used in the text.

The nature of the Monte Carlo method of simulation

The Monte Carlo method has the following important features which will be discussed in this section.

1. It employs mathematical models, composed of series of equations.
2. The method permits the derivation of answers without the need to solve the equations.
3. The method permits the rational representation of uncertainty.
4. The method can be used to explore the long term effects of a proposed policy or decision.

The Monte Carlo method is a mathematical approach to a problem in business or elsewhere. The business situation or problem is described as carefully as possible by a series of equations. Each of the equations describes a relationship between two or more factors of interest in the business, and together the set of equations represents the entire problem.

In many instances, the business problem is a complicated one. The set of equations which results may be very hard or even impossible to solve in the traditional algebraic fashion. The Monte Carlo method permits the analyst to obtain answers to these sets of complicated equations without solving them. Instead, the user of the Monte Carlo method tries out a large number of possible values for the variables in the equations, in a disciplined fashion we will discuss later, and an answer or set of answers is derived. The calculations associated with the running of a Monte Carlo simulation are lengthy and rarely attempted without the aid of a computer.

One of the reasons for the complexity of these models in a business setting is the uncertainty associated with business planning. Many of the factors in a business problem, especially the important factors such as future sales volume, are quite uncertain. In order to be of value to business planners, a model must be capable of representing this uncertainty with sufficient realism. The great advantage of the Monte Carlo method of simulation is that it permits the business planner to take account of such uncertain relationships in the building of his model. Let us now look at a very simple example of the Monte Carlo simulation method in use. The example is so simple that the method would not normally be used for its solution, but nonetheless it does permit a study of the basic method.

A businessman is confronted with the following problem. He wants to raise the price of his product by 10 percent. He believes there is a 50 percent chance of losing a single customer, who buys 40 percent of his output, but that no other customers will be affected. The product now sells for $100, costs $70 to make, and is being produced and sold at a rate of 1000 units per year. The manager wishes to make his decision purely on the basis of profit. Should he raise the price?

The profit margin presently is $30,000, representing a $30 contribution from each of the 1000 units. If the price were to be raised, and the big customer did not stop buying, the margin would be $40,000 (40/unit × 1000 units). On the other hand, if the customer did leave us, the margin would be only $24,000 ($40/unit × 600 units).

We are now in a position to perform the Monte Carlo simulation study of the problem. We know the profit margins that will arise in each situation. We must now take account of the probability function. There is a 50 percent chance that the customer will be lost, and, therefore, a 50 percent chance that he will remain. We must set up a synthetic experiment which has the same probability function as this, and sample from that experimental distribution. It so happens that tossing a coin would be a perfectly good substitute experiment: there is a 50 percent chance each of heads and tails. Let us, therefore, set up the experiment as follows. Let us toss a coin and say that if it comes down heads the customer will stay with us, while if it comes down tails he will leave. Then, we shall repeat the experiment many times, and write down the profit margin corresponding to the outcome. If the coin comes down heads, the margin is $40,000 but if it is tails the margin is $24,000. When we add all these margins together and take the average, we will be able to compare that average with the profit margin we are getting at the moment.

Suppose we proceeded to toss the coin 1000 times, and got 480 heads. This would give us an average simulated margin of $31,680, obtained as follows.

Heads 480 × 40,000	19,200,000	
Tails 520 × 24,000	12,480,000	
	$31,680,000	or $31,680 average

As the present profit margin is only $30,000, the manager should increase the price if he wishes to make the decision solely on the basis of profit expectations.

The reader may make the same investigation by analytical means, and find that the expected profit margin after the price raise would in fact be $32,000. The simulation approach will normally approach this analytical answer very closely. As was mentioned at the beginning of the problem, this example is so simple that one would not normally use simulation to solve it. The simulation method is intended for use in those large scale and complex situations where analysis will not work.

The significance of the 50 percent probability estimate must also be emphasized. This is a subjective estimate on the part of the decision maker. It is a critical element in the analysis, because if the probability of loss of the customer goes up materially, the correct decision will change to holding the price as it is. The probability of loss of the customer at which the manager would be exactly indifferent as to whether to raise the price or not turns out to be 62.5 percent. The reader may verify this algebraically if he so desires. The main point, however, is that the assessment of this type of probability is a new method of thinking for the majority of managers. There is no question that the evaluation of probabilities takes some practice before the average manager would feel confident in believing the results obtained.

In the above example, the probability distribution used was simple and determined by purely subjective assessment. In most practical applications of the simulation techniques, the distribution will be more complicated; a slightly more complex example is given later in this chapter. It may also be possible to determine the distribution by observation. If a substantial history of the uncertain event has been recorded, that history may be used to develop the distribution. For instance, firms wishing to study the payment delay patterns of their customers by simulation will undoubtedly be able to use the actual observed payment delays of prior periods as a starting point. Certainly, the creator of a simulation model should get as much factual data as he can, so that the model is as close to reality as possible.

Another important feature of the Monte Carlo method is that a model may be created with dynamic features. An analysis which considers only the short-term effects may be missing the point and dangerously misleading. A simulation model can be designed to carry its calculations out for a reasonable period into the future. The long-term effects of the assumptions built into the model and the special circumstances being investigated in a particular run of it can, therefore, be investigated thoroughly. As Dearden and McFarlan point out in their "Management Information Systems" this recursive feature of simulation models permits the analyst to observe trends and tendencies in a manner which would be tedious and tremendously expensive if attempted by hand.[1] In the field of accounting, a changeover from the FIFO to the LIFO method of inventory valuation provides a simple example. The immediate effect of such a change upon earnings per share may be quite substantial. However, if the business maintains a reasonably steady growth pattern and a reasonable balance between production levels and sales volume, the long-run effect of such a change may be quite insignificant.

For what kinds of management problems should Monte Carlo simulation be used?

As was mentioned at the beginning of this chapter, simulation is an approach to problem solving, not a specific problem solving technique. It is a method of thinking about and structuring a problem situation so that it can be handled; it is not a formula into which certain inputs must be plugged and from which the answer will be forthcoming immediately. For this reason, it would be inappropriate to provide a list of specific application of simulation; such a list would inevitably be incomplete. Instead, we shall consider the characteristics of a business problem which make the problem susceptible to solution by simulation methods. These characteristics are:

---

[1] Deardeu, J., and McFarlan, F. W., *Management Information Systems* (Homewood, Ill.: Richard D. Irwin, Inc., 1966), Chapter 5.

1. The problem is too complicated to be dealt with adequately by guesswork. This may arise because there are too many variables to consider, or because the long-term effects cannot be foreseen clearly.

2. No analytical model can handle the problem. An analytical model is one composed of equations which must be *solved* in order to reach an answer. The equations may prove insoluble.

3. The assumptions built into a possible analytical model are not realistic. Even if the equations are soluble, the relationships between the variables may not be appropriate to the situation. A straight line, for example, is not usually acceptable as presenting a demand curve.

4. Rules of thumb have proved unreliable. The shortcuts adopted when the calculations supporting the decisions were being performed by hand have oversimplified the problem and have proved misleading.

5. The amounts of money involved in the decision are large. The cost of creating a simulation model is considerable; there is little point in incurring this cost for a trivial decision.

6. Some of the factors in the problem are uncertain. The ability of the Monte Carlo method to handle uncertainty, provided that uncertainty can be described, makes the method relevant for many business problems.

7. The decision which is being simulated has implications for future periods. A budgeting model, for example, will usually have to be prepared for several months in advance. A simulation model can be used to compute the results for a given time period from the figures of the period before it and from additional data for the new period; the new results can then form a partial basis for calculating the next period's figures, and so on.

Most of the simulation models which have been created in corporations for management planning have been designed to help in production and inventory planning. In these fields, the variables are subject to uncertainty, but production managers are often able to specify the nature of that uncertainty with some degree of confidence. For instance, the manager might be unwilling to say that a particular project would take 30 days, but might be willing to say that it would take between 25 and 40 days, with 30 days as the most likely time. Also, the dynamic effects of a decision are very obviously important in production management. The scheduling of production is very much a matter of deciding which tasks to perform in which order. The effects of a given production plan over long periods of time are often of greater importance than their immediate consequences. Because of these two factors, and because production managers tend to be more familiar with numerical procedures involved in simulation than managers in other fields, simulation has been used in production more than elsewhere. It would be a mistake, however, to conclude that managers with financial responsibilities cannot benefit from using the simulation approach. Two examples are presented below illustrating particular problems in the financial planning field which were solved by using simulation.

The president of a medium-sized consumer goods manufacturing company wished to improve the quality of the sales forecasts used in the budgeting process. The present system called for each of the product line managers to prepare a sales estimate, and these numbers were then added together to give the total sales revenues expected for the whole company for the year ahead. Unfortunately, most of the company's products were subject to the same economic factors; if one of the sales managers estimates was too high, the other managers were usually too high also, and vice versa. This meant, of course, that the errors compounded one another, and that the total estimate could be seriously wrong. This, in turn, led to planning errors, either through the incurrence of excess costs by overproduction if the estimates turned out too high, or through the incurrence of overtime and extra material purchase costs if the estimates turned out too low.

Besides the problem of estimating total sales, some trouble had been experienced in predicting the timing of these sales. There was considerable uncertainty as to the months during which orders would be received, and the time customers took to pay the invoices was also variable. For cash planning, production planning, and general management purposes, therefore, a procedure for testing out the probable effects of various management strategies was wanted. A simulation model was decided upon and eventually constructed.

The model employed a probability distribution for each of the uncertain quantities mentioned above and carried out the calculations for a 24-month period. Output from the model included a cash budget, a production plan, and a purchasing schedule for each of the 24 months. Management has attributed yearly savings of $100,000 to the use of the model.

The second illustration involved a manufacturing company with sales of $80 million. The company's receivables had been increasing as a proportion of sales over recent years, and the company was running short of ready cash. Neither the company nor its more important competitors had been giving discounts for prompt payment; management was considering the introduction of such a discount system.

Four factors had to be taken into account in this problem. First, there would be immediate savings of interest because of the fall in the receivables balance. Second, there would be a loss incurred because of the effective price cut the discount would create. Third, there would be an immediate sales volume increase, because the new policy would attract customers from competitors. Fourth, the competitors would, after a delay, probably install a similar discount policy; some customers who had switched at the time of the company's policy change would probably switch back to their old supplier.

There were five important uncertain variables involved in this decision: the amount of the receivables reduction, the number of customers whose sales would be affected by the price cut through taking the discount, the amount of the sales increase, the delay before the competitors instituted a similar discount policy, and the number of new customers gained by the policy who would be lost when the competitors discount was installed. In addition to these factors, management had to consider the amount of the cash discount to offer, as a percentage of price, and also had to decide upon the number of days delay they would allow before the discount would expire.

As a result of a simulation study of the problem, the management of the company eventually decided to install a 12 percent seven day discount and have subsequently reported satisfactory results.

In each of the examples above, the features of the problem at hand were typical of simulation situations. The problem was fairly complicated, with several factors involved. Many factors were uncertain as to their impact. The decision involved much money, given the size of the company, and had intermediate to long term implications. Although attempts had been made, at least in the second case, to solve the problem analytically, these attempts had not succeeded, while the simulation gave an apparently reliable answer.

The steps involved in creating a simulation model

After a management planning problem has been perceived, and it has been decided that a simulation model might be useful in solving it, there are five steps which must be taken before results can be obtained. These are:

1. Decide the scope of the model, i.e., which variables will be embraced.
2. Analyze the importance of each variable; decide whether it will be included as a known quantity or whether it will be assigned a probability distribution.
3. Select decision rules for the model; relate the variables to one another by means of equations.
4. Generate the probability functions for the uncertain variables.
5. Assemble, test, and validate the model.

Scope of the model

The nature of the management problem is the prime determinant of the scope of the simulation model. The analyst, with the advice and consent of management, must decide which variables he is going to incorporate into the model and which he will leave out. This decision is not as easy as it may sound. For example, a simulation model may be proposed for studying the feasibility of a new production plant. Should the planned expenditure for marketing the product to be made in the plant be one of the variables in such a model? The sales-generating success of this marketing expenditure may be important in determining whether the new plant will be profitable. On the other hand, the model builder may elect to omit the variable, using only the expected sales level of the new product in his analysis. At any rate, the analyst must decide where he is going to draw the line.

Once it has been decided that a variable should be included within the model, the analyst must decide whether the values of the variable will be determined before the model is run or by the actual operation of the model itself. In econometric terms, this means taking the list of variables being considered in the model and dividing them into exogenous and endogenous groups. The values of exogenous variables are read into the model as data. They are used in the computations but are not affected in value by these computations. An endogenous variable, however, is one which depends for its value on the operations of the model itself. It is calculated on the basis of equations within the model, using exogenous variables and endogenous variables from prior periods as inputs to the equations. The "raw materials" upon which the computations will be based are normally treated as exogenous variables. These would include the probability distributions describing the uncertain variables and the assumptions which the management user wishes to test. In the cash discounting model discussed earlier, for instance, various levels of the percentage cash discount rate were read in as data and their effects on profit calculated; in fact, the rate was treated as an exogenous variable.

In contrast, the "answers" and most of the intermediate variables are normally endogenous. In a financial simulation, the objective may be to predict the amount of earnings per share or the amount of a bank loan than may be needed at some future time. As these would be computed by the model, they are endogenous by definition. Some intermediate variables may be either ex- or endogenous. For example, in a sales forecasting model, advertising expenditure may be treated as either exogenous or endogenous. In the former case, the advertising expenditure amounts would be determined in advance by the user of the model and fed into the model as data, there to be used for calculations. The level of sales anticipated in the model would be at least partially dependent on the amount of advertising expenditure assumed. If advertising were treated as an endogenous variable, however, the amount of advertising expenditure would depend on other factors within the model. For instance, advertising might be set by the model equal to a certain proportion of sales revenue in the month previous, or perhaps equal to a proportion of expected sales revenue in the current month. There are innumerable ways in which the calculations could be made, but the point is that when advertising is treated endogenously the model is permitted to calculate the variable value and the user must either trust the model's calculations or alter the model.

Clearly, it is important to decide which group a given variable shall fall into. If a modeler elects to make a variable endogenous he is obliged to specify the relationships upon which that variable will depend. On the contrary, if he makes it an exogenous variable, his model need only be capable of reading the values of the variable in and of operating upon them, without paying any attention to the way in which the number was obtained. The greater the number of endogenous variables the more complex the model will become, and the greater opportunities for error will exist. On the other hand, the more variables the model can handle internally the simpler the model will be to use and the greater will be its potential value to management if it is set up correctly. The cost of creating a model, including the cost of validating it, is likely to be proportional to the number of endogenous variables contained within it.

The certainty of the variables

The next decision to be taken in the planning of the model relates to the treatment of uncertainty in the model. The model designer may decide to treat any given variable as a known quantity or as uncertain. It is easier to treat a quantity as known, of course, but a major advantage of the simulation approach is that it permits uncertain quantities to be given due weight. The criteria for making this decision are the stability of the variable, the time in advance of use which it will be known, and the variable's significance to the problem. The pay rates of the employee group, for example, would be a stable quantity (contract negotiations being ignored for the moment) and would be known well in advance of use. There would be little point in treating this quantity as uncertain. As another example, the time to process a given job on a particular machine tool might be of interest in a production simulation. If the processing time was the same every time the job occurred, the quantity would be treated as constant. If the times were likely to differ significantly, or if the differences between the times was an important factor in the entire process being simulated, the decision would be to handle the variable as uncertain. One major steel manufacturing firm which uses simulation for many purposes has developed a rule of thumb for this decision. If a variable, in the judgement of a manager who has responsibility in the area, is likely to deviate by 10 percent or more from its median value more than one quarter of the time, the uncertainty should be treated formally by Monte Carlo sampling. If not, the variables median value is used as if it were certain to be accurate. As this rule has been in use without adjustment for several years, it presumably gives satisfactory results.

The equations which must be developed to interrelate the variables in the model are entirely at the option of the designer. There are no "rules" to be obeyed in this area. The objective, of course, is to pick a set of equations which can be relied upon to give accurate results, that is, an accurate representation of the behavior of the real system in the equivalent circumstances. How this is achieved is up to the model builder and his advisers. This very freedom of action can be dangerous. The management people working on the simulation must satisfy themselves that the equations make economic sense. Let us take a look at some examples.

$$AR(T) = AR(T - 1) - CASH(T) + SALE(T) - ADJUST(T) \quad (1)$$

Equation (1) above is a relationship[1] which might appear in any accounting simulation model. It states that the accounts receivable level at the end of period T is equal to the level at the end of the previous period $(T - 1)$, less receipts, plus sales, less adjustments (such as bad debts, returns, etc.) which have occurred during period T. By equations like this, we are able to carry the calculations of the simulation model as far forward through time as we wish, as long as we have the first accounts receivable value, and the streams of values for cash, sales, and adjustments.

$$DEMAND(T) = K_1 + K_2 \, ADVT(T - 1) + K_3/PRICE(T) \quad (2)$$

Equation 2 is taken from a demand model. The demand for the product in the period T is related to the expenditure on advertising in the preceding period $(ADVT(T - 1))$ and to the price charged this period $(PRICE(T))$. The K_i's are constants which establish the nature of the relationship. Equation (2) is stated in terms of certainty. In other words, once the amount of the advertising and the price are chosen, the demand is completely determined. In most business situations, this level of assurance is regrettably unattainable. Instead, the demand might be stated in uncertain terms as in equation (3)

$$DEMAND(T) = (K_1 + K_2 \, ADVT(T - 1) + (K_3/PRICE(T)))(R) \quad (3)$$

The equations are similar in every respect except for the presence of the variable R in equation (3). This is a number taken from a specially

---

[1] The subscript (T) in the equation indicates that the cumulative total of the variable at the end of period T is to be used. In the case of accounts receivable, $AR(T)$ means the total receivable balance at the end of the period. In the case of receipts, $CASH(T)$ means the sum of all receipts which have arrived by the end of the period.

prepared uncertainty distribution which we shall be looking at in the next section. By multiplying the previous estimate for demand by this uncertainty factor, we are able to depict the behavior of the demand function more realistically.

Probability functions

As we have mentioned, the possibility of dealing with uncertainty is one of the strengths of the Monte Carlo method of simulation. We must now consider how this is done. In an earlier illustration, the 50 percent chance of losing a major customer was simulated by means of a' coin-tossing experiment. Although most business uncertainties are more complex than that simulation, the basic principle behind the Monte Carlo method is the same in all instances. A probability function or distribution is assigned to the uncertain variable. Then, an experiment is devised to simulate that probability distribution. A sample is then drawn from the experiment, and the variable value thus obtained is used in subsequent calculations. The sampling and calculating steps are repeated as often as needed.

Let us now take a slightly more complex situation and consider how it may be dealt with in a simulation model. In the previous section, the uncertainty of demand given values for advertising and price was represented by the factor R in equation (3). Let us suppose we now want to build a description of R into the model.

The first step in creating a probability function is obtaining the views of the responsible manager. This individual must be asked what he thinks the chance of occurrence is for each range of possible values of the quantity. This is not an easy task. The manager is accustomed to dealing with this uncertainty by informal and intuitive means, not by writing his evaluations down explicitly. Even if this job is only performed roughly, however, the handling of uncertainty will have been placed on a more solid foundation than the purely intuitive methods used previously.

Let us suppose the manager decides that there are four chances in ten that the demand as computed in equation (2) will be within 5 percent of the right figure. In addition, he estimates that there is a one in four chance of the computed number being too high by anywhere from 5 to 25 percent. He also reckons that the number will not be more than 25 percent off in either direction.

We can describe this assessment in the following table.

Demand factor	Probability
75%–95%	one in four = 0.25
95%–105%	four in ten = 0.40
105%–125%	balance = 0.35
	1.00

We must next devise an experiment which possesses the same probability function as this. We employ a device called a random number generator, with which most computers are equipped. This random number generator is capable of creating a stream of numbers, all of them between zero and one, such that the numbers are statistically independent. This means that the value of each number generated is unaffected by the values generated previously in the stream. Every time we want a value of the variable under study, in this instance the factor by which demand will differ from the predicted level, we may use the random number generator to generate one random number.

The next step is to convert the random number into a value of the demand factor, so that the demand factor value can be used in subsequent calculations. In order to carry out this conversion, a graph like the one in Figure 25-1 is used, or a table containing the same information may be employed. The range of random numbers, from zero to one, is shown on the vertical scale. The range of values of the demand factor, from 75 to 125 percent is shown on the horizontal scale. Given any random number value, therefore, it is possible to read off a corresponding demand factor from the graph.

The slope of the line segments in the graph are derived from the probabilities we wish to represent. The probability table tells us, for example, that there is a 25 percent chance that the demand factor will lie between 75 and 95 percent. The lower left-hand line segment depicts this fact. It covers the 75–95 range on the horizontal axis, and the zero to 25 range on the vertical. The second line segment depicts the second probability estimate. It covers the demand range from 95 to 105 horizontally, and the range from 0.25 to 0.65 vertically. This vertical distance of 0.4 (0.65–0.25) is the probability desired for a demand factor in the 95–105 range.

In order to give the law of average time to work out, it is necessary to sample many times from the distribution, using a different random number each time. The result of such sampling will be a series of values of the demand factor, all in the range from 75 to 125 percent, collectively conforming to the probability distribution assigned by the manager. The remaining calculations in the simulation model are performed using each of the sampled values of the demand factor in turn as though it had actually been observed. For each sampled value, a corresponding value of the final answer will be computed. After frequent calculations have been performed, the various values of the final answer can be tabulated into a probability distribution for use in making the decision.

Assembly, testing, and validation of a simulation

The final assembly of the model from the parts created in the previous steps in an exercise in computer programming. It involves arranging

Figure 25–1
PROBABILITY DISTRIBUTION OF DEMAND FACTOR
The numbers on the vertical scale represent the probability that the
demand factor will be less than the corresponding number on the
horizontal scale.

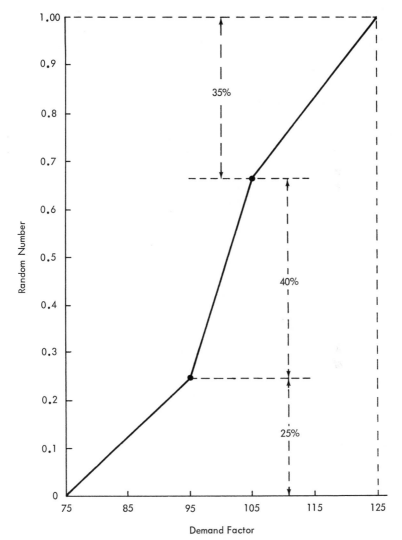

Demand Factor

the items in the correct order, and then writing the program so that
the appropriate model equations are called in where needed and the
various probability distributions sampled at the right times. This step,
although sometimes complicated, lies outside our area of interest in
this book.

When the first results are obtained from the model, however, the validation process can begin. It is very important that the management of the company—perhaps represented by the controller if the simulation is a financial one—be involved with this step. If the assumptions built into the model are not in line with the economic facts of the business, managers should not be surprised if the results derived from the model appear strange.

Validating the simulation model is simpler in financial simulations than in simulations of physical systems and military operations. In most organizations, there is a quantity of data already being collected on a routine basis by the accounting system and other routine recordkeeping procedures. Much reorganization of data may be called for, but the basic data are likely to be available for many management simulation applications. If the raw data are not available, a careful managerial review of the data collection procedure adopted by the model building group would be advisable. The corporate controller is in an excellent position to advise the modeling team on the availability of data they may use in preparing their models.

The validation of model results is usually done by running the model with some past actual input data (other than those used to create the model in the first instance) and by comparing the output with the known events which did occur. Mr. George Gershefski of the Sun Oil Corporation reported that a model designed for corporate financial planning in that company projected net income within one percent of actual for one year into the future when tested in this way.[2] Other reports have also been published of similarly convincing results of corporate financial models. The exact approach to the validation of the model must be devised with the purpose of the model carefully in mind. If management's previous best guess had been subject to a 50 percent error, it would be inappropriate if they complained about a 10 percent error in the results obtained from a model. The gain is obvious.

It is interesting in conclusion to consider an important paradox of corporate financial modeling. If the model produces results which are exactly what management would have expected, management will have little trouble in believing the model's results, but it will gain little from having the model around. It would have reached the same conclusions in any case. On the other hand, if the management decision proposed by the model differs from (and improves upon) the decision which management would have arrived at without the model's assistance, the model is contributing significantly toward the operations of the company. But in that event corporate management may have difficulty in believing what the model tells. In the last analysis, it is the company manager who must put the analyses of a model into practice. He is unlikely to do this unless he believes in the results, and he is unlikely to believe

---

[2] G. Gershefski, *The Development and Application of a Corporate Financial Model* (New York: Oxford University Press, Planning Executives Institute, 1968).

in the results unless he was intimately involved in developing the assumptions upon which the model was founded.

APPENDIX
Definitions of Mathematical and Other Terms

The definitions listed below are in their order of dependence; that is, a definition may include a term appearing before it in the list, but not a term appearing after it in the list.

Variable: An element in an equation, usually denoted by a letter, which may take on different values at different times and in different circumstances. Example: $X = 100$

Probability: The proportion of occasions, expressed as a fraction, upon which a variable is expected to take on a particular value is the probability of that value. Example: Probability of rolling a $6 = \frac{1}{6}$ (if die is fair)

Probability Distribution: A function stating the probability of each of the possible values of a variable. Example: the toss of a fair coin. The probability of heads is $\frac{1}{2}$, that of tails is also $\frac{1}{2}$. The sum of the probabilities in a probability distribution will always be one.

Uncertainty: If the probability that a variable will take on its most likely value is less than one, the variable is uncertain. Example: If the probability that $X = 100$ is 1, the variable X is certain. If the probability that $X = 100$ is 0.99, the variable X is uncertain.

Deterministic Equation: An equation in which none of the variables is uncertain. Example: Age = Current Date − Birthdate (all certain values)

Stochastic Variable: A variable which is uncertain in value, but which can be related to other variables by means of a probability distribution. Example: Sales = f(Advertising) where the function refers to the probability of sales variations in response to changes in the advertising expenditure.

Mathematical Model: A representation, expressed in one or more mathematical equations, of a real world object or system, either present or proposed. Example: Assets = Liabilities + Equities

Monte Carlo: A method of choosing a value of a variable, for use in a calculation, by drawing at random from the probability distribution assigned to the variable.

Problems

PROBLEMS

Chapter 1
Description of the controllership function

1–1. *Writing Off the QE2* (*The Journal of Accountancy*, August 1969). So that the Queen Elizabeth 2—new flagship of the Cunard Line—will be able to operate profitably during her lifetime, her book value was written down by nearly one third even before her maiden voyage to New York.

This accounting treatment is revealed by an examination of the 1968 financial statements of The Cunard Steam-Ship Company Limited, owner of the QE2, as reported in the June 28, 1969, issue of *The Accountant* (England).

The QE2 was included on Cunard's December 31, 1968, balance sheet at $48 million. Her total cost was actually about $71 million. (Both figures include an estimated $8 million of the purchase price not yet paid to the shipbuilder as of balance sheet date.)

The $71 million was reduced to $48 million in two ways. First a reduction of $1 million was made for an investment grant received by Cunard from the British government. Then, by action of the Cunard board of directors, another $22 million was written off as of January 1, 1968, to reduce the book value of the ship to its "economic value."

Sir Basil Smallpiece, managing director, indicated that "the effect of all these measures is that the company will start the year 1969 with a clean balance sheet. The Cunard Group is thus established on a firm financial basis for the future with no dead wood."

Depreciation of the QE2—at a straight-line rate over 20 years—will be provided on the reduced $48 million book value.

Comment.

1–2. " . . . *designing* and *operating* the records . . . *reporting* and *interpreting* the information . . . ," words that in the early pages of Chapter 1, denote four basic elements in the controllership function. Discuss manipulation in relation to these terms or as a possible fifth element.

1–3. "The controller is responsible for all quantitative information needed by management." Discuss.

1–4. "The tremendous capacity of the new computer made it possible for vice president of sales, Mr. A. B. Jones, to get the detailed information he had always wanted, that is profitability of each of the company's 4,200 products in each of 210 sales districts and broken down further by individual salesmen." Discuss.

1–5. The Wenatchee Apple Company, whose business is the purchase, storage, and sale of the famous western apples, had two large losses in 1971. The air-conditioning unit in one large storage building had failed, and repairs had not been effected in time to prevent considerable damage to stored fruit. A second loss resulted from the theft of 10,000 bushels of apples through the connivance of a watchman with a crooked trucking contractor.

The president of Wenatchee, having read that the protection of property is the function of controllership, blamed his controller for these losses. Discuss.

1–6. Probably the most important single figure series for investors and prospective investors is the 10 year earnings per share.

Northwest Airlines, in its 1971 annual report, shows both: A—Earnings per average share as reported each year, and B—Earnings per average share—recomputed after stock splits.

	A Actual	B Recomputed
1962	$3.97	$ .50
1963	5.73	.72
1964*	5.86	1.47
1965	9.99	2.50
1966*	5.81	2.90
1967	6.42	3.21
1968	5.47	2.74
1969*	2.55	2.55
1970	2.11	2.11
1971	1.01	1.01

* In each of these years there was a 2 for 1 stock split.

A stockholder studying the contrasting figures said: "It seems perfectly clear to me that the earnings under A were the *actual* earnings per share and therefore better accounting and reporting than the juggled figures under B." Discuss.

1–7. Northwest Airlines annual report for 1971 shows in its statement of earnings amounts for depreciation and amortization with reference to explanatory Note F as follows:

1970—$69,173,449; 1971—$77,245,465

Note F—Depreciation and amortization comprises three items. Discuss each of these in terms of the accounting problem involved and the apparent logic of the alternative which was used.

Provision for depreciation of aircraft and related flight equipment approximate $73,424,000 (1970—$62,993,000) and was computed on the straight-line method assuming 10 year lives and 15 percent residual values, except as to 747 jet aircraft as to which the life is 15 years and residual value is 10 percent.

Included in operating expenses for 1970 is the amortization of SST aircraft development costs of $1,100,000. Upon abandonment of the project by the United States Government during 1971, all such costs were refunded, and accordingly, $3,300,000 was credited to reduce depreciation and amortization expense for 1971 in accordance with Civil Aeronautics Board accounting requirements.

Boeing 747 aircraft training costs are being amortized over five years.

Chapter 2
The property control function

2–1.   The plant of the Eastern Brass Foundry was built on the bank of an abandoned canal which still held some fifteen feet of water. For many years it had been the tradition of the machining department to heave spoiled parts out of the windows into the canal when the boss wasn't looking. Contrast this handling the spoilage problem with the proper accounting in terms of breaking down the transactions in terms of its fundamental elements of authorization, custody, and record.

2–2.   Describe the "inflowing stream of monies and other values," and outline very briefly the principal techniques involved in their safeguarding for (a) an electric public utility, (b) a department store, and (c) a state university.

2–3.   Describe the "outflowing stream of monies and other values" and outline very briefly the principal techniques involved in their safeguarding for (a) a manufacturing company, (b) a bank, and (c) the Blue Cross of Michigan.

2–4.   Detroit Machining Corporation produced ten to fifteen tons of scrap metals per month which were sold to salvage dealers on quarterly bid basis. Salvage dealer Fulton had been the high bidder for some years and thus kept getting the business. Other dealers grumbled and could not understand how Fulton could pay his prices and stay in the business, which was very competitive.

Fulton's trucks called at the DMC plant whenever notified by yard superintendent Jones that loads were available. Jones himself ran the yard scale and made out the weighing report in ink, one copy to Fulton and one by company mail to the accounting office. Jones was Fulton's brother-in-law though this was not known to the DMC.

Discuss.

2–5.   Using graphic methods set up a flow chart for the business situation shown in Figure 2–1, but using punched card or EDP techniques. Read the text describing Figure 2–1 for clues as to hazards of error or fraud and provide for their avoidance in your chart.

Chapter 3

The function of legal reporting

3–1. While it may be proper to speak of the controller's legal functions, it would be misleading to say that the legal function of the corporation rests in the controller. Enlarge upon this distinction.

3–2. A speaker before a controller's group once said, "In the typical business there are more decisions of legal consequence made outside of the legal department than in it . . . ." Enlarge upon this remark.

3–3. "On most points we got along fine with the government boys at the hearing, but when it came to the depletion problem and we wouldn't budge off the 27½ percent the meetings practically broke up." This might well have been the report to his boss, of oil company controller Jones on returning from Washington after the House committee hearings on tax reform.
Discuss the implications.

3–4. In 1925, the biweekly labor-payroll entries for the foundry department of X Manufacturing Company were essentially as follows:

Wages expense-foundry	30,000	
Payroll accrued		30,000
Payroll accrued	30,000	
Bank		30,000

In similar journal entry form set up the biweekly payroll entries for X Manufacturing Company, giving effect to the impact of legal and social changes which have presumably become effective by January 1973.

3–5. Outline the reporting, legal and related, implicit in the January 1973 payroll situation envisaged in 3–4 above.

3–6. Inspect a number of annual reports of large industrial companies for evidence of reporting segregated profits by lines of business or classes of similar products to stockholders. Screen your findings against the provisions of SEC Release No. 8996.

Chapter 4

Implementation of the management concept

4–1. "Our CPAs tell us that our accounting system is fully in line with good accounting theory and that it is adequate as the source of income tax data and statements satisfactory to our bank creditors and stockholders.

"Yet we feel that our own management gets very little help from the system—that we are 'flying our business by the seat of our pants.' "

These statements were made by the President of E. & H. Cooper Company which employs 750 persons in the manufacture of varied lines of household appliances. As an accountant and management consultant what would be your line of approach to his problem?

4–2. The manager of the Grand Rapids Fair Department Store has for several years compared his annual operating figures with the Standards for Mid-West Department Stores put out by the University of Michigan Bureau of Business Research. The chief finding which causes him concern is that the items of supplies expense and employee sick leave expense continue to exceed the standard in spite of his annual diatribes on the subject to the department heads' and buyers' conference.

Discuss.

4–3. President J. A. N. Onder of Metal Parts Manufacturing Company called his controller into his inner office, closed the door and laid into him as follows: "Bill, this is the third quarter in a row that your report shows spoilage way high in the grinding department and you haven't made an inch of progress in getting it down to standard. Now I want *monthly* reports on spoilage from now on, and if you don't show some results pretty soon I'm going to have to look for a new controller."

What should Bill's course of action be?

4–4. A 1971 survey of small department stores brought out an interesting variety of treatments given to the recording of sales returns, which, with some simplification, can be summarized as follows:

a) One sales returned account for all departments, shown on the income statement as a deduction from total gross sales.
b) Sales returned broken down by department but no further detail available.
c) Sales returned broken down by department, with each department total supported in an analytical schedule by a breakdown as to reasons for return with captions as follows:

Goods damaged in delivery.
Goods did not operate successfully
Goods misrepresented by salesman
Customer changed his mind
Miscellaneous reasons.

The practice in some of the stores was to require the disgruntled customer to deal with some certain official or department under the title of "sales adjustments" or similar title. Other stores allowed individual salesmen to accept the return of goods (sometimes up to a certain limit only). The differences in the percentage of times each reason was given (where reasons were reported) varied remarkably from store to store, "miscellaneous reasons" going as high as 62 percent of the total in one instance.

Discuss the variations in techniques from the standpoint of accounting, reporting, and management.

4–5. Massee and Hilborn, selling through traveling salesmen show the following income sheet for July 1971:

	Product A	Product B	Product C
Sales	$100,000	$ 60.000	$40,000
Manufacturing cost of sales	50,000	40,000	15,000
Margin over manufacturing costs	$ 50,000	$ 20,000	$25,000
Marketing and administrative costs:			
Advertising*	$ 10,000	$ 6,000	$ 4,000
Salesmen's expenses†	8,000	4,800	3,200
Warehouse and shipping‡	5,000	4,500	2,200
Order and invoice handling§	2,500	1,000	1,000
All other marketing and administra-			
tive costs	12,000	5,000	4,000
Net product income	$ 12,500	$(−)1,300	$10,600

* Allocated to products in proportion to dollar sales.
† Allocated to products in proportion to number of salesmen's calls.
‡ Allocated to products in proportion to tons shipped.
§ Allocated to products in proportion to number of orders.
Note: All products are sold by all salesmen, though not all customers buy all three.
Directive: Advise Massee and Hilborn.

Chapter 5

Organization of the controller's department

5–1. Control of Acme Manufacturing Company, a medium-sized business with considerable potential, has just been taken over by R. L. Dixon, who will be chairman of the board and president. He commissions you to take the position as controller with a free hand to organize your own department and to bring in your own staff. Mr. Dixon has studied the "Ideal" Controller's Department Organization as shown in the text and approves it in principle, with the restriction that, for the time being, you may have only three persons at the assistant controller level and not more than twelve to fifteen supervisors.

With these limitations in mind, set up a revised organization chart for your department.

Mr. Dixon also asks you to give jobs somewhere in your organization to (a) a very brilliant nephew who has just graduated from college, majoring in accounting, and (b) an uncle who has had very wide experience in accounting but who lacks push, imagination, and ambition. Where would you place these two persons in your organization?

5–2. Three large businesses are described below. Though the three companies are of roughly the same size in terms of total assets, volume of revenue, and net income, their conditions are sufficiently varied that the pattern of decentralization of the controller's department may well vary in the three cases. Discuss the decentralization of specific subfunctions with reference to the essential differences in actual operations.

a)   A chain drugstore firm having 500 stores throughout the Middle West and South. Each store is set up close to the model, all but 25 have soda and light-lunch departments, all sell for cash only. Practically all purchasing is done centrally, though three subwarehouses are maintained for convenience and promptness in delivery.

b) A shoe manufacturing company with six plants in four states. Many models of shoes are produced in all the plants, though one specializes in women's high-style items and one in men's heavy work shoes. The labor force varies from 75 in the smallest plant to 350 in the largest. All plants are on standard costs, with standards set in the home office for uniform items and locally determined for the women's specialties and work shoes. All sales are made by a sales force operating out of the home office, and, while deliveries are made from the most convenient plant, customers' accounts are centrally controlled. Payrolls are handled locally by check against an imprest payroll fund. All major purchases are made by the home office, with most shipments direct to plants from suppliers.

c) A manufacturing firm which originated in the making of fine custom furniture in Grand Rapids but which has expanded by successive steps into standard household furniture through acquisition of a plant in Tennessee, another plant in Illinois which produces furniture exclusively for a large chain retailer, a plastic fabrics plant which produces coverings for the several furniture plants and for a considerable volume of the automotive trade, including seat covers for a chain auto supply company. The last acquisition was a small watercraft and sports accessories company. All ventures are operated as divisions except the boat company, which has kept its corporate identity as a wholly owned subsidiary.

Furniture sales are headed by a furniture sales manager who handles relations with the chain retailer personally and supervises two separate groups of salesmen for the "custom" and "standard" furniture lines. The plastics and boat companies have their own sales managers and sales forces. Purchasing is done independently by the several plants, except that the buyers for the furniture division cooperate very closely as agents for each other in certain standard procurements.

The company has been fortunate in having a controller at the Grand Rapids plant who has been exceptionally successful in selecting and training assistants to take very large measures of responsibility.

5–3. Superior Auto Parts Distributors had fifteen wholesale-retail branches in cities throughout the western states. In 1965 the Systems and Internal Audit Division headed by H. J. Pine set up a new decentralized accounts receivable–cash system under which the branch cashiers had considerable independence and responsibility. In 1968, the S. and I. A. Division auditor uncovered a considerable cash shortage at Branch 9 which had been developing since 1966 and had been missed in the 1966 and 1967 audits. This was explained by Mr. Pine of the S. and I. A. division as a "once in a million slip in the audit procedures."

In 1970 the company's outside auditors discovered another sizable defalcation in Branch 7. They also dug out the fact that the 1969 internal audit had uncovered "very questionable practices" in the handling of deposits in Branches 3 and 12, the report of which had never gotten beyond Mr. Pine.

Discuss.

5–4. If possible obtain organization charts of local corporations showing the placing of the controllership functions in the general organization and the organization within the controller's department. Identify the differences between these charts and the organization of the controller's functions as described in the chapters and illustrated in the "ideal" chart therein.

If possible discover and describe the differences in the local business situations which would necessitate or justify these differences in organization.

5–5. The Pierpont Hardware Company after 20 years as an independent business was taken over in a stock transfer deal by Michigan General Hardware in 1969. The entire accounting system of Pierpont was revised to articulate with the parent company. Louis Lavoie previously chief accountant of Pierpont was kept on as controller of what was now known as the Pierpont Branch of Michigan General.

Lavoie was clearly aware that he was henceforth functionally responsible to Michigan General Controller DeWinter, but that he was also to continue his eminently successful service at the branch.

In 1971 a very unfortunate circumstance developed when R. B. Smith, cashier at Pierpont, a nephew of George Smith the Pierpont general manager, was found to have embezzled $10,000 from the branch. The facts of the case were known to only three or four trusted confidential, local officers of the company. General Manager Smith fired his nephew, made restitutions of the $10,000 from his own private sources and asked Lavoie to keep the facts quiet, i.e., to not report them to the home office.

Discuss.

Chapter 7

The accounting plan

7–1. The owner of the Bay Delicatessen Shop of San Francisco is pondering the question of the advisability of continuing to import "exotic island fruits" with which he has been experimenting for a period of two years. Analyze this as a management situation with special reference to the problem of the impact that accounting data may have and the manner of producing such data.

7–2. An assistant controller, in the process of collecting information looking toward an extensive reorganization of the accounting and reporting plan, asked each department head to rethink his management problems and to tell him what basic information the department head needed to help him in their solution. Comment on the requests for information received from three department heads as follows:

1. The foreman of a foundry department: "I want information that will help me reduce costs of overtime labor."
2. The sales manager of a division selling 20 products: "I would like to know just how much of each salesman's travel expense should be allocated to each of our products."
3. The factory maintenance superintendent: "I would like to know the cost of labor and materials used for maintenance jobs in each factory department."

7–3. What should be the primary basis of classification and subclassification of sales accounts in the following situations?

a) The company makes four main types of products. It sells all four types of products both through brokers and through its own sales organization. The sales manager is responsible for all sales. He has one assistant who is in charge of the sales force, another who handles broker sales, and a third who deals directly with the government. The sales manager personally handles sales made to a large mail-order house.

b) The company sells a line of household supplies through a nationwide organization of house-to-house salesmen. It also sells the same products, through a different sales organization, to wholesalers for distribution through retails stores.

c) A tobacco company has 3 brands of cigarettes and about 100 brands of pipe tobacco. The products are sold (1) to distributors who stock wholesalers and retailers, (2) direct to one company for export, and (3) direct to one chain of cigar stores. All sales contacts with the exporter and the cigar chain are handled by one man, who reports directly to the vice president in charge of sales. The company does not employ salesmen in the ordinary sense of the term. There are four product sales executives in the organization, one for each of the three cigarette brands and one for all pipe tobaccos. Each product executive plans advertising and other promotional effort for his product, and each supervises a crew of missionary salesmen who call on retailers to promote that brand.

7–4. Country Hosts, a hotel chain, has purchased a controlling interest in the Briny Inn Hotel in a northern Michigan resort area. The chain plans modernizations and publicity to bring the inn up to a profitable basis, but it expects to keep the previous management and personnel in substantial control.

You are given the responsibility of reorganizing the chart of accounts for management usefulness. You are instructed to do this, if possible, without doing any unnecessary violence to previous techniques.

On arriving at the inn you find the books neat and in apparently good order with the following chart of accounts:

Account no.	Account title	Account no.	Account title
1	Cash	19	Expense and Revenue
2	Accounts Receivable	20	Restaurant Sales
3	Notes Receivable	21	Room Revenue
4	Prepaid Insurance	22	Interest Revenue
5	Rent Receivable	23	Miscellaneous Revenue
6	Restaurant Supplies	24	Fuel Expense
7	Coal on Hand	25	Laundry Expense
8	Room Supplies	26	Office Expense
9	Hotel Equipment	27	Wages Expense
10	Restaurant Equipment	28	Restaurant Supplies Used
11	Building	29	Room Supplies Used
12	Land	30	Insurance Expense
13	Notes Payable	31	Electric Expense
14	Accounts Payable	32	Bad Debts Expense
15	Accrued Payroll	33	Depreciation Expense
16	Meal Cards Outstanding	34	Phone Expense
17	Capital Stock Outstanding	35	Taxes Expense
18	Surplus		

It may help in your assignment to keep in mind two important considerations. Your changes must have clear advantage toward improved management usefulness to appeal to the home office and must still be simple enough to "sell" to the local management and bookkeeper.

Chapter 8

Manufacturing costs

8–1. What manufacturing cost figures may be useful in the following types of planning activities:
- a) Planning selling prices under normal competitive conditions?
- b) Planning whether to manufacture a certain product when the plant has idle productive capacity?
- c) Planning the volume at which the plant is to operate?
- d) Deciding whether or not to purchase a new machine?
- e) Deciding whether to make a certain part or purchase it from another manufacturer?
- f) Planning working-capital requirements?

8–2. One use of manufacturing costs is to "control." Name several persons, things, or operations that these costs may be used to control and state in each instance how costs are helpful in the control function.

8–3. Describe briefly a procedure that might be used to record each of the following in a company that prepares a monthly profit and loss statement but does not tie costs into its books.
- a) Issue of material.
- b) Labor performed directly on the product.
- c) Supplies used by Department A (which is one of several manufacturing departments).
- d) Transfer of completed product from the factory to the warehouse
- e) Sale of products.
- f) Return of product, undamaged, from customer for which he receives full credit.

8–4. Describe briefly the procedure that might be used to record each happening listed in Question 8–3 if the company used an actual job-order, cost-accounting system that was tied in with its general books and collected overhead costs by departments.

8–5. A standard cost system requires a more or less laborious calculation of standards and a set of variance accounts, neither of which is necessary in an actual cost system. In view of this, why is it frequently alleged that a standard cost system is simpler and involves less work than an actual cost system?

8–6. Discuss the uses and limitations of standard costs for
- a) Planning.
- b) Control.

8–7. What are the relative merits of charging payments for overtime labor to individual jobs versus including them as a part of overhead?

8–8. What are the misconceptions or fallacies that arise under these circumstances.

a) "A complaint of one sales department that its costs have gone up in spite of increased sales because the sales of another department have fallen off."

b) "A hasty conclusion by a sales executive that some product or territory which is 'in the red' on the basis of a territorial analysis of net profits is necessarily a drain on the business and should be eliminated."

Chapter 9
Operating costs in marketing and administration

9–1. In some situations, a budget is useful as an aid to the control of marketing and administrative costs; in other situations, a budget is virtually useless. With respect to each of the following situations, would a budget be useful? If so, what sort of budget standard would be most useful for expense control? What qualifications would have to be made in interpreting the comparison of actual to budget?

a) *Salesman's Salary and Expenses.* A salesman works out of the branch office of a large meat-packing company. He visits the retailers in his territory weekly and takes orders for products of his company. Prices are set by the branch office and are kept very close to competitors' prices; but for one reason or another, prices are not always identical with competitors' prices. Prices change frequently, sometimes daily. The salesman is paid a weekly salary plus his actual traveling expenses. Competition is very strong in the territory.

b) *Office Expense.* The manager of a certain department in an insurance company is responsible for the actual preparation of all insurance policies. There are approximately 100 typists in the department. The typist modifies and completes a printed insurance form to conform to the requirements of the prospective policyholder. Usually this operation involves filling in blanks on the form for names, addresses, amounts, beneficiary, etc., but occasionally additional sentences or even whole paragraphs have to be inserted. The manager must see to it that the work is done accurately and promptly and that costs are kept as low as feasible.

c) *Advertising.* The board of directors of a certain company have decided that the sales manager may spend 1 percent of net sales for advertising. All work in connection with advertising is done by the company's advertising agency; no employees of the company, except the sales manager, are concerned with advertising. The advertising campaigns consist entirely of magazine advertising in a variety of business and trade publications.

9–2. In general, there is more difficulty in setting useful control standards for order-getting costs than there is in setting standards for order-filling costs.

Distinguish as clearly as possible between these two kinds of cost, citing examples other than those listed in the text.

9–3.   Formulate guiding rules or general principles that can be used in connection with the following policy decisions:

a)   When a firm sells a number of products, under what circumstances should it change the price of one product (either lower it or raise it)?

b)   The market research division estimates that a proposed redesign of the product (including its package) will result in an annual increase of $100,000 in sales volume, with no change in selling price. What cost factors should be considered in deciding whether to go ahead with the redesigning plan?

c)   Under what circumstances should a product be discontinued, assuming that no new product will be added to replace it?

Chapter 10

Discretionary costs in marketing, research, and administration

10–1.   The table below shows certain facts about the selling effort of the Warford Corporation, a single product enterprise. The company has elected to sell to the machine tool manufacturing industry by direct visits by salesmen only. Comment on the facts given and devise the orders you would issue for further information. The product is advertised nationally in the trade journals.

Region	Number of possible buyers	Number of salesmen	Number of branch offices	Sales volume ($ millions)
Northeast	980	16	3	6.4
North Central	600	19	3	3.8
Northwest	150	0	0	0
Mid-Atlantic	300	5	1	1.8
Southeast	140	4	1	1.5
Southwest	290	1	0	0.6
Plains	200	1	0	0.3
Rockies	140	0	0	0
West	680	29	5	4.3

10–2.   Distinguish between "research" and "development." What is the essential difference between these two functions that often requires that they be treated differently for cost-control and cost-accounting purposes?

10–3.   Should the accounting system of a business be set up in such a way that management can obtain, from the account balances, the figures necessary to answer the policy questions raised in this chapter?

Chapter 11
Inventory valuation

11-1. Why does the "profit and loss" viewpoint generally take precedence over the "balance-sheet" viewpoint in connection with discussions of problems in accounting policy?

11-2. Give at least four different definitions of the term "Cost or market, whichever is lower" when used, without qualification, in an annual report to describe a method of inventory valuation.

11-3. What is the difference between "realization value" and "replacement cost"?

11-4. A certain company collected data on what its inventory value would have been under three different methods of valuation: first-in–first-out cost; replacement cost; and realization value (calculated on the assumption that the inventory will eventually be sold in finished form). The following tendencies were observed:

a) In years of rising prices FIFO cost was lower than realization value, and both were lower than replacement cost.

b) In years of falling prices, replacement costs were lower than realization value, and both were lower than FIFO costs.
Explain why these relationships occurred. Include in your explanation the probable relationship of cost to selling price in this industry.

11-5. Why is it desirable, from the "profit and loss" viewpoint, to write inventory values down to market when market is lower than cost?

11-6. Certain facts about the Morton Company, which manufactured and sold a single product, are shown in the table below. Year No. 1 was considered to be a normal year; year No. 2 was a year of high prices, and Year No. 3 was a year of low prices. Assume that the beginning and ending inventory each year consists wholly of raw materials.

	Year no. 1	Year no. 2	Year no. 3	Year no. 4
Sales, units..............	50,000	50,000	50,000	....
Selling price per unit (January 1–December 31)	$ 9.00	$ 12.00	$ 6.00	$ 9.00
Purchases, units	50,000	50,000	50,000	....
Purchases, cost per unit (January 1–December 31)	$ 3.00	$ 4.00	$ 2.00	$ 3.00
Inventory January 1, units.	10,000	10,000	10,000	10,000
Manufacturing costs.........	$100,000	$100,000	$100,000	....
Selling and administrative costs	$ 50,000	$ 60,000	$ 40,000	....
Additional costs required to process and sell ending inventory	$ 32,000	$ 28,000	$ 30,000	....

Compute the value of the ending inventory and the net profit for years Nos. 1, 2 and 3 under each of the following methods of inventory valuation:

    a)   First-in–first-out cost.

    b)   Replacement value.

    c)   Realization value (selling price less additional cost to make and sell).

    d)   Cost or market, whichever is lower.

Notes: 1.   Assume that the inventory on January 1 of year No. 1 was valued at $30,000.

2.   In calculating replacement cost and realization value, use the cost and selling prices that were in effect during the succeeding year, on the assumption that cost and selling price for the succeeding year were known at the time the inventory calculation was made.

11–7.   Consider the following factors about a specific company: relation of cost to selling price, inventory turnover, variety of items in raw-material inventory, percentage of raw material cost to total cost, length of the manufacturing process, policy with respect to inventory speculation, use of hedging. Under what circumstances would the LIFO method of inventory valuation provide a better estimate of the net profit earned by the company than the FIFO method?

11–8.   Should the controller urge the adoption of a method of valuation that is best from the standpoint of income tax considerations, even though he does not believe that such a method will best reflect the true earnings of the period?

11–9.   It has been argued that the universal use of LIFO would tend to even out the peaks and valleys of reported net profits that characterize business cycles and hence would promote the general welfare of the country. Do you agree? Why?

11–10.   It has been asserted that when a company uses LIFO, its income statement reflects price changes more rapidly than if it uses FIFO. Do you agree? Why?

11–11.   In the tables below are figures for two companies, which have been drawn up under certain simplifying assumptions, as follows:

    a)   Only one kind of merchandise is purchased and sold; 100 percent of product cost (i.e. Cost of Sales) is material cost.

    b)   As soon as one unit is sold, it is replaced in inventory by another unit, there is, therefore, no change in inventory quantity.

    c)   Sales volume each year is constant at 1,000 units.

    d)   Inventory turnover is 1.

    e)   Company A adjusts its selling price immediately and exactly for current changes in material cost. Company B prices at a markup of $1.00 per unit over the invoice cost of the specific units of merchandise being sold. Otherwise, the two companies are identical.

f) Selling prices and purchase cost change on January 1 then remain unchanged for a year.

1. Complete the tables so as to show the Gross Profit in each year for each company under FIFO and under LIFO.

2. Which method would you recommend for each company? Why?

Exhibit 1
COST OF SALES UNDER LIFO
(both companies)

Year	Inventory January 1	Purchases	Inventory December 31	Cost of sales
1.....	1,000 at $1.00	1,000 at $1.00	1,000 at	
2.....	....	1,000 at 1.50		
3.....	....	1,000 at 2.00		
4.....	....	1,000 at 0.50		
5.....	....	1,000 at 1.00		

Exhibit 2
COST OF SALES UNDER LIFO
(both companies)

Year	Inventory January 1	Purchases	Inventory December 31	Cost of sales
1.....	1,000 at $1.00	1,000 at $1.00	1,000 at	
2.....	....	1,000 at 1.50		
3.....	....	1,000 at 2.00		
4.....	....	1,000 at 0.50		
5.....	....	1,000 at 1.00		

Exhibit 3
GROSS PROFIT
(each company)

	Company A			Company B		
Year	Sales	Gross profit under FIFO	Gross profit under LIFO	Sales	Gross profit under FIFO	Gross profit under LIFO
1.....	$2,000	$	$		$	$
2.....	2,500					
3.....	3,000					
4.....	1,500					
5.....	2,000					

Chapter 12

Depreciation policies and methods

12–1. Stowbaw and Co. is a major construction company. At any given time, it has between three and five major projects in process. Total sales exceeds $40 million yearly. Most of the important assets of the business are construction machines, such as cranes, earth-movers, cement mixers, and specialized vehicles. Although these machines are robust, the treatment they receive on the sites tends to diminish their effective life. For example, mobile crane #188 was acquired in early 1969 for $67,000 and was depreciated using the straight-line method on the assumption of an eight-year life. By the end of 1972, it had become ineffective: It required so many repairs that it could not be relied upon. A similar but more modern crane was purchased in early 1973 for $92,000. This crane, #342, was slightly more sophisticated in operation, and, in the opinion of the site manager, somewhat less robust. Considering all factors, devise a depreciation policy suitable for cranes for the company, given that the experience with #188 was reasonably common and that some forty cranes were usually in service at any one time.

12–2. The controller of the Howell Company was one day presented with a problem relative to the recording of asset value and reserve for depreciation on machinery owned but not in actual possession.

The Howell Company was the sole supplier of an integral component part for the motor assembly used in one of the more popular makes of automobiles.

In October 1972, the company became involved in a labor dispute relative to wages and security benefits and was given notice by the officers of the labor union that, unless demands were complied with, a strike would occur in November. Demands were such that labor counsel for the company advised management to hold out against the workers. This plan of action was adopted with full realization that a lengthy work stoppage might result.

Immediately following the decision to resist the demands of the union, the president called a meeting of all officers, the sales manager, director of purchases, and the materials-control manager. At this meeting, it was decided, in order to prevent the shutdown of their customer during the strike period, arrangements would be made with other manufacturers to produce the required parts: One firm to perform the blanking operation on an automatic screw machine, another to perform a heat-treating operation, etc.

Under the direction of the vice president in charge of manufacturing and the director of purchases, these arrangements were accomplished. The Howell Company was to furnish the bar steel to the first operation at cost, and they were to ship to and charge the company performing the next operation, and so on down the line, with the company doing the last operation furnishing the Howell Company with notices of shipment to the automobile manufacturer and invoicing the company with the final cost of the part. Upon receipt of this information, the company billing department was to invoice the automobile manufacturer.

Negotiations between management and labor failed, and the factory employees were called out on strike in November, as had been threatened. Immediately, the above arrangements were put into effect, with raw material being rerouted from the steel mills and production starting to move.

Just at this particular time, the company was to take delivery of a new type of automatic screw machine which was to have performed the first operation on the product involved in this problem, and had received word this machine, valued at approximately $50,000.00, had been shipped the day prior to the strike and would arrive in a few days.

Naturally, with the factory idle, delivery of this machine could not be accepted, and it was decided, in order to obtain the increased efficiency that this machine could provide, that it should be sent to the firm performing the first operation. With the consent of this supplier, this was done, and the machine put to use.

When the vendor's invoice covering the purchase of this machine was received, these questions were presented to the controller for decision:

1.   Should the value of the machine be set up as a fixed asset immediately or deferred until the machine is actually received in the plant at the end of the strike?

2.   Should installation cost of the machine in our supplier's plant be paid by us and included in the asset value?

3.   Should depreciation be reserved currently or deferred until we put the machine into use in our plant at the end of the strike period?

4.   What disposition should be made of the additional transportation and installation costs when the machine is installed in our plant after the strike?

Chapter 13
The budget: Policies and procedures

13–1.   What is the relation between the "accounting plan" discussed in an earlier chapter and the "budget" discussed in this chapter?

13–2.   What use can be made of the budget? In other words, for what purposes are budgets prepared?

13–3.   Under what circumstances, if any, should a company budget a net loss for the coming year?

13–4.   Discuss the following statement: "Since many of the balance-sheet items are affected by sales volume and since sales volume is particularly difficult to forecast, it is a waste of time to attempt the preparation of a budgeted balance sheet."

13–5.   Discuss the following questions about each of the procedures described below: In what respects is the procedure a "budget"? In what respects does it fail to meet the qualifications of a "budget"? What are its strength and weakness?

a)   The company had 50 employees. It had no written budget of any kind. The president, who had been with the company for 20 years, claimed that he had no need for a budget, since he "had a pretty good idea" of how the company was doing and what its prospects were. He looked at all sales orders and invoices, and he examined the job cost sheets on which were recorded the actual cost of each lot of products manufactured. The company had an excellent credit rating, and responsible men in the community considered that it was well managed and profitable.

b)   The company had 200 employees. It had no budget, but it used a carefully worked-out standard cost system. Occasionally, the monthly income statements showed large variances from standard costs. The president commented: "I understand the significance of these variances because I know the current prices of materials, I know current wage rates, and from my daily trips through the plant I know how efficiently the manufacturing departments are operating, and how busy they are. I don't need a fancy budget." The company had an excellent credit rating, and responsible men in the community considered that it was well managed and profitable.

c)   The company had 2,000 employees. It had a budget department, responsible to the controller, which annually worked out a detailed, flexible budget for each manufacturing, selling, and administrative department. The budget for each department showed the expenses which that department was permitted to incur at all levels of operation; it was based on a careful analysis of all past expenditures in the department. A 50-page report, showing actual and budgeted expenses, was prepared monthly for management, and each department head received a copy of the page that pertained to his department. The company was in financial difficulty.

d)   A "flight plan" was made out for every flight of a major passenger airline company. This flight plan was prepared by the pilot and included the route he planned to take, the distance between each landing, anticipated altitude, a plan for an alternative route if weather should require a change, probable gasoline consumption and gasoline reserve, the forecasted weather conditions, anticipated speed and time of arrival and similar information about the flight. Of course, none of this information was in dollars. The pilot had to choose from routes prescribed by the Civil Aeronautics Authority, he had to conform to certain policies of the company, and he received technical advice and assistance from the company meteorologist; but the pilot was solely responsible for whether the flight was to be made and the particular route and altitudes chosen. The pilot signed the flight plan, which was initialed by the meteorologist and approved in writing by the flight superintendent, who was the pilot's superior. After the flight, the actual course, altitude, speed, gas consumption, etc., were filled in on the form, and the pilot was held accountable for differences between the plan and the actual happenings.

13–6.   Describe a procedure for budgeting the cost of goods sold item.

13–7.   Is there any significant difference between a flexible budget and a fixed budget that is frequently revised?

13–8.   Department 12 of the Hudson Company manufactured rivets and no other products. All rivets were identical. In August 1970, Department 12 made 4,000,000 rivets. The company used both a standard cost system and a flexible budget. Standard unit costs (per thousand rivets) were determined by dividing budgeted costs at an expected average volume by the number of rivets (in thousands) which that volume level represented. Certain cost information is shown in the following table.

Department 12	Actual cost August 1970	Standard cost per 1,000 rivets	Total standard cost August 1970	Budget August 1970	Budget formula
Direct labor	$10,500	. . . . .	. . . .	$12,000	$3.00 per 1,000 rivets
Direct material	22,000	$5.00	$20,000	20,000	$5.00 per 1,000 rivets
Departmental expenses.	9,500	. . . . .	. . . .	9,200	$6,000 per month + $0.80 per 1,000 rivets
Prorated general overhead	5,000	1.00	4,000	5,000	$5,000 per month
Total	$47,000	. . . . .	. . . .	$46,200	. . . .

a)   What was the expected average volume (in terms of rivet output) at which standard unit costs were determined?

b)   What was the standard cost of direct labor per thousand rivets? The total standard labor cost?

c)   What was the standard cost for department expense per thousand rivets? Total standard departmental expense?

d)   Explain as much of the difference between total actual costs and total standard costs as you can on the basis of the information given.

Chapter 14
Profit planning

14–1.   What is a "break-even chart"? Discuss the principal assumptions underlying break-even analysis.

14–2.   What uses can be made of a break-even chart and of the detailed analysis of fixed and variable costs that often underlies such a chart?

14–3.   In preparing a break-even chart, it is often necessary to use historical data. What are the limitations that must be kept in mind concerning the use of such data?

14–4.   List the principal reasons why the actual profit for a certain month may differ from the profit relationship that is shown on a carefully prepared break-even chart.

14–5.   What is the significance to management of the "break-even" point?"

14–6.   If a company has more than one product can they prepare a break-even chart for the combined operation? What are the major difficulties in the preparation of such a chart?

14–7. Two companies (A and B) sell the same product for $80. The variable cost per unit is $60 for both companies. Company A reduces the variable cost per unit to $54 and reduces the selling price to $76 per unit. Company B cannot reduce the variable cost per unit but is forced to adopt the selling price set by Company A. Each company sells 40,000 units. What effect does this change have on profits for the two companies?

14–8. What are the primary characteristics of direct costing procedures?

14–9. Discuss the statement that "different classes of costs may be relevant in making different classes of decisions."

14–10. You have an opportunity to increase sales by accepting a special order for a price that lies between the variable cost of the product and its full cost. Discuss the factors that should be considered in determining whether or not to accept the order.

14–11. During World War II the auto companies began selling cars to the federal government at a price below full cost in order to utilize some available capacity. This pricing practice has continued to the present. Is there any reason to doubt that this was a wise decision?

14–12. A small manufacturing company, making a single product which sold net for $1.20 per unit, estimated that under current operating conditions its variable costs were $0.40 per unit produced, its nonvariable costs were $900 per month, and its semivariable costs per month were as shown in the schedule below:

Production (units)	Semivariable costs
500	$ 500
1,000	600
1,500	700
2,000	800
2,500	900
3,000	1,000
3,500	1,100
4,000	1,200
4,500	1,300
5,000	1,400

a) Make a schedule of monthly costs at the various production volumes shown above by means of a table with the following column headings: (1) Production Volume, (2) Variable Costs, (3) Semivariable Costs, (4) Nonvariable Costs, and (5) Total Costs.

b) Construct a graph, with a line for each type of cost and total costs at each of the production volumes. Plot total dollar sales at the various production volumes, assuming that all units produced are sold. (Note that a column for sales figures may be added to the schedule prepared in A to give the same results as are shown graphically in B.)

(1) How many units does the company have to make and sell in a month to break even?

(2)   What is the amount of profit if production and sales are 3,500 units for a month? 2,000 units for a month?

(3)   If the company expects to produce and sell, over a normal cycle of good and bad years, an average monthly volume of 3,000 units, what will be the average monthly expected cost? The average monthly expected profit?

c)   Construct a second graph showing the unit cost of production at each volume of production. Draw in the additional line required to obtain the break-even point. (Note that a tabular schedule may also be prepared to show the same results portrayed by this graph.)

(1)   What is the break-even point?

(2)   What is the amount of profit per unit if production and sales are 3,500 units for a month? 2,000 units for a month?

d)   It was expected that the actual volume of production would vary from month to month but that the average monthly production over a series of active and slow years would be 4,000 units. At this long-run expected average monthly production volume and on the basis of the cost data shown in Section a, each unit would cost $0.925. In its cost-accounting system, therefore, the company valued each unit produced at a standard cost of $0.925. The cost "absorbed" by production in any month was found by multiplying the actual number of units produced by the standard unit cost, $0.925. The difference between this figure and the total of the costs actually incurred represented the extent to which the actual costs were "underabsorbed" or "overabsorbed." If, over a reasonably long period, the actual costs and the actual production volume met the long-run expectations, the underabsorbed costs resulting during months when volume was below 4,000 units would be offset by the overabsorbed costs resulting during months when volume was about 4,000 units; also, the total actual costs for the period divided by the total actual units produced during the period would come out at the average cost of $0.925 per unit. Draw in on the graph prepared in b above a line representing the amount of cost that would be absorbed at $0.925 per unit over the volume range from 0 to 5,000 units. This line may be labeled "absorbed into cost."

(1)   If 4,500 units are produced in a given month, what will be the amount absorbed into cost? If actual costs for the month are as shown by the total cost line for this volume, how much cost is over- or underabsorbed?

(2)   If 2,500 units are produced, how much cost is over- or underabsorbed?

e)   (1)   In the income statement, cost of goods sold was determined by multiplying the number of units sold by the standard unit cost of $0.925. Assume that during the first year of operation 42,000 units were produced at a total actual cost of $37,240 and that all units were sold at $1.25 each. What adjustment should be made to the gross profit to reflect the difference between actual costs and the computed goods sold?

(2)   Finished-goods inventory was also valued at $0.925 per unit. If only 35,000 units were sold of the 42,000 produced, would the adjustment to gross profit differ from that computed in 1? Compute the dollar amount of finished-goods inventory at expected unit cost and at actual average unit cost for the year, assuming that 35,000 units were sold.

(3)   Assume that during the first year of operations 30,000 units were produced at a total actual cost of $31,900 and that 5,000 units remained in year-end inventory, other conditions remaining as stated in 1 and 2 preceding. Compute the dollar amount of finished-goods inventory and cost of goods sold at both actual cost and standard cost. What accounts for the difference between the actual cost and standard cost figures?

Chapter 15

Planning and control of capital expenditures

15–1.   What are the responsibilities of the controller with respect to the planning and control of plant expenditures? What aspects of this problem are not his responsibility?

15–2.   Discuss how each of the following factors should be used, if at all, in a calculation that is prepared for the purpose of determining whether or not a capital asset should be replaced:
   a)   Standard costs
   b)   Depreciation expense
   c)   Book value of the asset being replaced
   d)   Interest on the new investment
   e)   Income taxes
   f)   Risk

15–3.   Many important factors involved in a proposed capital expenditure cannot be expressed in quantitative terms; hence these factors cannot be included in a mathematical calculation of possible savings or benefits. How can these intangible factors be taken into account in arriving at the final solution to the problems?

15–4.   Once a plant expenditure has been made, the costs are sunk—they are "water over the dam." Of what value then is a postcheck on the estimates of savings and profits that were prepared as a basis for the decision?

15–5.   Compare and contrast the following methods for ranking plant expenditure proposals:
   a)   Payback
   b)   Present value
   c)   Time-adjusted rate of return

15–6.   What method(s) would you use in evaluating a group of proposed plant expenditures? Why?

15–7.   Of what use is sensitivity analysis in plant expenditure evaluation?

15–8.   Compare probabilistic capital budgeting techniques (e.g., optimistic, most likely, and pessimistic estimates) with sensitivity analysis. Illustrate their similarities and differences.

15–9.   Distinguish between a capital budget and an operating budget. How are the two interrelated?

15–10.   Sitterman Inc.'s management group must evaluate three investment proposals, particulars of which are given below. Ignoring taxes and scrap values, comment on the relative desirability of the proposals. The target rate of return for projects of the risk class to which the three proposals belong is 18 percent.

Project	1	2	3
Investment at start	$11,000	$20,000	$30,000
Life in years	8	8	6
Net cash inflows at the end of each of years			
1 and 2	$ 4,500	$ 4,000	$13,000
3, 4, 5, and 6	2,500	7,000	6,000
7 and 8	1,000	6,000	. . . .

15–11.   Discuss the income tax considerations one should make when analyzing plant expenditure proposals.

15–12.   How do the various ranking methods discussed in the chapter relate to the amount of risk management is willing to assume? What ranking method would a "risk avoiding" manager tend to favor? Why?

15–13.   Discuss the concept of incremental (differential) cost as it relates to plant expenditure evaluation.

15–14.   What costs, if any, which are required for plant expenditure evaluation are not generated by the traditional accounting system? How can the controller aid in obtaining these costs?

Chapter 16
Statements and reports for management

16–1.   What are the essential characteristics of a good statement or report for management?

16–2.   What are the differences between a "control" report and an "information" report?

16–3.   In general, what conditions have to be met in order to justify the introduction of an additional control report?

16–4.   Should allocated costs be included in a control report?

16–5.   What are the advantages and disadvantages of using actual sales dollars, sales dollars at standard selling prices, and physical units (yards, pounds, etc.), respectively, as measures of sales volume? Consider the uses that might be made of each type of measure.

16–6. Make a list of the ways in which communication failure can occur between an industrial activity and the manager responsible, in the situation where the manager's sole source of knowledge of the activity is a report or series of reports. Comment on why each type of failure can happen, and on some points which can help to prevent it.

Chapter 17

Statements and reports for management (continued)

17–1. It has been said that the only ultimate justification for collecting figures is that they will eventually lead to action of some kind. If this is true, can there be such a thing as an "information" report?

17–2. What uses can be made of the information in a report that shows comparative profit and loss statements for the current year and for each of the preceeding ten years?

17–3. What possible qualifications are there to the validity of a comparison of current figures with those of prior years?

17–4. Shortly after he took over his job, the controller of a certain company recommended to the president that the company change its method of depreciation from a straight-line basis to a unit-of-production basis. The president objected on the grounds that this change would make future figures inconsistent with past figures and that it would, therefore, be difficult to use the past figures to disclose basic trends and useful comparisons. Is this objection valid?

17–5. What should be the responsibility of the controller with respect to nonaccounting reports? Should he prepare such reports and have direct supervision over them, or should he restrict his efforts primarily to accounting reports?

17–6. What constitutes a "venture," as the term is used to denote an activity within a corporation? Under what circumstances should "joint-activity reports" be used?

17–7.   Hamlin Company
  a)   Give a brief general description of the nature of the report shown in Exhibit 1 (Your description should be similar to the one that might appear in a company handbook that describes all reports used in the Hamlin Company.)
  b)   Explain, step by step, how the figure of $240 that appears under Burden, Volume, for Department F was probably calculated.
  c)   Which of the four departments apparently is most badly in need of further investigations? Why?

Exhibit 1
HAMLIN COMPANY

A. Increase or Decrease over 1960 Standard Cost, October, 1960

Department	Total std. cost	Material		Direct labor	Burden		Waste	Total mfg. var.
		Price	Yield, usage, and formula		Volume	Budget, etc.		
E	$ 25,200	$ 300	$ 300	$ 360*	$ 240	$ 600*	$ 60*	$ 180*
F	33,000	300	300	360	240*	450*	60	330
G	24,000	2,400	9,000	900*	480*	4,950*	3,600*	1,470
H	37,320	600	2,400	2,100*	720*	4,800*	1,560	3,060*
Total for October	$ 120,000	$ 3,600	$12,000	$ 3,000*	$1,200*	$10,800*	$ 2,040*	$ 1,440*

B. Increase or Decrease over 1960 Standard Cost, Year to Date—1960

Department	Total std. cost	Material		Direct labor	Burden		Waste	Total mfg. var.
		Price	Yield, usage, and formula		Volume	Budget, etc.		
E	$ 369,600	....	$ 7,200*	$ 800*	$2,400	$ 1,600*	$ 800*	$ 8,000*
F	484,000	....	9,600	....	....	1,600	800	12,000
G	359,200	$32,000*	48,000	3,200*	1,600*	8,000*	11,200*	8,000*
H	547,200	8,000	29,600	8,000*	1,600*	16,000*	2,400*	6,400
Total year to date	$1,760,000	$40,000*	$80,000	$12,000*	$ 800*	$24,000*	$13,600*	$10,400*

* Increase

Exhibit 2
REPORT ON DEPARTMENT COSTS AND VARIANCE
(month—November 1972)

Current month	(1) Actual	(2) Budget	(3) = (1) − (2) Variance	(4) Last month	(5) = (1) − (4) Variance	(6) Same month last year	(7) = (1) − (6) Variance
Direct labor	4250	3750	500	5630	−1380	3235	1015
Indirect labor	4680	4640	40	4670	10	4100	580
Materials	18385	16950	1435	19750	−1365	15185	3200
Supplies	875	1250	−375	1145	−270	960	−85
Power and variable overhead	1650	1390	260	1485	165	1295	355
Administration	2150	2150	0	2150	0	1750	400
Special items	432	0	432	625	−193	225	207
	32422	30130	2292	35455	−3033	26750	5672
Twelve months to date							
Direct labor	46480	46495	−15	45465	1015	39250	7230
Indirect labor	56150	56390	−240	55570	580	48750	7400
Materials	210350	177685	32665	207150	3200	143200	67150
Supplies	11280	13250	−1970	11365	−85	9870	1410
Power and variable overhead	17875	12750	5125	17520	355	10785	7090
Administration	25000	24850	150	14600	400	15200	9800
Special items	3050	300	2750	2843	207	13600	−10550
	370185	331720	38465	360113	5672	280655	89530

17–8.   Comment critically on the monthly report shown in Exhibit 2. This report is offered each month to the manager of the department. The upper half gives figures for a single month, the lower presents cumulative totals for twelve months. The budget figures are taken from a flexible manufacturing budget for the actual volume produced.

Chapter 18

Inventory control

18–1.   What is meant by the term "operating control" as applied to inventories?

18–2.   What should be the controller's responsibility with respect to the operating control of inventories?

18–3.   Formulate a set of policies that might be used as a basis for the operating control of inventories in a specific company.

18–4.   Distinguish between the two methods of controlling inventories—i.e., maximum and minimum limits versus the conversion of sales estimates into purchase requirements. Which method would be preferable for each of the following situations, or would some other method be preferable for either?

a)   The company produces only as orders are received. It manufactures a wide variety of metal products, usually to customers' specifications. Raw material consists principally of various sizes, shapes and alloys of steel.

b)   The company manufactures 200 styles of men's shoes which it sells to retailers. It is often possible to forecast total sales with reasonable accuracy, but it is impossible to predict sales of a particular style because of changes in consumer preference. Inventory consists of (1) about 20 colors and grades of leather and cloth and (2) about 200 items of "findings," which are the heels, nails, thread, laces, and other material common to all styles.

c)   The company manufactures automobiles. Which method should it use with respect to (1) motors which the company purchases (there is storage space for only three days' requirements of motors in the company's warehouse); (2) cigarette lighters, which the company purchases; (3) No. 0718 bolts, of which 16 are used in each automobile?

18–5.   What are the risks associated with an inventory that is too large? What are the risks associated with an inventory that is too small?

18–6.   The Glamour Cosmetics Company uses in one of its products a special grade of lanolin which it purchases from time to time as required. The average daily requirement for this material is 15 pounds. The interval from the placing of the order to the delivery of the material at the Glamour Company plant varies from 15 to 25 days. An examination of the company's records shows that the maximum production requirements for any 25-day

period will not exceed 475 pounds and that the minimum production requirement during such a period is not likely to fall below 275 pounds. The standard
order has been established at 900 pounds.

What maximum and minimum inventory points should be established under
these conditions?

18–7.   Exhibit 1 is a record of the orders and receipts of No. 2 pencils
for six months in the Sta-Fresh Biscuit Company, which had an office force
of 75 persons. This exhibit also gives a condensed record of issues. Actually,
an average of about 40 issues was made per month and the figures given
are the total quantity issued for each month. The company wanted to be
certain that it would not run out of No. 2 pencils. It was decided that
the former policy of ordering pencils monthly was inefficient and that henceforth they should be ordered only four times a year. No significant change
in the demand for pencils was foreseen. Determine maximum and minimum
limits and ordering quantities for No. 2 pencils.

Exhibit 1
STA-FRESH BISCUIT COMPANY
Activity on No. 2 Pencils

Orders		Receipts		Issues	
Date	Quantity	Date	Quantity	Month	Amount
March 1.	50 gross	March 4	50 gross	March	40 gross
April 1	40 gross	April 7	40 gross	April	35 gross
May 1	35 gross	May 6	35 gross	May	55 gross
June 1.	55 gross	June 8	55 gross	June	40 gross
July 1	40 gross	July 9	40 gross	July	45 gross
August 1	45 gross	August 5	45 gross	August	35 gross

18–8   (a)   Compute the most economical order quantity for purchasing
part X from the following details.

Cost to store one part for one day = $0.2/unit/day
    (including capital cost)
Cost of being out of stock = $2000/day
    by any number of units
Daily constant demand = 500
Purchase price per unit = $10
Delay between order and delivery = 1 day

(b)   Describe verbally a method for computing the most economical order
quantity if the assumptions in part (a) hold except that the delay between
order and delivery varies unpredictably between one and four days.

Chapter 19

Corporate strategy

19–1. In what ways can each of the following tools be used in corporate planning activities:

a) the computer
b) mathematical programming
c) simulation models
d) econometric models

19–2. Is long-range planning a line or staff function?

19–3. Peter Drucker once observed that management's attention should be focused more on the discovery of opportunities than on the solution of problems. Comment on this suggestion and, if you agree with it, suggest how management can organize their activities so that they can achieve this state of affairs.

19–4. LGW Co. has been earning an after tax rate of 20 percent on total capital employed while paying out 50 percent of earnings to stockholders. The firm's current debt-equity ratio is 1:2 and it can borrow money at an after tax cost of 5 percent.

a) Calculate the present earnings growth rate for the firm.
b) To what extent can management effectively control each of the determinants of the firm's earnings growth rate?

19–5. What is "financial leverage?" What is the significance of "negative leverage?" What are the constraints encountered by management as they attempt to employ financial leverage to their advantage?

19–6. Is there any inconsistency, in terms of long-run corporate strategy, between the following goals:

a) Maximizing the total earnings of the firm over its lifetime.
b) Maximizing the present market value of the firm's equity securities.

19–7. What objectives, besides long-run profits, might management consider in doing long-range planning? How should these other factors be evaluated? Why is profit-maximization not an appropriate operating objective from the point of view of those engaged in planning?

19–8. Some firms employ very little or no long-term debt financing. In light of the advantages of utilizing financial leverage, how do you explain such behavior?

19–9. A corporate financial officer has said, "We have a goal of earnings per share which we manage astutely every quarter." What is the difference, if any, between earnings management and earnings maximization? What are the implications of this difference for long-range planning activities?

19–10. What is the importance of the "planning gap" to the long-run planning activity?

19–11. What sort of background is desirable for a director of long-range planning?

19–12. What is the difference between strategy and tactics in terms of business planning? Who, in the business organization, should be primarily involved with strategic considerations and who with matters relating to tactics?

19–13. In what way can the "strategy matrix" be used by someone engaged in planning?

Chapter 20

Long-range planning for existing ventures

20–1. Should divisional objectives be developed by divisional management or established by corporate management?

20–2. What company or industry characteristics determine the optimal planning period?

20–3. What does the following statement, made about the railroad industry in 1960, suggest about the orientation of long-range planning activities? "I grieve to see the most advanced physical and social organization of the last century go down in shabby disgrace for lack of the same comprehensive imagination that built it up. What is lacking is the will of the companies to survive and to satisfy the public by inventiveness and skill."

20–4. Do you agree with this statement: "The activity that goes into the preparation of the five-year plan is of more value than the plan itself"?

20–5. In what way would the computer be useful in preparing long-range projections?

20–6. Discuss the following: "Perhaps the most important activity that management can engage in, from the standpoint of the long-run welfare of the firm, is deciding just what business the company is in."

20–7. The text states that for a long-range plan to be meaningful and intelligible it is necessary to make predictions of such factors as economic growth for the nation and industry, changes in prices for our goods and supplies, etc. Given the difficulty of making such predictions accurately, is there any point in proceeding with a formal planning process?

20–8. Since planning can be described as "preparing accounting reports for the future," it is natural that the firm's accounting staff should be primarily responsible for the preparation of long-range plans. Discuss.

20–9. What should top management do when it becomes obvious that they cannot meet the plans they have established?

Chapter 21

New-venture planning

21–1.   Assume that Company A is evaluating the possibility of acquiring Company B for cash obtained from a bond issue. Company A has calculated the present value of B's future earnings at a discount rate equal to A's target rate of return on net assets and found it satisfactory. Should Company A estimate the effect of the acquisition on future earnings per share? Why?

21–2.   Why are corporations so concerned with earnings per share figures?

21–3.   Discuss the merits of each of the following as possible discount rates for evaluating the present value of the future earnings of a potential acquisition.

   a)   the interest rate on borrowed funds
   b)   target rate of return on total assets
   c)   target rate of return on common stock equity
   d)   weighted average cost of capital

21–4.   Referring to Question 3, which rate would you use when calculating present value? Why?

21–5.   What are the advantages and disadvantages of the pooling method of accounting for a merger versus the purchase method?

21–6.   Company X is planning to merge with Company Y. What are the functions of each of the controllers involved in the planning process?

21–7.   Why are judgment factors so important in evaluating a potential merger or acquisition? Discuss the important judgment factors.

21–8.   Given the data, present value calculations, and earnings per share projections in the text example, would you make the acquisition for cash? For common stock? Explain your reasoning and preference.

21–9.   How does financial leverage relate to the evaluation of potential mergers and acquisitions?

21–10.   Companies may become "vertically" integrated via acquisitions. What is vertical integration? What type of new venture strategy is vertical integration indicative of? Discuss.

21–11.   Discuss the prerequisites for developing new ventures internally.

Chapter 22

Introduction to computers

22–1.   The sales records of Merko & Smith, Inc., have been computerized for some time. The billing of customers has been carried out satisfactorily for two years, and the recording of customers payments have also been dealt with satisfactorily. The senior sales management of the company have been less satisfied about the management information which has been produced by the computer system, however. No analytical reports have been generated by the sales system programs and the latter have had to be created manually, with inevitable delays, from the computer-printed accounts duplicates. The senior sales managers have been putting pressure on the systems group to install a completely new system to increase the management information output.

Before agreeing to this, the systems group leader has decided to explore how to meet their demands by adapting the present system. You have been presented with the following information and are asked to list all the managerial useful reports which could be developed from the data already stored in the system by adapting the programs without changing the data files.

The principal data files for the sales accounting application are the master file and the current transactions file. The content of each record in each of these files is as follows:

Customer Master File
    Customer name
    Customer account number
    Street address
    City or town
    State and Zip Code
    Credit limit
    Salesman responsible for the account (number)
    Balance at end of previous accounting period
Transaction File
    Date of transaction
    Customer account number
    Dollar amount
    Transaction type—sale, check, discount, etc.
    Product number
    Salesman number
    Quantity

Transactions are maintained on the current disc file for two months and are then placed on magnetic tape where they are stored for four years.

22–2. Visit a computer installation near you and either obtain or develop a chart of its components, similar to that shown in Figure 22–1.

22–3. The managers of Broad and Wall, Inc., are considering putting their order-entry and sales accounting procedures onto a computer. The company sells 10,000 products to 4,000 customers. Roughly, one tenth of the products and of the customers are replaced in the course of a year. The company already has an effective computer-based inventory accounting system in force, including a facility for finished goods. It would be advantageous if the sales system could feed data to the inventory system. Most of the customers are retail businesses. Broad and Wall have been in the practice of cycle billing their customers: that is, all customers whose last names begin A through C on the first working day of the month, D through E on the second, and so on. Credit terms of 30 days are granted to all customers and a 5 percent cash discount is offered those who pay within ten days.

Draw or describe a system flowchart of a possible procedure, including the above information and any other elements you would expect to find in the sales system of a major manufacturing concern.

Chapter 23
Internal control and audit in a computerized system

23–1. It has been argued that the auditor, whether internal or external, can discharge his duties perfectly by inspection of the inputs to and outputs from a computer system, without looking at what happens to data while inside it. Formulate your own position on this issue. Write a note refuting the alternative points of view.

23–2. Devise a procedure for verifying that a number has the characteristics of a date, e.g., 1973/08/24.

23–3. "When an accounting system is operated by means of a computer, it is essential to check and double-check every number that goes into the machine, both before it is fed in and while it is in. Then check it again when it comes out." Comment on the above remark, with particular reference to the difference between the need for checking with a computer and without one.

Chapter 24
Introduction to operations research

24–1. The Arbuckle Chemical Co., blends paints. There are two varieties of paint, deluxe and super. The difference between these lies in the proportions of base, smoothing compound, and thinner in the mixture. The coloration of the paint is identical as between the varieties. In the short term, Arbuckle has enough base to make 9,000 gallons of super or twice that of deluxe, enough smoothing compound to make 10,000 gallons of super or one-and-a-half times as much deluxe, and enough thinner to make 16,000 gallons of super or 12,000 of deluxe. The company did not expect to be able to sell more than 7000 gallons of super in the short term, however. The contribution per gallon of deluxe paint is $1.

a) What is smallest contribution per gallon of super that should induce them to produce any of it?

b) How much of each variety would you recommend they should produce if the contribution of super is $1.49? How about if it is $1.51?

c) Which constraints are binding on the profits of the enterprise if the contribution per gallon of super is $2.10. How much would it be worth to the company to loosen one of these constraints?

24–2. Implement your approach to a solution of problem 24–1 above on your local computer system. Use the built-in linear programming package; do not write one. Compare the output you receive with that you found by hand.

24–3. The Controller of Budgeon and White, Inc., was trying to decide which group of investment proposals from the available set to recommend to management for implementation in the current year. The management wished to limit the total of all capital investments to $750,000 and the amount of the earnings from the new project or projects in the first year was not to fall below $80,000. The treasurer had requested that the cash flow from the projects should be at least $200,000 in the first and $250,000 in the second year. At the same time, the company wished to maximize the rate of return on capital, so far as possible within the constraints given. The individual projects details are shown in the table below.

Formulate a linear programming solution of the investment decision problem. Assume that all the projects can be partially engaged in; that is, although the total investment for project A is shown as $375,000, it would be possible to scale the venture down to any lesser (but still positive) figure.

Project	Investment	First years accounting income	First years cash flow	Second year cash flow	Internal rate of return
A	375,000	35,000	50,000	45,000	37
B	217,000	42,000	166,000	50,000	25
C	105,000	10,000	60,000	60,000	31
D	230,000	35,000	88,000	105,000	26
E	504,000	123,000	45,000	197,000	38
F	125,000	22,000	40,000	55,000	24

Note: Unless you have access to a computer, you should formulate the solution only. Do not try to solve it.

Chapter 25

Simulation in financial planning

25–1. The sales demand at Joe's ice cream stand is a function of the temperature at Golden Creek Beach. The relationship is given by the equation where S is sales demand in dollars and T is the temperature in degrees Fahrenheit.

$$S = 1900 + 44T$$

Joe pays $35 for each canister of ice cream, and must place his order by telephone each afternoon for the following day. The weather is unpredictable, so the temperature on any day is unaffected by that on the day before.

Joe has kept track of previous temperatures, however, and found the following temperature range to probability of occurrence relationship.

Temperature	Probability
50–60	0.10
60–70	0.20
70–80	0.35
80–90	0.25
90–100	0.10

In addition to buying the ice cream, Joe pays fixed costs averaging $250 per day. The sales value of a single canister of ice cream, if completely sold, is $60, but no refund is allowed to Joe on unsold ice cream. Any unsold ice cream at the end of a day must be discarded.

Devise a simulation model which will help Joe decide how many canisters to order, assuming no information is available to improve his ability to predict the temperature.

25–2. Refer to problem 18.8 of Chapter 18. This presents an inventory control problem. Devise a simulated model, in a computer language of your choice, to carry out the analysis in part (b) of that question.

25–3. The level of pollution in the world depends on the rate of consumption of natural resources and on the rate of industrial growth. The rate of consumption of natural resources depends on the population and on the rate of industrial growth. The availability of food depends inversely on the population and inversely on the level of pollution. The population is constrained by the availability of natural resources.

Consider the interrelationships in the above situation. Write down the simplest possible model you can think of which would encompass them; do not be concerned at the moment that the model may not be accurate as a predictor. One of the tenets of good model design is that the variables in the model should include variables that are controllable by the decision maker; what is controllable in the above situation?

25–4. "There is no point in making a simulation model of a projected new activity or of its economic consequences—there just is no hope of verifying the model's output." Discuss and evaluate the above comment, with particular reference to the qualities of alternative methods of studying new ventures.

25–5. "The simulation approach to business problem solving is mathematically clumsy, difficult to verify, expensive to implement, and often extremely difficult to feed with the data required. In fact, about the only good thing about the approach is that there are times when nothing else will work." This remark was taken from a speech by a well-known advocate of optimizing models of the sort introduced in Chapter 24, Operations Research. Is it fair comment? Consider carefully the characteristics of the "times when nothing else will work."

Appendixes

Appendix A

4. Recording of Expenditures
5. Recording the Removal of Replaced Assets

SECTION V. DEFINITION OF CAPITAL CHARGES

1. Definitions of Proper Capital Charges to Authorized Orders
    a) New Equipment Purchased
        (aa) Trade-In Value of Old Equipment
    b) Construction by Employees
    c) Installation Charges
    d) Overhauling Costs on Used Facilities Purchased
2. Determination of Capital Charges in Special Situations
    General Limitation
    a) Revamping or Remodeling of Equipment
    b) Revamping or Remodeling of Buildings or Service
        Facilities
    c) Transfer of Equipment between Plants
3. Valuation of Plant and Equipment Purchased Secondhand
    a) Determination of Book Value
    b) Determination of Replacement Cost
    c) Income Tax Values

SECTION VI. PHYSICAL CONTROL OF PLANT ASSETS

1. Serial Numbering of Class I Assets
2. Authority for Physical Interdepartmental Transfers
3. Rotating Physical Inventory of Plant Assets

SECTION VII. OBSOLESCENCE

1. Information Required for Income Tax Claims for Obsolescence
2. Anticipation of Obsolescence
3. Partial Use of Obsolete Equipment
4. Limitations on Obsolescence Claims
5. Economic Obsolescence

SECTION VIII. MAINTENANCE OF PROPERTY RECORDS

1. Classification of Assets
2. Detailed Information on Property Records
3. Annual Trial Balances
4. Computing and Recording Depreciation
5. Disposition of Assets
6. Recording of Motors
7. Filing Property Record Sheets

SECTION IX. DEPRECIATION

1. Depreciation Rates
2. Depreciation on Additions and Removals

3. Depreciation on Fully Depreciated Assets
4. Depreciation on Assets Purchased Secondhand
5. Depreciation on Improvements to Leased Property
6. Depreciation on Idle Space and Equipment
7. Depreciation after Partial Replacement or Addition of Supplemental Equipment
8. Depreciation on Special Equipment
9. Adjustments for Economic Obsolescence

SECTION X. REPORTS TO CONTROLLER'S OFFICE

1. Annual Report of Changes in Plant Accounts
2. Capital Expenditure and Removal Authorizations
3. Quarterly Plant Account Summary
4. Analysis of Plant Accounts by Years of Expiration

Appendix B

1. Any repair or maintenance job which it is estimated will exceed $200 in total cost shall be covered by a budget order issued on no less an authority than the divisional Plant Manager. Actual expenditures on any such job shall be charged to the appropriate factory expense account as incurred, and shall also be recorded on the budget order, so that when the job is completed the total actual expenditures can be compared with the estimate. The $200 minimum for the application of this procedure may be lowered at the option of the divisional management.

2. On or before November 15th of each year each division shall submit to the Chief Plant Engineer for review and approval a statement of the maintenance program contemplated in the budgeted factory costs for the following year. For those plants which are operating under the procedure outlined in paragraph 3, below, for the handling of "major maintenance" (MM) jobs, this statement shall include a complete schedule and description of all such jobs. For other plants the statement shall include a description of any unusual jobs included in the year's program, together with the estimates of overall total expenditures for routine maintenance. No changes shall be made in the MM jobs scheduled for the year or in other significant features of the approved maintenance programs without the approval of the Chief Plant Engineer.

3. In order to avoid distortion of periodic cost and profit results, major maintenance expenditures in certain plants will be handled as special MM job orders, which will be charged into costs in accordance with the following procedure:

(a) During the first quarter, costs shall be charged each month with one twelfth of the total of major maintenance (MM) jobs for the year, as approved by the Chief Plant Engineer in accordance with paragraph 2, above.

(b) At the beginning of each of the remaining quarters of the year the monthly charge to costs for the quarter shall be determined by deducting from the total of the latest approved schedule of MM jobs for the year the amount already charged to costs since the beginning of the year, and dividing the remainder by the number of months remaining in the year.

(c) The monthly charges to costs, determined in accordance with subparagraphs (a) and (b), shall be offset by credits to a special Reserve for Maintenance account, and all actual expenditures on the MM jobs shall be charged against this reserve. At the end of the year any balance in the reserve shall be closed out as a year-end adjustment, by a debit or credit adjustment to the cumulative MM charge against costs, so that the total charge to costs for the year shall be equal to the actual expenditures. It is *not* permissible to carry over debit or credit balances in the reserve from one fiscal year to another.

4. The standard "Capital Expenditure and Property Record Procedure" defines the approved policy of the company with respect to the classification of expenditures between capital and maintenance and states in detail how the policy shall be interpreted and applied in specific situations.

5. (a) The titles assigned to maintenance jobs should be reasonably brief but should be accurately descriptive of the work to be performed. Such general terms as "repair," "change," "rearrange," etc., should be supplemented by more detailed descriptions, except on jobs under $100; and the larger the amount of the job, the more important it is that the description be fully informative. In some plants there are certain types of maintenance which are routine and repetitive in nature, and for these such general titles as "routine overhauling of cutting machines" will be acceptable. If so-called "blanket" orders are issued covering all minor repairs of a certain type to be performed during the year, the job title should indicate this, as, for example, "blanket order for routine overhauling of cutting machines." When general titles of this kind are used, a more detailed description of work actually performed should be kept for reference if required.

(b) If it is impractical to describe a job adequately in the title, a supplementary statement shall be prepared explaining the work in detail and indicating the reasons for charging to expense under the standard procedure.

6. (a) The Plant Manager in each division shall be responsible for the classification of jobs and the assignment of job titles. The Chief Accountant of the division shall be responsible for checking the classification see that it conforms to the provisions of the standard procedure, and for reviewing job titles.

(b) Copies of all orders over $500, together with any supplementary explanations prepared in accordance with paragraph 5-(b), above, shall be sent to the Chief Plant Engineer and to the Controller's Office for review of classification and titles.

7. Reports shall be prepared in each division each month showing for each maintenance job the authorized amount, the actual expenditure for the month, and the total actual expenditures to date. Copies of these reports shall be sent to the Chief Plant Engineer and to the Controller's Office.

8. The maintenance job orders for each year, and the stores issues, labor tickets, and other supporting data, shall be retained in the divisional files until notice is received from the Controller's Office that all income tax questions for the year have been finally settled. All or a part of these records may be preserved for a longer period, at the option of the division.

Appendix C

Present Value of $1

Years Hence	1%	2%	4%	6%	8%	10%	12%	14%	15%	16%	18%	20%	22%	24%	25%	26%	28%	30%	35%	40%	45%	50%
1	0.990	0.980	0.962	0.943	0.926	0.909	0.893	0.877	0.870	0.862	0.847	0.833	0.820	0.806	0.800	0.794	0.781	0.769	0.741	0.714	0.690	0.667
2	0.980	0.961	0.925	0.890	0.857	0.826	0.797	0.769	0.756	0.743	0.718	0.694	0.672	0.650	0.640	0.630	0.610	0.592	0.549	0.510	0.476	0.444
3	0.971	0.942	0.889	0.840	0.794	0.751	0.712	0.675	0.658	0.641	0.609	0.579	0.551	0.524	0.512	0.500	0.477	0.455	0.406	0.364	0.328	0.296
4	0.961	0.924	0.855	0.792	0.735	0.683	0.636	0.592	0.572	0.552	0.516	0.482	0.451	0.423	0.410	0.397	0.373	0.350	0.301	0.260	0.226	0.198
5	0.951	0.906	0.822	0.747	0.681	0.621	0.567	0.519	0.497	0.476	0.437	0.402	0.370	0.341	0.328	0.315	0.291	0.269	0.223	0.186	0.156	0.132
6	0.942	0.888	0.790	0.705	0.630	0.564	0.507	0.456	0.432	0.410	0.370	0.335	0.303	0.275	0.262	0.250	0.227	0.207	0.165	0.133	0.108	0.088
7	0.933	0.871	0.760	0.665	0.583	0.513	0.452	0.400	0.376	0.354	0.314	0.279	0.249	0.222	0.210	0.198	0.178	0.159	0.122	0.095	0.074	0.059
8	0.923	0.853	0.731	0.627	0.540	0.467	0.404	0.351	0.327	0.305	0.266	0.233	0.204	0.179	0.168	0.157	0.139	0.123	0.091	0.068	0.051	0.039
9	0.914	0.837	0.703	0.592	0.500	0.424	0.361	0.308	0.284	0.263	0.225	0.194	0.167	0.144	0.134	0.125	0.108	0.094	0.067	0.048	0.035	0.026
10	0.905	0.820	0.676	0.558	0.463	0.386	0.322	0.270	0.247	0.227	0.191	0.162	0.137	0.116	0.107	0.099	0.085	0.073	0.050	0.035	0.024	0.017
11	0.896	0.804	0.650	0.527	0.429	0.350	0.287	0.237	0.215	0.195	0.162	0.135	0.112	0.094	0.086	0.079	0.066	0.056	0.037	0.025	0.017	0.012
12	0.887	0.788	0.625	0.497	0.397	0.319	0.257	0.208	0.187	0.168	0.137	0.112	0.092	0.076	0.069	0.062	0.052	0.043	0.027	0.018	0.012	0.008
13	0.879	0.773	0.601	0.469	0.368	0.290	0.229	0.182	0.163	0.145	0.116	0.093	0.075	0.061	0.055	0.050	0.040	0.033	0.020	0.013	0.008	0.005
14	0.870	0.758	0.577	0.442	0.340	0.263	0.205	0.160	0.141	0.125	0.099	0.078	0.062	0.049	0.044	0.039	0.032	0.025	0.015	0.009	0.006	0.003
15	0.861	0.743	0.555	0.417	0.315	0.239	0.183	0.140	0.123	0.108	0.084	0.065	0.051	0.040	0.035	0.031	0.025	0.020	0.011	0.006	0.004	0.002
16	0.853	0.728	0.534	0.394	0.292	0.218	0.163	0.123	0.107	0.093	0.071	0.054	0.042	0.032	0.028	0.025	0.019	0.015	0.008	0.005	0.003	0.002
17	0.844	0.714	0.513	0.371	0.270	0.198	0.146	0.108	0.093	0.080	0.060	0.045	0.034	0.026	0.023	0.020	0.015	0.012	0.006	0.003	0.002	0.001
18	0.836	0.700	0.494	0.350	0.250	0.180	0.130	0.095	0.081	0.069	0.051	0.038	0.028	0.021	0.018	0.016	0.012	0.009	0.005	0.002	0.001	0.001
19	0.828	0.686	0.475	0.331	0.232	0.164	0.116	0.083	0.070	0.060	0.043	0.031	0.023	0.017	0.014	0.012	0.009	0.007	0.003	0.002	0.001	
20	0.820	0.673	0.456	0.312	0.215	0.149	0.104	0.073	0.061	0.051	0.037	0.026	0.019	0.014	0.012	0.010	0.007	0.005	0.002	0.001	0.001	
21	0.811	0.660	0.439	0.294	0.199	0.135	0.093	0.064	0.053	0.044	0.031	0.022	0.015	0.011	0.009	0.008	0.006	0.004	0.002	0.001		
22	0.803	0.647	0.422	0.278	0.184	0.123	0.083	0.056	0.046	0.038	0.026	0.018	0.013	0.009	0.006	0.006	0.004	0.003	0.001	0.001		
23	0.795	0.634	0.406	0.262	0.170	0.112	0.074	0.049	0.040	0.033	0.022	0.015	0.010	0.007	0.006	0.005	0.003	0.002	0.001			
24	0.788	0.622	0.390	0.247	0.158	0.102	0.066	0.043	0.035	0.028	0.019	0.013	0.008	0.006	0.005	0.004	0.003	0.002	0.001			
25	0.780	0.610	0.375	0.233	0.146	0.092	0.059	0.038	0.030	0.024	0.016	0.010	0.007	0.005	0.004	0.003	0.002	0.001	0.001			
26	0.772	0.598	0.361	0.220	0.135	0.084	0.053	0.033	0.026	0.021	0.014	0.009	0.006	0.004	0.003	0.002	0.002	0.001				
27	0.764	0.586	0.347	0.207	0.125	0.076	0.047	0.029	0.023	0.018	0.011	0.007	0.005	0.003	0.002	0.002	0.001	0.001				
28	0.757	0.574	0.333	0.196	0.116	0.069	0.042	0.026	0.020	0.016	0.010	0.006	0.004	0.002	0.002	0.002	0.001	0.001				
29	0.749	0.563	0.321	0.185	0.107	0.063	0.037	0.022	0.017	0.014	0.008	0.005	0.003	0.002	0.002	0.001	0.001					
30	0.742	0.552	0.308	0.174	0.099	0.057	0.033	0.020	0.015	0.012	0.007	0.004	0.003	0.002	0.001	0.001	0.001					
40	0.672	0.453	0.208	0.097	0.046	0.022	0.011	0.005	0.004	0.003	0.001	0.001										
50	0.608	0.372	0.141	0.054	0.021	0.009	0.003	0.001	0.001	0.001												

Source: Robert N. Anthony, *Management Accounting: Text and Cases* (4th ed., Homewood, Ill.: Richard D. Irwin, Inc., 1970).

Appendix D

PRESENT VALUE OF $1 RECEIVED ANNUALLY FOR N YEARS

Years (N)	1%	2%	4%	6%	8%	10%	12%	14%	15%	16%	18%	20%	22%	24%	25%	26%	28%	30%	35%	40%	45%	50%
1	0.990	0.980	0.962	0.943	0.926	0.909	0.893	0.877	0.870	0.862	0.847	0.833	0.820	0.806	0.800	0.794	0.781	0.769	0.741	0.714	0.690	0.667
2	1.970	1.942	1.886	1.833	1.783	1.736	1.690	1.647	1.626	1.605	1.566	1.528	1.492	1.457	1.440	1.424	1.392	1.361	1.289	1.224	1.165	1.111
3	2.941	2.884	2.775	2.673	2.577	2.487	2.402	2.322	2.283	2.246	2.174	2.106	2.042	1.981	1.952	1.923	1.868	1.816	1.696	1.589	1.493	1.407
4	3.902	3.808	3.630	3.465	3.312	3.170	3.037	2.914	2.855	2.798	2.690	2.589	2.494	2.404	2.362	2.320	2.241	2.166	1.997	1.849	1.720	1.605
5	4.853	4.713	4.452	4.212	3.993	3.791	3.605	3.433	3.352	3.274	3.127	2.991	2.864	2.745	2.689	2.635	2.532	2.436	2.220	2.035	1.876	1.737
6	5.795	5.601	5.242	4.917	4.623	4.355	4.111	3.889	3.784	3.685	3.498	3.326	3.167	3.020	2.951	2.885	2.759	2.643	2.385	2.168	1.983	1.824
7	6.728	6.472	6.002	5.582	5.206	4.868	4.564	4.288	4.160	4.039	3.812	3.605	3.416	3.242	3.161	3.083	2.937	2.802	2.508	2.263	2.057	1.883
8	7.652	7.325	6.733	6.210	5.747	5.335	4.968	4.639	4.487	4.344	4.078	3.837	3.619	3.421	3.329	3.241	3.076	2.925	2.598	2.331	2.108	1.922
9	8.566	8.162	7.435	6.802	6.247	5.759	5.328	4.946	4.772	4.607	4.303	4.031	3.786	3.566	3.463	3.366	3.184	3.019	2.665	2.379	2.144	1.948
10	9.471	8.983	8.111	7.360	6.710	6.145	5.650	5.216	5.019	4.833	4.494	4.192	3.923	3.682	3.571	3.465	3.269	3.092	2.715	2.414	2.168	1.965
11	10.368	9.787	8.760	7.887	7.139	6.495	5.937	5.453	5.234	5.029	4.656	4.327	4.035	3.776	3.656	3.544	3.335	3.147	2.757	2.438	2.185	1.977
12	11.255	10.575	9.385	8.384	7.536	6.814	6.194	5.660	5.421	5.197	4.793	4.439	4.127	3.851	3.725	3.606	3.387	3.190	2.779	2.456	2.196	1.985
13	12.134	11.343	9.986	8.853	7.904	7.103	6.424	5.842	5.583	5.342	4.910	4.533	4.203	3.912	3.780	3.656	3.427	3.223	2.799	2.468	2.204	1.990
14	13.004	12.106	10.563	9.295	8.244	7.367	6.628	6.002	5.724	5.468	5.008	4.611	4.265	3.962	3.824	3.695	3.459	3.249	2.814	2.477	2.210	1.993
15	13.865	12.849	11.118	9.712	8.559	7.606	6.811	6.142	5.847	5.575	5.092	4.675	4.315	4.001	3.859	3.726	3.483	3.268	2.825	2.484	2.214	1.995
16	14.718	13.578	11.652	10.106	8.851	7.824	6.974	6.265	5.954	5.669	5.162	4.730	4.357	4.033	3.887	3.751	3.503	3.283	2.834	2.489	2.216	1.997
17	15.562	14.292	12.166	10.477	9.122	8.022	7.120	6.373	6.047	5.749	5.222	4.775	4.391	4.059	3.910	3.771	3.518	3.295	2.840	2.492	2.218	1.998
18	16.398	14.992	12.659	10.828	9.372	8.201	7.250	6.467	6.128	5.818	5.273	4.812	4.419	4.080	3.928	3.786	3.529	3.304	2.844	2.494	2.219	1.999
19	17.226	15.678	13.134	11.158	9.604	8.365	7.366	6.550	6.198	5.877	5.316	4.844	4.442	4.097	3.942	3.799	3.539	3.311	2.848	2.496	2.220	1.999
20	18.046	16.351	13.590	11.470	9.818	8.514	7.469	6.623	6.259	5.929	5.353	4.870	4.460	4.110	3.954	3.808	3.546	3.316	2.850	2.497	2.221	1.999
21	18.857	17.011	14.029	11.764	10.017	8.649	7.562	6.687	6.312	5.973	5.384	4.891	4.476	4.121	3.963	3.816	3.551	3.320	2.852	2.498	2.221	2.000
22	19.660	17.658	14.451	12.042	10.201	8.772	7.645	6.743	6.359	6.011	5.410	4.909	4.488	4.130	3.970	3.822	3.556	3.323	2.853	2.498	2.222	2.000
23	20.456	18.292	14.857	12.303	10.371	8.883	7.718	6.792	6.399	6.044	5.432	4.925	4.499	4.137	3.976	3.827	3.559	3.325	2.854	2.499	2.222	2.000
24	21.243	18.914	15.247	12.550	10.529	8.985	7.784	6.835	6.434	6.073	5.451	4.937	4.507	4.143	3.981	3.831	3.562	3.327	2.855	2.499	2.222	2.000
25	22.023	19.523	15.622	12.783	10.675	9.077	7.843	6.873	6.464	6.097	5.467	4.948	4.514	4.147	3.985	3.834	3.564	3.329	2.856	2.499	2.222	2.000
26	22.795	20.121	15.983	13.003	10.810	9.161	7.896	6.906	6.491	6.118	5.480	4.956	4.520	4.151	3.988	3.837	3.566	3.330	2.856	2.500	2.222	2.000
27	23.560	20.707	16.330	13.211	10.935	9.237	7.943	6.935	6.514	6.136	5.492	4.964	4.524	4.154	3.990	3.839	3.567	3.331	2.856	2.500	2.222	2.000
28	24.316	21.281	16.663	13.406	11.051	9.307	7.984	6.961	6.534	6.152	5.502	4.970	4.528	4.157	3.992	3.840	3.568	3.331	2.857	2.500	2.222	2.000
29	25.066	21.844	16.984	13.591	11.158	9.370	8.022	6.983	6.551	6.166	5.510	4.975	4.531	4.159	3.994	3.841	3.569	3.332	2.857	2.500	2.222	2.000
30	25.808	22.396	17.292	13.765	11.258	9.427	8.055	7.003	6.566	6.177	5.517	4.979	4.534	4.160	3.995	3.842	3.569	3.332	2.857	2.500	2.222	2.000
40	32.835	27.355	19.793	15.046	11.925	9.779	8.244	7.105	6.642	6.234	5.548	4.997	4.544	4.166	3.999	3.846	3.571	3.333	2.857	2.500	2.222	2.000
50	39.196	31.424	21.482	15.762	12.234	9.915	8.304	7.133	6.661	6.246	5.554	4.999	4.545	4.167	4.000	3.846	3.571	3.333	2.857	2.500	2.222	2.000

Source: Robert N. Anthony, Management Accounting: Text and Cases (4th ed., Homewood, Ill.: Richard D. Irwin, Inc., 1970).

Indexes

INDEX OF AUTHORS

INDEX OF SUBJECTS